A ROCK TOO BIG

by

Arthur Barry

ArtySan Publishing

Table of Contents

I thank God for His unspeakably
beautiful Creation,
The Church of Christ

*To Him be glory in the church and in
Christ Jesus throughout all generations,
forever and ever. Amen.*
Ephesians 3:21

PROLOGUE

He put out the form of a hand and took me by a lock of my
head, and the Spirit lifted me up between earth and heaven
and brought me in visions of God to Jerusalem, to the entrance
of the gateway of the inner court that faces north, where was
the seat of the image of jealousy, which provokes to jealousy.
Ezekiel 8:3

Ezekiel's experience in being caught up between earth and heaven
is very intriguing. I find myself wanting to know what it is like to be
caught up between earth and heaven, but I don't think I want to be
dragged there by my hair. Probably the closest I will come to that is
to be caught up between the pulpit and the pew, which can be a hair-
raising experience.

If a Christian desires to grow in faith it would seem that a healthy
church would be an appropriate setting for that process, and not a
church that endures a division of fellowship. I have preached for six
churches and two of them have split over the doctrine of salvation.
I feel that I have actually learned some valuable lessons from these
heart-wrenching experiences, lessons that I may not have learned so
well if things had gone more smoothly. Some of us just have to learn

the hard way. I feel constrained to put these lessons in writing for the benefit of others who may be struggling with the questions that I have been forced to deal with. They are not new questions and many others, more able than I, have provided excellent teaching on this topic. It may be that we do not need another treatment of these questions about faith and fellowship, but perhaps I can shed light from a different perspective which will help some.

The scriptures that speak of the need to contend for the faith (Jude 3) and to test the spirits (1 John 4:1-6) are treated, by people of weak faith, in the same way that many treat the Old Testament scriptures. The God of the Old Testament is accused of being too harsh to meet the standards of the New Testament, and contending for the faith sounds too much like that Old Testament God. I have been in a Bible class where an individual was extremely reluctant to accept that Jesus actually raised a hand against anyone when he drove the money changers from the temple (John 2:14-17). I hope your jaw drops, as mine did, when you hear that. If your jaw did not drop then try this one. I once sat with three other preachers and talked about John the Baptist. One of them actually said he imagined that if John had the chance to do it all again he would probably not be so confrontational. Does that not cause at least a slight rise in your blood pressure?

It is important to realize that if you are looking for truth there is only one, whereas if you are looking for a lie then any lie will do and Satan has a seemingly endless stock of them. This work is concerned with the lie(s) about the Lord's Church. Many people are willing and able to take a clear stand on the nature and work of Jesus Christ and yet seem to be unclear, even confused, about the nature and work of His Church. As a result the popular teaching about the Church is that it is acceptable to have as many different kinds as possible and if you don't want to belong to any of them that is all right too. The emphasis on having a personal relationship with Jesus has become entrenched among most denominations. As a result their answer to the question, "What must I do to be saved?" is not "Repent and be baptized" (Acts 2:38). Their answer is, "Pray Jesus into your heart" (No Bible reference corresponds to this). Those who have fallen for these lies will likely reject those who argue for one true Church.

There is nothing more important to talk about than the truth of the gospel and how it needs to be proclaimed and protected. It is a simple matter of asking what God has revealed in the scriptures about the Church. The conclusions we find in the Bible might seem unlikely, but anyone who wants to be a Christian is forced to accept the most unlikely of all possible conclusions. The Bible tells us that God loved us enough to give His Son as a sacrifice for our sins, and then raised Him from the dead with the promise of also raising us from the dead. That is the gospel message and those who have obeyed the gospel are saved, and that means they are in the Lord's Church. It is this dimension of fellowship that causes us a lot of problems. Is salvation a function of fellowship, or is salvation just between me and God?

A preacher should be able to empathize with those who struggle with doubts. In fact all Christians are admonished to have mercy on those who doubt (Jude 22). Being merciful does not mean we are to wallow in doubt with those who doubt. All Christians are also admonished to contend for the faith (Jude 3). Contending for the faith does not mean we are to distance ourselves from those who doubt. If the Church lives up to these two requirements we will be fighting the good fight right between the pulpit and the pew. What a joyful struggle! What agitated contentment! Can you feel your hair being pulled?

Like the universe in which we live, the Church is a miraculous creation of God that transcends the wisdom of man. God's revealed will does indeed challenge us to accept conclusions that seem unlikely. Will we accept what the Lord has to say about His Church, that it is His Body and that baptism is the faith response that brings a lost soul into Christ? Or will we treat His Church as though He has created a rock too big for Him to move?

Chapter One

FLIMSY FAITH AND PHONY ARGUMENTS

I had been a Christian for some time when I first heard the challenge to the existence of God framed in the question, "Can God make a rock so big that He cannot move it?" I thought that was a clever question indeed. It is clever only because there is no satisfactory answer for the person of faith. A "yes" answer is just as desirable as a "no" answer to the one posing the question. Most questions can be expressed this way. A famous example is the husband whose enemy asked him, "Are you still beating your wife?" In the same way, one of my father-in-laws' old friends made a valid point when giving directions to an address in his neighborhood. When he explained which side of the road it was on he was asked if that applied to someone driving into town or out of town. His answer has become a classic around our household. "It don't matter which way you're driving; it's still on the same side of the road!" There are those who will not allow God to exist in any perspective but their own and for many that perspective demands that He does not in fact exist.

Churches of Christ are facing a crisis of faith. Many in the brotherhood harbor a desire to be like the religious groups around us and as a result are forsaking their first love (Revelation 2:4). This work is not concerned with those who wish to develop arguments against the existence of God. It is concerned with those who believe that God does exist and yet will develop arguments that essentially prove God has indeed created a rock so big that He cannot move it. As far as the nature and existence of God is concerned they are confident but when it comes to the nature and existence of the Church they are unable to accept what God has to say on the matter. The arguments call into question the biblical teachings about salvation and fellowship. The main point of contention in regard to salvation is whether a person has to be baptized to be saved, or not. In regard to fellowship, it is whether there is one, true Church on earth, or many.

One common argument against baptism is the case that is proposed that involves a hypothetical person who is dying in a desert. This person wants to be saved but there is no water available for baptism. Those who rely on this argument will maintain that God will waive the requirement for baptism when water is unavailable. In fact God must waive the requirement for baptism; He has no other choice. This argument will naturally further develop into the argument that baptism is not a requirement at all. Most denominations today have tossed biblical truth aside and embraced this conclusion. Despite plain Bible teaching about the oneness of the Church (Ephesians 4:4-6) all denominations embrace the concept that there can be many different denominations of the Church. This is an extension of the doctrine that claims everyone can have a personal relationship with God. If the Bible did teach that individuals can have a personal relationship with Christ, independent of others, then it would follow that groups of individuals can form churches that are independent of other churches. The Bible does not teach anything of the kind.

Until recently what the secular world knew as the Church was represented by Catholicism. Nowadays there is another frame of reference which has displaced, or at least gets equal attention with, the Catholic Church. This entity is commonly known as Evangelicalism and it draws members from most denominations, including the Catholic Church. Evangelicals seem to have all the big name preachers and when you hear about politicians courting the Church it is always the

Evangelical vote they are trying to win. It is easy to be beguiled by such an institution but it is an institution of men. Evangelicals subscribe to the teachings of men when it comes to salvation, church identity and membership, and Kingdom history. They generally believe that salvation is by "faith alone", and church identity and membership is left up to the preferences of men. As for the Kingdom on Earth it is yet to come. These are perversions of the truth.

Churches of Christ believe that salvation is secured when one is faithfully baptized in the name of Christ as the Bible teaches (Matthew 28:18-20; Mark 16:15,16; John 3:3-5; Acts 2:38; 1 Peter 3:21). We believe that the identity and membership of the Church is spelled out in the scriptures. Some specifics of that belief are that those who are baptized into Christ are added to the Church of Christ (Acts 2:47) and are expected to assemble for the Lord's Supper on the first day of each week (Acts 20:7; 1 Corinthians 11:17-21) and to encourage and love one another (Hebrews 10:25). The Kingdom on earth has been in existence since Jesus poured out his Spirit on all flesh (Acts 2) and began His reign on earth through His Body, the Church (Colossians 1:18; 1 Corinthians 15:25; Revelation 1:4-6). We now await the final consummation of all things at the return of the Lord in judgment. Every soul that lives needs to know that "...*it is appointed for men to die once and after that comes judgment*" (Hebrews 9:27).

There is a huge effort underway, by those who are attracted to denominational groups, to break down the barriers to fellowship between churches of Christ and evangelical denominations. To accomplish that objective they need to bring our biblical faith into conformity with evangelical theology. In other words, they must be willing to give up walking in the light for a place in the limelight. Some would bridge the gap by claiming that there are denominational groups that are in agreement with us about baptism. The hypothesis that supports this argument is that a person can be outside of the true Church and yet be saved by virtue of the fact that he or she has obeyed God's command on how to get into the true Church. This argument has to be classified as a non sequitur. The argument about the man in the desert, and the argument about God creating a rock too big for Him to move are also in this category. Any conclusions that might be drawn from these arguments are irrelevant because the arguments are fallacious.

You may be familiar with other arguments that are becoming popular as more people join the effort to change the Lord's church into a denomination like all the others. There is the argument that the Church of Christ is a denomination already because of its teachings that set it apart from others. We must indeed be careful that we are not just settling for being different, but the true Church, by definition, must be set apart. We are to be set apart by our devotion to the truth (John 17:17) and we should not apologize for that.

Another argument was framed by a brother who had been very instrumental in my conversion and early growth as a Christian. Years later, after our paths had taken us to different places, we met briefly and he explained to me why he had come to accept denominational fellowship. He told me he was not the person I had known in those early years, and that he now believed that people do not need doctrine, they need love. The doctrine versus love argument is completely false but it is also very popular. The fact is that Jesus has to command us to *love one another* (John 13:34). To use a concept from Star Trek, love is the *prime directive* for the Body of Christ. There is no love without doctrine, and vice versa.

We are familiar with the secular version of this philosophy, which blossomed in the sixties as the "Free Love" movement. Love and marriage no longer go together in the minds of many people. "What difference does a piece of paper make as long as we love each other?" many people ask in regard to marriage. "Do we really need to focus on the Bible, as long as we love one another?" cry the change-agents in the Church. In referring to the Bible we are actually talking about the teachings of the Bible and not the book itself. The book has to be read and applied for it to become the living Word of God. Are we to regard the Bible as simply a love letter? Is it not also the document that defines and authorizes a covenant relationship with God Almighty?

When we look at what God has mapped out in His plan of salvation it might seem daunting to us, but it is not our place to question His wisdom. We actually have to follow God's commands all the way. The question of whether or not a person needs to be baptized has been at the heart of two church splits I have been involved with. From that question arise other questions such as, "What is the Church?" and "How is it to relate to the world?" What God has to say about salvation and His Church is just too much of a stretch for the minds of many people these days. Perhaps we need to ask ourselves if Jesus would say of us,

> *"Indeed, in their case the prophecy of Isaiah is fulfilled that says: 'You will indeed hear but never understand, and you will indeed see but never perceive.'"*
>
> Matthew 13:14

There is no doubt that there is much that is impossible for men, but with God all things are possible (Matthew 19:26). We must not go beyond what is written (1 Corinthians 4:6). However, we must never be found guilty of implying that God's word goes too far and that He has made a rock that is beyond His ability to move. To be specific, I am referring to the failure to accept the reality of one true church in the world. Does God's Word allow for the existence of the Church of Christ? Nobody would argue that it does not. Does God's Word allow for the existence of Methodists or Baptists or any of the groups that men have named over the centuries? Huge numbers now argue that it does. I disagree.

Institutions of men have sought to sub-divide the rock that the Lord promised to build His Church upon (Matthew 16:18). Whereas God's plan called for one temple, these counterfeit plans have multiplex temples where the patron can pick and choose which church to attend to his or her heart's content.

When Satan offered Jesus all the kingdoms of the world (Matthew 4:8-11) Jesus declined his offer and immediately began to call people to the one kingdom of Heaven (Matthew 4:17). The Lord's plan has always been to move from many kingdoms to one kingdom, not the other way around. This one kingdom is:

- The kingdom prophesied by Daniel as being the rock that was cut out of the mountain but not by hands (Daniel 2:44,45).
- The rock upon which Jesus promised to build His Church. (Matthew 16:18)
- The rock of offense (Isaiah 8:14; Romans 9:33).

The Church is the Kingdom on earth (Colossians 1:13) and it is also the Body of Christ (Colossians 1:18). The Church therefore assumes the rôle of the rock of offense. To those who believe the scriptures, Jesus is a living stone and we are also living stones being built into His temple. But to the world He is a rock of offense (1 Peter 2:4-9). If the cornerstone of the temple is offensive, the temple is offensive. Jesus was clear in His warnings about that state of affairs (John 15:19-21).

The two Marys who went to take care of the Lord's Body after Jesus had been crucified and buried did not know how they would deal with the rock that sealed the Lord's tomb (Mark 16:1-5). That question did not stop them from going to take care of the Lord's body. That is faith in action. When they got to the tomb, the rock had been moved for them. That is God in action. Unfortunately, too many among us have decided that the rock will have to stay where it is because it is just too big.

The rock that seems to weigh too heavily on many believers is the mission that God gave to His followers. The Church is the body of Christ and as such we are to carry on the mission of Christ, which is to seek and save the lost. Luke 19:1-10 gives a biblical perspective for the relationship between those who are saved and those who are lost. Jesus came into Jericho where Zacchaeus lived and Zacchaeus climbed a tree so that he could see Jesus. Jesus responded by telling him to climb down because He was coming to his house. Luke 19:6 says that Zacchaeus hurried down and received Jesus joyfully. Jesus sums up this encounter with these words:

"Today salvation has come to this house, since he also is a son of Abraham. For the Son of Man came to seek and to save the lost."

Luke 19:9,10

Salvation came to Zacchaeus in the form of Jesus the Savior. Where is salvation today? Salvation is in the Body of Christ, the Church (Ephesians 1:10-23). The Church is to seek and save the lost (Matthew 28:18-20). Are the lost to seek salvation? Are there lost souls climbing metaphorical trees to get a glimpse of the Savior? Of course there are! The Bible plainly promises a reward for those who seek God (Luke 11:9; Acts 17:27). Was Zacchaeus saved when he climbed that tree, and, if he was, are all those tree-climbers out there saved today? Did Jesus really need to go to Jericho to save Zacchaeus? Do we actually have to make personal contact with lost souls today in order for them to be saved? Why am I asking these questions?

These are questions that are disturbing the faith of many people today. They are questions that are not found in the Bible and therefore can only be answered by using man's wisdom. The questions come from the mind of man and so do the answers to the questions. Rather than encouraging faith in God's word, they invite speculation. If we are looking for "Thus saith the Lord" then it is clear that the Church is a definite entity with a definite mission in a definite time and place. We must seek and save the lost, and the lost must respond to God's terms of salvation if they are to be saved. God asks us to trust Him to supply whatever is needed for us to get the job done. He does not ask us to speculate about alternative means for achieving the same ends.

God sent His Son to earth, to you and me. He did not wait in Heaven for an earth-born solution to man's problem. The two Marys did not stay in their room trying to imagine how the body of Jesus may have already been taken care of. Neither did they remain in their room stymied by the fact that a huge rock lay between them and their objective.

Lost souls can climb those trees all day long, but if salvation does not come to them they will just be out on a limb. The Bible is the story of God coming and doing what was necessary to provide salvation. The story, like God Himself, moves relentlessly from death to life. The reader is carried along, like it or not, on a tsunami of salvation. God has a plan and God reveals that plan. The world may reject the plan but faith will overcome the world (1 John 5:4,5).

Speculation says "I see a big rock. How can we find a way around it?" Faith says, "I see an empty tomb!"

Questions for Chapter One

1. Can the question of God's existence be settled by reason alone? Can it be settled by faith alone?

2. The question: "Can God create a rock so big that He cannot move it?," presents what is called the "omnipotence paradox." Can you formulate a similarly loaded question for those who only accept natural explanations for the universe? Eg. is there a "randomness paradox" or an "evolution paradox"?

3. The gospel message is full of conclusions that go against the normal flow of human thought. List the ways in which it stretches your thinking.

4. Do you see ways in which the Church, or yourself personally, may limit the power of God's Word? (Read Isaiah 55:1-13.)

5. Can you make a biblical defense for the existence of denominations?

6. Can you make a biblical defense for the doctrine of "faith only"? (baptism is not required for salvation)

Chapter Two

BREAKING BREAD OR BREAKING FELLOWSHIP?

I have been involved in two church splits that occurred twelve years apart, around the same time of the year. What follows is a recounting of discussions that led to the most recent split. Everything about this episode is troubling and the arguments I encountered, from people whom I loved and respected, just did not make sense to me. As I have pondered the causes of the split I have come to accept that the two sides were each approaching questions about salvation and fellowship from an altogether different faith perspective. I find that astounding and terrifying.

We met in hopes of defusing the crisis that had been escalating among us. It was a meeting of monumental significance no less so than the Yalta Conference that took place near the end of World War II, or Vatican II in 1962. After two sessions I felt my world shaken to the foundations again. We were not popes or cardinals or even Catholics, nor were we presidents or potentates or politicians of any sort, yet we delved into issues that carry eternal and universal consequences. No gathering of men in the history of the human race was ever called upon to discharge a weightier responsibility, and it showed on our faces and sounded in our voices. At the heart of our discussion was the heart of God, and it terrified each one of us as we began to glimpse the crossroads that lay in our path. If we could not find another path then there would be a parting of the ways.

This traumatic experience became the second of the two church splits that I had been involved with, and I can tell you that they do not get easier. If given a choice, I would rather have been in the shoes of John F. Kennedy facing down Nikita Khrushchev with the threat of a nuclear holocaust looming. No one would be hearing about our meeting on the nightly news, and there would be no spawning of innumerable tweets. The rest of the planet would be oblivious to the decision that was made that day, but we agonized as though we shared the burden of Pilate in deciding whether to crucify Jesus or set Him free.

At the root of this drama was the question of whether or not God created one true Church and, if so, do the scriptures adequately define that Church. I can break that down into the following formula:

Does fellowship equal or correspond with salvation? In other words, can a person be saved without being in fellowship with the Church (or vice versa)? Once you broach this topic, questions bubble up as though you have just opened a well-shaken can of coke. What is "church"? Are there degrees of fellowship, and thus degrees of salvation? Is it a process that provides maximum blessings for everyone no matter where they are in the process? Are denominations actually a part of the true Church but on some sort of spiritual fringe? Can the true Church outsource its duties to denominations? These are a few of the many questions which can get quite technical and extremely hypothetical. We shall look into some of them, Lord willing. Meanwhile back to the café…

One of the other men had preached a lesson that I had found disturbing. He had proclaimed that there are saved people in the denominations. People who were Baptists were specifically cited. The Church of Christ was compared to the Pharisee who thanked God that he was not like the tax-collector (Luke 18:10-14). The preacher explained that this is because we in the Church look down on other groups for their errant practices such as the use of instruments in worship and acceptance of women in leadership roles. He pointed out that in I Corinthians Paul addressed the Corinthians as brethren even though they exhibited a party spirit. In his opinion this was the same thing as modern day denominationalism and, therefore, Paul was setting a precedent for accepting denominations. I had taken this preacher aside and expressed concern about these ideas. So here we were, the four men that made up the male membership of our little group, sitting at a table in a popular local café, drinking coffee and reviewing the points of disagreement.

This meeting was the second time we had sat down together, and a café was chosen as the venue because the preacher I had confronted had refused to come to church with me. By the end of this meeting I would be faced with the conclusion that he was more comfortable going to church with his denominational friends than he was going to church with me. I knew we had differences of opinion on some pretty significant issues but he surprised me by breaking fellowship with me. What came as a huge shock, however, was that within one week I was anathematized by all who were in that meeting.

Let me put the arguments down as I heard them. A lost soul may encounter a denominational group and come to knowledge of the truth. That person may then get baptized and actually be saved though still not in fellowship with the Lord's Church (what I know as the Church of Christ). They urged me to accept the claim that if this preacher whom I was confronting should meet such a person as outlined above he would urge that person to come out of the denomination, but he would consider him to be saved whether or not he left his present fellowship.

Two questions immediately surfaced in my mind, so I asked:
1. What results had he had when he encouraged the people he referred to (he said he knew many) to come out of their denominations?
2. Why would he want to risk offending these people by telling them they needed to come out of their present fellowship if they are already saved?

These seem to be logical considerations, but I never got a clear answer for either question. I have to conclude that he had not actively pursued that approach. These questions speak to the issue of whether salvation and fellowship are interdependent. The main discussion centered on this issue and I found myself completely unable to accept the basic proposition of someone being saved apart from fellowship with the true Church. Over and over again we returned to this point as they tried to convince me that they were not disparaging the Lord's Church and supporting denominations. Over and over again I stopped them and said, "Such a person cannot exist. I cannot accept the proposition. How can this person learn the truth from someone who does not teach the truth?" Jesus words concerning blind guides apply here:

> *"Let them alone; they are blind guides. And if the blind lead the blind, both will fall into a pit."*
>
> Matthew 15:14

I was being asked to accept an argument that denies the existence of the God in whom I have come to believe. When we present arguments to an atheist it is not just a simple case of hoping to win an argument. We should be striving to convert this person to Christ. An atheist must undergo a complete shift in his worldview if we are to achieve our objective, and that means we must demolish the intellectual foundation of his life; in other words, we must attack his faith system.

> *For the weapons of our warfare are not of the flesh but have divine power to destroy strongholds. We destroy arguments and every lofty opinion raised against the knowledge of God, and take every thought captive to obey Christ...*
>
> 2 Corinthians 10:4,5

That scripture applies to false teachers as well as atheists. In the café that day I felt as though I was being asked to abandon biblical truth and dismantle my faith. These men were presenting hypothetical arguments and lofty opinions. To be in agreement with them I must accept a hypothetical God.

Let us return to the proposition that a man who has not made contact with the true Church may come to knowledge of the truth in some way. If he does not hear the truth from a denominational group, and I am convinced that he cannot, can he learn the truth independently by reading the Bible? This question seems concrete enough but, if this person has no contact with a true Christian, who is to know if he properly understands the truth? Who will test that spirit? We are speaking hypothetically once again. To many people the resurrection of Jesus Christ is just a rumor but we can actually provide eye witness testimony, from the scriptures, that God raised Jesus from the dead. The preaching of the cross must never be, "What if Jesus was resurrected?" Likewise, discussions about the salvation of any soul must never be prefaced with, "What if…?"

As for this man who is not in contact with the true Church, yet may come to an understanding of the truth, the only way to prove that is to talk to him personally. Some will say it is none of our business because it is between that individual and God. I consider that to be an extremely unchristian attitude. During our conversation at the café these men adamantly affirmed that it does not matter who baptizes a person as it is between the person being baptized and God. If that is true what are we to think about the following examples?

- The Ethiopian eunuch when God made him Philip's business (Acts 8:26-39)
- Paul, when God made him Ananias's business (Acts 9:10-18)
- Cornelius, when God made him Peter's business (Acts 10)
- The disciples at Ephesus, when God made them Paul's business (Acts 19:1-7)
- For that matter read again Matthew 28:18-20, where Jesus makes the salvation of the world the business of His disciples.
- If you are saved, ask yourself if you got to that point on your own. Aren't you glad that God sent real people and not hypotheses?

Even if we accept the hypothesis that a person can come to saving faith by independent study of the Bible we still have to ask how this hypothetical person will be baptized. Can a person who does not accept that baptism is required for salvation actually baptize someone else "in the name of Jesus Christ"?

I can find no biblical support for such a baptism. We would have to start stringing more hypotheses together to even make a non-biblical argument. Our mandate is to test spirits not develop hypotheses. If we ask the probing questions about salvation like, "Were you saved before you were baptized or when you were baptized?" we will find out for sure if a person has believed the truth or a lie. In my experience all denominational groups teach that God will save a person apart from baptism. Sadly, many members of churches of Christ are reluctant to ask the hard questions.

Back at the café, the men I talked with struggled to follow my reasoning. "Are you saying you are not saved if you are not baptized by a member of the Church of Christ?" they asked me. One of them voiced the concern that I was sounding like a Catholic or even a Gnostic. In the days that followed they refused to fellowship with me on the basis that I was adding requirements to salvation that were not found in the Bible. These questions form the heart of the discussion at the café and I became convinced that the men who mount these arguments have added avenues to salvation that are not found in the Bible. To them the idea of one true church which contends for one true faith was a *rock too big*. Their faith seemed to rest on speculative inventions of the human mind and not on the powerful word of God. God's word is not to be taken to a laboratory and subjected to batteries of tests. Unless I am gravely mistaken it is we who are being tested by God's word (Psalm 26:2; 2 Corinthians 13:5).

Is one true Church a hypothetical proposition? If it is then we must certainly entertain hypothetical propositions in regard to the discussion about who is saved. In God's Word, however, I find a very different kind of thinking.

*Now to him who is able to do far more abundantly than all that
we ask or think, according to the power at work within us, to
him be glory in the church and in Christ Jesus throughout all
generations, forever and ever. Amen.*

Ephesians 3:20,21

God does not need us to come up with contingency plans for His
plan of salvation. Instead of speculating about how to get around God's
Word, He encourages us to speculate about what amazing things He
might do in order to keep His promises. Please notice two things about
God's power from the passage above:

1. God's power will not be limited by what we think He can do.
2. God's power is at work in us!

Each one of us has to make up our own minds as to whether or not
we can trust God's Word in regard to creation. The alternative is to trust
the speculations and theories that have been proposed by scientists.
Are we here because of God's providential supernatural power or are
we here because of a long series of random natural events? The same
choice confronts us when we consider God's new creation, His Church.
Do we look for natural causes and explanations that we can understand,
or do we trust in His providential power?

*"The LORD lives, and blessed be my rock,
and exalted be my God, the rock of my salvation."*

2 Samuel 22:47

Questions for Chapter Two

1.   Are there any examples of hypothetical reasoning in the Bible that would lead us to accept hypothetical reasoning instead of a "Thus saith the Lord." in regard to salvation?

2   Are there biblical grounds for considering a person's salvation as being purely between that person and God with no need for another person to be involved?

3.   How do you understand the way Paul addresses the Corinthian church in his first letter? He calls them brethren, yet accuses them of indulging in a party spirit. Is this biblical grounds for honoring denominations?

4.   In our modern setting the term "Pharisee" is often used as a disparaging label for Christians who hold to a strict interpretation of the Bible. Read Matthew 23 where Jesus repeatedly refers to scribes and Pharisees as blind guides. Are they blind because they are too literal in their interpretation?

6.   Which of the following propositions, if any, would you consider to be hypothetical? Which would you consider to be biblical truth?

     a.   One true Church with many earthly variations designed by men.
     b.   One true Church which is replicated, according to God's pattern, all over the earth.
     c.   Salvation and fellowship cannot occur without obedience to the one Lord, one faith and one baptism (Ephesians 4:4-6).
     d.   One Lord and one faith are more important than the one baptism.

Chapter Three

INSIDE OUT

We have two cats that are basically indoor cats, but this past summer they both bailed out on us. Emma got out and immediately went "dark." For a month we rarely got a glimpse of her. Eventually she got tired of that and came back in. My wife, Sandy, is still trying to get her back into shape now. Elaine, however, refused to come back inside. The bizarre thing is that she lived on the porch and would hardly ever move off it. She was just outside our French doors and spent a lot of time with her face right up to the glass looking in. She cried to be fed and loved to be petted but we had to go out there to do that. When we opened the door she acted like she was going to come over the threshold but then she would turn away. Day after day, for weeks, she sat with her face up against the glass looking in waiting for us to come out to take care of her needs. When winter came she gave in and eventually came inside. Why did she want to live that way? Could there be some primeval current running in her blood that drove her to camp out on our porch? If she did not want to be inside, why did she stay on the threshold?

There are members of the Church who live their spiritual lives that way. They really do not like being in the Church of Christ, but they are afraid to leave it. So they take a position just across the threshold looking for something better to come along. In fact, they do see a lot that they like better elsewhere, but somehow they know they need to stay connected to the Lord's Church. We all need to be reminded of how Paul told the Galatians, in no uncertain terms, that they were being foolish if they thought they could begin their walk with Christ in the Spirit and then decide to switch to walking by the flesh (Galatians 3:3). They were dancing on the threshold of salvation and Paul had to be very direct with them. He began his letter to these people by telling them that he was worried that they were now believing a different gospel from the one he had given them (Galatians 1:6-11). As he exhorted them to be faithful he spoke some words that effectively placed a seal on the gospel he had delivered to them. As you read his words ask yourself if you would be willing to place the same seal on whatever it is you would tell another person when they ask you what they must do to be saved.

> *But even if we or an angel from heaven should preach to you a gospel contrary to the one we preached to you, let him be accursed.*
>
> Galatians 1:8

Paul was relentlessly persecuted because he preached the same message to Jews and to Gentiles. He did not require anything other than baptism as a response from Gentiles and that is the same response that he required from Jews (Galatians 3:26-29). What if he had eventually caved in to the pressure from the Judaizers? Would it have been that big a deal if he told Gentiles that they needed to be circumcised as well as baptized? He could have forged ahead with the ministry and won a lot more souls if he had just made that one change. What if he just got tired of fighting that fight? Just in case it ever did happen Paul sealed his message with those words to protect those who might be influenced by him.

Are you willing to make such a commitment to your message of salvation that you would demand of anyone that they should anathematize you if they ever hear you teach a different message? Perverting the gospel is a serious matter. Is it any less serious to tell someone that they do not need to be baptized to be saved than it is to tell someone that they need to be circumcised, as well as baptized, to be saved? If you were one of those Galatians it would have seemed perfectly natural, in their setting, to allow themselves to be circumcised. God had required it of the Jews in the past and Jews were the religious elite of their day. It would seem totally foreign if any of us today could be suddenly transported into their setting. We would be aghast if anyone told us we needed to be circumcised to be saved. I submit that if Paul could be transported into our setting he would be aghast when he heard the religious elite preaching that you do not have to be baptized to be saved and that it does not matter which church you belong to. Paul was resolute about guarding the Church from false teaching. We can certainly tell that from reading his letters. You can tell something else about Paul from his letters. He knew that he could not stop others from drawing disciples from the inside out, and it broke his heart (Acts 20:29,30).

So, good souls get caught up in this false teaching and they drift over the threshold. The true gospel is designed to be spread from the inside to the outside, of course, but the true gospel always calls people into the true Church. If you have obeyed a gospel but remain outside the true Church, you have obeyed a false gospel (2 Corinthians 11:4; Galatians 1:6,7). Even in the Old Testament God set up the terms of fellowship with Himself to include those who were not Jews. In Exodus 12:43 God says that no foreigner may eat of the Passover. However, in verse 48 He expressly stated that any foreigner or alien who wanted to partake of the Passover could qualify to do so. What was the difference between a foreigner who was allowed to eat the Passover and a foreigner who was not allowed to eat the Passover? Any foreigner who wanted to eat the Passover basically had to come inside. They had to be converted to the Jewish faith and for a man that meant that he had to be circumcised.

If a stranger shall sojourn with you and would keep the
Passover to the LORD, let all his males be circumcised. Then
he may come near and keep it; he shall be as a native of the
land. But no uncircumcised person shall eat of it.

Exodus 12:48

Foreigners tagged along with the Israelites, venturing in and out of
their camp as their own needs might require. They recognized the value
of having good relations with the Hebrew people but did not desire
to forsake their own heritage. The true church in the world today has
the same levels of interaction with those who are outside the Church.
There are those who do not belong and have no desire to do so. Then
there are those who like to have one foot in the Church and one foot
in the religion of their choice. Then there are those who have willingly
undergone the process by which they have been converted. They have
forsaken all other loyalties and put on Christ in baptism.

The Hebrew people soon lost all appreciation for their peculiar
identity. They were more enamored of what the gods of the people
outside their camp had to offer than of what their God had to offer. The
God who lived among the Jews told them not to mingle with foreigners
but the gods of the foreigners said that they should indeed mingle. The
gates of Jerusalem were to be opened on a limited basis and closed on
the Sabbath. That was to keep Jerusalem holy (special) and to keep
Jerusalem safe. When Nehemiah was overseeing the rebuilding of the
walls, after the return from exile, he was dismayed to see Israelites and
all sorts of foreigners bringing their merchandise to sell on the Sabbath.
He had this to say:

In those days I saw in Judah people treading winepresses on
the Sabbath, and bringing in heaps of grain and loading them
on donkeys, and also wine, grapes, figs, and all kinds of loads,
which they brought into Jerusalem on the Sabbath day. And I
warned them on the day when they sold food.
Tyrians also, who lived in the city, brought in fish and all kinds

of goods and sold them on the Sabbath to the people of Judah,
in Jerusalem itself! Then I confronted the nobles of Judah
and said to them, "What is this evil thing that you are doing,
profaning the Sabbath day? Did not your fathers act in this
way, and did not our God bring all this disaster on us and
on this city? Now you are bringing more wrath on Israel by
profaning the Sabbath."

Nehemiah 13:15-18

Tyrians bringing in fish! Can you imagine such a thing? Actually, it is hard for us to imagine what could be wrong with that. Since we are not Jews and do not observe Sabbath rules it is easy for us to miss the point here. God gave birth to the Hebrew nation and gave them a Law to guide them and protect them. The law was based on the fact that there was only one God (Exodus 20:1-3; Deuteronomy 6:4) but they were to be born, as a nation, into a world where all other nations on earth worshiped many gods. In the same way that many Americans believe that America can only stand as long as we stay true to our original Constitution, the Hebrew people were to stay true to their Law or they would cease to exist as a nation. Their faith in God would protect them if they protected their faith in God. If they kept God's commandments then God's commandments would keep them (Deuteronomy 11:26-28). The Sabbath was part of that protection (Exodus 20:8-11). During the Sabbath they were to disengage from their daily efforts to keep the world going and instead devote themselves to keeping their faith going. God's people need to understand that they must be devoted to one another more than they are devoted to the world. The same principle applies to the Church today. When Jesus commanded His disciples to love one another He explained why it should be so with these words:

By this all people will know that you are my disciples, if you
have love for one another."

John 13:35

God's people are in the world to impress God upon the world. Sadly, the tendency is to allow the world to impress itself on God's people. Christians are to be gatekeepers with the responsibility of making sure that the outside world does not overwhelm the Church (Nehemiah 13:19; Romans 12:2; Galatians 6:10). God does not take us out of the world but He does set limits by which we will remain holy and safe. The world is fully committed to "business as usual", but we who are the Church bear the responsibility of ministering to the world while remaining unstained by it (James 1:27). Nehemiah reminded his fellow Jews who were returning from exile of how their fathers had violated the Sabbath and how God was punishing them for that violation. There was a time when the gates were virtually off their hinges. Jerusalem was no longer safe because Jerusalem was no longer special. Jerusalem had been turned inside out.

So it is with the heavenly Jerusalem, the Church. Faithful Christians need to stand against those who would open the gates wide and welcome the world into the temple without demanding that they keep the New Testament commandments. Many wolves have gained entrance into the Holy City disguised as sheep (Matthew 7:15). The faith that Jesus sent into the world by the mouths of the apostles who had come out of the world (John 17:6) is designed to call people out of the world (Acts 2:38-40). Peter says it well in the following verse:

> *But you are a chosen race, a royal priesthood, a holy nation, a people for his own possession, that you may proclaim the excellencies of him who called you out of darkness into his marvelous light.*
>
> 1 Peter 2:9

By contrast, those who are false teachers are described as those who enjoy the favor of the world (1 John 4:1). The Church is the Bride of Christ, pure and spotless (Ephesians 5:25-27). We want everyone to join us but if they are to join us they must keep the same faith that we keep and that faith must be the faith that is found in the Bible. We want to keep the Church special and keep her safe so that there is a Church to come into when the lost come looking for that piece of Heaven here on earth. I don't want to see her turned inside out.

Questions for Chapter Three

1. On a scale of 1-10 how confident are you that you tell people the whole counsel of God about how to be saved?

2. Consider the following issues and put them in order of importance as to why people are attracted to the denominations.

    Musical instruments in worship
    Women in leadership
    Inclusiveness
    Biblical purity
    Emphasis on evangelism

3. Now put them in the order of importance that you personally assign to them.

4. Some difference in perspective between how we see the Church and how others see the Church is inevitable, but are we doing enough to clear up the confusion?

4. Are Christians supposed to participate in the Lord's Supper with non-Christians?

5. Membership is only for those who are born again (John 3:3-5). Does that mean the Church is exclusive?

6. Paul spoke of Demas who deserted him because he was in love with the present world (2 Timothy 4:10). What steps might Paul have taken to prevent Demas from leaving?

7. What steps should the Church take to keep its appeal for those who are in love with the world?

Chapter Four

THE ROOT CAUSE
(hitting the right nail on the head)

My first brand new bicycle was a Raleigh "Carlton". It was an unusual color, a sort of iridescent green with white mudguards. Bikes were something of a necessity in England back in those days, as many families did not own cars. I could barely sleep at night for a long time after I got that bike. I lay awake waiting for daylight and another chance to get out on the road again. Like most young boys I would spend lots of time cleaning and polishing my precious bike. We would congregate at one of our homes and break out the rags, chrome polish, spoke keys and grease for the wheel bearings. Then we would head for some distant place (usually no more than 10 miles away) with packed lunches that our mums had prepared for us. I do not remember ever feeling more liberated and exhilarated than I did when I had my own bike and knew how to take care of it. I could really make the bike shine, but when I took it out on the road I would always check the little pouch under the seat for one thing. I did not look for chrome polish or wheel bearing grease. I looked for the puncture repair kit. Whenever I happened to run over a nail and puncture a tire it made no difference how shiny and pretty the bike looked; I was stuck. I could sit by the side of the road and clean the bike, but that would be foolish. All the polishing in the world will not mend a flat tire. It is always better to ride on a clean shiny bike, but the root cause of my problem was a hole in one of my tires, and I was not going anywhere without a puncture repair kit. In any crisis it is important that we correctly identify the root cause of the problem and not waste time attacking incidental problems. We must hit the right nail on the head.

As we consider the threat to the integrity of the Lord's Church, we must make sure that we are addressing the root cause and not just the symptoms. Is the root cause the use of instruments in worship, for example, or is it a lack of love for God's Word?

As we consider this crisis of faith in the Church we might be tempted to disregard the root causes of our problems because they just seem overwhelming. Denominationalism has become a way of religious life in our society and it seems that very few people have respect for the truth of God's Word. Can we really expect to change any of this? Like Don Quixote we get distracted by windmills simply because they are easy targets. If we want to hit the nail on the head, then we need to make sure we are hitting the right nail.

Recently our local news carried an announcement about an "openly gay, non-celibate priest" at Cornell University who was campaigning for legalizing gay marriage in New York State. Though I am tormented by such physical and spiritual perversion I have to remind myself that no one will be consigned to hell simply because he or she is homosexual. Those who are exposed to God's fiery judgment will suffer because they "do not know God or obey the gospel" as Paul tells us in 2 Thessalonians 1:8. He also describes them as those who "refused to love the truth and so be saved" (2:10).

If I had opportunity to talk to this openly gay, non-celibate priest, my concern for him should be that he has not obeyed the gospel because he does not love the truth. His position on homosexuality is a symptom of such a problem, but it is not the root cause. Only if he can be persuaded to love the truth will he be able to see the error of his ways. It is also true that the most outwardly righteous person in the world will go to hell if he or she does not love the truth. My first reaction is to confront the homosexual about his behavior, but we all begin our walk of faith with an attitude change before any change of behavior occurs. It seems to be a more daunting task to try to change the attitude of a person who has embraced such deviant behavior than to change the behavior itself. So we attack his sexuality instead of his lack of faith.

My experience with church splits has taught me to try to focus on root causes and not to go attacking windmills. The doctrine that I am set to defend is the doctrine of Christ, which encompasses the doctrine of salvation in Christ, and the twin doctrine of the Church of Christ. There are problems with all sorts of doctrinal error in the world today, but much of it I would consider to be doctrine that is incidental to the doctrine of Christ. The root cause of problems in the brotherhood is not a love of instruments or of women in leadership, etc. The problems that hurt the Church arise from a lack of love for the truth. We are talking specifically about a lack of love for the truth about the Church. If someone promotes the use of instruments in worship, I see that as a symptom that all is not right with the spiritual health of this person. He, or she, simply does not love the truth. It may well be that this person's relationship with the truth is stunted because they have not yet heard the truth. This person may well repent if they are given an opportunity to hear the truth.

If a doctor sees a man double over with a pain in his stomach he does not immediately write out a death certificate. He regards the visual evidence as a symptom of some unseen problem. He investigates to find the root cause of the pain and applies himself, to the best of his ability, to bringing that person back to good health. That is how you cure the pain. Any doctor who signs a death certificate has to state the cause of death. If a person dies of stomach cancer he will not say the cause of death was stomach pain, he will say it was stomach cancer.

This work deals with teachings about the Church as it relates to salvation. How a person behaves once they have become a Christian is a vital topic, but we will not be going into detail about that. Instead we will focus on the aspect of becoming a Christian, which necessarily involves those who are already Christians reaching out to save others. Jesus sent His disciples into the world to make more disciples. In the first part of what has been called the Great Commission,s Jesus emphasized that.

> *Go therefore and make disciples of all nations, baptizing*
> *them in the name of the Father and of the Son and of the Holy*
> *Spirit...*
>
> Matthew 28:19

The final part of the command from Jesus lips was:

> *"...teaching them to observe all that I have commanded you."*
>
> Matthew 28:20

We need to be careful where we draw the line between what is required of a person to become a disciple and what is required to live the life of a disciple. Cornelius (Acts 10) might well have been judged as a man who was already doing everything he needed to do in God's sight, but he was not saved until he was baptized. Simon the sorcerer (Acts 8:9-22) serves as an example of one who, even after he was baptized, did not behave the way a Christian should behave. All of us know people who claim that they are good enough already without going to church. We have also heard those who claimed they were too bad to go to church. Both of those claims are false. The truth is that there is no one who is too good to be saved, neither is there anyone who is too bad to be saved. Conversion to Christ is a traumatic change for all of us but we need to be reminded of the difference between being saved and staying saved.

Also take note that much more could be said about the false teachings among the denominations. They have strayed far from scripture when it comes to soteriology (the study of salvation) by teaching that you do not have to be baptized to be saved. They have also corrupted the foundational teachings of ecclesiology (the nature of church) by encouraging the "church of your choice" mindset. When it comes to eschatology (the study of last things) the popular premillenial doctrine is completely anti-Christian. We will be focusing primarily on the connection between soteriology and ecclesiology. Another work may be needed to deal with the connection with eschatology.

The root cause of man's problem with God is that we take God lightly, rather than take Him at His word. One example in the area of ecclesiology will illustrate. Why have so many people become so comfortable with the idea that we can disparage the name Christian by taking some other name that says who we are better than Christian? Any time a person needs to find another name to identify his brand of Christianity, that person is not following Christ. I will go further and introduce the thought that tampering with God's identity by speaking our own words to define Him is nothing less than blasphemy. To blaspheme God's name is to take His name lightly, and if making up our own names for His holy people is not blasphemy then I don't know what is. How many new movements that have been started and named by men must arise before we get tired of trying to re-invent the wheel? The Lord got the Church right the first time.

I do not believe that the Lord told Mohammed to start another movement and call members Muslims because God's original movement had failed. Yet that is exactly what Muslims believe by the millions.

I do not believe that the Lord told Joseph Smith to start another movement and call members Mormons because His original movement had failed, but that is exactly what Mormons believe by the millions.

I do not believe that God told Charles Taze Russell to start what we now know as Jehovah's Witnesses or that He told any of them to make sure they separated themselves, by name, from other Christians. That is exactly what Jehovah Witnesses believe by the millions.

I do not believe God has called any of the so-called Christian denominations to distinguish themselves from His original movement, but that is what members of denominational movements believe by the millions. If God had done so that would have to mean that His original movement had indeed failed. His original movement is the one, true Church that was purchased with the blood of His Son. It is the Kingdom of His beloved Son. It will never fail. The only failure throughout history has been the failure of those who claim allegiance to the King but who do not take Him at His word.

> *You were unmindful of the Rock that bore you,*
> *and you forgot the God who gave you birth.*
> Deuteronomy 32:18

Picture a scene in hell where inmates are languishing in torment and asking each other, "What are you in here for?" I do not believe there will be any such conversations in hell. If we can imagine for a moment that there was, however, there will not be anyone answering the question, "What are you in here for?" with "I used an instrument in worship" or "I encouraged women to preach and teach". There will not be anyone who says they are in hell because they were homosexual and not even any person who says they are there because they were not baptized. If the question could be asked of every single inhabitant of hell, there would be only one answer from all of them:

"I did not love the truth enough to be saved."

We are all imperfect and can remember times when we have hammered our own thumbs instead of the nail. It hurts. The Lord's Church is often wounded because we pound each other when we should be pounding Satan. I have used two examples of issues that have divided us; instruments in worship and women in leadership. We must not take these things lightly but we must not think that these things define the Church. If we get the truth about the Church and salvation right first we will not go far wrong on these other issues.

> *But whatever gain I had, I counted as loss for the sake of*
> *Christ. Indeed, I count everything as loss because of the*
> *surpassing worth of knowing Christ Jesus my Lord. For his*
> *sake I have suffered the loss of all things and count them as*
> *rubbish, in order that I may gain Christ and be found in him,*
> *not having a righteousness of my own that comes from the law,*

but that which comes through faith in Christ, the righteousness
from God that depends on faith—that I may know him and
the power of his resurrection, and may share his sufferings,
becoming like him in his death, that by any means possible
I may attain the resurrection from the dead. Not that I have
already obtained this or am already perfect, but I press on to
make it my own, because Christ Jesus has made me his own.
Brothers, I do not consider that I have made it my own. But one
thing I do: forgetting what lies behind and straining forward
to what lies ahead, I press on toward the goal for the prize of
the upward call of God in Christ Jesus. Let those of us who are
mature think this way, and if in anything you think otherwise,
God will reveal that also to you.
Only let us hold true to what we have attained.

Philippians 3:7-16

Questions for Chapter Four

1. Paul told the Corinthians that he determined to *know nothing among them except Christ and Him crucified* (1 Corinthians 2:2). In his letter to them, however, he does discuss issues of morality and faithfulness. Why did he not deal with these things when he was with them? Why is he tackling them now?

2. Discuss the point made about the difference in changing a person's attitude and changing behavior. Do you ever modify your behavior without changing your attitude? Is it possible to change your attitude and not change your behavior?

3. Do you feel adequately acquainted with popular denominational teachings such as premillanialism? How does this doctrine affect the foundational teaching of Christ and Him crucified?

5. If a person loves the truth does that mean he or she does not sin? Is loving the truth the same thing as *walking in the light?* (1 John 1:7) Is it possible for a person to be saved and yet not love the truth enough to be saved? Is it possible for a person to be lost who loves the truth enough to be saved?

6. When we speak of one true Church, does that mean a church where every member is flawless in their understanding and obedience of all biblical teaching?

7. What is the difference between:
    a. Being saved by the power of the gospel (Romans 1:16,17) and
    b. Living in step with the truth of the gospel (Galatians 2:14)?

Chapter Five

GRACE ON LAYAWAY

Hope deferred makes the heart sick,
but a desire fulfilled is a tree of life.
Proverbs 13:12

When people doubt that God's word can reach its target, someone has to build a bridge to help God out. We go beyond God's word because we cannot see how God's word will go far enough. Quite simply, we sometimes forget what trust in the Lord is really all about. When that happens we tend to invent doctrines that do not meet the biblical criteria for faith (Romans 10:17). One popular idea has grace patiently waiting for the opportunity to save everyone at the final judgment. True faith recognizes that grace is unmerited favor that delivers power into the lives of faithful people. It is not an excuse to ignore God's commands and hope for the best when we die.

Abraham tried building a bridge or two before he finally learned to trust God's word. When he was a childless man waiting for the child of promise, he suggested to God that Eliezer would have to be the heir of his house (Genesis 15:1-5). Later on, when God named ninety year old Sarah as the mother of the promised child, Abraham was amused (Genesis 17:15-17). He suggested that Ishmael, his son by Hagar, would be a better way to go. After Sarah had given birth to Isaac, however, Abraham trusted God, even when God asked him to sacrifice Isaac (Genesis 22:1,2). If I had been Abraham hearing those words from God I would have been looking for a bridge to anywhere other than Mount Moriah. Surely that command was a rock too big? The Hebrew writer tells us that Abraham did indulge in his own reasoning as to how Isaac could be offered as a burnt offering and still fulfill God's promise to be the one to produce covenant offspring. The Bible tells us that Abraham concluded...

> *"...that God was able even to raise him from the dead, from which, figuratively speaking, he did receive him back."*
>
> Hebrew 11:19

Abraham never doubted that God meant what He said. To speculate on how God might go about fulfilling the awesome demands of His word is one thing. To speculate on how we can go about making His word less demanding is a very different thing. The very essence of faith is trusting that if God demands anything of us He will absolutely supply whatever is needed to get the job done, whether I see it or not. What do you do with a rock that is in your path that is too big to move? One solution is to leave it alone and go around it. Another common sense approach is to break it into smaller pieces that are more manageable. There are many who are more than willing to do that. As a result God's word has been perverted, and the Church has been divided. Almighty God has become a God of unlimited grace but diminished power. He has the will to love and save everyone but lacks the resources to carry it out. What He lacks in power He makes up for in grace.

Unfortunately, many now count on grace to be a feature of final judgment instead of something to be enjoyed now, God's trump card that He is holding till after the game is over. The further away we drift from the concept of one true church in the world today, the more we have to hope that God will just sort it all out when the world comes to an end. If the rock is too big and we have broken it down into many smaller, more manageable rocks, we just rejoice that we will see His mercy at judgment. This philosophy seems very much like what Paul warns the Church in Rome about:

"What shall we say then? Are we to continue in sin that grace may abound?"

Romans 6:1

According to this way of thinking, a smart person should spend a lifetime crawling to his or her destination alongside the railroad track, not expecting to actually board the train until he or she has arrived at the destination! Hear what the apostle Paul has to say on this matter:

Working together with him, then, we appeal to you not to receive the grace of God in vain. For he says,
"In a favorable time I listened to you,
and in a day of salvation I have helped you."
Behold, now is the favorable time; behold, now is the day of salvation.

2 Corinthians 6:1,2

The Word of God proclaims that grace and power come together, in the here and now, when God's people proclaim the gospel.

And with great power the apostles were giving their testimony to the resurrection of the Lord Jesus, and great grace was upon them all.

Acts 4:33

But he said to me, "My grace is sufficient for you, for my power is made perfect in weakness." Therefore I will boast all the more gladly of my weaknesses, so that the power of Christ may rest upon me.

2 Corinthians 12:9

> *Of this gospel I was made a minister according to the gift of*
> *God's grace, which was given me by the working of his power.*
>   Ephesians 3:7

What is this grace and power in aid of? It is all about the building up of the Church through the saving of souls. The Lord promised that the grace and the power to do just that would never fail His Church. But make no mistake: when He comes there will be no more grace for the lost and no more walking by faith for the saved.

Questions for Chapter Five

1. Do you associate grace with strength or with weakness? Does God want us to be helpless? Is grace a substitute for power?

2. Do you treat grace as a last resort? Do you know anyone who does? Will there be any more grace for an individual after that person dies than there is while that person is alive?

3. Was God's grace active in the account of Abraham sacrificing his son Isaac?

4. How does God's grace apply to a person who is dying in the desert who wants to be saved?

5. How does God's grace apply to someone who only knows denominational believers and has not been properly baptized?

6. How did God's grace apply to Jesus when He asked His Father if the cup could pass from him? (Matthew 26:39)

7. The apostle Paul was helpless and starving in the city of Damascus but he may as well have been in the desert. He could not go back to being a champion of the Jews and no Christian wanted any part of him. How did God's grace apply to Paul? (Acts 9:8-18)

Chapter Six

FIGHT, FLIGHT OR DELIGHT?

Let's be honest, sharing our faith can be a bit daunting. There is always the fear of getting in over our heads and ending up being embarrassed, not to mention rejected. Sometimes we just get tired of being on the other side of these theological discussions. If we are contending for the faith with family and friends it can get discouraging. The first disciples of Christ found themselves contending for the faith with the rulers and authorities of their day. Their very lives were forfeit, yet we read of examples where they did not back down. Even those who threatened them were amazed.

> *Now when they saw the boldness of Peter and John, and perceived that they were uneducated, common men, they were astonished. And they recognized that they had been with Jesus.*
> Acts 4:13

What they were not quite getting was the fact that not only had they been with Jesus, He was still with them! They had received the Spirit of Christ, as all Christians do when they obey the gospel. Christ is with us, and never more so than when we are contending for the faith.

It is true that baptism is required in order for a person to be saved and it is true that salvation and church membership are one and the same thing. Most of our religious friends reject both those truths, so we need the courage to contend with them for the faith. We might be tempted to tread softly and not ask the hard questions. When we have opportunity to talk about these teachings we must be aware that denominational members often use biblical words and phrases without a correct understanding of what those words actually mean. It is not enough to accept people in fellowship because they can quote the right words. We need to make sure they have the right understanding. I once witnessed a look of horror on the face of a mother when her daughter told her we had been studying about baptism by immersion. "You have been studying about what?" she asked three times and three times we answered her "Baptism by immersion." She finally relaxed and said with great relief, "I thought you were talking about being baptized by a Martian!"

Consider the fact that, to a great many people, the phrase "baptized into Christ" does not necessarily mean what it means in the Bible. Members of denominations typically believe they were saved before they were baptized. Some will even quote Romans 6:1-4 about being buried with Christ in baptism in order to be raised with Him without realizing that would have to mean that they were buried alive. It is crucial that we make sure that people are following biblical teachings of salvation instead of following traditions of men. For example, what if a person was baptized in a Baptist church with the words, "I baptize you in the name of Jesus Christ" Will that person be saved?

Christians are considered hypocritical if they only go through the motions and we should hold each other accountable when we simply mouth the words of faith but do not have our hearts in it. Isn't it at least as important to make sure that when a person obeys the gospel they are not just mouthing words? I believe we need to make sure that we ask the probing questions that genuinely test those spirits. For example, when Paul was concerned about the disciples at Ephesus who had been taught by Apollos, he asked them the question that goes to the heart of the matter, "Did you receive the Spirit when you believed?" (Acts 19:2) Paul tested the spirits and ended up baptizing those people "In the name of the Lord Jesus" (Acts 19:5). Does that mean he actually mouthed those words when those people were baptized or does it mean that he brought them to the correct understanding about being baptized into Christ? It is easy to become fixated on ending every prayer with the words, "In Jesus' name", but does that mean we have actually prayed in Jesus name? Words are extremely important, but shouldn't the emphasis be on what is going on in the mind? I heard a comedian describe a situation where a person was "mouthing off" and he asked this person, "Does your mind know what your mouth is saying?" I think of the outrageous things I sometimes hear coming from the mouths of young people in my daily work as a school bus driver. It is a good question for all of us to think about when we teach and when we pray and when we sing.

An extension of this discussion is the question of whether to baptize in the name of the Father, the Son and the Holy Spirit as Jesus describes in Matthew 28:18-20. Is it wrong to baptize only in the name of Jesus? The main concern should be that, unless the person has the correct understanding, they have not been baptized properly regardless of what words are pronounced at that moment. The words are not some sort of magical incantation. Paul baptized the Ephesian disciples again because they had not been taught about the Holy Spirit. They had been baptized in the name of the Father and of the Son, but not in the name of the Holy Spirit. When Paul baptized them in the name of the Lord he had put that right and satisfied the Lord's instructions from Matthew 28:18-20. The correct words need to be spoken *before* a person decides to be baptized if we are to have confidence in the baptism. The point also cannot be overlooked that Paul was not willing to let these people slide. He would rather risk offending them to get the job done right than to see them slide into hell.

Too often we approach denominational friends as though they are spiritual neophytes. That means that we cannot address sensitive issues with them in a direct way. Young children who are curious about where babies come from are usually told something like "Mommy and Daddy fell in love". They may even get the "Mommy and Daddy lay down together" explanation. Most children will venture as far as saying that kissing does the trick. To be sure love and kissing are involved, but if you are serious about producing offspring there is something else that is required, and it is not a stork.

It would be extraordinarily crass to give a very young child an explicit sex education lesson, so we more or less deliberately keep them in the dark till they are ready. That usually amounts to letting them find out for themselves. Why do we do that to our denominational friends? When it comes to sexual reproduction it is almost impossible to prevent human beings from figuring out the facts of life. When it comes to the facts of eternal life, however, I am convinced that it is asking too much to expect a person to figure it out for themselves. God certainly did not expect us to figure it out for ourselves. God sent His Son and His Spirit and His people into the world to teach the world about His offer of eternal life.

In dealing with the question "How am I saved?" the most popular answer is "Make Jesus your personal Lord and Savior." This statement is a valid statement, but how do you actually make Jesus your lord and savior? A restaurant waiter may just as well place empty dishes on your table and say, "Enjoy your meal!" Unfortunately, the standard answer from those who say you must make Jesus your lord and savior is that you must pray Him into your heart. That is like telling a young child that falling in love actually produces a baby. A majority of people in our world have embraced this kind of thinking, but when it comes to the truth about baptism in regard to salvation, very few people want to go there. As a result, huge numbers of souls have an incomplete understanding of how to be saved. If they have an incomplete understanding about salvation, then they are not saved. When they do look for an explanation of baptism they are told by their peers that baptism is something you do *after* you are saved. That is biblically untenable. Christians are called to *contend for the faith that was once for all delivered to the saints.* (Jude 3) and that means standing firm on the *one Lord, one faith and one baptism* (Ephesians 4:5). This responsibility is often side-stepped because of fear.

Psychiatrists tell us that human beings respond to fear in one of two ways; they either fight or run, and this is called the "Fight or Flight Response". What distinguished early Christians was their ability to respond to fear in a totally new dimension. In the book of Acts we read about the apostles being beaten and threatened because of their preaching about Jesus. What will their response be? Will it be *fight* or *flight*?

> *...and when they had called in the apostles, they beat them and charged them not to speak in the name of Jesus, and let them go. Then they left the presence of the council, rejoicing that they were counted worthy to suffer dishonor for the name.*
>
> Acts 5:40,41

Delight! Such is the response of people of faith when the religious elite bear down on them telling them that their faith is unacceptable. They do not call for an armed revolution; neither do they flee from the city, nor is there any hint of submission. I believe that the Holy Spirit can be likened, in one of its functions, to the function of adrenaline in the human body. The body's ability to produce adrenaline comes into play in the fight or flight response. A burst of adrenaline may enable a pregnant wife to lift a car that has fallen off the jack and pinned her husband. It may also enable the runner who is being chased by a bear to squeeze that extra bit of speed and endurance out of his heart and legs.

When Peter was told that he had to stop preaching about Jesus he did not back down. The fourth chapter of Acts begins with the account of Peter and John being arrested for their preaching. Peter had healed a lame beggar on the way to the temple and this frightened the Jewish leaders into the fight response. When they asked by what authority he had done this, Peter answered that it was by the power of Jesus' name and went on to proclaim that there is no other name given to man under heaven by which we must be saved (Acts 4:12). The Jewish rulers were impressed by the courage of Peter and John (Acts 4:13). The explanation for their boldness is found in the description of how Peter began his response.

> *Then Peter, filled with the Holy Spirit, said to them, "Rulers of the people and elders..."*
>
> Acts 4:8

Peter was filled with the Holy Spirit, which seems to be the spiritual equivalent of experiencing an adrenaline rush. There was no fight and no flight; only the delight of contending for the faith. This was a joy that overflowed when the Jewish rulers backed down and released them. You can almost hear Peter saying, "I didn't know I had it in me!" Their joy did not come from being persecuted, it came from being faithful. There is no faith without testing and none of us know just how fast we can run until we come face to face with a bear.

Unfortunately, this dimension of faith is being lost and growing numbers of people are afraid to test the spirits. People who do not have the Spirit of God learn quickly not to put other spirits to the test. The modern approach is to fellowship first and test the spirits later. Why are we afraid to ask those who believe they are saved if they have been properly baptized? It is because we know that if we do we risk alienating them. It seems preferable to many to believe that God's love covers everything and is able to produce offspring spontaneously. We don't actually have to do anything. As a result many people who have been taught that baptism and church membership is a matter of choice remain lost. Jesus, however, said that if we love him we will do what He asks.

> *If you love me, you will keep my commandments.*
> John 14:15

When Paul arrived at Ephesus and heard the report from Priscilla and Aquila, he took action. Apollos had been preaching in Ephesus and

Priscilla and Aquila had taken him aside to correct his understanding about baptism. This account is recorded in some detail in Acts 18:24-19:7. As a result Paul tested the spirits of some twelve disciples who had been taught and baptized. From the way Paul questioned them we find that he wanted to see if they had followed the teaching of Apollos. When he confirmed that they had done so he baptized them again. How many people today would care enough to make sure that those men were properly baptized? It is clear that it was very important to Paul, but a great many church members today will argue that it does not make any difference whether you understand all the facts before you are baptized. In other words the truth about receiving the Spirit when you are baptized is just an incidental detail. It is a strong warning that we have drifted doctrinally when we can sell the Holy Spirit so cheaply, as though it is nothing but a small bonus thrown in to sweeten the deal. Just toss it in the bag and they will find it eventually. We in churches of Christ may have gone too far in stressing that baptism is for the remission of sins and not putting enough emphasis on the receiving of the Spirit. Surely we understand why God wants our sins washed away? It is so He can live in us. The gospel is all about God living in us. The indwelling of the Holy Spirit is God's promise according to Peter in Acts 2:38.

1. Repent
2. Be baptized
3. Receive remission of sins
4. Receive indwelling of the Spirit

Apollos only taught up to the third point of this promise and that meant that those he taught did not have the Spirit. That means they did not belong to Christ and were not sons of God. (Romans 8:9-14). Paul was not willing to leave them without being properly baptized. They had not been adequately taught about baptism and, as a result, they had not been properly baptized. How many people do you know who need someone like Paul to care enough about the gospel to make sure they are properly baptized?

Too many are responding in the fight or flight mode when it comes to saving souls. They see a rock that is too big to move when it comes to confronting the traditions of men that have become so accepted. We need to recover the delight of contending for the faith. To contend for the faith is to contend with Satan for those souls who are lost.

So, what about the person who was baptized in a Baptist church with the words, "I baptize you in the name of Jesus Christ."? The only biblical model we have for the one baptism is where the person being baptized and the person doing the baptizing are in agreement with the Bible about what the one baptism is. Our example of a Baptist baptism cannot be found in the Bible. Search the scriptures beginning with the commands of Jesus and continuing with how the Apostles taught and practiced baptism. It all follows the pattern of faithful followers properly baptizing lost souls, which means baptizing them with the correct understanding.

Matthew 28:18-20	Apostles are to go, baptize, and teach.
Acts 2:38	Peter preaches baptism to receive the Spirit.
Acts 2:41	Those who received his word are baptized.
Acts 8:12	Phillip preaches, Samaritans baptized.
Acts 8:35-38	Phillip preaches Christ, Ethiopian baptized.
Acts 9:17,18	Ananias sent to Saul so that Saul can (1) see and (2) be filled with Spirit. Saul (1) regains sight and (2) is baptized.
Acts 10	Peter sent to tell Cornelius words by which he will be saved (Acts 11:14). Cornelius baptized (Acts 10:47,48)
Acts 16:14,15	The Lord opens Lydia's heart to hear what was said by Paul and she was baptized.
Acts 19:1-5	Ephesian disciples baptized again by Paul after he corrected their understanding about baptism.

In these examples we see the connection between water baptism and receiving the Spirit. We also see the connection between baptism and preaching. All this reinforces the fact that true baptism is required for salvation (Mark 16:15,16; 1 Peter 3:21) and true baptism demands true preaching.

Questions for Chapter Six

1. On a scale of 1-10 how much does fear prevent you from sharing your faith?

2. Is contending for the faith still necessary? Is it a good thing?

3. Can a person be a true witness to Christ without mentioning His name?

4. Why are we more comfortable talking about politics than talking about Jesus and His Church?

5. Have you ever felt the joy of overcoming your fear of talking about Jesus and His Church?

6. Which is the greater obstacle to true faith in the U.S.A right now?
    a. Progressive liberals in the government who want to eliminate all traces of Christianity.
    b. Traditions of men and counterfeit churches masquerading as God's representatives.

7. Which do you fear most?
    a. Telling the government you are a Christian.
    b. Telling those who belong to the "faith only" institution of men that they are not Christians.

Chapter Seven

KEEPING THE DREAM ALIVE

When Jesus promised to build His church He said He would build it "upon this rock" (Matthew 16:16-18). Peter had confessed that Christ was the Son of God and Jesus knew that He could now set his face to the cross (Matthew 16:21). Where there are those who confess Christ as Lord you will find Christ building His church upon their faith. That work began on the day of Pentecost following the resurrection of Jesus Christ (Acts 2).

If we track this idea of the rock prophetically, however, we run square into the rock that troubled Nebuchadnezzar in a dream he had. We read about this dream in Daniel 2. Was this dream beyond the reach of mankind? Well, if you were one of those whom Nebuchadnezzar called to interpret the dream for him it most definitely was an impossible dream because he refused to tell them what the dream was about. He demanded that they first tell him what he had dreamed and then they could tell him what the dream meant. If they could not comply with his wishes then they would be torn limb from limb and their houses would be laid in ruins. (Daniel 2:1-12). They insisted that he first tell them what the dream was so that they could then exercise their abilities. He, in turn, accused them of conspiring to lie to him till the times changed (Daniel 2:9). They complained that the king asked too much and that only "the gods whose dwelling is not with the flesh" could do such a thing (Daniel 2:11). For all of their boasting about supernatural abilities the magicians, enchanters and sorcerers were helpless. This was an impossible dream, a rock too big. And yet Nebuchadnezzar believed it could be done.

Nebuchadnezzar, true to his word, sent out a decree that all the wise men of Babylon be destroyed. Daniel was among that class of citizenry and he enquired as to the reason for the decree. When he heard the explanation he asked for an audience with the king so that he could show the interpretation of the dream to the king. Like the two Marys who went to the tomb of Jesus not knowing how they would move the rock from the tomb, Daniel committed himself to interpreting the impossible dream not knowing how he would succeed. He made sure to ask for the prayers of his three friends in this matter as they were all involved in this decree.

That night God revealed the mystery to Daniel. The rest, as they say, is history. Daniel did indeed interpret the impossible dream to Nebuchadnezzar after telling him what the dream was about. The explanation involved a sequence of four kingdoms, beginning with Nebuchadnezzar's kingdom. We learn from Daniel that the second kingdom was the Medo-Persian kingdom (Daniel 5:28) and the third would be the kingdom of Greece (Daniel 8:21). The dream culminated with an event which was to occur in the days of the fourth kingdom, which is the only kingdom not named in the prophecies of Daniel. We now know that this kingdom was Rome and Daniel has this to say about Rome:

And in the days of those kings the God of heaven will set up a kingdom that shall never be destroyed, nor shall the kingdom be left to another people. It shall break in pieces all these kingdoms and bring them to an end, and it shall stand forever, just as you saw that a stone was cut from a mountain by no human hand, and that it broke in pieces the iron, the bronze, the clay, the silver, and the gold. A great God has made known to the king what shall be after this. The dream is certain, and its interpretation sure."

Daniel 2:44,45

This is the first of several references to the kingdom of God in the book of Daniel. The message is unmistakable; God planned on establishing His kingdom on earth and He had a definite timetable that He was working to. If there was one word to describe this kingdom it would be "everlasting." Those who thought Nebuchadnezzar's dream to be an impossible dream to interpret hoped to defer their involvement till there was a change of times. The magicians just wanted to wait this one out till they could see what exactly was going to happen, but not Daniel. He jumped right into the providence of God with both feet. He did not try to keep one foot in man's world and one in God's world. Those of us living today have the benefit of hindsight to appreciate Daniel's foresight. The apostle Paul lived in the days when Daniel's dream was being fulfilled and he rejoiced that Christians could see these things written in the scriptures.

For whatever was written in former days was written for our instruction, that through endurance and through the encouragement of the Scriptures we might have hope.

Romans 15:4

The scriptures speak of the kingdom of God as a rock that smashes all the other kingdoms of the world. Daniel prophesied it would outlive all earthly kingdoms (Daniel 2:44) and Jesus promised that the gates of Hades would not prevail against this kingdom (Matthew 16:18). He referred to it as His Church and in Ephesians 3:10,11 Paul explains that the Church fulfills the eternal purpose of God.

Concerning this one true everlasting kingdom, many among us prefer to wait it out to see what happens next. What God asks of us seems to be too much for mortal men to comply with. That is because so many still have one foot in man's world when it comes to trusting

God's Word. We want God's everlasting kingdom to be like any institution of men, but the gates of Hades will prevail against any institution of men.

When Jesus told the apostles that they would be His witnesses in the entire world, they obeyed and it was so. They were to be emissaries of the Kingdom of Christ.

> *And Jesus came and said to them, "All authority in heaven and on earth has been given to me. Go therefore and make disciples of all nations, baptizing them in the name of the Father and of the Son and of the Holy Spirit, teaching them to observe all that I have commanded you. And behold, I am with you always, to the end of the age."*
>
> Matthew 28:18-20

If we are true to the scriptures then we must acknowledge that there are two commands in regard to baptism. We spend a lot of time emphasizing the command to be baptized (Acts 2:38) and so we should; biblical teaching about the salvation of a sinner demands that the sinner must be baptized to be saved. But that was not the first command that involves baptism. The first command is the one mentioned above from the lips of Jesus Himself when He sent the apostles into the world to make disciples of all nations. The first command involving baptism is the command to go and baptize. If Jesus had returned to Heaven immediately after His resurrection and never commanded the apostles to go into the world to baptize and teach lost sinners, then we could logically conclude that the whole world was automatically saved when Jesus came out of that tomb. The fact that Jesus did give what we call "the great commission" to the apostles proves that there is a specific job to be done by a specific people for a specific purpose. The mechanism of salvation was the process whereby disciples of Christ actively sought to make other disciples of Christ by baptizing and teaching them.

On the day of Pentecost, almost 2000 years ago, the rock that Daniel had seen in his dream became a reality on earth. The rock that was the kingdom of God was established by Jesus Christ on earth. The rock that was to smash all other rocks began doing just that. Jerusalem was the first to encounter the kingdom of Christ. After hearing the gospel delivered by Peter, 3000 Jews were baptized into Christ. In the days that followed, God's kingdom on earth grew mighty in word and deed. Then the Word went out into Samaria as those who became disciples also sought to make disciples by baptizing and teaching others. Within one generation the entire world had come under the power of the Lord Jesus Christ through the ministry of His Church (Romans 10:18; Colossians 1:6,23).

Given this level of success, it is hard to imagine that any Christian of that day ever stopped to ponder the "what if" questions that trouble us today. If God is approached faithfully He will provide whatever is needed in order for a soul to be saved. In fact my faith must demand that He provides the time and the materials necessary for the baptism of any sinner who wants to be saved. That includes the right person to do the baptizing and the water. If God says we must be born of water and the Spirit in order to see the kingdom of Heaven, then we must demand that God does not allow a person to be caught in a state of believing and yet being denied access to water for baptism. The rub is that I must also accept that I am one of those whom God has provided for the purpose of saving souls. Those who are in agreement with God about salvation are called to save others. The Church is God's rock of salvation and if you are a member you are living the dream of God.

Here is where we can all get caught up between heaven and earth, because heaven and earth come together in the ministry of Christ.

May you be strengthened with all power, according to his glorious might, for all endurance and patience with joy, giving thanks to the Father, who has qualified you to share in the inheritance of the saints in light. He has delivered us from the domain of darkness and transferred us to the kingdom of his beloved Son, in whom we have redemption, the forgiveness of sins. He is the image of the invisible God, the firstborn of all creation. For by him all things were created, in heaven and on earth, visible and invisible, whether thrones or dominions or rulers or authorities—all things were created through him and for him. And he is before all things, and in him all things hold together. And he is the head of the body, the church. He is the beginning, the firstborn from the dead, that in everything he might be preeminent. For in him all the fullness of God was pleased to dwell, and through him to reconcile to himself all things, whether on earth or in heaven, making peace by the blood of his cross.

Colossians 1:11-20

Jesus commissioned faithful people to do the work of seeking and saving the lost. They were to do it by going to where the lost were and making disciples of them. They were to do it by baptizing them and they were to do it by teaching them to observe all things that Jesus had commanded them. God's everlasting Kingdom had come to earth and it was unstoppable. People from all tongues and tribes and nations were rescued from darkness to walk in the light.

Then the seventh angel blew his trumpet, and there were loud voices in heaven, saying, "The kingdom of the world has become the kingdom of our Lord and of his Christ, and he shall reign forever and ever."

Revelation 11:15

Revelation 12 shows a vision of a woman that compares with a dream that Joseph had dreamed long ago (Genesis 37:9-11). Joseph dreamed that the sun, moon and stars bowed down to him. The interpretation was that his mother, father and brothers would serve him, and that did come to pass. This family was the nucleus of the Hebrew nation as represented by the sun, moon and stars.

And a great sign appeared in heaven: a woman clothed with

*the sun, with the moon under her feet, and on her head a crown of
twelve stars. She was pregnant and was crying out in birth pains
and the agony of giving birth. And another sign appeared in heaven:
behold, a great red dragon, with seven heads and ten horns, and on
his heads seven diadems. His tail swept down a third of the stars of
heaven and cast them to the earth. And the dragon stood before the
woman who was about to give birth, so that when she bore her child
he might devour it. She gave birth to a male child, one who is to rule
all the nations with a rod of iron, but her child was caught up to
God and to his throne,*

Revelation 12:1-5

The sun, moon and stars in Joseph's dream represented the family of
Jacob which was to become the nation of Israel. The woman in Revelation
12, who was clothed with the sun, moon and stars, is the Israel of God which
was to become the Church. The son who was born to this woman was to rule
the nations with a rod of iron. The son is Jesus, and He was taken up into
Heaven as Satan tried to destroy Him. Having lost that battle, Satan was cast
out of Heaven and down to earth where he tried to destroy the woman, who
represents the Church (Revelation 12:13-16). He was unsuccessful once
again so he went off to make war with the rest of her offspring, Christians
(12:17). The true Church will never be overcome by the gates of Hades, but
Satan can still pick off those members who wander away from the truth.
He prowls around like a roaring lion seeking whom he may devour (1 Peter
5:8). Those who wish to overcome Satan must do so by the blood of the
lamb and the word of their testimony.

*And I heard a loud voice in heaven, saying, "Now the salvation
and the power and the kingdom of our God and the authority of his
Christ have come, for the accuser of our brothers has been thrown
down, who accuses them day and night before our God. And they
have conquered him by the blood of the Lamb and by the word of
their testimony, for they loved not their lives even unto death.*

Revelation 12:10,11

The Kingdom has come. Satan could not stop it. No one can snatch a Christian out of the Fathers' hand (John 10:29) but any Christian can walk away. The one, true Church is still on earth but there are now many counterfeits. We must make sure we are walking according to the truth of the Bible and that we only fellowship with others who do the same. The dream of Joseph and Nebuchadnezzar is alive and well. Joseph's brothers ridiculed him because they thought his dreams were preposterous. "Here comes that dreamer" they said (Genesis 37:19). They still say that about those who believe what the Lord has to say about His one body, and one spirit, and one hope, and one Lord, and one faith, and one baptism, and one God and Father over all, and in all and through all (Ephesians 4:4-6). You will hear some celebrating "multi-faith" and "ecumenical" ministries that deny the Lord's command for one faith.

Do not accept the lie that kills the dream.

Questions for Chapter Seven

1. Why did God give the dream to Nebuchadnezzar instead of Daniel? (Daniel 2)

2. Why didn't God give Joseph's dream to all his family? (Genesis 37:9-11)

3. Is the Church the fulfillment of those dreams?

4. Did the dream say that the rock would smash other kingdoms to pieces or that it would be broken into pieces itself?

5. What does faith in God have to do with questions that begin with, "What if...?"

6. Are you waiting to see if the dream comes true before you commit yourself to the one true Church?

7. Why doesn't God speak directly to lost souls to tell them what to do?

Chapter Eight

PROCESSED CHRISTIANITY

King Agrippa, do you believe the prophets? I know that you believe." And Agrippa said to Paul, "In a short time would you persuade me to be a Christian?" And Paul said, "Whether short or long, I would to God that not only you but also all who hear me this day might become such as I am— except for these chains."

Acts 26:27-29

If you are reluctant to say that lost souls have to be baptized to be saved, but you cannot deny that baptism is linked with salvation, then the process doctrine is very attractive. This doctrine by definition is a bit vague but basically it says that a person has entered into the salvation process when that person believes. That is all well and good, but whenever I have heard anyone call on this doctrine, there has always been at least a strong suggestion that anyone in the process of salvation is actually saved. The process that begins with belief and ends with baptism is the process of entering into salvation, not the process of salvation itself. We need to distinguish between getting saved and staying saved.

Biological life provides us with a useful correlation for this discussion. There is a process for being born and a process for living. Even though a fetus is human life and it is wrong to abort human life, we do recognize that there is an actual event that launches human beings into the world where life is played out. Birth is the crux of life. We cannot take our place in the world if we have not taken our place in the womb in order to be born. The reverse is not the case, however. We can indeed take our place in the womb and yet never take our place in the world. The fetus is vulnerable to all manner of dangers that might prevent it from ever being born at all.

When a seed is planted, whether it is a biological seed or the spiritual seed of God's Word, we recognize that we now have potential life of one form or another. God's Word is the seed of spiritual, or eternal, life (1 Peter 1:23-25). I like to think that God views all human beings as potential eternal life. He sent His Son to save us all, because He loves us all (John 3:16) and He does not want anyone to perish (2 Peter 3:9). He obviously sees the potential in all of us. If a person is lost, there is always the possibility of being saved until the point of death. Something happens when a person hears the word of God. A process is initiated that is designed to bring a person into the kingdom of God and thus into eternal life. The process is complete when that person receives the Spirit of God. That is when we make the transfer from the darkness of the womb to the light of the Kingdom (1 Peter 2:9; Colossians 1:13).

Baptism is the crux of life in Christ. We cannot take our place in the kingdom of God if we have not gone through the process of being born again. Jesus said so when He described that process as being born of water and the spirit in John 3:3-5. The baptism that washes our sins away so that God can bestow His Spirit on us is water baptism carried out in the name of Jesus. If you have not come to that understanding then you are still in the womb and you need to get busy studying the scriptures, particularly the book of Acts. Being in that womb is no guarantee that you will take your place in the Kingdom of God. The spiritual birth process can be interrupted, just as in human life. Many are told to pray Jesus into their hearts once they believe and that they are saved at that point. Baptism is then tacked on to the process as something that is done after salvation. It is like some vestigial organ that once served a purpose but is now only for show. Let's be clear on this idea that a person can leave the womb and take his, or her, place in the kingdom of God before they are baptized. That is nothing less than spiritual abortion, because potential spiritual life is snatched prematurely from the womb.

Again, to lie about baptism is tantamount to spiritual abortion. Fortunately, the gestation period for the spiritual birth process is not fixed in scripture. The examples we read about all happen quickly. (Acts 2:37-41; 8:26-38; 10:42-48; 16:30-33) The apostle Paul stalled out for three days before he was baptized as he lay blind and hungry in Damascus. Once Ananias arrived, however, his words to Paul were, "And now why do you wait? Rise and be baptized and wash away your sins, calling on his name." (Acts 22:16).

There was always urgency about getting a person in the water for obvious, biblical reasons. If you are not too concerned with Bible reasoning, though, you will be comfortable simply getting a lost soul involved in the process.

If we accept that salvation, and by that I mean entering into salvation, is a process, then there is also this to consider. Isn't it true that condemnation must also be a process? The book of James gives us a process for sin:

> *But each person is tempted when he is lured and enticed by his*
> *own desire. Then desire when it has conceived gives birth to*
> *sin, and sin when it is fully grown brings forth death.*
> James 1:14,15

Is a person dead when he is tempted? He is being drawn into the process of death but is he dead? Notice that there is a point when death is experienced. There is temptation, then sin comes alive, then sin becomes full grown and it is not till this last stage that death enters the picture. Adam and Eve were told by God that they would die when they ate the forbidden fruit. They were tempted to eat the fruit and gave it some serious thought to the point where they did actually eat the fruit. When did death enter the picture? Was it when they were tempted? No, it was not. God actually banished them from the garden, and thus from the tree of life, after they had eaten the fruit of the tree of knowledge of good and evil. The fall of man can be viewed as a process, and we read about that process in Genesis 3. First they were tempted, then they yielded to the temptation and disobeyed God, then they felt guilty and hid from God, then God confronted them, then He punished them.

What about Jesus when He was tempted? Hebrews 4:15 tells us that Jesus was tempted in all points just as we are. Was He just as dead as though he was a sinner like you and me? No, obviously not, because He did not follow through with the temptation. In the same way we must not say that a person who is tempted to be a Christian is automatically a Christian. Consider the example of King Agrippa from the opening scripture in Acts 26:27-29. He was definitely being tempted by Paul's preaching but he was resisting the temptation. Any person must give it serious thought and decide if he, or she, wants to be born again by being baptized into Christ. Just as Satan encouraged Adam and Eve to take the step that actually brought death upon them, so he also encourages anyone who is tempted to be saved not to take the step that actually redeems them. If Adam and Eve had not eaten the forbidden fruit they would not have been separated from the tree of life. Up until the time when they ate the fruit they did not deserve to die. Up until the time a sinner is actually baptized they do not deserve to live.

Adam and Eve made the transition from being Garden dwellers to earth diggers as a direct result of an actual act of disobedience. Why is it so hard to accept that sinners make the transition from being earth diggers to Heaven dwellers as a result of one act of obedience?

Jesus of course is the Savior and He provided salvation for all by one act of obedience. He had prayed to His Father to take that cup from Him but God did not take it from Him. The Father needed more than the *willingness* of His Son to become a sacrifice. His Son had to actually die. If Jesus had successfully prayed His way back to Heaven, we would be without hope of Heaven.

The process took Jesus about thirty three years but it was that last day of his life that made the difference for you and me. Had God accepted Him back into Heaven the night before when He prayed in the garden, and asked to be spared that trial, we would be utterly lost forever. We could not be saved if He had not been incarnated, but we were not saved at His birth. He had to be resurrected from the dead in order for us to be saved, and for that to happen, He had to actually die. His incarnation was the preparation for His sacrifice, which He referred to as a baptism he had to undergo (Luke 12:50). We cannot be saved if we do not believe, but we are not saved when we believe. Belief is the preparation for our baptism. The one faith is all about believing that Jesus died for you and me so that we can have fellowship with God again. The one baptism is all about joining Jesus in His baptism. How can we ever feel that He is asking too much of us when He makes baptism the crux of salvation? Must we continually expect God to take that cup from us?

Questions for Chapter Eight

1. Some people can take a long time to make up their minds to be baptized. They may be eager to study and pray, and even come to church. They have been through all the Bible studies and can answer all the questions, but still hesitate to be baptized. Is such a person saved?

2. What should we be praying for while we wait for this person to be baptized?

3. Did Jesus have to die to be a sacrifice? Wasn't it enough to give up His home in Heaven and come to earth?

4. When Jesus washes our sins away, does He do it one sin at a time? Is it a process?

5. Did Jesus send Ananias to Paul to tell him he was saved or to tell him how to be saved? What would have happened to Paul if Ananias had refused to go?

6. The Bible was not available to most people for hundreds of years. Indeed it is still not universally available today. Those who were part of the first generation of Christians were saved without seeing any written document. Did God intend for the power of the gospel to shift from the people to the paper at some point? Can the printed word take the place of the implanted word? (James 1:21; 2 Corinthians 3:2-4)

Chapter Nine

THE THIRD PARTY

Does it matter who baptizes another person? If it can be argued that baptism is only between God and the one being baptized (I heard that very recently.) then there is no need for a third party at all. A person could quite properly baptize themselves, if that were the case. If it is true that the third party does not have to meet any particular qualifications, how are we to make sense of the examples of baptism in the Bible? Did God not care who baptized His Son? Could anyone in the crowd have baptized Jesus, perhaps even one of the Pharisees? Why didn't Jesus baptize himself? Why did God go to such lengths to get Peter into the home of Cornelius? Cornelius was a God-fearing man who seems to have been willing to do whatever God wanted him to do. It would seem to be a simple matter of speaking to him and telling him to get into the water, or perhaps one of the other members of his household could take care of it.

Most people are aware that there is this thing called baptism and that it has something to do with becoming a Christian. It is not a secret ritual that can only be understood by the initiated. The average atheist can probably give you as good an explanation of baptism as the average church-goer . Does that mean that the average atheist can baptize himself, or that he can get anyone, regardless of faith, to baptize him if he has a change of heart? It is hard to imagine that Cornelius was not already familiar with the Church and baptism. Yet God spoke directly to him and told him to send for Peter who would tell him "words by which you and your household shall be saved" (Acts 11:14). Why didn't God say the words to Cornelius Himself and cut out the middle man? It is hard for us to comprehend how much God desires to be with us, but in the gospel we learn that He achieved that in the flesh of Jesus Christ. Jesus went back to Heaven to pour out the spirit on all flesh (Acts 2:16,17). When the Spirit was poured out it came upon those twelve who were prepared and waiting according to the Lord's instructions (Luke 24:48,49). How are the rest of us to get it?

Jesus said the apostles were to be His witnesses in Jerusalem and Judea and Samaria and in the entire world (Acts 1:8). Witness is the key word because it speaks of someone who shares personal testimony of an experience with those who were not involved. In court a witness shares testimony with those who cannot be involved in an event which has already transpired. In the Kingdom of Christ a witness bears testimony to an event which is continuing to transpire and in which everyone is invited to participate. When people hear the gospel and obey it, they are baptized into Christ (Galatians 3:26-29). The event of the death, burial and resurrection of Jesus Christ, which transpired nearly 2000 years ago, continues to transpire every time a person is baptized (Romans 6:1-3). Living people get to re-live events in their past, but only Jesus Christ is capable of re-living His death, burial and resurrection. He promised to lay down His own life (John 10:15) but He did not hammer the nails into his own hands and feet. That action demanded a third party. When Cornelius called for Peter it was because he needed that third party who was authorized to help him lay his life down with Jesus. He needed a priest of God to prepare him to be a sacrifice. Accordingly, Peter went to Cornelius and baptized him.

Our question is, does the salvation of a soul require a third party or not, and if so, who is that third party to be? The biblical model does not allow for any random passerby to be called upon to baptize a sinner into Christ. It is a question of authority. A minister performing a wedding ceremony is called upon to pronounce a couple as being "man and wife" and he must prove that he has the authority to do so. He must officially sign the wedding certificate as authorized by the state in which the marriage occurs. Baptism that saves a sinner is baptism in the name of Jesus Christ (Acts 19:5). To say "I baptize you in the name of Jesus Christ is the same as saying "I baptize you by the authority of Jesus Christ."

Can a member of a denomination baptize by the authority of Christ if he does indeed acknowledge the basic fact of the gospel of Christ? Does it matter if he does not believe that baptism is for remission of sins to receive the Spirit? In other words, does it make sense that Jesus would authorize a person who changes His command, "He who believes and is baptized shall be saved" (Mark 16:16) into "He who believes shall be saved and then baptized"? How can anyone who is seeking true biblical understanding accept this proposition?

The scriptures definitely demand that a third party be involved in the baptism of a lost soul. The only biblical model we have, and beyond which we should not go, is the model that provides men who are authorized by Jesus for the work of baptizing others. That means that they are men who submit to the authority of Christ, which means they are obedient to His commands. When Jesus commanded His apostles to go into the world to make disciples of all nations,He prefaced His command with the following statement.

"All authority in Heaven and on Earth has been given to me…"
Matthew 28:18-20

Jesus was telling the apostles that He was authorizing them to carry out His bidding in the world. Later on Paul will remind the Thessalonians:

For you know what instructions we gave you through the Lord Jesus.
I Thessalonians 4:2

The apostles were faithful in carrying the teachings of Christ into the world; they also made sure that others could carry on that same work. Titus was one of those whom Paul trusted with the authority of Christ and to whom Paul wrote these words:

> *Declare these things; exhort and rebuke with all authority. Let no one disregard you.*
>
> Titus 2:15

Timothy was another man who was involved as a messenger of Christ and Paul makes sure that Timothy recruits other men who will also teach.

> *...and what you have heard from me in the presence of many witnesses entrust to faithful men who will be able to teach others also.*
>
> 2 Timothy 2:2

Men who are obedient to the gospel of Christ are authorized by the gospel of Christ to teach and baptize others. The best we can do, if we want a different model, is to come up with our speculative inventions that speak of the person who is on a desert island or some similar situation. If I convince myself that God has *another* way to save, apart from baptism, then it is easy to believe that those who teach the traditions of men for church doctrine are *another* third party. Nowhere in God's word will we find the authorization for the Church to outsource its duties to foreigners, even if they seem to be better at those duties than we are. Evangelistic zeal is a wonderful attribute but, while we are counting conversions, it is important to make sure conversions actually count with the Lord. We can get it right, and we must get it right. It is not good enough to pretend that those who teach that baptism is not necessary are close enough. There is no excuse for ignoring that person who has attended your church for years who was baptized as a Baptist. You and I have a responsibility to tell the truth, not just think it.

Once again I say that if you ask me about the dying man who wants to be saved but who is stranded in the desert I tell you that such a man cannot exist if the God of the Bible exists. If the God of the Bible says that a sinner needs to be baptized in order to be saved then He will not allow a sinner who wants to be saved to drift into a place where he cannot be baptized. The only circumstance that will thwart God's plan is when those who call themselves Christians deny the power of God's Word. God promises that His Word will not return void (Isaiah 55:11) but God's Word needs faithful people to obey it and to spread it (Romans 10:13-17).

When confronted with what seems like an anomaly we must remember Abraham's words when he was confronted with the most terrifying and confusing challenge to his faith. "The Lord will provide" was his answer to his son Isaac when he asked, "Where is the lamb for the burnt offering?" (Genesis 22:7,8). God had told Abraham to take Isaac up on Mount Moriah and offer him as a sacrifice. Abraham laid his son on the altar and was ready to put the knife to Isaac's throat until God stopped him. Why do so many who present themselves as faithful teachers and leaders in the church feel that they need to take the knife to God's Word to surgically remove, or correct, any anomalies?

Like it or not I am the third party and if you are a faithful Christian then so are you. If you are a woman, then you may well be at least as effective as any man when it comes to sharing your faith personally. Women are not permitted to participate in the *public* preaching and teaching where men are involved, however (1 Corinthians 14:34; 1 Timothy 2:12).

Judas was probing this concept of the third party when he asked Jesus a question one day.

> *Judas (not Iscariot) said to him, "Lord, how is it that you will manifest yourself to us, and not to the world?"*
> John 14:22.

Judas was trying to connect the dots between that small group of disciples and the rest of the world. Jesus had personally revealed Himself to them, but how could He do the same for everyone if He was going back to Heaven? Jesus answered Judas' question in John 15:26,27 by telling His disciples that they would partner with the Holy Spirit in bearing witness to Jesus. Jesus intended to show himself through the witness of His disciples. We must not pretend that there is still a question about how our neighbors and friends and family are going to be saved. We know the answer but sometimes lack the courage to be the third party. We would find the courage, as many of us still do, when someone reminds us who we are. The fire burns hot when we seriously return to the book and when we come together in the name of the Lord. It is never too late to fan the flame.

> *For this reason I remind you to fan into flame the gift of God, which is in you through the laying on of my hands, for God gave us a spirit not of fear but of power and love and self-control. Therefore do not be ashamed of the testimony about our Lord, nor of me his prisoner, but share in suffering for the gospel by the power of God, who saved us and called us to a holy calling, not because of our works but because of his own purpose and grace, which he gave us in Christ Jesus before the ages began, and which now has been manifested through the appearing of our Savior Christ Jesus, who abolished death and brought life and immortality to light through the gospel, for which I was appointed a preacher and apostle and teacher, which is why I suffer as I do. But I am not ashamed, for I know whom I have believed, and I am convinced that he is able to guard until that Day what has been entrusted to me.*
> *Follow the pattern of the sound words that you have heard from me, in the faith and love that are in Christ Jesus.*
> *By the Holy Spirit who dwells within us, guard the good deposit entrusted to you.*
>
> 2 Timothy 1:6-14

Questions for Chapter Nine

1. Are there biblical grounds for accepting that we can waive the requirement of baptism in certain situations?

2. Does baptism require a third party to carry out the baptism?

3. Are there biblical grounds for accepting that a person who does not teach the truth about baptism is authorized to properly baptize another?

4. Are there biblical grounds for accepting that a person does not need to actually hear the terms of salvation fully explained in order to be saved?

5. Are there biblical grounds for accepting that a person can be saved without being in contact with another person of saving faith?

6. Are there biblical grounds for trusting that God will provide whatever is necessary for the saving of any soul, in any place, at any time, if we trust Him and do His will?

Chapter Ten

HOW OTHERS ANSWER THIS QUESTION

Do others struggle with these questions about salvation and fellowship? Is it a heaven or hell issue for them, as I believe it is? Most Protestant denominations are, by necessity, very liberal on their stand about who goes to Heaven and who goes to Hell. They do tend to have serious doubts about groups who they categorize as cults, however. The churches of Christ fall into this category for some because of our strong doctrinal awareness.

Two well-known groups that are usually branded as cults are Jehovah's Witnesses and Mormons. They each claim to be the one true church ordained by God, but they do not have any definitive threat for those who are not members. My Jehovah's Witness friend once accused me of being a part of "reprehensible Christianity". When I asked what fate awaits someone like me I was surprised to hear that there are two hopes for the saved ones and nothing at all for the rest. Some will live in Heaven for eternity and some will live on a restored earth. But there is no hell, only annihilation for the rest. I ask myself why these people are so motivated to take this message to the world.

Mormons, likewise, believe they are the one true church. When you ask a Mormon if non-Mormon Christians are saved or lost the answer gets complicated. Mormons have seven different interpretations for the word "salvation" and everybody gets to experience one of them. Even the lost are saved a bit. Once again, I ask, why is this message so important for the world to hear? If a group of people distinguish themselves as being the one true church in the world, they should warn those who are not part of that church that they will be condemned at the Judgment. The Bible promises heaven to those who are members of the true Church and hell to those who are not.

To be clear on this subject, this author believes that if you are not in the one true Church you are condemned to eternal punishment. That is an awful conclusion that leaves me with a question. I will state it the way I was asked years ago by a young Palestinian studying at Manchester University in England. "If you really believe that" he said with genuine curiosity, "how can you sleep at night?"

That question has haunted me and I believe it is that haunting question that cripples the faith of so many. How can I be comfortable with the fact of my own salvation? If God's grace fills me with peace about my fate, shouldn't it fill me with terror in regard to the fate of the lost? We all need to ask ourselves if we are really acting according to the faith we profess. The answer must not be found by altering God's Word, however.

There are two fundamental adjustments that will make our own salvation more palatable. We can change the biblical view of sin so that, in our minds, more people are saved (Mormons). Or, we can change the biblical view of Hell so that being lost really has no significant negative consequence (Jehovah's Witnesses). These are lies but if I can convince myself of either of these lies then I can sleep at night. Ultimately, I must tamper with God's Word and that means I tamper with God's power and His grace, and that means I have to re-think church. Let us now see how the Catholic church has dealt with this conundrum.

Catholics have been known to be quite exclusive, but in recent years have softened their tone. Here is an extract from Vatican II (1962).

"The Catholic Church professes that it is the one, holy catholic and apostolic Church of Christ; this it does not and could not deny. But in its Constitution the Church now solemnly acknowledges that the Holy

Ghost is truly active in the churches and communities separated from itself. To these other Christian Churches the Catholic Church is bound in many ways: through reverence for God's word in the Scriptures; through the fact of baptism; through other sacraments which they recognize."

The non-Christian may not be blamed for his ignorance of Christ and his Church; salvation is open to him also, if he seeks God sincerely and if he follows the commands of his conscience, for through this means the Holy Ghost acts upon all men; this divine action is not confined within the limited boundaries of the visible Church."

How is that for covering all the bases? Of course, there are those who take the concept of one true church to an extreme and who believe that those who are not in it should die. Militant Muslims are an example. They do not want unbelievers walking around on earth, never mind in Heaven.

When it comes down to it any religion that espouses an eternal punishment for those who do not subscribe to that religion is going to be a hard sell. There are a couple of options for those who wish to maintain such a stance. You can make sure you have the power to enforce those ideas as did the early Roman Catholic Church in the past and militant Muslims in the present. Both groups have been willing to shed blood to get their point across. In some cases the blood is their own but the end goal is the death of non-believers. To maintain their religious purity they must purge the world of others. The second option is to love others and warn them about the coming wrath of God, hoping that they will join you yet knowing that they may well kill you. One person is willing to die to kill others and one person is willing to die to save others.

One other group must be considered before we leave this thought. Churches of Christ were greatly impacted by a movement that began in Gainseville, Florida in the sixties. This movement was initially called the "Crossroads movement" but later became known as the "Boston movement" and now is known as "International Church of Christ." The key theme for this movement is discipleship. I sympathize with their objectives completely but cannot accept some of their methods. They believe they are the one true Church and that hell awaits those who are not members, which is consistent. I have more in common with those of the discipling movement but here is why I am not a member.

1. They constantly promote the idea of saving the world in this generation. This kind of thinking is a wonderful sentiment but it cannot be a rule.

2. I have personally known members who seemed to develop a sort of lust for repentance and discipline. They became very unsettled if someone was not breathing down their necks and controlling their lives.

3. I have neither the personality nor the desire to start a world movement or any movement for that matter. Jesus already did that. Praise the LORD!

Questions for Chapter Ten

1. Does the Bible teach that Heaven is the reward for Christians and Hell is the reward for non-Christians?

2. Does the Bible teach that there are false teachers, also called antichrists or false Christians?

3. Are denominations part of the true Church or are they counterfeit churches?

4. Is it logical to claim to be the one true church and yet teach that members of other churches do not have to fear the wrath of God?

5. When are we to test the spirits?

      a.   Before a person joins the Church.
      b.   After a person joins the Church.
      c.   Before and after a person joins the Church.

6. Whose spirit should I test first? (2 Corinthians 13:5,6)

Chapter Eleven

WHAT ABOUT THE CAMPBELLS?

The case of Thomas and Alexander Campbell provides some interesting discussion here. We must be cautious about allowing any historical account to carry too much weight as, in reality, we may not be able to discern all the true facts that were in play. We are not talking about a biblical account but rather a tradition that has very good attestation. These men were very closely involved in the beginning of what is called the Restoration Movement in America. There is much debate over their views on baptism and, as I am not able to personally test those spirits, I must leave that to God. Nobody is going to be judged by either of the Campbells any more than we are going to be judged by Mother Theresa or any other well-known person who has been credited with righteousness by men. The Bible only allows for one comparison and that is the comparison between Jesus Christ and each one of us. When I compare myself with Mother Theresa I get to indulge myself in the concept that there are good people in the world and I can aspire to be among them. When I compare myself with Jesus I can only say, "I have sinned and I fall short of the glory of God." (Romans 3:23).

For the sake of discussion, however, is it conceivable that the Campbells, or anyone else for that matter, could have gone from

being lost to being saved by a process of self-study of the Bible
followed by baptism at the hands of a Baptist? The fundamental
question is whether or not there must be an unbroken chain of qualified
baptizers throughout history. Reasonable people would say that such a
proposition is unrealistic and that God's grace must afford other means
of salvation when circumstances demand it. Are we, then, to accept the
reasoning that God may have made a rock too big for Him to move?

The biblical model is for saved people to share their faith with lost
people. When it comes to teaching, Paul's instructions to Timothy are
plain. The faith is to be passed on by faithful teachers.

> *...and what you have heard from me in the presence of many
> witnesses entrust to faithful men who will be able to teach
> others also.*
>
> 2 Timothy 2:2

In the absence of any biblical instruction about a contingency plan
men have stepped forward with their own suggestions. To them the
answer is obvious: God will save a person who believes without that
person being properly baptized if there is no other way. This kind of
thinking is often verbalized as "baptism is necessary but not essential."
Those who doubt that it takes a properly baptized person to correctly
baptize another person will soon doubt that baptism is necessary at all.

What does faith answer to this question? First and foremost faith
must reject the notion that there has to be another way for God's will to
be fulfilled other than the way He said it was to be fulfilled. We must
not go beyond what is written (1 Corinthians 4:6). We must also reject
the idea that the Bible is unclear and that we must, therefore, allow
for variations in interpretation. Baptism is not just some theological
concept that causes spirited debate and division in the religious
community. Baptism is the crux of salvation which identifies the true
religious community, the Church. As we have already mentioned, many
simply invoke God's grace as the solution to these questions. But let
us be clear about the biblical teaching in regard to salvation and grace.

Ephesians 2:8 says we are saved by grace through faith. Grace demands faith and faith demands grace. Some seem to think that a lack of faith is that which demands grace. The faith we are talking about is that which comes by hearing the word of God (Romans 10:17). Baptism is mentioned 68 times in the New Testament and the scriptures clearly make it a requirement for salvation, along with faith, repentance and endurance of faith. Hear the word of the Lord:

> *"Truly, truly, I say to you, unless one is born of water and the Spirit, he cannot enter the kingdom of God."*
>
> John 3:5

The apostles obeyed the command of Jesus to go into the world and make disciples (Matthew 28:18-20). They baptized those who asked what they must do (Acts 2:37,38; 16:30-33). Those who received their teachings were baptized (Acts 2:41). Those who were baptized continued steadfastly in the apostles' doctrine and fellowship and in the breaking of bread and prayer (Acts 2:42). The Lord added those who were being saved to the Church (Acts 2:47). He did not add them to the Baptists or Methodists or Catholics because there were no such denominations. There were no denominations at all. There was just the one true church to which Jesus added those who obey the gospel. That Church still exists today despite the efforts to divide, dilute and destroy it.

If baptism is so important, why would anyone resist the proposition that two people could read the Bible and baptize each other correctly? If they both had the right understanding, wouldn't that work? There simply is no "Thus saith the Lord" that teaches about people being saved without being in contact with people who are already saved. Any argument that relieves me of the responsibility of personally sharing my faith and making sure that people are saved will come from the mind of man, not from God.

My position that a lost soul has to be baptized by a properly baptized person presents me with what seems like the possibility of a void in the flow of God's plan of salvation. I cannot personally verify that the chain of qualified baptizers is unbroken. Should I then build my own bridge across that void and just dispense with the true teaching about salvation? What I do know is that God has always been ready to provide such a person. If I doubt that, then I doubt God.

If there are any gaps in the continuity of God's mission to save mankind they are gaps in our faith not in His grace and power. We must never assume that His grace will accomplish what our faith will not attempt. At the very least we must insist that any baptism involves three people who are in agreement about baptism. The three are: The Lord, the one being baptized, and the one doing the baptizing. If there is any disagreement about the purpose of baptism, then one, possibly two, of the three are not truly heeding the scriptures. If that is the case then there will be only two persons involved with the baptism: the one getting wet and the one getting him wet.

In reality I know that the only people I can talk about are the ones with whom I personally talk. If I come in contact with a lost soul, it is my duty before God to make sure they hear the whole counsel of God. I cannot allow a person I have never met to change my faith that I must share with those whom I do meet. The same applies to you if you are a faithful child of God.

My position does not change the fate of anyone who has already passed from this world, but it might well make a big difference for those who are still living and who have not yet been saved. As human beings we are often influenced by concerns about loved ones who have passed away, but as Christians we should heed our Lord's command to:

> *"Leave the dead to bury their own dead. But as for you, go and proclaim the kingdom of God."*
>
> Luke 9:60

It is heart-breaking that there are so many who seem to be set in their ways, and those ways are just vain traditions of men. Do we give up on them? Would Paul give up? Would Jesus? No, they would not give up and neither should we. It is a fact that if we give up on trying to win them, they will eventually win us. There is no middle ground. When God gave the Promised Land to the Israelites He told them to wipe out the opposition and, when they failed to do that, God had this to say:

> *...know for certain that the LORD your God will no longer drive out these nations before you, but they shall be a snare and a trap for you, a whip on your sides and thorns in your eyes, until you perish from off this good ground that the LORD your God has given you.*
>
> Joshua 23:13

Christians today should be wiping out the opposition by converting them. By that I mean we should be contending for the faith (Jude 3) and taking every thought captive for Christ (2 Corinthians 10:5). If we stop to try and make sense of things that only God knows, Satan has achieved his objective. While we are trying to map out a reasonable scenario that is in harmony with human nature, we are falling away from the One who shares His divine nature with us. Satan sows seeds of doubt, such as the ones we are discussing, about the need for baptism and the need to be in fellowship with the true Church. We must not let Satan convince us that we have failed. If those doubts become the engine for our motivation we will fail. But, if we press on, faithfully trusting and obeying God's word, we will win.

The world will present all sorts of doubts and threats for us to process, but Jesus promises that He has overcome the world (John 16:33). I may be able to surmise that the Campbells got it right, but I cannot surmise my way into Heaven. I can spend all my days pondering and conjecturing about the fate of those who might find a Bible and read it and baptize each other, but God does not call us to ponder and conjecture. He calls us to seek and save the lost, and He tells us clearly how to do it. Even if we accept that we have been wrong, it is not too late to restore what is right.

Trust in the LORD forever,
for the LORD GOD is an everlasting rock.

Isaiah 26:4

I am painfully aware that my faith puts me on the hook and that is not a comfortable place to be, unless I am convinced that the one who hooked me is Jesus. Each of us needs to be prepared to face Jesus at judgment. If I am wrong, then Jesus is going to point to a lot of people who I would have thought are lost but who, in fact, are saved. Will that mean that I get sent to hell, then? I don't know for sure, but I know that if I get to the judgment and Jesus points to a lot of people whom I persuaded to believe they were saved but who are actually lost, that will be a very hard burden to bear. I am certain that He will send me to hell. If all these people who preach that you do not need to worry about proper baptism are wrong, then a lot of people will be going to hell who think they are going to Heaven. If I am wrong, it is my loss. If they are wrong it means the loss of countless souls.

"Not everyone who says to me, 'Lord, Lord,' will enter the
kingdom of heaven, but the one who does the will of my Father
who is in heaven.

Matthew 7:21

It is fear that prevents us from following the Lord. We are fearful about facing our neighbor or friend or family member with the truth about salvation. We do not want to offend anybody. What will it be like when we see them at judgment and the truth is no longer avoidable? The bottom line for any Christian must always be the saving of souls to the glory of God. Then we can sing with the angels as we view God's new Creation.

Oh come, let us sing to the LORD;
let us make a joyful noise to the rock of our salvation!

Psalm 95:1

Questions for Chapter Eleven

1. What effect do the Campbells (Thomas and Alexander) have on your faith?

2. Are there people who have genuinely influenced your faith in a positive way? Will you be judged by any of them?

3. Are there people you know who are no longer with us and you are not sure they were saved? Will you be judged by them? Will they be judged by you?

4. Are there people you know who are living and you are not sure they are saved? Do you have an excuse for not making sure?

5. Does God have a contingency plan to get the truth into the hearts of lost souls if the Church fails? Does God expect the Church to fail?

6. What would happen if you lived your life like the two Marys who went to take care of the body of Jesus?

Chapter Twelve

DOING RIGHT EVEN WHEN IT HURTS

For God alone my soul waits in silence;
from him comes my salvation.
He only is my rock and my salvation,
my fortress; I shall not be greatly shaken.

Psalm 62:1,2

Faithful children of God get hurt. The important reminder that we get from the scriptures is:

> *But let none of you suffer as a murderer or a thief or an*
> *evildoer or as a meddler. Yet if anyone suffers as a Christian,*
> *let him not be ashamed, but let him glorify God in that name.*
> 1 Peter 4:15,16

If we are willing to make exceptions to God's commandments for any reason, then we cannot honestly say that we love the Lord. It is true that each one of us is imperfect, but the Word of God is perfect (Psalm 19:7) and needs no changing. Paul is an example for us in standing firm in his doctrine regardless of how many arguments his detractors might present to dissuade him. In Galatians 2:1-5 he recounts a visit that he made to Jerusalem where he defended his doctrine that Gentiles did not have to be circumcised to be saved. There were those who argued against him, but Paul says,

> *...to them we did not yield in submission even for a moment, so that the truth of the gospel might be preserved for you.*
> Galatians 2:5

Who knows what kinds of arguments were presented to Paul or how many situations were invented in an attempt to demonstrate the weakness of Paul's position. I do know that the more determined a person is to win an argument the less discerning that person is about how he wins it. If the other person's argument cannot be denied, then at least perhaps someone can come up with an "exception."

This kind of thinking is what is called "situation ethics" and it is a very human response to situations that seem to be beyond our control. The same response is occurring among Christians today when it comes to the uniqueness of the church and the essential nature of baptism. We can imagine a scenario where someone is dying in the desert and who wants to be saved. Because we can imagine a situation that is beyond our control, we begin to make the necessary changes in the rules in the hope that we can gain control.

Let us review why we became Christians. Wasn't it because we found ourselves confronted by God's Word that proclaimed we were lost without hope unless we repented and were baptized into Christ? Wasn't all that because we had insisted on having things under our own control? Isn't it true that our lost state was a situation that was beyond our control? The gospel says we were dead in sin. How much control over death do dead people have? How much control do dead people have over anything for that matter? My escape from death could not have happened if I had not come to understand that I was powerless to escape by myself. I needed to be rescued, so Jesus came looking for me and called me out of spiritual death (sin) so that He can call me out of the physical tomb. (John 5:24-29). I cannot call myself out of sin but

Jesus can. Salvation occurs when a person hears the gospel and obeys it. That person will ask, "What must I do to be saved?" The answer is "Repent and be baptized in the name of Jesus Christ for the remission of sins and you will receive the gift of the Holy Spirit." (Acts 2:38) If it was left to my control I would be hopelessly lost, but God took control of the situation when He offered me forgiveness. God now has the control over my salvation, and I have the responsibility to trust and obey.

Those who attempted to get Paul to teach Gentiles that they needed to be circumcised to be saved found him completely unyielding. He would accept no exceptions for any situation because he wanted to make sure that the truth of the gospel was preserved (Galatians 2:5). Does this position clash with his position in 1 Corinthians 9:19-23? In this famous discourse Paul speaks of his determination to become "all things to all men." He even says he will become like one under the Law in order to win those under the Law. And again he says he does it for "the sake of the gospel." He gave a good demonstration of this when he had Timothy circumcised so he could assist him in his missionary work (Acts 16:1-4). Timothy was already saved but Paul knew that the Jews he was trying to save would not listen to what he had to say as long as he was accompanied by an uncircumcised Gentile. When Titus accompanied Paul to the council in Jerusalem where Paul defended the position that Gentiles did not have to be circumcised, Paul was proud to declare:

> *"But even Titus, who was with me, was not forced to be circumcised, though he was a Greek"*
>
> Galatians 2:3

Can you reconcile the following two statements?

- For the sake of the gospel Paul had Timothy circumcised.
- For the sake of the gospel Paul refused to have Titus circumcised.

Was Paul applying situation ethics? No, Paul was following the same pattern as when he in one place would accept a flogging, but in another situation would avoid a flogging. In Acts 16:23 Paul was flogged and thrown into prison when he was in Philippi. When he was in Jerusalem and Roman soldiers were preparing to flog him, he announced that he was a Roman citizen and they immediately backed off and left him alone (Acts 22:25). Why didn't he exercise that privilege when he was in Philippi? In fact he did announce his Roman citizenship but not until the day after he was flogged (Acts 16:37,38). I cannot say what Paul was thinking exactly, but I do know that the Philippian jailer and his household were baptized into Christ as a result of Paul's punishment (Acts 16:33). When Paul was imprisoned in Jerusalem, however, the outcome was to be a very different one. Paul had completed his work in that area and he would now be using his Roman citizenship as a ticket to Rome. He would continue to preach and teach about Jesus wherever he was.

Getting the gospel to as many people as possible was the unifying theme to all of Paul's actions. He would indeed adjust his behavior to suit the situation, but he was not seeking a better outcome for himself. When he had Timothy circumcised, and when he allowed himself to be flogged, he was looking for the best possible outcome for the gospel of Christ. When he refused to have Titus circumcised, and when he avoided a flogging, he was still looking for the best possible outcome for the gospel. It is a human tendency to change our behavior to bring about the most comfortable outcome for ourselves in any given situation. If Paul was thinking of himself, then his choices would seem completely erratic. He was not thinking of himself, though; he was thinking of the gospel and, in that light, Paul was totally consistent. Whatever situation he found himself in, he would never change the gospel. Paul practiced "salvation ethics"!

In our meetings we are good at promoting the idea of faith in God's Word, and we encourage each other to count on God's providence and to walk by faith not by sight. When we encounter extenuating circumstances, however, we often waiver and feel that we must bend the rules. Perhaps you have heard some of the excuses for doing so.

- "I fell in love with someone else's husband, but surely God does not want me to go through life in misery without him?"
- "I couldn't help it. He just made me so angry; I lost control and hit him"
- "I can't seem to earn enough money and always spend more than I bring in, so I got loans and now I am buried in debt. Can you lend me some money?"
- "I got a late start for an important meeting so I had to make up time by going over the speed limit."
- "I cannot believe you are saying that a man who is dying in the desert with no water around, who wants to be saved, will go to hell because he has not been baptized"

Daniel and his three friends were faced with "extenuating circumstances" and we rejoice that they did not waiver. They did not see the fire in the furnace (Shadrach, Meshach and Abednego) or the lions in the pit (Daniel). They saw Jesus in the furnace and Jesus in the pit. They walked by faith not by sight. They would not hearken to the winds and doctrines of men and refused to capitulate to the fear of what earthly rulers might do their bodies. They feared Him who could destroy both the body and the soul in hell (Matthew 10:28). They capitulated to their Creator. The fear of what our denominational friends and relatives might do is slowly crippling the Lord's Church. For too long we have been drawn into the doubting game and failed to give a positive answer to questions like the one about the lost soul dying in the desert wanting to be saved but unable to get to the water. For too long we have allowed ourselves to drift toward the conclusion that baptism is not always necessary and the church of Christ is not really unique.

The Sadducees tried to trap Jesus with a question about a woman who had been married to a succession of brothers who had passed away. They refused to believe in the resurrection and thought they had a home run when they asked Jesus whose wife she would be in Heaven. Here is how Jesus answered them:

> *"You are wrong, because you know neither the Scriptures nor the power of God.*
>
> Matthew 22:29

Those words are a terrible indictment on all those who play such trivial games with faith instead of making every effort to rightly divide the word of God (2 Timothy 2:15).

Let us review the answer of faith in God's Word again. If baptism is not necessary and the Church is not unique, then the God of the Bible does not exist. Talk to me about Daniel in the lion's den, not the lost soul in the desert. Remind me of God's longsuffering love and His covenant faithfulness and His inexhaustible providence. Don't talk to me about extenuating circumstances and rocks too big for God to move. Sing to me of Heaven; don't deal me a dirge from earth. Do right even when it hurts. God does!

Questions for Chapter Twelve

1. Does becoming *all things to all men* (1 Corinthians 9:22) mean we are to wallow in sin with sinners?

2. Does the gospel govern the way you behave personally?

3. If Paul were alive today, would he waive the need for baptism to please those in denominations who insist that one is saved by faith only?

4. How do we know that circumcision is not required today even though it was required under the Old Testament?

6. What does situation ethics say about baptism?

7. What does salvation ethics say about baptism?

8. If God practiced situation ethics how would He respond to the lost condition of mankind?

9. When was the last time you practiced situation ethics in regard to your faith?

10. Which situation would you rather face?
    a.   Loss of a friend for telling the truth
    b.   Loss of your life for telling the truth
    c.   Loss of a friends' soul for not telling the truth

Chapter Thirteen

CONCLUSIONS

"Church of Christ" says it all. This term, which Paul uses in Romans 16:16, tells us what it is and Whose it is. The Church of Christ is God's rock of salvation; therefore God can do what He wants with it. God has blessed us by revealing His plan of salvation, however, and Christians are called to trust His Word. There is only one source on earth to which we can go to verify the facts about Church and about Christ, and that is the Bible. Let's review, from the book of Ephesians, what the Church is.

The Church is the physical presence of God through His Son Jesus Christ as He dwells among faithful people by His Spirit. The living God shows Himself in living people. (2 Corinthians 6:16). These people include both Jews and Gentiles. (Ephesians 2:13-18; cf Acts 2:16,17) A popular denominational untruth teaches that the nation of Israel still has its own dispensation from God. The Bible teaches that in Christ there is no Jew or Gentile (Galatians 3:28). Premillenialism celebrates the distinction between Jew and Gentile.

Christ is the head of the Church which He purchased with His own blood (Ephesians 1:22,23; 2:13; cf. Acts 20:7). The Church is the Body of Christ (Ephesians 1:22,23), the Temple of Christ (2:18-22; cf. 1 Peter 2:9) and the Bride of Christ (Ephesians 5:22-32). The Church is also the eternal purpose of God (Ephesians 3:10,11). When people ask to change the name on the building from "Church of Christ", why not suggest changing it to "Eternal Purpose of God"? The two terms are synonymous. It is absurd for man to introduce his own names for God's eternal purpose.

All spiritual blessings are in Christ because that is where the Spirit is (Ephesians 1:3-14). Living souls are either in Christ or in sin (Ephesians 2:1-6). Sinners need to be sanctified, being cleansed by the washing of water with the word (Ephesians 5:26; cf. Acts 2:41; Titus 3:4-6). In order to be saved a person must be baptized into Christ, which means into His church (Acts 2:38,47). Salvation and fellowship are two sides of the same coin. You cannot have a personal relationship with Christ without having a personal relationship with His Church. If you take baptism out of the salvation event, you take the Holy Spirit out of the salvation event (John 3:5; Titus 3:5). If you take baptism out of the salvation event you take Jesus out of the salvation event.

> *Baptism, which corresponds to this, now saves you, not as a removal of dirt from the body but as an appeal to God for a good conscience, through the resurrection of Jesus Christ, who has gone into heaven and is at the right hand of God, with angels, authorities, and powers having been subjected to him.*
>
> 1 Peter 3:21,22

The Church is God's work of grace in the here and now (Ephesians 2:4,5). By the power of God's grace we can be raised to be with Christ now (Ephesians 2:6). God's grace works powerfully in the preaching of the gospel (Ephesians 3:7). While we walk by faith we receive God's grace. When Jesus comes we will no longer need grace.

> *And God is able to make all grace abound to you, so that having all sufficiency in all things at all times, you may abound in every good work.*
>
> 2 Corinthians 9:8

To be a Christian is to be one with Christ and thus one with Christ's Body. The Lord will not allow for more than one expression of His Body (Ephesians 4:1-6; cf John 17:21; 1 Corinthians 3:1-4). Many attempt to justify denominationalism by saying, "But we all believe in the same Lord." The Bible clearly warns that if you preach a different gospel you do not have the same Lord (Galatians 1:6-9; 2 Corinthians 11:1- 4). Likewise, if you do not hold to the one baptism you do not hold to the one faith and do not have the one Lord. (Ephesians 4:5)

The argument that Paul embraced denominationalism when he addressed the Corinthians must be rejected. Yes, they exhibited a party spirit and, yes, he addressed them as brothers (1 Corinthians 3:1-4). But Paul warned that anyone who destroys the temple will be destroyed by God (1 Corinthians 3:16,17). Next he warned against being deceived by their own wisdom (3:18-23). He continued to warn them not to go beyond what is written (1 Corinthians 4:6). It is true that in any congregation there are different levels of faith and maturity and the potential for division. To compare that state of affairs with full-scale denominationalism is disingenuous at best. Today there are separate groups championing separate faiths under different names. The preaching in the Church should always be focused on encouraging maturity and preventing division, and that is how Paul always preached. For men to stand before a congregation and use Paul's letter to the Corinthians to actually condone and encourage division is to go way beyond what is written. Such lies do untold damage to the Temple of God.

The Church preaches the truth in love (Ephesians 4:15) Doctrine demands love and love demands doctrine. Love is the bull's eye that the arrow of doctrine is aimed at (John 13:34; 14:15; Galatians 5:14; 1 John 2:5). If we believe in His love for us we must also love how He commands us. We must refuse to be carried about by every wind of doctrine, by human cunning, by craftiness in deceitful schemes. (Ephesians 4:14)

...for I find my delight in your commandments, which I love.
                                                              Psalm 119:47

99

Ephesians presents a staggering, majestic view of the Lord's Church. It is hard to take it in, but it is the truth. We must trust what the Lord has to say about His Church. We must not shrink back, because there is too much at stake. We must stay the course for the sake of souls that are not yet saved. We must trust and obey, to the glory of God. As human beings we can easily get caught up in the extremes of being too judgmental or too sentimental. Both of these extremes issue from a lack of faith in God's word. The legalist says it has to be done "my way" and the sentimentalist says, "God will take care of it for everybody."

Both are starved for God's grace. One shrinks the Bible down to bite-sized proportions that have no room for grace. The other tries to broaden God's word to cover all possible eventualities and thereby open up holes that have to be filled by human wisdom. Thus they nullify grace.

What do you make of the question about the lost soul who wants to be saved but who finds himself or herself in the desert, or on an island, or in fellowship with a counterfeit church? Do you think that it is reasonable to trust God to take care of sin and to supply whatever is needed? Or do you think it is reasonable to step in to God's shoes and make adjustments to God's Word?

> *For the word of God is living and active, sharper than any two-edged sword, piercing to the division of soul and of spirit, of joints and of marrow, and discerning the thoughts and intentions of the heart. And no creature is hidden from his sight, but all are naked and exposed to the eyes of him to whom we must give account*
> Hebrews 4:12,13

Does that sound like God is unaware of what is happening to that person in the desert? Do we really think we need to sharpen God's sword for Him by altering His word? Let's be honest and admit that our speculations and hypotheses have only served to blunt God's sword.

The Church must expect God to keep His covenant. The Church must not grow weary and expect God to find other means to accomplish

His mission on earth. In other words, God expects Christians to act as the third party between himself and lost souls and will not call upon unfaithful people or the Bible alone to be the third party. If I am going to call upon the Bible as God's message then I must accept that the Bible calls upon me to be the messenger.

When Christians walk by faith and not by sight then mountains get moved, mountains like the apostle Paul. He was on his way to crush the Church in Damascus but crumbled into a pile of dust himself while traveling the road to Damascus (Acts 9). Just a few days later he found himself being thrust into the heights once again, only this time he took his place among the peaks in a different world. He had moved from the kingdom of Satan to the Kingdom of Christ (Colossians 1:13) with no small help from a man called Ananias. Ananias was called upon to go to Paul and baptize him. All the empirical evidence that Ananias had available to him spoke to the fact that Paul would gladly murder him, but God told Ananias a different story about Paul. Ananias went to the house on Straight Street and found Paul, just as God had told him he would. As a result, Paul the persecutor of truth became Paul the preacher of truth. Ananias walked by faith, not by sight. Ananias baptized Paul.

When churches trust and obey God's Word without having to have an explanation of God's Word, then heaven and earth come together in celebration. Consider the Church at Thessalonica:

And you became imitators of us and of the Lord, for you received the word in much affliction, with the joy of the Holy Spirit,
1 Thessalonians 1:6

Restoration is a constant effort. I must make sure that I am not just pointing out error but that I am doing what I can to contribute to the restoration of the Church. Restoration within the Lord's Church may be a mighty movement that involves a lot of people and a lot of time. It might just involve me and my own walk of faith in this very moment. Every time we say no to Satan each one of us is restoring the covenant.

Every time we confront false teaching we are restoring the covenant for ourselves and for others. We live in this world where dirt gathers constantly so we have to be constantly diligent about removing the dirt. Studying the Bible does that, and going to church does that, and every act of Christian love and obedience is an act of restoration. Never doubt that God is still faithful to His covenant. No matter how many layers of dirt have accumulated, if you remove the dirt, the covenant is still perfectly new and pristine. That is why God is often compared to a rock. He is constant and, yes, immovable. Compared to other gods Moses declared:

> *Then he will say, 'Where are their gods,*
> *the rock in which they took refuge...*
> Deuteronomy 32:37

God is a rock because He saves.

> *"The LORD lives, and blessed be my rock,*
> *and exalted be my God, the rock of my salvation."*
> 2 Samuel 22:47

God and Jesus are One. Therefore Jesus is also the rock.

> *...all drank the same spiritual drink. For they drank from the*
> *spiritual Rock that followed them, and the Rock was Christ.*
> 1Corinthians 10:4

In a reference to the rock that we read about in Daniel 2, Isaiah describes the faithful people of God as being hewn out of the rock. There is continuity with the rock motif from God, through Jesus, to the Church.

> *"Listen to me, you who pursue righteousness,*
> *you who seek the LORD:*

look to the rock from which you were hewn,
and to the quarry from which you were dug.

Isaiah 51:1

The Lord promised that streams of living water would flow from His church Just as it flowed from the rock in Moses' day. (John 7:37-39; Revelation 21:10 - 22:1)

He made streams come out of the rock
and caused waters to flow down like rivers.

Psalms 78:16

There is nothing more precious or more powerful in this world than the one true Church of Christ. There is no greater adventure than the adventure of being a true Christian, and no greater reward than the reward that God offers to His faithful saints. The Church is the only true source of love and peace and joy. That is because of Jesus who is the Head of the Church.

Though you have not seen him, you love him. Though you do
not now see him, you believe in him and rejoice with joy that is
inexpressible and filled with glory.

1 Peter 1:8

The Church of Christ is the very heart and mind of God, seeking... always seeking... my heart and mind, and your heart and mind.

Questions for Chapter Thirteen

1. Does the Bible speak of one true Church or not?

2. Can you find the Church of Christ mentioned in the Bible?

3. Can you find the name of any of the denominations in the Bible?

4. What is the most important difference between the Church of Christ and all denominations? What do others perceive the difference is? If there are two different answers what are we to do about it?

5. What is the biggest threat to the health of the Lord's Church?

7. What is the biggest threat to your personal faith?

8. What is your answer to the question about a sinner who is dying in the desert but wants to be saved?

9. What is your answer to the question about the person who is in fellowship with a denomination and has not been properly baptized?

10. What is your answer to the Lord's prayer that all His followers be sanctified by the truth and that they be one? (John 17:17-21)

EPILOGUE

At the age of eighteen, in the village of Hazel Grove in England, I was feeling that I had outgrown my environment. Are there any eighteen-year-old males that do not feel like that? Had anyone told me that by the time I was twenty years old I would be married to a New York girl and I would be serving in the U.S. Navy, I would have thought they were crazy. Had anyone suggested that by the time I was thirty-four I would be training to be a preacher, I would have thought myself to be crazy.

I arrived in the U.S. in October 27, 1967 with not much of a plan for my future and a vision in my head of my dream girl. Within six months of arriving in the United States my life was shaken again when the Selective Service became very interested in me. By this time I had found a job and I had also found the girl of my dreams. When we found out that I was very shortly to be Vietnam bound Sandy agreed to come back to England with me. I broke the news to her mother one afternoon when I returned from taking her daughter back to college in Albany. She listened as I explained our plan. Then she told me that she understood and that they would support us in our new plans, which included getting married in England. I could hardly believe my luck as I processed her words, but her response was not merely verbal. Her non-verbal response amounted to one tiny tear. I simply thanked her and left, breathing a sigh of relief. Off down the road I went having accomplished what I had come to do and yet feeling quite undone and quite unable to follow through with my plans. I could not get that little tear out of my mind.

Years later I told my mother-in-law how that tiniest of tears had changed the entire course of my life. I decided to stay in the U.S but also made the decision to enlist in the Navy rather than be drafted. As I have often told people, I had met my dream girl and I have been in La-La Land ever since. Sandy and I were married shortly after I entered the U.S. Navy and we now have five grown children and twelve grandchildren scattered from New York and Pennsylvania to Illinois and Alaska.

We were twenty years old when we were married and twenty-six years old when we were baptized into Christ. We came into contact with the church of Christ in Endwell, NY. As I was encouraged to study the Bible for myself, I felt that I was coming alive in a wonderful new way. I began to accept that God had been active in my life even before I became a Christian, and that all these things had happened for a purpose. I was not saved until I was baptized, but I was baptized because God had provided a path that led me to that place in my life. God does that for people; He beats a path down between you and Him. It does not matter where you are, there will be a path and if, for whatever reason, you miss it, He will beat another path down. You may have moved on to another place but He will never stop providing paths that lead back to Him.

One aspect of what this book is dealing with is the question of how God uses the Church in this process. Is God beating a path down that will bring me into contact with that lost person? I found God when I found His church. My path crossed the paths of those who were already Christians. Is there a way for a person to be saved without crossing paths with faithful people? Not according to the Bible I read.

I have no idea how many other paths I had missed before, paths that might have taken me on a different trajectory while still arriving at the same place. I am also aware that God has continued to make corrections to my trajectory as I have strayed off course occasionally. At any time I could have, and still can, reject His guidance and go my own way. Some would say that only losers turn to faith in God. In God's eyes we are all lost but we are not losers. The world makes lostness final and irrevocable but God is always seeking the lost to bring them back to Himself. So I thanked God for bringing Sandy and me together and I thanked God for my dad's restlessness that brought us to New York in the first place. And I thanked God for the tear that sealed my fate in this grand adventure of life and faith, even before I was faithful.

There are many questions that I cannot answer. Many times I have seen events unfold in a way that I was convinced that God was opening a door, only to find that the door did not lead anywhere, as far as I could see at the time. I have also seen events unfold that did result in fruit for God's kingdom and I have not always been aware that a door had even opened. So I must let God worry about the details and keep preaching what I believe to be true from what He has shown to all of us in the Bible. God's story has been written, but mine is still unfinished. As a Christian I find great joy in two things I have learned:

(1) While I live on this earth I do not know what will happen between now and my departure. I find it exciting that anything can happen. As a Christian I can know that, whatever happens, God is working for the good of those who love Him and who are called according to His purpose (Romans 8:28).

(2) If I am faithful I can know I am saved and that means I can be at peace as far as what happens to me at the end of my life. My final outcome is perfection. I have the best of both worlds. God grants me that assurance and He is faithful. Just as surely

as that rock was rolled away from Jesus' tomb so death will be rolled away from my grave when He comes back for His faithful saints. All I have to do is remain faithful.

May we all strive for His purpose which he set forth in Christ:

...as a plan for the fullness of time, to unite all things in him, things in heaven and things on earth.

Ephesians 1:9,10

The message of the Bible is the stuff of dreams, but they are dreams from the mind of God. Impossible dreams come from the minds of men. God speaks prophetically, not hypothetically. There is nothing speculative about His plan of salvation. Jesus is at the right hand of God and He reigns on earth through His Spirit until His last enemy is put under His feet (1 Corinthians 15:25-28).

We must follow the examples of faith that are so abundant in the scriptures. We must see what God sees, not what men see. God saw a king when everyone else saw a shepherd boy, and he told Samuel to anoint David as king (1 Samuel 16:6-13). David saw the armies of the living God when everyone else saw Goliath, and David defeated the Philistines single-handedly (1 Samuel 17:1-58). A true Christian sees one true Church even though everyone else says it cannot be so.

May we all, with God's help, come together to contend for the faith that was once for all delivered to the saints (Jude 3). Such is the fellowship that comes from rock-solid faith which demands a rock-solid God who gives us rock-solid instructions on how to obtain rock-solid salvation in a rock-solid Church.

Trust in the LORD forever,
    for the LORD GOD is an everlasting rock.

Isaiah 26:4

CPSIA information can be obtained at www.ICGtesting.com
Printed in the USA
BVOW060228280212

283818BV00001B/7/P

LOUD AND CLEAR

The Grateful Dead's Wall of Sound and the Quest for Audio Perfection

BRIAN ANDERSON

ST. MARTIN'S PRESS 🙢 NEW YORK

LOUD AND CLEAR

First published in the United States by St. Martin's Press, an imprint of St. Martin's Publishing Group

LOUD AND CLEAR. Copyright © 2025 by Brian Anderson. All rights reserved. Printed in the United States of America. For information, address St. Martin's Publishing Group, 120 Broadway, New York, NY 10271.

www.stmartins.com

Design by Jonathan Bennett

Endpaper photo courtesy of Richie Pechner

The Library of Congress Cataloging-in-Publication Data is available upon request.

ISBN 978-1-250-31967-8 (hardcover)
ISBN 978-1-250-31968-5 (ebook)

Our books may be purchased in bulk for promotional, educational, or business use. Please contact your local bookseller or the Macmillan Corporate and Premium Sales Department at 1-800-221-7945, extension 5442, or by email at MacmillanSpecialMarkets@macmillan.com.

First Edition: 2025

10 9 8 7 6 5 4 3 2 1

For my parents and sister

Contents

Characters

BAND

Tom Constanten—keyboard
Jerry Garcia—lead guitar
Keith Godchaux—piano
Donna Jean Godchaux—vocals
Mickey Hart—drums
Bill Kreutzmann—drums

Ned Lagin—synthesizer/
  computer
Phil Lesh—bass
Ron "Pigpen" McKernan—vocals/
  keyboard
Bob Weir—rhythm guitar

CREW

Candace Brightman—lighting
  designer
Bill "Kidd" Candelario—roadie
Laird Grant—founding roadie
John Hagen—roadie
Clifford Heard—roadie
Ben Haller—lighting assistant
Dan Healy—mixer
Rex Jackson—roadie

Bob Matthews—equipment manager
  and roadie
"Big" Steve Parish—roadie
Richie Pechner—carpenter/
  roadie
Mark "Sparky" Raizene—roadie
Lawrence "Ram Rod" Shurtliff—
  crew chief
Joe Winslow—roadie

TECHS

Melissa Cargill
Betty Cantor-Jackson—recording
  engineer
Sal Cardinalli—Alembic
John Curl—Alembic
Janet Furman—Alembic
Dennis "Wizard" Leonard—Alembic

John Meyer
Tim Scully
Augustus Owsley "Bear" Stanley III—
  Alembic
Rhoney Gissen Stanley
Rick Turner—Alembic
Ron Wickersham—Alembic

MANAGEMENT

Sam Cutler

Rev. Lenny Hart

Bert Kanegson

Hal Kant

Richard Loren

Jon McIntire

Chesley Millikin

Ron Rakow

Jonathan Riester

Danny Rifkin

Rock Scully

FAMILY/OFFICE/LABEL/TRAVEL

Steve Brown

Gail Hellund

Eileen Law

Mary Ann Mayer

Rosie McGee

Bonnie Parker

David Parker

Courtenay Pollock

Sue Swanson

Alan Trist

SET

ONE

1

The Artifact

November 11, 2021. I stood in the rain when the truck rolled up to my parents' house on a Thursday morning. The driver parked the vehicle and opened the hatch.

"Where do you want it?" he asked.

"In the garage," I said, motioning up the driveway. "Thanks."

The courier hand-trucked the cargo onto a hydraulic lift and lowered it to the ground. The hundred-pound wooden crate looked like it held something ancient and fragile. I winced when the handler slipped while shouldering the load up the drive. A corner of the box thudded against the wet pavement.

Shipping this object freight to the Illinois suburbs had cost less than routing it to my Chicago apartment. Besides, having my parents present for the unboxing felt right, considering their own histories and what was inside—and all it went through to get here, its final resting place. The driver left and I inspected a boxtop label, bearing a brief content description: *1 black monitor, missing one large round speaker and two small round speakers.* I let my dad unscrew the crate open with an electric drill. We scooped away armfuls of packing peanuts and marveled at the payload, padded in shrink wrap.

I stuck my head inside. Using my phone's flashlight, I saw it, handwritten in black marker on the back of the monitor's remaining 12-inch JBL speaker:

G. DEAD

And stamped beneath, a date:

I curled my neck back out and got a headrush. The artifact held more surprises than I could have imagined.

The artifact is a one-of-a-kind hunk of junk, with a patina of scuffs, dings, worn
edges, adhesive residue, and frayed wiring. It measures 31 x 22.5 x 24 inches
and is constructed of 14-ply laminated Finnish birchwood painted matte black.
That one of its two 12-inch cones is missing lends the cabinet a winking robot
resemblance. Don't get me started on its dank interior odor.

The monitor now sits silently in my living room, and everyone in my family
has had a moment with it. I won it at auction, the piece with the lowest starting price among a Sotheby's sale of decommissioned items from the Grateful
Dead's Northern California warehouse. But it's invaluable to me, and I'll come
to suspect that the appraiser didn't entirely know what they had.

The handwritten *G. DEAD* and date stamped on the back of the 12-inch
cone suggest the sixty-four-pound unit was not merely "used on stage" at
some point in the band's three-decade history, per Sotheby's listing. The artifact was likely one of the vocal "fill" speakers used in the monumental concert
soundsystem that the Dead built and toured with in the early 1970s. Despite
its short life, the Wall of Sound, as this singular public address (PA) rig is
known, revolutionized the modern entertainment industry and encapsulates
a pivotal yet unexplored piece of musical, technological, and cultural history.
Not only did my artifact clock thousands of miles in these years, hauled into
and out of dozens of cities and venues in the US, Canada, and Europe. But the
soundwaves that flowed out of it also touched hundreds of thousands of people
who participated in the live experience of the Dead in a peak era, my parents
included.

More than Deadhead lore or an audiophile fever dream, the story of the
Wall is one of convention-breaking obsession and titanic human achievement,
featuring a group of individuals who risked their lives in the tireless quest for
"good sound." The Dead developed an unprecedented high-fidelity PA consisting of hundreds of speakers and dozens of power amplifiers stacked in columns behind the band. Not to be confused with the late hitmaker and convicted
murderer Phil Spector's music production formula, the Dead's Wall of Sound
was physically gargantuan; its assembled hardware weighed as much as a dozen
full-grown elephants, stood as tall as a school bus is long, and stretched the
length of a regulation basketball court.

The Wall was a manifestation of the 1970s age of extremes and experimentation. The system was a launchpad for the future of music and performance, and massively influential because it gave each individual player an unmatched command over their own onstage mix. "From a musician's standpoint," the late Phil Lesh, the Dead's bassist, wrote in his memoir *Searching for the Sound*, "the most endearing aspect of the system was the control the band now had over the actual sound heard by the audience." The band's sound crew "had eliminated the necessity for a front-of-house mixer, returning the responsibility to the musicians, where it belongs," Lesh said. "The soundman's job was now to monitor the sound in the hall and to report back if any adjustments were necessary." For instance, more vocals or drums, or less piano.

The idea was radically simple: Whereas conventional setups placed monitor speakers, which allow performers to hear themselves playing, in front of musicians, the Dead placed their monitors—like my artifact—*behind* the band, so they heard exactly what the audience heard. The point of the Wall, moreover, was to *eliminate* monitors, so it's not only that the monitors were behind the musicians. The PA *was* their monitors.

The Dead's rig was a technological feat but also a strenuous financial and human undertaking, requiring a crew of over two dozen roadies and sound techs and a fleet of semi-trucks to transport. The Wall eventually forced the band to go on hiatus, nearly a decade into their career. Tracking the rise, fall, and afterlife of this remarkable soundsystem, and the ambitions, machinations, and dramas that played out behind it, is a story about an inspired group effort; the relationships forged between towering figures in modern musical history and the eccentric and unsung characters around them; and what happened when rampant drug use poisoned the project.

The Dead are a uniquely American institution that remains equally beloved, misunderstood, maligned, and undeniable. How and why the Dead matter more than ever to millions of people of all ages around the world are touchpoints even for those who may not call themselves Deadheads, but who are interested in thinking about hearing and consuming music today. These are practices that are still defined by the Dead's enduring influence on generations of musicians and consumers, and their relationship to tech, performance, and fandom.

Meanwhile, surviving Wall personnel are in their seventies. Many have lived hard years, and are now experiencing health issues, from knee replacements to strokes to terminal illnesses, to say nothing of hazy memories. Dead & Company, the hugely popular revival project featuring longtime Dead members—

Bob Weir on guitar, Bill Kreutzmann and Mickey Hart on drums, plus a new guitarist, John Mayer—announced their touring retirement after a "final" stadium run in 2023, renewing interest in and appreciation for this era-defining band and their outrageous soundsystem. Then, in 2024, Dead & Company announced a thirty-night Las Vegas residency at the Sphere, the $2.3 billion state-of-the-art venue with a spatial audio system that may be quantum leaps beyond the Wall, but is a direct descendant of it. After the success of that run, Dead & Company announced another eighteen-show Sphere residency for spring 2025.

The Wall might have fallen silent a half century ago. But the system's reverberations only grow louder.

The array itself was a literal wall, sixty feet end to end. The system was made of nearly six hundred speakers and stood over three stories tall. The PA drew around 28,000 watts of power from forty-eight heavy-duty McIntosh amps. Dead sound crew members determined the rig could only be wired up using arm-thick military surplus cabling originally designed for plugging in docked ships to shore power.

The Wall's full support structure of custom staging and scaffolding, moreover, measured seventy-six feet wide by thirty feet deep at indoor venues, and over a hundred feet wide by forty feet deep outdoors. A rig of such magnitude necessitated that stages be equipped with a one-inch plywood floor, set ten feet above ground, bolted and tied to the scaffolding, because the force of such sound pressure could bounce the system by as much as a foot when the musicians pushed it. For the audience, the movement of enormous volumes of air created an effect of presence; they weren't just hearing the music but feeling it.

At its apex, the Wall weighed seventy-five tons. The operation required four semis and teams of crew members to leapfrog from city to city. Though there was just one system, the Wall had two identical scaffolding sets, so that when Crew A arrived with the PA at a given venue Crew B already had the frame assembled and waiting. Then they swapped places and repeated. They could often have the system up and running in about four hours, a feat of self-taught skill, scrappy innovation, and tightly choreographed teamwork. The price of the equipment, not including the $100,000 a month cost of transportation and labor, was $350,000, the equivalent today of over $2 million.

The highly specialized system's unique mechanism exemplified the Dead's famed close connection to their fans. With the bottom half of the Wall allowing the players to hear themselves onstage and the upper half projecting the sound out into the crowd, the performers and the audience, whom the Dead considered as much a part of the show as the band, all heard the same mix coming from stacks of speaker "arrays" at the musicians' backs. That the new technology allowed the band members to adjust their own individual mixes via customized control knobs on their instruments as well as their amps came at a time when sound mixers usually served as the middlemen between band and audience. The musicians could now take charge of the experience and respond to the crowd, note by note and beat by beat.

What about feedback? To eliminate the squealing noise that comes when an output signal (the sound of the Wall) is "fed back" into an input (the vocal microphones), the Dead's crack electronics team concocted two-headed microphones that canceled out the sound of the PA, so that all the audience could hear were the singers' voices. Such hacks were unheard of when PA tech was still in its infancy and fell short for touring bands like the Dead who wanted to play louder, to reach bigger audiences without sacrificing quality.

The Wall is a colossal character unto itself, the living, breathing megawatt protagonist in its own epic saga. Lesh, a lanky brainiac-type who fizzed with excitement, likened the system to "the voice of God." The Wall allowed the Dead "to get loud, clean sound at the back of the huge hall," Lesh said, "and supreme musical control, because we run everything from the stage." He described the PA as, simply, "apocalyptic" and said the experience of playing through it felt like piloting a flying saucer.

Weir, the dyslexic, spaced-out rhythm guitarist with boyish looks, has described the Wall as "the monster with a thousand screaming eyes" and has said that for as good as it sounded, the costs and logistics made the project untenable. The Dead often had to pay rent at two venues simultaneously, due to the leapfrogging scaffolding sets. A global fuel crisis was on at the time, too, so gas costs were astronomical.

Jerry Garcia, the understated guitarist and singer whose antiauthoritarian views made him a leader who largely refused to lead, could cut through the noise around the soundsystem in his characteristic way. As Garcia once told an interviewer before a summer 1974 outdoor Wall show, "It works—that's the thing about it."

The system was deafening. Sound level meters regularly hit 120 decibels onstage with the Wall, about as loud as a jet engine at close range. Ear protection was an afterthought. All of the band members, and likewise the crew, would later experience some degree of hearing damage as a result of sustained exposure to amplified music at such ear-splitting levels.

Yet the sound it reproduced was so fine, like confronting the sublime, that you would hardly know. Forget "turning it up to eleven," as the timeless *Spinal Tap* bit goes. The Wall packed so much power that its volume knobs didn't need to be dialed past two, Dennis McNally, the band's former longtime publicist and author of *A Long Strange Trip*, a history of the Dead, told me. The sound the Wall projected was so clean and distortion-free that it could be heard clearly, with no wind degradation, from a quarter mile away outdoors. Ask anyone who saw the band perform during those storied years, especially in 1974, whose jaws dropped at the rip-roaring yet crystalline audio, and they'll tell you there has been nothing quite like the Wall, even if the music industry and the state of live concert technology have since surpassed it.

The Dead might've achieved something pristine in the Wall era, but under the hood the vibe was coming unhinged. The early days of touring with the soundsystem were imbued with a collective mentality driven by the pursuit of something greater—and psychedelics. Yet by the summer of 1974, the situation reached a coked-up breaking point. Some of the Dead's road crew depended on substantial quantities of stimulants purely as fuel for the physical and mental grind of traveling with and maintaining the Wall. This undercut the "all for one, one for all" spirit that had got them there in the first place.

"The stresses and strains associated with large scale touring... were starting to create cracks and crevices in our unanimity of purpose," Lesh later said. The band's crew "was twice as large as it needed to be, and could be quite surly." As Weir has said of this time, the roadies were "drowning in mountains of blow." By an ill-fated and under-attended European run that fall, when the band failed to break even, many party members carried knives—as much tools as for drug use, and also to intimidate greedy promoters during shakedowns.

After clocking just forty shows with the full system in 1974, a decision to stop touring was made by group consensus among the band, management, and the entire crew, as such matters were largely always handled in Deadworld. Yet the idea to stop first came down from the upper ranks of the Dead organization, on its way to becoming one of the top forty biggest corporations in California. By 1975, the PA was being disassembled and most of the roadies and other band employees were out of work.

But the Wall was so technologically groundbreaking in its short run that it still thrums decades after its physical dissolution. Though simultaneous sonic innovations were popping off elsewhere, albeit on smaller scales, around this same time—notably in the lofts and clubs of gay underground dance scenes in New York City and Chicago—the Dead's sphere of sustained influence in the realm of audio is astounding. Through this exceptional rig, the Dead gamely leapt into uncharted sonic territory and set the bar for distortion-free, hyperrealistic, three-dimensional sound reproduction as we now know it. That's why their PA remains an icon of a past sonic gold standard, both on stages and beyond. Unraveling this legacy brings us into the Dead's world, and the Dead into ours.

The Wall was temperamental. Speakers and tweeters blew left and right. The phase-canceling mics regularly failed and produced vocal mixes that have been criticized as sounding "tinny." But the monolithic PA has cast a long shadow across the musical landscape. The Dead pioneered the stacking of speakers in curved vertical arrays that "throw" sound over the audience, now industry standard from stadiums and arenas to auditoriums to beer-soaked clubs.

The audacity of the Dead to push their system as far as it could go—and then some—has also had a conceptual and aesthetic influence on Wall-like rigs used by the Allman Brothers Band and German krautrock icons CAN, to Southern California punks Black Flag and arena funk rockers Red Hot Chili Peppers. More recently, Grammy-winning rock groups like the War on Drugs have shouted out the Dead's Wall. So too do working musicians like Sean Yeaton, bassist in the critically acclaimed New York punk band Parquet Courts, revere the Dead's rig. "The Wall of Sound represents to me the absolute mold of live audio presentation," Yeaton told me.

An attempt is even underway to faithfully re-create the PA. Anthony Coscia, a guitar maker and Deadhead from Connecticut, is building his own to-scale working replica of the soundsystem. The idea came to him during the pandemic, and he began building a functional model in earnest in 2021. He's about halfway there, and financing the project largely out-of-pocket. His "mini Wall of Sound" quickly went viral, making the front page of the *Wall Street Journal*. Coscia has since notched a handful of public demonstrations of the quarter-scale version. "I didn't have any doubts that the community would embrace the project," Coscia told the *Journal*, "but I think I misinterpreted how big the community is." Surely a few of the over one million people who've seen his project on Facebook alone likely were born *after* the Wall came down.

One such Deadhead, born in 1975 when the band was on hiatus, has taken a reverence for the Wall to a deeper level. Bob Gendron, a music journalist, has an intricate black-and-white tattoo on his right arm of the system's curved center vocal cluster. The tattoo is based on a widely seen photograph of the cluster, packed with dozens of 12- and 5-inch speakers and looking like an insect's eye, taken during soundcheck at a May 1974 show. "I've had a couple of people that have seen it and they're like, *Holy shit, that's the Wall of Sound*," Gendron told me.

But outside of rock and roll fetishism, many millions are touched by this soundsystem, and by extension the Dead, in our everyday lives in subtle and profound ways. The band continued for twenty years after the Wall era, forever altering musical history and the very fabric of modern society. The story of the Wall dials into the significance of these social, artistic, cultural, and consumer frequencies too. The basic technological underpinnings of noise-canceling headphones, AirPods, and assistive hearing devices, for instance, were refined through the Wall. "The hearing aid tech industry may owe the Grateful Dead a long overdue thank you," according to the American Academy of Audiology, a leading professional organization of hearing healthcare experts.

This story also taps into the Dead's ever-widening network of influence on media dissemination and consumption. As the Wall came alive, the Dead up-ended established models of content and idea sharing, foretelling today's notions of "free" everything, from streaming to social media. In the early '70s, hardcore fans began sneaking their own portable recording kits into shows to capture live sets, in the hopes of bringing home the experience of the Wall. The Dead knew this was going on and took a stance that tacitly approved of, then fully embraced the practice, inadvertently nurturing a worldwide distribution network for boot-leg cassette tapes that just might be the original viral marketing campaign.

The Dead's brand of what Garcia called "hip economics," moreover, where money is kept circulating among "the family" or "the community," opened a universe of possibilities for others in the do-it-yourself tradition. Against the odds, the Dead got rich along the way. Despite their countercultural spirit, the band grew into one of the most successful live acts of all time, smashing atten-dance and sales records. They did so by serving as the antidote to studio-signed bands that churned out radio hits. A later-era sleeper single, "Touch of Grey," did crack the top ten on the *Billboard* Hot 100 chart in 1987. But their live show was always the main event. By the mid-'80s, the Dead regularly drew tens of thousands of people to their performances, and just as many ticketless folks hung in the parking lot—a fractal-like bazaar scene and subculture in itself.

The band had entered the "Mega Dead" era and typically sold around two million tickets a year. They filled football stadiums and had a private Learjet chartered for their roadies, well into the '90s. Then, under the suffocating pressures of fame, the oppressive machinery of touring, and the isolating hole of opiate addiction, Garcia died in August 1995, and the Grateful Dead entered a new phase of existence.

Like Garcia himself, the Wall was so renowned during its brief life that it has become a meme. As of the early '80s, Lesh was referring to the '74 PA, not yet known as the Wall of Sound, as the "rocket gantry system," owing to its resemblance to the complex of service platforms and rigging around a rocket's launching pad. By then, the PA had already entered the band's secret-handshake iconography and visual universe, and the soundsystem is still a part of the Dead's legacy stage dressing. Lesh performed as Phil Lesh & Friends in front of a mock "Wall," constructed of corrugated cardboard, at the Skull & Roses Festival in Ventura, California. During summer stadium tours, Dead & Company have included odes to the soundsystem in their light show. Since Dead & Company formed and began touring in 2015, the group has sold around four and a half million tickets and grossed over $430 million, and has likewise become an attendance record–breaking stadium act.

"Name another band in the history of the world where a soundsystem was something you would remember fifty years later," Chris Coyle, Dead & Company's lighting designer, told me. Without fail, projecting the Wall's likeness behind the band is one of those moments, Coyle said, when from his vantage point in the crowd, "you get to see all the phones get up and start taking pictures."

Now more than ever, the Wall reflects something back at all of us—something exhilarating and uncanny, awe-inspiring and absurd, a triumph that simultaneously captures a mythic past and gazes into a radical future.

This story is personal. My parents both orbited the Dead, and each other, in various capacities in the 1970s, including at legendary Midwest Wall shows. In the '80s, their paths crossed and the two bonded over a shared affinity for the band. Now in their seventies, they represent a generation of Deadheads, stand-ins for the sociopolitical archetype of the working-class hippie-stagehand in a scene that was inclusive and progressive for the time, but still largely white, straight, and male dominated.

Throughout the '70s, Mary Ann Crosby, my mother, was associated with prominent concert promoter Howard Stein through a connection at the now defunct

Flipside Records in Chicago. Beginning in her late teens, mom worked shows by heavies like Black Sabbath; Hawkwind; the Who; the Kinks; King Crimson; Genesis; Emerson, Lake & Palmer; Mahavishnu Orchestra; Procol Harum; Traffic; Jefferson Starship; Ten Years After; Deep Purple; New Riders of the Purple Sage (featuring Garcia on pedal steel guitar); and of course, the Dead. She also baked goodies. Once in Madison, Wisconsin, while roaming backstage at the drafty, ten-thousand-seat Dane County Coliseum before a "proto"-Wall show in 1973, she bumped into a bespectacled man in jeans, a black sweater, and cowboy boots. It was Garcia, with his infectious laugh, nimbus of curly dark hair, and bittersweet-sounding singing voice. She offered a cookie. Garcia smiled, took a bite, and "seemed to be really tickled for me to stumble upon him," she told me.

My father, Mark Anderson, started catching Dead shows in Chicago in 1969, when he was nineteen. Their music "was so feral and exploratory," he told me. "Wide open, like the times." The band's evocative lyrics drew him in, "and allowed room for thought," he said. Before long, the wider scene became attractive: "Band members' philosophies, traveling Deadheads, and recognition of other like-minded souls each had their allure," he said. "At the time, finding other kindred spirits was a challenge." He went on to do seasonal grunt work for UltraSound, the band's preferred PA provider, founded in 1978 by Dead-adjacent audio engineers. Part of an indispensable Midwest local union crew, my dad helped the band's roadies rig up, or "fly," speaker arrays at Dead shows in forty-thousand-capacity outdoor "shed" amphitheaters throughout the '80s. He even handled the ornate Afghan-style stage rugs the band played on. Made of synthetic rather than natural materials, the rugs couldn't hold a static electrical charge that might otherwise affect the overall sound.

As bit players in the Dead's Wall era, my parents' journeys loom large in how they passed on that legacy to my older sister, Elizabeth, and me. "We just explained and showed what it was about the band that we liked, not that you should like them," my dad told me. There is a certain percentage of people in each generation who "get it," who the band speaks to, he said. "It seems as though you and Elizabeth are in that percentage."

I've been captivated by the Dead soundsystem my entire life. My first concert? The Dead at Alpine Valley, Wisconsin, in 1989, when I was three—long after the Wall. The sold-out gig drew forty thousand ticketed attendees and another twenty thousand revelers in the lot. Dad worked the show, setting up stage technology as an UltraSound contractor in his low-profile, band-issued local crew shirt and sticky access pass. One of my earliest flashes of memory is of Garcia gently kicking a balloon that had landed onstage during the show. I also remember that four-year-old Elizabeth and I were unsure about the Dead's experimental "Space" jam in their second set. Our little brains couldn't make sense of the sound of the band "going underwater," as mom always describes it.

During family road trips in the '90s, Elizabeth and I listened as our folks told stories—live Dead tapes always soundtracked the drives—about independently seeing the band before either of us was born. The Dead had built a mountain of speakers called the Wall of Sound that was loud but clear and *blew people's minds*, including theirs. In the backseat, my sister and I would side-eye each other in wonder and laugh.

I first wrote about the Wall in 2015, in a feature for *VICE* that was pegged to the band's fiftieth anniversary and only scratched the surface of a deeper story that has completely consumed me since. The twist is that an actual, physical part of that soundsystem has dropped into my own life.

The journey branches out from a birch tree that grew to maturity in Finland. One day in the early '70s, that tree was felled, stripped, cut into sheets, layered three-quarters-of-an-inch thick (14-ply), and then shipped to the West Coast of North America.

Richard Pechner grew familiar with Finnish birch. A carpenter and amateur photographer who worked for and toured with the Dead from their early days through the end of the Wall, Pechner can remember picking up loads of the material at MacBeath Hardwood, a lumber import company in Berkeley. With his red-framed glasses and smoky cackle, Pechner, now in his seventies and living in Hawaii, is just one of the characters from the Dead's scene who feel ripped from a madcap Thomas Pynchon novel. I showed Pechner a picture of my artifact not long after I acquired the piece. He guessed that he could have cut out the front board, "or I could've glued the box together," he said.

At one point, the Dead were buying up whole shipments of Finnish birch as the band's DIY worldview collided with a yearning for better live sound. Standard audio gear in the mid-to-late '60s was still primitive pre-war technology, down to the guts of the instruments, and "mostly looked like what you'd see in a club because they were playing smaller venues," Pechner said. "As things got bigger people started realizing that you needed sound reinforcement—you need a PA system." The whole rock scene at that time, he added, was under similar constraints in terms of how to put on a good performance. "But the

Dead in the beginning were always trying to figure out how to do it themselves, mostly because of the inconsistency when you'd tour." The Dead's refusal to accept this standard reflects the countercultural, almost punk-like attitude braided into the band's subversive identity.

This search for ingenuity explains their new choice of wood, determined by the heads at Alembic, a still-active Bay Area electronics and instrument company so intertwined with the Dead in the late '60s and early '70s that the two collaborated on what became the Wall. Alembic professionals like Ron Wickersham, Rick Turner, Augustus Owsley "Bear" Stanley III, John Curl, and Sal Cardinalli discovered that a dense variety, like birch, would give them better control of the speaker's output. The material was ultra-rugged, an added benefit for road life. MacBeath was only getting so many pieces of Finnish hardwood at the time—and the Dead needed *a lot* of it to accommodate their fledgling PA. "We'd say, *we want them all*," Pechner said. So the importer would notify them when fresh shipments arrived. "We'd go right over and buy it up and bring them back to San Rafael."

That's where so much off-road scheming, conceptualizing, and sheer forging of the Wall transpired. San Rafael was the longtime home of Dead headquarters, about a half hour north of San Francisco. The incorporated outfit settled into an office space at Fifth and Lincoln in 1970. The band, enjoying increasing levels of financial success and playing to bigger crowds as their touring with Alembic's early iteration of the Wall ramped up, then started their own in-house record label in 1973. Now, they could release their music themselves and, crucially, maintain artistic control, a bold move when a band's commercial success and reach were still bound to an outside record label contract.

This couldn't have happened just anywhere. Northern California was an incubator and harbinger for what was percolating nationwide even before Vietnam War protests began in the late '60s. "There were obviously other places where things were going on—Detroit, Chicago, New York—but it seemed like the Bay Area had a unique kind of convergence, that one was feeding the other, back and forth," Pechner told me. "You had [novelist] Ken Kesey down at Stanford being given LSD by the government. You had politicos at UC-Berkeley that started the free speech movement. And in the Haight-Ashbury, the default was it was the lowest-rent neighborhood in San Francisco."

The Haight, where the Dead lived communally in a Victorian three-flat at 710 Ashbury, attracted people who lacked the resources to live in more affluent neighborhoods. Pechner was there, helping schlep the band's gear to and from

710 when they were playing now-legendary free shows in San Francisco's Pan-handle and elsewhere around this time. The Dead were just one of the groups playing an emerging form of electrified psychedelic rock, but became *the* one, and arguably, the last left standing of a generation.

Against this crackling and technicolor backdrop, an expanding misfit's crew of psychedelicized roadies and sound techs tinkered on the PA, both on and off the road. They were gruff dudes with names like Lawrence "Ram Rod" Shurtliff, Donald "Rex" Jackson, Mark "Sparky" Raizene, "Big" Steve Par-ish, Clifford Heard, Bob Matthews, Joe Winslow, and Bill "Kidd" Candelario. With success came bigger and better gigs but also increasingly compartmen-talized divisions of labor. The crew always functioned well enough to get the job done, though members grew siloed, irritable, emotionally toxic to each other and those around them, and at times even physically confrontational and violent over equipment turf wars and heavy drug use that came to a head under the Wall. "They'll tear your flesh off," Garcia later told one inter-viewer, speaking of the band's "merciless" roadies. "They can be extremely painful."

Meanwhile, Garcia, Weir, and Lesh got to plug into, play their instru-ments, and sing through this extraordinary soundsystem. Likewise the band's then pianist Keith Godchaux and backing vocalist Donna Jean Godchaux, a husband-and-wife combo, as well as Kreutzmann, the burly drummer who had a taste for blow and got punchy when he drank.

But it was people like Pechner, Parish, Raizene, Candelario, Curl, former Alembic amplifier technician Janet Furman, recording engineer Betty Cantor, longtime Dead live mixer Dan Healy, and a constellation of other heads, who were in the room during this signal moment. They built and refined the Dead's PA by hand while the collective's sonic ambitions, together with their recording capabilities, grew higher. Their behind-the-scenes experiences are as enter-taining as they are harrowing—a romp full of close calls, all-night hauls, and run-ins with cops, fire marshals, Hells Angels, and international drug smug-gler Deadheads. They are the original roadies who trailblazed technological innovation on the largest scale ever seen at the time. "It was a *lot* of work," Candelario told me decades later, "and a lot of driving."

If not for them, the Wall would've never been, and its experimental legacy wouldn't endure. Without the Wall, a generation of engineers and audio freaks wouldn't have coalesced on the West Coast to explore their most out-there ideas through soundsystem R&D for the Dead, the only band then willing to throw cash at such heady pursuits—which, in time, became the standard audio setup with which any concertgoer, anywhere, is familiar.

"The money was always there to build stuff and learn stuff that you needed to learn," said Candelario, who started working with the Dead in the late '60s as a teenager and remained part of the crew and merchandising arm to the end. "Nobody ever said, *Don't do that.* Everybody always said, *Hey, it's not done yet!* We could fabricate whatever we wanted. We could build whatever we wanted." If it had something to do with improving the music, funds were available.

Our world has been radically shaped by the Dead, regardless of one's own relationship with the band. And their fabled PA of the early '70s is perhaps the most striking example of that outsized influence. "The Wall of Sound is this incredible expression, and part of this much, much *bigger* expression of the Grateful Dead at their absolute most ambitious," Jesse Jarnow, co-host of the *Good Ol' Grateful Deadcast*, the official Grateful Dead podcast, told me. "That's the legacy, in the most real artistic way. Pushing your DIY independent system as far as you possibly can. Pushing away from the mainstream of the music industry, away from major labels, away from standard factory gear. Really doing everything yourself."

If we are all at least a little bit Dead, then the Wall is a prism that refracts the light from every angle. Yet the rig did not fall from the clear blue sky. The system was a yearslong endeavor. A progression. "Somebody's put a lot of time and effort into studying that and into figuring out how to make those cabinets, so that they had the integrity that they have," Healy told me. "We built that system, the Wall of Sound, from the ground up, from scratch." The Wall was a *before* and *after* moment. In Healy's words, "a kind of a Holy Grail."

I wanted to understand how it all came together, to place other surviving bits of that soundsystem, like my artifact, and learn the stories of fellow keepers of the Wall. But in order to track down "where they're buried," as one such keeper, the senior roadie Parish, put it to me, I had to first follow the signal back to the beginning.

2

The Mother Rig (1964–1966)

The sounds that emanated from 2338 Santa Catalina Street in Palo Alto in the early 1960s went unrecorded. But James "Sully" Sullivan, a neighborhood kid, remembered that those playing music at the single-story house "had a basic rhythm going," he told me. "Definitely loud. It was amplified."

The group of adolescent boys not yet calling themselves the Grateful Dead took form in this low-slung suburban garage in the predominantly Black and blue-collar "East Paly" of 1964. They had help from Ruth Marie, mother of giddy Garcia, an acne-scarred folk and bluegrass picker who played guitar and sang in the upstart band. She purchased the earliest soundsystem for what became the Dead: a pair of top-of-the-line Klipsch speakers.

Along with those built by Altec-Lansing and Stromberg-Carlson, two other audio companies of that era, the Klipschorns were some of the best high-fidelity speakers available to everyday consumers. A pair of the speakers, based on acoustic-horn technology originally designed for auditoriums and movie theaters, took up about a third of the average living room, like a warship's tuba-shaped ventilation ducts.

"The Klipschorn causes more *OOOing* and *AHHHHing* than any high-fidelity loudspeaker on the market," read a 1965 advertisement in *Audio* magazine. The loudspeaker came in a range of hardwoods and "contains three carefully matched horns...developed and combined with only one thought in mind: the finished product must offer the closest possible identity with original sound."

Garcia had never entirely forgiven his mother, a nurse and bar owner, for remarrying after his father died when Garcia was five. Still, he depended on his mom's support—and this mother rig was the origin of the Dead's quest for audio perfection.

"She came up with a present for him, when she saw his band was starting to gel together," Steve Parish, who was not yet in the scene but would become Garcia's guardian roadie, told me. It was a simple, rudimentary practice system, "but it was still a step up from anybody else at that time. It was a *big* deal to have a PA."

That was just one facet of Garcia's sound-soaked upbringing. At Ruth's downtown San Francisco tavern, her preteen son had absorbed music from the jukebox and a portable radio that became a fixture plugged in his ear. Young Garcia discovered blues and early electric rock and roll records by Black guitarists like Chuck Berry and Freddie King. Recordings by Carl Perkins, the Crows, John Lee Hooker, Jimmy Reed, Muddy Waters, Jimmy McCracklin, B. B. King, and other R&B heavies also turned Garcia on to certain sounds, tones, and "textures," like the repeating slap of an echo chamber, that imprinted deeply into his own psyche and sonic sensibilities.

Garcia's stepfather, moreover, kept mandolins and various stringed instruments around the house, and even electrical instruments, amps, and a tape recorder—novelties at the time—were accessible to him at home. The middle-register signature of woodwinds, the clarinet in particular, seized Garcia. "That sound is very present in my ear," he later said. Some people can recall smells, Garcia explained, whereas "I can hear a sound and all of a sudden it will transport me to places."

One instrument he was decidedly not drawn to back then? The accordion—like the one his mom gifted Garcia on his fifteenth birthday. He convinced her to exchange the squeezebox for a Danelectro guitar and a small amp. Garcia didn't know how to tune an electric, but learned to pick and play on it anyway, "tuned to an open tuning that sounded right to me." Someone eventually showed Garcia how to properly tune the guitar and finger three basic chords. "It was like something gave me the key to heaven," Garcia later said. He *had* to make that sound. "It was like a disease with me."

Garcia experienced other life-altering episodes in this pre-Dead era, like discovering cannabis. He enjoyed getting high, working at his guitar, and hanging with Laird Grant, a neighborhood buddy Garcia made after Ruth moved the family to suburban Menlo Park. Grant would become the Dead's founding equipment manager and roadie, schlepping band gear and helping run an ever-evolving soundsystem.

The five-string banjo, it turned out, was a perfect vessel for Garcia's burgeoning and obsessive, all-consuming nature. As Garcia had been getting into bluegrass records around this time, he thought to himself, "God, what is that sound? I gotta make that sound." Garcia decided to try a hand at the stringed instrument in 1962, when he was twenty and taken by "that incredible clarity ... the brilliance" of the sounds it made.

So Garcia bought a used banjo from a local seller with the last name Kreutzmann, whose son was named Bill. (Garcia and young Kreutzmann would soon be jamming together.) A year later, Garcia nabbed Best Banjo Player at the Monterey Folk Festival, where he performed with his Bay Area friends and fellow pickers Robert Hunter and David Nelson. Bob Dylan, who had not yet "gone electric," also played the fest. Garcia, upset over Dylan's amplified acoustic guitar, later recalled splitting not long into Dylan's set, which Hunter blamed on the shoddy PA sound.

On May 24, 1964, Garcia arrived at the temple of bluegrass—rural Indiana—at the Brown County Jamboree, or Bean Blossom, a festival put on by mandolinist Bill Monroe, considered the godfather of the genre. The stop was part of a cross-country journey Garcia embarked on with his friend Sandy Rothman, and the two recorded a tape of themselves and others picking at the fest. Too bad the electronic hum made the audio unlistenable.

Yet it's clear that Garcia was a "taper" in the heady early '60s, road-tripping across the South and Midwest with a banjo in one hand and an audio recorder in the other. "I used to be a bluegrass music freak, and I spent a lot of time taping bands," Garcia later told *The Golden Road*, a Dead fanzine. "I loved being able to do it, and I loved having the tapes afterward and being able to trade them around."

Young Bob Weir, a girl-crazed class clown who soon joined up with Garcia, his guitar instructor at a mom-and-pop shop in Palo Alto, Dana Morgan's Music, was likewise a budding taper. Weir was known to record guitarist Jorma Kaukonen's early Bay Area coffeehouse performances. Already, a preoccupation with capturing audio recordings of live gigs was taking root in their circle.

Meanwhile, at coffeehouses like the Boar's Head in San Carlos, another of Garcia's friends and musical collaborators was making noise of a different sort. Ron McKernan was a soulful, booze-drenched crooner who played a Vox Continental organ and a beat-up acoustic guitar. He had been drinking hard since the age of twelve, and was now a greasy, stocky eighteen. In addition to performing his own material and blues covers, he played harmonica with the

Zodiacs, another pre-Dead iteration of the band that mainly gigged at Stanford fraternity parties.

The default leader of that short-lived group, Troy Weidenheimer, played guitar and would signal a key and a groove as the others fell in. On drums was Kreutzmann, who had already been gigging around with local matching suit–style Bay Area rock bands. Garcia played bass, and later spoke about the influence the Zodiacs' open format had on his own mode of playing "free."

Sully, the neighborhood kid, was close to the white-hot core of what were likely some of their first, bumbling practice sessions at 2338 Santa Catalina— then the residence of the McKernans, a middle-class family of five. As a young teen, Sully befriended Ron's kid brother, Kevin. He rode his bike to their house, smoked weed with Kevin, and heard his older brother's band "makin' noise" in their garage, through this earliest PA. "They were just a bunch of young guys lookin' to hustle chicks," Sully told me.

Around the time the Zodiacs had run their course, McKernan, Garcia, and now Weir focused their creative efforts into yet another precursor Dead band. Mother McCree's Uptown Jug Champions had notched their first gig at the Tangent, a Palo Alto coffeehouse, in January 1964. Known to also rehearse in the Garcia family's garage, Mother McCree's featured McKernan on harmonica, Garcia on banjo and guitar, and Weir on jug and washtub bass. Bob Matthews, a friend who became an integral member of the Dead's sound and recording crew, briefly played kazoo in Mother McCree's.

But for months, McKernan, now nicknamed Pigpen, had been pitching Garcia on the idea that they start a band that played electrified rhythm and blues. They could pretty easily adapt a lot of the jug material they were already playing. "Let's *do* this," Pigpen would say, citing the Beatles and Rolling Stones as inspiration. Garcia came around to the idea by autumn of 1964. The Warlocks were born.

May 5, 1965. On a Wednesday "family night" at Magoo's, a Menlo Park pizza parlor, Pigpen, Garcia, Weir, Kreutzmann, and an acquaintance, Dana Morgan Jr. (on bass), plugged into the mother rig. Having made their debut at Menlo College the month prior, this was only their second gig.

No tapes of that first public performance at Magoo's, or of two more mid-week shows the Warlocks played at that brick-walled club that May, are known to exist. Only the haziest of memories remain of these gigs, other than the place had predictably bad acoustics. The band was sometimes crammed at the front of the space, and other times into a corner, "no stage, no nothing, flat on the ground," recalled Garcia's buddy Grant, who was present at Magoo's.

But a thumping sense of their first PA, and the frenzied excitement of experiencing their nascent sound, can still be gathered from other firsthand accounts. "The first night at the pizza place, nobody was there," Garcia later recalled. But when the Warlocks played Magoo's again the following week, "there were lots of kids there." By their third gig at the restaurant, between three and four hundred people had turned up, mostly local high schoolers. Crowds spilled onto the street. "People were freaking out," Garcia remembered.

Take Phil Lesh, who attended the band's third-ever show. Then taking classes at the nearby College of San Mateo, and worshiping the likes of Charles Ives and Karlheinz Stockhausen as a student of classical and avant-garde musical composition, Lesh later underscored the physicality of the young band's sound. "The music was so loud, even outside, and the groove so compelling, that I just *had* to dance… only to be blown back against the wall," Lesh recalled. At Magoo's, one had to navigate through "an almost palpable sea of sound."

Buzz was building around the group. "Some say that it was Garcia's idea to turn Mother McCree's into an electric blues band, but Garcia told me it was Pigpen's idea," Lesh later said. "At first he wanted to electrify the jug band, but then changed his mind, saying, *No, let's get a drummer and make it a blues band.*" Contrary to popular Dead mythologies, Pigpen was arguably the group's original instigating force and front man. "Pig was our first lead player," Kreutzmann later said. "Before Garcia had all the spotlights at him, Ron was our boy, he did it all."

Lesh was intrigued. For someone like him, who at the time was not actively practicing music, that Pigpen and Garcia were going in this new direction was "a very exciting development," he said. "I couldn't wait to hear Jerry play electric guitar." What was novel, after all, was precisely that: "Amplification of instruments and voices enabled nuances that once would have been lost in the noise floor to be clearly heard," said Lesh, "and developed further in a seemingly infinite progression."

He sat up front that night at Magoo's, close to the stage, transfixed. Later that evening, Garcia encouraged Lesh to try his hand at bass—Dana Morgan Jr. wasn't cutting it—and become a member of the group. In addition to Pigpen's commanding stage presence and Garcia's inspired playing, Lesh was apparently also impressed with Weir, whom he had met at a party earlier that year. Weir, Lesh realized, "had progressed so far and so fast on guitar that he was now the rhythm guitarist in the new band." Lesh didn't need much convincing to take up Garcia's offer. This pivotal moment illuminates the centrality of three-dimensional sound in the Dead's cultural history, an opening bell chime in the run-up to the Wall.

On top of the Klipsch rig, the band was using loaned gear from Dana Morgan Sr.'s local music store, which had played after-hours host to their first practices as a five-piece. Seventeen-year-old Sue Swanson, an early friend of the band who likewise caught them at Magoo's and elsewhere around the mid-'60s Bay Area, hung around the shop at these sessions. She was invited by Weir, a classmate from school. "Talk about ground floor," she told me. Swanson remembers the literal wall of sound: Instruments were hung around the showroom, like the cymbals that resonated from the ambient sound pressure of the band practicing. Swanson's lasting memory of these early jams is not of the music but the volume, and how the whole place seemed to vibrate, especially the sandwich-like hi-hats. "While they're playing this music all that stuff is *rattling*," Swanson said.

Guitars, amps, a sparkling new gold Ludwig drum kit—they had it all. "One cool thing I have to say about Dana," Kreutzmann later wrote in his memoir *Deal*, "he never asked for the gear back" even after his son had been replaced on bass by the fast-learning Lesh. By other accounts, by late spring 1965, Morgan Sr. apparently decided he "hated the noise they were making" so he sold all their instruments.

With Dana Jr. now out, the band nonetheless had to find a new practice space. They made some use of the rehearsal room in the back of Guitars Unlimited, a Menlo Park music shop where Garcia and Weir both now happened to work. At one standout Warlocks practice at Guitars Unlimited, "Jerry turned on the lights and we crowded in the center of the room," Lesh recalled. "Pig stomped out his cigarette and ran some scales on his organ as Bob, with a distant look in his eyes, tuned up his guitar, and Billy, nattily dressed as always, sat ramrod straight at his drums and rattled off a few warm-up flourishes." Lesh plugged in his bass, "and tentatively plucked a few notes." They were playing on borrowed amps, "and it would be several months and a few gigs until we would score some of our own, thanks to the generosity of Jerry's mom."

In the meantime, they jammed for the next seven hours. Lesh was so hyped on playing an electric instrument, and with this particular group of musicians, that he couldn't fall asleep that night. "It felt as though the electricity flowing through the instrument had permanently amped up my aura to a new intensity," he said.

On June 18, the Warlocks played their first gig with Lesh at the teen rock club Frenchy's, in the Bay Area town of Hayward. Swanson transported the band members in her own car and the band stumbled through their set of Chuck Berry, Beatles, and Stones covers, coming across "wooden" sounding, "real stiff," Lesh remembered; they didn't get paid that night. Then again, as Garcia later said of their sound at that moment in time, the band's "most endearing quality was how rough and raunchy we were. Noisy."

They leaned into it in order to fill set times as they became a band. When the Warlocks landed a six-week residency at a bar in nearby suburban Belmont called the In Room that September, they pulled five nearly hour-long sets a night, six nights a week. At the In Room, "there was no shortage of meth, alcohol, or loose women," Kreutzmann recalled. "That was the vibe. Real angular. Cigarette smoke filled the air." On a good week, the In Room gig earned the band around $800. As Garcia later said in an early issue of the official Dead Heads newsletter, during the In Room run the band "developed a whole malicious thing, playing songs longer and weirder, and louder."

The band was out there, thanks to the various mind-altering chemicals already propelling their groupmind. They often had spent the daytime hours dropping acid and gonging around the peninsula before showing up at the In Room, smoking a couple joints in the back parking lot, and extolling the LSD experience—that its effects were like peeling back layers of an onion, and that it gave you the ability to "see right through people." Psychedelics allowed the band to think outside the sonic box, watering the seed of an idea from which the Wall sprang.

In Room co-manager Dale O'Keefe recalled that the band held it together for sets one and two on a given night, but that by set three things would start to get strange, and by set five they sounded downright "barbaric." Larry, the In Room's towering glass-eyed bartender, by contrast, couldn't get enough, and wanted them to turn up even louder. It was there the Warlocks gained confidence while playing at increasing levels of volume. "We learned to trust each other—and played longer," Lesh said. "We learned to make music out of feedback, out of noise, if you will—and the walls melted (or so it seemed)."

The band also tuned in to structural and environmental characteristics and first learned how to leverage, and riff on, such site-specific quirks—an attention to the microcosmic-macrocosmic model of sound that guided them through the Wall. In Belmont, night trains ran along nearby tracks on a set schedule. The band didn't let the rumble stop them in their tracks, nor did they try to fight it by overpowering the noise with their own. Instead, they synced up and played along with the locomotive lurch. Out of this improvisation came "Caution (Do Not Stop on Tracks)," one of their first original numbers, which happened to also be a straight rip of Them's "Mystic Eyes," a popular song at the time.

For Steve Brown, a record industry head, the experience of seeing the band in those days was "love at first sound." Brown distinctly remembers picking up on the early boost the Warlocks had gotten from Garcia's mom. They were "able to get a PA that was something more than what other people were using at the time," Brown told me. He can remember thinking, *Oh, these guys are getting serious.* He had already gotten to know the musicians; an early fan and friend of the band, Brown has been called a proto-Deadhead. He soon became the first fan to tape-record a live Dead gig, and later spent time in the soundfield at Wall shows as a band employee.

Brown had caught the Warlocks at Magoo's, but seeing them at the In Room was something else. "They had Phil, so that made a difference in the way that the whole sound was," Brown recalled. The In Room was a good club to see them perform in the mid-'60s because the band essentially had their own wing within the building. "It was the second kind of 'L' shape from the bar area, which made it nice to have their own space," Brown said. "The songs they did were going more into rhythm and blues and sounded really great, as far as the sound in that room when they were playing."

But the general state of live concert sound reinforcement was still primitive. Unlike today, the musicians didn't have monitor speakers; they couldn't hear themselves playing over the sound of their own amplifiers. Club-size venues like the In Room largely were not equipped with soundsystems, meaning all the sound of the instruments came from the amps themselves. If a venue had a PA, it got placed in front of performers, traditionally just a single small speaker to each side of the stage. Such early systems were fashioned not for electric instruments but for speaking and singing, and often drummers played acoustically—that is, not amped. Vocal microphones got jacked into instrument amps, leaving singers straining to go as loud as the rest of the band was playing. Any semblance of a "mix" was rudimentary, balanced roughly between the settings of individual instrument amps.

This made playing to twenty people, let alone hundreds or thousands, no small feat. Achieving even halfway decent sound that people in the back, as well as the musicians, could all hear was a wall in and of itself that needed to be overcome. The state of the art in mid-'60s live sound sometimes was able to squeak by in small rooms, though in bigger and/or high-ceilinged ones the acoustics were often bad. At one gig the Warlocks played around this same time at Pierre's, a San Francisco club that was entirely brick and concrete with tall ceilings, the space was far longer than it was wide. The inferior sonics, coupled with the band's ripping PA, assaulted the unsuspecting crowd.

Cutting through the dark, seedy air and smoke back at the In Room, the music the Warlocks played was likewise "just about as loud as any kind of a club that wasn't really made necessarily for a concert," Brown said. "That's what everybody was kind of falling into at the time." But at the Belmont bar they had a "nice little stage," which upped the overall production value of the gig. "It was more getting toward where we were headed, as far as the kind of music performance situations that gave a better sound and a little more privacy."

Sam Salvo, another In Room bartender, similarly recalled the Warlocks' residency in terms of a *before* and *after*. "Even their crew had this wild energy about them," Salvo later wrote, "and they all seemed to be in their own world." When the band took the stage, he added, "some people just listened like they were just another band, but most people were in awe." The Warlocks "were loud, outrageous, very good, and ahead of their time."

Elsewhere that autumn, the band hit the studio for the first time. On November 3, the Warlocks changed their name—for a single recording session—to the Emergency Crew, and hastily cut a half dozen tracks, mostly covers, as an audition for Autumn Records. Nothing came of that rough-sounding demo; for Weir, the highlight was finding himself in the storage room next door, among another band's gear. Weir was envious of their fancy Fender Showman amps—if only he could replace his Bandmaster, a less high-end model, with one of those.

The band then changed their name again. That same month, flipping through LPs at a local record shop, Lesh is said to have landed on a single by another band calling themselves the Warlocks. In all likelihood these other Warlocks were a band from Texas who later changed their name to ZZ Top, and not the Warlocks from New York City who soon renamed themselves the Velvet Underground.

One dark and stormy night thereafter, Garcia pulled a dictionary off the shelf at Lesh's apartment, randomly flipped it open, and there it was, leaping off the page: Grateful Dead. They had their name. "It's just a loaded phrase," Garcia later said of the common motif in folklore, wherein a deceased individual's spirit confers benefits to the stranger who gave them a proper burial. "It looks good in print, it sounds good—it's got a sort of euphoric thing going for it."

Now the Dead, and their PA 1.0, had to face their biggest test yet.

December 4, 1965. The band was set up in a Victorian-style house in San Jose, plugged into speaker columns that Lesh recalled being so big you could lie down inside the subwoofers. On hand was an aspiring magazine publisher named Jann Wenner, a twentysomething who would soon launch a new monthly music publication with a story about the band. They played uncomfortably loud that Saturday. The host of the party later tried to make the band pay the electricity bill. So much for the first appearance of the Grateful Dead.

The high-quality LSD circulating had something to do with the way the night had gone off, and how the sound was perceived. That San Jose gig marked the second of a dozen or so Acid Tests, mind-expanding, psychedelic-fueled, audiovisual happenings that took place over the coming weeks and months on the West Coast, from Portland to Los Angeles. The Tests were organized by the author Ken Kesey, enjoying the success of his breakout novel, *One Flew Over the Cuckoo's Nest*, and his troupe of Merry Pranksters. The events occurred before lysergic acid diethylamide, or LSD, was criminalized in the US, and served as a model for the Dead's Wall project—and beyond.

The Dead were the de facto Test house band. Participants gained entry by paying one dollar, drinking LSD-spiked fruit punch, and tripping out with fellow travelers—and "passed the test" if they made it through the end of the night. The idea was to summon a hive mind through drugs, sound, light, and improvised music, and the Pranksters brought their own soundsystem too, making all kinds of disorienting sonic feedback loops. "When the Dead were playing through their own equipment, that sound was washing around the hall," Kesey later said of these early Tests. "Nobody had ever heard anything like this—where they were part of the ambience of the sound."

Not infrequently, the band members were too high to perform more than a few notes during the Tests. (Except for Pigpen—he stuck to the bottle and didn't even smoke weed.) The happenings "are a great training ground," Rock Scully, the Dead's soon-to-be manager, later wrote in his highly fabulized, ax-grinding memoir *Living with the Dead*. "After learning to play against all that insanity, the Grateful Dead can play anywhere. Nothing will ever faze them again."

The single thing that kept the whole operation from descending into complete chaos was this white-knuckle "professionalism," wrote Scully. Through the end of the Wall, he herded the band by plane, train, helicopter, and auto-mobile, and also in a press and promotional capacity, as he spiraled into his own opiate addiction alongside Garcia. But through rain, snow, sleet, and the pitch-black of night; through busted fan belts, intense acid trips, blown speakers, and fried amps, "we are always there on time and never (totally) blow a gig," Scully said.

The elusive individual supplying the namesake psychedelic for the Acid Tests, and the greater Bay Area and beyond, had recently introduced Scully to the band. That would be Augustus Owsley Stanley III, an eccentric Kentucky-born chemist and amateur audiophile whose hairy chest earned him the nickname Bear. He rewired more than just the Dead's perception of reality. Deep-pocketed and by all accounts extremely horny, Bear was on a crash course to becoming the Dead's first official "soundman," and a key Wall architect. Bear's then part-ner in chemistry, a reclusive PhD student named Melissa Cargill, would later talk about Bear's personality in terms of a relentless drive to be in control and "gain mastery" of his interests and to "penetrate into things."

Over the next two years, Bear manufactured loads of LSD with help from Cargill and others he recruited into his clandestine Dead-adjacent mobile acid lab. His reputation already preceded him on the streets of the emerging counterculture. Without Bear, the journalist Jay Stevens later wrote in *Storming Heaven: LSD and the American Dream*, "the Acid Tests probably would never have taken place, for the simple reason that LSD was too difficult to obtain."

The first time Scully saw the Dead, at a December 10 benefit for the Mime Troupe at the 1,300-capacity Fillmore Auditorium in San Francisco, he was trip-ping on Owsley acid. About an hour into the Dead's set, Scully recalled, the room was "breathing deeply, like a great sonic lung from which all sounds orig-inate and which demands all the oxygen in the world."

The following night, December 11, as the band waited around cranked on LSD at the Big Beat Acid Test in Palo Alto, they got held up by Bear. In a sign of things to come, Bear "scurries around connecting wires and plugging in amps," Scully claimed. "Five minutes into the Dead's set there is a big flash of light and sparks begin flying. A few people, thinking this is part of the show, cheer." Bear managed to patch things together but then—*flash*—another blow-out, Scully recalled. "We want to *play*, man," Pigpen apparently snapped, "just jam the fucking thing together." Bear simply stood there, "wide-eyed and fro-zen in the posture of inner debate," as Scully remembered.

Bear eventually got the system up and running and the band kicked into their set. In front of the low stage was seventeen-year-old Florence Nathan, a future Alembic employee who would create tie-dye speaker screens for the band's PA, run equipment orders, and help prepare extensive gear lists for international tours. But she can't say if she enjoyed or knew the songs they performed that night, or even if they played them proficiently. "I'm not all that sure the band could have told you either," she later wrote in her memoir *Dancing with the Dead*.

Later that Saturday, according to Scully, Bear told the band that Scully was going to be their manager. "You guys sure played pretty," Scully said, square-like, to the group. As he left the Big Beat event, he crawled into the back of the band's first dedicated equipment vehicle. By then, "all our gear pretty much fits in Kreutzmann's station wagon," Scully said. The Dead were barely scraping by, yet Bear was soon leveling up the band with top-flight gear, Scully recalled, using earnings from his side business. "He's our patron. He's making so much money from making LSD he can afford to bankroll the Dead," Scully said. "He is willing to do it as long as we do it on his terms." There among the drums, mic stands, assorted amps, and the mother rig—emblazoned with a fresh green GRATEFUL DEAD tag—Scully passed out.

Bear later disputed even being present that night, saying in interviews that the first time he saw the Dead perform was at the Muir Beach Acid Test on December 18. *That* happening was held up the coast in a log cabin that normally hosted weddings. A thirtysomething journalist named Tom Wolfe immortalized the Muir Beach Test, and the Dead's earliest soundsystem, in a generational and genre-defining work of immersion journalism, albeit an overwritten one filled with racist and other sketchy stereotypes.

The band "piled in with their equipment," Wolfe reported in *The Electric Kool-Aid Acid Test*, and began to play. "The Dead's weird sound!" Wolfe wrote. "Submarine somehow, turbid half the time, tremendously loud but like sitting under a waterfall, at the same time full of sort of ghoul-show vibrato sounds as if each string on their electric guitars is half a block long and twanging in a room full of natural gas."

The sound shattered Bear's realm. He couldn't *not* be a part of what the band was onto, and he remained an inspiration—and sometimes foil—to their sonic pursuits for decades. Simply hearing Garcia play was enough to push him "to go to work for the most amazing group ever and have a fabulous time of it," Bear later said. "I just hitched a ride and tried to make a positive contribution." What he brought to bear on the Dead's audio efforts, up to and through the end of the Wall, always pointed back to the "as above, so below" worldview. The ancient occult expression was the bedrock of Bear's belief "that whatever happened on any physical, emotional, or mental level while he was tripping was not a fantasy," Robert Greenfield wrote in *Bear*, a biography.

Five minutes. That's how long the Dead played at Muir Beach, as Garcia later recalled, in an interview at the band's San Rafael office that featured a guest appearance by Bear; "Long enough to impress the shit out of me," Bear chirped. Garcia's guitar that night, Bear said elsewhere, "seemed to come out of the universe and try to eat me alive." He ran out of the lodge before the Test had ended. Freaked out on his own supply, he peeled off in his car and crashed into a ditch. Bear was not hurt, but thoroughly rattled.

The same could be said for mom Garcia's PA. The Klipsch boxes eventually got a boost from a pair of midrange speakers built by the band's crew and powered by a Sansui amp. But after about a year, as they gained popularity and played out more, the band upgraded to a higher-quality system of primarily Fender gear. The old Klipsch speakers were eventually placed in storage at the Alembic shop until Garcia later asked the crew to gift the boxes to their biker friends at the Richmond chapter of the Hells Angels. The mother rig will make a nice party stereo system at their motorcycle clubhouse for the next fifty years.

3

The Lead Sled (Or, Owsleystein) (1966)

January 22, 1966. Pigpen was the only band member to decline one of the white capsules offered to the Dead that Saturday night. The group was loosening up at a friend's apartment near the Longshoremen's Hall in San Francisco, about to play the biggest Acid Test yet, a three-day affair billed as the Trips Festival.

Forget the acid manufactured by Swiss pharmaceutical giant Sandoz Laboratories, a variety of the psychedelic with which anyone in the Dead circle was acquainted. "No, this is new Owsley," their friends said. "This is what you want."

Bear's all-encompassing influence came on quick. The band was playing through new Fender equipment they acquired after mothballing the mother rig, but the Dead were about to hook into a stereophonic setup owned by Bear, the hirsute scion of a mid-South political family. He had hit it off with Phil Lesh at the Fillmore Acid Test on January 8 and was soon running the band's system.

The Dead had begun to experiment with feedback and unleashed squalls of noise at the Fillmore. "Extremely loud distorted tones wrenched from the speakers by electromagnetic interaction between the musical notes perceived by the pickups and the magnetic fields of the pickup, speaker, and amplifier," Lesh said. Rock Scully, who attended the Fillmore Test, was again taken aback by the band's sound and music. He "had the distinct sensation that the roof was lifting off."

Bent on working with the Dead, Bear got to talking with Lesh and asked how he could help. The band didn't have a proper sound technician, the bassist explained. Bear, who had a knack for audio through prior service-related ham radio and television experience, liked the sound of that. His own home at the time, a cottage in Berkeley, was an audiophile's sanctum, a hideout "filled with the most fantastic gear," Scully recalled. "All these amazing toys." As Scully would say decades later, "I should have seen the 75 ton 'Wall of Sound' coming as far back as Owsley's sound lab in Berkeley in 1965."

In his living room, Bear wired up a personal stereo system beyond what even serious high-fidelity aficionados at the time could have fantasized about ever owning: a set of massive Altec-Lansing Voice of the Theater speaker horns, originally designed for movie houses.

"If I could not be at a live show, next best was listening to music at Bear's," Rhoney Gissen, another of Bear's partners in chemistry, who also lived with him on and off into the 1970s, later wrote in her memoir *Owsley and Me.* "He modified his home audio system by exchanging the components of the amp and preamp with precision parts he ordered from an aircraft manufacturer," wrote Gissen. "He changed the type of cables and the wiring of the connectors. He had the best speakers—JBLs with the cones exposed. He even altered those, adding a subwoofer to increase the amplitude of the bass. His placement of the two tall speakers was calculated to optimize the quality of the sound." Already shining through were two concepts that helped make the Wall: souping up hardware and attention to acoustic directivity.

In that Berkeley cottage, Bear first laid out his vision of achieving three-dimensional sound—a sonic North Star that guided the band's haul to the big rig. "The concept of a stereo PA system is so ahead of its time," Scully recalled, "that it will be almost ten years before they start using it in movie theaters."

So by the Dead's Trips Fest appearance, Bear later claimed, he was their soundman. After sampling some of his latest batch of acid, his strongest vintage yet, the band entered the Longshoremen's Hall, a hexagonal concrete structure shaped like an umbrella. They would have a "great" Test, Bill Kreutzmann said of the night he remembered first meeting Bear himself.

Longshoremen's was the first sold-out Test. An estimated six thousand heads turned up over the course of the weekend, with musical accompaniment from the Dead and the not yet Janis Joplin–fronted Big Brother and the Holding Company. "All helplessly stoned, all finding themselves in a roomful of other thousands of people, none of whom any of them were afraid of," Jerry Garcia later recalled of the Trips Fest. "It was magic," the guitarist said.

At no point in history had more people tripping assembled in meatspace. One attendee, a local head named Dick Latvala, could recall the sights and sounds "very, very vividly," he later said. "But there was so much else going on there, it wasn't like I noticed the Grateful Dead as being an entity separate from any of the other things going on." Still, Latvala was hooked. "My passion—compulsion, I should say—with the Grateful Dead started in January of '66."

Wolfe, the dapper immersion journalist, was again present. His *Electric Kool-Aid Acid Test* offered a further snapshot of the Dead and their PA, devoting a chapter to the Trips Fest. "The mothers of it all were the Grateful Dead," Wolfe wrote—and Bear was indirectly responsible. "He started buying the Dead equipment such as no rock n roll band ever had before," including "all manner of tuners, amplifiers, receivers, loudspeakers, microphones, cartridges, tapes, theater horns, booms, lights, turntables, instruments, mixers, muters, servile mesochroics, whatever was on the market." The band's sound, Wolfe added, "went down so many microphones and hooked through so many mixers and variable lags and blew up in so many amplifiers and roiled around in so many speakers and fed back down so many microphones, it came on like a chemical refinery."

The writing is provocative, but Wolfe's might not be the most sound depiction of the band's system at the time. Tim Scully—no relation to the band's toothy and bowl-cut manager—was then a twenty-six-year-old UC-Berkeley dropout and acidhead who assisted Bear with painstakingly setting up the Dead's new-fangled PA in this era, and told me his memory disagrees with Wolfe's Trips Fest description. The rig at that event "was the Pranksters' soundsystem," Scully said. They had a mixing board made by sound synthesis pioneer and early synthesizer icon Don Buchla, according to Scully, as well as a tape deck that Kesey and his friends typically had wired into a figure-eight loop, plus their own set of mics, amps, and speakers.

Tim Scully was new to the mix but got on well enough with Bear, who had realized he needed an extra set of hands if he was going to steer the Dead's rig, and was now grooming Scully. "He was a bright kid," Bear later said of Scully, who had been majoring in mathematical physics and made a quick study. "He knew enough about electronics and how to wire two or three parts together, and all I knew basically was what I had learned through being an electronic technician in my Air Force period," Bear later told David Gans, oral historian, author of *Conversations with the Dead*, and host of the long-running nationally syndicated *Grateful Dead Hour* radio show. "I knew we had to do something because the technology was so primitive it seemed like it was holding the music back."

When Bear first heard about Tim Scully from a mutual friend, he wasn't looking for a student in acidmaking, as Scully later wrote in an essay about his time with the band. Rather, Bear "was fascinated by the Grateful Dead and wanted to find an electronic designer and technician who could implement some of the ideas he had for the band." Scully hoped that if he passed this other kind of acid test it could open doors to an apprenticeship making LSD. "In my mind," he wrote, "working for the Grateful Dead was an extended job interview for a position as Bear's lab assistant."

The Trips Festival was a trial for Scully, and he and Bear were soon fabricating the finest audio gear imaginable for any band at the time. On the side, their underground laboratory produced some of the most famous varieties of LSD ever created, like Orange Sunshine, Blue Cheer, and White Lightning. "Once Owsley came in a *lot* of things changed," said Steve Brown, the proto-Deadhead who saw the band at Magoo's and the In Room and also caught their Trips Fest performance. "Especially the Lightning he was giving away," he told me. "Good for taking a few and dancing with the walls the rest of the night."

Here is where the narrative begins to blur. The marginalia and sonic residues of this early history are full of question marks, strikethroughs, and asterisks surrounding certain dates, locations, chronologies, and timelines. After all, the Dead were taking LSD and other psychedelics regularly (often as a group), and so too were many of those who attended any of their shows back then.

"My memory has a lot of holes in it," Tim Scully told me, a caveat that could apply to nearly everyone in this story. In books and, later, on the internet, he'll find contradictory recollections from other individuals who were likewise present in one state of mind or another at any number of these same events, which occurred nearly six decades ago now. "I found that almost everybody's memories, including my own, are subject to error, morphing over the years, and fading," he said. To pinpoint exact dates, times, and places, Scully tends to put the most credence in contemporary written records—concert and Acid Test posters, namely. "I've tried to use those as anchors to tie down the stories that people tell."

Back at the Longshoremen's Hall, getting ready to play, Lesh crawled to his instrument and rose to his feet. "The Ouroboros of sound has manifested onstage in the form of hundreds of wires and cables presumably connecting every electronic entity in known space," he recalled. "The energy generated by three to five thousand linked and synced minds is playing havoc with our conventional electronic gear; the amps are frizzing and frying, sometimes emitting piercing ultrasonic shrieks like the beacon in *2001: A Space Odyssey*. But curiously, it's almost benign; no one is being shocked."

That's when the amps reportedly cut out. Hallucinating, Lesh turned around "to see a plug leap out of its socket and scurry across the stage like an arachnoid rubber band," he recalled. "And then another! And another!" The image is seared in his memory: The energy level in the hall was apparently so high that their equipment power cords surged out from the electrical outlets. But then, as quickly as it all went haywire, the system hummed back to life. "The amps are working now," Lesh said. "No one knows why."

In the entirely concrete hall, the band's raging sound resonated throughout the bodies in the crowd precisely because the building's acoustics were suboptimal. The effect was liberating. "We've played a lot of things that were almost as wild," Garcia said at the time, "but I don't think there has been anywhere I felt as personally free." With coverage in local and regional publications like the *San Francisco Examiner*, *Chronicle*, and *Daily Cal*, plus nationals like *Newsweek* and *Time*, the event marked the opening note of what became a din of global media attention on the burgeoning West Coast psychedelic rock scene. Before long, the media became obsessed with the Dead's growing soundsystem too.

Later that night, Bear drove Gissen back to her apartment. Shifting in the front seat, Gissen realized she had been perched on "some sort of machine" that was the size of a Cracker Jack box and housed in a black leather casing. "That's part of the Grateful Dead's new approach to sound," explained Bear, clearly excited. "It's a condenser microphone. I'm making live recordings with a state-of-the-art soundsystem that captures the transformative moment of expression and creation with the audience who are also high on my LSD."

Meanwhile, Kesey approached the band. The author was evading drug charges and dressed incognito. "You guys are going to be more famous than you realize," Kesey said.

February 12, 1966. Six months earlier, the Watts neighborhood of Los Angeles had exploded in civil unrest. But on this night, in a hot and grimy warehouse, the Dead performed at yet another Acid Test.

The Dead were in LA for about a week when the band and Kesey and the Pranksters, who had followed the Dead down the coast, threw that Watts event (though technically, it happened in neighboring Compton). Bear, whose jury-rigged and cumbersome experimental PA was especially delay prone during setup, was in rare form. At Watts, everybody who turned up got screaming high as his soundsystem came together.

The Dead had embarked on a half-baked mission to scope out the music business in the entertainment capital of the world. They found a pink stucco mansion at 2511 Third Avenue to hole up in. Bear covered rent and footed the grocery bills, in addition to paying for the gear he procured for the band. The vacant three-story "pink house" would be their austere home base during this LA sojourn. "The idea was, I guess, to rehearse, write new material, develop the soundsystem, and play some gigs," Lesh recalled.

The Dead and their expanding family—roughly a dozen people—might have already been a unit with no "leader." But 2511 Third Avenue was Bear's house. Garcia's then wife, Sara Ruppenthal (they were separated at the time), later said that it was as if the band was held "in captivity" by their soundman at the pink mansion. Ruppenthal didn't join them, yet described the place as having "perverse, evil vibes."

Bear was their "benevolent dictator," as Florence Nathan, who soon went by Rosie McGee and traveled south with the band—she and Lesh were dating—put it. He lived in the attic with Melissa Cargill, his acid partner and girlfriend, and tended to look down on most others who weren't men. There was always money for him to pour into the band's sound gear, though there were never any funds for the women's "excursions or materials for hobbies or any other interests," McGee claimed. "It's certain we all lost brain cells from doing nothing but smoke dope and take acid, cook, clean, do laundry, and hang around with the guys."

The house's wide-open living room was big enough to hold all the band's gear. "Big speakers and all," Tim Scully recalled. The soundsystem now centered around the hulking pair of Altec Voice of the Theater speakers that originally were Bear's home stereo, which he transported from Berkeley. He had purchased the speaker horns just prior to seeing the band perform at Muir Beach.

Despite him later likening it to "about the ugliest hi-fi system" going at the time, the Voice of the Theater kit served as the Dead's new soundsystem. It was initially a two-horn setup, "one horn on each speaker—a bottom and a horn on each side," Bear later explained, though they quickly added two more Altec horns to the system. The rig started with just a single McIntosh 240 stereo tube amplifier, but as they settled in LA they soon added an additional three Macs—the beginning of a storied and enduring relationship between the band and that audio company, whose amps powered the Wall.

They set the four amps to mono, meaning they now had a dedicated amp for each of the electric instruments: keyboard, bass, and a pair of guitars. Mounted to a sheet of thick plywood, this line of amps became known as "the lead sled." The name seemingly derived as much from the "sledding" style of arranging gear as the weight of the transformers in the amps; metal handles were affixed to each end of the lead sled, for easier transport.

The exact origins of the nickname are murky. Blair Jackson, author of *Grateful Dead Gear*, an overview of the band's equipment, told me he first heard Bob Matthews, the onetime Mother McCree's kazoo player and soon-to-be Dead sound crew member, refer to a "lead sled" when talking about the band's PA from that era. This fleet of amps powered the giant Altecs, combo woofer/horn speakers—now four altogether, for each of the amps—that broadcast the sound of the instruments and drums.

The lead sled was loud enough, Lesh recalled, "to bulge out the sides of the house when we cranked it." The Dead let their soundman take them where he may. "We were cautiously delighted when Bear became interested in applying his alchemical forces to our sound, a development that turned out to be a mixed blessing in many ways," Lesh said. The group had a shared vision of the ecstasy of song and dance being a sacred rite, according to the bassist, and proportional to that framework Bear yearned to create a soundsystem. "His ideal was musical sound undistorted by the artifacts present in the sound-reproduction system—the entire signal path from pickup through preamp through power amp to speaker. Only the vibrating string and the vibrating air had purity," Lesh wrote. "Everything else was compromised and must be made transparent. A noble goal, and one we endorsed gladly."

To put it another way, as Kreutzmann later wrote of the Dead's time with Bear in LA: "Somehow we were placed inside his dream of building the perfect soundsystem for a live band."

When Bear was nineteen, he nearly shattered an eardrum in a pool diving accident. He jumped off a high board and landed hard on the water on one side of his head.

Partially deaf in one ear as a result, Bear claimed to be able to "see" sound. He saw it emanating from the Dead's curved speaker horns while high on his own supply of acid, watching the band rehearse in the pink house and perform around LA. To him, the sound was akin to "interacting waves of color." This sensation of "total synesthesia," wherein one sense (hearing) is experienced through another (sight), shook him. *This is not what I expected it to look like,* he thought to himself. *I've got to remember what this is doing.* "It was completely three-dimensional," Bear later recalled, "and ever since then that's how I've viewed sound—having real dimensionality that changes as you move around in a space."

The Dead and the Wall were a vehicle for Bear to conjure the physical manifestation of that feeling. In that sense, the group's fur-chested sound guru "kind of saved them from being a nothing band that would just sort of fade into the darkness," John Curl, then an engineer at Ampex, told me. "A lot of bands did."

Resurfacing this seeing-sound story in interviews over the years, Bear drew a direct line from that experience to his "original vision" for the Wall, as Kurt Torell, an associate professor emeritus of philosophy at Penn State University-Greater Allegheny, noted in a 2019 essay on synesthesia published in the scholarly journal *Dead Studies*. "There is evidence that certain members and crew of the band were quite self-conscious about thinking of sound and music in visible, three-dimensional, and synesthetic terms," Torell wrote, "and deliberately sought to foster that perception in the audience through the music and its amplification." That rings clear across a patchwork of concerts and events where Bear's innovations met the Dead's audience head-on, laying groundwork for the technological skyrocket that was soon to launch.

A more recent psychological term could reasonably be applied to Bear's synesthetic sensibilities, meticulous and persistent nature, and seeming inability to pick up on certain emotional cues: neurodivergence. "He had charisma without having social skills," the late Steve Silberman, a Deadhead, science writer, and author of *Neurotribes: The Legacy of Autism and the Future of Neurodiversity*, once told me. "He was a very powerful advocate for his own ideas." Years later, Silberman, who saw the band perform with the Wall, spent a few days with Bear at a Dead scholarship conference, and came away convinced "Bear was on the spectrum, and in the best way."

It's not just synesthesia, although that phenomenon is also overrepresented in people on the autism spectrum, said Silberman, who co-authored *Skeleton Key: A Dictionary for Deadheads*. It's also that autistic people are often hypersensitive to distortion; bothered by "unclean signals," one could say, in a range of ways. The idealized PA that Bear had in his head became a reality exactly because of his aversion to such corrupted signals. The Wall, then, "was a massive team effort to eliminate intermodular distortion," Silberman said, a technical term used by Bear and others in the Dead's sound ranks. "I think the Wall of

Sound was one of the greatest achievements of the neurodivergent community that ever happened," Silberman said. "It was a collaboration between neurotypicals and neurodivergent Bear."

This is someone who attempted to communicate with the gear. Something in the way Bear formed bonds with nonhuman entities, as evident from these earliest days of the band and through the Wall years, is relevant to both him holding up gigs and likely being autistic, according to Silberman. "People on the spectrum often have unusual attachments to nonhuman things," he said. "Owsley had audio equipment."

That can explain the stories of those who variously witnessed Bear dropping to his knees, hugging speakers, sobbing, and talking to the electronics, as if trying to coax something out of the hardware. *I love you, you love me*, he'd whisper through tears. "Owsley had a lot of beliefs that were questionable, but in his mind, they were unquestionable truths," Kreutzmann recalled. When the Dead first went to Bear's place in Berkeley, "he told us he could talk to electronics, mentally talk to them, like people talk to plants," the drummer claimed. Near as Kreutzmann could tell, "they actually listened." Agonizingly, in some cases. Other times, Bear was met with radio silence. Yet "if something was wrong with the sound, he'd sit there and really talk to these machines," Kreutzmann said.

Trust. That's what it came down to. One of the key reasons why someone like Silberman believed that autistic people form such attachments, say with audio gear, is precisely because human behavior is unpredictable and not reliable in a way autistic people might prefer or need. "It must have upset Bear very much when his nonhuman friends *also* turned out to be unreliable," Silberman said.

Decades later, Bear would talk about one's supposed ability to interact with "inanimate equipment" under the influence of N,N-Dimethyltryptamine, or DMT. A naturally occurring hallucinogen, the so-called spirit molecule quickly gained popularity among the band and crew. Somebody would be smoking DMT backstage, or behind the band's growing backline of speakers and amps, and suddenly *everyone* together would begin experiencing the music getting louder and more "strident" with a "certain tonality to it," Bear later recalled. But then the PA would freak out. The tubes in the band's amplifiers "would get red hot and burn out half the time and it would tear the voice coils out of the speakers," Bear said. "Yet we couldn't make it do that ordinarily."

They got the sense there was "some bad karma" associated with using DMT, as Steve Parish, who linked up with Bear and the band over the next few years, wrote in his memoir *Home Before Daylight*. "It seemed like whenever we smoked it around the stage, something weird would happen to our equipment," he wrote. "Amps would go out and things would explode whenever we messed with it during a show, so we became very wary of it."

Plus, the mere whiff of DMT can trigger an instant flashback, enough to temporarily render even a seasoned head into a puddle. Before long, the Dead—stand-ins for the freewheeling psychonaut lifestyle—did something almost unthinkable for, well, the Dead. A group bound by seemingly one rule, which was that there were no rules and that life was, in Garcia's words, all about "having fun" and "getting high," banned smoking DMT onstage. *Anything* for good sound.

Meanwhile, back at the Watts Acid Test, the makeshift venue was "probably the scuzziest place I ever had to play," Lesh recalled. Overheated and parched attendees pulled from the only source of drink that night: the high-voltage LSD barrel. Bear, for one, vividly recalled another captivating instance of "seeing" sound flowing out from the Voice of the Theater horns—and Wolfe, once more, took in the scene. It is the final such performance the journalist documented in his *Electric Kool-Aid Acid Test*. In the book's titular chapter, Wolfe observed the heavily dosed heads who had immersed themselves in a sensory onslaught in the industrial warehouse that night. "I looked around," Wolfe wrote, "and people's faces were distorted ... the band, the Grateful Dead, was playing but I couldn't hear the music."

Here again, Tim Scully told me that this isn't the most faithful account. "Although it's been quite a while since I've read his book," Scully said, "I remember thinking at the time that it didn't sound very much as though he was there at the Watts Test." The band was still playing through Fender amps, according to Scully, who nested himself in one corner of the warehouse. High on supercharged LSD, he manipulated a spread of new electronics gear, like power amps, preamps, and tape recorders, that Bear brought special for the event.

Scully had been tinkering on the system with his friend Don Douglas, who briefly drove the band's equipment truck and promoted their LA gigs, and was likewise along because he wanted to make LSD with Bear. Scully and Douglas "put together the beginnings of the system" for that Watts Test, Scully recalled. The individual electric instruments each had their own preamp, power amp, and theater speaker. (A preamp boosts electronic signals coming off the instrument's pickups, which convert the vibrations of the strings into an electronic signal, before sending them to a power amp. This remains a crucial stage in the "signal chain" of an idealized distortion-free sound.) The PA component itself ran on separate preamps, power amps, and speakers.

At Bear's urging, Scully also custom built a central preamp and distribution system. This first-of-its-kind, shoebox-sized unit had simple controls for treble and bass and for mixing stereo monitor channels. The preamp got mounted in a hard case to protect it during transit, as things got banged around a lot. "All their amplifiers—everything, the guitars—all plugged into this black box that Tim had," Bear later said. "And then out of the box it went into the amplifiers and then it went into the speakers."

The Dead's mixing station, where Bear could be found "turning the dials like Baron Frankenstein," as Rock Scully recalled, often was hooked up stageside. This was still a time before "front of house" sound booths had been established in a "sweet spot" out in the audience. But in another bit of foresight on Bear's part, Tim Scully's centralized preamp also housed a tape deck. The Dead could now easily and regularly record their own performances and practices.

They quickly realized that the system needed more low end, in what will be a perennial concern in the life of the Wall. Added at the last minute to the Watts PA was a "super bass" speaker that Bear had acquired. Driven by a 400-watt amplifier, this hefty unit had an extremely low response in the low frequencies that coupled booming sub-100 Hz audio into the floor. "You could feel it in the ground some distance away," Tim Scully recalled.

This system was a pain to haul around, and setting up the Altec horns also took precious time, because those cabinets were similarly unwieldy. "The Voice of the Theater speaker boxes were huge," Rock Scully recalled. "Four of them would just about take up an office." The fragile horns quickly proved ill-equipped to withstand the wear and tear of a working band, namely their being so prone to blow fuses and overheat that the Dead carried spares wherever they went. "We couldn't trust any promoter to provide us with enough electricity or clean electricity," Rock wrote, "so we also had these huge, incredibly heavy transformers that were just monsters and needed sledding." The Dead only grew increasingly preoccupied with power as the Wall materialized.

Making it all go was thankless work. "The logistics of packing up all the equipment, loading it in the truck, unloading it, hauling it up or down stairs, unpacking it, laying cables, taping them down, setting up mike stands, and testing everything, made the job of getting ready for the band to play a major production," Tim Scully recalled. "This was a source of friction with the band because this made it impossible to be spontaneous."

Despite Bear's best intentions, the intermittent reliability issues were a constant bummer, adding to the operational "nightmare" that was schlepping around so much equipment, and setting it all up only to tear it all back down. Their lead sled took a hit, presaging the beatings Wall gear would weather in the years to come. "None of us understood the abuse the equipment would have to withstand—everything from being immersed in Coca Cola to getting dropped down stairways," Tim Scully wrote. "Of course, some of the reliability issues may have owed something to everyone being stoned on acid while setting up and operating the equipment." That appeared to involve the audience too. "At a couple of Acid Tests," Tim Scully recalled, "it seemed that a psychic connection developed between the crowd and the soundsystem, and this feedback overloaded the speakers, blowing them out."

The lead sled was fitful. "Bear and Tim's ambitions vastly overshot their knowledge," Dennis McNally wrote in his Dead history. Band and crew alike confronted a steep learning curve around acoustics and soundsystems in the lead-in to the Wall, a reality to which Bear, ever the uncompromising presence, would not immediately bend. "The combination of stonedness and Owsley's demand for perfection at all costs resulted in endless repetition and delay," McNally added.

At the Watts Test, Bear and Tim Scully had just converted all the band's guitars. That was in order to play through the "hi-fi" system that was now their amp backline, explained Lesh, who remembered Bear going on at the Test about how the path to "better sound" was in low impedance. (That's a technical term in acoustics for achieving as close to distortion-free sound as possible by the flow of electrons facing as little resistance as possible.) "My instrument was the last to be so altered," the bassist recalled, "and in our shortsighted excitement at the thought of being able to play through the new system, we had left all our other amps behind in San Francisco." The conversion mechanism involved the rudimentary external black box that Bear had Scully build, which got plugged in between a given instrument and the preamp and amp stages. Lesh looked on in despair at the soundman and his apprentice crouching near the amp line, doing surgery on this centralized preamp.

"As I watched them struggle with wires the size of a thread and a soldering iron like a Polish sausage, colors dripping off of them like big drops of sweat, it slowly dawned on me that my bass wasn't going to work and that we had no other way to amplify it," Lesh said. He refrained from kicking them. "No sooner had I drawn breath to let forth a screech of dismay than Bear had screwed the cover back on the box, and we were ready to go."

But after one or two songs, Garcia decided he was done for the day. "I'd wanted to play so badly," Lesh recalled, "and it had actually sounded good in that awful place." For Kreutzmann, that short and dusty gig was memorable for being the first time the drummer ever got weirded out while playing stoned.

By dawn, police surrounded the building. No noise complaint was lodged, given no one actually lived anywhere close to the dilapidated venue. None of those emerging from inside appeared to be inebriated either, so there ultimately wasn't much the cops could do, though one of the Pranksters got arrested. Spooked, the Dead, and others who had passed the Test, scampered into the morning light.

As the weather warmed that spring, the Dead rehearsed, rehearsed, rehearsed inside the pink house.

The band pushed the lead sled during these sessions, honing their craft for public stages. The Dead often sounded rather "awful" live back then, admitted Richie Pechner, the soon-to-be band roadie and speaker cabinet maker. (Pechner was still about a year out from falling in; his entry point, Danny Rifkin, was a San Francisco State University dropout and friend of Rock Scully's who arrived as a guest at the pink house, and soon became the band's co-manager.) The Dead "always brought it," Pechner said. But they were running up against mounting technical limitations. That had as much to do with the band being unable to hear themselves over the sound of their own speakers as it did with the fact that, in 1966, there was still no such thing as a musical PA.

The Dead, being pioneers of the form, first had to learn how to get a "tight" sound out of Bear's system. "Compared to the average run-of-the-mill speaker, it sounded OK," Bear later said, speaking of his old Altec set. The kit went loud—and Bear wanted as much. Yet "it wouldn't get loud enough."

There in the living room, Cargill helped Bear dial in the Voice of the Theater speakers and what was an initial dual-channel 80-watt McIntosh amplifier. They also had to modernize all their equipment and really work at beefing up the low end. For Bear, that "was the focus of attention, right from the Acid Test days," he later said. "The bass guitar didn't have the same standing or power, no matter what kind of gear you used, it just didn't have the ability to reach out and grab— it's much harder to get that much power at lower frequencies." At the time, they were hitting bass-related snags because the amps and speakers available on the market simply weren't efficient enough.

So they went shopping. A conservative estimate of Bear's total spending on audio gear in LA, including various McIntosh amps and preamps and Sennheiser microphones, comes to over $20,000 today. He typically paid in cash. "I don't have all the receipts for all of the equipment that Bear bought," Tim Scully told me. "But the ones that I have are consistent with the system getting put together in L.A. in early February 1966." Bear covered most of the rising costs associated with the lead sled, which certain band and crew members also referred to as the Owsleystein rig (a combination of "Owsley" and "Einstein"). Scully claims that select electronics they used were paid for out of his own pocket, despite him having no recollection of making salary.

Some of Bear's ideas could be executed using this sort of off-the-shelf, albeit higher-end, equipment. The Dead's soundman looked to his assistant to synthesize the whole rig. "He wanted me to do the technical work to pull the system together," Scully said. Among his Bear-assigned tasks, Scully made tons of high-quality cables from high-quality connectors. He also provided monitors, turning around some speakers to face the musicians—perhaps the first time this had ever been done—"so the band could effectively hear themselves as they played" and adjust their levels accordingly. These are humble beginnings, but already still more shades of the Wall are coming through.

A few of Bear's ideas Scully did think were particularly worthwhile. Namely, reducing hum and other unwanted noise by swapping out the high-impedance, unbalanced connections between the instruments and their amplifiers for a low-impedance, balanced line; replacing low-quality mic connectors and wiring with good-quality, low triboelectric—a kind of contact electrification—noise cables and connectors as a way of cleaning up overall signal quality; and upping the overall sound quality by swapping the low-fidelity Fender amps, which had limited power, for the high-fidelity McIntosh vacuum tube–powered amps, which had sufficient "headroom" to circumvent "clipping," a form of distortion.

Clipping occurs when noise signals surpass whatever voltages the electronics are designed to handle; it's what happens when an amp is "overdriven," a common occurrence in electrified rock music in 1966. That March 12, at the Pico Acid Test at the Danish Center in LA, for instance, Bob Weir noted the popping noises that rang out of the "funky" PA. "Even mildly distorted sound wasn't acceptable to Bear or to Tim," remembered McGee, who was present that night, "so they'd turn the volume down just enough to prevent it."

That wasn't the only sort of clipping the Dead encountered that spring. For a fly-on-the-wall *Los Angeles Free Press* profile, their first proper media interview, reporter Steve White dropped by the pink house on March 19, as plans for a UCLA Acid Test fell through. The place was alive. Even at this early stage of the band, the whirl of crew-family was described, in White's word, as "ant-like"—a comparison that stuck as the Wall scaled up.

In the den, the entire band stood around waiting to hear a tape. Enter Bear, "the Dead's engineer and electronic genius of the group," who was busy setting things up, White wrote. A bank of a half dozen Voice of the Theater speaker cabinets, one for each instrument, ran the length of the wall, and "behind and around us are microphones, stands and instruments," White wrote. "The engineer is dickering with a phantasmagoria of plugs, dials, and switches."

Bear explained how they operated at about 110 decibels—as loud as a jackhammer, power saw, or symphony orchestra—and that all the speakers had 330 watts coursing through them. "I changed all the instruments from high to low impedance. That way we get pure sound," Bear told White, pointing out the four McIntosh preamps in the rig—one for each instrument, enabling them to mix with more precision. "We got Super Basses, vacuum sealed for the lows and basslines," Bear added. And they monitored the system with an oscilloscope, allowing them to keep a gauge of the amplifiers during a show. "We do continuous mix, as we play," Bear said. "That way you get recording studio quality in live performance."

He hit play on the tape. It's the Dead's new single, set to drop days later, though ultimately never released; Side A was the traditional "I Know You Rider," which the Dead performed for the remainder of their career, and the flip was "Otis on the Shake Down Cruise," a song that shortly got nixed from their repertoire. White took it in: "Pure sound—sound that makes you giggle that anything could be that loud," he wrote. The effect was enveloping, "that kind of loud heavy sound that drives you toward the speakers," only neither dissonant nor muddy. "Crystal clear, even at this volume."

Later that night at the Carthay Studios Acid Test, where the would-be UCLA Test had gotten moved, White clocked co-manager Rock Scully standing beside the Dead's speakers. They met eyes and Rock mouthed the word: *s o u n d.*

March 25, 1966. At the Dead's LA Trouper's Club show, Weir, facing around a hundred attendees, blew out not a speaker but his pants seat. When he wanted his sound tweaked, he side-shuffled over to Tim Scully, who was stageside at the oscilloscope mixing station, monitoring for clipping.

When the night was through and expenses paid, the band pocketed a cool $75. It was a fitting conclusion to the Dead's last Los Angeles gig—for now. The Bay Area was the Dead's scene. Everyone wanted to go home.

But what really ended the Dead's LA jaunt was Bear and his controlling ways. "It became a burden at shows because, as our soundman, everything had to be perfect before we could start," Kreutzmann recalled. "Not our idea of perfect, but his. And he was constantly experimenting with new ideas for better sound, which were all fine experiments, but all too often they delayed our start time."

And not just by minutes. Garcia later recalled Bear's system requiring "so much paraphernalia" to work properly that at every gig, they spent five hours setting up the system and another five hours tearing down. "Hands were breaking," Garcia said, "and we were getting miserable, and the stuff never worked. Sometimes it was so weird; we got some far-out stuff on that system. It had its ups and downs." In the end, they didn't get much "done" in LA, per se. "But we had some barn-burning trips," Lesh concluded.

Bear, for his part, felt that ultimately no one could define exactly what the system had to do. The band members would say, "*Well, I play the guitar and want to hear a sound. What kind of sound? Well, you know, the right sound.* The musicians couldn't talk about it," Bear later said, "and I hadn't a clue." Bear just knew that whatever existed there was too archaic. In pursuit of louder, clearer, more powerful sound gear, they went as far as they possibly could in 1966. "We tried and tried and tried," Bear said, "made all kinds of stuff, and tried centralized." The system grew such that it "required a separate pilot over there controlling things while the band was playing, which was unsatisfactory."

The proof was in his sonic journals of Dead performances. "I could play you tapes that would make you cringe, they're so bad," Bear recalled of these earliest recordings. "Any one of them could sing on his own okay, but they sounded terrible together, and I think part of that was that the technology of onstage monitoring was pitiful." Bear thought it was crucial that musicians be able to clearly hear themselves so as to vocal blend. "But once they were onstage with the instruments going, each one would hear something else and they'd all be off key," he said. "It was sometimes painful." That's why Bear insisted the band do soundchecks whenever possible.

They did the best they could with the tools they had. But those tools were inadequate, which said something about the state of society and the world, according to Bear. "I thought it was absolutely disastrous that we were building rockets that could deliver atomic bombs to destroy entire cities," Bear later said, "and musicians were playing on something that looked like it was built in a garage in the '30s."

Bear and the band eventually went their separate ways. "It could have been my personality and the sound not being what they had anticipated," Bear admitted. "But back then I still had a lot to learn." He and his crew will return to making LSD more or less full-time. The Dead's sound team, moreover, had become a liability. So long as Bear and Tim Scully were present, Weir later said, the Dead were "a bust waiting to happen." But the looming threat of drug enforcement authorities notwithstanding, they all knew more about sound engineering, event production, and the power of mass media than they did before they came to LA. The Dead will carry those lessons.

Tim Scully's time with the band ended that July, and Cargill, Gissen, and Douglas all peeled off in the coming weeks and months. As Scully later told me, "the extended job interview was over." Douglas, the equipment truck driver, had been willing to help build the Dead's electronics, but considered himself to be of little use. He too decided that it was time to move on.

But Bear remained a driving force behind the band's ever-a-work-in-progress PA. "It's a tribute to a man, the book that you're doing," as "Cadillac" Ron Rakow, an ex–Wall Street financier who soon entered the picture as another Dead manager-type, told me. "If you got Owsley's trust and he liked you, he would go to the end of the world for you," Rakow said. "He was a soft, gentle, wonderful being, or a ferocious intellect that crushed any opposing intellect. It was pretty far out."

The spirit of Bear's early system will carry through to the end. "By amplifying and manipulating the sound," as Torell wrote in his paper on synesthesia, Bear set the band on a course to enhance "the materiality of the music, and hence its visible, tactile, and three-dimensional objective quality." As the Wall slowly came alive, they learned how to further control the Dead's sound as if they were painting with their instruments and voices, playing Ping-Pong with notes, or molding the sonic envelope like an immense slab of clay. The band could sometimes "appear to push the sound out toward the audience like a wall, and then abruptly cut it off," Torell added, "or allow it to decay so as to create an impression of falling or moving forwards or backwards, and thereby a sense of distance, three-dimensionality, and motion."

When Bear's system wasn't acting up, it was something to behold. His PA produced "what nearly everyone agreed was some of the cleanest and most powerful sound that anyone had heard from a rock 'n' roll band," Blair Jackson wrote in his Dead gear overview. "He got them thinking about the inadequacy of the prevailing live soundsystems of the day, while pointing at possibilities for improving the state-of-the-art." The band was fond of the clarity and sheer power of his rig. And thanks to the tape deck Bear installed—a first for any rock group—they grew a quick appreciation for the ability to go back and review recordings of past performances and rehearsal sessions, to study and better understand the band's progression as it was unfolding.

In a matter of months, at such a formative time for the band, Bear had leveled up their whole operation with his own funds. "He had furnished the band with the best sound equipment that money could buy," Robert Greenfield wrote in his biography, "and then worked tirelessly to ensure that their sound onstage would be second to none."

The souped-up PA had a clear effect on members of the audience too. Rifkin, now co-manager, recalled one powerful show in this era. "We had these big Voice of the Theater speakers and I hurt my back carrying them," said Rifkin, a beanpole figure. "I remember standing in front of Pigpen at this gig and he blew my mind—he kind of made me dance and got my back healed."

The Dead rolled into their first stop back in San Francisco on April 22, back at the Longshoremen's Hall. They had some time to kill. Unsurprisingly, the PA was giving all kinds of feedback during setup. When Bear's experimental soundsystem worked, "it was really good—the best in the world," Pigpen later remarked. "But it wasn't too often." As Bear and Tim Scully addressed the problem, the band again posted up at their friend's nearby apartment.

To reach the next stage in their ascent of the Wall, the Dead had to not throttle persnickety Bear as he sorted out a replacement system. They still had shows to play—a gig was a gig. In the meantime, according to Garcia, they quietly thought that if Tim Scully "was able to work on it long enough and get enough parts made, we would be able to have a working system."

But then the band did something they hadn't done before. They left California.

SET TWO

4

The Good, Old Reliable
Soundsystem (1966–1967)

The band was late pulling into Vancouver the last weekend of July 1966.

The Dead came to the British Columbia Trips Festival at the PNE Garden Auditorium to play their first ever out-of-state gigs, only they got so high on acid they forgot they had a show that night. Laird Grant, hauling a half ton of equipment in Tim Scully's converted green Sunshine cookie truck—upgraded from Bill Kreutzmann's station wagon—was also in a jam. The hang-up involved one of the passengers having a prior drug conviction. Canadian border authorities stopped the van.

Band and gear all somehow arrived at the venue that Friday evening, though the apparent stage height had Jerry Garcia demand their equipment be moved away from the edge. Some audience members attempted to scale the stage front, too, enough bodies that the structure shook. Once the Dead plugged in, after grinding Bear delays, and began to play, the sound wasn't all there. The fest was really a "very complex light show," Garcia recalled, so "a band would only get to play maybe one set a night and it would be a short one."

Over the summer, the band had clocked some two dozen shows using Bear's cutting-edge albeit finicky PA in and around the Bay Area—and in sonically unforgiving venues, like Harmon Gym in Berkeley the weekend of May 7. Gymnasiums are highly reverberant and often a tough sell for live concert sound. That was true in 1966, though cavernous gyms presented even greater problems for the Dead into the Wall era. *Chronicle* music writer Ralph Gleason and Jann Wenner, the soon-to-be founding editor of *Rolling Stone*, both attended the Harmon gig. As Joe Hagan reported in *Sticky Fingers*, an exposé of Wenner and his magazine, the pair "walked up to the loudspeakers on the stage and stuck their heads close to hear Garcia's spidery guitar playing."

Other days that May and June, the Dead and their system stood on plywood on the grounds of the band's new digs. They had secured a short-term rental at one in a litany of "powerspots"—an esoteric geophysical concept that fascinated the band—on the emerging roadmap of Deadworld. Coming up from LA, Rosie McGee and Melissa Cargill saw a newspaper ad for Rancho Olompali, a stately yet crumbling Victorian spread on seven hundred acres in present-day Novato, in unincorporated Marin County. For the Dead, this was an idyllic and mystical temporary base of operations in the band's communal era.

At Olompali, the band jammed whenever they wanted. The site was still isolated enough back then that they didn't have to worry about the noise bothering anyone. "All our gear is set up on a flat stage in front of the big house and anybody can play at any time," Rock Scully recalled.

Meanwhile, the Dead's business model shifted as the band gained popularity and their tolerance with Bear, and his "Topsy-like" soundsystem, grew thin. As McGee remembered, there was a gradual transition "from Bear-funding to band-funding of other expenses"—food and the like. "But it took a while." Nothing was ever quick with their outgoing patron and sound guru, so really, Olompali was a rolling sesh. "It was like one continuous six-week party," Kreutzmann said. "Bear was with us so we had acid and a PA system."

Before an impromptu Dead jam at one legendary LSD-soaked Olompali party, Rhoney Gissen recalled Bear placing Sennheiser microphones on stands low to the stage. She and others "approached the stacks of speakers and stooped to feel the vibrations of the diaphragms," Gissen said. "We put our heads so close to Garcia's mic that the tone changed. If I could have put my ear right up to the guitar strings, I would have done it. I would have crawled into the amplifier."

Bear still had Tim Scully tinkering on the system for the moment. Cargill, the ultra-reclusive chemistry prodigy, also continued playing some kind of a role with the PA. "I'm not sure what she did," Sue Swanson told me, "but she was always in there fiddling with stuff and helping out." Swanson, for her part, now helped produce the first iteration of a Dead newsletter—the zine-like *Olompali Sunday Times*. As for Bear and his rig, Swanson, newly eighteen, said she always loved the curious little man who hardly ever met you with his eyes when he talked. "He was a very strange character. I sort of kept my distance."

In any case, "I'm sure it took forever for it to set up." Swanson and others called the glacial pace at which the Dead's sound visionary toiled "Bear time."

Elsewhere, the Dead went through their first proper recording experience. They had booked time with aspiring recording engineer Gene Estribou, who built a studio on the top floor of his San Francisco home. Bob Weir recalled humping their gear up so many flights of stairs leading to the space. The band still had their amplifiers, weighing a hundred pounds apiece, bolted to a thick plywood sheet. Weir shouldered the load with Bob Matthews, whom, as one of the band's resident electronics experts, they called "Knobs." One night at the studio, after the Dead had played the California Hall on May 29, he sat entranced, watching the tape reels spinning. "I'm the guy who's going to record the Grateful Dead," Matthews told Weir. "I'm the guy in the family that's gonna do this."

But when the Dead hit Vancouver that July, it was déjà vu. "Bear had some great ideas," Matthews, who joined the band on that trip, later said. "But it was difficult for him to remember that the show starts at eight, so you have to be prepared and you have to be able to make decisions."

After five agonizing hours spent loading out of that gig, the Dead hung around Vancouver for another week. "I do remember that we set up the soundsystem in a park and the Dead played a free pop-up concert, which was fun," Tim Scully told me of his final Dead outing. The band played two more scheduled shows in town, at a club called the Afterthought, on August 5 and 6. Bear taped those performances using the 10½-inch reel-to-reel recording deck he insisted be a permanent fixture in the Dead's early system. But when they listened back to the live recordings, the sound was spotty. It was abundantly clear Bear's system wasn't cut out for touring.

"It never quite worked," Garcia later recalled. "It was really bringing us down. After going through a zillion weird changes about it and screaming at poor Owsley and getting just crazy behind it," he explained, "we finally parted ways."

Back in California, everybody was bummed about the sound problems they ran into and with Bear's controlling nature. They were tired of "muddy sound compounded by interminable delays while Bear tuned the system to be *just exactly perfect*," Phil Lesh said. "Bear, for his part, was reaching his limit with our constant grousing."

Besides, the band now eked out enough of a living to exist without a patron, so they talked it over with Bear. He told them to go to Leo's, a local music shop. "Pick out whatever you want," Bear said, "and send me the bill." The Dead weren't expecting such an outgoing act of generosity. Their new rig, mostly Fender and some Sunn equipment, cost him $4,000, the equivalent of nearly $39,000 today. Essentially, Bear "bought us some regular single-minded equipment so we could go out and play," Garcia later noted. Enough with the bleeding edge. "Good, old reliable" gear, in Garcia's words, worked for them.

Bear sold the Altec Voice of the Theater horns, and a single McIntosh amp, to one Bill Graham. A brash up-and-coming concert promoter, Graham helped set a lasting stage for the Dead and their Wall. Soon, the Altecs got repurposed as the house PA for the Fillmore, the San Francisco ballroom that clipboard-toting Graham had begun booking.

By that point, Bear, Cargill, Gissen, and Tim Scully spun up their Point Richmond LSD lab, and soon relocated the underground chemistry operation to a suburb of Denver, Colorado, to throw off the feds. They brought a reel-to-reel and a cassette player and "we had special tapes that the bands had given us to use while we were making the LSD," Gissen said. "Owsley put on the Grateful Dead. Tim had wired together a preamp and amp and assembled bass speakers that Phil had once tried for his guitar." The in-house system "sounds great."

Bear then played a tape of Blue Cheer, a Bay Area band that took their name from his eponymous batch of LSD. That power trio was reportedly the world's loudest band at the time. Blue Cheer's own affiliate audio heads, like the Dead's, blazed a path along a similar forefront of sound technology.

Come Labor Day, the Dead were officially without a soundperson.

The first time Dan Healy saw the Dead perform, opening for their friends the Quicksilver Messenger Service at Graham's Fillmore that summer, the sound did not grab him.

"I'd been mixing in the studio and knew what good sound was, and what was coming off that stage was not good sound," Healy, an audio engineer, later said. Public-address systems for rock shows still basically did not exist—just a small speaker box to each side of the stage, if that. After that Fillmore gig, Healy, then working for Quicksilver, ribbed Garcia and Lesh, whose amp he fixed earlier that night when it stopped working. Their soundsystem, Healy told them, "really sucked."

Garcia challenged Healy, saying something to the effect of, "Put your money where your mouth is."

"You're on," Healy replied.

When the Dead played the Fillmore again about a month later, Healy and a new PA—the next version in this early Wall development phase—were ready and waiting. In the weeks leading up to that gig, Healy sought out kit at the major Bay Area audio providers that rented gear. "It was equipment from a few different companies, so I wanted to make sure it was all hooked up so that things were compatible," Healy later recalled. He piled in with all this stuff a few days before the show and got to it.

Venues like the Fillmore, the Matrix, and the Avalon formed a network of aging San Francisco ballrooms that hosted rock shows. Even though they were in various states of disrepair, these old ballroom spaces were hotbeds of acoustic inquiry in the mid- to late '60s. They attracted other heads in the Dead's broader scene who likewise chased better sound and pushed the state of the art in live concert production.

At the Avalon, audio engineer Bob Cohen forged one of the earliest—if not the first—monitor systems in the history of live music, as well as a basic noise-canceling headphone technology that he later sold to the National Aeronautics and Space Administration. Cohen had help from seventeen-year-old Betty Cantor, who worked concessions but wanted to get more involved in other aspects of putting on a gig.

Cantor soon met Matthews and Healy, helped co-found Alembic with Bear and others, and worked for the Dead, serving as the legendary recording engineer behind some of the band's most celebrated and widely heard performances, including those featuring a precursor Wall. One of her Dead tapes was entered into the National Recording Registry of the Library of Congress, on the basis of its historical and cultural significance to the American experience. But for now, Cantor helped Cohen set up the microphones on the Avalon's stage and ran cables, soaking up everything she could. "I was always looking for something more to do," Cantor told me.

The need for social ritual merged with electronics at these dance halls. Electrified sound "*commands* attention," said Chet Helms, who booked the Avalon. If band and audience were once two distinct entities, then the Dead's soundsystem now fused them into a single organism. The rig brought crowds into the same envelope of sound as the musicians. As above, so below; microcosm, macrocosm.

Back at the Fillmore, a few weeks after first seeing the Dead and Garcia challenging him to improve the band's sound, Healy was nearly set. He had rearranged all the power connectors to accommodate the rented gear that he lugged into the hall, making this "huge" soundsystem for the band. "It was a horrible-looking monstrosity," he recalled. "But when the gig came—BAM!— you could hear the singing." They sounded great that night.

And so the Dead got to work, playing through this more conventional gear and integrating a new soundperson in Healy. Between shows, Healy hit Mc-Cune Sound Service, then the main source of hi-fi equipment in the area. He met other early career audio engineers like John Curl and John Meyer, the latter of whom worked at McCune; Curl and Meyer also soon both fell into the orbit of the Dead and the Wall. Healy rented loads of gear from McCune, blew it all up, and then rented some more, as the Dead's system got tweaked and refined and grew larger. He eventually pressured McCune to effectively tell the equipment manufacturers themselves to do better. When Healy returned gear he rented for experimenting with the band's PA, the electronics were shot. This forced the Altecs and JBLs of the 1960s to then make a higher-quality product, because now it was even more about dollars and cents.

Yet here was someone with plenty of plainspoken wisdom to share within the family. "Healy is a fantastically good teacher," Garcia later said. "He's the guy who taught everybody in the crew. He's got a good way of being able to talk about any number of technical things without losing you."

Healy not only helped make the Wall a reality but also held down the band's live mixing post for the better part of the next three decades. In his words, "the rest is history."

October 6, 1966. LSD had just been declared illegal in California. At a rally in the Panhandle, hundreds gathered to watch the Dead play that Thursday. The band's gear was driven in on a flatbed truck. An electrical extension cord appeared out of a nearby apartment window and got strung up and over the street and down into the park, powering the impromptu free event.

The Dead walked over from 710 Ashbury Street, their new communal headquarters, which Danny Rifkin happened to be leasing. The band had a presence at the three-flat for the next two and a half years. Among 710's many visitors, the Federal Bureau of Investigation came looking for the band's old soundman, who the Dead were still friendly with, and various "underground" characters. (Bear, Cargill, and Tim Scully occasionally dropped by 710.) The agents knew all their names, and the bureau continued monitoring the Dead through the Wall era.

Across the street from 710 was 715 Ashbury, where two eventual Dead employees, Swanson and Ron Rakow, both lived. Rakow had recently clicked with Rifkin and Rock Scully—and shortly thereafter, with Bear. Rakow told me he was then introduced to Garcia. The guitarist admired Rakow's hustle, despite his business acumen coming under suspicion by many Dead family members. Among other questionable ventures, that same year Rakow endorsed a cutting-edge new loudspeaker design called Circlephonics, then in early developmental stages; he brought in some $40,000 from investors, but the technology never materialized.

Three days after meeting Garcia, Rakow recalled, Rifkin and Scully explained to him that they talked with Garcia and wanted to know if Rakow could help them acquire more of the standard hi-fi equipment the Dead were using. "Will you lend us nine grand?" they asked.

Rakow knew the Dead needed the cash but considered the chances of being reimbursed slim. "Instead of being a sucker I'd rather be a patron—I'll just give you the money," he told the band. He claims he gifted them the nine grand, equivalent today to over $85,000, "and they did what they did with it."

Through various streams, then, funding and resources started pouring into the Dead's post-Bear soundsystem program. But these were still meager days. "We take almost any gig we're offered," co-manager Scully said. "With the money we're getting—three hundred to four hundred a night if we're lucky—we can't go much out of the Bay Area." The group's finances got pooled; everyone took a $25 weekly allowance, and "musicians and employees all made the same amount," the economist Barry Barnes later wrote in *Everything I Know About Business I Learned from the Grateful Dead*.

Yet the women of 710 were the exception to receiving any kind of monetary stipend, part of a tradition of gender non-parity that extended through the Wall. Women largely still got assigned domestic roles in Deadworld—cooking, cleaning, and rolling joints. As they assumed other less visible though no less important duties while the Dead and their soundsystem grew, they had to advocate for their fair share.

In just a few years, the band was earning a few thousand dollars per well-paid show. By the early '70s, when the Wall was further scaled up and they started seeing real success and employees shared in the wealth, the Dead pulled in tens of thousands of dollars on big stadium gigs and festivals. But even those figures won't cover the organization's ballooning overhead, as the band's rig, including labor costs, accounted for an ever-growing percentage of every Dead dollar.

Back in late 1966, they remained nothing if not hungry for equipment. "The band has this voracious appetite for gear," co-manager Scully wrote of the time. "Garcia wants a new soundsystem, doesn't want to deal with these crummy house systems in theaters anymore. And it's true that if we're going to play bigger places, we need more gear, *and* a more powerful PA, *and* bigger trucks to haul it." For the moment, their equipment was schlepped in Grant's pickup.

No one individual was at the wheel, as it were. The Dead were a "tribe" that made decisions communally. But a group dynamic had taken shape that informed the band's approach to its PA on the road ahead. "Jerry may be tribal elder, but he doesn't make the decisions," Scully said. "The most he'll do is back ideas to his liking. Still, it's Jerry's nod that is always needed to get the tribe moving in one direction."

Rifkin, now road manager, had pull too. The San Francisco State dropout was already a moral pillar in the Dead's scene. His opinion could change the band's mind if he felt strongly about something. He was also drawn to an ideology that epitomized so much about the Dead's Haight-Ashbury tenure: *free.*

Becoming millionaires was never the band's primary goal. Improving as musicians and bettering the sound was their aim. "The Dead have always poured money back into the scene in the form of sound and lights and musical instruments," Healy later said. Even into the '70s, when band members, crew, and office staff alike earned modest salaries, whatever money remained in the pot always got allocated for band gear and pursuing sonic excellence.

But in late September 1966, the Dead signed their very first record deal. They were staid old Warner Bros.' first rock group and given a $10,000 advance—the equivalent of around $96,000 today—and an 8 percent royalty. The contract made no mention of publishing. "We're not trying to be famous or rich," Garcia told one interviewer. "We're just trying to make our music as well as we can and get it out, because there's a demand for it, to some extent."

More than anyone, perhaps, during this initial period of business and commercial creep, Rifkin made the free model palatable for the band as being aligned with its sound approach. The seed was planted when one Emmett Grogan, representing a local activist group called the Diggers, whose core doctrine was the concept of *free,* dropped by 710. Grogan apparently asked Rifkin and others: Why don't the Dead similarly "play free"?

That's exactly what the band did in the Panhandle the day California criminalized acid. Among the heads assembled in the polo fields that afternoon was

Richie Pechner, a prospect of both the Diggers and the Dead crew. Pechner was then eighteen and asked by Rifkin, a friend of his, if he was available to pick up the band's gear at 710 in a rented flatbed, and then drive the load to the park. Pechner can't recall who rode with him and the Dead's equipment. Possibly Matthews? Whoever it was carried a credit card.

The experience represented yet another leveling-up of their whole scene. The sound was "pretty raw," as Pechner recalled of that October 6 Panhandle gig. "But enthusiasm was very high." The way Garcia saw it, the playing was *pure* in the streets. The only person who seemed to express reservations about this more guerrilla approach was Grant. At these early free open-air performances, the occasional spectator would want to hop onstage and the Dead's founding equipment manager had to intervene. Already, the band's crew was gaining a surly reputation that would precede them.

But when the band gigged this way, "everything came together with a certain grace that seemed almost like divine intervention," Kreutzmann later wrote. "We played because we wanted to play." Looking back, "it was probably genius marketing, because massive crowds gathered once word spread," Kreutzmann said. "Every one of those shows expanded our audience."

January 14, 1967. Two flatbed trucks were backed end to end and lashed together. Audio gear from various Bay Area bands got cobbled into a soundsystem that filled most of the makeshift stage at what was billed as the Human Be-In. This "gathering of the tribes" was yet another free event, including buddy bands the Jefferson Airplane and Country Joe and the Fish, at which the Dead performed. Twenty thousand heads turned up that day in the Panhandle.

"Bear had freely distributed his White Lightning acid throughout the crowd," McGee recalled. So when the band was about to begin, "the crowd was already well into the groupmind that would characterize Dead audiences from then on." But during their opener, the power cut. Someone apparently kicked loose a generator cord. When the electricity eventually got restored, the generator was guarded by a Hells Angel. The Dead ended up playing a tidy three-song set.

Days later, the band was set up on a different stage—a cavernous recording space in Los Angeles. They entered RCA Studios to make their debut album for Warner's, quickly cutting fifteen tracks with producer David Hassinger. Save Pigpen and Weir, everyone was popping various amphetamines. "You can hear the Dexamyl humming through the album," Scully later said. The zippy song versions, all tunes they had road tested, reflected such "production aids."

The band was known for their volume back then, which clashed with outside studio engineers who Weir later recalled were adamant that playing quietly was the only proper way to record. The resulting self-titled album, released that March, didn't capture the band's full sonic range and presence quite like the Dead's live experience. "It didn't fill out the same way," Weir said. As Lesh later put it, *Grateful Dead* feels rushed, "hyper" even, like "sound and fury buried in a cavern." Garcia grew similarly critical of *Grateful Dead*, finding the "speedy" and "crude"-sounding record a difficult listen. But around the time of its release, the guitarist said it "sounds like one of our good sets."

Meanwhile, the Dead and Healy were getting into electronic sounds and devices to a degree they hadn't ever been. "We've been mostly just working on getting better at our instruments," Garcia said at the time, "and the electronic stuff is stuff that you discover playing at enormous volumes in the big auditoriums. Pretty soon your guitar is feeding back and there's this insane sound coming out of it and you find that by fiddling around the right way you can control it to a certain extent and that becomes part of the way you play." Ignore it, and "it just gets louder and louder and takes over the entire thing." Riffing on this idea in a separate interview that year, Garcia spoke of the band's sonic questing in terms that blinked in neon: "It's more important that it be clear than loud," he said of the ideal Dead sound. "It would be nice if it were both loud and clear."

But then the Dead experienced any band's worst fear. Their equipment vehicle was stolen—with everything in it—one night around the release of *Grateful Dead*. The next day at 710, Garcia gave a wide-ranging interview with Randy Groenke (a former banjo student of Garcia's) and was seemingly at peace about their gear and transport getting swiped. Garcia said it was "pointless" to worry about the theft. "Maybe there's some sort of spiritual due that we paid because we're being successful," he told Groenke, "that means that now somebody can steal our equipment and not feel guilty about it."

Mid-interview, the house phone rang. Rifkin, one room over, answered the call and received good news: The Dead's vehicle had been located. Cruising back alleys near the band's new Potrero Hill practice space, Grant and Bear found the band's gear, all 1,300 pounds, safe and sound. "What luck!" Garcia laughed.

Then as now, vans and trucks were a fixture in the hidden infrastructure of touring. As the Wall got rolling, the Dead went through many more transport vehicles, of all shapes, sizes, and models, to accommodate their soundsystem manifest. Despite everything at times conspiring to work against the band's fleet and crew, the Dead won't forfeit a single gig due to a lack gear in all their years on the road.

To help thwart future van and equipment thefts, beginning in the late '60s, the Dead leaned on their "dependable" relationship with local biker gangs. "We're hiring a couple of Hells Angels to guard our warehouse, now that this stuff has been stolen," Garcia told Groenke. Yet the Dead were asking for it during their stint rehearsing at the decrepit Potrero Theatre. As Caroline "Mountain Girl" Garcia, at the time married to Ken Kesey, recalled, "I think a lot of equipment got stolen in that period."

San Francisco was undergoing a crush of media attention, tens of thousands of visitors, and the sketchy behavior and darker energy that come with heroin, cocaine, and speed. As Scully recalled, "there is a definite shift from the psychedelics and experimental drugs to the hard-drive drugs. A lot of the momentum of the Haight had to do with methamphetamine."

So one morning that spring, the Dead left 710 Ashbury and headed north. The band's office still functioned out of the house, but the individual musicians, crew, and family members eventually settled, one by one, in Marin County. The departure marked the end of one era and the start of an even stranger and wilder new one.

The Dead and their rig made for a ranch on the Russian River near the town of Healdsburg. A friend of Kreutzmann's, whose family owned the secluded vacation spot, offered the Dead space. "We accepted gladly," Lesh recalled, "with the caveat that we'd be bringing our gear."

At the river's edge was a covered sundeck, where the Dead set up their equipment. The platform put them at a perfect vantage to watch kayakers paddling downstream—and to inundate them with weird noises. The band faced their speakers toward the water, and when paddlers passed in front they were hit by low-level feedback, "just subliminal enough to catch their attention, while Pig and Bobby muttered strange imprecations into the mikes," Lesh said.

Other times, they cranked their rig to 110 decibels and made animal sounds, creepy vocalizations, or approximated Martian-speak. "I don't know if any kayaker actually fell over from the shock of what sounded like a giant eighty-foot bullfrog or anything," Kreutzmann later said, "but we sure tried."

These prankster-ish sonic hijinks contained portents of extremely far-out things to come, like the Dead's harsh experiments in "Feedback," a kind of forerunner to the eerie noise of "Space." (That is the name given to the slot of free-form sonic dialoguing in the second set of the typical Dead show, when the band entered a musical *space* with no walls.) They had a box called the Insect Fear Device, Scully said of this time, "that you can plug the guitars or microphones into and play or sing through it and it makes all kinds of unearthly sounds."

There are even glimmers here of perhaps the most ahead of its time and overwhelming Wall application: a collaboration between Lesh and Ned Lagin, a friend of the band whose work of computer-assisted ambient "biomusic," called "Seastones," was part of the same continuum of sonic experimentation as "Feedback" and "Space." During set breaks at select shows the Dead played with the full Wall, Lesh (on bass) and Lagin (on modular synth and computer) pumped massive tones, drones, blips, and blorps at unsuspecting audiences. At one of the final appearances of the Wall, at a hometown show at the Winterland Arena in late 1974, some head in the crowd can be heard on an audience tape screaming: "He-e-llllp!"

For the time being, the Dead got some writing done along the Russian River too. At another woodshedding session in Healdsburg later that summer, "Dark Star," perhaps *the* Dead song, emerged. The band's first collaboration with Garcia's picking pal turned lyricist Robert Hunter, "Dark Star" is less of a "song" and more of "an approach, a platform for exploration, a gate swinging open to *the zone*," or that plane where the band and crowd "travel" together, according to *Skeleton Key*, the Deadhead dictionary.

But first, they embarked on their grandest adventure yet.

June 1, 1967. The crowd murmured at the Tompkins Square Park bandshell in Manhattan, site of the Dead's East Coast debut. The band plugged into their rig and began to play.

The sheer loudness of their sound initially overpowered the audience. Yet every few minutes, "someone comes up to me with their notes: *When do we get a chance to speak?*" Scully recalled. "I say we have this hard-and-fast rule. The microphones and the soundsystem are ours and they are for playing music only."

Such requests don't interrupt the indoor show the Dead played a few nights later at the hip Café Au Go Go, a rectangular cave-like downstairs club on Bleecker Street. Garcia, for his part, had recently said he hoped "to go there

and just turn up real loud and play real loud. Lethal doses." But the night before their first gig of a weeklong booking, Lesh shuddered, "knowing that it will
be painfully loud for everyone, especially us." The band played "directly into
a brick wall at point-blank range, and the ambient noise and bounce back were
deafening," Lesh recalled. "We didn't really need a PA; the stage monitors
would have done the job just fine."

The first Café gig, on June 6, was passable, despite the rough acoustics.
The crowd "soaks up the sound and it becomes bearable," Scully remembered.
"However, the racket from the wall is so loud that it bounces all the way up
the stairs." The band's sound hit the Garrick Theater, immediately next door,
where Frank Zappa's band, the Mothers of Invention, was also in town for a
run of shows. Zappa, Scully claimed, "is a jerk about the whole thing. Instead
of coming down himself, he gets the manager and *demands* we turn our amps
down." The two bands were reportedly forced to stagger their sets. The Dead's
sound, noted a *Time* magazine stringer present that night, was "sensory, piercing right to the blood, and you become one with the music."

Later that month, back on the West Coast, the Dead stood in front of a
rented backline of all new Fender gear, about to perform at the Monterey International Pop Festival. The three-day fest was filmed and eventually released
as a movie, though the Dead did not agree to appear in the film. Their slot at
the highly publicized industry event marked "the inauguration of the Grateful
Dead tradition of always blowing the Big Ones," recalled Lesh.

Tens of thousands of people turned up that weekend in Monterey. Security was light by Sunday afternoon—Scully and Rifkin had dosed the two
guys working as stage guards. Later that evening, the Dead played a lackluster
three-song set, sandwiched between the Who and the Jimi Hendrix Experience.

"After the show, there's a million and a half dollars' worth of amplifiers sitting
on the stage," Scully claimed in his memoir. In his retelling, they commandeered
their artist friend's merch van, backed the vehicle "right up to the stage, and
load it with what we need." They took around a dozen Twin Reverb amps, plus
assorted speaker boxes and power amps provided by Fender and its then parent
company CBS. They left a note, promising to return the gear.

The Dead then departed Monterey with this "liberated" heap of amplifiers and speakers, performing for free back in and around San Francisco. At
El Camino Park in Palo Alto, for instance, at another free outdoor "Be-In,"
the *Stanford Daily* reported that the Dead "were the highlight of the afternoon." Some four thousand people turned up that Sunday, July 2, among them

Sully—the neighborhood kid, now a teenager, who overheard the amplified foundations of the band through the mother rig in the McKernan family garage.

But the Dead's managers were seemingly conflicted. What if they simply kept the pilfered Monterey kit? "What if," moreover, became a mantra for the band's approach to its Wall program, and nearly everything else within Dead-world. Scully claimed that the band even replaced a few blown vacuum tubes once they were done using the amps, though not long after they arranged for a drop in downtown San Francisco. "Don't expect to find any of us hanging around," Scully wrote to the Monterey-Fender team. "So long, folks, and thanks for the loan!'" The Dead returned all the kit but for one amp, which went missing in the shuffle.

The Dead's earliest sound reinforcement trials had finally seemed to level off. Now boosting the band's own Fender gear was an assortment of amps and speaker cabinets purchased from Kustom and Sunn, both leading audio companies at the time. That's when they returned to Canada.

At the outset of a Northeast tour later that July and August, alongside the Airplane, the band rolled into Ontario for a six-night run at the three-thousand-plus seat O'Keefe Center (now Meridian Hall). They hit immediate snags. "The soundsystem had a buzzsaw noise in it, probably caused by one of the light dimmers," Lesh recalled. The buzzing noise was so great it overwhelmed even the Dead's loud music, which partly explains why the band played poorly that night. "Also, for the first time, Jerry and I started grumbling to each other about the music," Lesh said.

Weir was spaced out on LSD, not keeping up. Garcia and Lesh confronted their rhythm guitarist, a target of frequent dosings by crew members, and told him to get it together. "The band was in complete turmoil," Dennis McNally wrote in his band biography. Garcia "was ready to fire Weir for his insensate playing."

Yet to experience the band live, the local *Globe and Mail* reported, produced a particular sensation. Neither volume nor intensity, "but noise." The feeling was not unlike "a jet taking off in your inner ear, while the mad scientist was perversely scraping your nerves to shreds."

The Dead and the Airplane then played a pair of free shows in Montreal. The first was at Place Ville-Marie, a downtown city center flanked on three sides by high-rises. "It's clearly going to sound horrible," Scully said, sizing up the spot. An estimated twenty-five to thirty thousand heads showed up.

"We have to carry in the gear by passing it over the heads of the crowd," Scully recalled. "There is no place to get on and off the stage." Both bands played for roughly an hour, their sounds becoming almost tactile bouncing between the walls.

Later that Sunday, at the World's Fair exposition across town, the Dead and the Airplane played at the Youth Pavilion. The enclosed space was meant to hold a hundred bodies, tops. The Dead's high-decibel music "reached over the walls of the enclosure and pulled in curious fairgoers," McGee wrote. A forward rush of bodies crushed those up front. Somehow the Dead, after stopping briefly, made it through their set with no one getting hurt.

Swinging through Millbrook, New York, the Dead then pit stopped at the estate of multimillionaire Billy Hitchcock, heir to the Mellon oil fortune whose sister was then dating Rakow. East Coast psychedelic figurehead Timothy Leary and his crew had recently holed up at the compound. "The Grateful Dead are part of the equation—the audience, you too," Bear, along for the trip in no official capacity, told Leary. "I call it the feedback loop. If the band hears themselves perform, they complete the loop." The band performed for Leary and the psychedelic elite in the living room, though little is known about the midweek house show.

From there, the band was en route to Michigan, to notch their first ever shows in what became a key Dead market and an essential proving ground for the Wall: the Midwest. But once they returned home that August, after shows in Detroit and Ann Arbor, the Dead underwent a first wave of personnel change within their emerging crew. These internal shifts and family expansions had deep and long-lasting impacts on where all functions of the band, and their rig, went from here. The changes began where the road crew itself started. Sometime after Monterey Pop, Garcia's childhood buddy Grant, the band's original roadie, announced he wanted out. So he quit. He and Garcia remained friends, and soon Garcia was making enough money to set up Grant with his own farm.

One day at 710, a few months after Grant's departure, a young man from up north arrived at the Dead's door. He stood a stocky five-foot-seven, rode in on a Harley, and was all piercing, ice-blue eyes under a mat of bushy blond hair. He didn't talk much, other than to say that Kesey had sent him. "Name's Ram Rod," he said. "I hear you need a good man."

Lawrence "Ram Rod" Shurtliff became *the* Dead roadie. A crew member's crew member, he represented the true conscience of the band and was indispensable to the operation for decades to come. A farm boy who frequently wore cowboy boots and a poncho, a throwback to his youth in the East Oregon high desert, Ram Rod had calloused hands and was practically ready-made to handle the band's amps and speakers. He had a strong block-and-tackle sense of spatial logistics, picked up from his time packing truckloads of watermelons back home. Ram Rod set the mold for many of the Dead's future crew members, in that he might have had a gruff or standoffish exterior but on the inside was capable of being immensely compassionate to those around him. And more than that, as the consummate roadie, he knew the gear—he knew the sound.

Ram Rod soon rose to the position of crew chief and went on to be one of the longest-serving employees of any musical group in history. When he did speak, people listened. As Garcia later put it, Ram Rod was the Dead's "highwater integrity marker."

But for now, Ram Rod split time between Haight-Ashbury and his hometown of Pendleton, Oregon. Though boasting a population of only around fourteen thousand residents at the time, Pendleton provided another four farm-strong future Dead roadies. Ram Rod soon recruited a murderer's row of childhood friends and regional acquaintances, beginning with Donald "Rex" Jackson and followed by John Hagen, Clifford Heard, and Joe Winslow. The "Pendleton boys" were rough-and-tumble, a product of their own making. "It wasn't like we hired them," Garcia later remarked. "They invented themselves—kind of like the band, really."

Then early that October, 710 got pinched. Pigpen and recently sober Weir; managers Scully and Rifkin; Matthews, the equipment guy, in the living room opening a box of new speakers when California Narcotics Enforcement Bureau officers appeared; and a half dozen friends, including Swanson, McGee, and Pig's partner Veronica "Vee" Barnard, were booked (and soon released) on drug charges. Wenner immortalized the bust in the first issue of *Rolling Stone*.

A couple of weeks after the raid, the band, along with Big Brother and Quicksilver, brought all their gear into Winterland Arena, plugged in, and clapped back. That autumn night, the decaying and cavernous 5,400-seat former home to the Ice Capades staged a "Marijuana Defense."

"The audio evidence is incomplete, but everything you need to know about the state of the Grateful Dead's collective musical consciousness in the late fall of 1967 is right here, a benefit concert for themselves," Ray Robertson wrote in *All the Years Combine: The Grateful Dead in Fifty Shows*. The band was still figuring out how to play "The Other One," which Weir and Kreutzmann wrote together, for instance, yet the song was already a "raging beast," Robertson said. And through their screaming rig, "the sheer power of the thing and the musical tension throughout are sizzlingly palpable."

The sound, and the message, was clear.

December 1967. A four-vehicle caravan crawled onto I-80. The Dead were headed out to play shows in New York City and Boston.

They were a bona fide touring party. Healy ran sound. Matthews equipment managed the PA. Joining them was Rakow, who had an International Harvester van to help haul gear. The band had also recently bought their own Dodge Metro van, and at a prearranged location outside Sacramento met Ram Rod and Hagen, who drove down from Oregon in Ram Rod's Dodge Ram. Ram Rod, Hagen, and Pechner were all out for their first time as road crew. "There was this hierarchy of status of responsibility that was always prevalent," Pechner, who was not yet full-on with the band, told me. "If you were the runt or the new guy, you'd kind of be a little behind everything else."

When the band and crew made it to New York, the grind had only begun. That winter of 1967 into 1968 was "bone-marrow-chillingly cold," Lesh recalled. When the Dead played a few gigs at the dilapidated 2,400-seat Village Theater on Second Avenue (soon to be rebranded the Fillmore East by Graham), Kreutzmann and Mickey Hart, who had joined the band as a second drummer, played with gloves to keep their hands warm. "The crew built a fire backstage so they could keep *their* hands warm," Lesh added.

Such hardscrabble gigs were illustrative of the raw spaces and shows a working band like the Dead, equipped with an always-evolving load of sound equipment, took on in this era. But the mood chilled further when the band booted their PA guy between gigs. "Matthews is fired," Swanson, who had flown out along with Garcia, informed Ram Rod one day during that East Coast run. "You're the new equipment manager."

Matthews, himself just eighteen, was let go for refusing to set up Hart's drum kit. A Brooklynite who relocated to work at his estranged father's Bay Area drum shop, Hart had recently befriended Kreutzmann. When Hart first saw the Dead live at San Francisco's Straight Theater earlier that year, their opening set captivated him by its very volume. The sound was "oceanic," as he later described it, "with waves crashing and currents flowing—all I could really hear was the guitar and bass—and loud!" The sensation that night was "this amazing wall of sound swirling around," Hart has said elsewhere. Joining the band on drums during the second set at the Straight was an experience Hart likened to being "whipped into a jet stream." With the introduction of a second drummer, the Dead could now venture into polyrhythmic space and beyond.

Only here they were, a long way from home in the dead of winter, and the crew's most senior member had a problem with the band's newest player. Meanwhile, the band entered Century Sound, a recording studio in New York, to continue tracking their second album for Warner Bros., *Anthem of the Sun*. After Warner's had relented to letting the band do their follow-up record themselves, Lesh and Garcia, nudged on by Healy, landed on a concept that merged live and in-studio tracks into a trippy audio collage. That was an approach to making a record that no one else had taken to that point.

During initial *Anthem* sessions earlier that month in LA, Hassinger, again in the producer's seat, rolled up to American Recording to be reminded of who he was working with. The entrance was blocked by heaps of sound equipment that the band had ordered from Studio Instrument Rentals. The band went in and out of several other studios while recording the record, including Sunset Sound in Hollywood. As will happen a number of times during the making of *Anthem*, the band got thrown out of Sunset for smoking weed, as Scully recalled, "in quest of that elusive sound we hear all the time onstage."

The Dead had developed an attention to sonic detail in highly controlled environments that was just as aggressive as their approach to sound in more open-ended concert settings. Garcia, in particular, "had this undying belief that if you hear it quiet and it's good, it will sound good live," Scully said. With Healy, the band's live sound mixer, now in the recording booth, the *Anthem* studio experience was a headier trip than the last.

The end result contained a comical number of edits. "All over the fucking place," Garcia later said. Not only was *Anthem*, released in July 1968, the first rock album to blend live and studio tracks, it was also the first to stitch together all songs on a given side into one flowing and continuous work—two techniques that countless artists and bands follow to this day. The Dead's second LP was likewise the first ever to feature editing devices from the film world, like jump cuts and montages.

But between recording sessions in New York City late in 1967, the Dead loaded up their gear and drove to Massachusetts. On December 29, they pulled into a subterranean parking garage on Boylston Street in Boston. The Psychedelic Supermarket was an underground venue, yet another concrete club with the acoustics of a cinder block in a succession of venues with bad sound that paved so much of the way for the Dead in their approach to the Wall. If only the band and crew had known what they were going to be up against.

"We got there and we were going, *Well, somebody shoulda told us!*" Pechner said of that pair of Boston gigs, the final shows the Dead played that year. "You start figuring these things out by having the situation present itself. Maybe we should send somebody to take a look *before* we go so we know what to do, if we need to change things or bring stuff." They soon began putting that idea into practice as the Wall took shape; the Dead helped define the art of "advancing" a gig or a tour—sending one or two people out ahead of the rest of the band and crew to check out venues and report back on any potential headaches.

A kind of process in this era organically evolved around the band and crew, both with each other and the soundsystem. "You could just see it getting more specific, in terms of what needed to be done," Pechner told me. And the underground Supermarket, with its low ceilings and columns placed every forty or so feet, "was indicative of the limitations."

One person, at least, was pleased with those shows. "I've been trying to get people to dance for two months," promoter Ross Laver told *MIT Technology Review* after the gigs. "This is the first time it's happened. It's great." But to the Dead and their entourage, the sound was brutal—loud trebles ricocheted off the walls and ceiling. Playing in such an unsatisfactory environment dampened the band's enthusiasm, Pechner said. When the sound wasn't great, the musicians walked offstage and said, "That was like a trainwreck." Or, "We got feedback from *this*," or, "*That* wasn't working," or, "I couldn't hear the piano."

Such gripes and hard-earned knowledge had begun to percolate. *All* the sonic pain points the Dead encountered back then, according to Pechner, were the driving force that ultimately went into developing the Wall, where the musicians basically said, "We have to have this, we have to have that; I gotta hear this, I gotta hear that."

As 1967 rolled over to 1968, the band's rig still wasn't that well developed. "It was mostly the backline—and not a PA," Pechner said, considering this was a time when clubs supplied their own basic systems. "That alone was one of the things that drove the Dead to make their own PA, because it was always hit or miss depending on what the venue had."

Through the noise, their path to the Wall cohered. But no amount of advance scouting could have ever possibly prepared them for what was coming down the line.

5

The Righteous PA (1968–1969)

The Dead had gigged a lot for a young band, but still hadn't toured.

In early 1968, they undertook their first proper two-week trek in DIY fashion, with shows in Seattle, Eugene, Portland, and Ashland, alongside Quicksilver. Scully was their advance man, talking with officials and anxious locals. The Dead offered up intense volume. A review of their January 29 gig at Portland State College noted how the saturating sounds that blizzardy Monday night were so loud "we could see and feel the music."

After the last stop of the Northwest tour, on February 4 at South Oregon College, the band caught an early flight home. But the Dead's roadies got tied up when police pulled over their van heading back to San Francisco.

The roadies were ordered to unpack all six thousand pounds of gear, which the cops inspected item by item, before clumsily attempting to repack everything while the crew waited and watched on the roadside. "This is the very beginning of that kind of harassment," Scully recalled. "And there is a *lot* of shit to search through! Not only the sound equipment, which is growing almost daily, but all the recording gear."

Yet the joke was always on authorities and their "hard foolin'" drug-sniffing dogs. Steve Parish, still a year or so from joining the crew, later claimed that the roadies were bonded by an "unwritten rule" that the equipment shall never be used to transport drugs. But another soon-to-be party member would be particularly skilled at smuggling contraband within the band's soundsystem, a technique that continued through the end of the Wall. The PA was, first and foremost, a vehicle to achieve amazing sound. But the rig also was a perfect vessel for surreptitiously moving stashes.

"I could hide anything," said Candelario, then a seventeen-year-old East Bay head who saw the Dead in the Panhandle and entered the band's scene around this same time as a roadie and Alembic's first employee. "I was the guy everybody came to," he told me. There were all kinds of nooks, crannies, and easily fashioned secret compartments in the gear, Candelario said. "I had special amps with big transformer boxes that I could hide crap in." Until then, finding nothing, the police let the Dead's roadies be on their way.

But once back in San Francisco, the recent death of a Dead hero, the Beat poet and Prankster Neal Cassady, hung over their camp. That February 14, the Dead shared a bill with Country Joe at the 2,800-capacity Carousel Ballroom, dedicating their second set to Cassady. The Carousel was a new Ron Rakow–instigated venture that aligned the Dead, the Airplane, and Quicksilver as a business triad aiming to compete with Bill Graham.

"As Valentine's Day began, the Grateful Dead quippies"—short for equipment handlers—"brought the equipment to the Carousel and stacked the stage with tie-dye speakers and amplifiers custom designed by Bear," recalled Rhoney Gissen, who attended the gig with the band's erstwhile soundman. Once the gig was underway, "the sound was clear and balanced," said Gissen, seated in the sound booth with Dan Healy and Bear. At set break, "Phil announced his praise for the venue and the sound."

Later that same gig, Lesh, distracted and mourning Cassady, entered a state of what he called "total brain-sag." Lesh stopped playing, trying to make sense of what was happening. "Even worse," he said, "I suddenly noticed that Jerry was *glaring* at me from across the stage—something that never happened before."

Afterward, hoping to slip into the night unnoticed, Lesh ran into Garcia backstage. Garcia collared his friend. "You play, motherfucker!" Garcia snapped, shoving aside Lesh, who tripped and tumbled down a staircase. Garcia apologized to Lesh a couple of days later. "Sorry, man," he said. "I don't know what came over me."

Moods lifted that spring, peaking in another guerrilla-style free show the band played on March 3 in the Haight. A pair of flatbed trucks, Lesh recalled, pulled "tight and close," and a roadie bridged the two beds with a piece of plywood. Out came the drums, which got nailed to the stage. Some half dozen electrical extension cords "sail through the air" out of a window of the nearby

Straight Theater. They plugged in their power strips, fired up the amp line, and began tuning their instruments.

"We rip off our standard warm-up licks, set volumes (loud!)," and away they went, Lesh said. "Of all the free shows we played during the time we lived in the Haight," he later said, "this is the Grateful Dead's finest hour." The sounds of that historic gig lived on thanks to Steve Brown, the record industry head and proto–Dead freak, was one of the earliest Dead audience recordings and the seed of a tree that only branched out from there, alongside the band's PA.

The band still rehearsed at the abandoned and easily broken into Potrero Theater. At the very least, "we could play loud and long there during the day," Lesh said. More than once, Lesh claimed, the Dead blasted hunks of ceiling insulation clean off using low-frequency feedback. The band's Potrero tenure was a crucible through which the Dead forged what ultimately stands up as some of the most creative material of their entire career. Taking inspiration from time signatures of Indian and other non-Western musical traditions, the Dead, especially drummers Kreutzmann and Mickey Hart, began applying frameworks and structures that really no one else had considered using in a rock context. They could only emerge from these sessions with a song like "The Eleven," arranged in 11/8 time.

Hart had touched on such themes in an interview with the University of Oregon's *Daily Emerald*. The band was clearly questing to articulate the sonic apex they chased as a unit. The operative phrase was already in use in the context of recording producer Phil Spector's maximalist studio production formula, featured on tracks like "Be My Baby" by the Ronettes. (Spector and the Dead are not known to have met.) But in the *Daily Emerald*, Hart talked about working within a "wall of sound" the Dead created, and how at gigs they tried to build their wave to flood every inch of hall space. "We can work with fantastic volumes, but we can also bring it down, lately, and still keep the wall," Hart said. It's not so much sheer volume as it was the reality that they were moving together as a band that gave rise to the "wall."

But the Dead soon found themselves soundperson-less, yet again. That summer, Healy joined back up with Quicksilver, who he toured with over the better part of the next three years. A familiar face resurfaced in his stead.

Busted on drug charges in late 1967, Bear kept a low profile with his chemistry and audio pursuits. At "Tab House," the residence in Orinda, California, that

Bear, Melissa Cargill, Gissen, and Bear's artist friend Bob Thomas established after returning their lab to the Bay Area, "the first thing Owsley and I did was set up the soundsystem," Gissen recalled.

Bear had grown partial to monophonic sound, a key shift in his thinking around what became the Wall. "For him, purity was greater in mono sound—a single audio signal sent to more than one speaker with all speakers reproducing the same sound, no splitting," Gissen said. He also further expounded on his maintaining sonic journals of shows. "Recording live music is where it's at," Bear said, pressing play on a live Dead recording from his tape stash. "There's feedback—an electric connection between the audience and the musicians. When it works, it's one harmonious voice vibrating in rhythm. Nobody has figured out how to record live music. We can do it!"

In the meantime, Bear had also begun hot-rodding amplifiers and steadily designing and building out the Carousel's rig. "If we lease the Carousel, I can build an electronics shop here," Bear had said at an initial deliberation between the Dead, the Airplane, and Quicksilver. "I need a place to work on the soundsystem and the guitars."

Bear could throw himself anew into the Dead's sonic pursuits, as the band, part owners of the ballroom, played there often. "The machines would blow up or there'd be feedback and he'd be saying, *How could you fail me?*" Hart later said of Bear. "He personalized it way beyond rational thought. He was asking things of them and expecting results." Hart claimed he and Lesh had a special relationship with Bear that ran counter to Garcia, who "thought [Bear's] madness was sometimes ruining our moment, whereas I thought it was in the name of science." Bear "was more of an idea guy," Hart added. Healy, by contrast, "was a seat-of-his-pants guy who actually could make things happen."

Engineering the Carousel soundsystem invigorated Bear. His right to travel had not yet been revoked, "but he could forget about his legal problems in the music," Gissen said. Moreover, "with the business aspect of the Carousel under control" thanks to Rakow, Gissen assumed she "was part of the sound crew and listened carefully to Bear's ramblings." The musicians, Bear explained, *had* to hear both themselves and the house mix. "We will build the best soundsystem for the musicians at the Carousel," he said, "with monitors that have the same quality as the house speakers."

Bear's audio equipment filled the Carousel's stage, sound booth, and provisional shop in the balcony. "He rejected the modern solid-state equipment in favor of heavy tubes," Gissen said. He claimed tubes were superior, "providing the most power, and power was the driving force of rock 'n' roll. Even with distortion, the sound was saturated and steady." Bear outfitted his booth with a mixing board, an oscilloscope, a tape recorder, and a workbench for soldering. "His goal was to modify the sound equipment with state-of-the-art electronics using tubes and modern Mylar," Gissen said. "He was opening up all the equipment, tearing out the old resistors and capacitors and replacing them with new components. He told me everything had to be unsoldered and resoldered."

In the upstairs workshop, Bear then taught Cargill and Gissen how to do just that. Cargill naturally took to soldering, while Gissen struggled. Moreover, down on the stage, "Ram Rod and Rex had lined up the amps and were unscrewing the casings with a long automatic screwdriver. I tried it and made them laugh out loud," Gissen said. Meanwhile, Betty Cantor and Bob Matthews, both now also working at the Carousel, sorted through cables, "opening the connectors to see if anything needed soldering," Gissen recalled. "Could I find a role with the Grateful Dead family? Not soldering, that was clear." She felt burned that Bear ultimately did not seem to want her on the audio team. "I thought, if I couldn't be part of Bear's sound crew, I'd die."

At the Carousel's sold-out opening that March, "while the Airplane was playing, Bear was still working on the Dead's electronics, running back and forth from the sound booth to the stage," Gissen recalled. After the Airplane, "Bear still had not finished setting up the Dead's equipment, and I started to worry. I wondered, why couldn't he be on time? Why did his drive for perfection cause so many problems?" Eventually, the Dead went on. "But Bear was still fiddling with the equipment as the band began to play," she said. "He moved between the drummers to reposition the mics. Nothing could distract the band once they started, but I felt in the way. I had to stop following him around." The music that night "was louder than I thought, which I learned when I tried to talk," Gissen said. "The sound was wonderful ... and even I was feeling it."

As Bear reintegrated, the Dead's sound team and road crew entered another feverish phase of expansion and specialization. At the Carousel, Bear started collaborating with Matthews on beefing up the soundsystem. After getting clipped from the Dead's equipment crew in late 1967, Matthews returned to San Francisco and started spending time with Cantor. As the Carousel got going, Cantor slung hot dogs for one Jon McIntire, who ran concessions, and apprenticed herself to Matthews on the sound front.

Matthews and Bear, Gissen claimed, were "eager" to teach Cantor how to work the soundsystem. Soon, "I was jealous and insecure," Gissen said. Matthews certainly had "ulterior motives" with Cantor, though their ensuing romantic partnership did not undercut her quickly growing into an ace engineer.

Through their connection with Bear, Cantor and Matthews soon joined forces with Ron Wickersham, then an audio engineer at electronics company Ampex, and luthier Rick Turner. Within a year or so, they started Alembic and began working closely with the Dead. As Matthews later recalled, he and Wickersham and Turner each headed up a different division. "I did recording and PA," Matthews said, "Ron did the electronics, and Rick did instrument manufacturing." By the early '70s, Alembic essentially existed to serve the Dead. The company's building a prototype Wall was critical in proving that the wildest theoretical acoustic concepts underlying the system could be brought to life on an epic scale.

But the next crew member to come fully aboard with the Dead in 1968 was Rex Jackson. Brash, confident, handsome, and with a larger-than-life, horse-riding air about him, Jackson possessed a "drive to express some spark," his fellow Oregonian and soon-to-be Dead roadie Joe Winslow said. Yet Jackson, all long brown hair and Stetson hat, was "frustrated in how to do it."

Still, Jackson and the other Pendleton boys embodied "a real can-do energy," the Prankster Ken Babbs later said. "These guys didn't shirk any of the heavy work, but would always get it done, which wasn't always easy because in those days it was still a psychedelic journey," Babbs went on. "But they were all part of the same team, and they made it a better team."

The Pendleton unit ushered a strong cowboy sentiment within Deadworld. They also began to actually build the band's various systems and speakers, the earliest iterations of wooden boxes that evolved into ruggedized yet finely tuned cabinets like my own artifact. "It was a devotional type of roadie-ism that was kind of neat to see," Mountain Girl, Garcia's partner at the time, later said. "I think that feeling disintegrated, over cocaine."

The story of the Dead and the Wall is intertwined with a late '60s and early '70s chemical shift. Coke's toxicity ate at the exploratory, ungated psychedelic whimsy and "good" judgment that had united band and crew. And it's no co-incidence that this marked change occurred as the Dead became a true road outfit.

There wasn't a ton of funding at this point, and what money the band did make was routed back into the purchasing of instruments and gear and advancing their soundsystem. But blow could always be procured. The drug's teeth-gnashing "influence on people's attitudes and personalities, when they are doing a lot of it, exacerbated the separation and changes people," Rosie McGee later said. "The whole scene was coked out."

There were still dank weed, Bear's LSD, and routine dosings attached to the Dead and their rig. The band was "literally born out of a psychedelic prank," admitted Kreutzmann, who later said he did not condone anyone being dosed without prior consent. "Therefore, certain things were just woven into our DNA."

But increasingly, lines of white powder were chopped up atop speaker monitors or taken into bathroom stalls for discreet bumps. Cocaine was used "simply as a stimulant to keep people who were working very, very long hours going," Dennis McNally told me, "but that's crew guys. I don't believe that Bear or any of the designers were using it to stimulate their creativity of building the Wall of Sound."

Candelario is one of a few crew members who claimed they never touched the stuff. "I didn't do cocaine," he told me. He preferred coffee for powering through all-night drives, or a couple polite afternoon drops of acid "so you were kind of wired" for load in, setup, soundcheck, and showtime. Candelario, for his part, was working odd jobs at the Carousel. One day at that ballroom, he recalled, Bear handed him a box of connectors and a pile of mic wires, and asked, "Can you make these into cables?"

"Sure," Candelario said.

"You did a good job on those," Bear later told him, inspecting Candelario's work. "You are the cable guy from now on."

Such fine motor skills belied Candelario's middleweight boxer's build and that he could be acerbic, even downright ornery. He wore various hats, like so many Dead crew members, but excelled in fabrication. "If it needed welding," he said, "I could do it." Candelario's father kept a portable welder/welding machine out front of their house, and if his son misbehaved he faced "driveway punishment." *Weld all of these pieces together*, his old man ordered. All manner of pipe and metal, cut into angles and such. "It was good training for fabricating later on," Candelario admitted. "You had to just jump in and get it done," he added, "instead of worrying about where the coke guy was."

In these Carousel days, Ram Rod, now Dead crew chief, likewise handed a grip of busted cables to Candelario, who fixed them. "Hey," Ram Rod told him, "you're on *my* crew now." Ram Rod himself was already learning from Bear, as

Garcia later recalled. "But it's one of those things where you learn stuff from Owsley sort of by osmosis," Garcia said.

Meanwhile, holed up in the Potrero, the Dead steadily worked on a new album. "Sometimes I'd just hang around outside and listen, maybe talk to some of the guys on the crew," said Parish, a towering teenager from Queens who worked security at the World's Fair pavilion in Flushing Meadows Park and New York–area clubs. He had done time at Rikers Island for possession before visiting San Francisco, staying with a friend who lived near the Carousel. The Dead roadies, he noticed, "seemed to be family, brothers-in-arms with the boys in the band. They were united in some great cause."

But as the crew solidified and the soundsystem continued to grow, loosely affiliated characters seemingly always hung around the Dead's offices and shows. This revolving cast of well-to-do, jet-setting Deadheads, known as the Pleasure Crew, had the money, resources, and connections to support a purely party animal lifestyle, a liability for the band and, by extension, their PA. Pleasure Crew member Kenneth "Goldfinger" Connell, notably, was an early West Coast acid distributor and weed smuggler, believed to then be flying tons of cannabis into the States. With the exception of Peter "Craze" Sheridan, who did occasional stagehand labor on the early Wall, the Pleasure Crew did not carry speakers or fix broken amps. "Where there's booze and dope, there's hope," Sheridan was known to say.

Bear, who detested alcohol and cocaine and feared what hard drugs could do to the band's scene, would have nothing to do with the cadre of affluent hangers-on. Some of these individuals, known entities to the FBI and various law enforcement agencies, attracted unwanted attention. When the touring hiatus got called at the end of 1974 and dozens of band employees got laid off and the Wall got disassembled, there were murmurings that it was to get the heat off their backs.

Years later, Healy recalled being thrust into this era when officials told them that they were playing either too late, or too early; too loud, or not loud enough; or that they were drawing too many people into one area, or blocking streets. "It got to be the cops versus us," Healy has said. "And that's where all the 'fuck the band' stuff and 'tear down the Wall' stuff came from. Unfortunately, a lot of that ended in throwing the baby out with the bath water."

With the Pleasure Crew present, another bust was waiting to happen. Connell alone posed a serious risk to the Dead's operation. "Goldfinger was undoubtedly being trailed by Feds," claimed Sam Cutler, the Dead's soon-to-be road manager.

Yet Connell and other Pleasure Crew members traveled with the band, had a hotel suite in whatever town they were in, brought copious drugs, and loved to gorge themselves on bacon after gigs. "And no one knew how they got there," Lesh later said. But if the Pleasure Crew had a "generalissimo in chief," he added, it was Rakow.

The former Wall Street financier had recently convinced the Dead, the Airplane, and Quicksilver to create a vague partnership under his direction. "This was Rakow's first real leadership role with us," Kreutzmann, wary of outsiders trying to burn the band, said of the Carousel. "That's probably why I don't remember most of it." At one point, there was talk of moving the Carousel stage, an idea Bear called a "waste of money." The acoustics throughout the hall were considered good. But Rakow proceeded anyway, hiring carpenters when the operation was hemorrhaging money.

Rakow did help generate genuine financial opportunities for the Dead and also briefly played a more active role with the equipment crew. He assisted in winding up and tying cables, leaving them "for Ram Rod to weave into the load," Rakow told me. But to many insiders, it was always unclear why Rakow, who had a snake oil salesman's charm, was ever "hired" to control anything to do with the band's money, let alone sound. "I think he believed in his get-rich-quick schemes," Kreutzmann said, "he just didn't have the know-how to see them through."

The Carousel, through Rakow's stewardship, still served as an early incubator for some of the band's most influential roadies and audio and recording techs. The Dead's involvement in that venture was essentially "an attempt to bypass the middlemen of promoters and hall rentals, and enjoy all the benefits themselves," wrote Barry Barnes, the Deadhead economist. Though short lived, the Carousel was very much a people's space too, for a time housing offices of the Black Panthers. "With the Carousel as our community playground," said McGee, "our gigs felt more like huge parties than the running of a commercial enterprise designed to make money."

Wherever and whenever the band now performed, their extended family, herself included, was an onstage fixture, grouped behind the amp line. Which is where they found themselves one spring afternoon in New York City, between the band's gear and a brick wall.

May 3, 1968. Columbia University's campus in Manhattan was on lockdown. Students were striking over the school's ties to the US military and proposed construction of a nearby segregated gymnasium. Access to the private Ivy League school was now restricted. That's when the Dead emerged from an equipment truck at the Columbia union loading docks that Friday and made for a patio in the library quad, before cops or school officials thwarted them.

The band scrambled to pull off a stealth gig just inside campus. They quickly set up all three tons of their equipment. Student strikers immediately got turned on at the sight of a powerful PA, despite being told by the Dead that the rig would be used only for music. "The politicos take one look at our soundsystem and go crazy," Scully recalled. Seemingly everyone had "an important announcement." In the span of a minute, Bob Weir, then twenty-one, claimed that he had to tell off five individuals. The crowd–band dynamic at Columbia presented "a bit of an odd situation," McGee said. Some of the people in the audience weren't familiar with the Dead and were clearly more keen to leverage the PA to make speeches.

The interruptions continued into the Dead's set. According to firsthand accounts, university administrators cut power to the soundsystem not long into the band's performance, only to plug the rig back in, fearing a riot.

"We were always in the middle of those kinds of conflicts," Garcia later said. "There was a while there when every tour...somebody would fuckin' turn off the power, would shut us down." And "you have no idea what it's like," Garcia added, "building up and all of a sudden the power is gone." That made the Dead furious. They never considered themselves to be a political band, Garcia said, but authorities "associated us with danger." The moment officials "started seeing people freak out, they thought, 'Okay, that's it. We're not going to let this go any further.' Boom."

When that happened, "we were perfectly happy with our regular amplifiers," Garcia reflected. Yet oftentimes, officials wouldn't let the Dead play. In fact, "that's the evolution, really, of our whole soundsystem and our power... with those big fuckin' things that clamp onto the main trunk route," Garcia said, referring to the mainline connection that found a place in the Dead's electricity supply for the growing Wall. That feature spun out of the cord getting pulled at college gigs in the late '60s. "We want something that nobody can fucking turn off, ever, you know? It was like they drove us to it."

After power was restored back at Columbia, the sound of the music took over. Watching and listening from behind the band's backline, McGee remembered the moment the Dead roused the hundreds who had gathered. "The guys won them over," she said.

One head in the crowd was Janet Furman, then a junior who earned an electrical engineering degree from Columbia a year later. That was her first time seeing the Dead. "It was possible to get right up close," Furman told me. "I had a great time. Did I have an inkling that I was gonna have my path cross with them later in life? No." But Furman was considering a music industry career, and possibly moving to California after graduating.

The Columbia show was one big "prank," in Lesh's words, executed with precision speed to a largely student audience in a more dire headspace than the band. "We play a short set, pack up, and split," Lesh recalled. The caper clocked in at under two hours. According to Kreutzmann, the Dead "probably fared better" a few days later in Central Park, where they played another free gig alongside the Airplane and the Paul Butterfield Blues Band. A *New York Times* review of that May 5 gig reported that the Dead "are extremely driving, amplified, and hirsute."

Yet the days of the guerrilla Dead gig were numbered. "It's a shame that the institution of the spontaneous free concert has fallen prey to economic realities; it was one of the most satisfying manifestations of our collective transformation program," Lesh later said. As the Dead brought the model of the unannounced outdoor gig from San Francisco to the rest of the country, "there would usually be a very enthusiastic and receptive, if not large, audience." They had their rig to thank for that.

Back home, the Carousel spun out.

The jointly owned ballroom closed that June, due to a loose admissions policy and the venture, under Rakow's direction, falling into financial disarray. Graham soon took over the space, rebranding it Fillmore West, and booked the Dead for five nights in late August. The band was preparing to record their third LP for Warner's, *Aoxomoxoa*, and hoped to practice the material before a sizable crowd. Graham said Bear, who the promoter always had it out for, could simply leave his equipment set up during the venue changeover.

The band had formally asked Bear if he wanted to rejoin as their soundman, while Healy went back to working with Quicksilver. Bear met them at the gutted Potrero, where the band continued rehearsing songs for *Aoxo*. "Everything was primitive," Bear recalled, "so I went to work for them again and started improving the gear." He would implement what acoustic knowledge he had gleaned in his time away, aiming to bring the Dead's whole rig "up to snuff."

The band's own dynamics were in a state of upheaval. "Jerry was definitely emerging as the undeclared leader," Lesh said. "As much as we all loved playing with one another, everyone's primary music bond was with Jerry." And yet Garcia maintained that there wasn't any one leader among them. As he later told one reporter, "everybody is the leader when it's time for them to be the leader."

These revolutions occurring across the Dead's realm were reflected in thrillingly bent and leaderless live sonic experiments. The band's utilizing feedback as a musical element, Lesh later claimed, was originally (mostly) his idea. "There we were with these electronic instruments, and it was starting to be obvious to me that they could function in that kind of manner," he said. Despite feedback being difficult to control, their instruments were "tonal" insofar as the sounds they produced typically have harmonic structures like tonal notes. Still, the waves were harsh and loud. "Feedback" was "performed" live sporadically for two or so years, until the Dead came to explore other terrain through their instruments and the full Wall.

At one confrontational Friday night gig that June 14 at Graham's Fillmore East in New York City, the Dead, ping-ponging between the coasts in this era, opened with "Feedback." Squealing, unrelenting noise leveled an unsuspecting audience. One head remembered people begging mercy of the band. "Enough! We can't handle this anymore," they said. The band broke and left the stage. But then the audience urged them to reconsider. The Dead returned and played the rest of the show.

"Feedback" blasted from the Dead's system throughout that summer. On August 4 at the Newport Pop Festival in Costa Mesa, California, photographer Jim Marshall stood on the outdoor stage and snapped a now widely seen photo of the band members turned away from the crowd. The band held their instruments up to, or scratched them against, their backline wall, producing distortion and noise. The title "Feedback" itself "is neither innocent nor accidental," Ulf Olsson, a comparative literature instructor at Stockholm University, Sweden, wrote in *Listening for the Secret: The Grateful Dead and the Politics of Improvisation.* "The players are feeding back the signal produced by their instruments into the electrical circuit formed by amplifiers and PA system." By turning their backs to the audience, in order to face their amps and speakers, the band called further attention to this very act of "feeding back." The practice "is a form of short-cutting of rock music, which in a way is the system that the band is feeding back into: there is no pulse, no melody, no chorus," Olsson said. Within the Dead system, "feedback is a counter-signal within a system of power relations."

Elsewhere that summer, still more new faces appeared to help get the band's affairs in order. They had recently signed on a dedicated road manager, Jonathan Riester, who had been working at the Carousel. Riester was now another advance man dealing with promoters and ambivalent townspeople, securing the band's compensation at gigs, and handling other day-to-day aspects of travel for a growing touring party and three-plus tons of gear. Riester stipulated that the band likewise hire McIntire, whom they also knew from the Carousel. McIntire was first tasked with straightening the band's business files as the Dead's office vacated 710. He sorted through whole shopping bags and wastebaskets bursting with three years' worth of bills and receipts.

From out of this chaos of paperwork, McIntire and Bert Kanegson, whom Riester had also stipulated be hired as another manager type, puzzled together a kind of financial State of the Band. "That took quite a while," recalled McIntire, who opened a new San Francisco Dead office. But before long, a Deadhead phone technician tipped them off: Their line was tapped by the FBI, who were "convinced that the Grateful Dead are a front for a sinister acid-making cartel bent on corrupting the world's feckless youth," according to Scully. The managers eventually joined the others in San Rafael, the final location of the Dead's offices.

In the meantime, the band settled into a new rehearsal and equipment storage space in Marin, the site of some of the most significant conversations and R&D into initial Wall building blocks. Early that September, Kanegson scouted out the Pepto-Bismol–colored warehouse south of Novato near Hamilton Air Force Base. "Loud rock 'n' roll could not disturb the military planes taking off and landing day and night—and we never complained," said Gissen, who joined Cargill as secretaries for the band's management. Setting up shop, Bear and Ram Rod "pushed the amps into different positions, chasing the sound, their ears bent to the speakers," Gissen recalled.

While the band rehearsed in the back room, the Dead's prodigal soundman doubled down on his ultimate audio project. Bear "hoped to produce the most purely transparent musical sound yet by analyzing and tuning the sound as the band played," Lesh said. In the development of modern sound reinforcement, Bear's basic concept will be a paradigm for what is now done automatically in real time with computers. Bear himself went down as the first engineer to deliver live sound in stereo, as well as having a hand in the invention of stage monitors. He wanted to now resume purifying the entire signal path, which began at the instruments themselves.

In that path Bear schemed up for the Dead, low-impedance electrical pick-ups (on guitars and bass) flowed through specialized cabling, which carried the signals through customized preamps and hi-fidelity power amps that were similarly all low-impedance. To that end, Bear and the Dead's expanding tech-crew circle started building more of their own speaker cabs, each tuned specifically to each musician's respective instrument.

Bear's incessant need to adjust levels during setup and soundcheck once again delayed gig start times. But when he wasn't live-mixing Dead shows and rehearsals or schooling those in earshot on the subtleties of mono, Bear, a pestering and oftentimes punishing presence, occupied a tin shed behind the pink warehouse, hyper-focusing in a coontail hat, paisley shirt, and round wire glasses. Under a leaky roof, what Bear had been thinking of as an in-house mechanism for distilling the best ideas and talents flowing through Deadworld to their purest, elemental forms, as an alembic would, took form. This process would allow the band's assorted heads to then use those raw materials to build new and better stuff, both for the Dead and other musicians and groups in their broader circle. Bear converted the shack into a makeshift shop and acoustical laboratory, and soon brought in Ron and Susan Wickersham.

The Dead and Bear had recently met Ron, a quiet Indiana-born electrical engineer, at Pacific High Recording in San Mateo during *Aoxo* sessions. Wickersham's employer Ampex, which held the patent on stereo, had newly installed at Pacific High Prototype #2, the second in a pair of what were then the world's only 16-track recording decks. (In the mid-1950s, Ampex had made the first breakout videotape recorder, and now it had spawned the multitrack recording process by merging its video transport technology with audio heads.) As was often the case, the band was at the right place and time to go to another level. They came into Pacific High one day, fiddled with Prototype #2, and said screw it. Armed with the new 16-track rig, they redid the record from scratch.

"The end result was dense and cumbersome in places," Kreutzmann recalled, "and all that studio time cost us a fortune, but we were experimenting on the sonic frontier, exploiting cutting-edge technology."

In the shack behind the pink warehouse, after Bear poached Wickersham from Ampex, they dug into solving the band's sound equipment troubles. They yearned for a truly dependable PA, to be freed of the shoddy sound provided by promoters that so frequently hampered live performances. "The attitude of the Grateful Dead was always If it won't work, throw money at it, even if we were broke," Lesh said. Scully, in particular, "simply couldn't say no to himself or to anyone else," Lesh claimed. Perhaps because of that mentality, until the Dead's first commercial "hit" record in the late '80s, none of the individual band members, much less crew and staff, earned more than a cost-of-living salary. In what Lesh called "true communal fashion," all their money went into the proverbial pot and was then distributed into the various buckets of furthering their trip.

From the beginning, "every one of our moves was powered by deep waves in the group unconscious," Lesh said. That groupmind had a significant bearing on where their collective dollar went. As the band grew, an increasing hunk of the pie went toward the Dead umbrella organization's overhead, from paying salaries, to covering the costs of advancing gigs and tours, and purchasing office supplies. But mostly, the money got spent on gear.

On paper, then, the sonic solution appeared deceptively straightforward: The Dead should make their own soundsystem and take it with them on tour. To get them there, their techs needed more space to work on the PA off the road. Before long, Bear and the Wickershams relocated into one of the Novato warehouse's large side rooms, now used for gear repair and assorted builds and construction projects. Bear "was a pack rat and saved everything—duplicates, triplicates, qua-druplicates," Gissen said. "In his endless quest for better-quality sound, he had amassed an arsenal of equipment and needed quippies to schlep it."

Turner, the luthier, stepped into the picture in this same era. He was equally instrumental in designing what became the Wall, and had been live-mixing the Youngbloods, a Bay Area band that McGee was moonlighting for as a kind of manager and secretary. She noted the instrument he made for the Young-bloods' bassist, "and thought that Phil and the Grateful Dead crowd would be interested in what I was up to," Turner told me. "So she arranged a meeting." In Novato, Turner started hanging with Bear, Wickersham, and Matthews, who had since made amends with the Dead. "That was sort of the technical crew," Turner recalled, plus Cantor and the band.

Initially Bear-funded, Alembic wouldn't incorporate for another year. In time, Turner and Wickersham became the dominant forces behind the company behind the Wall. The relationship between those two individuals, Bear later recalled, was "not what you would call totally compatible signs. One's a dragon and one's a sheep."

The venture's first project? Hot-rodding Lesh's Guild Starfire bass, known as "Big Red." Bass was perpetually problematic from a mixing standpoint, as low-end notes tend to get lost while the highs "cut" through. Thanks to Turner, in particular, Lesh's bass earned the distinction of carrying the first "active" electronics ever installed on a stringed instrument, now standard practice in amplified music. Even more far-out, Lesh recalled, was the quad pickup the Alembic techs installed on Big Red, which gave the bassist the ability to send, or "throw," a note from a given string to a separate cluster of speakers within the PA. But until the development of the full Wall, Lesh wouldn't be able to take full advantage of that feature.

For the time being, the band and crew continued down the road, enduring high highs, low lows, and assorted fits and starts, technological and otherwise. But sometimes, just when things looked darkest, came a glimmer of clarity. And these hard-won and incremental gains boosted their collective spirit.

Take an unlikely pair of performances in Ohio that fall. The venue for the first scheduled gig, the six-thousand-capacity Veterans Memorial Hall in Columbus, was "huge, cold, and hollow-sounding," Lesh recalled. That Friday, November 22, the band ran a quick soundcheck. By showtime, around three hundred people had arrived in support of the band. The Dead, through the pursuit of better sound, were earning hardcore fans who showed up to see them play, despite everything. Garcia counted into "Morning Dew," a cover of an antinuke folk song by Bonnie Dobson. "I know from the first chord that it's going to be a good night," Lesh recalled, "in spite of the feedback from the PA."

The Dead had nothing booked the following evening, so they made the spontaneous trip to play in Athens, a seventy-mile shot down US 33. And with a new member too. The band had recently brought in keyboardist Tom Constanten, a friend of Lesh's, to fill out the sonic palette and pick up Pigpen's slack. The group's original frontman could still whip crowds into a frenzy, but began flubbing his organ parts as his alcoholism worsened.

Constanten played his first show with the band that November 23 at Ohio University. As he realized, the big issue during his brief tenure with the Dead was primarily a matter of amplification. His stage rig had a pair of Leslie speakers, but Constanten wanted two more of the cabs, to compensate for Garcia's searing guitar sometimes being picked up louder than Constanten in his own mics. The ambient noise level of the band's guitars had been "jacked up" by Alembic hot-rodding their instruments, which involved replacing all the stock individual components with the highest-quality gear, Constanten later recalled. His Hammond B-3 keyboard would often be overwhelmed in the live mix. "While I was with them," Constanten said, "Jerry was going through four

Twin Reverb [amps] turned up to ten—hard to imagine, but they built upward from there."

For the rest of the band, that impromptu Rust Belt gig was a model of "what if?" energy, and an instance where the Dead left yet another receptive audience in a choice position. As Lesh put it, "hanging from the walls."

By 1969, pieces of the Wall started to make sense, in terms of having crowds hear what the band heard. Break down the difference between the microcosmic environment of the stage and the macrocosmic environment of an auditorium or hall, and leave no differentiation between onstage monitors and the audience.

Yet most Dead insiders still couldn't comprehend a defining Wall characteristic. One fateful day that year at the Novato warehouse, during an informal meeting of certain band and tech crew members, Bear hit them with a wild idea, as Turner recalled.

"You know," Bear said, "the solution is the PA system has to be behind the band."

The others looked at Bear like he had lost his mind. "He was crazy, but he was always way ahead of everybody," Turner told me. Placing the whole of a soundsystem *behind a band* was then an unheard-of idea, so Bear's comment represented another leap forward in the Wall's evolution.

A battle raged between the band's backline and the stage monitors—sometimes referred to as "foldback" speakers—meaning the musicians had to listen to different sound sources. (Nowadays, in-ear monitors, of which the Dead eventually were early adopters, can deliver a desired mix to the dome.) Bear's vision was a line of speakers that included the monitors and got placed behind the band, to eliminate that conflict between competing sound sources such that the musicians and the crowd all heard the same thing. The key was the phase-canceling microphones that Alembic engineers designed to prevent feedback caused by the sound of the Wall picked up in the vocal mics.

They encountered the concept at the Fillmore East, where in-house sound techs Chris Langhart, John Chester, and Bob Goddard worked a crushingly loud Blue Cheer gig and flashed on the idea. The Dead played the Fillmore East a total of twenty-seven times and did something at Graham's New York hall that they never did anywhere else: willingly used the club's own soundsystem. That the band chose to perform through the Fillmore East PA, designed and built by Chester, speaks to the live concert sound work done there.

Traveling around the country, the Dead picked up signals, according to Ben Haller, who worked lights at the Fillmore East and soon joined the Dead's lighting crew. "The Dead heard about the concept—everybody did," Haller told me, of the feedback cancellation technique. "Bear and Alembic were always snooping around."

That was part of a shared and idealized Dead belief formulating: Sound should be delivered to audiences on par with a quality hi-fi home system. Even a casual concertgoer is familiar with that standard today, but it was still beyond where most any band was at in their own sonic journeys back then. That meant distortion free: loud, clear, and clean. Along the way, Bear and other technical people in Deadworld also worked out how stacking speaker cabinets in a certain way allowed them to deliver different sound pressure levels, to account for the physics of projecting their music across bigger stages, venues, and audiences, without sacrificing quality. Again, common practice today, but not so in the late '60s and early '70s.

For now, a soundsystem design that placed the entirety of the amp, speaker, and monitor line at the musicians' backs was difficult for the others to grasp. But the premise was intriguing enough that Bear's pitch at the Novato warehouse—that the PA go behind the band—wasn't dismissed outright. "We sort of filed it away," Turner said.

In the meantime, the Dead and their crew and techs registered when things clicked by crowd reactions, as the band set its ambitions on performing to more people. "The fans were definitely driving the band," said Richie Pechner. "When the band played well you could tell it was one of those nights. And when they didn't, more likely than not it would be a technical issue." The goal was always "to try to make it so every show had the highest quality," Pechner told me. "It was all about the sound. They were obsessive about it."

The Dead clocked over 140 dates in 1969, more gigs than any prior year in their existence, and setting a pace of a hundred-plus shows a year into the '70s. The band's equipment weighed some eight thousand pounds by this point. Aside from guitars and bass, the rig included a couple of Fender amps and JBL boosters; a modest PA, likely a mix of Sunn and Acoustic speaker cabinets; Pig's portable Vox organ; a pair of drum kits, plus some gongs and congas; and a few Ampex MX-10 dual-channel tube mixers stacked in the audience, or front of house.

"It was a very simple PA," Candelario told me. The rig was a three-way crossover, meaning the sound was divided into three segments—there were 15-inch speakers, 375 drivers, and high-frequency horns. "It was generally stacked up like a square on the stage," Candelario said. "Very primitive. This is before we learned about line arrays." What they didn't know back then is that "we should've stacked it in a column."

Occasionally the band flew domestically with all this kit to play one-off shows in other cities. Michael Lydon, a founding *Rolling Stone* editor, once witnessed the Dead and crew catching a commercial flight in the late '60s. "In the cargo area, a huge rented truck pulls up with the Dead's equipment, ninety extra pieces of luggage," Lydon recalled. "Like clowns from a car, amp after amp after drum case is loaded onto dollies and rolled into the jet's belly." The passengers realized that the band was holding them up; the Dead realized too, only "they dig it," Lydon wrote.

But the Dead and their caravan still primarily traveled by ground. That meant refusing Bear further privileges after he got a traffic citation in Chicago on tour that January. Driving erratically en route to a pair of shows at the Kinetic Playground on the city's north side, Bear was pulled over and detained. Authorities let him walk once the appropriate city officials were paid off. The gig had been successful enough to nearly cover the cost of "grease," bribery being another gear-turning element included in internal Wall tour budgets. That was the end of Bear's time behind the wheel.

January 24, 1969. Ram Rod, John Hagen, Jackson, and Candelario had rolled Prototype #2, the new Ampex deck, into the Avalon Ballroom for a three-night run of Dead shows. Recording engineers Matthews and Cantor then captured 16-track live tapes of some of those performances—the first time this had been done successfully. (They had done multitrack recording weeks earlier, on New Year's at Winterland, though that tape didn't turn out.)

To pull it off, Wickersham, urged on by Bear, had invented a microphone splitter, a new technology enabling them to produce high-quality live tapes. The splitter carried a given microphone or instrument signal to the PA and to the machine's recording inputs with no degradation. After all, "many of the tools we take for granted today in electric music didn't exist in 1969," Lesh later said. "Back then, they occasionally had to be cobbled together on the spot."

On the second night at the Avalon, they tested the recording rig, which included fourteen microphones placed onstage for capturing all the instruments plus the PA/recording split. The band played its opening sequence of songs "for all it was worth," Lesh recalled. They were hyped when they came offstage, saying, "That was the one!" and "I don't believe it!"

What they did not know was that Bear had been crouched beneath the mixing board as the band was "happily playing along," fiddling with an input card, according to Lesh. "I can't seem to get anything from the number thirteen line driver," Bear mumbled to himself of what happened to be Weir's guitar channel.

Out in the recording truck on set break, asking their techs to roll playback, the band discovered that not a single note of Weir's had gotten laid to tape. "We turned on Bear like a pack of rabid wolves," Lesh recalled, "reducing him nearly to tears within minutes. We all felt as if we'd played one of the finest sets ever, only to be betrayed by the very tools we'd just brought to life."

The next night, they managed to capture a few keeper tracks. Enough was forgiven for them to repeat the 16-track recording process at the Fillmore West later that month and into March. They rolled tape over a four-night stint that some now believe to be the greatest run of shows the Dead ever performed. *Live/Dead*, released that fall, drew heavily from these two batches of tapes.

The idea behind the live album was to place the listener in the audience. *Live/Dead*'s recording setup was "simple," Matthews later said. Thanks to Wickersham's PA splitter box, there was no signal processing between the same onstage mics going straight into the tape machine's input channels—the electronic signal was pure. Mixing *Live/Dead*, Matthews explained, they opted to not re-create a spatial environment from the onstage perspective of the musicians, but rather the feeling of being *within the hall*. In some respects, Matthews and Cantor were stand-ins for the "audience." By exploiting time itself, through audio delay and reverberation decay and "in a very musically defined and tuned manner," Matthews said, they added a dimensionality to the record "that makes it feel like it's in a real space."

Live/Dead carries a timeless clarity and primal presence. A big part of that staying power resides in Cantor's perception of sound. The underrecognized recording engineer later described her hearing like Bear's sense-swapping synesthesia. The positive effects of using psychedelics, namely "good LSD," were key to Cantor realizing her own "ability to get clear," she said. "That's how I describe things," Cantor explained. "I see the sound. I hear the tiniest of stuff." Tripping on acid, especially Bear's, "has enabled me to find that within my brain."

What she and Matthews and Bear did with *Live/Dead* encapsulated what the

Dead were about in capturing live sound, as well as the experience between artist and fan being a big, inclusive thing. "The Dead were always a live act," Cantor told me. To represent them properly, they had to go back and forth with Warner Bros., forcing through the idea that "what they *really* are is a performance act—they're not really oriented to the studio."

And to have the end product sound that good? Nobody approached that back then. "No one was doing it 16-track," Cantor said. She remembered folks from Wally Heider's 8-track recording studio, the dominant live recording service in town, giving them grief. "They came into our truck to make fun of us because we didn't have a board or any gear. They were laughing at us." But Cantor said, "Our shit sounds so much better than yours!"

In setting up that system, the Dead's techs first tried using various microphones that did not give them enough signal, which is why they ended up routing the mics "direct" into the machine and upping the transformer level, or gain. The effort was "an experiment that worked out really well, and ended up being a very clean system," Cantor said. "It's part of why it sounds the way it does— it's so present. It's just a microphone and the tape." She couldn't say "what Bear was fiddling with, or what Phil thought Bear was fiddling with, because Bear *didn't* fiddle with the electronics while things were happening," Cantor claimed, referring to Lesh's confrontational anecdote. "Ron Wickersham? Now, he would be somebody that might be fiddling with something." *Live/Dead*, in any case, redefined what it was to make a live record. The album's version of "Dark Star" is also widely considered one of the all-time takes of that defining Dead song. Cantor and Garcia both said as much.

Back in Novato, the band practiced, practiced, practiced. Gail Hellund, a friend recently brought on as an additional band secretary, could not take phone calls over the noise. "Whoever you are, you'll have to call back," Hellund said into the receiver. "The band is rehearsing."

Next to Hellund, in the other storefront office room, was still another new face: the Reverend Lenny Hart. A preacher and devout Christian, Mickey's Bible-toting estranged father had convinced the Dead to let him "manage" the band's finances, and almost immediately folks were suspicious of his motives. But the Novato warehouse was a powerspot of creativity and collaboration too, despite the Reverend's presence. "First everything breaks down, and then it's built back up; it's distilled into the right thing," Bear later said of the founding and thinking behind Alembic. "We were trying to take all of the technology and all of the experience and put it in a vessel. It was also the concept of the vessel, the concept of a place where it could be done."

The Dead and crew, plus the Alembic team and heads from the broader scene, bumped into one another at the pink warehouse, with Bear usually serving as catalyst. Healy, technically working for Quicksilver, recalled visiting the Alembic lab in Marin to hang out and tinker. "All of us would go out there to try building our own guitars, pickups, and amplifiers," Healy said. "Garcia would come in and tear his guitar apart in the afternoon. It was a great place."

Yet the band was not open to formally partnering with the new company. At the time, the Dead hoped to streamline operations and detach their rehearsal space from Alembic's instrument repair work and a new PA-for-rent the company began building. "The Dead really weren't interested in doing [Alembic] as part of the Dead, especially with Lenny Hart," Susan Wickersham, Alembic's first bookkeeper and Ron's partner, later claimed. "He wanted to cut off all the expenses."

Bear, for his part, was uninterested in a financial stake in the company he effectively started. He loathed business. "Bear's thing was always that he was trying to solve specific problems, which appealed a lot to me, because that's the way I liked to work, too," Ron Wickersham later said. "And he tended to relate to the player's vision of what needed to happen."

Aside from hot-rodding and customizing instruments and electronics for the band, Wickersham and people like Curl, another Ampex engineer freshly poached by Bear, focused on refining the band's sound chain. Wickersham has said that Bear was "interested in developing a much better live soundsystem for the Dead," and figuring they needed more reliability and consistency, was the one advocating that they use JBL loudspeakers for the PA. Bear, moreover, walked, sometimes even ran, around a space, determining the right sound coverage. Wandering a hall with him was a kind of schooling for the Dead's assorted sound techs. "Running around, listening everywhere," Wickersham later told me. "You don't hear anything at the sound desk, as far as how to build a better system."

Every detail demanded attention. That explains why Bear was also "hypercritical about building mic cables, how to coil up the mic cables," Wickersham has said. "You respected every piece of gear." Take the power amplifiers of the day, specifically the Dead's burgeoning use of modified McIntosh 75 tube amps. "We used to carry around crates of tubes," Wickersham said. "The McIntosh circuit gets more power out of these certain tubes than you get out of any circuit." With those tubes, they reduced feedback, "so they recovered from clipping faster and sounded dramatically better."

As Alembic established itself and the Dead became its main customer, the company began building custom guitars and basses according to the specifications of the individual musicians. Alembic techs similarly threw themselves into the band's soundsystem, modding out the stage boxes, cabs, horns, monitors, cables, and other existing components, before making entirely new ones in-house from scratch. McGee, who worked as an equipment purchasing agent at Alembic, recalled how Ron Wickersham would present to the Dead prototypes of whatever sonic thingamabobs he and Bear and Turner and others had cooked up. Often, this led to Alembic doing modifications before putting whole assembly lines in place, replicating those ideas across similar gear in the band's arsenal.

But there was still no formal billing arrangement, so the Wickershams weren't getting paid for the work. The couple clocked hundreds of hours with no compensation. Susan had been logging their time and confronted the band's management. She and Ron were tired of working as hard as they were only to be perpetually broke.

"We never got a single paycheck from the Grateful Dead," she later claimed. Bear gave her a few hundred dollars here and there, but "it was not a paycheck." So one afternoon she bought a pack of Rediform invoices and billed the Dead for her and Ron's time. The company's first-ever invoice, she noted, was to Lenny Hart for some amps they had recently redone. On that payment, she opened Alembic's first bank account. As Ron later said, "Alembic was forced to be founded in a way."

That was a chaotic time for the Dead, especially with finances. Constanten had a unique window into the band in a vulnerable moment, as his entry coincided with the beginning of the Reverend Hart administration. It was clear to the band's new keyboard player that even with money beginning to roll in, they were still figuring out how to run their business, a growing component of which was their PA. "The economics of that were kind of curious because the sound equipment added a lot of weight to bring on the plane," Constanten later said. "I remember for a while, the gigs were scheduled so that the band would fly and the road crew would drive a van, and somehow it worked."

That April, the Dead embarked on a college tour. Merely stepping foot on a campus remained a charged gesture. But at one weekday afternoon outdoor gig, at Washington University in St. Louis, the band's sheer volume, not political statements, made waves. Noise complaints were called in from blocks away.

May 29, 1969. The Dead were booked in the Robertson Gymnasium at UC Santa Barbara. That Thursday night show was indicative of the tensions, growing pains, and territorialism now relative to the band's sound reinforcement.

A *Rolling Stone* cover story noted how internal incompetencies had screwed up the band's travel arrangements. They drove to Santa Barbara only to be told by the promoter that they could not use their own PA. Instead, they had to play through the soundsystem of the opening act, singer-songwriter Lee Michaels (to be more widely known by his 1971 hit single, "Do You Know What I Mean?"). Ten songs in, after about forty minutes, Garcia unplugged his guitar. "Sorry," he told the audience, "but we're gonna split for a while and set up our own PA so we can hear what the fuck is happening."

Backstage, an argument among the band and crew escalated. If they were unable to play through their PA, Garcia fumed, then they were doing the fans dirty, not "righteous." The least the Dead could do was refund the audience. Or, they could tell off the promoter and have the roadies continue setting up their PA so that they could put on a *real* show. "Where's Bear?" Garcia shouted.

Their soundman lay on top of the amplifiers, belly to the rafters. Bear, whom Garcia once jokingly called "Satan in their midst," was drifting further out, high on his own LSD supply, talking to amps and claiming to receive terrifying signals. At one gig, "I was hanging on the curtain because I couldn't get away from the amps," he later recalled, "which sounded to me like the explosion at the end of the world. I could smell the smoke of the universe as we knew it collapsing, and I didn't want to leave because I was too afraid." Admittedly, he'd been "taking too many things and I blew it and just got carried away."

Hearing his name called out that night in Santa Barbara, Bear got up and approached the band. "Are you in this group, are you one of us?" Garcia reportedly screamed. "Are you gonna set up that PA? Their monitors suck. I can't hear a goddamn thing.... How can I play if I can't hear the drums?"

"Let's just go ahead," said Pigpen. "I can fake it."

"I can't," Garcia shot back.

"It's your decision," said Pigpen.

"Yeah," Lesh chirped, "if you and nobody else gives a good goddamn."

Struggling to form words, Bear said that properly setting up the Dead's PA would take a good two hours. He then turned and walked away.

"Owsley's an arrogant, egomaniacal motherfucker and I love him dearly," Riester, the road manager, later said. Riester claimed to be the only person among them who ever took a swing at Bear, before a show at the Avalon. "Don't let Owsley fuck with the system," Lesh and Garcia told Riester at soundcheck. "It's perfect." Later that evening, when they returned to play, a soldering iron crackled as Bear futzed with the gear. "He changed it all!" Riester said. "I flipped on him and punched him in the chest really hard."

The situation did not come to blows at the Santa Barbara gig, though by the time Bear disappeared that night the band's roadies were onstage dismantling the Dead's partially set up PA. The house lights flipped on and the crowd dispersed. "A good night, a potentially great night," *Rolling Stone* reported, "had been shot by a combination of promoter burn and Dead incompetence."

A week later, at the Dead's June 7 show at Fillmore West, it wasn't Bear but Goldfinger who injected chaos. The Pleasure Crew fixture had likely spiked a punch bowl that Bear had already electrified with his LSD. Pretty much everyone present that evening tripped *hard*. "Once on stage," recalled Lesh, "everything seemed somewhat familiar, even though the instruments and amplifiers (not to mention the other musicians) were grinning at me with alien features superimposed on their own."

Bear was furious about the overdosage. After the gig, he "continued to methodically pack up the equipment," as Gissen recalled. But then some of those who partook began disappearing, though the missing all eventually resurfaced unharmed. They simply wandered off tripping and somehow found a way through in one piece, which is not unlike the story of the Dead itself. "I suppose we can only be thankful that our luck continued to hold," Lesh later said.

Then there was Pigpen, a drinker's drinker and never one for psychedelics. For now, he was "coming on strong as the show closer," Lesh said. When Pig took lead, "the grooves get fatter," or *fur-lined*, as they described the sound. "Each beat has just a little more weight and the space around it is more vivid," Lesh continued, "the textures get leaner, and the give-and-take between the individual band members (as well as the interplay between Pig and the band as a whole) becomes sharper, more pointed, and faster."

Parish was soon watching over Pig's drinks onstage. The Dead had recently linked up with Parish at a pair of shows the band played that July 11 and 12 at the World's Fair site in Queens. The shows were put on by another rising East Coast promoter, Howard Stein, who soon branched into the Midwest through an operation with which my mom became associated. Parish recalled fraternizing that weekend with Ram Rod, Hagen, and Candelario, "three wild and crazy guys who formed the nucleus of what would become the greatest road crew in rock and roll history," he said. But it was Cliff Heard, a "ne'er-do-well and a troublemaker," who extended the invitation to California. "You can work for the band and stay with me," Heard told Parish. "It'll be great."

Meanwhile, other soon-to-be key players in the Wall story were also emerging. Candace Brightman first met Parish around this time at rock shows at the Fillmore East and the Capitol Theater in Port Chester, New York. A self-taught lighting designer, Brightman had just started in the business, and she and Parish clicked immediately. The first time she saw the Dead, moreover, "it sounded like nothing I had heard before," Brightman told me. She won't be brought on in an official capacity until the early '70s, but eventually embodied a bright spot in the darkness for the Dead's system.

Some 3,400 miles away, gaunt and goateed Cutler, then managing the Rolling Stones, was already acquainted with loud music, as well as the logistics being carved out around putting on a truly big show with passing sound. When the Stones played a free outdoor concert at London's Hyde Park in 1969, "to accommodate an unprecedented number of PA speakers, we included separate scaffold towers in the stage design," Cutler later wrote in his memoir, *You Can't Always Get What You Want.* That gig drew an estimated quarter to half a million people. Cutler worked alongside WEM, then England's largest PA system company, on calculating the load weight so the stage would support the rig.

Cutler was familiar with the Dead's soundman too, or at least with Bear's acid. At a recent Blue Cheer gig in London, where a roadie for the notoriously loud band slipped him a hit of Owsley's LSD, Cutler noted how that power trio had toted their own PA. Not many bands did so in what were still early days for rock music, in Britain especially, Cutler said, "and I was amazed to see that Blue Cheer traveled with a soundsystem they had brought all the way from the States and that they had onstage monitors." This kind of sophisticated gear appearing in England made for "a bit of a revelation." Later, after Cutler got to know—and work alongside—the man himself, he was energized by Bear's always aiming for excellence, "a far-out state of affairs he described as *boss*," Cutler said. "Boss meant the best equipment, the best instruments, the best stage set-up, the best PA. The best of everything was his primary concern." Except hard drugs.

Yet the increasing recreational usage of amphetamines was coming on stronger in Deadland by August 1969. "As the people in our scene got into the daily use of cocaine with steady encouragement from accommodating dealers, our environment definitely got colder, less friendly and decidedly less mellow," McGee recalled.

The uptick in coke tracked with a coarsening of the all-male road crew. They might have never treated McGee badly, for one, even at the peak of their "testosterone/cocaine obnoxiousness," she said. But "as more people with agendas tried to get close to the band at gigs," McGee explained, "the crew got more protective and exclusionary, and they closed ranks with increasingly macho attitudes." The social pressures on the crew from the outside were considerable the bigger the operation got. "Everyone is gonna be your fuckin' friend," Winslow, of the Pendleton unit, once said. The road "turns you into gristle."

But the crew and the musicians were humbled by the band's biggest flop yet, an outdoor gig in front of four hundred thousand people one dark and stormy night that month in upstate New York. As Garcia later recalled of the Dead's appearance at the Woodstock Music & Arts Festival, they were in for "the ultimate calamity."

August 16, 1969. Clouds formed over dairy farmer Max Yasgur's property in Bethel, New York. Yasgur's six hundred acres were hosting masses of young people at what had now been declared a free three-day festival. Backstage that Saturday afternoon, Ram Rod and Bear got a bad feeling.

The Woodstock setup involved several wooden turntables ("cookies") arranged for swiftly rotating various bands' gear on and off the thirty-foot-high stage. Bear and Ram Rod knew the rigging would not withstand the weight of the Dead's equipment, all eight-thousand-plus pounds of it. As Bear later claimed, their warnings to the stage manager weren't taken seriously.

If only they hadn't been ignored, then maybe the Dead wouldn't go down as the band that broke the stage at the most famous and widely dissected live musical event in history. But after the roadies had loaded the Dead's equipment on the back-facing half of one of the cookies, sure enough, the platform collapsed under the weight of their gear. That took time to sort, though there were extra sets of hands to help move the Dead's rig piece by piece, around to the stage front. That included Parish, who wasn't yet working explicitly for the band but was rather "little more than a hired hand at Woodstock," he said.

The Dead did not go on until after midnight, so delayed was the event on their account. Now that it had begun to rain, their soundman insisted that an electrical grounding issue be fixed before the band hit. Bear was frantic as the makings of a potential mass electrocution unfolded. The top of the Woodstock stage, covered in sheet metal, was wet. Orbs of blue lightning rolled across the surface, as Lesh recalled, when the band opened with "St. Stephen," a track off the recently released *Aoxomoxoa*. The vocalists got jolted when they approached their microphones. Garcia later recalled his guitar giving him "incredible shocks" that night too.

All the while, the band played into a void. "Not only is it pitch black in front of the stage, but the PA is so loud that we can't get any sense of *auditory space*," Lesh recalled. All they got was the sound of their amp line, the vocal monitors, drums, "and a huge roar deeply penetrated by [an] all-conquering sixty-cycle hum." Some helicopter radio chatter was also being picked up through Lesh's instrument. Disorienting, to say the least. "The sound on stage was damn near impossible to work with," Kreutzmann remembered. "We couldn't hear each other."

That's when the power went out, plunging the scene into pitch-darkness, save a couple of work-lights and the small status bulbs that still shone on the PA amplifiers. Rain continued to fall and the wind whipped. Bear scrambled, causing more delays trying to fix things and get the sound exactly perfect. He plugged cables in and set up microphones on stands, with Ram Rod shadowing him. Without saying a word, the two worked to keep it all together.

But now people could be heard screaming, as the stage structure vibrated and slid in the mud. A backing screen behind the Dead had caught a heavy gust and was being pushed askew, at a diagonal to the band's amp line, like a giant sail. "Garcia and Weir—all those guys—when they're in front of people and they're high and there's *fear* in the air," Scully later said of Woodstock, "they become fearful too."

In the meantime, the PA continued to buzz like a "demented ten-ton insect," only the band's amps were still dead. The stage seemed to have stopped moving, though, and like that, the amps powered on. But once the Dead resumed playing, they had no idea if the PA was even sending music out to the people they still could not see, Lesh explained. "Hum is all we hear from that direction."

They bailed after a few songs. Garcia was first to leave the stage and practically threw his instrument at Ram Rod. Bear, too, was bummed and apparently cornered Lesh, complaining about their set being too short—the soundman had just about worked out the kinks in the system. The Dead once again "seemed to find ourselves unerringly in the crosshairs of chaos," Lesh said. Woodstock won't be the last time that unholy trifecta—inclement weather, technical difficulties, and poor timing—confronted the Dead either.

A fresh line of thunderclouds loomed as the Dead got helicoptered out of Yasgur's farm, en route to New Jersey. They switched into cars at Newark Airport, bopping quickly back into New York for a connecting flight out of Kennedy Airport. The band was going home. As they barreled across town, the sky opened up with biblical energy when a bolt of lightning and a clap of thunder hit perfectly in sync. If only the Dead's soundsystem rolled like that, Constanten cracked. "Now that's the PA we need."

December 6, 1969. Unlike at Woodstock, the Dead played a heavy hand in organizing another massive free outdoor gig, this one on the West Coast to a crowd of an estimated three hundred thousand people. They even loaned most of their own in-house PA, via Alembic, to the cause.

The concert site had been moved from Sears Point, a raceway in Sonoma County, to one at Altamont in neighboring San Joaquin County, over difficulties in securing an event permit. Bear and Ram Rod, Jackson, Hagen, and Heard comprised the Alembic crew for the event and, along with Cantor and Matthews, helped set up the whole system of amps and assorted speakers and run sound. Prior to the advent of widely available multichannel models, for live mixing the Dead stacked their trio of MX-10s, giving Bear the dozen inputs required for the stereo PA. "They went out there and built the infrastructure, the stage, the speaker towers," Gissen said.

When Sears Point backed out with under forty-eight hours to go, the Novato warehouse, fifteen minutes away, became a makeshift planning center. The concert was to include performances by Santana, the Flying Burrito Brothers, Jefferson Airplane, Crosby, Stills, Nash, and Young, the Dead, and the Rolling Stones, the Dead's co-conspirators. At the time, the Stones were filming a movie about themselves and thought a free gig would make for a splashy ending.

Cutler was there as plans changed. He and the Stones "called some of the shots," Kreutzmann recalled, while Scully—and by extension, the Dead—"called some of the shots." Between the two groups, "there seemed to be this natural feeling of collaboration," Kreutzmann said, "even though the two bands represented two very different camps." According to Cutler, it was Bear, together with the band, family, friends, and Stones lighting designer (and Altamont co-planner) Edward "Chip" Monck, who ultimately decided that it still was possible to pull off the show on schedule.

The Dead, for their part, had just learned a hard lesson in timing, trucks, and transporting sound equipment that September at the New Orleans Pop Festival. The promoter, Bear later recalled, refused them access to a vehicle for schlepping their gear from the airport to the venue. "It's your problem, mate," Bear told the promoter when the Dead's stage rig was late showing up.

The PA for Altamont, by contrast, was melded from different local systems, namely the Dead and Alembic; Bob Cohen of the Family Dog; and Quicksilver, through the Dead's old soundman, Healy. In the scramble to move equipment to the raceway, McCune Sound, the audio provider that rented the equipment for Sears Point, refused to further loan any gear for the show. The Dead offered up, among other kit, their never-before-used Buchla-made banana-shaped bass cabinets, newly stenciled with thirteen-point lightning bolts—Bear's design, meant to differentiate the band's gear on stages.

Bear and the Alembic crew tore down the equipment at Sears Point and packed the load out to Altamont, some seventy miles southeast, by truck and helicopter; other gear was airlifted from the Novato warehouse to Altamont. (Now that they were chartering helos, Alembic often got stuck with the tab.) Calling for even more equipment, Bear was the last person to leave Sears Point and he wouldn't sleep until he and Healy arrived by truck at Altamont at dawn. Alembic's Ron and Susan Wickersham likewise worked all night, wiring cables together at the Novato shop.

The scene at Altamont grew bleaker by the minute that Friday, December 5, on the eve of the show. Dead road manager Riester had backed his stake-bed truck, full of band gear, to the stage, low to the ground and still in a state of being assembled. Under work-lights, Riester and the Dead/Alembic crew unpacked and got to it.

Barely three feet high and located at the bottom of a brambly hill, the stage setup spelled trouble. "We needed some kind of security to guard the stage," Kreutzmann later said, only "nobody hired security." This was a free show, after all, and that was where the Hells Angels came in. At every free Bay Area gig, their motorcycles were fixtures near stages, while the various club members (mostly) kept their composure and even looked after lost children and watched over the band's power lines and generators. Involving the Angels, the thinking went, could be critical to successfully pulling off the gig without incident.

Considering the Dead played such a key organizational role, it was believed that the Angels would maintain a sense of order and calm at Altamont. The Dead were the bikers' favorite band.

Somehow, "a loose kind of deal was struck with them where they would do things like make sure nobody rushed the stage in exchange for free beer all day," Kreutzmann said. "Everyone approved it, or allowed it, one way or the other," the drummer added. "Either we're all to blame or else nobody's to blame."

High on a strong batch of Orange Sunshine LSD, Bear, Healy, and dozens of other equipment handlers from around the scene worked through the night. Rigging up the PA was a matter of wiring the combined bricolage of tens of thousands of pounds of different kinds of gear into a single unit, no simple task given the circumstances and altered states of mind. As Cutler recalled, "these guys built the sound, the back-line, and the whole show at Altamont in less than thirty hours!"

The entire crew were running on little, if any, sleep. "The circadian rhythm was destroyed," recalled Gissen, who got helicoptered in that evening among other family members. "The set up was the hardest I'd ever seen." Plus, Bear had been unable to make and distribute his own special batch of LSD. "There was no free acid at Altamont, because he was too busy working sound," Gissen later said, likening Bear's crawling over the system that night to an ant in a colony. "I would say that's one of the reasons it failed: no LSD."

The following morning, on the outskirts leading into the grounds, police turned away the Wickershams. They were lugging all the cables they made the night before and took the roundabout way by car into the site—over fields and then rolling slowly through crowds to the backstage area. There were instruments and speaker connectors waiting for them. Alembic's 16-track recording console had similarly been hauled in to record the show.

After Santana's opening set, witnesses on- and backstage took in a crush of bodies down in front. They watched increasingly drunk, dosed (on another non-Bear batch of LSD), and belligerent Angels prospects assault attendees around the foot of the stage. The onlookers were reportedly baffled by the turning-violent vibe. Yet there was a gig on and work to do: Cantor can re-member carrying speaker monitors that had gotten stuck out in the crowd at Altamont during setup, and a Hells Angel being a sort of bodyguard while she off-loaded the cabinets. "Just put 'em on the edge of the stage here," she said, "because the bands can't hear themselves."

The documentary crew that was rolling film, to be later released as the concert film *Gimme Shelter*, caught the exact moment during the Stones' set when Angels went for Meredith Hunter, a Black concert attendee, who had brandished a handgun. After Hunter was stabbed five times and then beaten by the biker club prospects, a couple of concertgoers tried to carry his body to the front of the stage to draw attention to what happened. Cantor, keeping a close eye on the Dead/Alembic equipment, "watched in shock."

The bikers then pulled Hunter's body stageside and underneath Riester's stake-bed truck—the back of which Garcia's partner, Mountain Girl, and others now hid inside. This was "the very truck we were going to put our equipment in to take it back to our sound studio," Scully said, "but we'd have to pull the body out from under it first and we don't want to do that."

Before the Stones had even ended their set, the Dead got choppered out of the raceway. That weekend in late 1969, the Dead did something they won't make a habit of over the course of their career: They bailed on a gig last minute—and not once but twice, in the span of just a few hours. The band had an aftershow scheduled later the night of Altamont at the Fillmore West. But really, how could they go on?

6

The Tie-Dye Rig (1970–1971)

January 1970. Sam Cutler lay low at Jerry Garcia's Bay Area home. One day after Altamont, Garcia "grudgingly agreed that there was some responsibility on the Dead's part," Cutler said. "I could sense his embarrassment about his own family's role in what had gone down."

The Dead were about to traverse more maneuvering and scaling-up of their organizational chart. The operation became further entwined with ambitions for a soundsystem that now weighed ten thousand pounds and was transported in a dedicated eighteen-foot truck. "Jerry knew that apart from the fact that they had the sound together and the playing was good, the rest of it was chaos," said Cutler. The Dead sought even higher-quality production values. "They wanted their own light and sound on the road," Cutler said. "Well, all of this costs money."

Cutler grew the Dead some 500 percent over the next three years, working closely with bookers and the band's big prototype Wall, a colorful rig with amps and speakers adorned in tie-dye screens first made by Rosie McGee. As Richard Loren, a friend of Garcia's and another soon-to-be Dead agent-manager, later said of Cutler, "he'd intimidate the promoters and he got the Dead more money than they'd ever gotten before, which they needed for the soundsystem."

By then, the band's management was a kind of beast alongside its PA. At "the apex," Cutler said, was Reverend Hart. Then came dapper assistant manager Jon McIntire, all long blond hair and pearly whites. Post Altamont, the Dead needed an experienced road and tour manager, as Jonathan Riester and his stake-bed truck were on their way out. That January, Garcia asked Cutler, exiled from the Stones, if he wanted to travel to Hawaii for a pair of shows. "I needed a vacation and a job," Cutler said. Like that, Cutler "became a member of the Grateful Dead family."

The band performed that January 23 and 24 at Honolulu's Civic Auditorium, a two-thousand-capacity indoor venue, alongside the Airplane. The Dead halved their rig for the Pan American round-trip flight, given they weren't making serious money just yet. As the *Honolulu Advertiser* reported, the Dead had arrived in town with "5,000 pounds of Alendic [*sic*] sound equipment."

The scale and novelty of the Dead's soundsystem, incubated in-house by Alembic, was becoming an object of fascination for journalists and music critics, who often cited the size and weight of the rig in their coverage of the band. "We would get newspaper reporters in different cities come and hear it," Ron Wickersham told me. "They weren't necessarily that much into the music but they would be amazed at the performance in these essentially reverberation chambers that had no acoustic treatment." This captivation and attention to detail from the press is a sonic string in the historical record, supplementing the band's own internal technical documents and gear inventory lists in tracking the staggering show-by-show growth of the Wall.

Cutler clocked his first real working gig with the Dead on February 4, at the Family Dog on the Great Highway in San Francisco, alongside Santana and the Airplane. A reporter from the *Yonkers Herald Statesman* caught the Wednesday night gig, when members of the Dead and the Airplane returned to the cramped stage after their respective sets. They then launched into an hour-long jam that blew the room out into an all-enveloping auditory space.

"By the time Grateful Dead leader Jerry Garcia brought the jam to a triumphant halt, members of the audience were straining on tiptoes toward the shattering wall of sound," the journalist, Robert W. Neubert, noted. "When the jam ended, most of the crowd was emotionally and physically exhausted." That might be the first documented use of the term "wall of sound" by a member of the press to describe the airwaves being pushed out of the Dead's PA. Neubert had the moniker for the system, popularized later by Deadheads, beat by a few years.

But the first order of business, as far as Cutler was concerned, was establishing a rapport with the band's crew. "They were absolutely central to making the whole touring thing work," Cutler later said. "A good equipment guy could take at least a few weeks to train, if not months, and they were hard to find."

And while the band members all knew how to use their gear, few of them could properly set up their rigs without help from a skilled hand. As such, "equipment guys were well looked after," Cutler said, "and their opinions noted and acted upon."

There was already a Dead-ly communication style among them, which Cutler quickly picked up on. Ram Rod, in particular, was known to look you in the eyes as he spoke out of the side of his mouth, lips curled inward, and in short sentences, "in what can best be described as a conspiratorial whisper, regardless of how mundane the topic being discussed." Rather than shouting over blaring music, the crew chief had learned that others could hear and understand what he was saying if he talked at a volume considerably lower than the ambient noise level, pitching his voice under. "Now he talked softly all the time," Cutler said, "and consequently he was heard."

Conversations flowed between Cutler, Ram Rod, Clifford Heard, and others, behind the scenes of this on-ramp stage in their drive to the Wall. Their extended dialogues concerned the art of transporting a ballooning load of people and equipment over vast distances. They had their load in/load out routine down, though their processes and workflows necessarily refined further as literal tons more gear got added to the system. "They wanted high fidelity," Cutler told me. "The best that could be achieved." The Dead would spend millions of dollars to that end.

Not only did the PA take hours to set up but there was always some technical issue or another to troubleshoot. Earlier that February, at a Monday night show at the Fox Theatre in St. Louis, Bear was in rare form. The gig, days after members of the Dead, including Bear, got busted on drug charges at a New Orleans hotel, started an hour late, as the *St. Louis Post-Dispatch* reported. (The first of the three New Orleans gigs was Constanten's last with the band.) Bear "prowled about the stage," the reporter, Harper Barnes, wrote, "twisting knobs, cursing microphones, and scowling at loudspeakers." He had "built most of the Grateful Dead's massive array of sound equipment, but he was unhappy with the theater's public address system." Bear "must have adjusted everything properly because the sound was just fine, blasting clearly into the far reaches of the second balcony."

Bear time. "Owsley was a pain in the ass because he was such a perfectionist," Cutler told me, "but a lovely man." That perfectionism was infectious: As their whole trip got more "professional," there was never a moment with the PA, Cutler claimed, where everyone went, *Right, that's it, we've got it.* The rig could *always* be better. "The soundsystem was a constantly evolving process," Cutler said, "just like the Grateful Dead's music, just like the Grateful Dead's songs."

On the average early '70s road night, Cutler collected the band's pay "with cash and a smile." Meanwhile, Rex Jackson and Heard, built like "brick shit-houses," took lead in breaking down however many tons of equipment the Dead were hauling before loading it all into the truck. Then the crew would be "rolling up literally thousands of feet of cables," said Cutler, who chipped in. "Sweat poured from us as muscles we hadn't used before were asked to do work that surely no human body should," Cutler said.

The load was cumbersome. Initially, the Dead had no road cases for their McIntosh amps, which each weighed nearly 130 pounds on their own; those were still housed in the cardboard boxes in which they came from the factory. Those amplifiers eventually were transported in ruggedized Zero (Hallibur-ton) flight cases, adding to the overall load weight. "As we were building the Wall of Sound, we had over seventy Mac 2300 amps," Steve Parish later said. "In order to travel with them safely in trucks, we originally found army surplus cases that were military spec. We bought three of those and they fit a Mac 2300 perfectly." The cases got painted in easily identifiable orange and purple. "They served us well."

Moreover, speaker boxes like my artifact, which they soon started manu-facturing in-house and adding to the soundsystem, each weighed over seventy pounds. Those units, fitted with the preferred JBL speaker cones, typically got stacked in the same column within the two arrays—to either stage side—that comprised the band's stereo PA at the time. That stacking got done not so much by labeling the boxes individually, say by number, but according to the highly organized nature of the road crew's truck unpack/load in and load out/truck pack logic. In the end, Cutler claimed, they got the load out down to two hours.

They often then drove through the night to the next gig. "That's back in the days when gas stations closed at nine o'clock," Bill Candelario told me. They worked in shifts. Everybody on the crew drove a tank of gas, then switched. "We were always telling that last person, *if it's starting to get dark make sure you fill up before your shift is over*," Candelario said. Never pass an open gas station and *not* get filled up.

Their caravan rolled on.

The Dead had played enough to have become a "full-range band," as Garcia used to like to say; their repertoire covered a swath of American music. They notched 142 gigs in 1970, not including the considerable number of free shows the band played that year. But while the band's performance level remained high, the climate around them became what Parish likened to a "pressure cooker," as the Dead racked up gigs and miles—and fed a PA that stretched out, projecting their sounds louder and clearer.

The Dead were now officially on-boarding Parish. Then nineteen, he had accepted Heard's invitation to come to California. The Dead had become "something they never really explicitly aspired to be: a hard-working, professional, career-oriented band," Parish later said.

Parish rolled with Ram Rod, Heard, and Jackson, who "were different," he said. "And they knew it." Heard, in particular, "acted and reacted straight from the gut, consequences be damned, and as a result he could be difficult to work with." Most Dead sound and equipment crew members, and also some of the musicians, had issues with Heard, a hot head with a feared right punch, who kept a bushy mustache and wore wire-rim glasses under a trucker hat. Heard and Jackson were known to get into physical fights.

Ram Rod took in Parish. The newbie spent a lot of time with Ram Rod in this era, soaking up knowledge and hanging around Alembic's new warehouse space on Judah and Ninth in San Francisco, "in which we built a massive public address system and recording studios," Parish said.

But the schooling came from all sides. Though still off working for Quicksilver, Dan Healy, whom Parish called an electronic whiz and "something of a guru" to the Dead crew, taught Parish about electricity and the purchasing and fabricating of speaker cabinets, and first showed him how to work a Fender amp. Bob Matthews was likewise knowledgeable, albeit more high-strung and difficult to glean pointers from—he "had sort of a snotty attitude about the technical aspects of the business, as if they [the sound crew] were engineers and we were merely hired hands—they were the brains, we were the brawn," Parish said. Bear was a good teacher, too, "but his escalating legal problems had driven him out of the picture."

Meanwhile, acid. At "virtually every performance" in this era, several of the band members themselves played stoned on LSD, and "those of us on the crew routinely worked while we were high," Parish claimed. "It was just part of what we did." That LSD acted like a stimulant "allowed those of us on the crew to stay awake and work long hours, tearing down sets and packing away equipment and driving to the next town for the next show," Parish said.

Such was life in Deadland. Within the band's widening circle, the notion of "work," let alone earning a living wage, was difficult to square with the realities of an outside "straight" world. Increasingly, the Dead had to interface with that world. As their soundsystem grew more complex, they needed to draw increasing amounts of power from the grid and meet various local and site-specific structural codes, noise ordinances, and labor laws that differed by city, state, and country.

Garcia expressed that precarious sentiment that year in an interview on fame and playing music professionally. Music gets people high, "and everybody should be able to get high," he said. "The rest of it has to do with dealing with the externals, like what's there to work with." Namely, "a theater here, a multi-purpose room there, this PA, this approach to advertising and economics."

Simply put: "all that shit."

February 13, 1970. The Dead were back at Graham's Fillmore East, with support from the Allman Brothers Band, from Macon, Georgia. The three-night run grossed $55,000, the equivalent today of over $455,000. The press was taken by Garcia's "crystal clear" guitar tone. The gigs are considered some of the best the Dead ever performed, but the Friday show, the second night, became legendary thanks to a subset of their growing fanbase: tapers.

Taping live performances was in the Dead DNA. A recording deck had been a fixture in their soundsystem since the "Owsleystein" days. Steve Brown's partial recording of the Dead saluting Haight Street then kickstarted the practice among the band's followers. East Coast taper Les Kippel boasted that he was the second person to ever record a Dead show, and later claimed that one "Legendary Marty" Weinberg from the Bronx "was the first person, bar none, to record a Grateful Dead show." In truth, Kippel was likely not in the first ten audience members to record Dead shows, and there were Bay Area tapers, like Harry Ely, who probably had the East Coasters beat. Still, the compulsion to document live gigs was in the bedrock of the band, their PA, and some of their most hardcore devotees.

A secret "basement tape" of the Dead playing through their colorful ten-thousand-pound system that February in New York City took on mythic proportions. The recording was made by John Chester, who ran house sound for Fillmore East. His capture of that night's performance will "serve as a keystone for all Dead tape collectors," wrote Dennis McNally, the Dead publicist and biographer.

The "Chester Reels" came from a surreptitious patch straight into the sound-board. These quality recordings were some of the first to be shared among Deadheads, after one of Chester's assistants, Alan Mande, dubbed the tapes. Mande then bequeathed Bob Menke, another first-generation Dead taper, with copies. That this Dead tape trading tree grew apace with the band's expanding PA was hardly coincidental. Fans quested to preserve the live performances that made the Dead a shared sonic experience with the audience in meatspace, through a connective tissue–like soundsystem.

Predominantly young men, tapers smuggled their own stealth recording kits into gigs, including microphones and portable tape decks, to "bootleg" performances. They did so with the Dead's tacit approval for years, and eventually a first-of-its-kind audience taper's section was established at shows. But band and crew initially were ambivalent about persistent "taper geeks" jockeying to pitch their rigs, typically forty to seventy-five feet out from the stage, or "in the mouth," in taper-speak. Jackson would pace the aisles, spot mic cables, and cut the wires with a knife, stowing them in his own bag. Bear gained a reputation for ripping tapes from fan decks and destroying the recordings.

The Dead performed around 5,500 hours of live music throughout their career. One potential peril of allowing audience members to record every last note of the band's music won't be the "off" gigs, which came with the Dead territory, but the "clams"—flubbed notes, botched parts, missed starts, transitions, finishes, and other imperfections. These clunkers are in the tapes. Likewise the sonic residue of blown amps and tweeters, speaker hum, "hot" mics, unwanted feedback, melting amps, cranky monitors, and side-talk that also marked the taper record as the Wall came alive. Such were the messy, unpredictable noises of real-time progress during the band's searching for the best live audio through their constantly morphing rig.

For tapers, it was essential to try and bottle the signals, warts and all, for enjoyment, dissection, and sharing long after the band and their giant soundsystem loaded out and left town. By 1970 and 1971, tapes of the band's shows were circulating widely in college networks. "In what remains the best decision we never made, allowing tapers to record and trade our shows essentially usurped the function of studio records with live performances," Lesh later said. No two were alike, so "every show that went forth and multiplied itself on the trading tree was another advertisement for our live shows."

A month after Chester's secret recordings, on a return trip to the East Coast, the Dead played a pair of shows at the Capitol Theater in Port Chester. Those

March 20 and 21 gigs, put on by the promoter Howard Stein, encapsulated what was then the total Dead experience. During a backstage interview before the second night's gig, Mickey Hart talked with *Zygote* magazine about the interplay between sound and light in the band's live presentation. The described sensation harkened back to the synesthesia flowing through the Dead's collective antennae: Rock and roll light shows were still an emerging artform, Hart said, but what the Dead were after, as far as a visual component to their shows, was akin to "stimulating the actual sound with waves of energy and colors." A review of that second night's performance, also published in *Zygote*, noted the "rhapsodic quality" of the Dead. "Waves of sound," the write-up added. "Ever-changing textures."

Back on the West Coast the following month, the Dead shared a bill with one of their heroes. The Miles Davis Quartet opened for them over four nights at the Fillmore West. Band and crew were too timid to approach Davis, except Garcia; the two rapped about music, enjoying each other's company. The trumpeter was dabbling in amplified music, recognizing the Dead as playing a kind of electric jazz. Garcia admired how Davis manipulated silence, an influence clearly heard on recordings of most any "Dark Star" the Dead performed through the end of the Wall. One of the more striking aspects of the Wall, in fact, was just how pin-drop quiet the Dead could play against such a giant backline.

In the meantime, the band was hacking through monitor feedback problems. During an acoustic set on April 18 at the Family Dog, the band ribbed their soundman.

"C'mon, Bear," Lesh said early in their set, between songs. "Turn up the monitors on the guitars."

"They were good when we started," Garcia remarked. "Now you can't hear 'em."

"Quit dickin' around and turn 'em up, up, up, up," Lesh said.

"Listen to the man," Bob Weir chuckled. "We make the rules around here."

Lesh spoke up again after another song: "Turn up his guitar, will ya?"

"There go the guitars again," Garcia said. "Where are they?"

"God damn it, Bear," Weir said, "will you get it on?"

"The guitars are off again, off again, off again," said Garcia. "We can no longer hear them in the monitors at all. They are as though invisible. Unheard. Unstruck." After another song, "Still can't hear the guitars," Garcia said. "We're just gonna ... wait."

Weir had an idea. "I'm gonna move my whole setup out that way, away from the monitor speakers per se," he said, "that way maybe we can get some level." Weir can be heard shuffling his rig. "I hate moving equipment around," he said, off mic. "It's beneath my station." After yet another song, Weir dug in: "Hey, Bear! How come they keep going away! Does anybody have a tomato?" During a feedback squall, Weir joked, "That's the Bear solo."

The band still brought the noise. Later that month, during a pair of shows the Dead played at Mammoth Gardens, a former ice rink in Denver, on April 24 and 25, a *Colorado Springs Sun* reporter noted how the band "built to an excruciating climax, and then caught its breath to build to another, and another, wave after wave, crescendo after crescendo." Full-tilt, "primal" Dead.

The direction the band was taking in its songwriting and studio approach is a different story. *Workingman's Dead*, their new album, had a stripped-back sound. Reeling from Altamont, the band focused on semi-acoustic tunes, "the kind of music they had started playing long before they were the Grateful Dead," the longtime San Francisco–based journalist Joel Selvin wrote in *Altamont*.

Released that June, *Workingman's* was also born of being ripped off. Reverend Hart got fired around this time when enough people realized he was stealing from the band. Hart absconded with some $150,000, the equivalent today of over a million dollars. "The business response to Lenny's financial piracy was a considerable restructuring of the band's management," McNally said. Scully assumed more of a promotional role for the Dead, and less band manager, which became McIntire's job. Cutler now steered as road manager, and soon Dave Parker, who had played with Garcia and the pre-Warlocks jug band, and his wife Bonnie came on to bookkeep.

The Dead wanted to move on, as Parker later explained. But still more experienced manager types were hired after the elder Hart left them broke, beginning with Hal Kant, a world champion poker player who helped the Parkers clean up the mess. The band's unpaid bills amounted to a hundred and fifty grand in debt, "and they were in the hole even more than that to Warner Bros.," Parker said, "because they had taken so much in advances on records that didn't sell very well." Post-Reverend, salaries were kept at a few hundred bucks a week for the band, "although they would also get money for instruments and recording equipment if they needed it," Parker said. The sound came first—always.

Around this same time, the Dead vacated the pink warehouse in Novato and began renting an old Victorian at Fifth and Lincoln in nearby San Rafael. The band and crew moved into a rehearsal space on Jacoby Street, blocks away. That semi-shared space quickly turned into a "dust bowl," Richie Pechner, who had prior carpentry experience and was now beginning to help cut and assemble the band's cabinets, told me. "It wasn't a commercial woodshop," Pechner said of the facility, which lacked a dust collection system. The space "had those big roll-up doors and when we really got into cutting wood we'd just open the door and let the breeze take most of the dust out." Piles of shavings accumulated otherwise, and the finer particulate seeped into the band's instruments and electronics. "You could see it was not well thought out, like a lot of things," Pechner said.

The other ambient influence behind *Workingman's* dustier, simpler songs, was blow. Closing track "Casey Jones," with its recognizable "Driving that train / high on cocaine" refrain, is a tune that Garcia later called a "pretty good musical picture" of what that drug is like. "A little bit evil. And hard-edged. That singsongy thing." The *Workingman's* recording dynamic was likewise a little bit evil, hard-edged, and singsongy, despite the mellower sound the band was taking. Over a quick five days at San Francisco's Pacific High Studios, with recording engineers Cantor and Matthews at the reels, the Dead laid down the set of new songs.

Cocaine had become a "common wash" for all things in Deadworld. To reach Bear's vision of one unified backline of amps, speakers, and monitors, the winding path was riddled with bumps of the best drugs money could buy. Pechner recalled one "early Wall of Sound" show at the Fillmore West in this era, as the Dead were set to play through the tie-dye rig to three thousand rapt heads. "We were having trouble with the monitor system from the beginning, getting it to work correctly," Pechner told me. During setup that day at the Fillmore, someone on the crew hollered to those in earshot: "Monitor meeting!" When Pechner and a few others assembled around one of the monitors, a bindle of white powder appeared and some lines were drawn on the cabinet top. They each hunched over and took a sniff.

There were more "monitor meetings" where that came from, Pechner explained, "although the issues with the monitors behind the band continued to be a problem." Those were still early days for amphetamines being widely accepted and eventually ubiquitous in their collective drug diet. "It signaled the beginning of the end of the psychedelic phase, as these harder drugs tended to be counterpoint to the acid and weed," Pechner said. By the end of the full

Wall run, consumption was "off the charts," he said. "You could see personalities change."

The *Workingman's*-era Dead also gathered at another powerspot. The "Pondareister," named after outgoing road manager Riester, was a rural Marin horse ranch rented by Hart. At points, Rock Scully, certain Hells Angels, and Pleasure Crew members all lived at the drummer's place. Cutler also briefly resided there, as he molded the road crew that would one day scale three-story scaffolding without harnesses, with heads full of who-knows-what, servicing the band's magnificent soundsystem.

Others, including Heard and Parish, lived at yet another communal ranch, this one called Rucka Rucka, not far from Hart's place. For a moment Rucka Rucka was the center of social life in the Dead's scene, Parish said. Weir's then girlfriend, Frankie, kept those living there in line, according to Parish, who witnessed Eileen Law give birth to her daughter with Jackson in a back room that summer. A friend and soon-to-be Dead employee, Law helped grow the band's official mailing list, keeping fans informed through communiqués packed with hand-drawn schematics and detailed information about the state of the band's soundsystem, finances, and tours.

On a more typical day at Rucka Rucka, Heard, Jackson, and Parish were up around 9:00 a.m., "and we'd begin loading this old silver Metro with gear," Parish recalled. About an hour later Ram Rod rolled up, and the four of them drove to San Rafael, "where we'd help the band set up." Between gigs, they rehearsed songs for their follow-up record, a sonic companion to *Workingman's* called *American Beauty*.

Then one morning, a kind-looking stranger with long, wavy blond hair and a backpack full of tie-dyes came walking up the road.

Courtenay Pollock had just moved to San Francisco from New York. He lucked into a living arrangement down the way from Rucka Rucka. On his first day in town, Pollock dropped by the residence, hoping to sell some of the colorful tapestries he'd been making for the past year. Frankie Weir, who took Weir's last name despite the two never marrying, showed him inside and asked to see his wares. Soon, "these trucks pull in and these rowdies tumble out and rumble through the house," Pollock remembered. "They stop in the middle room," where Pollock had displayed some of his tie-dyes.

"Far out, man," one of them said. "You can do our speaker fronts."

"I'll make it happen tomorrow morning," another chimed in.

"Who are you guys?" Pollock asked.

"We work for the Grateful Dead," they said. It was Heard, Winslow, and Jackson.

The following day, Pollock again walked up the road to Rucka Rucka. Weir drove by and offered him a lift. Pollock said he was going to the ranch; that was his place, Weir replied. "These are great," Weir later said, inspecting Pollock's tie-dyes. "I'll make sure it's all in motion for you."

The next morning, Pollock rode with Weir to the San Rafael office. They sold the rest of the band on Pollock creating a cohesive tie-dye stage set for the soundsystem. Not individual panel fronts like those currently adorning the rig, but a complete tableau. Pollock was soon down on Front Street, where the band had moved its rehearsal space, away from the sawdust at the Jacoby Street shop, and began measuring the cabinets.

To that point, the tie-dyeing of the band's backline had been purely aesthetic. "To give something colorful to look at for the audience and for the band members when they turned around," as McGee told me. According to her, Matthews first flashed on the idea of covering the band's amplifiers and cabs with craft store "psychedelic" fabrics—before then, front-facing "grilles" were black or silver, as many are still today. McGee tie-dyed shirts as a hobby, and then "had the idea of replacing the store-bought fabric on the speaker cabinets with tie-dyed ones." She made a test batch.

By then, McGee worked as Alembic's receptionist and booker of the company's new in-house studio. Not only that, "I purchased the wood and electronic items needed for the manufacture of Alembic products," McGee said, "at first restricted to pickups, preamps, speaker cabinets and the electronics needed for the many custom conversions they did on existing basses and guitars." So when Pollock was asked by Jackson, Weir, and the rest of the group to create a set of tie-dyed mandala-style covers for the band's soundsystem, McGee was "happy as a clam to turn over the Alembic speaker cover commissions to him."

Pollock liked McGee's first-generation screens. "Her dyes lasted real well, they stood the test of time," he told me. But by the time Pollock took over, McGee's screens had faded. "Rock and roll is tough on fabric," he said.

The screens were now a visual extension of the sounds flowing from the Dead's PA. "An actual, physical visual extension of the music," Pollock said, chiming with the Dead's broader synesthetic tendency. "That's why it was so successful." For him, and indeed for many others who've taken LSD, the trip experience "is really in my own inner sight." Through the Dead's rig, then, "it was wonderful to have the opportunity to put color, form, and geometry with psychedelic potential where you're creating imagery out of abstraction."

This was only the outset of the Dead's shaping that visual interiority as much as the soundscape at their shows, through their megawatt PA and accompanying stage dressings. But already this enters heady terrain around audiovisual processing and the subtle interplay between sound, color, and light leading into the Wall.

As Kurt Torell, the associate professor emeritus of philosophy at Penn State Greater Allegheny, wrote in his essay on the Dead and synesthesia, sometimes the sheer broadcasting of a sound out of the band's PA "through increasing and decreasing volume created the impression that the sound emanated from a vanishing point to envelop an empty space, geometrical or otherwise, and then dissipated." That's a sensation McGee's and then Pollock's tie-dyes began stretching out and enhancing like levels in a hidden architecture.

On rarer occasions, "the sheer density of sound and the progressive playing of notes might foster the impression that the physical reality outside the listener, or the atmosphere itself... was somehow being cut or ripped apart to reveal some kind of transcendental reality behind it," Torell said. Stare a hole through the rig-spanning mandala as the band itself "ripped," and one just might come out a changed person.

Sometimes, Lesh's bass, the drums, and rhythm even synced with "the manipulation of volume to give the impression of something collapsing toward a vanishing horizon," Torell added, "as if into a well-like hole or tunnel that progressively unfolded in turn with the passage of time and in advance of the *heard* sense of the present *location*." The scarabs and singularities in Pollock's designs provoked this fractaling, boring sensation, unfurling as the soundwaves moved through spacetime.

Still other times, "all of the sounds of the band collectively worked together," and given an amplified boost, produced an Escher-like corkscrew of impressions: "intersecting gears, interlocking shapes and mechanisms, spinning axles and disks, silvery spindles, and flywheel and pulley-like objects," Torell said, "where only their intersections and subsequent divergences might be constituted by the sounds themselves, while the gears and interlocking mechanisms and shapes themselves were perceived as existing only beyond the sound, and therefore only implied by it." When *that* happened, Torell continued, "the sound would merely circumscribe and imply the existence of those gears, axles, and flywheels beyond the sounds themselves, where the sound served merely as a kind of cradle and visible portion of the gear that otherwise might remain hidden from view." As above, so below.

For Pollock, the opportunity was beyond his wildest dreams. "It was wonderful to have that exposure on the big stage," Pollock told me. "Back in those days, nobody knew who did the tie-dyes."

Yet nobody seems to recall the public unveiling of Pollock's first stage set. "You may have seen a photo," Pollock told me, of the only known scrap of visual evidence of that show, which had to have been sometime in the second half of 1970. "It's just a snapshot with a low-end camera. It's got a kind of a purple-burgundy curtain behind the stage."

The venue was likely a couple of hours' drive south of San Francisco. (The gig was quite possibly August 5 at San Diego's Golden Hall; some credit the photos to an Emerson and Loew.) "I had already measured everything," Pollock told me, "designed my blocks of stacks where Garcia had a full stack, Weir had a full stack, and Phil had just two side-by-side bass [cabs] that made another big square." Pollock created a mandala for each. Where there were four blocks, he folded the material so that at the point where the shapes came together they had to be framed. He included two- or three-inch pleats so that the very edge of the part of the front-facing side of the screen was the "center line," he said. "That matched up perfectly." Colors came easy: "Bright and psychedelic for Garcia, more reds," Pollock said. "Weir was in his very mellow period...so he got all kinds of greens and blues. And Lesh, being a Pisces, he got blues with purples—watery."

But at that first gig, Pollock sweated for hours backstage while installing the cabinet fronts. "Joe Winslow was running those things out from the stage one at a time," he recalled. Pollock had a little configuration drawn up, showing what was what within the full design. "And this is the upper left corner of Garcia's stack?" Winslow would ask, the two of them studying the diagram. "I had everything pieced out and ready," Pollock said. "I thumbtacked them into position so that I could remove the tacks if I had to make any adjustments, and after I was happy with it then they were stapled in and taped over so that now they're really fixed in there. So Winslow was running them back out, putting them on that amp—or whatever it was," Pollock recalled. They finished just in time for soundcheck.

Pollock continued creating tie-dyes for the Dead in his home kitchen for the next few years. With seemingly each show they played, he had increasing surface area to cover onstage—first wider, then higher, as the band stacked the emerging Wall.

By 1972, the system's low-end component alone was powered by eight huge Alembic speaker boxes per side, each with a pair of 15-inch JBL cones. That's according to Dennis "Wizard" Leonard, an East Coast head who soon entered the Dead scene as a recording tech. "The boxes were like big Fender Bassman boxes," Leonard told me, alluding to the size and shape of the units. Plus, there were Garcia's and Weir's respective stacks, themselves growing apace. The rig also included four JBL ninety-degree horns on either side of the stage, replete with 2440 midrange compression drivers, as well as—for the highs—2410 drivers. The monitor "wedges," typically serving as guitar foldback speakers, were JBL D110s mounted low on stands. And a stack of chained Ampex MX-10s still served as a front-of-house mixing station. "It was really simple, actually," Leonard has said, "but very hi-fi."

The two arrays each flew Pollock's expanded continuous tie-dye grilles, so "they could be set up that way," Leonard said. "That was a rare occasion!" In most any photo of the Dead's rig from this time, the speaker boxes were clearly never assembled exactly the same way twice—in fact, the system was evolving precisely that way, customizable to any setting. Pollock, especially, had to accept that reality. But after only a few months of steady mixing the ultravivid, highly toxic hot-water aniline dyes of the day and creating his Dead speaker cover designs at home in Marin, he started getting dizzy and winded. That's when Pollock noticed the pit stains on his shirt: His sweat was coming out turquoise.

Meanwhile, out on tour, the grind was just as colorful.

Union hours and codes allowed only limited windows of time for Dead roadies to enter venues and unload gear. "They often have to get up at five, get over to the hall, and they've only gotten into town two hours ago, traveling all night, one guy driving, the other guy sleeping," Scully said. Then they had to deal with "surly" local stagehands. "If you don't grease them, forget it!"

These dynamics and growing pains were, again, reflected in the sounds coming off the stage in this stretch of the band's PA adventure. The Dead's May 2 performance at Harpur College in Binghamton, New York, was an era-defining "event," with an acoustic followed by an electric set. But requisite technical difficulties kicked things off that Saturday.

"How 'bout some hearing tests?" Garcia said into the mic, addressing Matthews, mixing front-of-house. "Can you people hear these guitars?" Garcia asked the restless audience. Feedback shot through the vocal mics. "Hey, Bill," he asked, "can you hear the guitars?"

"Aaahhhh!" Kreutzmann cried.

"Guitars louder in the monitors please, Bob," Garcia said. "Woo hoo," went Garcia. "We can still have more guitars in the monitors, Bob."

"Fat monitors!" Lesh said.

"Okay, that's good," Garcia decided.

"Have at it," Matthews said.

Later that night, during the electric set, the Dead performed "Feedback" one last time. Feedback itself was no longer embraced like it had been since the band's earliest days. The harsh noise hindered where the Dead hoped to go with the Wall-to-be, something their slide rule–wielding audio engineers were tasked with scheming up ways around.

The following day, at Wesleyan University in Connecticut, the Dead soundsystem sat in tense silence at a free gig arranged by the Black student community. A Black Panthers rally happened to also be taking place in nearby New Haven. By then, the FBI's Dead file noted their friendly run-in with Huey Newton, founder of the Panthers, on a flight to New York to play the Fillmore East that same year.

Yet the roadie Heard, "not known for his liberal racial views, objected" that Sunday at the Field House in Middletown, as McNally later reported. Heard only reconsidered the situation "at the point of a .38 being shoved in his stomach." (It is unclear who brandished the handgun.) According to one bystander, some Wesleyan students then started giving Kreutzmann trouble. Cutler, who had instructed the band and crew not to power up the PA, relented. The Wesleyan show produced what is considered one of the all-time worst Dead audience recordings.

The day after, the Dead rolled into the Massachusetts Institute of Technology in Cambridge for a pair of gigs and got off to a more auspicious start. The band was greeted by Ned Lagin, who was studying at MIT and had caught the band for the first time the previous December at the Ark in Boston. "They were all hanging around their amplifiers for two hours before they were supposed to start playing," Lagin told me. But then they started. In a word, they were "remarkable."

Lagin wrote them a letter, expressing an interest in what they were doing and explaining a bit about what he himself had going on. "Then my friends and

I got the idea to invite the Grateful Dead to do a concert at MIT," Lagin re-called. "I helped organize that. They all drove their own vehicles at this point...and Garcia had a rented station wagon with his amplifiers in the back." Garcia hadn't responded to Lagin's letter but had told Lesh about him. Now, here he was.

Between shows, Lagin invited them to a performance of an 8-track, four-tape-recorder piece of his that he had booked at the MIT chapel, "this circular, cylindrical building," Lagin said. "I set up eight speakers around that circle, and we sat in that circle—a bunch of MIT people and friends, and Mickey and Jerry and Phil—and they listened to my electronic music composition."

"This guy would really like to play with a 16-track recorder, I'm sure," Gar-cia said.

"I'm sure he would," Lesh said. With that, Lagin got invited to California.

A *Tech Review* write-up favored the Dead's free outdoor show on May 6 over the paying indoor concert the following night in Dupont Gymnasium. The first date was part of nationwide campus strikes in response to Ohio National Guard troops killing four unarmed college students at Kent State University. "The audience's kinetic energy was damped by the cold" that night, the *Tech Review* reported. As such, "the music was for listening, and hence better." The Dead stood "behind a gaggle of microphones, behind them two eight-foot coffin woofers, clusters of speaker horns."

A more carnal scene is said to have played out days later before a gig in Atlanta, and is illustrative of how far the band went for their sound personnel. Though some dispute Bear's presence in Georgia, on the eve of the show at the Sports Arena, Kreutzmann and Lesh reportedly smoked a joint in their hotel room, watching Bear and his girlfriend have sex, when the cops barged in. (Bear remained a free man for just a few more weeks, before he was shipped to Terminal Island, a low-security federal prison, on one old and another more recent drug charge.) The officers asked the Dead's drummer and bass player to intervene. "He's our soundman," Kreutzmann explained. "If I get him to stop, we'll have terrible sound tomorrow night."

As it turned out, the airline had left the Dead's equipment behind in Boston. The band played that Sunday night gig, to an estimated two thousand heads, on loaned gear from the Allman Brothers, whose drummer, Butch Trucks, had been assembling the first version of that band's own soundsystem. At the en-core, members of the Macon group joined the Dead for a jam that culminated with Pigpen lighting a cherry bomb under his organ. "A perfect audile [*sic*] exclamation mark for this most profound musical/community statement," read a review in the underground newspaper *Great Speckled Bird*.

Once reunited with their gear, at the very next show, on May 14 at Merramec Community College in Kirkwood, Missouri, monitor troubles undercut an opening acoustic set. Before the New Riders of the Purple Sage, a Dead-adjacent country rock outfit that frequently opened for the band, took the stage to perform the middle block (followed by the Dead's closing, electric set), someone—possibly Cutler—called for backup: "Can Bob Matthews come up on stage and sort out the soundsystem which isn't working."

When not beset by sound problems, the Dead were reminded that their stacked-up exploits in pursuit of loudness and clarity were not happening in a vacuum. On May 16, the band played an outdoor concert on a hot Saturday at Temple University in Philadelphia, the second of four acts, including Cactus, Steve Miller, and the Hendrix Experience. Years later, Kreutzmann recalled the Dead opening for Hendrix and "watching him blow the house down afterward," the drummer said. "That band was so fucking loud. They played with a wall of Marshall stacks behind them, and it's funny that I should call them on that because of where we went with our own soundsystem a few years later. They got there first."

Later that month, the Dead and all their gear loaded onto a plane. For the first time, they crossed the Atlantic Ocean.

The Dead got sent by Warner's on a one-shot promotional UK gig for *Workingman's*, to establish their lore and position themselves as an "in-demand" act in the future. The trip included a single performance at the Hollywood Festival, on a farm in Newcastle-Under-Lyme. Other acts included Traffic, Mungo Jerry, and Black Sabbath, a Birmingham four-piece likewise pushing the limits of volume.

That Sunday, May 24, was rainy and cold. Backstage, a dosed BBC2 documentary film crew member trailed Garcia, who motioned toward Ram Rod, Jackson, and Matthews, huddled and setting up mic stands. "Here's the crew you want—these are the guys that do the real work," Garcia said to the camera operator. "The rest of us just hang around. Of course, they're camera-shy buggers."

Backed by their tie-dyed rig, the Dead were then nagged by amp problems for most of their set. But late in their performance, at the peak of "Dark Star," Lesh recalled, "all of a sudden this jet plane bifurcates the sky." A vapor trail appeared, and within an instant everything had changed. The impression that the band sometimes could steer events in the sky, including the weather, with their sound was already becoming part of the mythos and allure of the Dead as a live act.

But Garcia was not entirely psyched on their overseas debut. While the Hollywood Festival house monitoring system gave previous bands trouble, Ram Rod and the Dead's handlers had adjusted their own monitors to create a "complete shell of sound," Garcia said. "All you could hear were the least hearable frequencies, super-low things, and stuff coming out really weird," he explained. "It was starting to get good; we were getting used to the sound of it, and the feeling of it, and the people were starting to get enthusiastic." Yet in a festival situation, "it's kinda hard to get it on. You can't compete with the outdoors."

After returning to the States, the band and rig boarded a train due west. Tour promoters had chartered a fourteen-car Canadian National Railways locomotive with sleepers, lounges, and a well-stocked bar. As June turned into July, the Dead, the Band, Buddy Guy, Janis Joplin, the Flying Burrito Brothers, and others embarked on what's billed as the Festival Express, traversing Canada and stopping along the way to perform.

The gigs offered a snapshot of the Dead's evolving system, the media's fixation with it, and reactions to the sound itself. At the CNE Grandstand in Toronto on June 27, the music "flowed from the delicately balanced sound machines perched high atop towers entangled in a maze of electrical wire," the *Spectrum*, the University of Buffalo student newspaper, reported. As for the Dead's set, "their moments in this concert will last for a long time," which got "burned on a brain already numbed with fatigue, dope, and constant music."

On July 1 in Winnipeg, an estimated four to five thousand heads turned up for twelve hours of music at the outdoor Fairgrounds. The promoter's biggest problem was "how to keep their performers and equipment from blowing away in winds which gusted up to 40 m.p.h. throughout the day," the *Winnipeg Free Press* reported. During the marathon gig, "technicians clambered about on steel towers, tying down sound equipment and warning festivalgoers to stand clear in case anything should break loose." The wind was an elusive atmospheric factor the Dead's road and tech crews needed to overcome, as much for the quality of the sound as the safety of those in proximity to the band's speaker stacks.

By Calgary, the final performance stop of the train tour on July 4 and 5, the seismic rig made some attendees physically uncomfortable. Tiers of amplifiers emitted "solid layers of sound which could crash and crush your mind," the *Calgary Herald* reported. The Dead did "the Nashville bit"—an allusion to *Workingman's* countryfied direction—along with "some heavy, free-form rock which had the ground trembling." At times, their sound "was so wild and so loud it left people near the speakers a little light-headed."

But then the rig and most all the Dead's touring personnel went back out on the road for the remainder of the summer. The crew had committed to work the Medicine Ball Caravan, a "traveling Woodstock" film that Warner's had pumped nearly a million dollars into and which the Dead dropped out of at the last minute to continue writing *American Beauty.* The Caravan crisscrossed the country, pulling over for smaller-sized gigs that featured appearances by B. B. King, Jethro Tull, Alice Cooper, and Joni Mitchell.

Alembic provided the PA and recording capabilities for those outdoor stops. Taking cues from the early Dead playbook, the crew positioned a flatbed, backed up the truck and off-loaded the low-end speakers, and then stacked the horns on top. These sound and recording techs, McGee said, were already "experienced road warriors and fearless at pulling together technical scenarios while higher than kites." On the Caravan, McGee "really bonded" with the Wickershams, Matthews, Cantor, and Turner, plus Candelario and "the new guy" Mark Raizene, both of whom now worked for Alembic.

Raizene was a former stagehand at Chicago's Kinetic Playground, where my father first saw the Dead in 1969. In April 1970, at an outdoor Dead show on a family farm in rural Poynette, Wisconsin, Raizene chatted with the band's "kwipment krew" and helped set the stage after the organizer flaked. That Sunday, Matthews told the chipper Raizene that if he wanted to work for the Dead, he had to move to the Bay Area. A week later, Raizene was in San Francisco. When he walked into Alembic, he told me, Matthews, Wickersham, Turner, and others were going, "Who the fuck is this?"

"Figure out if you wanna hire me or not," Raizene said.

After a week without pay, they signed him on. Deciphering Bear's idiosyncratic wiring system took a minute. "It was color coordinated and all this other weird stuff," Raizene told me. "It wasn't like, *put this in here, and put that in there, and run this over here.*" At the time, Bear "had these big, crescent moon–shaped speaker cabinets," Raizene said, referring to the Buchla units used at Altamont. "They weren't pieces of shit but they weren't very good either. It was like the start of how we were gonna start stacking stuff up and do it when we eventually moved behind 'em."

By the time Raizene had a handle on Bear's color-coded arrangements, the Dead were renting the new system Alembic was building. "So I went to run the stuff when they'd go out," he said. When the band eventually decided to purchase that system, "I went with it. That's how I got hired on with the Grateful Dead."

Not long after Raizene came around, back on the Medicine Ball tour, he and Candelario were heading south into Los Angeles, down the San Gabriel Mountains. Raizene operated a six-wheel Bobtail truck loaded with a generator, something the Dead/Alembic carried—a backup power supply—through the end of the Wall. Candelario drove a similar six-wheel truck loaded with Alembic gear.

Before taking off, Candelario told me, he gave Raizene a heads-up: Once they got to the crest of the mountain, *do not* take the vehicle out of compound low gear—rather, let the engine take care of the braking. But as Candelario recalled, "he takes it out of gear and he goes by me freewheeling, his brakes are on fire." Candelario zoomed in front of Raizene and let him come up to the back of his truck, slowing him down. "It was gnarly," Candelario said. "He easily could've crashed."

Meanwhile, that September the Dead began tracking *American Beauty*. "They had sat around in a circle and rehearsed this record, so they were ready to go when I got them," audio engineer Stephen Barncard, brought in on the sessions at Wally Heider Recording, later said. The ten-song, semi-acoustic album included perhaps their most iconic tune, "Truckin'," a kind of mission statement for the band, crew, and Deadheads.

Here, Scully later said, is when "the craziness begins." Momentum from *Workingman's Dead* and *American Beauty*, released and well received in the same year—*Beauty* dropped that November—helped sustain the Dead for the next twenty-five years and beyond. The back-to-back success of *Workingman's Beauty*, as this era of studio output is known, also brought critical changes to the Dead's overall functioning and growing soundsystem.

"Things on the Dead financial front were looking brighter," Cutler recalled. "I would arrive home with the funds from one tour and drag myself into the office to organize the next one. There was a constant and unending demand for funds from the organization, which seemed to be growing exponentially, and the only way to satisfy this demand was by doing gigs." At the time, the Dead still (mostly) used in-house sound and lights, but the changes they underwent in this moment, their investment back into a blossoming rig, which required more crew members to handle, exemplified their insatiable hunger for new gear. It demonstrated just how deeply committed they were to producing the best possible experience for audiences.

Magic. That's how David Crosby described live Dead. "Magic is doin' it so well that you get it up beyond mechanical levels," Crosby told *Rolling Stone* that July. "Magic is making people feel good and stuff. Magic is, if you're high on psychedelics, having a great big love beast crawl out of your amplifiers and eat the audience."

But then tragedy struck. That September, Ruth Garcia's car went over a hillside while she was out driving in San Francisco. She died of her injuries. That Garcia, now twenty-eight, had not fully reconciled with his mom, who had furnished the band with their first soundsystem, ate at him. She was sixty.

October 31, 1970. The sounds coming off the stage at Stony Brook University in New York were just as frightening as any audience costume at the second of two Dead shows.

Ballrooms had been fertile ground for rock and roll, but increasingly colleges were in play—universities had budgets. That fall, booking agent Ron Rainey helped organize a low-budget campus run. The Dead chanced it, using local in-house PA systems. Bear was now serving time at Terminal Island, so on most tours in this stretch Matthews mixed front-of-house while Cantor ran recording and assorted sound duties. But at Stony Brook, Matthews seemingly wasn't behind the boards. Both early and late sets were mixed by hapless students in over their heads.

Night one hadn't been a bomb. A review in the student-run *Spectrum* noted how Ram Rod, "the Dead's whiz kid," could swap out a blown speaker "quickly and efficiently." The Stony Brook *Statesman* compared the experience of spending the night with the Dead with "birth trauma" or skydiving. "You just have to be there at three in the morning when you find yourself totally overwhelmed by all the sound, your body resonating," the *Statesman* reported. Then, "from within all that sound, Garcia comes through with a few notes from somewhere and you know that there's somebody way up that's paying attention."

Night two took a turn. "Hey, man, turn the microphones up," Weir said to the front-of-house mixer. "Leave 'em right there. Don't touch the fuckin' things. Don't touch the fuckin' things, man, cause you don't know what you're doing."

"Mister Soundman, sir," Pigpen said, "can I have a little more main in the monitor if it's at all possible? If I don't get it the way I want it, I'm going to rip off your head and shit in it." A near-riot later broke out among gatecrashing fans.

The following month, at the Park Sheraton Hotel in New York City, Weir struck a different tone. He talked up the band's advancement of their scene with a reporter from *Creem*, a scrappy Detroit rock magazine. "Not just our family but the hippie craftsmen and artists," Weir said. "And we have electronics crews who are exploring new horizons in sound, and video for that matter too. And they need support, and we're just about the only people who can give it to them."

Days later, during a November 23 Hells Angels benefit show at New York's Anderson Theater, Weir expressed an alternate sign of appreciation for their crew. He gave the occasional middle finger "to the stoned out soundmen in the balcony," the *East Village Other* reported. "They didn't have the monitor loud enough or something, and there was a feedback problem. And Garcia just kept on smiling."

That was another thing the Dead had to contend with during their ascent of the Wall: Jerry Garcia of the Grateful Dead, already famous and presumed by many to be the "leader" of the band. That year, Garcia was asked in an interview if he saw himself, and by extension the Dead, as some kind of guiding light for their followers. "Fuck, no," he said. "We're just musicians. On a good night our music will be clear and won't scare anybody and won't hurt anybody." Still, to some Garcia was godlike, and the Dead a religion.

Crowds of devotees and curious newcomers alike now met Garcia and the Dead when they came to town. "It's like a statesman returning to his people," read a *Chicago Daily News* review of their November 27 show at the Syndrome, an indoor venue then booked by the promoter Stein. Their music "builds to a peak, spreads out in all directions, comes back into focus and begins again, driving harder and reaching higher." One attendee called the sound the band made the "closest possible thing to Nirvana," and described the show as "more of a religious happening than a concert."

My dad, then twenty years old, was one of the six-thousand-some-odd heads who caught the Dead at the Syndrome that Friday night. He was hooked. "I don't consider that I left anything behind to follow the band," he told me, speaking of this era. "But on a show-to-show basis, it's a different story." There was always something he should have been doing other than seeing them.

Unbeknownst to him, my mom, still a high schooler—one town over—was likewise getting in deep. She soon caught her first Dead show, at Chicago's

3,800-capacity Auditorium Theatre, and was then following the band's gigs for a few weeks at a time, through a connection under Stein's production company via some friends of hers who worked at Flipside Records. "I was able to help them backstage at the concerts they promoted, including Grateful Dead shows, and I just got swept into the whole scene," she told me. "I did leave behind a more stable and secure lifestyle in the '70s because I wanted the freedom to go anywhere when I wanted."

By 1971, the band no longer had to take every gig offered. Everybody in the Dead's camp welcomed this gear shift, except Garcia. He played out virtually every "off" night, mostly in his never-formally-named group with piano and keyboardist Merl Saunders. At Bay Area clubs like the Keystone, Garcia and friends used the Dead's backline. Garcia alone was playing through four Fender Twin Reverb amps. "The open-backed amplifiers just shred your ears," Scully said.

Come spring, the Dead upgraded their rig once more, the ignition sequence of a technological skyrocket. It was a "momentous financial decision," Lesh said. "Since the soundsystems we'd been using everywhere (usually provided by the house or by the promoter) were so problematic, we bought the Alembic PA that Bear and Ron Wickersham had been developing for use locally and took it on the road with us." With this bespoke system, "bigger equaled better, louder, and cleaner. Bear's goal was, as always, sound that was transparent, clean, undistorted, and very loud."

Through the rig, they implemented some of their incarcerated soundman's most outrageous ideas. This system, Lesh said, "was to grow and evolve into the fabled 'Wall of Sound.'"

Before he went to jail, Bear said he believed, based on the opinions of speaker manufacturers and other tinkerers in the Dead's circle of sound techs, that they could build an integrated system wherein each instrument would have its own amplification.

Bear's hunch was that this was possible through the acoustical concept of point source. That's when a speaker system produces, from a single source, the full range of sound. In this case, each of the six musicians was given a PA, with their own respective channels and loudspeakers deployed individually, to achieve optimal coverage depending on the space the band performed in.

As Bear later explained, "the big system" comprised six independent ones, and was simply an eleven-channel PA—the bass alone had four channels, and the drums three. By putting all volume control directly at the fingertips of the players onstage, they mixed themselves. "To the extent that they could properly hear what was going on and to the extent that they were communicating with each other and with the sound technicians who were wandering around in the hall," Bear said, "was to the extent that the mix was perfect and the sound was perfect."

For the time being, the band still relied on venues to supply certain components of sound reinforcement gear, or the money to purchase or rent such equipment, as they built out and refined the Alembic PA for the road. But the guarantees the band required of promoters to come and perform through the customized system were already apparent in the Dead's contract rider language.

"The Grateful Dead will provide all audio equipment for $750," read a handwritten note atop an American Federation of Musicians of the United States and Canada agreement for a March 14 gig in Madison, Wisconsin. (The Dead were a union band.) That's equivalent to around $6,000 today. A similar AFM rider for a show at the 5,200-seat Auditorium in Providence, Rhode Island, the following month, stated that the "EMPLOYER" (the promoter) was responsible for provisioning a "soundsystem." The Dead's contract further stated that if the rig provided wasn't up to the band's standards, then they wouldn't play.

The PA furnished by the promoter should be "capable of providing clear, undistorted evenly distributed [vocal] sound throughout the audience area" at 115 decibels, the agreement read, and, as measured using a sound pressure meter, within a frequency range of at least 100 to 10,000 Hz (cycles per second). That meter reading was to be taken thirty feet out from the front of the stage. Sound pressure level drops were not to exceed six decibels for every hundred feet thereafter. Loudness *and* clarity.

The soundsystem, moreover, must be equipped with a dozen "high quality cardiod [*sic*] dynamic low impedance" microphones. Additionally, "loudspeakers shall be located in such a position as to retain the illusion that the sound emanates from the performance area." The Dead specifically would *not* accept "visable [*sic*] central clusters of loudspeakers in the middle of arenas," then a typical house PA configuration. It was also fully anticipated "that the soundsystem supplied will consist of multicellur [*sic*] or sectoral high frequency horns and suitable high efficience [*sic*] bass units." But *not* "sound columns and other types of PA horns." The Dead still hadn't come around to the vertical (linear) array concept.

Finally, the provided soundsystem needed to include at least a pair of high-quality monitors for the performance area. "These speakers should be movable on stage," the spring '71 AFM contract noted, and "are to be full frequency response units and shall have a volume control separate from the main house system." The contract listed some "major suppliers of rental" PA systems like Clair Bros., a prominent East Coast audio company, as well as McCune Sound. "These people have frequently worked with us," read the contract. "They understand the needs of the artist in order to make the finest presentation of your show."

At that April 21 Providence gig, the sonic membrane between the band and audience was right out of the Acid Tests. "After they take my ticket I walk through the doors to the side of the stage and up to Garcia," one head later recalled. The two shook hands. "Would you let me sit behind the amps?" the fan asked.

Garcia stood to begin the show. Ram Rod moved a stack of equipment cases, "and I head through and I go around the amp," where they claimed to receive a few drops of LSD on the tongue from an eyedropper of Bear's acid. After the second set had ended, before the encore, the musicians filed through a gap between amplifiers. "The combination of energy from the fans, the energy coming off the guys and Bear's secret sauce, had me peaking again," the attendee said.

As the crew broke down the gear later that night, Lesh reportedly sat on an amp next to the fan, who admitted, "That music is all I need to make me happy for life."

"That's exactly how I feel," Lesh said.

While the new rig came together, the Dead's road party solidified further.

Ram Rod, Jackson, and Heard now comprised the band's dedicated tech crew. Hagen ran point for the New Riders. Matthews mixed sound, and his equipment team included Candelario, Raizene, Winslow, and Parish, who came on full-time that spring. His starting salary was $70 a week. "It seemed like all the money in the world at the time," Parish said.

That April run was the "new" crew's first proper tour as a unit. That was also the band's first bus outing, though mostly the roadies still rode the equipment trucks. Parish and some of the other crew also began pulling double duty as security, "to block and tackle the occasional psychotic who got some bad acid and wanted to run onto the stage naked and begin humping an amplifier." One night not long into Parish's tenure, a nude fan leapt into the band's zone and landed on a power box, obliterating a connection; standing six foot five and weighing 250-plus pounds, Parish handled the guy before Garcia even noticed. On another occasion, a young woman stumbled up and knocked a power plug, blacking out half the stage.

At a band gathering in San Rafael that year, Garcia had told the crew, "We'll take care of everything in front of the amps. You guys take care of everything behind the amps," Parish said. "What he meant was this: *The band plays. Everything else is up to you.* At least that's how we interpreted it." The crew "felt we owed it to the band," Parish added, "to the equipment, and, yes, to the fans, to maintain a sense of order around the stage." That gear, "the Wall of Sound and everything that went with it," Parish said, "was our lifeblood. We built it with our own hands and therefore we felt a personal connection to it."

The stage was a fragile "bubble" that had to be protected. That extended to the typical load in/setup, now that the Dead owned the Alembic PA. "Most of the guys on the crew weren't real big on drinking," Parish said, as "you couldn't work as hard as we worked if you were drinking. Setup was generally the sober part of the day for us anyway, although on occasion we'd break to have a joint, to take the edge off." Otherwise, "the work was too hard, the consequences too severe. We were climbing and working, and we depended on each other not only to make the show a success, but to make the job safe." Amphetamines, though? "Like everyone else on the crew," Parish said, "I used speed less as a recreational drug than a tool that allowed me to work eighteen- and twenty-hour days that were a normal part of our life."

Meanwhile, back at Alembic headquarters late that spring, McGee assembled a serialized gear inventory for the Dead's upcoming trip to the French countryside, scheduled for June. That detailed manifest, or carnet, "would allow the mass of band and sound equipment to enter and leave France more or less intact," said McGee, who joined McIntire in advance of the band, the crew, and the load. A sixteen-person entourage and a stripped-back three and a half tons of equipment—106 individual pieces—needed accounting for.

Raizene, Ram Rod, and Jackson then "got everything straightened around, the right cases for the numbers on the equipment," Raizene told me. At the airport, "I'm dumping all this crap right straight into the plane. We get on and fly off to Europe to do that festival."

The gig the Dead were slated to play, a free fest at the Rodeo Ranch at Auvers-sur-Oise, was rained out. "But the band and crew were already on the plane and wouldn't learn of the cancellation until they landed," McGee said. "Festival or no festival we couldn't be separated from our gear, so it was essential that we get a truck." Raizene and Hagen guarded the gear at the small Orly Airport that Saturday. McGee, fluent in French, secured a loaner vehicle, paying two of the men from the rental company to assist the Dead roadies in loading the gear. "It was fun to watch the smaller French guys try to lift the 130-pound McIntosh amp road cases," she said.

But once they had departed for Hérouville, site of a sixteenth-century château—the onetime home of the composer Frédéric Chopin—where the band would be staying, the truck started giving them trouble. Raizene later recalled the vehicle being "an odd articulating hybrid, almost like a fifth-wheel box truck," which made operating the weighted-down vehicle difficult. Plus, the truck had so little power that they struggled to make it over the initial highway grade.

"This truck's gonna kill us!" yelled Raizene and Hagen. "We gotta get another truck!"

"All right, all right!" McGee shouted over the road noise. "We'll figure something out."

At the first exit, McGee asked around and eventually a local agreed to let them borrow his vehicle. It was "a relic of a stake-bed truck," McGee recalled, "but it seemed to be running well and the tires were good on it." After Raizene and Hagen "decreed it would probably get us the remaining fifty kilometers to Hérouville and back, we made the deal." McGee, Raizene, and Hagen pulled up to the château later that night, rig in tow, to applause.

"Six thousand miles is a long way to come for nothing," read a *Zigzag* review of the Dead's weekend in France. Attempts were made to quickly put together a gig at a "suitable venue" in Paris; there was even "talk of taking the entire entourage and 3 1/2 tons of equipment to the Glastonbury Fair" in England. "What finally happened must have been one of the most amazing events at which the Grateful Dead—or any other band for that matter—have ever played."

The following day, the Dead and their rig, flying Pollock's vibrant full-set mandala dyes, assembled on the château's back lawn for an impromptu four-hour performance to locals. "We played and the people came—the chief of police, the fire department, just everybody," Garcia told *Rolling Stone*. All "had a hell of a time." A film crew produced a legendary recording of the night's performance, some of the finest moving outdoor color images of the rig in this era.

By late June, the band's business outlook was looking brighter still. "The Dead's finances had been straightened out and the continuation of our journey was assured," Cutler said. "People in the band pursued their own musical projects and the crew began to assemble the 'wall of sound.'" But not until they visited their imprisoned audio visionary.

August 4, 1971. The Dead and a pack of roadies were tripping on LSD as they pulled up to the gates at the federal correctional facility at Terminal Island, off San Pedro, California. Inside their truck was a streamlined soundsystem. Entry guards performed only a casual inspection.

"We had a manifest," Raizene told me. "They got bored and said, *just bring this shit in and set it up and shut up.* And we did it." They were told not to mingle with prisoners. But "a few of them would come up and we'd start talking," Raizene said. "It was no big deal."

The Dead came to boost the spirits of inmate Augustus Owsley Stanley III. In an Oakland jail, waiting to be transferred to federal lockup, an inmate had jumped Bear and broke his nose. In standard-issue felon button-up khaki shirt, dungarees, canvas belt, leather shoes, and a buzz cut, Bear now spent good portions of his days inside a cell kitted out with high-fidelity and electronic gear, smuggled in with help from accomplices—anything to keep him occupied during his time at what he described as "a walled prison with a yard in the middle." The complex is situated next to a naval base and ringed by a high-wire fence. Armed guards posted in observation towers watch the prisoners' every move.

"I've visited with bands in various different configurations to lots of different prisons, and Terminal Island was I think the most oppressive feeling," Cantor told me. "Man, something about that place." Cantor herself later talked about sneaking in live soundboard tapes for Bear to study behind bars at Terminal and again at Lompoc, a medium-security federal penitentiary to which he would be transferred. But back then, she said, "we wanted to give Bear some music, you know?"

The band and family missed him, no matter how much Bear could be at times. At a gig the Dead played on July 2—their last at Graham's Fillmore West, which the promoter soon closed—Lesh dedicated "That's It for the Other One" to "our friend Owsley, who's in jail." So that Wednesday in August in Southern California, the Dead pulled off a private gig, just for Bear and his friends on the inside.

After being let through the gate, the Dead and crew began unloading gear outside the prison library. Not a single guard stopped or hassled them. "It's funny that they left us alone," Candelario told me.

Bear was given "free range" for the occasion. He helped ready the stage and the system with assistance from a seasoned felon named Bob Nichols, whom the Dead later put through trucking school to haul the band's post-Wall rig. Bear clearly missed being out with the Dead. During the setup, he said to Parish, "I've got to come back on the road with you." Others, like Weir, had too much going on to chat with Bear. "We got a little time with him, but I didn't get a great hit on what it was like to be in prison," Weir recalled. "I was too busy getting the gig together."

They blew the place out. "We brought in sufficient speakers to do a show for two or three thousand people," right there in the outdoor exercise yard, Cutler told me. (Terminal Island holds around 850 male inmates.) "It wasn't very difficult," Cutler said. "We set up a little stage and the band played and everyone loved it. It was a good opportunity to say hi to Bear." The stunt doubtless "did him a world of good, mentally and emotionally."

The Dead played twenty songs for their on-again, off-again soundman. "A lot of times we play concerts and get people breaking in," Garcia cracked early in their set. As he told *Rolling Stone* that fall, getting to see and perform for Bear at Terminal Island was "just great." Garcia called their original soundperson a "hero" responsible for bringing "a really solid consciousness of what quality was to our whole scene. And that's been the basis of our operations since then: being able to have our equipment in really good shape, our PA really good."

A soundboard recording of the party-like prison gig is remarkably high-quality, despite some nagging bass distortion, fuzz, and early equipment snags. Before "Hard to Handle," an Otis Redding cover, for instance, there's some off-mic chatter to do with "power going out in a monitor," or a piece of gear that "blew up," Weir says. The caper was a testament to the force of ideas Bear represented to the band; he got behind the boards that afternoon too. "He's out there mixing the shit, right?" Raizene told me, laughing. "Of course."

Until Bear's release and reentry, the band tore down the road with the Alembic system, applying and testing his ideas show in, show out, as the PA evolved—and as the songs themselves likewise grew. Take *American Beauty*'s "Sugar Magnolia," which didn't initially whip up crowds. Robert Hunter, now fully in as band lyricist, recalled the moment that changed.

"The first time that song ever came off was in Chicago," Hunter said, likely referring to the first of two nights the band played at the Auditorium Theatre later that August. "Bob Matthews was at the soundboard at that time, and he went off into the audience or backstage or something like that, and there was nobody there at the sound booth." Hunter slipped in and, right as Weir sang the "sunshine daydream" refrain, punched it. "There was a thing that everybody should be at the same level—including the voices, which tended to get lost—so I just cranked it up," Hunter said, "and the audience just sat up, and then they had the reaction to it at the end that they've had ever since."

Raizene, a Chicagoan, has similarly fond memories of that hometown Auditorium show. "The place sounded so damn good," he told me. "Loading in was kind of a bitch because it was down this alley, to the stage entrance. We weren't using the big trucks yet—we were using smaller box trucks." He invited his mother to the gig and met her out back of the Auditorium near that stage entrance.

My parents were both present that night too, although they still didn't know each other. "It was a gorgeous, ornate venue with great acoustics," my mom recalled. She worked the show via Howard Stein Enterprises and entered the building through that same alley door.

The Dead "are heroes precisely because the band makes music to live in, which is entirely different from music one goes to listen to," the *Chicago Daily News* reported. "When those in the audience manage to dance despite immovable chairs, it's fairly obvious the customers are glad they came." At times, "the approving roar of the crowd alone was louder than the music volume of many lesser bands."

August 26, 1971. At Gaelic Park in the Bronx, the Dead performed outdoors for three-plus hours to fifteen thousand heads at a mini rock festival staged by Stein. Behind-the-backline images taken that afternoon by photojournalist Chuck Pulin offer another unique window into the Dead refining their system.

The images are deceptive. Some of the Fender Twin combo cabinets onstage hold no speaker cones, apparently removed to eliminate the rattle of the amplifier tubes. The band still drew from the "brains"—the actual amplifier portions—of those units, and wouldn't fully start using McIntosh amps for their instruments until the following spring, thus "marking the beginning of the Wall of Sound."

That's according to Mike Wald, a tech-inclined Deadhead and guitar player on a decades-long quest to build his own "Jerry rig" that replicates Garcia's tone. Wald, more widely known as Waldotronics, has accumulated his own deep stash of Wall-centric knowledge, archival material, and artifacts.

"The instruments went from tube combos to hybrid setups with the Twin preamps tapped," Wald has said. At Gaelic Park, the rough size of Garcia's rig was the same stack he had used up to that point, only by the end of 1972 and early 1973, it began to be configured vertically. The rest of the speakers added to his full Wall system "took other amps and were the sound reinforcement for the venue," Wald said. "It was a LEGO set built up from the band's base setup from those Twin tube combo amps."

The next stage in the evolution of the Dead's system was to similarly turn the rest of the horizontally arrayed gear, as visible in the Bronx photos, "vertically," Wald said, "for a better throw and spread," both acoustical terms for propagating soundwaves from a single source. But for that Gaelic gig, "this is the setup reengineered to a hybrid setup for a huge sound." The sound bridged the microcosm of the stage and the macrocosm of the audience. The "band-to-fan-to-band electro-chemical process" was on full display, the *Village Voice* reported. The Dead "came home to the cheers of the fans."

That September, the Dead surpassed another milestone in their unlikely journey as a "popular" act. They earned their first certified gold album with a self-titled double live LP, variously known as *Skull and Roses* and *Skullfuck*. Once again recorded and produced by Cantor and Matthews, the album compiled eleven tracks performed around the Bay Area and in New York City that spring. The liner notes contained a far-reaching call to action in an analog age: *Dead Freaks Unite: Who are you? Where are you? How are you?* Drop a line at the Dead post office box address and the band would keep you connected to their goings on.

Warner's gave the band a sizable budget for promoting the live record, including around $100,000—the equivalent to around $771,000 today—to cover radio simulcasts of over a dozen shows that fall. Noticeably absent from those gigs was Pigpen, whose health continued to deteriorate. That September he was admitted to the hospital with hepatitis and a perforated ulcer. His bandmates donated blood.

As Pigpen convalesced, it's a miracle that none of the rest of the band or crew ended up hospitalized (or worse) for job-related injuries. The margin for error was razor thin. Now working for Alembic "ruggedizing" the Dead's Fender and McIntosh amplifiers, Janet Furman, who moved to California after graduating from Columbia, once came dangerously close to getting fried. She got zapped with four hundred volts while fixing an early Wall amp in a dark backstage area before a Dead show in this period at Winterland. "I got the shock of my life,"

Furman told me. "It threw me ten feet backwards across the stage." Not only did it leave her in pain, she said, "but I was embarrassed."

Winterland was perhaps *the* powerspot in the Dead's Wall geography. Which is fitting, because the venue's sound wasn't great. "A huge dirigible hangar of a building," Lesh later said of Winterland, "it had the kind of acoustics that admitted of only one approach—play *really loud.*"

The arena was especially harsh on bass frequencies, which irked Lesh. But under these challenging conditions, the Dead found creative ways through to better sound. "That's where we cut our teeth," Healy later said. "I was raised in the worst tub going, so by the time I had to venture into bigger halls around the country, I'd lived for so many years with that, the rest of it was a piece of cake." Another Graham venture, Winterland won't become the Dead's main Bay Area performance center until 1973, by which point the million-plus-dollar Alembic PA had grown to thirty thousand pounds and required a forty-foot semi-truck to haul.

Fall 1971 brought some personnel shifts too. Hart, in part distraught over his father's malfeasance, had voluntarily exited the band earlier that year. The single-drummer Dead played lean and mean, turning on a dime, even as the sophisticated architecture of sonic hardware surrounding them became ever more complex. Meanwhile, Keith Godchaux, a shy piano player with sad eyes, clocked his first show with the band on October 19 in Minneapolis, at the Northrop Auditorium at the University of Minnesota. The band's equipment, all 150 pieces and $100,000 worth, had gotten delayed at the airport; the road and sound crew got the system assembled only minutes before showtime.

An uncredited black-and-white photograph from behind the backline, during setup, has the balance of a Renaissance painting. Garcia, Lesh, Weir, Kreutzmann, and Matthews stand in a circle, looking down at Ram Rod, kneeling and working on an amplifier. In the foreground, back turned and seated cross-legged, is an unidentified stagehand staring at some sort of power supply block. Behind them all, stacked five Alembic cabinets high, is part of the baby Wall—one of the two arrays that formed the stereo system. They had clearly started tilting upward some of the high-end tweeter boxes to project the sound into the farther reaches of the house. The image contains all the mundane technical conversations and servicing of the band's rig that most concertgoers simply weren't privy to.

The band played for nearly four hours that night, "building the sound and the levels of the songs," the *Minneapolis Star* reported. From that gig forward,

Godchaux's touch came to occupy its own sizable stage presence within the fledgling Wall. "Keith liked to play on grand pianos and, once he got comfortable with us, he brought a Steinway on tour and it sounded great," Kreutzmann later said. "Our technology had finally gotten to a point where we could bring a grand piano out with us, and mic it in a way that would do it justice. We had to isolate it from the other sounds on stage. That was a big deal at the time," and it was Healy who "basically invented the technique for that."

At virtually every stop that fall tour, ticket demand overran venue capacities—these were mostly still modestly sized clubs and amphitheaters. "The Grateful Dead has become incredibly popular and we can't play a small hall anymore without having three thousand people outside wanting to get in," Garcia said at the time. "We have to play shows like some military campaigns just to make sure the equipment guys don't have to be fighting thousands of people to save the shit."

As a goodwill gesture toward those who couldn't score tickets, the Dead managed to get their shows aired on local FM radio stations in many of the towns they hit. This, in turn, further fueled the Dead taping scene. High-quality recordings of the shows on that tour were heavily traded, even flipped into bootleg records.

"The band has its groove together on stage," Scully, who was involved in efforts to quash album piracy, later said. But since Bear had gone to jail, something else became clear. "Our soundsystem has fallen into sad repair," Scully said. "It's in very fatty shape." At a November 14 gig at Texas Christian University in Fort Worth, the band paused early in the first set, due to technical difficulties with the rig. "Grateful Dead Standard Time, folks," Weir told the crowd.

The following month, the Dead performed a four-night run at the five-thousand-seat Felt Forum in New York City. Healy happened to be performing in town as a folk duo with singer Darlene DiDomenico and stopped by the Forum. "The setup was terrible, the sound was terrible, the whole production was muddy, the music was all fucked," Healy later said to Scully. "It had all degenerated to nothing. I was appalled." The touring party vibe was off, too, he said. That first night at the Forum, Kreutzmann punched out Bear's stand-in, Matthews.

Such sonic "atrocities" would not stand. Healy dropped what he was doing and made his intentions clear to Garcia, Lesh, and Ram Rod. "I'll see you on the [West] Coast when this tour is up," he told them. "I'm restaking my old turf."

7

The Alembic PA (1972–1973)

April 1, 1972. Fifteen thousand pounds of equipment sat inside flight cases at customs at JFK in New York. The gear was heaped "in this huge bonded warehouse, like the last scene of *Citizen Kane*," Rock Scully recalled.

An agent consulted the carnet. The Dead's crew, handling the band's gear, and Alembic, overseeing the PA and recording equipment, assembled the manifest for a return trip overseas. Rosie McGee, Alembic's purchasing agent, remembered the "intense collaboration" inventorying the seven-and-a-half-ton load. The gear needed to be itemized in one document, "and the daunting task of preparing it fell to me," McGee told me. She worked with Ram Rod on compiling the band's portion. "It was a chaotic and imperfect process, and I had to impose a hard deadline on making changes. I fully understood that there was no way the carnet could have been more than mostly accurate." If customs opened the "wrong" case? "Beg forgiveness," McGee said.

The overwhelmed agent was the first in a line of baffled customs officials, venue and hall techs and stagehands, and fire-code auditors across five countries over the next few weeks. "In the end they inspect one box and one speaker cabinet, get fed up, and say screw it," Scully recalled.

The Dead's Europe 1972 tour was their longest yet. Releasing a live record would help offset expenses, so they packed a 16-track deck. That unit was "as big as a wall," said Scully, and installed in a mobile "studio" truck, where Betty Cantor and Bob Matthews, alongside Alembic recording techs Janet Furman and Dennis Leonard, rolled tape during the shows. Select captured tracks were later released as *Europe '72*.

Their touring party counted forty-nine people: seven musicians (Keith Godchaux's partner, Donna, now sang in the Dead), five managers, five office staff, ten equipment handlers, four drivers, and over two dozen others. "Fuck it," Jerry Garcia had said. "Everybody goes."

The Dead also had, for the first time, a lighting rig and designer aboard. As Candace Brightman later told me, she saw Garcia and keyboardist Howard Wales, performing as a duo, earlier that year on the East Coast. "After the show, Garcia asked me if I'd do their Europe '72 tour," Brightman said. She accepted the offer. Brightman's rig fit into the crew's system as the piece that was then always "first in, last out" at every venue, because the lights had to go up before anything else could be put in place. Her playing off the band and their sound mixer helped them transcend the sum of their parts and mesmerize Wall audiences. "Candace Brightman was probably very likely the most fantastic, greatest lighting director that ever walked the face of the earth," Dan Healy later said.

The Dead had reached an inflection point on their path to audio perfection. "The Grateful Dead now believe that in order to hit the big crowds they're playing to, they *need* a wall of sound," Scully said. "Born in Owsley's brain and materialized by Healy," Scully continued, the immense PA was already an essential piece of their live gigs. Phil Lesh's stacks alone would peak at thirty-two feet tall, the height of a standing bass wave. "Soon I was spending a fucking fortune on this stuff," Scully said, namely amps, monitors, speakers, and even a computer for the delay—part of the phase-canceling mic setup. "They're wondering where all their money is going, and I'm telling them, 'Look up!' We're buying thirty-two feet in the air of speakers and amps and scaffolding."

Behind the rising Wall was a logistical knot. "How many guys is it going to take to move this stuff and set it up?" Scully said. "We have to figure out how to get it up there without breaking backs and what insurance costs are going to be and where we can get the pneumatic hoists and cables to put the system up. You can't get a union guy anywhere in the United States"—much less early 1970s Europe—"to do this kind of backbreaking precision work." Plus, now that they used the Alembic PA, Scully said, "we have kids throwing things at the speaker towers and then we have to figure out a way to cover them. This is when we get the psychedelic coverings made."

The Wall represented a "radical, radical change," Scully continued. "The

existing systems we encounter all date back to our parents' generation and before."
And the spaces the Dead now performed in "don't want to hear about us bringing
this mountain of scaffolding for the Wall of Sound." Already, by Europe '72, "it
is *tons* of fucking gear," Scully said. The rig was constantly "getting bigger and
bigger and heavier and heavier. So much doggone stuff it is out of hand."

On April 6, the eve of the tour kickoff, the Dead ran a soundcheck at London's Wembley Arena, the first stop. "Above the diminutive figures on stage,
towered a massive gantry supporting lights, speakers, screens, etc.," read a
Melody Maker review. The place was a boomy warehouse with a huge steel superstructure. "It sounded just like playing in the shower," Allan Arkush, a former
Fillmore East stage crew member and friend of the Dead, later recalled.

So Scully and some of the tech crew rented every curtain and parachute in
town and draped them along the length of the hall, in hopes of "deadening" the
hollowed-out space in time for opening night. They folded the parachutes in
half, hanging them festoon-like from the rafters in tiers of nine by three—as
if the Dead were in a big-top tent. "It was a brilliant stroke," co-manager Jon
McIntire said. "The sound wasn't great," he admitted, "but it was handleable in
comparison to what it would have been."

Then the venue's heating system kicked in, right as "the PA was tuning into
the building," Bob Weir said in an interview later that year. The parachutes
dislodged, floating down from the ceiling. After opening with "Greatest Story
Ever Told," from his forthcoming solo record *Ace*, Weir told the audience,
"We've got a couple of technical difficulties, of course, to work out."

A few songs later, Lesh addressed Mark Raizene. "Hey, uh, Sparky," he said.
"Take out a little more five hundred. Five hundred. Just one notch." (Lesh was
asking for a change of equalization—take out a dB or two at 500 Hz.) A voice
yelled off-mic: *Woo!*

The band played for nearly three hours. "Standing, nodding in time, without theater or histrionics, almost waist-deep in monitor speakers," the *International Times* reported. When the Dead returned the following evening for
the second Wembley gig, the place was packed. "The parachutes were all up,
and the sound was beautiful," Weir recalled. Late in set two, before "Dark
Star," feedback whined through the PA. "That there's the Alembic solo," Weir
cracked. But the audience was "really appreciative, enthusiastic, warm," he
remembered. "It really blew my head."

At the next gig, on April 11 at Newcastle City Hall, the Dead played to
a sell-out, 1,500-seat crowd. A *Shields Gazette* reporter "counted 35 speakers

covering the whole of the stage and most of the raised levels at the rear of the stage." But despite the Dead's loudness, "it was powerless." For hours, "this U.S. band stood before dozens of their entourage at the back of the stage and played complacent, uninspired music before a capacity audience." The Dead, the *Gazette* warned, "will lose a lot of friends if they persist in this attitude for the rest of their British tour."

April 13, 1972. The Dead and all their gear were crossing the North Sea by overnight ferry to play three gigs in Denmark. Stepping off in Copenhagen, at the first of two shows at Tivoli Gardens, technical difficulties crept in. After *Workingman's* "Cumberland Blues," about midway through set one, Weir took the mic.

"We have an equipment breakdown," he said. "We're going to fix it shortly and be right with you."

"Bullshit!" shouted a head in the crowd.

"That guy must be from America," Lesh said.

"If we was to get high between songs," Garcia said, in exaggerated beatnik, "isn't that all right?"

"Hell yeah!" the head shouted back.

"Thank ya!" Garcia said. The equipment issue—whatever exactly it was— got resolved. The band dove back in.

Two days later, on April 16, at Stakladen at Aarhus University, the Dead played to around eight hundred people in a low-ceilinged cafeteria. "The center figure is Jerry Garcia, whose guitar playing moves to the outer limits," the *Aarhus Stiftstidende* reported. "The characteristic west coast sound is not absent, but it has matured. Hallucinogens are no longer needed—The Grateful Dead takes nourishment in the realization. All these influences seized the whole hall, and the clarification spread. It was less music than it was close interaction with the audience."

The next day, the Dead returned to Tivoli Gardens to tape a live performance for a national television broadcast. According to Scully's tour journal, the band was about to begin its set but the camera operator couldn't spot the emcee. "Can't find him because he's right behind Garcia's huge amp," Scully wrote. To be seen over the backline, the host stood atop a garbage can he had emptied onto the floor. Steve Parish entered the frame as the band was introduced. On the playback monitor, "all you see is a big fist coming sideways through the screen, *CRUMP!*"

Parish later claimed to have simply pulled the host down. The dumped trash drenched the band's equipment cables in discarded milk, orange juice, and water.

One did *not* disrespect the Dead's sonic space like that, a hardcore mindset as the Wall ascended.

On to the Beat Club in Bremen, Germany, for another television show on April 21. A soundcheck recording that Friday captured the incessant gear problems, hyper-specific mix requests, gentle ribbings, and technical tweaks that marked this push-and-pull moment. Feedback shot through their monitors during "Loser," a track from Garcia's recently released solo record *Garcia*. Adjustments were made, and for the next ten minutes they continued checking the sound, teasing songs, and chattering off-mic. At one point, Lesh gave his own feedback to a crew member: "It sounds like crunchy granola!"

There was a ninety-minute limit on their actual set and no in-studio audience, but bodies had still gathered to watch. "Now that there's all these people around here, you can crank up the monitors," Weir said into the mic during brief banter as final pre-show adjustments were made. "Healy, turn them up a little bit, see if we can get by without a ring, 'cause there's a lot of people standing around."

"Sure ain't ringing too much," Lesh said.

"It sure ain't ringing," Weir replied. "We can get a little more louder."

"Protect yourselves, gentlemen!" Lesh cracked.

"OK, turn it down just a hair," Weir instructed Healy. "OK, that's much better than it's been, leave it."

"You might even run my microphone down a little since I'm well known for shouting," Lesh said.

"This fellow over here hollers," Weir clarified.

"That's 220 cycles a second—closer to 200," Lesh hooted. "Take out two more."

"Don't take too many out, man, that's my range," Garcia chimed in. "Don't try and make it perfect, man. Don't try and cut all the ringing out of it. Just turn it down a little bit overall."

"Actually, it's OK," Weir said. "Let's just play."

"Wait a minute, we gotta fix the organ," Garcia said. "Will you turn on my microphone?"

"If anybody back there ever feels like boogieing, now is the time," Lesh said. "Keith's gonna bring the piano, and it's a really nice piano."

"Turn up the monitors a little," Weir said. "They're not ringing at all."

With that, they were ready. "OK, we're rolling," Garcia said.

The band kicked into "Bertha," an uptempo *Skullfuck* track. They played nine songs over the next hour and a half; only one made it to air.

At the next stop, on April 24, the Dead hit the Rheinhalle in Dusseldorf.

"No reaction, period," Scully journaled. "Baddest gig nightmare ever." But a few heads were taken by the band's sound and influenced by their approach to building the Wall. That included Karlheinz Stockhausen, the electronic composer whom Lesh idolized and who attended the gig with some of his students. "They're the *only* ones that have a clue what the Dead are doing," Scully said.

Elsewhere in the audience that night were members of CAN and Kraftwerk, two of the most influential German bands of all time. The CAN camp was especially captivated by the Dead's mountain of speakers, a picture of which they studied afterward. CAN engineer René Tinner did not attend that show, but later explained that the Dead's rig inspired them to "take up that spirit of having a wall of sound behind the band."

Tinner and CAN scrounged up any loudspeaker they could and mounted them together in a unified backline. Taking a cue from the "as above, so below" principle that continued guiding the Dead and Alembic through the Wall, the Germans similarly stacked a kind of PA atop their backline. "So the arrangement on the stage was more or less...just for the band, and of course the audience, which was close to the stage," Tinner later told the official *Deadcast*. Microcosm, macrocosm—the performers and the audience all heard the same thing. "The band was so relieved at the introduction of this system because there was never any monitor problems anymore," Tinner said. CAN used this setup for the rest of their career. The Wall-like sound system, albeit much smaller in scale, featured prominently on the cover of their *Live in Stuttgart 1975* record.

In the meantime, the Dead arrived in Frankfurt for an April 26 gig at the Jahrhunderthalle. But rolling up to that 4,800-capacity venue, they realized the entrance was too small to bring in the load. "And if we can't get the equipment in, the band can't play," Scully wrote. "Everything has to be taken apart and pulled through sideways. You know, do we put it up on end or do we cut it in half? The crew, needless to say, is not happy." It was a problem that only intensified as the Wall formalized. "Sometimes we had to use the sledgehammer to get the stuff in there," Parish told me. "And it absolutely wasn't making us popular in some places."

European venues posed additional challenges. In Frankfurt, the distance between the loading dock and the stage was the length of a football field. "There was no way to come from the loading dock to the truck with all this stuff," Parish said. "The ramps were not what we should've had, at that time. Steel ramps came a little bit later for us. So we had to use forklifts to load the trucks. You can't use a ramp—there's no room to forklift the stuff in." Facilities like the Jahrhunderthalle "would build these makeshift ramps," and "as soon as we rolled over them, they'd collapse sometimes. That was dangerous shit, man. You don't wanna get killed putting up gear. It could happen."

At the Jahrhunderthalle, Bill Candelario almost ate it. "They had these big trolly carts that were about twelve feet long and three or four feet wide," Healy remembered. "One of these had all of the speaker cabinets on it—thousands of pounds." Candelario stood on the ground between the loading dock and the truck, shuttling stuff, when the cart got away, rolling down before its wheels dropped off the dock end, pinning him between the tailgate and the edge of this cart. "I thought it was going to cut him in half," Healy said. "We ran there, grabbed it, and pulled it away from him, and he just walked away. I thought, 'This is where Kidd gets it.' It was a miracle that he didn't get hurt. I saw a bunch of those."

But once they had all the equipment loaded in and set with levels checked, the Dead knew they were in a superior-sounding space. "Absolutely magnificent," as McIntire recalled of the Jahrhunderthalle, designed by prominent postwar German architects Kraemer and Sieverts. The musicians were affected by "the spectacular acoustics of that hall," McIntire said. As far as he could tell, "they were able to hear themselves better than they normally could. Phil was totally stoked on it because he knew exactly what was happening there."

The in-person sound of the band playing that Wednesday night seemingly could not be contained. The Dead were "faster than a speeding speed freak... more powerful than their 16-track recordings... able to leap tall speakers with a single bound," reported *Stars and Stripes*. "Not only were they turned on, but the audience was turned on and tuned in to their brand of cosmic rock."

April 29, 1972. Uglier reminders of Germany's recent past lurked beneath their next stop, the Musikhalle in Hamburg.

During setup, Leonard needed a microphone "snake," the main power cable. At the time, Leonard would run the snake in, up and over and around, to get Cantor's recording route to the stage, and then brought the lines out to Healy, who handled conversion power. In the Musikhalle's basement, Leonard learned that one of the local stagehands flew in Hitler's Luftwaffe. "These guys would have thrown me right in the oven, Dennis Leonard from the Bronx," he later said. He asked them about the snake and, to his surprise, "they were totally cool."

The gig started slow that Saturday night, but once the Dead slipped into a "Dark Star" that ran thirty minutes, "it turned into musical chaos," *Flash* magazine reported. The crowd "could hardly calm down." By the end of the gig, "the audience stood almost as one on the velvet armchairs and yelled for an encore. But it wasn't until a few minutes later when the light in the hall went on again and the roadies started dismantling the system that you knew that the Dead wouldn't be coming back."

The Dead were on to Paris, for a pair of gigs on May 3 and 4 at the Olympia Theater. "Hallowed ground," Scully said of the two-thousand-plus-capacity venue, built in 1892, "but with insufficient electricity." A cheat sheet, headed EUROPEAN ELECTRICITY, was included in the thirty-some-odd-page informational packets given to touring party members, denoting the variance in volts and cycles by country. Across the continent, Europe is 50 cycles (Hz), whereas the US is 60 cycles (Hz). France, specifically, was 220 volts at 50 cycles (Hz), or 110 volts in more remote areas.

Power was an issue for the Dead through the Wall's end. Many of the venues and buildings they performed in, especially European ones, could not reliably provide enough clean juice for the system. Basically, electricity comes in three phases, with a neutral in the center, and a ground. Typically you want three-phase "Y" power, as Ben Haller, who joined as a lighting tech, told me. At the Olympia, Haller explained, the generator split the rotation into three power-generating sources, only in Paris it's four-phase, five-wire. In other words, it pulled power off in four places in the rotation, and at a slightly lower voltage. "And if it only came off on one point," he said, "the generator would strain and relax, strain and relax."

Haller and Healy grappled with electrical power conversion. "He did it for the sound, I did it for the lights," Haller said. "OK, you get that side, I get this side," the two would say, opening a venue's power box. "We'd work it out— trying to cram sound and lights together." The lights produced an audible hum, due to their carrying a flickering load. "We had to be at least ten feet away at all times with the cables," Haller explained. "You could cross at ninety-degree angles. But Dan and I had to work very carefully together to make sure a lighting cable never got near a sound cable."

The Dead's techs had recently installed transformers in the rig. That way, "we didn't have to have inverters there," Candelario told me, speaking of their backline and the persistent Euro electricity problem. "All you had to do was turn the switch on the transformer to get the right power." That was still "before we had code," Candelario said. None of their amplifiers or electronics carried the third "pin"—it wasn't in the electricity panel. So they drilled a hole into the ground by the panel, pounded in a rod, and connected it to the stage so that none of their people got shocked.

The Wall was grounded. "We started that," Candelario said. "Everywhere we went we ran a ground rod." Years later, Candelario's brother, working for the manufacturer Thule, passed through some of these same venues, and old-time union electricians said, "The Grateful Dead put that in." The rods were still there.

Helping wrangle the "thousands" of cables wiring the Dead's system, co-manager Ron Rakow had a view into this renegade power supply network, an outgrowth of the band having the cord unplugged over the years. "They were all the same length so they were all the longest length," Rakow said of the cables. "They were heavy. And then there was the *very* heavy one."

Because they stopped using venue-supplied electricity "early in the game," Rakow said, Bear had earlier gone and "designed a cable in sections that we could take apart, so that when we rolled 'em there were a whole bunch of small sections." This cable then went down through the building, into the city's electric line. "With a little meter he had, he found out which one was that," Rakow said, of Bear's tapping the municipal grid. "We would put a clamp on that network," reaching through the sheathing, into the little wire that carried the electricity. "*That's* what we played on, because the buildings were not dependable," Rakow told me. "That was the solution. And I had to wind the cable."

Back above ground, behind the backline, sat the Dead's gray A/C distribution block, secretly hooked into the given city's power supply. Marked DANGER: HIGH VOLTAGE and slapped with a Europe '72 tour sticker, this wood-mounted metal panel was the transformer that allowed for easy flips of the switch. Matthews built the unit.

The Dead "became the first band to tie into the main electric panel," Parish later said, speaking of that piece. "This had to be done with high-quality construction and reliability. It also afforded us some control over the authorities shutting down the show if we ran a little overtime. Having our own distro provided all these benefits to us and we used it for the next decade." With "Garcia," "Weir," and "bass" labeled in black marker on their respective breaker switches, the box proved a dependable route of electricity to the Dead's stage amps.

At a given venue, "they either give you an extension cord, which is miserably, hopelessly inadequate, or else you have to learn how to use the power that's in the hall," Healy told me. "We had these big, fat cables that connected directly to the service entrance and came out to the stage, and then it broke into various subpanels and breaker panels and stuff. We had the equivalent, and portable, wiring for, like, a dozen houses," he added. "It became a matter of, *If you wanna have it then you gotta build it and bring it with you because you can't expect to find it somewhere where you go.*"

So despite "insufficient electricity" back at the Olympia in Paris, the band prevailed. "A Dead show is indeed an astonishing musical escalation," *Best* magazine reported. Calling the Dead's appearance there (and in London) a "triumph," may the reviewer "recommend them to you if you really and very simply want to get off"?

Meanwhile, an idealistic male fan hassled the band as they left the Olympia, following them back to their hotel. The youth punished them for not taking a stronger stance in their political consciousness, including access to gigs. Whatever happened, he asked, to playing for free?

May 5, 1972. After the Paris gig, Parish was on a mission.

Earlier that night, they all took LSD. Parish, Ram Rod, Rex Jackson, Joe Winslow, Candelario, and Raizene were left to break down the equipment. Only they were too high, lying on their backs onstage and unable to speak, except for Parish, he later claimed. He rolled up cables and dragged speakers off the scaffolding, over a wet cobblestone walk, and out to the truck, on loop for the next three hours. When the rest of the crew came to, they helped with the remainder of the load. By 3:00 a.m. they were ready to go.

When a show was over, "that's pack-out, everybody leaves," Parish has said. "And you've got to still take the stuff. That's when you've got to keep your dignity." He admitted to doing coke "a few times" after shows, before loading out, "and indeed it did provide an electric rush that made me feel like Superman. It also made me edgy and nervous and even a little bit nauseous. I'd be tossing equipment around, grinding my teeth, sweating."

The crew had an altogether different relationship with the gear than the band. "When you're driving the stuff at night, all the equipment's back there and it's talking to you in a different way than it talks to them when they're playing on stage," Parish said. "It teaches you how to put it, over years—to learn what you can put what way, or it'll break and you won't have it when you need it at a show. You have to come to this place with it, and it tells you that, too."

But in the predawn Parisian darkness, as the road crew left for a rendezvous with the band at their next gig in Lille, near the border with Belgium, the truck seized up. There was something in the fuel tank. Sugar, possibly. Or urine? Water? Soil?

The Dead had been sabotaged. One of the other equipment handlers, who returned to the hotel after the Olympia gig, dumped ice cream from their window, nailing the "French revolutionary type" who was berating the band. As they slept a few hours before leaving for Lille, the kid poured a foreign substance into the gas tank of the Dead's equipment truck and stuck a potato in the exhaust pipe. "The truck breaks down," Scully recalled. "Equipment never leaves Paris."

The band was dismayed. When the time came for the Lille gig, "our gear— amps, guitars, drums, PA—was still several hours behind us in a quickly rented backup vehicle," Lesh said. Garcia "insisted that we do the right thing," Lesh added. The Dead would soon stage an impromptu makeup gig in Lille.

First, they headed *back* to England, catching the last ferry spot after a breakneck LSD-fueled ride across France. A notorious customs agent in Dover then asked to "see something" in the equipment truck: one of Candelario's fake amplifiers holding their weed stash, strategically packed at the very front of the vehicle. "I wanna see this amplifier," the agent said, inspecting the Dead's carnet.

"Sure, no problem," said Raizene, who pulled out that particular McIntosh 3500. There was a fan on the back of the unit. Raizene could see through the vent that the towel shoved inside, containing the drugs, was loose—Clifford Heard had earlier taken some buds and not resecured the contraband. Raizene quickly flipped the amp over and said, "here's the numbers."

"This checks," the agent said.

Raizene shoved the amp back in the case and threw it aside. "What's next?" he asked.

"Alright, boys, thank you very much!" the agent replied. Relieved, they repacked and hit the road.

On May 7, the Dead entered Wigan, for a Sunday appearance at the Bickershaw Festival. It had been cold and wet all weekend. In such conditions, Candelario told me, Garcia would say, "Hey, come here, put your hand on my strings and touch the microphone." Knowing the roadies and techs had done everything properly, Candelario would touch the guitarist's strings and mic—no zaps. "It was like, 'oh, you want *me* to get shocked,'" Candelario said.

But as the Dead hit, the skies brightened. The band played for four and a half hours to fifteen thousand heads. It was still chilly, so much so that "we had those huge Calor gas heaters on stage," Weir told *New Musical Express.* "The smell was getting to us and the heat was actually altering the molecular structure of the strings causing us to go out of tune. I was pleased when they broke down and we were able to play in a naturally frozen condition."

The conditions were bearable thanks to the sound quality. Namely, "the deep rumblings of Phil Lesh's bass chords and Bill Kreutzmann's drumming, the cutting guitar rhythms of Bob Weir, and most dramatically of all, Garcia's superb lead," *Melody Maker* reported. "The weird little phrases he played, with their bell tone and uncertain symmetry. The vital flames of feedback, beautifully controlled." The Dead's had been a "sensational" set, "a worthy antidote to a weekend of mud."

Next up: the Netherlands. An *NRC Handelsblad* review of the sold-out May 10 gig at Amsterdam's Concertgebouw gushed over the state of the San Francisco band's complete audiovisual package. "Although musically the group is somewhat overrated here, in technological terms the Americans completely surpassed all previous pop groups," the review read. "A soundsystem stacked towering high and wall-wide turned out to be excellently tuned to the hall. With flawlessly functioning lighting equipment, even of a king-sized format, the group was sprayed with refinement with bright hues and twilight mists."

Adding to that color was the Concertgebouw's fresh $250,000 gold leaf flake job. Around the hall, gaffer's tape held down the Dead's cables. "Go to fold up cables after show and roll up yards of gold leaf with them," Scully journaled. "Whoops!"

The following day, at Rotterdam Civic Hall, "Dark Star" continued its transit alongside the band's growing system. That was the longest performance of that piece, clocking in that Thursday at 48 minutes, 38 seconds. By 1973, the pace of "Dark Star" further slowed, resulting in the song's "dreamy" period that fall and winter. The track is the "largest scale work in the Dead's repertoire," per *Skeleton Key*, the Deadhead dictionary, and between 1972 and 1974 it took the band far out. Like the Wall through which that song's soundwaves beamed, "it sometimes reaches truly monumental proportions."

The crew then experienced another close shave in Belgium, en route to the Lille makeup gig. Border agents asked them to open the back of one of the trucks. An official consulted the carnet and requested to see a certain item, Candelario recalled. "They looked at us like it was *our* job. And I said, 'No, it's your job, you're the customs agents. You wanna see something you're gonna have to get in there and find it.'" Besides, Candelario told me, "there was no way they were ever gonna find anything I had stashed in the gear."

By the time the Dead pulled into the Lille Fairgrounds on Saturday, May 13, no one suspected anything. "This was before social media, so it was 'catch us if you can,'" Kreutzmann recalled. It was cold and overcast. The stage was exposed but for the scaffolding tarps covering the left and right speaker arrays. The tie-dye fronts Courtenay Pollock produced back home—now wearing a hazmat suit and no longer sweating turquoise—popped against the sky. "There was a little bit of rain but it was certainly psychedelic," Kreutzmann said.

Three more stops to go. On May 16, the Dead played Radio Luxembourg. Their performance got broadcast at a million and a half watts to roughly sixty million listeners, according to the event organizer. The station's theater had only 350 seats, and a brief scuffle broke out between security and fans who were unable to get inside.

"On a colorful stage and in front of a surprisingly not even fully occupied hall, about two dozen community members of the Grateful Dead sat down next to the musicians and their instruments and amplifiers," the *Luxemburger Wort* reported. As the band performed, "Garcia often let a very delicate lead guitar be heard, but the sometimes too loud volume of the whole group shouldn't be able to excite us beyond measure." The tens of millions of at-home listeners "were given a far better sound quality than those present in the hall."

Matthews did some quick math. Totaling the watts of power the Dead were working with, he estimated that the band's performance "was the single largest radio transmission of a single source ever," as Scully claimed, perhaps somewhat dubiously.

On to Munich. That's where it all went black.

May 18, 1972. Munich Fire Department inspectors hassled the Dead crew as they assembled the soundsystem at the Kongressaal Deutsches Museum.

According to the head inspector, the transformers in the Dead's amplifiers did not meet the Munich Fire Code, Scully recalled. "At first, we patiently attempt to explain that our amps aren't listed in their book because they'd been *custom-made for us*," he journaled. "They can't believe that these unshorn guys in Harley T-shirts can possibly know what they're doing." The marshals ultimately could not lodge "any legitimate objection to our equipment."

But they claimed that a rig of the Dead's magnitude *could* still pose a fire hazard. So they doubled their crew, Scully recalled, from forty to eighty firefighters. At least one got stationed outside each dressing room. Typically only band, crew, and family were permitted behind the Dead's amp line, and yet a half dozen more fire brigadiers posted in that zone, "an unflinching phalanx of gloom," Scully said. Another half dozen stood beside the mixing board. "And each Fire Troll, I'm not kidding, has his own bucket of sand. And should there *be* a fire, they're going to *dump these buckets of sand on our sound equipment,* the great multimillion-dollar electronic Pyramid of the Dead."

Meanwhile, the band, crew, and most everyone else in the Dead's entourage were coming up on LSD. At the hotel earlier that day, "who shows up," Scully wrote, "but the most infamous Haight-Ashbury smuggler of them all: Ken Connell." Goldfinger had escaped the "dire" Hanja prison in Athens, Greece, so the Dead were skittish about his presence, considering the warrants out on him in a dozen countries. Traveling on a German passport, he arrived toting a big suitcase. Anything inside this "medicine chest" was yours under one condition: You had to first take a hit of acid.

Goldfinger then had an idea. The Pleasure Crew fixture bought ten cases of Bavarian brew, and dosed the firefighters en masse at the venue. Later that evening, just before the gig had ended, the lights went out. One of the dosed firemen had reportedly flipped over Garcia "smoking a huge, fat, badly rolled hash joint, which is coming apart and spilling burning chunks of tobacco and hash onto the stage," Scully wrote. On top of Garcia's amplifier were a second joint and a pair of cigarettes, all lit. "Smoke is curling up into the kleig [*sic*] lights, ashes are cascading off the amp, and the amp itself is slowly simmering away," Scully said. So the firefighter heaved one bucket of water—not sand—over Garcia, and a second at his amp. "Everything stops, the whole place goes pitch-black. The audience begins flicking lighters and lighting matches, which, of course, drives the fucking firemen even more bonkers! And that was it, no more juice. Luckily, the band had played a couple of hours by then so it doesn't, thank God, develop into a riot."

There was, however, "one more little glitch," Scully added. The Dead's transformers might have had shut-off circuits, but the resulting surge of electricity "is so massive it backs up into the municipal power system, and we end up blacking out half of Munich that night."

Scully's tales and sometimes fuzzy chronologies need always be taken with skepticism. Other Europe '72 party members could not specifically recall, but didn't rule out, the "Munich blackout"—again, memory banks are variously charred and full of holes. Haller, the lighting tech, does remember that gig "turning into a stink." He claimed to have padlocked the electric panel late in the show because unfriendly venue staff "were trying to kill the power," he told me. They didn't have bolt cutters and couldn't remove the lock. Things were tense for a moment, but the concert went on. "I don't remember the power going out," Haller said.

But at least one individual later corroborated much of what Scully wrote in his journals. "Garcia pulled out a big fat spliff, lit it, had a wonderful toke, then carefully placed it on top of his amplifier," Sam Cutler said of that Munich stop. "The fire marshal totally lost his cool and before anyone could stop him grabbed a bucket of water and dumped it over the amp. Half of Munich was plunged immediately into darkness." Transformers could be heard popping across the city's electrical grid that night, Cutler claimed.

Days later, the Dead returned to London to conclude the tour with a four-show run at the Lyceum Strand. "Although the first set was somewhat repetitious, the high points were still very high," read a *London Times* review of the first gig, on May 23. The Dead "confirmed their unique status...and they play it through a superb soundsystem designed to their own specification in San Francisco."

They were peaking. "As the music floated over in waves from the front of the stage and percolated into the crowded, labyrinthine maze of corridors and iron balustrades," *Sounds* magazine reported, the crowd "sat there gripped with wonderment that a band should fill the whole of the hall, not just with its music, but with its very presence." Yet the intensity of the Dead's sound was not ruled by volume. "There are whole areas of space which are implied rather than hammered out," *Sounds* noted.

Not everyone was so taken. At the final Lyceum show, the last night of the European run, Cutler got his mom into the gig, seating her next to Matthews in the mixing box. After the Dead's first set she "berated the musicians for playing music that was loud enough to be life-threatening," Cutler recalled. Then she demanded to be taken back to her residence.

The Dead headed home too.

Back in the Bay Area, the band was stoked that Bear was being released from prison and "coming back to join the sound team," Lesh said.

Bear was discharged that July, after completing two years of a three-year sentence. Out on probation, he had already relinked with the Dead by the time they arrived at the Berkeley Community Theater on August 21, on the first of a four-night run at that 3,500-seat venue. "The Dead can come down to a whisper and still keep it moving," *Rolling Stone* reported. "That they make it appear to be so effortless is a tribute to their ability"—and to a rapidly refining soundsystem indebted to Bear's initial acid-enhanced visions.

His return resonated with Lesh. The bassist experienced sound through a similar kind of synesthesia as Bear's, seeing music "as notes on spaces, sometimes colored, paisley, sometimes fragmented, and sometimes whirling notes and treble clefs with little feet running around them." But Bear's latest reentry would not be as seamless or unobstructed as in the past. "With Bear's return, we had three really strong skill sets working together," Lesh said. "Matthews/Betty mixing the real-time house sound; Healy the supremo hands-on troubleshooter and acoustical analyst; and Bear the wild-eyed radical visionary idea man." The problem was, "each of them wanted some of the other's turf." Healy, a bespectacled and fast-talking audio geek who "had sworn to upgrade the soundsystem ASAP," and Bear, notably, both wanted to mix in real time.

"Unlike Bear, who did not have the crew's confidence, and Matthews, who was easily distracted," Dennis McNally wrote in his Dead biography, "Healy was an effective leader, able to take some of Bear's inspirations, as run through the design minds at Alembic, and make them work on the road." Healy's insistence on quality seeped into the very buildings the band operated in, and he and Ron Wickersham were soon creating renderings of structural designs and plotting room acoustics.

"Before a tour," Healy told me, "I would spend *days* doing architectural drawings and drawings about how to set the scaffolding up. How to configure it so that the speakers would be set properly so that no matter where you were, if it was an old theater and you were in the balcony, you heard just as good as if you were downstairs." He and the Dead's techs shared that information with hall and arena staff, like at the Civic Center in Springfield, Massachusetts, where the band performed that October. The drawings greatly improved the acoustics of that space.

The touring Dead's social work structure had morphed into something unrecognizable to Bear. To him, developing, schlepping, setting up, and tearing down the soundsystem had become "isolated." All tasks, save sound mixing, used to be shared among the crew—at least that's how Bear saw things. But Matthews had established distinct and separate roles that Bear, whose laser-like single vision was a strength and a flaw, later described as "compartmentalized."

When the band didn't put him in charge of the sound crew, after he asked to be reinstated in that position, Bear claimed he was relegated to a parcel of his prior domain. As if to say, "here's a piece of your job back, just a taste—now stand over there," he recalled. Each crew member, in fact, was now "fiercely defending his little territory," Bear said. "There was no 'I can do this, you can do this, you can do that, and we can switch around' kind of thing. No, it was 'This is mine, this is yours, this is mine.'" The scene had been "an almost tribal thing of everybody sharing in all the work and all of the obligations, and helping each other like a bunch of brothers." But then "all of a sudden I came back and it was like the union and the management."

The road and sound teams now performed their discrete functions as the Dead were onstage. Acceptance was "by far the single most difficult thing for Bear," Robert Greenfield wrote in his biography. That was still an "exciting" time, Bear later admitted, "although I was having some problems with the crew, many of whom had come to work after I had gone, and resented my efforts to improve things on stage and with the equipment." The attending problems, "of getting those who did my job while I was away to back off and allow me to return to my work, eventually inspired me to design the Wall of Sound." Yet "these hassles did not interfere with my ability to mix, and the band played some fine shows during this period."

In the meantime, alcohol and cocaine sharpened the perceived conflicts and tensions among the group. And this at times toxic, misogynistic, and physically intimidating working environment only heightened around the growing Wall, which supported subterranean break rooms built into the scaffolding, below the stage of the seventy-five-ton PA. That's where band, crew, and family could all get polluted.

"The Dead stage has a maze of hallways underneath it, an incredible nether-world of cables covered with rubber padding so that you don't trip over them," Scully later said. "The only way out to the audience is usually from under the stage." Other areas were "like little clubhouses you can go down into. Nitrous oxide isn't allowed on the stage, but no one said anything about *under* it. When the band isn't playing, you can hear the gas running and the people laughing down there."

Some of the resulting behavior, were it to occur today, would be scandalous. But back then, it was just part of the trip, not that that makes it any worthier of tolerating. That included how much people got paid. Before tours, Brightman and Haller, who told me he regularly scouted venues, went to the bank for advance money in the form of prepaid credit cards. "She got a three-thousand-dollar Visa and I got a ten-thousand-dollar one," Haller said. "And she's my boss."

Contempt for women also colored who got the glory and for what. "It never mattered to me to get credit until other people take credit from my work," Cantor told me. To this day, she has not earned a cent from her recordings of the band's performances that have since made the Dead organization serious money. Cantor's reels are still being released, most recently under the *Dave's Picks* series; taking its name from Dead archivist Dave Lemieux, the series succeeds *Dick's Picks*, the beloved and long-running line of vault releases helmed by the original archivist, the late Dick Latvala. "You can't just be assertive without being a bitch when you're a female," Cantor said. "I think guys are just as much bitches as girls, as far as that goes."

The band largely allowed this culture of abusive behavior and unfair working conditions to fester by never fully policing their entourage. "That was one of our big downfalls, not taking a stand with the crew," Mickey Hart later said. Co-manager Danny Rifkin and crew chief Ram Rod were "the great spirit of the Grateful Dead, the real souls," Hart said, "but some of the other guys have other agendas." The drummer got along with Heard, and even with Candelario, "before he turned into a monster... Me me me. He wouldn't step outside of his area code to help."

The diminutive Bear, for his part, struggled to reintegrate into this chillier and siloed scene, especially after losing a lot of his sense of humor behind bars. Candelario later told journalist David Browne, author of *So Many Roads: The Life and Times of the Grateful Dead*, that Bear "would get these brilliant ideas, but the road was not necessarily the place to make that happen or test that out." Bear had taught Candelario so much about audio and the pursuit of better sound, "but we were more mechanized and more uniform when he came back out, and it was hard for him."

Here was somebody who seemingly was always watching and voicing his beliefs. Furman remembered being at the Alembic shop one day after Bear's return, "working away on some project, and I'd realize he was standing right behind me, looking over my shoulder," she told me. "If I did anything that was, to him, questionable he would call me on it. He was very opinionated about everything. He had loads of great ideas and I had all the respect in the world for him. But he was sort of this omnipresent person. I kind of felt like he was breathing down my neck sometimes."

Bear himself was under close watch. Years later, Susan Wickersham recalled how the feds staked out Alembic's shop, then at 60 Brady Street in San Francisco. Her upstairs office provided a view of the lot where company personnel parked, and "for a couple weeks there was this tan Grenada with government plates sitting in the parking lot with a couple guys in suits," she explained. "They sat there all day long watching the building," inside which the Dead's sonic tinkerers passed afternoon joints and constructed the million-plus-dollar hi-fidelity analog Wall. One day, Alembic's receptionist called to Susan: Two FBI agents were there and wanted to speak with her. They came upstairs and introduced themselves.

"Do you know an Augustus Owsley Stanley III?" they asked.

"Bear, yes," Susan said.

"Do you know his whereabouts?"

"He's doing the studio later today," she explained. "He works here on an album." (At the time, he was editing *Bear's Choice*, a soon-to-be-released live record featuring tracks recorded in early 1970 at the Fillmore East.) Just then, Susan got a phone call; it was Bear. "Are they there?" he asked.

"Yeah, we've got two hours—we can book some time for you," she said into the receiver. They'd already worked out the coded speech. The agents had no idea.

"They're looking for me," Bear said, hanging up.

The agents handed Susan their cards and said to be in contact if she heard from Bear. They spent the next few days stationed in the lot. "It was a weird time," she said.

Aside from his reputation in the LSD underground, and the constant surveillance that came with it, Bear's contributions to the Dead's sound game were already consequential, despite his now diminished role. He claimed the Dead, under his guidance, were the first to institute onstage monitors. If the Dead weren't technically *the* first—Blue Cheer was—then they were definitely early developers and adopters of that technology.

At Alembic's shop, moreover, Bear and Wickersham developed the concept of "noising" a venue, which they then field tested before gigs with Healy's help. There was often a thirty-to-forty-minute window after the system was assembled and wired up, wherein the arenas the Dead increasingly filled would be awash in a roaring hiss, like a heavy rainfall or wind: white noise, the sound of a particular frequency, projected through the PA. (Pink noise, also used in these sessions, is white noise with reduced high frequencies; pink has a lower pitch than white.) Then a cutting-edge B&K harmonic analyzer evaluated the noise, showing on a computer screen those frequencies that bounced, lingered, or dispersed, so that the band's techs could adjust levels, speaker positionings, and venue treatments accordingly.

The ideal result? A harmonically *flat* room, an acoustically balanced blank slate. The profile of an empty hall is much different from one containing thousands of bodies, of course, but noising gave the Dead's techs, and generations of sound mixers to come, a solid baseline to work from.

Such breakthroughs left an indelible mark on the live concert and sound reinforcement industry. Noising tools, in particular, "led to the use of sound-deadening material (stage curtains and the like) in many of the arenas we were now playing," Lesh said, "while the concept itself spread out, to other bands and sound companies, and was continually being refined and upgraded by all." Decades on, "every self-respecting sound company has a completely computerized multichannel audio analysis system as an everyday component of its PA."

Money and resources for high-tech acoustical gadgetry had continued pouring in while Bear was away. In the band's naivete, they thought they could take control of every aspect of their collective trip "without falling prey to the infighting and dissension that comes with the territory," Lesh said. Yet by following their group intuition, they found a way through the noise to reach an unlikely sort of signal.

Cutler played a particularly huge role for such a nontraditional outfit. That May, Cutler founded Out of Town Tours, essentially an in-house booking agency that counted the Dead and adjacent acts on its roster. Out of Town occupied an office a few doors down from the band's Fifth and Lincoln space in San Rafael, where Cutler created "an alternative power base to the band itself [that] would, in the end, spell disaster for him," McNally wrote in his Dead history. But Cutler's "aggressive improvement of their money-making ability over the previous two and next two years would make some dreams possible."

While some were rising in this game of jockeying inside Deadworld, other long-standing figures were falling. That June 17, the Dead played at the Hollywood Bowl in Los Angeles. Pigpen could never quite keep up with the band's increasingly improvisational jamming, though his presence was noticeably diminished that Saturday. He did not sing, played congas on only a few tunes, and his occasional organ parts were quiet in the mix. A *Los Angeles Herald-Examiner* review noted the spaced-out sonics and exploratory playing that found Pig, a bluesman, out of step. During a second set jam, the band "pushed the piece into a writhing vortex of atonality. After their trip into the whirlpool of sound they pulled themselves back out again."

All but one.

As summer 1972 rolled along, the band—sans Pig, who stayed home—made an East Coast run.

The stops were getting bigger, from four-thousand-seat theaters to small stadiums. Yet the Dead were still not averaging $5,000 per show, while employing almost two dozen individuals and operating with a monthly overhead soon pushing $100,000, or close to $740,000 today. At clubs like Bill Graham's old Fillmore East, the Dead had "become a stable, economically functioning band," McNally said. But now promoter John Scher booked them in the region. With his help, they were destined to become a colossal act at Roosevelt Stadium.

That's the decrepit twenty-four-thousand-capacity former ballpark in Jersey City, New Jersey, where the band played on July 18. "Seated well to the front and side, so that one bank of tie-dyed amplifiers half-hid Jerry Garcia," were music critic Robert Christgau and a friend, who "felt so wasted" a half hour into the second set they moved back. "For a while we sat far from the stage in the lower grandstand, and discovered an unsuspected peace there," Christgau reported. "We missed Pigpen and his blues, though."

Back on the West Coast, at an outdoor show in front of twenty thousand Deadheads in Veneta, Oregon, on August 27, a film crew captured the band's performance. The Veneta tapes were later released as the live concert film *Sunshine Daydream* (2013). The visuals featured behind-the-scenes action shots of the Alembic crew, roadies, and various management personnel, eventually making for a "Who's Who" montage. The implication was that these folks were indispensable, as evidenced by a time-lapse of them building the rig, Pollock's dyes caught in spectacular moving color. For that event, the band's techs and the film crew devised a novel approach to time syncing using an onstage master clock. "That was an early sound thing," Ron Wickersham told me.

The gig itself that hot afternoon—triple-digit temperatures had their instruments going out of tune—was an instant classic, exemplary of the year 1972 being a "sweet spot" in the band's trajectory. "In short, this is peak era Good Ol' Grateful Dead," read a retrospective piece on the performance in Veneta published decades later in *Aquarium Drunkard*, the respected online music magazine.

But on September 3, at a gig at Folsom Field at the University of Colorado at Boulder, storm clouds gathered as the Dead took the stage. Balls of lightning crackled around the sound equipment. "But the band went right on playing while standing in two inches of water," John Perry Barlow, a childhood friend of Weir's who joined as another Dead lyricist, later recalled. Somehow, "nobody got electrocuted." The Dead's supposed ability to "control" or alter the weather truly became the stuff of lore. "After hours of rain," McNally reported, "one shaft of light appeared from the black clouds, and within a few moments the entire cloud cover peeled back like magic."

Two weeks later, on September 15, the Dead hit the Boston Music Hall. The sold-out gig started an hour and a half late due to equipment setup delays, the *Boston Globe* reported. As it turned out, the Dead's trucks got held up en route to Massachusetts. Rakow, fearing a riot, phoned Senator Ted Kennedy, who transferred him to then governor William Weld. Weld dispatched a dozen police cars, sirens blaring, to escort the Dead's load down the highway.

But with high highs came low lows—and Bear time. At another gig that fall, at which Matthews failed to show, Bear recruited some college-aged kids to help load out the mixing gear. They supposedly absconded with half the band's system, Bear later recalled, while the mixing board ended up in a nearby dorm room. Arriving at the next town, the crew got word and, realizing they had no PA, blamed Bear.

Bear regarded himself as a central Dead figure, almost a member of the band. But the crew no longer deferred to him as such, if they ever fully did. (As Candelario told me, "Owsley likes to think he invented everything.") So one of the roadies picked up Bear and threw him across the room, into a water cooler. It is unclear who that was—Raizene told me he collared Bear a few times, but could not recall this particular instance. Bear was rattled. "These are my tools, and it's my job, and you're accusing me of messing everything up? I didn't steal it," Bear said. "The problem now is to make this show happen, not to blame me, physically."

By the Dead's show on September 21 at the eighteen-thousand-capacity Philadelphia Spectrum, Godchaux's rig was glitching. The piano system was a component of the Wall that Bear obsessed over. Before "Black-Throated Wind," another song from Weir's *Ace*, Weir addressed the crowd. "Courtesy of our wizard-like piano amplification system," he said. "There you have it. That was a good one."

Later that month, the Dead played a free outdoor concert at American University in Washington, DC, and met head-on audio weirdness of a different sort. Thirty or forty yards out from the stage was a campus radio station tower, and apparently when Garcia plugged into his amplifier, the sound of the radio station boomed "loud and clear," Scher, the promoter, later recalled. "It sort of freaked everybody out. They made a sort of announcement, 'we've got some technical difficulties.'" After half an hour, Ram Rod figured out how to prevent the radio waves coming from Garcia's amp.

The gig must always go on.

October 1, 1972. The Dead had the night off. Bear and Garcia caught Black soul-jazz singer Roberta Flack's gig in a six-thousand-seat ice rink in Massachusetts. They wanted to check out the new house PA of one Dinky Dawson, founder of Dawson Audio Services and former soundman for Fleetwood Mac, for whom he'd been building a custom system.

Bear and Garcia "were transformed by the concert, my soundsystem reproducing Flack's music with such clarity and crispness, even in the potentially overwhelming space," Dawson wrote in his memoir *Life on the Road*. During a cello solo, "Garcia's mouth hung agape, until he was distracted when some of the ice that was under the floor of four-by-eight plywood sheets behind us made a sharp cracking sound."

"What was that?" asked Bear. "Have you figured out how to project sound behind us too?!"

"One of these days we'll get to quad," Dawson laughed, "but right now I've got to be content with what I've got."

"I'll tell you what you've got," said Garcia. "You just cracked ice with a cello solo!"

Bear asked Dawson how he'd done that.

"It's no secret," Dawson replied. "If you use the right speakers in the right boxes, you will have the same results."

In that moment, Dawson claimed, Bear made a fateful decision. "He would build a system for the Grateful Dead that was based around my principle," Dawson said. Over the next couple of months, Bear and Healy regularly checked in "to ask questions as their own construction began on a system that they eventually called 'The Wall of Sound.'" Yet the pair "discounted a critical piece of my advice," Dawson said. That was to avoid relying upon standard PA speakers, "and instead utilize either home equipment or self-designed gear like mine."

The end result, according to Dawson, was that the Wall "always sounded heavy, and devoid of the smooth warmth that purred through my speakers."

That cost the Dead, Dawson added, "as constant adjustments and overhauls of the speaker system nearly bankrupted the band." Yet "The 'Wall of Sound' still outperformed any other system on the road at that time (except for mine, of course!)." The Dead "deserves major credit as a leader in the field of concert sound reproduction and high marks for attempting to give their fans a much better concert experience."

But first, the Dead's project had to scale. "They wanted to play bigger and bigger shows," Bear said. They asked him, "'What can we do? Do something.' I was the guy who started rock and roll sound," Bear boasted, "and I said, 'You can build something big, but you may not like it. It will take a lot of design work.' But they were game and they went for it."

Dave Parker, the band's financial manager, was on the inside of these scalings. By 1972, the Dead were debt free and, for the moment, "things were going okay," Parker said. Now the band "wanted to develop the soundsystem, and an enormous amount of money went into that," he explained. Back then, "the state-of-the-art hadn't developed to the point where you would have good sound in arenas and stadiums. They wanted to play smaller places, but it was tough to make any money doing that because their travel expenses were so high."

Bear "helped inspire them to what could be done," Parker added. "There was a sense of going for the best." They could have all taken bigger checks, but instead spent hundreds of thousands of dollars on equipment. "It was driving me nuts, because Bear was very good on the conceptual, but I thought a lot of money was being wasted," Parker said. He and Bear were sometimes at odds, "because he'd have a vision of some fantastic thing he'd want to do—'Replace all this!'—and I was trying to deal with the resources that were actually available."

Meanwhile, Wickersham gathered an informal PA "consulting committee" in late 1972. "A lot of that was very distasteful, engineering wise," he later told me. "Arguing with financing. It wasn't technical at all. So other people participated in all that. But that let me concentrate on the pure goals. Owsley was in and out of favor, especially with some of the people on the crew. They didn't want him around."

The all-male committee included Wickersham, Bear, Healy, Turner, Raizene, Cutler, and John Curl, who held an office at Alembic's shop. "We tried to break it all down and address every area we could, because it wasn't like there was a single thing wrong with the instruments, microphones, or recording gear, the live PA, and all that," Wickersham has said. And while there were some "eureka" moments, "you kind of had them because you were contributing to the group."

At issue, Wickersham added, "was that live music's dynamic range is so much greater than what you get from recorded music." To achieve the dynamics of a live symphony orchestra, or a rock and roll concert, "you have to approach it differently than the way it was being done at the time." And to play a system "really loud," the Dead's early '70s sound team learned, "you can't mix the stuff together and have it intermodulate. This destroys the clarity," said Wicker-sham.

As they got in with folks like Curl and John Meyer, another Dead-adjacent audio engineer involved in the band's various systems, they had to scrap all they knew and begin again. "Garcia understood that," Healy said. "And we proposed to build the Wall of Sound, which was to be an experimental lab." They called it a breadboard, "lifted from an old phrase from making experimental radios," Healy said. "The object was it could be configured in any conceivable way—so we broke it all down into individual pieces and then when you went to play a show we could configure it in any fashion that we wanted." Dovetailing with that "was for the first time ever designing the soundsystem to match the venue you're in."

Healy further claimed that by this time they "bottomed out all the research" done beginning in the 1920s at Bell Laboratories. That's the New Jersey–based industrial and scientific research company behind many sonic standards, including vacuum tube advancements and the development of the transistor, the digitization of sound, and the invention of the decibel, the logarithmic unit of sound measurement. The Dead's sound people even approached the JBLs and Altecs of the early 1970s, asking if the companies wanted to get involved in their project. But the manufacturers, already selling existing products faster than they could make them, apparently told them to get lost.

A "whole renaissance" in sound started around 1970, according to Healy, and by 1974 the Wall, a system for which many individuals took credit, was fully up and running. "It was a fantastic, incredible scene, and anybody who ever had a chance to witness it, that's a once in a lifetime event," he said. The Wall "proved beyond any shadow of a doubt that it was time to go forward and time to adopt new ideas, and time to stop holding onto the history and get with the new stuff." But as they stared down 1973, the Dead's PA stacks were too short.

When Meyer, another fast-talking audio geek in glasses, first got to know the Dead, Bear told him about their complications with the speaker columns. No matter what they did, Bear said, they were unable to get the music to the balconies.

"I know," Meyer told him, "because they're not tall enough."

"What do you mean?" Bear asked.

Meyer began walking Bear, and the rest of the crew and band, through the acoustical engineering concepts undergirding what the Dead were expressing in their pursuit of the best sound imaginable.

"This is mathematically known, what you guys are doing," Meyer told them. "You're not really researching something that's never been done. You're implementing it in a much bigger way than the theory; I mean, no one has really implemented this." They would "either have to build columns all the way to the ceiling or we'll have to curve it." That ultimately informed the Wall's piano and vocal clusters, "curved arrays with lots and lots of drivers on them to kind of get a wider dispersion," Meyer told me. Curved speakers were a first in the music world, and the Dead were at the forefront.

There was something of a handbook for many of these core principles. RCA and Princeton University inventor and engineer Harry F. Olson's *Acoustical Engineering* (1957), then out of print, was considered a foundational text in the fundamentals and practical applications of modern acoustic science. Meyer had a copy from a previous job in hi-fi stereos. The Dead learned of the text and asked about procuring a copy.

"This is all calculus and differential equations—it's not an easy read," Meyer said. "Unless you guys have the math, it's not gonna be much good." But he didn't mind sharing the text. "I just gave them my book and they made copies of it." As Turner, who made significant contributions to calculating ideal dimensions—based on the cube root of two, at ⅓ octave—for Wall cabinets with "smooth" response and no "internal reflection," told me: "We each had Harry Olson's bible."

Effortless. The sound they were after "didn't hurt your ears," Curl, who occasionally joined the band at shows, helping set up and tear down the system, told me. "It was *really* loud, because most of the energy was up in the bass region," yet "we didn't add a whole lot of extra distortion because the drivers were overloaded or stressed." They clocked onstage sound levels at 120 dB, about as loud as a jet engine, though "it wasn't harming your ears, comparatively speaking. It was just loud music. We always thought that loud sound was not such a bad thing—it just was when it wasn't *clean.*"

The Wall was "kind of like a big hi-fi," Curl said. At the time, he didn't know if it was doable, practically speaking, on the scale the Dead hoped to achieve. He just told them, "You want it done? OK, we'll do it." And they did, "and we made it work," Curl told me. He, too, noted how reluctant JBL, in particular, was to receive any of the Dead's technical knowledge and feedback. They hoped to share insights with the audio manufacturer in the interest of advancing the state of the art. But when confronted with problems, JBL "asked me what rock did I come from under," Curl said. "They did not like me telling them what's wrong with their speakers and what could be fixed."

So the Dead's techs "just replaced the horns," Curl said. That's how the top of the Wall's curved centerpiece, specifically the dozens of 5-inch cones comprising the "highs" of the suspended honeycomb vocal cluster, came in. "We found that if we used enough of them in parallel we could emulate a whole body of horns," Curl explained. All the 5-inchers carried the same signal, and the "side guys" would push against their neighbors, coupling the individual speaker drivers, which increased directivity and overall efficiency. "We were getting something for almost nothing by using a whole array of these," Curl said. "That's one of the main things the Wall of Sound changed to."

The Dead started using Electro-Voice tweeters, a brand of high-frequency loudspeaker, that extended "the highs" out to 20,000 Hz, the theoretical limit of "perfect" human hearing. "It was effortless and very, very low distortion," Curl said. At the time, JBL made a similar product but it had too much distortion, so the Dead's techs decided against using it. "We switched from all JBL to put the Electro-Voice tweeters on top."

They still needed more cabinets to properly stand up their new and improved PA. *Lots* more cabinets.

Everybody had an idea about how to do this.

"It was a collective kind of a movement," said Richie Pechner, now cutting wood at a heightened clip at the San Rafael shop. But from a technical standpoint, if Alembic said to do something, it got done. Turner and Wickersham, particularly, "had the expertise to kind of vet some of this stuff," Pechner said. "Once it was decided, we had carte blanche to put it together. Of course, from the band's point of view they wanted it finished before tour. There were a lot of long days, late nights, cranking out the cabinets."

So many long days and late nights, that compensating Pechner, among the Dead crew paid hourly in cash, was soon discussed internally. Handwritten minutes from an upcoming "tech meeting" included agenda item "Richie's pay," regarding "work to be done on cabinets. Salary?" That ultimately was decided in Pechner's favor. Healy advocated for him.

This got down to the 14-ply Finnish birch that Pechner and other crew acquired to make the PA. An ex-con who worked on high-pressure cement forms, including the Bay Bridge, apparently hipped the Dead to the material. "There were all kinds of people around, contributing stuff, that was what worked pretty great," Wickersham said. "The goal was to get the sound really good... so any ideas got listened to and tried."

The laminated birch variety, available from importers like MacBeath Hardwood in Berkeley, was steel-strong but significantly lighter. The wood could also be cut using a consumer-grade SKIL saw. The ex-con reportedly mentioned this to someone affiliated with the band, "and wham bam, we got a bunch of birch and we're makin' cabinets out of it," Haller, who claimed to be privy to that decision making, told me. Though he couldn't recall that individual's name, Haller said that somebody within the Dead's sound crew "confessed that's where they got the idea." Haller's Uni-saw, recently acquired at a local trade show, got installed, among other tools, at the Dead's workshop. (The Dead reimbursed him the $800 he paid out of pocket.) His saw, along with one owned by Candelario, was used to cut the birch into hundreds of cabinet sides and speaker fronts. They soon also purchased a Rockwell Uni-shaper to do the mortise cuts to hold the pieces together.

For stress testing boxes, "we actually took a first couple and went out in the parking lot and we'd see how high we could throw them in the air," Haller said. "When they'd crash down most of them survived really well. It redefined how we built them."

The material is truly durable, as the structural soundness of my artifact attests. "You knock on it and it's *hard*, you know it's not soft wood," Curl said. "Moving, loading, unloading, dropping, it survives all that." Fourteen-ply was about as thick as you could get for birch back then, which made the material all the more attractive because the Dead "were hoping to get the walls so strong that the resonances of the cabinets would be minimized," Curl added. "They were heavy but they were practical because they were rugged, and they would stack well."

Around that time, JBL cones became refurbishable. Now, when things got damaged "we could actually repair our own speakers," Curl said. Candelario and Raizene, among other roadies, used to do a lot of this manufacturing and restoration work. Curl remembers the powerful glue scent permeating

Alembic's multilevel shop: "You could smell them getting high, probably, on the fumes."

The soundsystem itself still typically resided in two arrays, at stage left and right, and at center stood the band and their amplifiers. But the Dead began adding more speakers to center stage, for both monitoring and other instruments. Bear, Wickersham, and Curl soon also added a second dual-dynamic mic to the vocal setup, followed by a third dual-condenser version. This last piece enabled them to stack all the onstage PA speakers atop the guitar amps and monitors at the band's back and not be bombarded with feedback.

"That is all the Wall of Sound is," Mike Wald, who is reverse engineering (MWOnline) Garcia's tone, has said. "A PA system stacked on top of and behind the band, serving as both the band's monitors and audience's PA system." Any amplifiers visible onstage were either for each individual player's amp monitor or that of another instrument, such that the volume controls were at their fingertips. The remainder of the PA speakers were powered by behind-the-stage amps "monitored and controlled" by Alembic hands.

The Dead now fully used McIntosh power, another significant leveling up of their rig. They bought dozens of 2300s through the end of the Wall, fanning out to area suppliers, as the amps were still hard to find. The audiophile, rather than commercial, sound gear was both low distortion and roadworthy.

"One time I had ten amps showing up into San Francisco," Raizene told me. He can't recall to which supplier the Macs got shipped, but "Bonnie Parker was with me and I had thirty grand in my socks, in my boots, because you either had to pay cash or certified check. I didn't know how much this was gonna be, and I didn't know how much was gonna show up." At the loading dock, Raizene began moving the hundred-plus-pound amps into the equipment van.

"You got a certified check?" the salesperson asked.

"Cash," Raizene said.

The rep brought Raizene and Parker into his windowed warehouse office. Workers on forklifts puttered by, gawking at the Dead roadie counting out the bills. "Holy shit!" the rep remarked. "What do I do with thirty fuckin' grand?"

"No problem," Raizene said. "I'll take the money and the amps and bring ya a check tomorrow."

Some of those solid-state amplifiers, distributed throughout the system, were nicknamed: Loretta, Laura, Louanne, Maggie, Maui, Mona, and "Low Blow," tagged in black marker below each unit's glowing blue output meter.

These are "the potent 300-watt transistor amps that soon become the backbone of the Dead's system," Blair Jackson wrote in his gear overview.

One of the Dead's first 2300s helped power the Wall's midrange vocals. A circular red notice slapped on the amp's side served as a motto for the Dead's sonic flight-taking: JET FUEL ONLY. Another Wall-era 2300 was Garcia's "Budman," named after the Budweiser sticker Ram Rod placed on its front panel. As Parish explained, Healy had "figured out how to take a line out from Jerry's guitar amp, first into a McIntosh 350 tube amp during the early Wall of Sound set up." After the 2300 debuted in 1971 and the Dead began buying up the amps, Budman was "the one that Jerry liked the best and he played through it for years." That tracks with a Deadly mantra, in line with Bear's attachment to inanimate objects: *All amps have personalities.* The phrase was scrawled on an internal Dead "EQUIPMENT" list.

Leonard, the Alembic recording tech, helped dial in these amps, and recalled the band's willingness to explore what was available to them. Lesh "was always into trying new things," Leonard has said. "Bobby was, too. He was always futzing around, using the latest and greatest." But Garcia? "I always got the impression he was very happy just using his [Fender] Twin," Leonard said. At the time, Garcia played a Twin into a 2300—Budman.

The Dead had the cash to actualize these soundsystem dreams. In 1972, they grossed $1.4 million, the equivalent of over $10 million today. Many people "ate the pie," as the band put it, but by 1973, 18 percent of every Dead dollar was being allocated to gear and equipment, i.e., maintaining the PA. ("Purchase and maintenance" and "support" accounted for 14 and 4 percent, respectively.) That would be like Apple spending nine-tenths of its total income strictly on R&D, "knowing that they could never make it back," McNally told me. "The point was this Holy Grail. God knows, Jerry talked about it. They all talked about it."

They endured one last harrowing trip to cap the year. Late that November, the Dead were en route to a pair of shows at the Hofheinz Pavilion in Texas, on a run through the Plains. The amphetamine-fueled overnight drive to Houston from Wichita, where the Dead had just performed at the Century II Convention Hall, followed a straight road with a single turn. Parish and Raizene were in the Ryder truck full of gear.

Before dawn, Parish lost control of the wheel at the turn. "You gonna slow down?!" Raizene shouted. The truck landed on its side in a muddy field. As the vehicle and gear sank into the soft earth, the two roadies wriggled themselves free.

Raizene spat out mouthfuls of dirt, and assumed that when the rest of the band and crew reached the wreckage, they'd assume the two roadies were dead.

Healy, driving in a rented car with his wife Patti, Jackson, and Garcia, rounded the turn and saw a tie-dyed speaker grille in the road. "What the fuck is that?" he said. Then he saw another grille. Then a cabinet. And another. "I get all the way around the corner and I see this Ryder truck upside down, with the shit scattered, out in this big grassy field," Healy told me.

Parish and Raizene were unscathed. From then on, the Dead's crew got better pay, accommodations, and treatment. The gear also survived, a durability marker of the new custom-built equipment. "We stopped and helped everybody pick it all up," Healy said, "got another truck out there, loaded up, took it to the gig, set it up, and played the fuckin' show."

February 9, 1973. At their first show of the year, in Stanford's Roscoe Maples Pavilion, the Dead jacked into a rig unlike any before. They opened with "Promised Land," a Chuck Berry cover. But immediately things went sideways.

The Dead's crew had arrived days earlier at the campus gymnasium to load in and assemble that latest version of their experimental soundsystem. Noise tests ensued. Bear now believed stereo privileged only certain listeners; mono, which essentially equalized all seats in the house, was better. The alchemy-minded soundman's rig was proof. By concentrating all the sound at a common point, "all the wavefronts would be like a single person speaking," Bear later said. "No matter what it did in the room, it would make sense."

When the doors opened that Friday and heads filled the seven-thousand-plus-capacity Pavilion, a handsome spread of high-sophistication wooden cabinets made in-house by Alembic techs and fitted with 5-, 12-, and 15-inch JBL speakers greeted them. At the heart of the system was an array of Electro-Voice tweeters, modified by Healy, Bear, and Matthews. Along with $20,000 worth (around $146,000 today) of new amplifiers and assorted kit, the array was calibrated to generate pink noise—evening out the highs and lows, producing distortion-free sound on the level. Sully, the childhood friend of Pigpen's younger brother, remembered entering the gym that drizzly day and being taken aback by the "towering" rig, he told me. "Nowhere near the entire Wall but it was a good chunk of it."

On the first note, *all* those new tweeters, which Healy had installed in the PA, blew up. "I smoked out $12,000 worth of speakers just like that!" Healy recalled. "I thought, 'Oh God!' But I think the most that was said was, 'Nice going, asshole.'" (Wickersham has maintained that this specific experiment had nothing to do with the actual developing of the Wall.) Still, they needed to remix on the fly that evening.

The *Stanford Daily* noted "some technical difficulties" throughout the opening set. "The vocals were almost inaudible for the first few numbers," the *Daily* reported. "The players accordingly turned them up, but they were still a bit hard to hear. Also disappointing was the fact that the audience could only rarely hear Keith Godchaux's piano work," to the point one forgot Godchaux "was there at all." Even late in the first set, "bugs were being worked out of the system."

After the band's midshow break, Weir addressed the tinkering, troubleshooting, and tweaks to the rig happening behind the scenes. "You don't know how hard it is making all those little adjustments back there in the dark, seeing double," Weir told the crowd.

Making the situation more precarious was the gym's spring-loaded floor, meant for basketball games. As so many people bounced to the music, so too did the stage—and the huge PA. "They had to stop at one point," Sully said. He can remember the stacks swaying.

Indeed, when the crowd danced in sync with the beat, "the monster speaker towers, which . . . reached halfway to the rafters, were rocking so violently that they might have fallen if they had not been also suspended from the rafters," the *Daily* reported. Yet the sounds that flowed through them made up for the delays. "After seeing 8,000 people get off on their music for nearly five hours, I see no reason to complain," the *Daily* reviewer concluded, "but only to ask, 'how soon are the Grateful Dead coming back?'"

That gig, the band debuted seven songs that appeared on their next two studio albums, *Wake of the Flood* and *Mars Hotel*, released later that year and in 1974, respectively. But the Stanford blowout really illustrated their "move fast and break things" mentality toward audio pursuits. "It's fair to say that the Grateful Dead's soundsystem was always in a state of flux," Blair Jackson, the Dead journalist, later said, yet changes came rapid-fire in 1973.

The Dead's rig was now the center of an accelerating homegrown worldbuilding project. Not far from their San Rafael offices was a stable of craftspeople and contractors who made and serviced the band's instruments, amps, speakers, and various electronics. The Dead conveniently also were located close to a local carpet store, where they could buy scraps for deadening insulation inside cabinets like my artifact. (Rug padding, they realized, is more effective than fiberglass at reducing "internal reflections" at low frequencies.) But Alembic's rising status stood apart. That company was already one of the highest-end instrument and speaker manufacturers out there, and essentially existed to further the Dead's trip.

In the meantime, the Dead did something else unthinkable in that age. "We already owned our own soundsystem," Lesh said. "Booking and travel were in-house. It seemed as if being our own record company would be worth a try." Garcia had already alluded to the band starting a label as another extension of their scene, and a means to separate themselves from the status quo in music distribution. "We're not interested in competing with the rest of the record world," Garcia told one reporter. Grateful Dead Records and Round Records, their boutique label for Garcia's solo and adjacent releases, were born.

After Stanford, the Dead inventoried all their gear for "insurance purposes." The total estimated value came to $154,983, or roughly $1.1 million today. A detailed internal list, headed "GRATEFUL DEAD EQUIPMENT INVENTORY," included an organizational code key that paired five "uses" (band members, monitors, PA, booth and testing, and lights and electrical systems) to a corresponding location within the system (line, tower, spare, raw stock, booth, and stage lighting).

The manifest ran to four bulleted pages. There were 30-plus McIntosh and Fender amps, over 150 PA speakers of various sizes, gobs of assorted microphones (including the new dual-cap, feedback-canceling vocal mics), connectors, hardware, and instruments like "Big Brown." Lesh's new "Alembicized" Guild Starfire quad bass had a dedicated channel for each string and over a dozen knobs, controlling everything from bandwidth to frequency response, to resonance and filtering. Such pricey innovations "allowed the band's instruments to be as loud and clear—not to mention weird—as the soundsystem," wrote Barry Barnes, the Deadhead economist. Valued at the time at $5,000, or around $36,000 today, Big Brown's improved electronics "really did have the ability to send each string to a different stack of nine speakers," Turner said. "And it actually did get used that way in the Wall of Sound."

But the only way to know for sure was to road-test their singular new creation. The second week of February, the Dead packed up their million-plus-dollar, thirty-thousand-pound load into a forty-foot semi-truck, booked for a Midwest-Plains run through the doldrums of winter.

February 15, 1973. Snow blanketed Madison, Wisconsin, when the Dead pulled into the Dane County Coliseum. All that separated some of the ten thousand heads who caught the band that night, and the ice rink beneath them, was a thin tarp. "It must've been cold," Candelario told me.

My mom, then nineteen, made the 150-mile drive up from Chicago. Now performing day-of odd jobs for Howard Stein Enterprises, she encountered Garcia pre-show backstage and offered a baked good from a batch she made. "Bringing cookies was customary," she told me. The reputation had her nicknamed "Cookie Lady," as penned onto her promoter-issued access pass.

That Thursday evening marked the first Alembic PA proper tour date. That winter run, moreover, was the proving ground for this early Wall. And the finicky rig being dialed in at Madison would've been lost to time if not for a rare taped pre-show soundcheck.

"I gotta hear more of myself," Weir said during "Jack Straw," a Weir-Hunter track from *Europe '72*. The next song, *American Beauty* opener "Box of Rain," Weir again spoke into the mic: "Turn up Donna Jean and myself."

"Hey, hey, hey, hold it!" someone shouted—Garcia or Lesh, possibly, though it is hard to say with certainty. The band stopped, took a beat, and started from the top.

"That was just a test," Weir said. "We're checking it all out to be sure everything is plugged into everything, alright?" he added, to light cheers.

The Dead played for four and a half hours that night, including the standard half-hour set break. "Between songs, they relaxed, adjusted dials on the mass of electronic equipment that surrounded them, and tuned and retuned their instruments," the *Capital Times* reported. The audience "at first seemed ready to fly off to screaming ecstasy, but the easy tone...relaxed them."

Through a widely circulated audience recording, the show became yet another arterial branch in the tape trading tree. At a million-plus listens, it is in the top three most listened to of over seventeen thousand Dead recordings on the Internet Archive. That San Francisco–based digital preservation project houses hundreds of hours of unofficial live Dead recordings, some 26 terabytes' worth. Between 2001 and 2008, one Archive user claimed, the Madison tape was the most downloaded Dead show.

"Dane County 2/15/73" is considered a go-to "starter tape." The recording serves as a gateway for those familiar with the "live" Dead element, who are open to deepening their sonic engagement with the music, the ambience of "the hall," and the band's ever-shifting and magnificent rig. The "Dark Star" that night was "exquisite," per *Skeleton Key*. That jam built into a melodic run from Lesh, before the band segued into *Wake*'s "Eyes of the World," a peak, and then brought the room back down with "China Doll," which would turn up on *Mars Hotel*. This kind of Dead "is hard not to like." That the gig went off in the frozen Upper Midwest made it all the more sweet.

But at the next stop, the St. Paul Auditorium on February 17 in Minnesota, "the evening was not without its problems," the *Minneapolis Star Tribune* reported. There was "amplifier trouble, the Auditorium's poor acoustics, and some in the audience who refused to clear the aisles and passageways." At one point, "a man leaped on stage, knocked over a microphone, and was dragged off by a guard. All this did not appear to dampen the enthusiasm of the audience, however." The Dead's appearance that Saturday, to around nine thousand heads, was the first ever live performance at that venue. "You can have the Rolling Stones," read a review in the local *Star Tribune*. "Give me a Grateful Dead concert every time."

Days later, at Chicago's International Amphitheater on February 19, the Dead donned tailor-made Nudie suits, a cosmic-cowboy look to match the sound pumping from their finely tuned rig. "Chicago was an important gig in one of America's major cities," tour manager Cutler said, yet "what an awful venue!" Given the South Side location was "in the middle of the stockyards, the whole place stank of slaughter and old meat."

My dad was there that Monday. "Missed work that day and the next," he told me. The New Riders opened. Yet no complete tape of the show exists. Back then, live recording of the band by their own crew was somewhat haphazard. Post Europe '72 and until 1974, Candelario ran two-tracks at most Dead shows, but was now also attending to Godchaux's piano rig. (Cantor, meanwhile, recorded from a mic-split feed.) Reels might go unflipped as the band performed, losing music to time, if something more urgent needed Candelario's attention in the moment.

"I have only found a cassette of Bear's that had a very stunning, if not shocking" run of songs, Latvala later said of "Chicago 2/19/73." (Despite being paroled, Bear traveled with the band and rolled tape.) The medley went from "He's Gone" into "Truckin'," off *Europe '72* and *American Beauty*, respectively, into a jam, into "The Other One" into "Eyes" and finally into "China Doll." This block of music, Latvala said, "simply has to be heard to understand how good things can get!"

Then the Dead were off to the University of Illinois at Urbana-Champaign, two hours south, for back-to-back nights at the twenty-thousand-plus-seat Assembly Hall. The shows each drew around seven thousand heads. In his "Best of '73" listening notes, Latvala wrote that the second sets from both nights "are fucking fantastic!!!" But the second date, February 22, was the clear standout. Moreover, "allowing for equipment hassles that were quickly remedied the sound was very good," the *Daily Iowan* reported.

On to a sellout show at the ten-thousand-capacity Fieldhouse at the University of Iowa on February 24. Candelario first scouted the venue for a Dead gig in 1971, when their rig was quaint, comparatively. Now, after two years of dizzying growth and development, they worked with something exponentially larger and more complex.

"Backstage looks like [Citizen] Kane's basement," wrote Dave Hellund, the *Daily Iowan* reporter. "A huge clutter of empty equipment boxes, spare amps, brief cases and tool boxes. The Dead brought two trucks full of equipment," as much as any other act that had ever played the Fieldhouse. "The roadies manage to know where everything is. An amp goes out and they find and replace it in two minutes. The malfunctioning amp goes backstage for repairs by flashlight." The road crew, he said, "don't start drinking until a couple of hours into the show. By then the controls are set where they want them and only an actual failure will need attention or an inexplicable case of feedback."

Hellund's fly-on-the-wall piece portrayed a culture clash within the crew. Whole sections of his review are devoted to them. That shows how big of a reputation the Dead crew had already gained, something unique to the band at that time. "The roadies are pros," Hellund wrote. "They know how to set up a stage, how long to talk with a stage crasher before picking him up and dumping him off the back, how to handle a persistent photographer." The Dead's roadies were famously camera-averse, especially Bear; he and other crew insisted that the flashes disoriented the musicians onstage.

There were two varieties of Dead roadie. "One is the ex-football jock who does a lot of lifting, climbing, and crowd control," Hellund wrote. "This is the type that asked me to step out in the parking lot to settle a difference of opinion concerning camera angles." The other type was older, "a little burnt out," and of the "electronic genius" type. "Where the first type said 'get the hell out' ... the second said it was dangerous to be under the loudspeaker platform."

The Dead played for five hours that night, including set break. "Being close to the stage is like playing against the Dead," Hellund concluded. "They're a better team and it's a joy to watch competence in action. But when you're getting beat bad, after a while even competency gets to be a drag."

At the penultimate tour stop, the Pershing Municipal Auditorium in Lincoln, Nebraska, the Dead performed to a sellout crowd of over six thousand on

February 26. "Compared to a number of currently hot rock groups, the Grateful Dead sound almost calm," the *Lincoln Journal* reported. "They do not indulge in super-electronic pulsating music, but in purer sounds." That Monday night show drew mixed reviews, though "for stoned and straight alike it was A Concert. No warm up group, no comedy, very little rest for the performers," the *Journal* added. "It was the Grateful Dead, in quickly and out with a flourish on the exceptional finale of an exceptional 'Not Fade Away,'" a Buddy Holly cover.

By the last stop, at the Salt Palace in Salt Lake City, Utah, on February 28, "from start to finish the show was first cabin," the *Salt Lake Tribune* reported. "The soundsystem was elaborate, the light show by [local visual artist] Heavy Water was super, and the warm up band, The New Riders of the Purple Sage, was magnificent." That was the last gig the band played while Pigpen, forced off the road due to his ailing condition, was alive.

Pigpen, who was working on new solo material, now lived alone. He died of a gastrointestinal hemorrhage on March 8. Five hundred people turned up for his party-like wake. Ron "Pigpen" McKernan was twenty-seven.

Garcia was torn up over losing their first lead player, and even considered ending the band right there. He felt that they wouldn't ever be the same. Lesh was devastated too, but as he later said, "I didn't yet comprehend the magnitude of the hole that had just been blasted in the Grateful Dead."

Meanwhile, business boomed. "Pigpen's death was juxtaposed against the backdrop of the Grateful Dead's rising success," Kreutzmann later said. And the bigger it all got, "the less I paid attention to it." Things had gotten to a point where "our managers had managers," the drummer added.

Now with their own company and in-house label, the incorporated Dead of 1973 were poised for liftoff, looking and operating unlike most any other "band" around. Rakow had convinced the First National Bank of Boston to create a financial umbrella, whereby the bank would approve and underwrite some eighteen independent Dead-selected record distributors throughout the US.

Once the distribution deal was finalized, Garcia described the venture as "the most exciting option to me, just in terms of 'What are we gonna do now that we're enjoying this amazing success?'" he said. "The nice thing would be not to sell out at this point and instead come up with something far out and different which would sort of be traditional with us." Garcia might as well have been talking about their PA.

That spring, the band's mailing list grew exponentially too. An initial 350 people had responded to the "Dead Freaks Unite" call in late 1971. But letters now poured into the Dead's office by the hundreds every week. The band had to beef up the lines of communication, keeping fans informed of goings-on with the soundsystem, among other components of the machine. After the band announced an upcoming slate of stadium gigs, their San Rafael post office box was inundated with letters from upset fans. Stadiums are not known for quality sound, let alone intimacy. The Dead heard their concerns and soon issued something of a response in hopes of dispelling worries. But in a characteristically frank and self-deprecating manner, the band compared itself and its rig to a snake eating its tail.

"The pursuit of quality presentation of our music, with more and more people wanting to hear it, has led us into larger and larger halls with an ever-increasing array of equipment," they wrote in the "State of the Changes—How the Dragon Uroborous (Giga Exponentia) Makes Us Go Round and Round" issue of the official Dead Heads Newsletter. "Ambiance comes in different sizes. We like a small hall, and so do you, and an outdoor gig in the sun, and a large hall when it can be made to sound good." Few halls larger than six thousand capacity, moreover, "aren't sports arenas with novel acoustic and environmental puzzles."

Eileen Law, a band friend, took charge of the mailing list not long after the Dead Heads organization, first run by lighting crew member Mary Ann Mayer, went live. She opened all the fan letters, handled the ever-expanding guest list of dozens, sometimes hundreds of names at hometown shows, and "does fifty other things, and generally occupies the same essential moral position as Ram Rod does on the crew," wrote McNally.

Mailing list signatures were now collected at shows, in the soundfield, typically toward the side or back. That is where one could find Brown, then working full-time for the band, helping Rakow run their label. A compact and affable presence wearing long brown hair and aviator sunglasses, Brown occupied the "FREE STUF" stand at tour stops throughout 1973 and 1974. Hometown friends of the band made the wooden structure; the booth was adorned with Pollock's tie-dyes and had painted lettering that read, "GRATEFUL DEAD COMMERCIAL MESSAGE." Fans who visited the booth could get the "free little posters that had to do with the [latest] album or just nice Grateful Dead stuff," Brown told me. "They were proud to be at a place that had the biggest speaker system anybody had ever shown on a stage," he added. "If they got there early enough and saw people working on the thing and setting it up, they were pretty impressed."

That year, Brown signed up, by hand, nine thousand new names to the mailing list. By the end of 1973, the list totaled twenty-six thousand contacts, and by 1974, peak Wall, it grew to forty thousand. After all, the hierarchy of the Dead's scene was horizontal. At the center was the band. Crew and family made up the next layer out. A huge portion of the following layer, occupied by a million-plus people around the world, was physically opened through the soundsystem.

"Configurations of speakers and amplifiers change almost as rapidly as we move from gig to gig," the Dead explained in an upcoming newsletter edition that included a highly detailed yet homey schematic of their rig. The sheer physics of projecting sound "dictate that any given increase in the size of a hall requires an exponential rate of increase in equipment capability to reach everyone in the hall with quality-at-volume."

The accompanying image, a two-page foldout rendered by Mayer, depicted the PA as arranged at one outdoor Bay Area show that May. It was the first such technical drawing of hers of the soundsystem to appear in the band's direct-to-fans communications. Mayer's diagram was an instant keepsake and entry into the Dead's iconography, alongside the Steal Your Face, or "stealie" logo, which debuted in 1971. Her visual was a striking example of the size and shape of the Dead's PA always varying by venue.

Internal gatherings were now being called to address technical concerns. "At meetings we'd discuss sound, where we were sober in the daytime," Parish told me. "The whole thing was a topic we discussed in every forum we could possibly do to learn it, and to get real serious about it." At the typical "tech meeting" in this era, often dozens of heads, from band members to engineers to roadies, convened to talk through all things Dead PA, instruments, and the making and maintaining thereof.

By then, the main PA was still a stereo system. "The speakers on the left and the right sides are handled completely separately," Turner told *Guitar Player* at the time. The front-of-house booth held the Ampex MX-10 mixers, a pair of Altec Acoustic-Voicette graphic equalizers (part of their "noising" component), and a Nagra 2-track tape machine, for capturing audio of the concert. The part of the PA that the audience heard was all controlled from this booth in the back of the hall.

Each of the four singers now also had a pair of Sennheiser microphones, stacked three inches apart, one atop the other. Run out of phase, they effectively canceled background noise. "Any sound that goes equally into both mikes disappears when the two signals are added together," Turner explained, "so that all you have left is just the sound of the voice, since the singer is only singing into one of them." Along with their pink noising "every hall they play in, the Dead eliminate any audibility or tone quality problems that crop up." The monitor system, moreover, was powered by four 3500 amps, with outputs running to around a dozen JBL A12 "footlight-type" cabinets, plus some stage-side speaker stacks.

Ram Rod, Healy, and Raizene "head the actual equipment crew," Turner said. "It takes them, and about eight other people, four hours or so to set it up. A lot of the original designing was done by Bear." Turner shouted out a "kind of a consulting committee," including Wickersham, Matthews, Curl, Bear, and himself. "All of us work on it from time to time," he said.

The Dead played seventy-three shows in 1973. They hauled the rig into civic centers and basketball and hockey arenas, pursuing nothing but sonic excellence. At an indoor gig on March 24 at the Spectrum in Philadelphia, the system reportedly "fizzled out" fifteen minutes into their opening set. "We want to give you an absolutely perfect show and this is not perfect," Weir told the audience. "So we're going to go back and fix it, so we can give you a perfect show—thank you." They came back out three more times, working out the kinks, and resumed the show after forty-five minutes. "It was like having a pair of headphones on your head in your bedroom!" one attendee recalled. "Clear as a bell, no feedback, no overload."

At football fields and a series of outdoor "mega-gigs" elsewhere that year, crowds were so huge that the band's techs had to figure out how to project good sound over vast distances. The Dead's engineers were the first to successfully demonstrate digital time delay, a practice with which most anyone nowadays is familiar. The band was locked in on creating the highest-level, yet most accessible, experience for the hordes coming to see them play.

"They had an ethic about the person in the backseat, the far back," Alan Trist, one of Garcia's oldest friends and now head of Ice Nine, the Dead's publishing arm, later said. The person in the deepest reaches of the venue, indoors or outside, who had paid the same money to see the Dead as anyone near the stage, was worthy of experiencing the same-caliber sound, Trist said. "I think that's indicative of everything they did right there."

May 13, 1973. Mother's Day. The Dead returned to Iowa for a Graham-produced outdoor afternoon show at the State Fairgrounds in Des Moines. The venue had camping space for ten thousand people, an ideal, centrally located setting to host the country's number-one-grossing live act, thanks to Cutler's hustling. Deadheads "never miss a Sunday show," and "Des Moines 5/13/73" is precisely why.

But when Candelario, Parish, and Ram Rod entered the Fairgrounds two days beforehand, an error on the venue's marquee greeted them. "They spelled Grateful Dead wrong," Candelario remarked. "G-r-e-a-t-f-u-l." The local promoters quickly corrected the sign.

Midwest Deadheads came out in droves. Twelve thousand advance tickets sold for $5 a pop, many purchased at pre-Ticketmaster Ticketron kiosks at regional record and head shops like the Chicago Flipside location my mom frequented. Another three thousand tickets, at six dollars apiece, moved at the door. The band bagged $35,000 in total gig income, shelling out $11,836 in expenses, including $250 for "sound." Total profit, after road costs, came to $23,164, around $166,000 today.

Boosting the band's own colossal soundsystem was a supplemental PA component rented for that show from Heil Sound, an audio provider based in St. Louis. Bob Glaza, an Iowa head who attended the show, remembered the chatter around the rig and the Dead's crew. "Everybody was talking about all these speakers piled up on top of each other and the semi-trucks full and all the people it took to assemble it," Glaza later said. The system that day wasn't so loud he couldn't think, "but I do remember that the sound was pretty amazing."

First, the Fairgrounds stage had to be Deadified, now a routine problem that soon prompted them to carry dedicated Wall staging and scaffolding. The sixty-by-sixty-foot concrete slab in Des Moines stood six feet tall, so as the stage got built sound "wings" had to go up front to support the two side arrays. In a Dead profile in *Rolling Stone*, Parish explained that within the divisions of road crew labor at the time, he handled the stage-right PA tower, and Winslow oversaw stage left. But at the Fairgrounds, they couldn't place all the speakers on the structure ahead of time. That would've obstructed views of the Saturday night races that ran until 10:00 p.m. Graham and the band apparently sat in the grandstands and enjoyed the roar of motorsports with ten thousand locals. The crew resumed setting up the rig afterward.

The Dead's roadies had already confronted a powerful thunderstorm at dusk that destroyed the elaborate stage roof. The covering was contracted out to a Missouri company and constructed of thousands of half-pound fiberglass panels screwed together and affixed to a wire frame. The high winds loosened the panels, whipping them airborne. The flying debris reportedly forced the Dead crew to seek shelter. In the end, a black tarp got lashed to the scaffolding above the playing area.

But by daylight, the local promoters beheld the system built overnight. The rig still flew a couple fading Pollock dyes on some of the musicians' amplifiers, toward the middle of the stage. One of the co-promoters later called the system "the world's largest home stereo, outdoors," because "it looked like speakers you'd have in your living room—except there was a mountain of them."

The band gave a marathon performance that Sunday. They clocked thirty-three songs, at a total playing time of four hours and twenty-one minutes, over three sets—one of the longest gigs the band ever played. Some minor technical difficulties kicked things off, naturally. "It may well take us a few minutes to get everything kinda evened up here," Weir said after a go-to "Promised Land" opener. "Bear with it." A dozen songs later, Weir cracked, "That was an elaborate ploy to test the monitors."

The weather largely held. "It turned out, most of it was beautiful," Steve White, the co-promoter, later said, "which early May in Iowa is not a guarantee." But for a moment, thunderclouds rumbled in again.

"At times the subject of the jam was the weather," the *Des Moines Register* reported. During the second set, the band worked through "Looks Like Rain," from Weir's *Ace*, and followed up with *Wake*'s "Here Comes Sunshine." But at around 4:00 p.m., "things turned ugly." The temperature dropped. A brisk wind picked up. Light rain began to fall.

There was only so much clear plastic sheeting to cover the more sensitive electronics and instruments, leaving much of the PA, mounted on side scaffolding, exposed. Standing on the wet stage, Garcia experienced electrical shocks. The *Register* described the gathering that day as combining "elements of circus, a convention of Shriners, and a department store shopping crowd three days before Christmas." Only some fans began to bail.

But as the band segued into the final chorus of "Here Comes Sunshine," exactly that, and more, played out: The sun parted the clouds, revealing a rainbow in the east. The crowd's frenzied swell and release is audible on recordings of the Fairgrounds performance. A palpable are-you-seeing-this excitement comes through the singers' voices too.

A set of color photographs preserve this impeccably timed aerial phenomenon. The images were captured by Larry Kasperek, then studying photojournalism at the University of Missouri. Kasperek ventured from far afield to roughly front and center. He distinctly remembers the crowd "freaking out" over the rainbow, "responding with an ovation that lasted for a good ten minutes." Raising his Nikon overhead, Kasperek aimed at the arcing spectrum of light, and pressed the shutter release.

"I didn't think it was a very good picture," Kasperek told me. "It's slightly overexposed and I didn't have a wide enough lens, really, to include the stage and the rainbow. If you were facing the stage, the rainbow was completely ninety degrees to the right."

Kasperek was more amazed by the speaker stacks and pristine audio. "It was *loud*," Kasperek said. "But I did remark to myself that it is the best concert sound I've ever heard." In a word, "pure." The only other show Kasperek can recall having as good of a soundsystem was when he saw Frank Zappa, who once had his manager tell the Dead to quiet down.

I've pored over Kasperek's Iowa '73 photos. They offer a glimpse at the efforts of a collective figuring things out as they went. Like other visual artifacts of the Dead's PA in this era, the Fairground images illuminate one step along their path, considering that the constant prototyping, iterating, scrapping, rebuilding, and reconfiguring defined the band's audio approach. "Everything was always changing," Healy, the Dead's mixer, told me. "Nothing was ever the same two gigs in a row."

Familiar faces are hidden in Kasperek's images, or just out of frame. My dad, then twenty-three, stood a dozen people deep in front of the stage-left array, in a sea of hair and suntanned bodies. I first spoke to him about that day while reporting an initial feature story on the Wall for *VICE* in 2015, published around the Dead's fiftieth-anniversary concert in Chicago (where another rainbow appeared). "Given how long ago it was and my positioning in the audience—close, on one side—it's difficult to recall many specifics," he said. But the sound was so fine, given it was an outdoor show, that on "a very threatening day, the sun came out!"

My mom remembers it clearly too. She attended the show as a guest via Flipside and can still picture the floodlights that burned all night as the Dead's crew repaired the stage and assembled the PA. During the performance, she watched from a viewing stand on the opposite side of the stage as my dad. A friend gave her grief for having a backstage pass. "Crosby!" her buddy, a speck in the crowd, yelled between songs. "...Fuuuck yoouu!"

My parents continued to narrowly miss each other at shows over the next few years. But that they were both at that Fairgrounds concert, moved by the rainbow and the soundwaves flowing out of a once-in-a-lifetime rig containing many key Wall components, seems fated. "Legendary show," my mom told me. "Blew the minds of all the attendees."

As a journalist, editor, and wannabe audiophile, I obsess over any photo of the Dead soundsystem. But Kasperek's images set me on an even deeper journey. What I picked up early, through my parents, is that what made the band's system special, possibly even still unmatched, was the loudness *and* the clarity. With age, I've developed a further appreciation for what that meant—be it sunshine and rainbows or otherwise.

No mention of such atmospheric wonders made the press at the time. The lone review of the gig in the *Register* noted an overall mellow, rather than ecstatic vibe, a testament to the band's ability to play the crowd, not the weather. Yet the event in the sky was so in sync with the sound that some thought it was part of the production. "How did you guys make that rainbow come out over the stage?" one maintenance technician asked the local promoter the day after the show. A *double* rainbow even appeared in the Dead's third set, during "Sugar Magnolia" and lasting through a "Casey Jones" encore. Facing east, the band repeated the closing refrain while the colorful arcs faded.

A patchwork of collective memory, or non memory, lies behind every town, venue, show, PA configuration, overnight drive, and space between. Some in the Dead camp remember nothing of the sort happening that day. Candelario, for instance, said his mind was elsewhere. "I wasn't there to look around and see that kind of stuff," he told me. "I was there to do my job." But that doesn't make it any less real. For someone like Brown, the dust shook off when I asked him about that specific show—and the rainbow. "Well, of course," said Brown, who would've been holding down the FREE STUF booth in the soundfield. "That's the Grateful Dead's magic."

What is clear is that the musicians were taken by the moment. After "Here Comes Sunshine" had ended, Garcia, who had walked to the stage edge for a better sky view, looked at his bandmates. "Wow," he said. "I didn't know we could do that!"

May 20, 1973. The Dead pulled into the University of California at Santa Barbara campus stadium. Wickersham and Turner, holding down Alembic's shop that spring, came to witness the new system. The Sunday afternoon gig along the central coast was the rig's second outdoor appearance, the first being in

Des Moines. Conditions were more pleasant than in Iowa, though the Alembic heads clocked the Pacific breeze.

Already with this early Wall, "at an outdoor gig, it could sound like you were in front of studio monitors, it was so clear," the soft-spoken, wizard-bearded Wickersham has said. But in a field report written for the band at that show, Wickersham noted that this other, naturally occurring kind of air movement is a big factor when quality audio, to say nothing of performer, crew, and crowd safety, is at stake. Sound is but vibrations in the air. When that air is disturbed, even slightly, so too is the sound.

"In Santa Barbara, light winds cause the sound to blow away from the intended destination," Wickersham wrote. The "beam" of sound projected over the stadium's walls got swept at a hill some eight hundred feet away, at a forty-five-degree angle to stage left. The Dead and their techs encountered, and had to clear, such site-specific hurdles as the system and the crowds grew. By then, Wickersham has noted elsewhere, they were focusing on directivity, "another aspect that comes later into a fundamental part of the bigger Wall of Sound." Without uniform directivity across frequencies, "the sound decays at a different rate."

The New Riders opened that gig. Considering the rig was so dialed into the Dead's exacting standards, while also changing by the show, most bands had difficulty working with the PA. "It was not an easy system for other people to play through," Turner told me. "Not even the Grateful Dead."

So whenever they played with other groups, two separate systems were available. The Dead had their own experimental rig. A more conventional sound-reinforcement configuration, of stage-right/left sound wings and speakers and floor monitors, was also assembled and operable for any openers who weren't "sports" enough to go through the Dead's arcane system. "Other bands were scared to death of the Wall of Sound," Healy told me. "It was its own beast. It was so unconventional that nobody really had any way of getting used to it," he said. "It's like an ugly dog—you had to know it to love it." In a word, "anathema."

When bands opened for the Dead in this era, the conventional system would simply be turned on, and vice versa when the Dead then played through their Wall. "The two of them didn't really work together simultaneously," Healy said. "Just imagine two complete different setups, because we didn't really have sound wings. Our sound wings were behind us." The Wall was effectively "one big sound wing."

For now, the Dead performed another three-set marathon gig to some twenty thousand heads. The vibes were again mostly mellow, and the Santa Barbara gig pulled in $22,980 for the band, around $165,000 today. As far as the average listener was concerned, the Dead overcame any breezy barriers too. "The sound at the outdoor site seemed OK," one head recalled.

But at some point, the Dead dodged a close one. One witness remembered the cabinet "busting up when it hit the stage." The speaker reportedly fell from the stage-right PA stack "and crashed too close to a child" for comfort, according to another witness. (A group of kids sat near Garcia's feet, a still not uncommon sight at Dead shows at the time.) That attendee claimed a crew member then "climbed the scaffolding with a knife held in his teeth."

Raizene can recall the incident vividly. He was then responsible for tying all the speaker columns to the scaffolding with rope using a particular knot. "At the end of the day I'd just pull and all the knots up the stanchion would cut loose and the rope would fall to the floor," Raizene told me. But the stage preparation at Santa Barbara was especially "tough," he said. "I had amps blow up, I was fixing some shit before the gig. We were set up but I couldn't get to roping. I never did that again, of course." He leaned on Ram Rod. "I got so much going on," Raizene explained. "Can you take care of Garcia's stack?"

"Yeah," said Ram Rod. "No problem."

Fast-forward into the Dead's set. As Garcia was playing, a cabinet indeed vibrated loose and fell toward one of the kids. "If she had been a foot or two over to one side, where the cabinet came down, she would've been killed," said Raizene, who scrambled up the scaffolding—the roadie with the knife in his mouth. "Next thing I know, here comes Ram Rod right behind me. He's nailing all the cabinets together." The fallen cabinet was a Fender Twin. "It hit the floor and all that's left was the front board holding the speakers, while the rest of it was laying there," Raizene said. No more parts of the Dead's PA are known to have crashed down that afternoon.

"I'm sure something like that might have been happening," Healy, who worked closely with Raizene, told me. "A lot of this stuff is legendary rumor." If you were there that afternoon in Santa Barbara, Healy said, you were more likely going, *that wasn't that big of a deal.* "I know that a couple of times cabinets have fallen. But to the best of my knowledge they never hit anybody."

Yet everyone in the Dead's camp could now agree, as the system scaled, that one of their core "creeds"—that crowds were as much a part of the show as the band—had become too treacherous. A new rule came down, Healy said, prohibiting the audience from gathering onstage. Though there were always exceptions, "we stopped it," he said. "There was too much at stake—it was too risky," he concluded. "That was part of the responsibility of keeping the place safe. We're there to play music; we're not there to hurt people."

The day after Santa Barbara, Wickersham and Turner visited Kezar Stadium, a sixty-thousand-capacity outdoor football arena in San Francisco. The Alembic heads noted that wind would again be an issue, so they equipped the Dead to try something new for their May 26 hometown gig.

The PA arrangement that Saturday afternoon was immortalized in Mayer's first schematic, published that summer in the Dead Heads Newsletter. A legend deciphered the electronic mass. There are the 15-, 12-, and 5-inch JBL speakers housed in the Dead's custom cabinets. There are the amps—2300s and Fender Twins. For the PA itself, there are (from top to bottom) the tweeters, high mids, low mids, and lows. There are monitors and extenders for each individual player too. Again, still a stereo configuration, "but we did have some line arrays in the backline," Turner told me of "Kezar 5/26/73." The system was beginning to coalesce behind the band.

Not pictured in Mayer's schematic? The stacks of speakers in Kezar's soundfield, a prime reason why that gig was "maybe the culmination of the stereo PA," Wickersham later recalled. "One of the big innovations there was having delay towers before digital delays existed."

According to Wickersham, Curl acquired some Philips-brand chargecoupled device chips, which "was digital shifting but the charges were analog, so the signals weren't digitized." By putting several of those chips together, "we could sample at a high enough rate to get the high-frequency not decimated, and then record it on the little electrostatic charges that went down the shift registers and made a delay." With help from Healy—who claimed he essentially invented the practice, at least in their scene—and others, they stacked concentric rings of delay towers in the crowd, accounting for the distance the sound needed to travel to cover the seas of spectators.

The Dead were operating on the cusp of the digital age that cool, sunny, and windy day. So too were the particularities of their phase-canceling differential microphone setup, by then fully integrated within the traveling system. Bear took credit for pushing for the Dead to use this setup, which actually went back to Olson, the RCA engineer whose "Bible" the band's techs studied. Olson called the technology a "di-pole microphone."

The arrival of the artifact on November 11, 2021. BRIAN ANDERSON

The artifact in the author's living room. BRIAN ANDERSON

The mother rig, the earliest speakers in Dead history. The two Klipsch horns were purchased by Garcia's mom for her son's band in the mid 1960s. This small PA was eventually supplemented by a pair of speakers built by Dead roadies and a Sansui amp, as pictured. SOTHEBY'S

One side of the Alembic PA on May 13, 1973, at the State Fairgrounds in Des Moines, Iowa. Among those in attendance were the author's parents. When it looked like rain during the show, the clouds parted and a rainbow appeared. COURTESY OF LARRY KASPEREK

ABOVE: Invoice from Quality Control Sound Products, an early Wall spin-off company, to the Allman Brothers Band, for work done on custom Dead-inspired soundsystem gear, dated September 25, 1973. COURTESY OF RICHIE PECHNER

RIGHT: Roadie Rex Jackson forklifts Alembic PA cabinets up to crew chief Ram Rod Shurtliff during setup at Northwestern University's McGaw Hall in Evanston, Illinois, on November 1, 1973. CHARLES SETON

TOP: The Dead and the Alembic PA at Feyline Field in Tempe, Arizona, on November 25, 1973.

MIDDLE: A portion of the upper level of the Alembic PA's unified backline for gigs at the Boston Music Hall in late November and early December 1973. This marked the first time the entire system was stacked behind the band— a momentous occasion.

BOTTOM: Dead pianist Keith Godchaux in Boston, with visible rack of McIntosh amps and custom speaker boxes, in late November and early December 1973.

TOP: Dead bassist Phil Lesh, backed by still more speakers, tweeters, and a rack of McIntosh amps, in late November and early December 1973 in Boston. Note the early version of the phase-cancelling mic component. COURTESY OF LARRY INVER

MIDDLE: Dead drummer Bill Kreutzmann and (seated) Lesh, kicked back against the Boston rig, in late November and early December 1973. COURTESY OF LARRY INVER

BOTTOM: Dead lead guitarist Jerry Garcia walks off in Boston, late November and early December 1973. COURTESY OF LARRY INVER

TOP: The Alembic PA as seen from behind in Cleveland, Ohio, on December 6, 1973. This marked only the second time the Dead's roadies and techs assembled an early version of a center cluster on a wooden platform using individual, fanned-out speaker stacks. (The first time was in Cincinnati, days prior.) BEN HALLER VIA JOHN POTENZA

BOTTOM: Ron Wickersham's corresponding handwritten notes for the "Cleveland from behind" photo. BEN HALLER VIA JOHN POTENZA

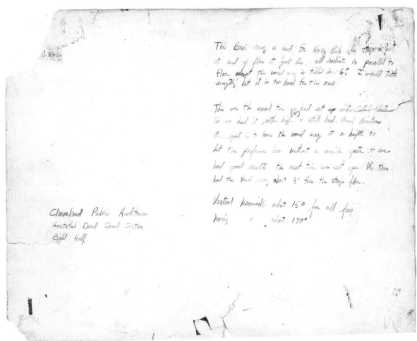

TOP: The stage-left portion of the Alembic PA as seen in Cleveland.
BEN HALLER VIA JOHN POTENZA

BOTTOM: Wickersham's corresponding notes for the "Grateful Dead Sound System—
Right Half" photo from Cleveland. BEN HALLER VIA JOHN POTENZA

Dead roadies rolling dice ahead of a gig at Winterland in early 1974. Counter-clockwise from top: Rex Jackson, Dan Healy, unidentified woman, "Big" Steve Parish, Richie Pechner, Bill "Kidd" Candelario, Joe Winslow, and unidentified man. BEN HALLER VIA JOHN POTENZA

RIGHT: Invoice from Quality Control Sound Products to Pomona Electronics for 750 banana plugs, shipped in late February 1974 to San Francisco's Winterland Arena, to wire up the nearly there Wall.
COURTESY OF RICHIE PECHNER

BELOW LEFT: Roadie Rex Jackson's Quality Control Sound Products business card.
COURTESY OF RICHIE PECHNER

BELOW RIGHT: Roadie and carpenter Richie Pechner's Quality Control Sound Products business card.
COURTESY OF RICHIE PECHNER

INVOICE

SHIP TO QUALITY CONT. SOUND PRODUCTS
WINTERLAND HALL
POST & STINER STREET
SAN FRANCISCO, CALIFORNIA 94100

Manufacturers of electronic test accessories

NO. 013020
PAGE 1

CUSTOMER NO. 47195

SOLD TO QUALITY CONTROL SOUND PROD
292 JACOBY STREET
SAN RAFAEL, CALIFORNIA
94901

POMONA ELECTRONICS
A Subsidiary of ITT

1500 East Ninth Street
P.O. Box 2767
Pomona, California 91766

Telephone: (714) 623-3463
TWX: 910-581-3822
D-U-N-S 00-824-2547

CUSTOMER ORDER NO.			F.O.B.	INVOICE DATE	DATE SHIPPED	VIA UPS	VIA PP	COD	PREPAID COD CHECK NO.	OTHER	SALESMAN
VERBAL RICHARD			POM	3/11/74	2/28/74	X					014

QUANTITY ORDERED	QUANTITY SHIPPED	QUANTITY BACK ORDERED	ITEM NO.	DESCRIPTION	PRICE	AMOUNT
750	750	0	02390	MDP-ST BLACK	.57	427.50
				SUBTOTAL		427.50
				POSTAGE		3.02

PD 6/17/74
CK#1012

TERMS: 1% 10 Days — Net 30
Deduct this amount if paid within 10 days.
4.28

TOTAL 430.52

This is to certify that merchandise covered by this invoice has been produced in accordance with the Fair Labor Standards Act of 1938 as amended.

CUSTOMER'S COPY

PLEASE PAY ON THIS INVOICE AS NO STATEMENT WILL BE SENT UNLESS REQUESTED.

QUALITY CONTROL
SOUND PRODUCTS INC.

292 JACOBY STREET
SAN RAFAEL, CA. 94901
(415) 453-9884

JACKSON
(415) 457-1830
(MESSAGES ONLY)

QUALITY CONTROL
SOUND PRODUCTS INC.

292 JACOBY STREET
SAN RAFAEL, CA. 94901
(415) 453-9884

RICHARD PECHNER
(415) 457-1830
(MESSAGES ONLY)

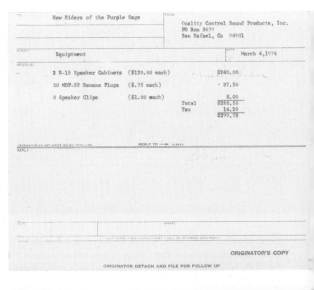

ABOVE: Tallying up a Quality Control Sound Products order for work done for the Dead in 1974.
COURTESY OF RICHIE PECHNER

TOP RIGHT: Quality Control Sound Products invoice to Dead-adjacent country rock outfit New Riders of the Purple Sage, dated March 4, 1974.
COURTESY OF RICHIE PECHNER

BOTTOM RIGHT: A "Cosmic Bear" 2x12 Wall cab—marked one of four—dated May 9, 1974.
COURTESY OF MARK PERLSON

ABOVE: The Wall in Reno, Nevada, on a windy May 12, 1974. This marked the first time the Wall proper was assembled outdoors, and the first time the just-completed modular center cluster was "flown" using suspension cabling and electronic winches. RICHIE PECHNER

BELOW: First proper preshow soundcheck through the full Wall, May 17, 1974, in Vancouver, British Columbia, Canada. RICHIE PECHNER

LEFT: Cutting speaker fronts was a near constant activity at the Dead's workshop on Jacoby Street in San Rafael, California, circa 1974. RICHIE PECHNER

RIGHT: A one-of-a-kind technical drawing of the Wall, likely done up by a roadie for the purposes of loading in at a particular venue in 1974. The schematic is initialed by Lesh ("PL") and signed by Dead rhythm guitarist Bob Weir, whose hand likely also labeled the individual stacks.
COURTESY OF RICHIE PECHNER

BOTTOM: The Wall beams the Dead over a soundfield occupied by thirty thousand spectators on June 8, 1974, at the Oakland Coliseum. The Beach Boys opened this gig but, like many bands that shared the stage with the Dead in this era, opted to play through their own PA, not the Wall.
ALVAN MEYEROWITZ/
RETRO PHOTO ARCHIVE

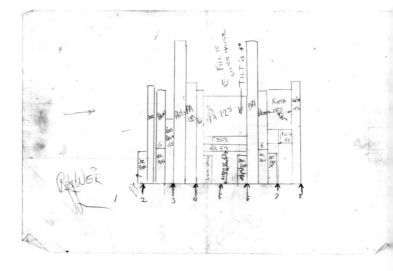

ABOVE: The backside of the center cluster at the Hollywood Bowl on July 21, 1974.
COURTESY OF JERRY HOGERSON

AT LEFT: The view from behind an amp rack on July 21, 1974, at the Hollywood Bowl.
COURTESY OF JERRY HOGERSON

BELOW: The center cluster on July 21, 1974, at the Hollywood Bowl, 1974.
COURTESY OF JERRY HOGERSON

One of the phase-canceling microphone consoles on July 21, 1974, at the Hollywood Bowl. COURTESY OF JERRY HOGERSON

Ned Lagin and Lesh performing "Seastones" on July 21, 1974, at the Hollywood Bowl. COURTESY OF RALPH BOETHLING

Lagin soundchecks his computerized rig at Roosevelt Stadium in Jersey City, New Jersey, on August 6, 1974. At top left, note the hanging black scrim covering most of the Wall. COURTESY OF NED LAGIN

LEFT: An early Wall cab from Weir's rig, now owned by James "Sully" Sullivan, a childhood friend of the late Kevin McKernan, whose older brother, Ron "Pigpen" McKernan, was the Dead's original instigating force and frontman. BRIAN ANDERSON

RIGHT: An early Wall cab from Garcia's rig, also now owned by Sully. When he inherited the cabs, plus a few McIntosh amplifiers, from the Dead after Pigpen died in 1973, Kevin McKernan, repurposed the speakers for his short-lived psych rock band Osiris, and drilled the two port holes in an attempt to further the sound. BRIAN ANDERSON

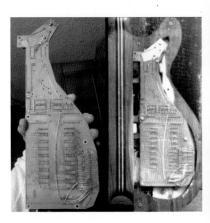

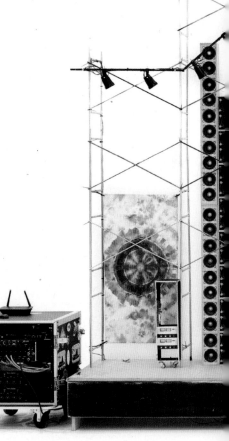

TOP LEFT: A unicorn McIntosh 3500 amplifier used in 1972 and 1973 in the Alembic PA, and again in 1974 within the Wall as part of Lesh's bass rig. Note the partially covered red "Joe" sticker—at the time, the roadie Winslow oversaw the side of the stage that included this amp. COURTESY OF BOB TSEITLIN

TOP RIGHT: The inner circuitry of Lesh's quadraphonic "Mission Control" bass, which functioned as part of the Wall. COURTESY OF JASON SCHEUNER

LEFT: A Janet Furman designed Alembic F2B preamp from Lesh's Wall rig. COURTESY OF JASON SCHEUNER

A McIntosh 2300
amp from the Wall.
COURTESY OF JASON SCHEUNER

The quarter-scale version of Anthony Coscia's Mini Wall of Sound. The psychedelic banner
designs were created by Matt Siebecker. COURTESY OF COURTESY OF ANALOGR

The half-scale version of Coscia's Mini Wall. COURTESY OF COURTESY OF ANTHONY COSCIA

THE ALEMBIC PA (1972–1973)

But differential mic tech really first came from the military sector, used by fighter pilots and other aircraft personnel. "The engines were really noisy… so that was the only way they could communicate," Meyer has said. One microphone received engine sound, then removed from the signal of the other microphone, which picked up engine sound and the voice of the pilot, so that only the voice carried through the transmission. Today's noise-canceling headphones are rooted in this same concept.

In the Wall, Bear later explained, the technique was in fact a means of eliminating leakage, or "spill," into the mics, though it did also help cancel feedback. Soon, he and the Dead's techs had swapped the Sennheisers used for the dual microphones in favor of instrumentation mics from Brüel & Kjær, a Danish audio electronics company, that they modified further to fit the full system.

"Nobody has really repeated the experience because it did have these weaknesses," Curl told me. "It changed the sound of a person's voice a little bit, because part of the sound of their voice would go into the subtraction part of the mic. Not just the loudness of their voice. But a certain range of their voice—total range—would change the sound of their voice." For a guest musician like Bakersfield country icon Waylon Jennings, who opened for the Dead at Kezar, "if they didn't know how the mics worked, often they would sing between the mics and cancel themselves out," Curl said. "They'd be going loud then soft then loud again, and modulate themselves and not realize it." Jennings, someone the Dead idolized, was dancing, almost, between the two mics with his harmonica. "Poor guy," said Curl. "He didn't know."

The Dead experienced technical difficulties of their own that afternoon. "They definitely had equipment problems, which I don't think ever got solved during the whole gig," Mike Dolgushkin, a Bay Area head who helped create *Deadbase*, the widely consulted live setlist guide, later said. "But musically, they managed to transcend that."

The press ate it up. "Superb Sound at Kezar," read a *San Francisco Chronicle* headline. "The dust whirling off the running track occasionally mixed with clouds of pot smoke, but mostly it was huge amplified sound that filled the air," the *San Francisco Sunday Examiner & Chronicle* reported. The band "utilized more than 150 separate loudspeakers for amplification, ranging from six inches to three feet in size." That the attempt at using an additional set of midfield speakers—the time-delay towers—was "less than successful" owed to such technology still being first generation.

Yet another review of the Kezar gig, published in the *San Francisco Phoenix*, noted the ten-foot-high stage that "dominated" the stadium. "On each side towered banks of speakers which provided the most impressive sound that I've yet heard outdoors," said Betty Golden, the *Phoenix* reporter. "It came through loud and clear and was heard many blocks away." Garcia's guitar "pierced the air high above the band's lush backing. The crowd danced, picnicked, and strolled around the stadium feeling good to be surrounded by an ocean of loud music."

The *New York Times*, in a piece published around this same time, was similarly awed, calling the Dead "unique, completely unmistakable, something soft and lustrous even at its most hard-driving moments." The result "owes a great deal to years of electronic fiddling which have culminated in the most polished, custom-fitted, and dynamically 'clear' soundsystem in current use."

Rhoney Gissen recalled the Dead "trying out Bear's new system" at Kezar, a crossroads in her own tenure. She had enrolled in zoology classes at San Francisco State. As Starfinder, her and Bear's kid, followed his dad around as he tended to the sound, "I found an out of the way spot on the stage to study during the breaks," Gissen said. At one point, Garcia sat next to her. "I told him my plan of going for a career in science," she said. "He liked it and encouraged me." She went on to start her own orthodontics practice, with "a fully equipped dental lab to fabricate orthodontic appliances," Gissen wrote in her memoir, the closing line of which reads: "Helping Owsley build the most powerful soundsystem in the universe, I had learned to solder."

Days later, as the Dead prepared for East Coast shows in June and July, Wickersham issued another technical report. Addressed to Parker, the Dead's bookkeeper, Wickersham's memo detailed the more than a half dozen new audio projects then underway, and those individuals assigned to them. There were the difference-condenser microphones (Bear and Curl), different preamp for dynamic microphones (Curl and Furman), mixer for monitors (Furman with Lesh, Bear, Curl, and Healy), delay line "bucket brigade type" (Curl), Phil Lesh guitar system (George Mundy, an electronics engineer), PA array (Wickersham), and maintenance (Leonard).

These various projects all left paper trails. A good deal, though not all, of that historical record is currently housed at the official Grateful Dead Archive at the University of California at Santa Cruz. One can chart the band's sound engineers' real-time thinking and problem solving around the system as it was in mid-1973 in a grip of internal sketches now kept at Santa Cruz. They include some notes and quick math regarding the specific stages built for the band's upcoming shows in Washington, DC, and upstate New York.

One of those hard-to-decipher calculations features a miniature drawing, in blue pen, of the LEGO-like speaker array. The back-of-the-envelope sketch has marginalia and asides verging on the metaphysical, while echoing the "seeing sound" synesthesia baked into the Dead's sonic DNA. "Dense knots," one reads. Another says, "floating galaxies in the retina."

June 9, 1973. The Dead trucked into the nation's capital. Over two scorching hot days at RFK Stadium, home to NFL games, eighty-three thousand heads received the sounds of the Dead and the Allman Brothers.

A proper Dead/Allmans collaboration was long brewing. The Allmans had previously bailed out the gear-delayed Dead in Atlanta, letting them play through their rig. The two bands were then booked on the debut of Don Kirshner's *Rock Concert* television program in 1972, but the Dead walked because the network wouldn't let them run their own sound. Now, the Allmans would be playing through the Dead's big new system.

When advance crew members arrived at RFK that Wednesday before the weekend gigs, their work was cut out for them. Rig construction for that event produced a PA larger than anything the Dead, or any band, had used to that point. A Wall prototype was on clear display.

Like the PA itself, a delay system was a custom fit. The band's curt itinerary on the eve of the first show read, simply, "A day of tests." Buddy Thornton, a former NASA Marshall Space Flight Center radar engineer who soon joined the Brothers' own in-house sound team, recalled Wickersham and Healy taking slide-rule measurements that Friday. They were determining how far from the stage to position the delay speakers, large black cabinets, in the stadium's bowl.

The Dead's system was "a monster," Thornton later said. "I'd never seen anything that big; they had some side fills but they had those big stacks with Phil's bass rig and Jerry's." This was "the Owsley Stanley design, I guess." How none of the Dead's speaker towers came tumbling down was beyond Thornton. "I didn't see any real bracing but a lot of the things they did, and the Brothers too, were kind of defying gravity at the time."

Site-specific sonic quirks at RFK centered around a hole in a wall. The stadium's exposed vertical concrete rear wall produced "bounce back," so they physically tilted the system. Today, this could be accomplished by adjusting the phase, à la radar, but back then tilting was the way around that echoing effect. "Then we had delay towers that were tilted up, and so they went out and hit the wall," only there was a sizable hole in the middle because that back section of the venue had partially covered seating, Wickersham explained. "We could get rid of the reflection out through the hole by doing it that way."

But again they narrowly evaded potential disaster. As Haller, the lighting tech, recalled, a net—a "shade cloth"—hung over the playing and backstage areas. Once the shows got going a Dead crew member lit bottle rockets, setting the covering on fire. Embers dripped onto the equipment. (On some audience recordings, fireworks zipped and popped during the Sunday performance.) "That place could've gone up in flames," Thornton later claimed.

With no fire extinguisher on hand, a tipsy Ram Rod thumbed an open bottle of Heineken—the Dead and crew's preferred brew—and started to slosh the fire out. (Cases of Heine's sometimes got placed atop the half dozen or so McIntosh amps powering the vocal and piano clusters, an economical way of stabilizing the Wall's electronics racks.) Soon, all the roadies were shaking up bottles and spraying beer. The fire did go out, but some of the Dead's gear got drenched. "The equipment smelled a little bit and stuck together a bit after that," Haller told me.

The second day at RFK might also be *the* longest Dead show, if one includes the ending jams featuring both bands. Total Dead stage time: 4 hours, 40 minutes, 47 seconds. "The oppression of the muggy heat lifted as the music took over," the *Baltimore Evening Sun* reported, as thousands "enjoyed the remarkably good quality sound that the phalanx of about 300 speakers provided." Lesh, notably, took flight with his quadraphonic bass, throwing his four strings to separate clusters.

But with higher speaker stacks and sonic peaks came larger and more unpredictable crowds. The potential for negative energy encroached around the periphery of some of the band's shows, like outside RFK after that Sunday performance, when a woman reportedly was raped, at either knife or gunpoint, under a bush. "Problems start to creep in," McNally told me, speaking of the Dead's position at the time. In a cruel irony, the band "makes things so nice and cool for people, whether it's sonically or in terms of the experience of the show, that you attract more people and then things get out of hand."

June 22, 1973. The Dead were back on the West Coast for a gig in Vancouver at the seventeen-thousand-plus-capacity PNE Coliseum.

The band's "reputation is probably now at its height," the *Vancouver Sun* reported. "The Coliseum was not set up for your local neighborhood band. There was a huge, black curtain serving as a backdrop for what looked like 200 expensive McIntosh speakers [*sic*] and banks of complicated blue dials and lights." The performance itself was "low-key and laid back—and very quiet, belying the towering ranks of speakers that looked more like a pseudo-*Hair-West Side Story* set than a soundsystem," read a *Vancouver Province* show review. "The Dead, at last. Very fine."

Two days later, heading down the coast, the Dead hit Portland's twelve-thousand-capacity Memorial Coliseum. From where an *Oregon Daily* reporter sat in the back of the hall that Sunday night, "the sound of the Dead's new soundsystem was excellent." They did have trouble hearing some of the vocal harmonies. "But it was really nice to hear a good system for a change."

Latvala, the band's original archivist, paid special attention to that performance in his 1973 show listening notes. The Portland gig "contains one of the most exciting segments of G.D. music that I have ever witnessed," Latvala wrote. That would be the "Dark Star" that goes into a jam, into a drum solo, then back into a jam, then *back* into "Dark Star," then into another jam, then into "Eyes" and finally "China Doll." This sequence "is worth finding," Latvala said.

The following weekend, after a stop in Seattle, the Dead arrived in Los Angeles, booked for three sold-out nights at Hollywood's Universal Amphitheater. They were the first act to appear at the new venue; originally a fully outdoor space, a roof was installed later after noise complaints. There was a curfew in place and that first show of the Dead's run, on June 29, is believed to have ended around 11:00 p.m.

Those who arrived early that Friday reportedly witnessed an unconfirmed pre-show performance by Lesh and Ned Lagin, the electronic musician and friend of the Dead from Boston who had periodically been sitting in with the band. The pair, according to one attendee, were onstage fiddling with "a couple of bays of black boxes and got these machines going and they played an atmospheric music, not recordings." They appeared to be "responding to each other in the moment." Though Lagin told me he has no memory of that occurring, the performance would have been another leap in the evolution of Lagin's computer-assisted work "Seastones."

What is certain about the *actual* Dead show that night is that the band played for some three hours. One head recalled being thrown by the "Test me, test me, test me…" line from first set opener "Bertha." "Why testing?" they thought. "The sound seems OK!"

The next day, June 30, marked another event in the sky coinciding with a Dead show and the rig at its core. The solar eclipse might not have been in "totality" during the band's performance that second night in Hollywood. But the passage of celestial bodies was a fitting synchronicity, while a reporter named Cameron Crowe clocked more recent songs like "Eyes" standing out from the Dead's standard fare.

"They're a little more sophisticated in terms of structure than our other ones," Garcia told Crowe. "But they're Grateful Dead all the way. I mean, they sound like The Grateful Dead." Much like ever-shifting configurations of the PA itself, show to show, "all the tunes are very different from each other and the ones that preceded them as well," Garcia said.

One attendee that second Universal night remembered the pristine audio even from their far-away positioning. "We were third row from the back, but it didn't matter," they recalled. By the third and final night at the Universal, July 1, the rig was fully dialed in. "I seem to remember big stacks of amps and speakers," another head remembered. Still another individual present in Hollywood was even more blunt: "The sound was perfect."

Not all were sold on the band's LA run. "The Grateful Dead on stage are disappointing at best," the *Daily-News Post* reported. "Though the Universal soundsystem is the best have ever heard [*sic*] on stage (indoor or outdoor), the 'Dead' produced very little that was worthy of such a fantastic system." The band also "didn't address the audience once or even acknowledge our presence," the reviewer added. "During the applause after each number they turned their backs on the audience and fiddled with the knobs on the amps. If that's the best they can do, I hope, 'The Grateful Dead' stop performing live."

But the biggest gig, requiring the most massive assembly of the Dead soundsystem to that point, was bearing down.

July 28, 1973. Neither rainbows nor eclipses were reported over Watkins Glen Raceway in upstate New York. That's where the rig brought the sounds of the Band, the Allman Brothers, and the Dead to six hundred thousand people, long recognized as the largest-ever audience gathered for a pop festival. The single-day event, billed as the Summer Jam, exceeded Woodstock.

That was a time for drilling into issues related to the Dead's now fifteen-plus tons of soundsystem gear and other equipment. "Intended or not, all of the technical developments, especially as they applied to the PA, were making it possible for them to put on their prime gig" of the season, McNally wrote in his history of the band. Dead co-manager McIntire, for his part, apparently thought the idea of doing a show so large was "playing with fire."

That month, Alembic published a PA-heavy brochure bearing the jumbo-sized title, "The Grateful Dead's Sound: Or, 'Could You Turn Up a Little? We're Having Trouble Hearing You in the Next Valley.'" With the attention the company now enjoyed, Alembic offered some eye-watering numbers behind the soundsystem it was continually building for the band, as the rig was typically arranged at mega-gigs like Watkins Glen.

A ten-person crew now handled the three-hundred-plus speakers and forty amps that spilled out of the forty-foot semi. The rig ran on 24,000 total watts of "quadramped" stereo power. To either side of the stage were two vertical stacks of a dozen 15-inch woofers—Lesh's bass extension speakers. Weir's and Garcia's respective guitars, as well as Godchaux's piano, each had between six and eight 12-inch speakers. Sixteen 15-inch woofers, twenty 12-inch low-mid-range speakers, sixty-four 4-inch low-midrange speakers, and more than forty tweeters formed the "quadramped" PA system for drums and vocals.

The monitor system was now positioned behind the band in four columns, consisting of 12- and 5-inch JBL speaker cones and banks of tweeters. The monitor segment alone ran on 4,000 watts. Yet they were inching toward doing away with that arrangement. "Instead, the entire system will stand as one towering 30' wall of speakers behind the band," the brochure read, and by next year surely the Dead will "write a song about the PA." Alembic was using the occasion, and its affiliation with the band, to pitch its services more broadly. "We will design you a soundsystem like the Dead's" that would be "guaranteed to shake the foundations of every building on your block when you practice in the garage."

Watkins Glen was nothing if not exemplary of the lengths to which the Dead, and Alembic, pursued sonic perfection. "The Grateful Dead were in charge of the sound," Cutler, who was involved in organizing the show, told me. "It was quite a revolutionary soundsystem."

The Band, for their part, wanted nothing to do with the Dead's PA, presumably opting to play through the "conventional" system setting. But Thornton, now working on the Allmans' sound, got called ahead to a meeting at a Holiday Inn in Elmira, New York, to interface with the Dead's crack sound crew, including Bear. Healy motioned him into the hotel conference room, where immediately, in terms of engineering, he was impressed. The Dead's techs had raceway blue-prints pinned around the walls of their makeshift nerve center. The prints showed where the stage would be, and how they were going to dig the trenches and lay cable out to the delay towers. "I knew how to read blueprints," Thornton told me, "and I was looking at these things like, *Man, this is a helluva gig they're planning here.*"

Once the show got underway, Thornton noticed Bear, tripping on a batch of LSD he made for the event, lying atop a cable pile. Bear himself later men-tioned Watkins Glen with respect to using psychedelics and supposedly con-trolling amplifiers and the soundsystem through telekinesis, something he claimed to be able to do: "Hooking it up to a whole sea of people," he said, "like one mind." After first grasping how the human ear processes sound, Bear had "matched the PA systems into that," which, according to him, no one else appeared to be much interested in. "Except I can't train anybody in it," he said, "so when I'm gone, it's gone."

Watkins Glen was epochal. That was especially true for the Dead and their team of "scientists and sound engineers who, under Owsley's vision and Healy's leadership, were trying to create the next advancement in live sound presentation, for the benefit of our audiences," Kreutzmann said. Not many other bands back then had salaried employees dedicated to this kind of work. As a result, "some of the ideas and practices that we came up with are now industry standards," Kreutzmann added, like "calibrating each individual venue. Our sound guys even sold various venues our sketches and diagnostics of their room's acoustics."

Graham's FM Productions constructed the staging and backstage fencing for Watkins Glen, a job two people worked on full-time for half a year. "The stage was one you dream of as a roadie," Allmans' crew member Joseph L. "Red Dog" Campbell wrote in his memoir *A Book of Tails*. "About 20 feet high, 80 feet wide, and 60 feet deep, with 25 foot PA wings on each side. A monster stage."

A few hundred feet out came the first concentric ring of delay towers. Healy had arranged an equipment rental for the digital delay line—a model DDL 1745, the world's first such audio device—through local supplier Eventide Clock Works. "They were extremely grainy and noisy-sounding," Healy told me of this first generation of delay units. So he augmented them with Dolby noise-reduction systems, used in recording studios to this day to eliminate tape hiss and other unwanted noise and acoustic anomalies. "It was successful," he said, "but it was too new of a technology and the electronics just weren't pro-gressed enough" to the Dead's liking.

Still, Healy frequently used those Eventide units "because it was a matter of adopting new ways of doing things," he said. "Eventually second generations came out that were quieter and sounded better, and then a third generation came out and pretty soon they got to a place where they sounded really, really good, and I didn't have to use any special preparation. I could just hook 'em up and set the time delay."

That figure can be calculated simply by knowing time and distance. But "to fine tune it down to absolute, *absolute* perfection," Healy said, "you have to perform a form of listening test." Healy would go out into the field, "past the stage and the first row of delay towers… and you would put test impulses through the soundsystem. Then I had a system that I had contrived that used an oscilloscope that I could compare time and distances with." From there, Healy could "microscopically adjust the delay time until the time distance was erased out of it."

Healy was joined by Raizene during this listening test at Watkins Glen, positioning the towers just so. They had pink noise going through the stage system and used a dB meter to measure the sound's loudness at a certain distance, recalled Raizene, who drove a truckload of gear cross-country with Winslow a week before the gig.

"How many milliseconds do you think it is from here to there?" Healy asked.

"Eighteen," Raizene guessed.

Healy looked at the meter. "You're pretty damn close!"

"Yeah? What's that?" Raizene asked.

"Twenty."

Raizene had a "pretty good" time at Watkins Glen. But it was still a job. "I wasn't there for sex and drugs and rock and roll," he told me. "I was there for the damn sound." And he was dialed in: The millisecond range he'd gut-checked with Healy tracked with a soon-to-be-published *Rolling Stone* profile of Alembic, in which Turner further traced that delay system's path.

At Watkins Glen, "the sound from the stage speakers is doubled two hundred feet from the stage by four delay towers," Turner said, "with speakers wired to the stage amps but with a 0.175-second delay built in, so that by the time the sound from the stage speakers reaches the tower area through the air, the signal broadcast from the towers will be synchronized with it." Positioned radially two hundred feet farther from those towers—four hundred feet out from the stage—were another half dozen towers, followed by still a half dozen more towers two hundred feet beyond that. "Sixteen delay towers in all, plus the main PA," said Turner.

The setup for this "last of its era" event was staggering. Curl was likewise among those in the Dead's camp who spent the week leading into the show on-site rigging the PA, including the delay towers. "We had to bury the audio cables out to the mixing shack, and all that," Curl remembered.

Intermittent rain fell that weekend, creating muddy conditions that never make a larger-scale outdoor production easy. "Those kinds of big shows were always confusing," Candelario told me. "Getting your gear up on the stage, and getting it covered up in case there was rain, and preparing for the show—making sure you had done everything you were supposed to do." Back then, Candelario said, "I set up the booth for Healy, ran all the snakes, and then set up stuff on the stage."

That's where he and Parish and others assembled last-minute speaker boxes. "At Watkins Glen we were building the cabinets on the stage the first day we got there," Parish told me. "We worked all day and night, putting insulation in the cabinets, porting them, doing everything."

Meanwhile, Furman lifted off on a different trip altogether. Her efforts above and beyond the call of duty made that legendary event possible. At the time, the Dead's preferred 2300-model power amp was made in small batches and difficult to source on short notice. "The Dead would need a massive amount of amplification to reach all those people," Furman said. The day before the show, the band realized five more of the "giant" 2300s were needed to drive their sound across what had temporarily become one of the largest cities in New York. Cutler handed Furman $6,000 in cash and said to go find what they needed "any way I could."

Conveniently, there was a McIntosh factory in the nearby town of Binghamton. "We were already backstage at the concert, and every road in the area was clogged with concert traffic," Furman said, so Cutler chartered a helicopter. Before long she was airborne. The factory was closed for the weekend but Furman had tracked down the owner at his home. About a half hour later, the pilot landed at the Binghamton airport, where she and the McIntosh man rendezvoused. Press waited for them—it wasn't every day that a helo touched down in those parts. Flashbulbs popped. Reporters shoved microphones at Furman's face.

"They asked me what the helicopter landing was all about," she told me, "as if they didn't realize that six hundred thousand people were gathering a short distance away." Furman tried to tell them, "but I'm sure my explanation was mumbled and not very informative." The helicopter's engine was running, so there was a ton of noise. "I was unprepared for so much attention," she said. "I didn't think it was my place to be a spokesperson for the entire event."

With six grand wadded in her pocket, Furman and the McIntosh rep drove in his station wagon to the factory. He sold her the five amps off the production floor. They headed into town, where the helo was cleared for liftoff, and transferred the gear. The tiny chopper reportedly strained under the combined weight.

"We had a very scary moment as we took off, coming within inches of crashing into a high-rise building," Furman recalled. But they cleared the structure and doubled back for the concert. "In the moment I landed, delivering the goods," Furman said, "I became an instant hero." Four of those amps went to Lesh's new quad bass rig. "That was kind of the beginning of the Wall of Sound concept," Furman has said elsewhere, "of each musician, each instrument, having its own soundsystem so there would be a minimum amount of intermodulation between them."

All three bands then ran a public soundcheck. As Lesh later recalled, the Dead didn't want to be one-upped by the Band or the Allmans, who had just done their respective checks. "We went up and had a blast doing two short sets," Lesh said, "playing about two hours and sounding a lot better in the cool of the evening than we did the next day, when the overnight rains combined with the midsummer heat and humidity had rendered the speaker cones soft and soggy."

Dyed-in-the-wool Deadheads speak in hushed, reverent tones of the "Watkins Glen Soundcheck Jam," a standout twenty-minute improvised musical passage the band explored that night before the actual concert. "I'm still kind of astounded at what they did," Silberman, the *Skeleton Key* co-author, once told me. Silberman was fifteen that summer and went on to see a hundred-plus Dead shows. He traveled solo by bus to Watkins Glen from New York City, and was immediately taken by the delay towers, which he'd never seen before. Then, that Saturday evening, the Dead kicked into their test under Brightman's lights.

"It was very tightly organized on instrumental themes," some of which recalled parts of "Eyes," Silberman told me. "A very focused jam. At the same time, it was kind of quiet. It wasn't just a thundering locomotive." Silberman could listen to such "summer '73 jams" all day, and even later worked with the Dead on a proper release of a soundboard recording of the Watkins Glen check. "At the same time that they were developing this incredible soundsystem," Silberman said, "they were finding a middle ground between structured playing and space. They did that better than anybody else."

The next day, the Dead opened the marathon show. They "played listlessly in the heat, perhaps fearing what might happen if they encouraged the crowd to do more than sway," McNally reported. A water truck hosed down a crush of fence-hoppers. According to Weir, the mind-boggling scale of the event had the Dead "rattled." Winslow, tripping on LSD, later recalled the sensation of being trapped, as if the Watkins Glen stage was "our only reality."

A functioning PA needed to broadcast good sound, not just for the band and the audience's pleasure but as a matter of public safety. When a few hundred thousand people gather together, "if the soundsystem goes down then you lose control and people can get killed," Healy told me. "The importance of that is number one. Absolutely, the soundsystem *must* stay on regardless."

At Watkins Glen, the PA, and the delay system, stayed on and made good. "When you sit on stage and you're watching the people, and they're clapping in time to the music, it would be a wave that went away from the stage," Haller recalled of the view from behind the band. "Everybody said, *why aren't they clapping in unison?* And we realized they were clapping at the speed of sound." The delay worked.

The Dead's playing was more than decent too. "It's actually a pretty good show!" Silberman told me. "It's just not astonishing like the soundcheck. I think it's releasable and it's beautiful." The soundcheck jam remains the only officially released recording of the Dead at Watkins Glen.

After the Dead's set, Curl bumped into Bear backstage. Bear handed him three LSD capsules synthesized from different batches he had made. "This is what I've decided you should have today for this special occasion," Bear said. Curl ate the first dose. A half hour went by. Forty minutes.

"Not much had happened," Curl remembered. "I'm fairly calibrated to stuff," he told me. He ate another dose. "The second one, unfortunately, was *really* strong," he said. "I wound up not being very comfortable, and here I was onstage as the bands were playing." He looked out at over a half million bodies, to the horizon, and saw a sea of snakes. (Bear later reported experiencing similar serpentine visualizations at Watkins Glen, enhanced by the undulating hills that spread out from the stage.) "I'd done LSD before and plenty of it at times, but I don't like being overdosed," Curl said. He scrunched his body inside an empty cardboard packing box somewhere backstage. "Loosely," he recalled, "but so I had a defined space." He rode it out.

During tear down and load out came more heroics. Curl and other exhausted crew members had the impression that they'd all return to the hotel that night for some rest, then pack up the system the following day on their way out to a pair of Roosevelt Stadium shows with the Band. But the crew were told that they were responsible for packing up the entire system before the band even left the stage. "They surprised us," Curl said. "Very unprofessional." The truck was backed up to the stage, so they wouldn't have to drag any gear through the mud. Yet they were in no shape to be handling so much heavy equipment.

That's when someone—Curl can't recall exactly who—produced what looked like an ounce of blow. "A *pile* of cocaine," he claimed. "They just put it out, on top of maybe a loudspeaker cabinet." They each took a snort and got to it.

"Pretty soon we were, like, throwing those speakers at each other." Curl laughed. "We dove through that goddamned truck in record time. And then we sat there for a long time because we were trapped with all these people who were trying to leave all at once because the gig was over." By this point, it was morning. The band had long since been choppered away; eventually the helicopter scooped up Curl and the rest of the crew. They grabbed their stuff from the motel before being taken to the airport, en route to Jersey City. Curl has never been so tired.

"It was battle fatigue," he told me. Like a lot of the crew, Curl, then in his early thirties, was still young and in relatively good shape. But waiting at the airport, he couldn't keep his eyes open. "I'd just fall asleep literally sitting in the chair."

Back in San Rafael, post Watkins Glen and Roosevelt Stadium, the Dead stacked cash.

"The band was making a lot more money," said Hellund, the secretary who now worked for Fly By Night, the Dead's in-house travel agency. The Dead were then one of the two biggest touring bands on Earth—they and Led Zeppelin each sold $5 million in tickets in 1973. Hellund remembered Fly By Night's Frankie Weir and Cutler entering the Out of Town office after big shows and tallying earnings. "Wow," they said, "this is really different."

According to Watkins Glen co-promoter Jim Koplik, the Dead were paid $117,500 for that gig, equivalent to $835,000 today. The Summer Jam's massive draw earned them a $25,000 bonus. The place got trashed. "But we made money," Koplik said.

Wherever the Dead now went, devotees turned up in increasing numbers. "It was really fucking obvious that people were starting to follow the band around," Brown, present in the Watkins Glen soundfield at the "free" booth, has said. Some of those fans, tapers specifically, were growing emboldened. That October, *Rolling Stone* ran yet another piece on the Dead, about the burgeoning free tape exchange network across the country, most notably in New York City. By then, a half dozen US cities played host to such Dead exchanges.

"There's nothing like a Grateful Dead concert," as the Deadhead saying goes. But there's also nothing quite like a good recording of one from the crowd's perspective. "An excellent audience tape can give the listener more of a 'feel' of being at a show than a soundboard tape," wrote *Skeleton Key*. "The sound on the very best audience tapes is faithful to the Dead's PA ambience," which the audiophile journal *The Absolute Sound* once called the world's "finest large-scale High End audio system."

The band members themselves were mostly always cool with taping, a departure from prevailing attitudes toward ownership and what is now called intellectual property. "The shows are never the same, ever," as Garcia later said. "When we're done with it, they can have it." Whatever initial attempts were made to root out those in the crowd capturing performances eventually fell away. The tapers "were a self-regulating community, operating according to a shared ethical code," said Barnes, the Deadhead economist. "This type of thing is what turned Deadheads into a group apart, loyal to one another and to the band—and eager to share tapes and spread the word about the Dead."

Community is what the band really sold. "That is our main product—it's not music," Barlow, the band lyricist, later said. Indeed, by September 1973, the mailing list ran to 25,731 names and counting. A benefit of their in-house label was that the band netted higher returns on sales. This enabled them to allocate a specific budget for the fan club mailers, which were issued periodically to that point, and went out quarterly or biannually for the next decade.

Meanwhile, the band spent the remainder of that summer at the Record Plant in Sausalito, recording *Wake*. But by the first week of September, the Dead had packed up their load and hit the road again.

The kickoff to an early fall tour, a pair of shows on September 7 and 8 at Nassau Coliseum in Uniondale, New York, was a bust. Thirty-nine people were arrested, mostly on drug possession charges, and for years the Dead steered clear of that Long Island venue with a heavy police presence. "While I am not inclined to believe that musical considerations outweigh social ones," one reviewer wrote, "it is a shame that with a group as good, and as popular, as the Grateful Dead, the sound never has a chance of success at the coliseum."

Conditions were more favorable at the next stop, the College of William & Mary in Virginia, where the Dead were booked for two nights on September 11 and 12. "Unlike most modern concert bands, their approach to live performance is the reproduction of their distinctive sound," the *Richmond Mercury* reported. "This priority puts staging and appearance far in the background. Their live appearance is in fact an invitation to the whole Dead 'trip'... through the most advanced soundsystem that has ever been used in this area."

The Dead's rig, the *Mercury* added, "is a marvel of space-age electronics." The system "converts the impulses from electric guitars and drums into a form of technical-music magic." Garcia's guitar "comes through with clear distinctive notes even in intricate high-speed strains." Lesh's Alembicized Guild bass "is not heard as much as it is felt. It forms the 'bottom' of the Dead sound like a soft, warm blanket." And "through technical genius, the drums sound like assorted cannon fire muffled in an infinity of towels. The serene harmony of the rhythm guitar completes the song of the Dead."

After a stop in Providence at the Civic Center, the band was on to Syracuse, for a pair of shows on September 17 and 18 at the War Memorial. Ahead of the first night's performance, Weir talked with the Syracuse University radio station. The Dead had gotten themselves "into a sort of spiraling thing where we had to have a lot of employees and a huge overhead and this PA that we've been building," Weir said. "In order to pay for it all, we had to play bigger places, and in order to play bigger places and get decent sound we have to buy a bigger PA, and in order to buy a bigger PA we have to make more money and play bigger places."

"At one point, you made the decision to play large halls," co-manager McIntire chimed in.

"We did do that," Weir replied.

"That is when we started increasing the equipment," McIntire said. "That decision came first, and that was caused by the fact that we would draw [more] than the small halls could hold, and on the East Coast we were having trouble." The Dead "were being forced into large halls, so we increased the soundsystem to come up with that."

That McIntire was live on air, talking alongside a band member, was telling. "Danny Rifkin's moral authority had a longer influence on the Dead than Rock [Scully's] rakish inspiration," McNally said, but McIntire was "the man who would best define the band's management in terms of quality and understanding of the band's mission." McIntire now "represented the pursuit of excellence as against the piratical quest for size, glamor, and cash" that fueled Cutler, his rival. As Healy once told me, "I had the most faith in McIntire."

Up first at the War Memorial that Monday and Tuesday night was singer-songwriter Doug Sahm and his backing group, who opened that East Coast run. "They used the Dead's soundsystem and their music just didn't mix with such a big system," *The Press* reported. "Bad notes prevailed." But by the time the Dead went on, "it was fantastic. The sound mix was excellent with their new custom built Alemdic JDL [*sic*] soundsystem including over 300 speakers," *The Press* noted. "From ninth row center, the clarity was superb."

From there, the Dead were off to a pair of shows at the Philadelphia Spectrum on September 20 and 21. Ahead of the performances, Garcia spoke with the *Philadelphia Daily News*, gesturing at an ultimate sonic powerspot. "Symbolic of the Dead's continued concern for their music is their refusal to play big halls unless staging and sound conditions are optimum," wrote Jonathan Takiff, the *Daily News* reporter. At the Spectrum, the Dead were surprised to discover what Garcia described as that venue's intimacy and sonic warmth, not often qualities found in that kind of room. If only the Dead had a similar space accessible to them, and their fans, at all times. "I have a fantasy of building our own place to perform," Garcia told Takiff. "Then we could really perfect the sound."

But the band's rig gave them problems in Philadelphia. "Not helping much in the inspiration department," Takiff wrote in a separate review of the first Spectrum show, "the band's huge soundsystem malfunctioned all night, burying Bill Kreutzmann's drums," and likewise Martín Fierro and Joe Ellis, who played saxophone and trumpet in Sahm's band and joined the Dead onstage at a few stops that run. "Poor sound harmed the debut of the Dead's latest musical meandering."

Then came the flying discs. Before the band kicked into a "Big Railroad Blues" opener the following night, Frisbees were already clipping the speaker arrays. "Hey, ah, folks, do us a favor," Lesh addressed the crowd. "Don't throw your things at the stage. We need our loudspeakers."

Before long, the Dead would hang a huge black scrim in front of most, though not all, of the full system; the bottom of the Wall was left exposed, so the musicians could adjust the levels of their amps. This helped obscure the rig, to keep the listeners' attention on the music, not the gear. But the screen also shielded much of the equipment, especially the fragile circular paper domes at the center of each individual speaker, from objects whizzing out of the crowd.

For now, the Dead hit the Civic Arena in Pittsburgh for a gig on September 24. "With no chairs on the arena floor, it was sardine tin time again in front of the stage (which was laden with about 24 tons of equipment, the same soundsystem the Dead used at Watkins Glen)," the *Pittsburgh Press* reported. Yet "it was an extremely low-profile show ... like sitting at home listening to your stereo."

At the last early fall tour stop, on September 26 at the War Memorial Auditorium in Buffalo, the PA was again already creating buzz. The Dead's soundsystem "will be placed on 30 foot towers," read a show advertisement in the *Spectrum* newspaper. "It is the newest and most modern sound equipment ever used by a group indoors."

Fourteen thousand heads filled the Auditorium that Wednesday night. A *Buffalo Evening News* reporter sat "in the high seats at the far end" of the hall and was most blown away by Brightman's work. They enjoyed "the wonderful intricacies of The Dead's lighting (continuous). The bandstand was bathed in all the fascinating hues of a mistuned color TV, red musicians and purple stage, orange stage and green musicians, iridescents glowing on silhouettes in the darkness."

The Dead's lighting team, under Brightman's direction, could *really* drive the life cycle of a show. "Candace had a good feel for what the audience could use—the bumps, the rhythmic changes, going down to a cool color," Haller, then Brightman's assistant, told me. "You sometimes build, build, build," Haller said, "but then you have a low point toward the end of the show and then you build out of it to your encore. You gotta do that with the lights." The Wall, after all, "was more than just sound," Haller said.

The economic engine of the Dead grew brighter and hotter as that tour wrapped. According to the band's September 1973 operating statement, total (rounded) income for eleven shows came to $250,000, or the equivalent of $1.7 million today. Travel expenses were $55,000; equipment costs, $20,000; $18,000 for salaries; $6,000 for office expenses; $9,000 for legal; and $3,000 got spent on payroll taxes. Before partner draws, profits came in at $110,000. Partners ended up taking $33,000. The Dead went home with $77,000, or over half a million dollars by modern standards.

Yet in only a matter of time, the Dead will have burned through those earnings.

October 19, 1973. The Dead pulled into Oklahoma City for a gig at the Fairgrounds Arena. That Friday show began the final two-month haul of their milestone year, beginning in the Plains and Midwest, followed by a run of shows in the West, before closing out with another East Coast tour in November and December.

This stretch coincided with not only the most critical stage yet in Wall growth and evolution but the music and playing likewise entered uncharted terrain. Latvala, one of the most dedicated Dead listeners of all time, later said he could "stay in the winter of 1973 forever."

Earlier that October, a letter from the promoter of the Oklahoma City gig reached Cutler. The contract included a breakdown of event expenses, quoting $2,000 for "GD sound and lights," $400 for electrical hookup, $600 for stage-hands, and $1,000 for "set, stage and curtain." (That letter also quoted $2,000 for sound and lights at the next show, in Omaha, put on by the same promoter.) The Oklahoma stop featured prominently in another *Rolling Stone* article, pub-lished the following month, on the business of the Dead. The reporter, Charles Perry, offered the deepest dive yet into the band's soundsystem and those who kept it running on the road.

Compared with Marin home life, "the cast of characters is reduced to the basic touring party of 23," Perry wrote. There were the six musicians, a road manager, and the sixteen-member crew. There was co-manager Rifkin; the "boys room," a.k.a. the "office" of the Dead's gear crew, including nine sound "quippies"; and Mayer, the former Dead lightshow operator now working with Law on the fan club and newsletter and slinging T-shirts at gigs. Then there were the drivers who operated the forty-footer that transported the sound gear. Rounding out the en-tourage were Brightman and three lighting techs—the roadie Heard was briefly absorbed into the lighting team, after a feud with Jackson boiled over that year.

"It seems an immensely large crew, but the Dead's system is immense," Perry wrote. The equipment weighed around twenty-three tons, "all of it needed if the Dead is to have the sound they want: a sound that will fill an arena clear to the back at any level of volume, from a whisper to a fortissimo you can feel in your kidneys, but completely clear and distortion-free." According to Perry, the Dead were considering doing away with relying on "this titanic accumulation of amps and speakers." Cutler told the reporter that the path the band's operation had taken over the past year was a result of overspending in the previous one.

"There's the matter of growing demand too," Cutler said, "but the Dead are sup-porting, directly or indirectly, 40 or 50 people." Monthly overhead was $100,000, "and that's forced us into the larger halls," Cutler added. "There don't seem to be any halls in the country between about 6,000 capacity and 10,000, so the band has been forced to provide sound equipment for those gigantic ice rinks."

The Dead's "ant-like" crew wasted no time. By 9:00 a.m., the Dead's two equipment trucks were backed to the Fairgrounds stage. The bass speakers came out first, lifted by forklifts—or sometimes by hand, depending on hall structure—and placed inside the scaffolding. For that particular gig, a dozen of those 15-inch speakers got mounted to either stage side. "They couple when we stack them vertically," Healy told Perry that morning. "More volume."

By 10:30 a.m., all the 12-inch speakers had similarly been hauled out of the truck and stacked. Banks of thirty-two 12-inchers were mounted to both of the arrays and "slightly fanned out for sound dispersal," Perry noted. Atop those went two banks of 5-inch speakers—thirty-two to each side—housed in semi-circular cabinets the crew designed specially for horizontal dispersion. "The two banks are aimed with a sight level at different parts of the grandstand for complete sound coverage," Perry reported, "then tied into place." Two dozen tweeters then got stacked atop those, followed by fifteen speakers of varying sizes, for guitars and piano, placed on both towers. The vocal monitors had also been arranged onstage, interspersed with amps. These combined hundreds of speakers "keep the musicians in tune," Perry wrote, "and make up for the missing area of sound coverage right in front."

Come late morning, the entire rig had to then be wired up. "Now comes the puzzle of tracing the miles of coiled cable from the right amplifier to the right speaker," Perry said. The power onstage ran separate from that which went to the more than three hundred scaffold-mounted speakers, and came through a military-grade cable connector meant for hooking up ships to power at port. Healy motioned at the arm-thick cable, the lifeline that carried in all the juice. "This would power six blocks of tract homes," Healy told Perry. "It's 600 amps, three-phase. And we started out with just two extension cords. Now just our power equipment alone would fill a pickup truck."

That fit into the Dead's steadily ruggedizing the rig. At Mike Quinn Surplus, Fry's Electronics, and other Bay Area shops, the band's techs and roadies purchased the assorted built-tough parts that made the Wall nearly indestructible. From empty machined aluminum server racks, originally designed for aircraft electronics but perfect for holding McIntosh amps; to the orange-and-purple Anvil road cases that protected the gear in transit; to that super-thick cable that delivered all the Dead's power at shows, "We've got to have equipment that's waterproof and destruction-proof," Healy told Perry. "It's got to be rock & roll specs, which are tougher than military specs. We know, because a lot of this surplus falls apart on us."

From here—early afternoon—two large military lockers opened and out came the Genie lights, "telescoping towers powered by air pressure that will support the stage lights and the black backdrop," Perry wrote. The lighting rig had its own eighteen-foot van, driven by Winslow. There are a combined forty-eight lights onstage, between the Genies and those on the scaffolding. Near the arena's roof are four additional promoter-provided followspots, operated by local union crew who took cues from Brightman, who sat wearing headphones in the booth below.

By 3:00 p.m., all 459 speakers were in place and powered up. The band ran soundcheck and set their volumes. "When the quippies have adjusted level knobs to the musicians' satisfaction," Perry said, "the musicians go back to the hotel for dinner and the quippies finish lashing everything into place for the concert."

Around showtime, Candelario took his place on the floor, a hundred yards from the stage, in the mixing and recording booth alongside Healy and Brightman. Backstage, any number of people attempted to slip messages to Garcia, who had stage fright and whose fame pulled in strangers and hangers-on. But soon the band was playing.

"I guess we can say with confidence that things take on new meanings on 10/19/73 in Oklahoma," Latvala wrote in his "Best of '73" listening notes. The gig contained yet another instance of a "top version ever" of "Dark Star" into "Morning Dew"—and don't forget "the jam within this incredible medley, of course!"

The sound in the hall was sublime. "I thought the Dead was going to blow the roof off of the building," remembered one head, who claimed to be studying architecture at the University of Oklahoma. "It was so loud and Phil was so powerful, there were moments of pure fear, and I loved every moment of it," despite thinking that the band might have done structural damage. The Dead's roadies and engineers always complied with local weights and measures officials, who made sure their rig was up to building codes. But as that attendee recalled, "The floor was shaking and the columns were shaking, and my head was shaking!"

Then came tear down, pack up, and the all-night drive to the next town. "Ram Rod packed real good," Raizene told me. "Jackson was OK. But I could pack that thing in—you couldn't even get a cat hair in between the speaker cabinets. Stuff 'em real tight, that way they didn't move around." They had a saying, Raizene added, that served as a timesaving work motto back then, be it loading in or out: "Hit 'em with the shit and split."

Two days after Oklahoma City, at the ten-thousand-capacity Civic Auditorium in Omaha, Raizene and the rest of the roadies rose early to do it all over again. A local crew "and the band's 25-member entourage worked from 8 AM Sunday to build a 90-foot stage across the end of the auditorium, with 30-foot towers on either side to hold speakers and lights," the *Omaha World-Herald* reported.

"The volume wasn't overpowering, however; only enough to overcome the arena's notoriously bad acoustics." Another reviewer that evening "counted more than 400 speakers on stage." The spread of Alembic cabinets, given a catalyzed polyurethane finish for increased ruggedness (perfect for match striking), and electronics "was probably the most impressive array of equipment yet to accompany a rock concert."

On October 25, after a gig in Bloomington, Minnesota, the Dead returned to the Dane County Coliseum in Madison. The band played to a crowd of 9,100, in what Latvala later called "one of the all-time, out-of-this-world kind of shows," of which he couldn't speak highly enough. The second set "does you in," Latvala said. The "Dark Star" into "Eyes" into "Stella Blue" is "where the action is! There are 'jams' surrounding these songs that contain some very, very scary and unbelievable playing. A bass sound that Phil employs here will pretty much have you seriously thinking that this might be too much!"

Two days later, at the State Fair Coliseum in Indianapolis, the crisp power of the system had one head, walking around the space, surprised at "how clear it sounded without being really loud." But before the Dead even took the stage that night came more airborne disturbances. "In the spirit of friendly cooperation," Lesh told the crowd, "we'd like to request that you refrain from throwing Frisbees toward the stage." That year, they had already lost around two hundred speakers to Frisbee strikes.

There were other hazards, too. "We went through speakers at a monumental rate in the Wall of Sound, because there was no protection in front of them," Healy told me. "Sticking them up, stagehands' hands would go through the cones." Other times, the toe of a roadie's shoe might accidentally puncture a paper dome. (This likely explains the busted paper dome on the remaining 12-inch JBL speaker in my artifact.) "The attrition rate was so high," Healy said, "that we couldn't keep sending them back to JBL." So the Dead enrolled Raizene and Leonard in that company's "reconing school" in LA that year, to learn how to fix the speakers themselves.

The Dead blew through so many cones that the tech crew devised "special aluminum milled clamps," according to Alembic's recent brochure. The recognizable rectangular fasteners held the cones in place—most of the speakers were "infinite baffle," with no ports in the cabinets. The clamps had a quick-release function. When a speaker went down at a show, most any of the crew would scale the scaffolding "like monkeys," as Pechner put it. "You'd go up and somebody would bring the speaker [up the backside] so you could pull the one out, hand it to 'em, and pop in the other one." All without damaging the cabinets or causing delay.

"I invented that," Candelario told me when I showed him a photograph of my own artifact. "The clip." The 12-inch speaker cutouts in the cabinet I own still carry the milled clamps. "The one that JBL makes wouldn't hold a speaker in and they'd break," said Candelario. "So I came up with that idea."

In another memory, someone at Alembic, possibly Bear, had the original clamps made locally at Willy Stryker's Fabrication. Then one day in San Rafael, Raizene bumped into two brothers who were looking to open a rehearsal and recording studio, which eventually became Hun Sound. One of them, Raizene recalled, was a master machinist. Raizene happened to have one of the aluminum clips on him and placed the part on the table in front of them.

"You think you can make these?" he asked.

"How many you want?" one of the brothers inquired.

"I dunno," Raizene said. "A couple hundred."

"No problem."

The brothers had access to milling machines at Victor's Iron Works, another fabrication shop in San Rafael. They went and "whipped 'em on out," Raizene told me. The clips have a little "foot" on the backside, so that when you tightened them it was like a fulcrum, pushing down on the speaker so it wouldn't move. The vibrations that Garcia, especially, was putting through the cabinets "would've loosened just about anything, except for those clips we had made up," Raizene said. Garcia's extreme "phonics and sonics" were known to crystallize his speaker's aluminum domes—one of the reasons the Dead had switched over to mostly paper caps. "You'd touch 'em and they'd fall apart," recalled Raizene.

Back on the road in late October, the Dead plugged in for the first of two nights at Kiel Auditorium in St. Louis. Much of the show was "devoted to experimentation in far-out sounds," the *St. Louis Post-Dispatch* reported. Flanking the onstage sound equipment was even more gear, "piled high as an elephant's eye and surrounded by almost enough scaffolding to paint the stage ceiling. There were bright green decibel meters everywhere," referring to the front-facing panels on the McIntosh amps, "not merely so impressive from ground level as they were from the balcony." Ditto the Dead's "excellent lighting system, which from the clouds made the stage look like a scene from a science fiction movie." The Dead "has a lot invested in light and sound, but the group does not depend on gimmicks or ear-splitting volume in its music. The quality is there."

By the end of the Dead's performance the following night in St. Louis, they were cooking. "All around the people crowded into the spots where they could get a view of the band between the piles of amplifiers and speakers," reported the *Daily Illini*, the student paper at the neighboring University of Illinois. The *Daily* writer scored a sweet sightline to watch Garcia riff on the traditional "Goin' Down the Road Feeling Bad," now a staple in the Dead's repertoire of covers.

"The gentleness of the group's sound captivated the consciousness of approximately 9,000 fans each night," read another review of the Dead's '73 Kiel shows, published in *The Current*, the University of Missouri at St. Louis student paper. "The richness of the group's tone was enhanced by the two thirty-foot sound towers which aided the Dead's sound in adequately penetrating the auditorium."

Pack up, load out, and another all-night burn. The Dead were off to suburban Evanston, Illinois, north of Chicago.

November 1, 1973. The Dead were booked at Northwestern University's McGaw Hall, a hangar-like space that normally hosted college basketball games. Candelario advanced the venue, and seemed astounded to see the seven-thousand-capacity hall, all hard surfaces—an acoustic nightmare. Years later, he described McGaw to me as "that spaceship-looking place."

Organizers with Amazingrace, a local music and arts collective that put on the Dead's McGaw performance, recalled Candelario's "we're gonna solve this" attitude. "Put up some parachutes," he told them. "This will make a better sound." The order was a throwback to the Europe '72 tour, when the Dead crew first strung up parachutes to absorb sonic reflections. The Amazingrace organizers similarly bought a dozen parachutes and rented a cherry picker to hang the treatments in the rafters.

Like many Dead shows to that point, any hangups were over what administrators thought would be a violent bunch of drug-crazed hippies. Amazingrace's interfacing with university tech support staff was easy. "It was like dealing with two entirely different organizations," Amazingrace's Darcie Sanders told me. "The suits, their only concern was property damage. They didn't care about noise, they didn't care about technical issues."

Sanders and her fellow organizers received the Dead's rider a few weeks out, before final university clearance—not uncommon in those days of down-to-the-wire deliberations around the band's gigs, especially at colleges. The rider requested cases of Heineken, naturally. The document also noted specifics regarding electrical power and was concerned about the stage size, particularly the load-bearing stanchions underneath, and access to the building.

But university power plant and equipment department personnel notified the organizers that the electricity in McGaw would be insufficient to power the soundsystem, even with the Dead's own supply. They would have to bring cables in from elsewhere on campus—including the town hospital where, years later, I was born—to get electricity behind the forty-by-eighty-foot stage.

The Dead's caravan arrived that Thursday afternoon at a small side door at McGaw, through which all forty-eight thousand pounds of equipment needed to quickly pass. That was a late start for an operation that got going early on show days. Meanwhile, the fire marshal requested that six thousand chairs be strapped together, for fear of fans throwing the individual seats. When the crew backed up the main equipment truck and lowered the loading ramp, a roadie, wearing a shirt that read *Don't worry—it's rented*, came down in the forklift and immediately pushed aside some forty rows of chairs.

Before long, Garcia had shown up. It being the day after Halloween, the guitarist wore "a little pig nose," recalled Jeff Beamsley, another Amazingrace organizer. The roadies were working, yet "he's hangin' in there, showing some respect, appreciating what's going on, and also kind of supporting all of us who are running around trying to get everything done."

That was typical of the guitarist back then. "Garcia was there a bunch early in the morning," Raizene, himself an early riser, told me. Garcia arrived basically when the crew did, and started noodling his guitar and talking shop. Seated onstage next to the stacks, he wouldn't necessarily assist the crew in moving or adjusting any of the gear, but exuded positive energy and was genuinely curious about and engaged in their job. "You play through this shit, you wanna see if it works," Raizene said. "You don't have to ask him twice."

The somewhat unlikely Northwestern event produced a rich visual record, including documentation of this pre-show window. Under house lights, Charlie Seton, a photographer then a Northwestern student, floated around the hall, popping off shots of the space coming together and the crew assembling the gear. One of Seton's black-and-white images, taken on his trusty Canon F-1, captured either Jackson or Winslow in a cowboy hat, forklifting a speaker cabinet up into the receiving hands of Ram Rod near the stage-right tower.

"It's like I shot those photos to order for you," Seton told me. He doesn't remember getting hassled. "You can see I was in there, next to the forklift, to take the picture." Then again, time was tight so there wasn't a lot of discussion at that point, before the doors opened and over six thousand attendees, including my dad, streamed in. According to organizers, the Dead crew had maybe three or four hours to get everything in and set up. Decades later, Seton licensed some of his McGaw images for the fiftieth-anniversary reissue of *Wake*, first released in mid-October 1973; the reissue included a half dozen previously unreleased live tracks from Evanston.

No known full recording of the Dead's first set exists. But consensus among most of the Amazingrace crew, and others present, is that the sound in the room that night was "terrible," as one organizer put it. The band could hear themselves fine, but out in the hall the acoustics weren't great, despite the parachutes. "If you got six feet away from the stage," another organizer told me, "it was muddled."

Yet Flawn Williams, still another Amazingrace organizer, thinks the sound that night was better than most people remember. "There was precious little in the way of stage monitors happening," Williams told me. "Part of the magic of that back wall was that they were playing through those things and that's how they were hearing one another. They had a vocal section up in the middle of that wall, and then they had a separate instrumental set for each thing."

The Dead's differential mic setup, moreover, "remains an amazing technical solution to monitor feedback problems," said Williams. The idea has since been imitated: the Crown audio company, a subsidiary of Samsung-owned Harman Kardon, for instance, eventually released a line of microphones with a similar contraption, only built into a single mic. "I was pretty amazed that [the Dead's rig] worked the way it did," Williams said.

To pull off the operation in what amounted to a B-29 aircraft hangar was exceptional for the time. "Given the complexity and the sheer number of cabinets that they were working with, and they had to come in in small enough sets that the forklift could bring 'em through that standard door, that they got that infernal thing assembled and cabled in the time that they did was just remarkable," Williams said. He also noted the pair of tape machines "tucked in the support structure of the stage." The Dead's recording techs could start one machine with a fresh reel right before the tape on the other ran out. Provided nothing else needed tending to when it needed to be flipped, they could record a five-hour show, as stipulated in the band's rider. Williams later taught music recording at Georgetown University, using "Evanston 11/1/73" to illustrate how the art of live concert taping developed alongside the evolution of sound-reinforcement systems like the Dead's.

The McGaw performance came shy of that allotted three-hundred-minute block. The Dead had no other shows for another week—their next engagement was a three-night hometown run at Winterland, now considered some of the finest shows of this era. But the caravan packed up and left that night, as quickly as they blew in. Hit 'em with the shit and split.

November 17, 1973. The Dead were ripping another university basketball arena. But by intermission at the band's Saturday night show at UCLA's Pauley Pavilion, Matthews was looking ahead.

The Dead were slated for three nights, from November 30 to December 2, at the Boston Music Hall. In the UCLA locker room at set break, Matthews flipped around the coach's chalkboard. He quickly gathered the band members and began to draw out the plan for Boston.

Like Candelario and other Dead crew in this era, Matthews advanced venues. "I would go out to promoters who wanted to do a show," Matthews, all stern resting face and blond ponytail, later recalled. He would show up at a concert organizer's office with the band's two-inch-thick technical rider, casually drop it on their desk, and ask, "So, you think you're ready to do a Grateful Dead show?"

Days prior to the UCLA appearance, Matthews had scoped out the Music Hall in Boston. It was obvious that the ornate venue's fifty-seven-foot-wide proscenium would not hold the band's current eighty-five-foot-wide setup. As a workaround, the entire soundsystem, Matthews explained backstage at Pauley, would need to be mounted behind them.

"We're this far out, and here's the width of the stage," Matthews said, sketching the Boston plot. "We can do this show if we take these wings and put 'em back in common ground with the amp line," which, comprising the core of their instruments and stage amplifiers, spanned fifty-four feet, not including the two sound towers. But now that the phase-canceling mics were in play, they could drop the side arrays altogether by simply stacking the system up high behind the amps in a straight line, putting all the sound at the band's back. That between-set markup session in the UCLA locker room was a clear "a-ha" moment. "That was the birth of what became the 'Wall of Sound,'" Matthews later claimed.

But before the band left for the East Coast, they hit the Denver Coliseum for a pair of shows on November 20 and 21. "The road crew had begun setting up the 20-foot sound towers and banks of amps and multicolored lights in the cavernous Coliseum at 9 AM," the *Straight Creek Journal* reported. The exact number of speakers needed for a given show hinged on venue size and shape. But at a facility like the Coliseum in 1973, the Dead were likely integrating into their standard eighty-five-foot-wide stage plot something like 150 speakers

THE ALEMBIC PA (1972–1973)   209

and however many dozens of McIntosh amps needed to power those custom cabinets. Garcia, freshly shaven, arrived with his entourage that afternoon in Denver "and helped set up the equipment for the soundcheck."

After doors, Frisbees sailed around the Coliseum as the crowd waited in anticipation. "On stage, various people popped in and out of the dark hole behind the amps like groundhogs casually watching the over-anxious crowd rise whistling and shouting," the *Journal* noted. That first night was still "a bummer," and "only 5,000 people arrived for the show." The following evening, a Wednesday, had a fuller crowd, though not a sellout. Opener Earl Scruggs, a banjo player, and his bluegrass band "could not be heard over the magnificently muddled soundsystem," the *Journal* reported. But by the time the Dead came on, "infinite care had been given to guarantee the best possible sound for themselves and their audience. They wanted to hear each note, and they wanted you to hear each note, for they do not hide behind cacophonic effects."

The Dead had previously turned down the Coliseum "because of its poor acoustics," the *Journal* added. Bill Graham apparently convinced them that the venue "could be conquered, so they agreed to an indoor concert. They made a heroic effort to present the clarity their music demands. But the Coliseum remained unconquered." Yet once the band had gone on that second night, "they'd brought their center of good feeling on stage with them and made it a special place: subdued in blues, yellows, oranges, the harsh red and eerie green from the sound equipment gave the stage a spaceship effect. From their space-stage, they sent out waves of mellowness into the crowd with noticeable effects."

By Sunday, after the band's stop to play an under-attended gig in El Paso, Texas, stormy skies again threatened. At their November 25 outdoor show at Feyline Field, a minor league baseball stadium in Arizona, Haller, the lighting tech, can remember scaling the scaffolding and helping to stack one side of Lesh's two towers as conditions bore down. "The show got started two hours late, due to the weather, which held up the start of putting the soundsystem together," according to one local report. "The Dead carries its own soundsystem and the total package weighs about 23 tons. Now that's a lot of stuff to get unpacked and put together."

Plastic tarps got draped over most of the gear. "Looked like serious rain on the Wall of Sound," one head remembered. But during a first set "I Know You Rider," when Weir sang "The sun will shine in my backdoor someday," the sun came out.

The PA at Tempe could rattle your insides. "The sound from the 'big wall' was so loud you could feel it in your kidneys," remembered another attendee. "But it didn't hurt your ears." That otherwise chilly and windy afternoon was far hairier for some nude concertgoers, tripping on mushrooms, who reportedly jumped from the sound tower.

November 28, 1973. Garcia joined Hart, still on Dead leave, at the San Francisco Palace of Fine Arts, for an event billed "An Experiment in Quadraphonic Sound." At that one-off performance, while the band's equipment was trucking to the East Coast, Garcia hooked his guitar into an ARP Odyssey, an early electronic keyboard, and produced way-out noises.

That adventurous midweek event is now considered an early version of "Space." Hart will actively explore that sonic terrain in the second set at Dead concerts for years to come, once he's officially back post Wall. But Lagin and Lesh also both joined that day. The Palace of Fine Arts set was another "Seastones" precursor, including the first live tape mix of Lagin's abstract biomusic piece broadcast in quad.

But fast-forward forty-eight hours, to night one at the Boston Music Hall. "We started late," Matthews recalled. The center of the stage floor at that intimate three-thousand-seat venue could not hold the weight of the rear system, now unified behind the amp line. Yet at the proscenium there was enough support, so they ended up removing the first eight or nine rows of seating and constructing the stage out front.

Meanwhile, the semi carrying the Dead's equipment got delayed, when the hired driver, battling a drug problem, "completely fucked up," Parish told me. They dispatched Heard to rescue the gear. "Good thing we put one of our guys in there," Parish said, "because we just didn't trust anybody to do anything in those days without us." The truck rolled up to the Music Hall at 5:00 p.m. that Friday, way past due. Heard had a noticeable black eye.

"What surprises await us?" recalled one attendee, Michael J. Sanditen. The curtain opened to reveal an empty stage; people stared, mouths agape. "Soon, Ram Rod and crew appeared on forklifts delivering steel scaffolding and the necessary tools to assemble a skeleton frame for the scaled down 'Wall of Sound,'" Sanditen said. Over the next three hours, "we watched as the crew set the steel, hooked up the pulleys, ran the ropes, placed the planks, hauled in and set up the speakers, lay the wiring and plugged in the guitars and amps."

Bear was on one that night, over the tilting of the second level of speakers now behind the band, angled to cover the upper and farther reaches of the hall. But Candelario found himself in a particularly precarious position during setup. He hung from wires over the audience, joining a cluster of speakers together using braces and a two-by-four. A roomful of Deadheads watched his every move. "It was a real nerve-wracking performance," Candelario later recalled.

After the mic stands got placed, Lesh appeared and addressed the crowd. "Let's hear it for the crew getting us set up in time for you tonight," he said. "You see, we thought we were supposed to be here tomorrow night. We've been playing a lot of skating rinks, multi-purpose halls, convention centers and it's nice to play someplace other than a shithouse."

The show began around midnight. The Dead opened with a triumphant fourteen-and-a-half-minute "Morning Dew," more or less as a soundcheck. "As you can see we're still making some adjustments up here," Weir said after that song had ended. The crowd had gone off: "I can still recall the pent up enthusiastic release of the audience," said Sanditen, who returned to the Music Hall on December 2, for the third and final night.

Yet adjustments to the soundsystem continued through the rest of that Boston run. Stage chatter during Sunday's performance made clear that even as the Dead were standing up their ultimate soundsystem program, there were always technical nitpickings and tweaks to be made. Weir needed Raizene, then running the vocal system, to make some modification or another. "See if this one's working yet," Weir said in between opening set songs. "Turn it up, Sparky. It's still not very much there." Raizene himself later spoke highly of that gig, telling me that the Boston run indeed represented a breakthrough.

The second set that Sunday night also featured a feedback jam, "as Bobby, Jerry, and Phil literally climbed up to the amps and speakers to create whatever spontaneous sounds possible using just their own raw equipment," recalled Sanditen, who wrote about his experience seeing the Dead. His essay later got reprinted in volume 14 of Latvala's *Dick's Picks* series, featuring select recordings from these Boston '73 shows, taped by Candelario. On the audio, the presence of the PA is undeniable.

"That was the major leap forward in proving that the Wall of Sound could work," Turner later told me of the Boston stand. Key to it were the differential mics: "The major effect of that was not so much that it canceled feedback, which it did to a certain extent, but it got rid of backline bleed into the vocal mics," Turner said. "Whatever you wanted in the PA was what was in the PA. What you didn't want in the PA wasn't there. That was a major cleaning-up of the sound right there." When it worked, it worked "fantastically well," he added. "When it doesn't it's a problem. But we were the ones out there figuring it out."

At their Music Hall finale, wrote a *Boston Globe* reporter, the band's "new seven-ton set up"—an obvious misprint—"above and behind them, provided the clearest audio reproduction this writer has ever heard." The Dead "are to be commended not only for the joy spread through their exceptional music but also for their conscious efforts to present rock in an intimate and relaxed atmosphere." Never miss a Sunday show.

The Boston configuration was recorded for posterity and as a reference for people like Pechner on the manufacturing team, who began morphing that setup into the final product back in San Rafael. Haller, carrying a Rolleiflex, popped off a shot of the system at the Music Hall from up front near stage right, looking across the unified backline. The band likely even hired a separate local photographer to take another full, wide shot of the rig.

At center stage, a defining Wall component had been taking shape over the past weeks and months, as the system melded behind the band. In the traditional Dead narrative, the public debut of the Wall, with its curved vocal array, is often dated to the Bay Area in March 1974. But in the official Dead archives, I found technical drawings created by Wickersham for the band's December 4 stop at the Cincinnati Gardens. The designs clearly depict the early center cluster "sandwitch [*sic*] plans."

Within days of the Boston run, Wickersham had penciled up the diagrams and specs to scale on graph paper. His sketches noted the size, shape, and acoustic spread, or "throw" (in degrees) of the vocal cluster, comprised of individual speaker stacks fanned into a curve, at that specific Ohio venue. It's a small subtlety in both the band's chronology and their development of the Wall. But that they were slotting in key parts of the system earlier than typically believed shows how nimble and ahead of the curve the Dead's sound and road crews were.

Frisbees flew around the Gardens that Tuesday night while the crowd waited for the system to come alive. It was two years to the day since Healy saw the band on the East Coast and decided to "restake his old turf." Yet the show started more than an hour late due to technical difficulties. "Took forever to set up the Wall of Sound," one Cincinnati head later recalled. "Phil came out, alone, with a glass of wine, and proceeded to yell about the promoters." Lesh reportedly then turned around, looked at the rig, and said something to the effect of, "I think this is getting ridiculous." The show got going around 9:00 p.m.

"The music poured out of the speakers and was VISIBLE," another head remembered. "A river of colorful notes." Others present that evening got the impression that the rig was swaying. One recalled the musicians looking at the system, "and maybe it was me, but it seemed that it was moving."

Midway through that show, part of the PA took a hit. Lesh "blew out a row of speakers, sending technicians scrambling across catwalks 15 feet in the air in mid-song," the *Dayton Daily News* reported. "But despite the delays and technical problems, the Dead, as was to be expected, put on a crowd pleasing performance."

The overall quality of the rig surpassed what that echo chamber–like hall was used to. There was "a bank of speakers 32 feet high, angled and tilted in just the right ways to provide the best sound, all held in place with aircraft cables, custom suited to the acoustic situation at the Gardens," the *Cincinnati Enquirer* reported. The effect was "loud, clear, with the echo almost completely eliminated. Pity all the good equipment was of so little use." But the sonic clarity was still not lost on the audience, according to a separate review of the show. "The 'Dead' cleared the air when they hooked up to a good part of their 23-ton soundsystem," the review noted, "and had everyone clapping after their last two numbers."

By December 6, at the Cleveland Public Hall, the Dead did it again. Wickersham dashed off some remarks about the system on the back of a pair of black-and-white photographs, taken again by Haller during setup in front of and behind the PA, a rare vantage from which to observe this early Wall. In the back-facing photo, Ram Rod was turned away, toward a stage-right amp rack; standing above on a wooden speaker platform, Parish held a loop of cables and seemed to look directly into the camera.

"Cleveland from behind," Wickersham wrote in loopy, sloping scrawl. "Power amps are MC2300 except for the tweeters which are MC3500." Speaker cables all ran individually to each transducer for the 12- and 15-inch units, and to each group of four of the 5-inchers and tweeters. They used double banana Pomona Electronics plugs, a kind of connector they now were purchasing by the hundreds, "which are the only inexpensive (also the mated pairs) that have a low enough DCR," or dynamic compression range, Wickersham wrote. "We use 12 gauge wire in short runs. All the rows are sealed in the voice array. The open-backed cabinets are for the guitars because the musicians like the sound better.

Very little cabling was in at the time this was taken but they have about 100 wires come down from that vocal array. Those missing 12-inch speakers at the sides," Wickersham explained, regarding an empty "bay" of stage-right cabinets, "should be there but the rigging couldn't hold them." The levels for each amplifier rack, he added, had been set using the scope that was by then a permanent fixture in their toolkit.

On the flipside, Wickersham took in the spread of electronics from the audience's standpoint. "This basic array is used for hockey rinks when stage is put at end of floor at goal line," he wrote on the back of the corresponding front-facing Cleveland photo. "All radiation to floor except the vocal array is tilted down 6°. I would tilt everything but it is too hard for the crew." That was the second time they had deployed the center cluster, "so we had it rather high and still had vocal monitors." Their goal was to dial in the vocal array to a height that allowed the musicians to hear without a monitor system, and they had "good results" the next time they set up—in Durham, North Carolina, days later. "We then had the vocal array about 9' from the stage floor," Wickersham added. "Vertical beamwidth about 15° for all freq[uencies]. Horn beamwidth about 170°."

The sound and playing that evening in Cleveland were hot. "That's a goddamn keeper, that gig," Raizene told me. But the vibe turned when members of the Dead crew clashed with stagehands and Teamsters who were now to be expected at the band's Rust Belt gigs. The local crew had it written in their contract that they would move the gear to and from the truck and stage. Load in that day was smooth, but now the Dead's crew ignored the locals and broke down and loaded out the bulk of their own stuff, as they always had.

"I'm packing the shit up," Raizene told me. Meanwhile, Heard "overloaded his handtruck on this kid," a stagehand being broken into the union. Raizene could hear Heard berating the local crew member. "I'm in the back of the truck," Raizene recalled, "and I see two guys lookin' at me. They've both got windbreakers on and their hands in their pockets," a sign they carried .38s under their jackets. One of the union heavies even brandished their piece at Parish that night, when 150 Teamsters arrived with baseball bats after Jackson threw a beer can at and began to fight one of their men.

"What's going on?" Raizene asked the pair in windbreakers.

"There's some trouble here," the more senior boss said.

"Take it easy," Raizene said. He proceeded inside and up to the stage. "You shut up and get the fuck outta here," Raizene told Heard. Then he turned to the kid who'd been targeted. "Don't worry about that asshole—I'm the one you gotta worry about," Raizene said. "You were doing fine."

Back outside, Raizene approached the guys in windbreakers. "OK, he's gone," he said. "Are we gonna have any more problems?"

"I dunno," the boss replied.

"If we do, you come find me and I'll straighten the shit out," Raizene said.

"Where you from?" the boss asked.

"Chicago," Raizene replied.

"OK, no problem."

December 8, 1973. Another day, another town, another venue, another power issue. If energy had always been a concern for the Dead's rig, then the West being under a recently enacted oil embargo during the Arab-Israeli conflict directly impacted the soundsystem as it phased into the Wall. And not just on the resultant pain the Dead's new truck drivers, Moe and Jimmy, felt at the gas pump.

In the week ahead of the band's Durham gig, there was debate over the footprint of a Dead show that feels prophetic. At issue was the lighting of a Christmas decoration in the student union at Duke University, where the band was to perform in the 9,300-seat Cameron Indoor Stadium. The union defended the light display by asking the Dead to abbreviate their show, saving the energy required to power the decoration. "It was explained that in five minutes the Grateful Dead's extensive amplifying system would expend as much energy as that used by the holiday tree's more than 1,000 lights for 24 nights!" student Holly Hemsworth wrote to the editor of the *Duke Chronicle.* "Can we afford to have a Grateful Dead concert, given the energy crisis?"

Yet the Dead had already signed a contract for the Saturday concert. "Therefore the union cannot cancel because of the energy crisis or they would lose $20,000 and a lot of student popularity," Hemsworth said. "However, they have stated that they would write the Dead, requesting them to cut back their amplification system."

During the setup in Durham, where the center vocal cluster was mounted nine feet off the stage floor, Garcia chatted up a carpenter on the local crew. The hired hand helped build the stage, and Garcia talked to him about the material that formed the body of Wolf, his new custom guitar. (The name derived from a wolf decal recently placed on the instrument, built by luthier Doug Irwin.) "He was cool enough to take time to tell me about the rosewood on it," the stagehand later recalled.

As the soundsystem itself came together, the carpenter clocked Bear directing the Dead's own men onstage. "There were different versions of big sound systems" in development at the time, and the stagehand claimed that the Dead's engineers and sound techs, plus the crew erecting the giant speaker arrays, coined a moniker for the Durham rig: the Two Towers. The Dead's performance that night, for that matter, was "fabulous." No energy spared.

Off to Charlotte, for a poorly attended Monday night gig at the seventeen-thousand-capacity Coliseum. Feedback squealed from the PA when the band plugged in. From the stage, someone who sounded like Parish yelled, "No, no, no, no!" Something was up with the dual-cap microphones.

"Hey, Jerry," Healy, at the front-of-house booth, said over the monitors. "Say something."

"Ha-ha," Garcia laughed. "It's gone. Hello?"

More feedback.

"Hello? Turn Jerry's microphone up," Lesh said.

"I think the problem is that one of the out-of-phase ones . . ." Garcia began to explain, his voice coming in and out.

"Turn up Jerry's microphone!" Lesh said, louder.

"Woo!" Garcia said. "Woo!"

"Turn it up," Lesh said. "Up. Turn it up. Mine's the one that's feeding back," the bassist said, turning to Garcia.

"Let's see if this works or not, now," Weir said after some final adjustments.

The band clicked into opener "Bertha" and were off. One attendee that December 10, from a front-row spot at Garcia's feet, behind a row of cops, remembered a theatrical flourish at the encore. During "Casey Jones," an individual scaled the speakers with a fire extinguisher and blasted "smoke plumes" like a chugging locomotive—not the first time this happened, either. "The smoke blasts obviously surprised the band," they said, "especially Lesh."

On to Atlanta's Omni Coliseum, another indoor athletics arena that typically hosted basketball and hockey in addition to concerts. At the time, "you now had all these multi-purpose rooms that weren't available for rent long enough to build the system," Wickersham has noted. "Sometimes we'd need two days to set up the stage. You can't put those speakers on the floor of a hockey rink. They have a basketball floor that they put over the ice, with insulation. You've got a protective covering over that so you're not messing up the basketball finish." Place the soundsystem on top, and the Styrofoam padding would be crushed. "So we had to have a scaffolding company build a bridge out to the sides. How are you going to do that when you've got a basketball game one day before?"

Ahead of the gig, Weir spoke with the *Atlanta Journal Constitution*'s Kathy Tilley. The guitarist talked about conjuring what Tilley called "good vibes" by "delving into the mysteries of music and electronics to deliver that music to the masses." The rig was "nearing perfection," Weir told Tilley. "It's sounding real good but we are not satisfied. So onward, ever onward." The Dead would unleash its new configuration, featuring thirty-six-foot-tall speaker stacks and thirty-eight tons of assorted equipment, Tilley reported. "If it works," Weir smiled, "we can make one of those hockey rinks sound real good."

One head in the crowd that evening said that the Omni's acoustics were actually "outstanding," enhanced by the quality of the Dead's system. Years later, they could still hear the "crisp licks" from Garcia's "Eyes" solo.

The following week, the Dead made it to the Curtis Hixon Convention Hall in Tampa, Florida, for a pair of near-capacity shows. These were the final Dead performances of 1973, a towering year for the band on every front, most notably their unrivaled rig. Around 5,700 heads were present "to experience the custom soundsystem and cosmic improvisations" that Tuesday night, the *St. Petersburg Times* reported. The band's sound crew had scoped out the "acoustic properties" of the auditorium weeks prior. "The advance men decided they would bring a 40-foot semi-trailer with 15 tons of equipment on it," the paper added.

That might seem like a misprint, considering the rig's total weight approached forty tons by then. But what few photos exist of that gig do show what appeared to be a smaller version of the system, slimmed down into something like the stereo setup the band had been playing through most of that year; the center cluster soft launched over the past few gigs went back to the lab, seemingly. This reconfiguration was determined by the Dead's techs to be most suited to the venue.

They still had piles of gear. "This equipment included literally hundreds of speakers, amplifiers, and exotic accessories such as the oscilloscopes used for tuning up," the *St. Petersburg Times* noted. Another review, published in the *Tampa Times*, found the musicians standing "between two mountains of speakers on the biggest rock and roll stage Curtis Hixon Hall has seen in years and years." Banks of Dead amps reportedly pumped out more wattage than what was then the most powerful radio station in all of Florida.

A few songs into set one that first night, Weir had to fill dead air while the crew corrected some technical difficulties with the piano system. And then later in the show, during a noise freakout section of "Dark Star," Garcia signaled to one of the crew, barely audible over the dense overtone waves of feedback and drone that Lesh knobbed from his quad bass. "There's a blown speaker in here somewhere!" Garcia shouted off-mic. "We've got a blown speaker!" The challenge for the Dead was "to blend their electrical potential into memorable music," read the *St. Petersburg Times* review. Still, the show was "never draggy and often brilliant."

Night two at Curtis Hixon came to occupy a special space in the live Dead canon. Two decades later, Latvala selected excerpts of Candelario's master two-track recording of that performance as the inaugural *Dick's Picks*. As Latvala told Gans, the *Grateful Dead Hour* host, around the compact disc release of that first volume, there were a good five other "great" shows from this late-1973 stretch worthy of being picked to begin the series. "But 12/19 had this version of 'Here Comes Sunshine' that just kills me," Latvala said. The rendition of that *Wake* track "will raise the hair on your arms."

For now, the rough-and-ready Dead, backed by their high-flying system, were headed home. In that December East Coast run alone, the band spent $2,718 on "equipment purchases," $959 on "lighting expense," $108 on "stage construction costs," and $3,450 on "outside labor" from Wickersham and Pechner. Total gig income for that final month of 1973 came in at $160,996, while total expenses ran to $87,406. Total profit: $73,590. That's the modern equivalent of around $500,000.

The stage was set.

SET
THREE

8

The Wall (1974)

January 1974. At an unofficial Dead tech gathering, Mark Raizene claimed to take matters into his own hands.

"I was at this meeting with Ron Wickersham, John Curl, Rick Turner, and I think Bob Matthews," he told me. "They had these plans all drawn up—blueprint-like—for a center cluster."

Minutes taken that month at a separate, full-band meeting in San Rafael sketched their sonic ambitions for the year and beyond, including construction of a cluster of speakers in the middle of the system, replacing the stacks of individual cabinets. As Dennis McNally wrote, "It was the final element in building the Wall of Sound."

Those minutes stated that they needed "grids for speakers" and two forty-foot trucks (one promoter provided): "Will 2 40 footers help unload & load faster? Need 9 [person] snake." The "Modular Unit," moreover, was "not to happen until 1975. With less gigs this year, modularization isn't as easy to have much collateral to receive loan" from Crocker National, the Dead's local bank at the time. Key to actualizing that speaker grid was "Bread-boarding," the old circuitry phrase for making experimental radios; "consistent array and tilt parameters"; modularization design; and financing and upkeep, given the Wall was itself like a rolling experimental laboratory.

"During the next 2 or few months," the minutes continued, "check into documenting an itemize [*sic*] equipment list and review." In addition to dependable setups, "Bear needs to follow up on modular process and how it's doing; Need to decide on Final Set-up (will have 2 sound experimentation gigs; Winterland + 1 more)."

A formal "tech meeting" was also called for later that month. Two dozen Deadfolk attended *that* quorum, which covered stage scaffolding and roofing, "amplifiers checked out," and "plastic molded grid—design needed," presumably for the smaller piano cluster. They discussed scouting venues, including in Montana, where the Dead hadn't ever gigged, and also the equipment truck "fuel situation" and "pads." Sam Cutler, having laid the groundwork for an upcoming spring tour, acquired the forty-footer with air-ride suspension for smooth transport.

Back at the more unofficial "meeting" at which Raizene said he was present, the techs were of the opinion—in his memory, at least—that the vocal cluster, designed to disperse full-frequency sound from the centerline in a 120-degree arc, was out of reach. This would explain the year-plus timeline on modularization. But Raizene looked at the drafted plans. "It's 1974, man," he said. "We can *do* this shit, no problem."

Raizene took the specs to Victor's Iron Works, the Dead-friendly fabrication shop in San Rafael. Along with Willy Stryker's, another local shop, this is where the curved cluster was forged. Raizene "hired those guys on to build the internals and make the top pieces, where the tweeters and the 5-inchers were," he said. "They were steel, and all that."

After hours, Victor's master welder Gene Peretto opened the shop to Raizene, Dan Healy, and other Dead crew. "He helped me," Raizene said of the compact Peretto, who wore a skull cap, boiler suit, and glasses. "I'd show up about four in the afternoon and we'd start working, 'til about two or three in the morning, building all the stuff. Then the next day, I go off doing my own thing and they went off doing their regular business." Until late afternoon, when they'd do it all over again.

At one of these off-hour sessions, Richie Pechner photographed Peretto and Raizene, in a Dead crew T-shirt and jeans. Pechner crawled inside the cluster's empty frame, capturing Raizene's determined expression as he fastened the grid's rigid trussing to its wooden top. "That's how it got built," Raizene said.

Neither Ron Wickersham nor John Curl could recall Raizene insisting their design was doable and taking off with the plans. But they could also both believe that it happened. "It sounds reasonable," Wickersham told me. "That crew really did a good job taking something that was proven to work and converting it into something that became portable." Bear, moreover, later shouted out Raizene for his work on the cluster.

Meanwhile, Raizene claimed to have also purchased the Wall's construction-grade framing, based on plans drawn up by Dead-friendly engineers. Raizene bought the bracing from Safway Scaffolding for $13,000—around $88,000 today—plus a few hundred hardwood sheets for the custom stage for $7,000. "It represents the finalization of what Bear started back in the '60s," Raizene said. "Our equipment was getting so heavy with the amplifiers. And the promoters would charge three to five grand a gig for staging. Some of the staging had concrete on the scaffolding, and our equipment was going through the deck. So I said, *Fuck this shit.* I got the money to buy our own staging and set it up for two trucks to leapfrog the gigs."

To keep the apparatus balanced and actually tied down to the rest of the scaffolding that went to the ground, a second setup was built behind it. "Not as tall—about half," Raizene said. "Let's say you use five sections of scaffolding to get the height you want; you use two to three sections behind it, that was all tied to the main scaffolding, the Wall itself, and the backpiece, and it hooked up to the stage below, to the scaffolding on the ground. And we'd have all our amplifiers and stuff inside of that in the racks." To further support the rig, they hooked a lattice of stainless steel guy-wires to the scaffolding that then got staked into the ground some feet behind the stage. As Raizene put it, "That fucker wasn't going *nowhere.*"

As if to demonstrate the tiered structure's sturdiness, Raizene packed a hammock that year. "When everything was all set and cool and they were playing," Raizene told me, "I put it behind Garcia's [rig] and I'd step out there and hang out there in the hammock, thirty feet above the ground listening to music. If you couldn't find me on the stage, if you looked up there I was. Behind all the equipment, in the scaffolding."

Elsewhere behind the scenes, Cutler got fired. The split had to do with the Dead not wanting to give their Cockney tour manager a 10 percent cut, "by working with another party for half that rate," as David Browne reported in *So Many Roads.* To that point, Cutler had supported their soundsystem plans. "You don't think, 'I don't know about that,'" Cutler explained. "You think, 'Good for them, let's go for it.'" But Richard Loren, Jerry Garcia's personal manager since 1972, later insinuated that the system Cutler helped grow, by landing the band bigger shows and more cash, was ultimately his undoing. (Raizene, moreover, told me Cutler was withholding money from the band that he'd supposedly collected from promoters, now that the Dead didn't need to pay to use staging.) That was especially true given the rig cost as much as it did, such that pulling off mega-gigs was a requisite for paying for itself. In early 1974, the Dead asked Loren if he would be their booking agent. The high-energy East Coaster accepted.

The Dead clocked thirty-three performances across the US and Canada, plus a short European run, with their full soundsystem that year. That's a steep drop from grinding out a hundred-ish gigs annually since the decade got going. But rig-wise, the 1974 shows were an apex. "It takes being able to understand what commitment is," Healy later told me, reflecting on that epic "guts on the line" year. "We didn't dance around the maypole and pick daisies. It's not that way. It wasn't a village in that sense. It was *way* more hardcore. It was hardwrought from a lot of blood, sweat, effort, and brains. A lot of skinned knuckles."

The fruits of their labor were all part of the progression. "We're hearing the real balance, not a product of vocal monitors or any of that stuff," Garcia said in an interview that year. "Our other system"—the Alembic PA—"was okay. It was a step toward this direction, just like this is a step toward another direction—more, better," he said. "That's our trend, to make it as good as can be made. What that means is we're probably going to manufacture the components of the thing, because we're at the point where what's available in the market is not good enough anymore."

Under the same roof, plans were underway to build even more systems and speakers like theirs—for others besides the Dead.

January 23, 1974. Rex Jackson, Pechner, the Dead-adjacent carpenter Sal Cardinalli, and one Richard Iverson all signed on the line. The signatures formalized their new speaker company's articles of incorporation, drafted over weeks and months of back and forth with California's Office of the Secretary of State and now carrying the county clerk's gold seal. "The name of this corporation," Article I stated, "is QUALITY CONTROL SOUND PRODUCTS."

The moniker was both incredibly specific and delightfully vague. "We were getting stoned and kicking it around," Pechner told me. "One of the things that was always true with the Dead was quality. I think we always started with that word, and were trying to put together an acronym or some way of doing it. But then the word 'sound' had to be in there because it was a speaker company." As far as the state cared, they were legit.

That the address and phone number on their stark business cards matched the Dead's Jacoby Street shop shows how interlinked the two entities were, despite a new degree of distinction. Per Article II, Quality Control formed to "engage primarily in the specific business of the design, manufacture, distribution, and wholesale-retail sale of sound equipment." That included, but was not restricted to, "producing sound by electronic or other means, transmitting electronic audio waves, creating currents and frequencies in the transmission of soundwaves and to further engage in audio, as well as visual, sound mechanisms."

Increased attention was now on the suite of more or less in-house services continuing to expand around the Dead. "There was all this chatter about, 'Oh, this band, they're really starting to draw people and they're getting successful and hiring,'" Pechner said. The push behind Quality Control "was in all that kind of energy," as the company spun off from the Dead's PA. "It came out of the building of the Wall of Sound," Pechner said. But in this fabrication and growth frenzy, the carpenter-roadie recalled that Quality Control was *really* established to clarify what work was being done and for whom.

"We were starting to cross the line with Grateful Dead on doing stuff for other people," Pechner said. "It was kind of an unclear chain of command." They were using Bill Candelario's table saw, for instance, and Ben Haller, who likewise gave his Uni-saw to the cause, soon also started an informal "tool of the month" club—billed to the band. "There was all this comingling," Pechner said. "But Ram Rod thought that we could sell these systems to other bands," essentially mini Walls, modeled on the rig they were continuing to build for the Dead. Ram Rod considered himself "the perfect emissary to do that because of his position," Pechner explained. With this new entity, "we tried to formulate a way to do that and get a little separation."

Pechner's impression was that certain individuals in the Dead office questioned how time was being spent. "You could see that our ambition had to take a different format if it was going to continue," he said. "We were thinking, 'This could be a whole new thing! We could be making PAs.' Of course, you can't expect your employer to pay for your outside activities. I think that's when it kinda came to a head." That was the impetus for creating Quality Control: to split the two and also capitalize on the association with the band, "to have this new company producing product that was previously produced only for the Grateful Dead."

He and Cardinalli, who had already been building Alembic cabinets and installing studio flooring at that company's space, were not touring, per se, with the Dead. (Jackson and Iverson, by contrast, always joined the band on the road; Iverson was Ram Rod's alias, used on paper and when pulled over by police.) At the time, "we were making the cabinets in the shop on Jacoby Street that was rented by the Grateful Dead," Pechner said. "We didn't know very much about what we were doing." Dead tours went out with manifests that included cabinets they had recently made, and those boxes got worked into the system. "It was kind of this transitional period, which basically ended that year when the band decided to take time off," Pechner said. "This was all heading into that."

Before the company was even officially established, Quality Control had done work for at least one major client. Pechner shared with me a cache of never-before-seen documents related to the short-lived, Wall-inspired speaker company, including original hand-drawn product specs and diagrams, receipts for materials, time logs, bank and partner correspondence, checks, and legal markups to the articles of incorporation. In those documents, I found a "cabinets and equipment" invoice for $6,797.10—the equivalent to $47,000 today.

The September 25, 1973, tab from Quality Control was addressed to none other than the Allman Brothers.

The Brothers soon began fabricating their own such cabinets, fashioned on the Dead's, in an old cotton warehouse turned woodshop in Macon.

That's according to Buddy Thornton, the former NASA radar engineer who first encountered the Dead's crew at RFK and Watkins Glen. Thornton had since been tasked with building the Brothers a system. He was impressed with what the Dead were up to, "as far as the delays and how they were aiming the system," Thornton told me. The roadies and engineer types behind the Dead's big rig were "brilliant." Thornton likely even met the Quality Control crew, but admittedly doesn't remember it too well. "I saw Healy and Wickersham more often than anyone," he said. "We didn't have a lot of interaction." But reviewing the invoice to the Brothers, "I distinctly remember going out to San Rafael, probably at their shop, and ordering some of this stuff," he explained. "That was the beginning of our system."

The Brothers purchased sixteen A-15 speaker cabinets, identical to those in Phil Lesh's stacks, likely used by Lamar Williams, then bass player for the Brothers; twelve B-12 cabinets, like the boxes in Garcia's stacks; twenty-four hot-rodded JBL K-120s, probably housed in the B-12s; a thousand feet of Belden-brand cable wiring; a hundred banana plugs; and labor, for patch cords, plug modifications, and delivery. "That was our first contract," Pechner told me.

The Macon soundpeople took note of what materials Quality Control used, like 14-ply Finnish birch. "We bought a trainload of that stuff," Thornton said. "We used it to build our cabinets too." The only difference was that theirs were ported, rather than enclosed, meaning each contained a hole to help equalize pressure between the inside and outside of the box. But here was another early and tangible instance of the Dead's hi-fi audio project making waves, clearly informing Thornton and the Brothers' tech and equipment crew, similarly composed of scruffy dudes in denim and T-shirts with nicknames like Gyro, Red Dog, and Twiggs. "That was the inspiration," Thornton said. "I don't know if it's plagiarism but techies talking to each other, if something works they're gonna use it."

It's like how the Dead picked up on the phase-canceling microphone setup demonstrated by the old Fillmore East's in-house techs. Just as Wickersham, Bear, and especially Curl devised a similar contraption for the Dead, Thornton likewise attempted to implement the same thing into their own rig. "But Gregg Allman and Dickey [Betts, Brothers co-founder and guitarist] didn't know how to use the two mics," he said. "The only way that thing is gonna work is if your point source is directly on the one mic, and the other mic is sensing the out-of-phase signal over the background noise. I never got it to work with those guys."

But Thornton and the Brothers' sound team were so taken by the Dead's doings in the broader audio realm that they additionally purchased Alembic kit in this same era. "We bought some of their preamps," Thornton said.

Those were blue, rack-mount units with tubes, originally designed by Janet Furman. Through her prototype, a player "could plug a guitar into one or both pre-amps, and the outputs would drive a rack-mount stereo amp," according to a history of Furman Sound. That's the thriving company—yet another spin-off audio business—Furman soon started, bringing ace solderer Melissa Cargill with her and leaving Alembic and the Dead largely behind. "This was a revolutionary concept at the time," she said. "Previously, only studios used racks for fixed, permanent installations." The appeal of musicians having equipment racks, as the Dead had in their Wall and ever after, "took a few years to catch on," she added, "but this is where it all started."

After inventing this preamp equalizer, Furman made twenty herself, mostly for friends. Her first "sale"? A gift to Garcia. Alembic later sold this model unit as the F-2B—F for Furman. "I didn't sit there wiring up a production run," she told me. "Someone else would have done that. I don't remember who, but possibly Susan Wickersham."

The F-2B is the very equalizer that Lesh, in particular, had multiples of in the Wall, and that Thornton had acquired for the Brothers. Even beyond the Dead's immediate realm, Furman's creation is renowned: David Gilmour, guitarist and co-vocalist of Pink Floyd, another contemporaneous band in notorious pursuit of audio perfection, later called the F-2B his "secret weapon" in the studio. Practically every professional recording rig today has a Furman preamp, which essentially enables a control of tone of onstage equipment on a level you'd get in a studio setting.

The Wall, then, was a roving system and a place of research and development, incubating technologies that still ripple today. The Dead's rig "represents an innovation in live sound technology," Thornton said. Moreover, "I know a lot of people refer to people like myself, and Wickersham and Healy—all that whole Alembic crew—as roadies, and when you call someone a roadie it's like an image of schlepping equipment, loading and unloading trucks," he said. "A lot of folks don't understand that some roadies are not just schlepping equipment. They're actually designing and making cutting-edge technology, at that time anyway."

But back in Macon, Thornton had a limited budget. "We had four guys on the sound, including myself, buying parts and blowing speakers and replacing things," Thornton said. Unlike the Dead, the Allman Brothers "invested a lot of their money in other things, like private airplanes and . . . real-estate deals that didn't work out." Eventually the band split up.

On the opposite coast, the Quality Control team upped the, well, quality of their sound products, as they simultaneously tended to the Dead's Wall. Refinements and gains in either track fed into the other.

"We did various things to improve the design," Pechner told me. For cabinet construction, "instead of using a butt joint," whereby one piece of wood is simply placed against another, "we dadoed that joint." That's the carpentry term ("dado") for a sturdy channeling joint used in cabinetry, where an adjoining piece of wood is then secured. "Then we glued them up as one unit, so they were pretty strong," Pechner said. "They were a huge improvement over anything anybody else had. To my knowledge, I don't think any of them ever broke or failed. There were some that got dented or scratched, but they were pretty much bulletproof."

Another invoice I uncovered in the Quality Control documents—what I call the Pechner Papers—is dated February 28, the day after the company's paperwork was officially filed with the state. Pomona Electronics had shipped 750 of the black MDP-ST-model banana jacks to Winterland, which aligned with a three-show run the Dead had just wrapped at the first of the "2 sound experimentation gigs" mentioned at the New Year's meeting. That hundreds of those jacks were being acquired in a single buy underscores the enormous complexity of the band's system.

"That was to try to standardize the connection," said Pechner. "Previously, if you had a JBL speaker cabinet it would have one of several types of connectors to get into it. What we systematically did with the Wall was uniform all the connections. There was only banana plug connection—no RCA or XLR," he said, referring to two other types of electrical connector. "We said, 'Nope, we're gonna use these.' So everything got that connection, including the amps [which] had to be modified to take the other in. We were trying to make it dummy-proof, because we were a bunch of dummies and things were always getting fucked up."

At the typical Winterland show in this era, like those on February 22 through 24, the Dead's crew were fabricating cords in the hours leading into a gig. "That was a constant activity," Pechner said. "'Oh, I need a thirty-foot cord,' so somebody would bust out the soldering iron and get some wire and get the plugs and make it up. That was one of the jobs of the roadies—to produce that stuff. I did that. We all learned how to solder."

On night one at Winterland—the Dead's opening gig of 1974—all those banana plugs Quality Control had shipped to the venue got hooked into the system, flush on the backs of the cabinets. In black-and-white photos Pechner took that Friday afternoon, the vocal array had clearly coalesced at the center of the rig but still comprised individual speaker stacks. They were awaiting the completion of the two-piece center cluster; Raizene, Healy, and others were not yet finished assembling the modular array. A smaller-scale arrangement of speaker stacks had also been assembled as a second fanned cluster, above Keith Godchaux's piano at stage left. There were a *lot* of cabinets on display.

"I mostly remember how intense it was in getting the changes implemented into the setup," Pechner said. "The band expected improvement each time. Some things worked and other things didn't," which was to be expected given the always in-progress toiling that went into evolving and perfecting the system. "With so many moving parts and no real script to adhere to, it's incredible that we pulled it off without any catastrophic loss," he said. "Winterland was home for us so that helped.... The sound was definitely improving, with the clarity and separation becoming more apparent with the changes."

Those modifications would've been apparent to anyone in the crowd who had previously seen the band. "I lived pretty close to Winterland and liked to watch them load in whenever they played there and maybe be lucky enough to catch a soundcheck," one head recalled. "I remember noticing a lot more speaker boxes than usual being unloaded from the truck."

That individual claimed to have then snuck into the venue with a few others. There it was, "the giantest Grateful Dead soundsystem ever!" they said. "Just boxes and boxes of JBL's in various sizes stacked to the ceiling! It was as though they had been listening to our innermost wishes as our appetite for volume and clarity was voracious and insatiable." When the amps got turned on, a short somewhere in the power chain emitted an eardrum-rattling "*POP!*" But just as the interlopers were "getting comfortable and looking forward to the band getting up there to try out this new rocketship, Steve Parish noticed us and immediately came and physically removed us."

A soundcheck tape recorded before that show emphasized the "sound experimentation" in "sound experimentation gig." Rig-specific crosstalk got picked up during the check, especially in the gentle, vocal-forward *American Beauty* track "Attics of My Life."

"... There's just no level on them compared to the band," Lesh said at an instrumental break.

"We need low end," Bob Weir said.

"Come on!" Lesh snapped. "Run 'em up, goddamnit! Who's running the amplifiers back here, anyhow?"

"There's the guy that's gonna run 'em up for us," Weir said, presumably at one of the crew.

"Hold it," Garcia cut in toward the end of "Attics." "Did somebody put a limiter on the monitors? Wait a minute." Off mic, a dog barked.

This bit about "the monitors" is especially revealing. In a written statement, vocalist Donna Jean Godchaux told me that performing through the Wall was "a major challenge" for a singer. "Those little bitty monitors were trying to compete with a giant wall behind us," Godchaux said. "Difficult." There may have been no foldback "wedges," yet there was an ear-level set of dedicated vocal monitors that acted as such in the system. "As you fine tune it and get it together," Parish told me, speaking of that Winterland soundcheck, "that became a thing about really hearing the vocals as good as we could for those guys. That was what you were overhearing right then, when that was starting to evolve."

Decades later, when Candelario's complete concert recording of February 23, night two at Winterland with their nearly-there Wall, was released as *Dave's Picks Volume 42*, the cover paid homage to the mighty PA. The psychedelic illustration featured a skeleton steering a tall ship carrying the Dead's soundsystem through the flooded streets of San Francisco.

On February 24, Graham introduced the band, saying, "This is a peaceful Sunday night with the Grateful Dead." Listen to Candelario's master two-track recording of that third Winterland gig, later released as *Dave's Picks Volume 13*, and the clarifying aspect of the PA is unquestionable. The Dead's techs had so finely tuned the system to the hall's acoustics that the sound filled only the spaces that needed covering. As Healy later told me, another part of the theory of the Wall "was to set it up so that 100 percent of the sound only went to 100 percent of the audience, and nowhere else."

That was strikingly clear even during the band's more exploratory passages. That evening's twenty-nine-minute "Dark Star," which Lesh has said is "always playing somewhere" and simply tapped into, may not have been "the most spectacular or aesthetically radical 'Dark Star' the band ever played," according to Ulf Olsson, the critic who wrote about the Dead and the politics of improvisation. "They do not take it out to absolute atonality and distortion—not until twenty-four minutes have passed," wrote Olsson, who did not attend the show. Like anyone else, he can listen to recordings thanks to Candelario, Betty Cantor, Jackson, Bear, and fan tapers who documented these and other shows over a half century ago. The music played that particular evening at Winterland, Olsson said, "cuts through the body, torments it, reminds it of another life that is at hand—in the music itself."

From the mid-'60s on, the Dead's improvisations had always been enabled by an increasingly higher-quality PA. Throughout the history of the band, the elaborate jams "depended on superior soundsystems," Theodore Gracyk later wrote in *Rhythm and Noise: An Aesthetics of Rock*. After all, "improvisational rock was hardly possible when the musicians had no stage monitors and the cheap amplification system distorted the music into a dull roar, with a sound mix that put the tinny vocals out front."

After expenses, the Dead made out of those Winterland gigs with $29,567, the equivalent of over $197,000 today. And "for the purposes of distributing profits from this gig," read a show earnings report, "no equipment or lighting expenses were charged against the profits." The money had to feed the soundsystem, considering that the equipment, staging, and scaffolding now weighed a combined forty-plus tons. That was soon to include Lesh's new quad "Mission Control" bass, a fully functioning part of the Wall thanks to Turner and others at Alembic. One time that year at Winterland, recalled Raizene, Lesh was playing that very instrument during soundcheck, bouncing notes around the venue.

"I'd really like to hear what..." Lesh started.

"Gimme the damn thing," said Raizene, plonking out notes while Lesh walked into the auditorium to fully experience the sound.

"Damn," Lesh said.

Raizene then messed with some of the eleven knobs on the bass, for controlling different sounds and tones. Lesh returned and said, "That works pretty good, doesn't it?"

"Fuckin' A!" Raizene hooted.

Aside from that instrument's electronics, "the thing was a work of art and easier than hell to play," Raizene told me. "I cranked it up for him a couple of times, so it would just sort of feed back. It was far out."

By then, Lesh's "Big Brown" bass already accounted for $250—around $1,600 today—of the band's monthly gear bill, per a two-page internal document, "March Equipment Costs 1974." That list included payments to San Rafael Carpet for speaker insulation, like the horsehair rug scraps lining the insides of cabinets like my artifact; Victor's Iron Works for "jack plugs, filter covers, handbook"; Willy Stryker's for "shop welding—PA"; "Mac California," for "front panel center cluster-Sparkie [sic]," for the black scrim; Zac's, a local parts supplier, for "PA"; Leo's Music for assorted equipment and supplies; and additional payments to Alembic for "PA consultation and supplies."

A slew of individual purchases were also tallied into those gear expenses, mostly on locally sourced PA components and assorted tools and kit (and labor, in some cases). Ram Rod, Raizene, Candelario, Winslow, Jackson, Parish, Bear, Curl, Healy, and Cardinalli all bought stuff and filed receipts with the band. Total equipment costs that month came to $22,779, around $150,000 today.

That was just one tranche alongside rising travel, salary, and office expenses, and even the cost of the musicians' union dues. A general "Grateful Dead Operating Statement" for March 1974 put total income at $452,237, around $3 million today. This other numbers-heavy Dead document listed $17,379 under "equipment costs"—$7,116 for "PA expense"—and stated that after $125,302 in expenses, the band-business profited $326,935 that month.

Not explicitly mentioned in these spring expense sheets? Quality Control. But in the arc of Dead developments, the fledgling speaker company, with a modest $743.59 (around $4,900 today) bank balance by the end of that March, "led to separating the PA from the band, in terms of how they toured post lay-off," Pechner said. "It became an outside entity completely. But this is how it started, when we decided, 'We can make this stuff and then sell it to other people.' I don't think we had realized we could've toured it. I don't think anybody had thought that far ahead."

March 23, 1974. The Dead's yearslong pursuit of audio perfection had come to this moment. The band was set for the second of the "2 sound experimentation gigs," at the Cow Palace, outside San Francisco. The Saturday night event was simply billed "The Sound Test."

The crew had arrived at the 16,500-capacity venue the day before the gig to construct the imposing mass of equipment, which had swelled in cost to over $350,000—some $2.3 million today. "We attacked it like a group of killer bees," Candelario recalled. There were now a dozen-plus columns of variously sized speakers, 480 in all, held in place by scaffolding bolted to the custom staging. Combined, Garcia and Weir had thirty cabinets; Lesh had sixteen a side. The very tallest columns rose forty-five feet above the stage. The system essentially beamed nearly fifty-foot-tall notes over the band and into the soundfield. Despite so much air being moved above the musicians' heads, they weren't immediately overwhelmed by all that power, meaning onstage sound pressure levels for the Wall sometimes measured lower than out in the hall. Yet even in the crowd, one could hold a normal conversation. The sound was that inoffensive.

For the first time, too, an indoor venue physically accommodated the Dead's load. "That was my real sound experiment, for everything," Parish later told me of the Cow Palace show. "I felt that was where we really had the elbow room and the space to do it."

Twenty heads had been present at yet another band meeting on March 14, ahead of the Sound Test. "Not ready to say yet what the final setup will be," read minutes, giving an update on modularization. "There will be a shape of center clusters, movable stacks, and the packaging will be different making it easier to setup." But Raizene, Healy, and others needed a little more time to complete that job, so the middle vocal rig for Daly City was still composed of individual speaker stacks. At that meeting, under "Gigs," the assembled talked additionally about how, save the New Riders, "the PA isn't compatible for other groups." They discussed "ways to get around that (interfacing setup, 2 stages, etc.)."

Then, the following afternoon, a "Mike" called the Dead's office and left a message regarding "soundsystem—Palo Alto" for "Ron." It's unclear if that meant Rakow, or, as likely, Wickersham. But the point remains: The sound was at the top of their groupmind. Money was, too, which always tied back to the Dead's PA. On March 13, another call had come into Dead HQ, from a Bank of Boston representative. That year, the bank used the term "cult" to describe the Dead, when the financial institution registered that the band's dedicated listenership meant the Dead and their in-house record distribution were a sound business bet. Yet the rep "wanted to discuss problems" and left a message for Rakow.

That month, while recording *Mars Hotel*, tensions were also building between band members. "But much of this comes from the pressure of running their own business," Rock Scully said, which involved flying to record pressing plants to ensure quality control, "and not seeing each other—not practicing that much."

They worked in a San Francisco studio with the capacity to sync up two 16-tracks. "As the band's soundsystem seemed to be testing the mid-seventies attitude of 'more might be nice,'" said Steve Brown, who was present at these sessions, "it was not surprising to find them filling up almost all thirty tracks with something." But the Dead always struggled in controlled environments, in contrast to the full sonic spectrum they could now cover live with their Wall. "We can play down to the level of a whisper, and we can play as loud as twenty jet airplanes," Garcia said that year. "So the expressiveness of our music is limited by recording."

In the meantime, even he and his bandmates were on weekly stipends. "The Dead have kept themselves poor from the beginning by putting money into sound," Wickersham told local reporter John L. Wasserman in a piece titled "The Dead: Committed to Sound Perfection" that was pegged to the Sound Test. "This project has been underway for about seven years," Wickersham said. "I've only been into it for about five and it's not finished yet. It's an ongoing study. Each performance is not only a musical performance but a sound performance."

The Sound Test drew in a cross-section of Deadworld. Shuttles went to and from the Dead's office and the Cow Palace. Guest lists ran to a combined 150-some-odd names. The core "Band and Crew" list noted twenty individuals (and plus-ones). A separate "Employees and Wives—Automatic Backstage & Special Seating" list accounted for dozens more, including familiar faces from earlier in the Dead's sonic journey like Laird Grant, the band's first-ever roadie and equipment manager. Also listed was Sue Swanson, who experienced the young band's wall-rattling sound and would later serve as the Dead's chief technology officer and webmaster, when the band's legacy moneymaking blossomed online. Cardinalli, the Alembic/Quality Control carpenter, got in too. Turner and Wickersham also were listed (with a plus-one and -two, respectively). The gig was not one to miss.

For a month, the Dead had run ads for the show on the local Top 40 radio station, overselling the event. When the band took the stage, the musicians passed through a dummy Wall speaker into the space in front of the solid backline. But as the gig started, seconds into "U.S. Blues," from *Mars Hotel*, the Wall balked. Garcia's guitar volume dropped suddenly after his first few notes. Is there anything more Dead-like "than their state-of-the-art, astronomically expensive soundsystem immediately screwing up and Garcia's guitar going missing during the opening song of the night?" said Ray Robertson, author of a micro history of the band in fifty shows.

The quick-acting crew had the issue sorted before long, and the band proceeded into a lengthy first set. "With speakers that reach as high as a three-story house, even in as uninviting a concert venue as the Cow Palace," which primarily still hosted livestock conventions and sports, "the music is loud and clear and rich," wrote Robertson, who did not attend the gig. And "not just to the audience, but to the *band*, an indispensable ingredient if the goal is symbiotic playing."

Moments in set two were less than symbiotic. When the band false started "Playing in the Band," something was off with Weir's vocals, an issue because he sang lead on that song. A minute or so in, as the tune fell apart, Garcia played the ominous theme from Chopin's "Funeral March."

"Wait a minute," Lesh said. "Sorry, sorry, sorry."

With no monitors in front of them, they were totally exposed—a direct line back to the Acid Tests, where no boundary existed between band and crowd. *Everybody* was in the soundfield, along for the ride. "The Wall was a very concrete manifestation of the idea that the band and the audience were the same," Steve Silberman, the Deadhead science writer, told me. "It was cosmic democracy."

Yet the band had broken what for so many groups is the number one rule of live performing. "Even the most-novice garage band knows that if something goes wrong on stage—speaker or microphone malfunction, a busted instrument, whatever—you're never supposed to stop playing," Robertson said. But doing precisely that, and having the crowd cheer them on until the problem got resolved, was just like the Dead.

"How 'bout it," Weir said as his mic came back on. "Ah, there it is. A thousand pardons, folks. We'll try it one more time."

The rest of the Sound Test went off without incident. The Dead "plays on and on, like they can't get enough of their brand new toy," Robertson wrote. Firsthand accounts speak of an acoustic environment with no dead zones—anywhere in the audience, the sound was "just exactly perfect," as Weir and others used to say. "Had no idea what I was looking at," recalled one head, whose friend shouted "Look at that soundsystem" repeatedly. "It was definitely an impressive event."

Another head remembered sitting cross-legged on the floor for that entire show, tripping on LSD. "No one tripped over me or was bothered by my non-verticality," the attendee said. And fortunately, "the soundsystem was amazing! The music came from every direction with pinpoint clarity. It was everywhere and anywhere all at once." When the show ended and Graham ordered the house lights turned on, the seated fan realized they had spent the whole evening facing the rear wall, with their back to the stage. "It didn't really matter where you were inside the Palace or what you did that night or what you saw. There was audible musical magic in the universe."

Yet another awed attendee similarly glimpsed the rig afterward. "That's when I first saw the magnitude of the 'Wall of Sound.' It truly went from wall to wall and to the ceiling," they recalled. "The speakers went right into the cloud of hazy smoke." Still others in the crowd that night called the Wall "absolutely historic," and said its qualities were "embedded in my soul" and had "shaped my life." As one Deadhead explained, "the Sound Test did such amazing things to my blown-out head I almost forgot I was an oiled sardine."

Weeks after the gig, a friend of David Gans, with whom he had also attended the Sound Test, acquired a tape of that show. At the gig, "it was just incredible how great the sound was," Gans, the future *Grateful Dead Hour* host, told me. Notably, during "China Cat Sunflower," "when they get to the bridge and they hit this giant E chord, Phil hit a note that caused the entire room to rattle." Gans then sat at his friend's place and listened back to the audience recording, and "when they got to that note in 'China Cat' it caused distortion on the tape too. That's a memory that just sticks out in my head."

The Test was a turning point in Gans's own collecting and trading of Dead tapes and also in the life of the soundsystem's moniker. In the days following the Cow Palace, the *San Francisco Chronicle*, alongside a black-and-white photo of the rig, printed the first known reference to the Dead's "Wall of Sound." It remains unclear if one of the crew, perhaps, was overheard using that nickname in Daly City, or if the *Chronicle's* photo editor can be credited. It didn't stick immediately—but it would, given enough time.

Years later, the Sound Test was released as *Dick's Picks Volume 24.* Dick Latvala, who likewise first got heavily into collecting tapes in 1974, tapped Bear to write liner notes about the Wall. "I told them before we began I was sure it could be done, the technology was available, but I was also sure they would not like it once they were locked into using it," Bear said. Yet the system represented "the first successful use of line arrays in large-scale sound reproduction. All of our lines were mounted tightly together as a single unbroken wall." Modern line arrays, by contrast, "are hung in isolation as two single, separated, multi-element line arrays. This arrangement will not radiate a cylindrical wave. Our only multi-element arrays were multiple-line clusters." The Wall was precisely that: "a radiating wall. The entire surface was working, the lines and clusters combining to produce a kind of sound no modern system can duplicate."

The differential vocal microphones, featuring pairs of B&K instrumentation mics, for that matter, "caused a loss of low frequencies in the voice," Bear admitted, "but it did limit spill quite nicely." Had the differential design been pushed further, they might well have "eliminated" that tinny sound that came from losses in the low frequencies. But each musician now had control over their instrument levels, and could likewise dial in their own vocal settings. "It was a system which needed no sound man," said Bear.

Besides Healy, Bear was synonymous with "sound man"—and long insistent on that being *his* role. But in "realizing this system," Bear shouted out Wickersham, Curl, John Meyer, Matthews, and Healy for their technical expertise, and also said that "virtually everyone in the crew had some part in constructing this monster." The Wall, Bear claimed, "was arguably the best large venue system for amplified music ever."

The first show post Sound Test was supposed to then take place at the University of California, Davis, only a familiar problem arose. The band was "unable to fit its new soundsystem on stage," the *California Aggie*, the campus paper, reported.

So the Dead again did something they hadn't done yet. They stacked the full system outside.

May 12, 1974. The Washoe Zephyr, a seasonal daytime wind that barrels across western Nevada, blasted the backside of the Wall. The system was assembled on an outdoor stage "like some huge beehive racked up on a scaffolding" at Mackay Stadium in Reno. The Dead were in town for another afternoon Mother's Day gig marked by a curious aerial phenomenon. The gusts rocked the just-completed suspended center cluster.

A tech meeting was called at the Dead's new San Rafael rehearsal space on Front Street in the week before Reno. The promoter's crew and the Dead's people then spent two full days erecting the stage and soundsystem. One could imagine the anxiety leading into the gig. This first time they "flew" the modular array is a milestone and the stuff of lore. "It was like a hurricane!" Brown recalled of conditions that day. "I thought it was going to collapse. 'This is really bad!' I was scared. It was untested." Hundreds of speakers, "being put up with University of Nevada stagehand help."

Kreutzmann, whose drums sat on a riser directly below the two-ton vocal cluster, ran out from underneath. The speakers "were hung from one single winch and if something went wrong or if the speakers ever broke free, I would be flat as a penny on a railroad track," he said. Kreutzmann insisted that the rigging be supported by two more winches, "for extra insurance." At his request, the crew also hung the cluster from the corners, not just down the middle, to better stabilize the load and prevent swaying anytime the wind blew.

The cluster itself was beyond ruggedized. The two pieces were given aircraft-grade wheels with four- or five-inch casters. The treads were a kind of Teflon material, and each wheel alone could take thousands of pounds. Rifkin, who stepped away from co-manager duties but now helped handle onstage mics and cables, once had his foot run over by accident; the weight of the cluster nearly severed his toes. Arriving at a venue, they rolled the unit onto the end of the truck, where a forklift took it down and brought it to the stage. Their contracts that year denoted specific forklift brands—Hyster, Clark, Yale—that the Dead knew would withstand the job. "Nothing else would do," Sally Mann Romano, a friend of the band who began working for the Dead office, later said. "The wrong stage construction would have meant the stage would have fallen in and people would have died."

Once off-loaded onto the stage, the cluster got rolled into position and raised using electric chain hoists. Out in the audience, Healy, having predetermined the right elevations, helped guide the unit into place at the proper level. He even had one-tenth-scale models of the Wall's bracing and speakers, and before tours "would set it up and then translate it all to real, full size," he told me. He got venue blueprints and drew the Dead's entire rig on top. "I would plot where all the speakers went and the nature of how the scaffolding would look, for each and every show."

Pechner remembered Kreutzmann sizing up this scene onstage at Reno, after the cluster was raised. "When we engineered how to fly the Wall of Sound, we'd already figured out that it had to be two halves, because making it one cabinet was unwieldy," said Pechner, who also took color photos that day. "But because we put wheels on it then we figured we can just take the two, mate 'em together on the stage, and then lift 'em into place." Kreutzmann was uneasy. "He goes, 'You gotta move me out,'" Pechner said, "which required the stage being deeper, because he didn't want to sit under it."

They had recently gotten a catalog from the industrial supply company Grainger, which had an office near the Dead's shop. "I looked up these winches that could lift two tons each, so we figured out we can lift it, but we also had to angle it," Pechner said. "So we put a third one on the front so once it's up, tilt it wherever you want. They had wire remote controls so we just flew it like that." Nowadays, "everybody flies that stuff," he added. "It's all hung [with] winches. But I gotta think we were one of the first to do that."

The cluster had large eye hooks that the hoists attached to. The heavy-duty hooks went through the top of the grid, into the truss framework, which was really what held all the weight and kept the cluster from breaking apart. (The load was too heavy to have been just a box; if they had done that and tried to lift by the lid, the lid would've ripped off.) "I think that was probably the most potential for danger," Pechner said. "But because it was so over-designed, one lift—one of those winches—was twice the capacity, double what the load was." A single winch could've lifted both cluster pieces into place, and they had three. "When we'd get it in position we just put a hard line on it against the scaffolding, so it couldn't go anywhere. It was pretty secure."

Raizene purchased the cylindrical winches, which weighed eighty pounds apiece and were roughly the size of a table-top microwave. "We'd get it set up, then we'd figure out, with pink noise, the angle" for the cluster, he told me. Typically that was in the 4 to 6 degree range, as seen in a one-of-a-kind technical drawing I found in the Pechner Papers. Signed by Weir and Lesh, the sketch depicts the Wall at an unspecified 1974 show, though the handwritten "tilt is 4°" and "fill to cover house" arrowed at the cluster were prescriptions for that given venue. The drawing, replete with scaffolding bay numbers, was likely made by Weir and one of the crew, for the purpose of setting up the gear.

"Then I used these safety wires to make sure that if it did go for some reason, it wasn't gonna go very far," Raizene said, of fastening the cluster. "Because Kreutzmann said, 'Hey, I'm right underneath this shit!' I said, 'Don't worry. It's not gonna slip. If it does, I'll let you know.'"

Building the structure was a matter of protecting the PA from the elements, and also protecting the audience—and the band—from the PA. Unlike other sound reinforcement companies, "we never had a system come down ever, once," Healy told me. "We went out of our way." And Raizene "would be the person that was adamant about that. Everybody understood. Nobody disagreed. Nobody argued with him. It was just a question of who was gonna take initiative to do it." So much of the Wall "was the initiative of the people who were responsible for making it work," Healy added. "A monstrosity like that does not work itself. There was no possible way to make it user friendly. It was very quirky, like building a jigsaw puzzle each show."

But at Reno, another kind of fear struck the air: that what was billed as "the most powerful soundsystem in the world," though not necessarily the loudest, would draw noise complaints, resulting in a court order to shut the show down. That morning, the promoter, university officials, and local police met and "encountered the sound problem," the *Reno Evening Gazette* reported. The head of student union activities first raised the possibility of "the rock sound" triggering a petition, likely among local residents, against the concert. "If we're served with an order to shut it off, we'll have to shut it off," the university police chief told the *Gazette*.

No such order was served, though the Reno gig started an hour and a half late. During a quick soundcheck, Weir reportedly singled out the one speaker that wasn't working right and needed adjustments. Some fans waiting outside the stadium's entrance said they could see Lesh's test notes fluttering in a decorative water fountain. "If we could be half as loud as this wind, we'd be doing alright," Lesh told the crowd as the band tuned up. "Anyone know what time the Washoe Zephyr pulls out of town?" he asked once the show was underway. Lesh later called the sound at Reno "a brilliant stroke," and "absolutely clear and coherent from a quarter mile. And *loud*."

For some in the crowd of an estimated ten thousand heads, the gusts that afternoon appeared to come out of the Wall. Kreutzmann, for his part, would one day call the system "the pinnacle of the great Owsley sound experiment." But it was disconcerting that the enormous load was "all assembled and disassembled on a daily basis, leaving much room for fault."

The cluster held that first flight. Out in the soundfield, the gusts could momentarily carry the sound away, though the gig was still a "stereo buff's dream," the *Gazette* reported. At the very back of the field, one head swore they could hear a loose nut in Kreutzmann's kickdrum pedal, the "transparency" of the PA was that amazing.

At one point, a farmer tractored up, and Parish talked to him out back. "He came from three miles down the road," Parish told me. "He was working in his field and he heard the sound of the show completely. He came over to see what was going on because it was so loud." Yet, if you stood onstage in front of the rig as the band played you couldn't hear it, really, owing to most of the air blowing above the musicians' heads, boosted by the zephyr. "It was mind blowing," Parish said. "Trying to make that PA work in the confines of what you'd call the metaphysical world was difficult. It pushed everything to the limits, as it took us along with it. We thought we controlled it, but it ended up controlling us in a lot of ways."

May 14, 1974. With a handful of "warm-up" Wall shows down, the Dead had ironed out most of the initial system kinks. Entering Missoula, for the only gig the band ever played in the Big Sky State, they were poised to expand their sonic campaign. Some might even say this was the *real* "first Wall of Sound show."

Seven thousand heads packed Harry Adams Field House at the University of Montana that Tuesday night, the first of a six-date summer Pacific Northwest run. "The Grateful Dead is audible to the very last seat when they perform," the *Montana Kaimin* reported ahead of the gig. "The group uses 459 speakers that usually take about 12 hours to set up."

Walking into the Field House that evening, Mark Parker, later of Yellowstone Public Radio, immediately locked on to the rig. "The first thing I saw was this huge bank of speakers almost to the ceiling," Parker recalled. By then, the Dead's caravan was up to four trucks, hauling roughly seventy-five tons of equipment. Their 1974 contract rider, dubbed "The Book," held eleven sections of technical information, from electrical requirements to grounding, to stage and stage-related structures. One of the various accommodations indoor venues had to meet? Concrete floors.

The crew was hitting its own rhythm, a feat given the Wall, including staging and scaffolding, took as many as twenty-six road members and fourteen hours to assemble, in some cases. They followed a routine that they had been refining for years: Day of show, they began at 8:00 a.m. and spent the next two hours getting all the gear on stage; by midday, they had the speakers stacked and broke for lunch. By 4:00 p.m., the whole rig was wired up with the amps running. By 8:00 p.m. the gig would have begun, and the band then played until 1:00 a.m. Pack up and load out by 4:00 a.m., then travel through the night to begin again the next day, in a new town.

"I don't know how anybody else could've ever done it," Parish told me. "We were so used to not sleeping and eating." Yet they were young and strong and "able to pull it off." Parish likened the *Odyssey*-like esprit de corps among the Wall crew to iron men on wooden ships carrying supermassive cargo and speedrunning the setup. "People always tell me, 'Well, you guys had two crews and you had two sets of equipment,'" Parish said. "Horseshit. We had one fuckin' Wall of Sound. The only thing we did was have a skeleton crew to set up the scaffolding—you had to have that exactly right. We had to have a couple of guys that went ahead. When we did one-nighters with that thing, we were men of steel."

To motivate them, Hunter, one of the band's lyricists, began writing sea shanties. "He wanted me to teach them to the crew when we used to put up the Wall of Sound, because we used to haul 'em up with line and block," Parish has said. "The other guys wouldn't get into it, but it was 'Lift that bail...' kinda thing." When he wrote for the Dead, Hunter told the *Oakland Tribune* that June, the words "must (within limits of course) speak for all of us, the community and the equipment guys too."

At any given gig, Healy now carried what was effectively a full electronics shop to keep the Wall running. "Every show I would have to completely rebuild amplifiers and stuff," Healy told me. "I had inventory and parts. Spare transistors—I'd buy them hundreds at a time," he said. "There wasn't anything that had to do with sound and electronics that we couldn't repair or deal with when we were on the road." Not infrequently, they were modifying and fixing stuff within the Wall just minutes before a show started. "It's like an extremely sophisticated race car," Healy said. "It's never quite ready." To win the race, "you have to spend continuous time giving it attention. There's always something that makes it better, always something that it needs, or that needs correcting. We tried to stay on top of it all."

This on-the-spot work demanded a level of acrobatics across the Wall that happened almost completely in the dark, if the show was indoors and underway. Candace Brightman, controlling the lights, would obscure the system. "You only want to hear the music, and in the darkness sight doesn't get in the way of your listening," Brightman later said. "In general, don't make a statement—let the band carry the show." Working closely with Healy, Brightman's own rig and approach to light emerged alongside the band's sonic evolution. Lighting the musicians so they could still make out the crowd, or even straight-up spotlighting the crowd, she further dissolved any barriers remaining between the Dead and the audience.

Back in Missoula, the setting was exemplary of why the Dead even needed to have their own PA over a given house system. Visible in the upper left corner of yet another photo of Pechner's is the Adams Field House PA, a small circular cluster of eight ceiling-mounted speaker cabinets, which wouldn't have cut it for the Dead. The band's "wall of speakers," the *Missoulian* reported, "made the music loud, but not a blare." Their rig "is the most innovative and experimental system in the world," as each band member had their own individual PA that "tied into the whole."

Here again, there wasn't a bad seat in a house not known for stellar acoustics. "At every other arena show I'd heard, the only decent-sounding place to be was right in front of the stage," attendee Milo Miles wrote decades later in an NPR piece pegged to the *Dave's Picks Volume 9* release of that Missoula recording. "Awed by the Wall of Sound, I walked all around … and it was like Jerry Garcia was picking guitar right next to me."

Not only was the Wall visually overwhelming, but it was as if a giant stereo system had been set up. "Best sounding show ever," yet another attendee said. Listen to a recording of that gig, and the separation and total clarity between the instruments can be hard to articulate in words. "What you hear here is what we heard then," the fan added. The Dead reportedly could even be perceived across campus that night, where the sound was still "sensational."

If the Cow Palace Sound Test had been just that—a "trial"—and Reno subject to conditions that demanded a different kind of focus, then "the Wall of Sound really starts here" in Missoula. That's according to one reviewer's comment under the show's recording on the Archive. They have a point. The Dead's operation by Montana was clearly dialed in after a gauntlet of shows over the past months, and only climbed higher into the summer, experimenting with unheard-of sonics.

But when the band, who got paid $20,000 for the gig, returned for an encore, someone in the crowd threw a plastic beer stein toward the stage and beaned Weir. The band played "One More Saturday Night" and split.

May 17, 1974. The Dead had returned to the PNE Coliseum in Vancouver. Up in the scaffolding, some roadies made adjustments. Under house lights before doors opened, the band let loose.

At the first several Wall road appearances, there had been no chance to run full pre-show PA tests with the musicians. "We weren't able to get it set up in time for the band to come out and do a soundcheck," Pechner told me. "Literally, they were opening the doors and we'd be up there still, plugging stuff in. The band would be chirpin' in the background. 'I wanna plug it in, I wanna test.' Didn't happen." The first few songs of the band's opening set often amounted to a kind of soundcheck. But in Vancouver, they had enough of a window.

"A phone call went to the hotel," Pechner said. "Hey, you guys wanna do a soundcheck? We've got forty-five minutes before doors open." So they came over and plugged in. "Zen," Pechner remembered. "Not only was the band not in show mode, they were in rehearsal mode, so they were dicking around." If you wandered into the empty hall, you realized how "powerful and clean" the sound really was. "It was fucking unreal," Pechner said. "I don't think there was ever a moment where you had that kind of opportunity. Phil would go string to string, and you could *see* it."

The effect was extraterrestrial. Pechner likened it to the five-note "light" theme—*buh, buh, buh, buh, buhhh*—beamed from UFOs in Steven Spielberg's *Close Encounters* (1977). "You couldn't see the lights, but it would go around like that," he said, of Lesh's quad bass noodling each string to its own stack. "He would just roll it and you'd go, *What the fuck, man?! This really is cool.*"

They had reached still another milestone. Pechner can remember talking with Ram Rod and others at Vancouver, "all congratulating ourselves at actually, finally, getting our shit together," he said. "It was the best soundsystem, like having your home stereo turned on for the first time and going from mono to stereo, and hearing separation and the tones and the intricacies of what they could do." And the show hadn't even begun. "It was so overwhelming. They turned that up, just trying to test it to see how much they could pump through."

Pechner walked into the soundfield, framed the band and PA onstage, and began taking pictures. One of Pechner's wides of the Wall that afternoon is another defining visual document of the system. "Talk about being fortunate," he said. "I was there as a roadie and I happened to be a photographer. At the time there was a lot of negative photography vibes." Yet his camera had its own Halliburton case, which all individual crew members were issued at Ram Rod's behest. Pechner chronicled that entire Pacific Northwest run and licenses his Wall images to this day.

Minor technical hiccups still arose from the system during the actual show. "Truckin'," for instance, was "Bobby-flubbed," according to one "Vancouver 5/17/74" memory, "and has mic dropouts (that came with the fickle and unreliable Wall of Sound). But the end jam is fine."

Two days later, at the Portland Memorial Coliseum, the band took the stage fifteen minutes late—no time for a check before doors. The sound was only "so-so" that night, and "the acoustics of the building didn't do the soundsystem justice," one head recalled. One had to be close "to really hear the vocals, and good instrumental separation."

Before "Truckin'" in the second set, Weir addressed the audience. "We're having technical difficulties, as you might have assumed," he said. But the band–crowd energy was still "enormous" that evening, despite the acoustics and the cops turning on the house lights and pulling the power a little after midnight.

At the next Pacific Northwest stop, the Hec Edmundson Pavilion at the University of Washington in Seattle, on Tuesday, May 21, the Dead faithful "came to hear the band, they came to see the Wall of Sound, they got what they came for," Robertson wrote in his fifty-show microhistory. Notably, the Dead clocked the longest-ever "Playing in the Band" that night: forty-six and a half minutes. That was no coincidence. Everything in Deadworld, from the music to the playing to the soundsystem, was peaking in late spring 1974. The sound, as one attendee recalled, was "so clean and clear."

On May 25, the Dead returned to the Campus Stadium at UC Santa Barbara, site of the falling speaker incident. The Great American String Band (featuring Garcia) and vocalist Maria Muldaur, of "Midnight at the Oasis" fame, both opened the gig. Fog hung in the area in the days preceding the event. Over concerns about setting up the rig on the eve of the gig, a "decision was made to tarp the entire Wall for protection from the elements," Pechner recalled.

In color photos he took of that show, the blue sheeting is like a hood over the scaffolding superstructure.

Meanwhile, fans camping in the field next to the stadium watched the rig come together, when suddenly, the grass sprinklers turned on. John Conroy, a photographer on assignment with the promoter and the university, had arrived earlier in the week and also watched the Dead's advance team build the stage, now a kind of "island" ten feet above the audience. By Thursday or Friday, "as they kept stacking speakers and hanging things from up high," Conroy told me, "it was like, *Are you kidding me? What is this thing?!*"

Covering the setup, Conroy and a buddy had posted up in the venue's rear bleachers. They could see a man walk off the stage and toward the back, rolling out a big tape measure. Conroy was popping off shots when the guy ran up and grabbed him by the throat.

"What are you taking pictures of?" the man asked.

"I'm just hired to take pictures of the setup," Conroy said.

"Give me that film!" the man demanded.

Conroy had two cameras and gave the man the film from the one with nothing on it. The man turned and left.

"Do you know who that was?" Conroy's friend said. "That was Owsley Stanley."

Conroy has photographs of that moment—pictures Bear himself never knew about. "At that point he was on parole and I don't think he was allowed to be with the band," Conroy said. "He didn't like being photographed, I know that."

That afternoon, Bear's associates, Turner and Wickersham, also ventured deep into the soundfield, to listen. "It was just incredible with the full system," Turner told me. He and Wickersham walked a good half mile out from the stage, "and it was clear as a bell. It was just phenomenal. It was really quite amazing." Because they weren't mixing everything through a single set of speakers, "the intermodulation distortion was really low. In that sense, it was like the effect of a large pipe organ." The Wall was a kind of instrument that could be played.

Such simple in-the-field listening tests were not yet common practice among rock and roll bands, much less the nascent pro sound industry. "Most other people never go far away from their system to hear what their system is actually doing," Wickersham told me, speaking of that site-specific walk with his then business partner. "They miss that—or just give up on it."

Filing into the campus stadium once gates had opened, still more fans were struck by the sight of the system. "That fucking Wall of Sound that reached up to Heaven," one head recalled. Another individual, settling a few dozen feet in front of the stage, was "astonished to see that monster soundsystem... looking like a giant Martian hieroglyphic."

When the Dead came on that unseasonably hot Saturday, the sun reportedly broke through the haze. Chuck Nagel, who then worked special orders for JBL, caught many Wall shows, but counted Santa Barbara among the top. "We shipped a hell of a lot of speakers," Nagel recalled. "Nothing like JBL and McIntosh for a little power. When they did their wind up it would literally move the crowd."

The festivities were documented by one "Russ D." on regular 8mm color film with no sound—the only moving images of an outdoor Wall show, and its kaleidoscopic crowd, known to exist. One fan, along with some friends, had positioned themselves "dead center" on the lawn, and later wrote that the show "was definitely the most incredible (and memorable) Dead concert ever for us, being the first time we ever saw, heard, and felt The Wall of Sound monster." Another attendee, lying on the grass and chewing peyote, noted that "the clarity of the sound was amazing even at 50 yards away."

At set break, the Dead's sound crew pumped the Beatles' *Sgt. Pepper's Lonely Hearts Club Band* through the Wall. As Wickersham told me, even intermission music played over the PA got applause. The fidelity was *that* good. Once the band returned, the crowd was again "bathed in crystal clear sound that could crack like close thunder," yet another head recalled, "or drop to the quietest nuance of Jerry's little pinkie on the fretboard."

One of Conroy's other photos from that daytime show, snapped from a helicopter looking down on the event, gives a sense of scale like few other images of the Wall from this era. The rig itself, off to one side, doesn't dominate the frame; what *does* is the mass of humanity—some twenty-three thousand people—to which the system broadcast good sound. "You could pick out one instrument and hear it crystal clear," Conroy remembered. "And the vocals were so sharp. It was quite amazing."

Even better? No speakers fell that day.

At an early June band meeting, the Dead aggressively plotted the rest of their year and into the next. They discussed approximate August dates to begin shipping gear out for a European Wall run, an outrageous task even by Dead standards. They hoped to then continue touring the States that autumn, with a proposed "couple of nights to cover loans," maybe in November and one on

New Year's, and another the following March. "Can Matthews run PA," minutes read. "Richie on the road."

But more immediate concerns were also addressed, like the roof for their next show, at the Oakland Coliseum on June 8. The Graham-promoted concert was billed "A Day on the Green" and featured a four-act bill: Bay Area rock band Commander Cody and His Lost Planet Airmen, who had opened the recent Vancouver show; the New Riders; the Beach Boys; and the Dead. Thirty thousand heads turned up for the all-day event. Tickets were $8.50 advance, $10 at the gate. Music started at 10:00 a.m.

The weather cooperated, easing any stage roofing concerns. In the highest sections of scaffolding, splashes of color marked the occasion. The band and crew had moved on from the trippy speaker covers made by Pollock, which ultimately weren't allowing enough air through, and over the past months a few stragglers on the band's amps were removed. "That was when they nixed the idea of maintaining the tie-dye screens," Pollock told me. Really, the Wall "was too big, too intricate." Preserving the cohesive mandala-like design over such a huge and ever-shifting surface "wasn't practical—there'd be so much damage all the time. Seventy tons of equipment. It's *a lot*."

But Pollock, now working for the Dead's label, was known to string psychedelic banners from the Wall's bracing, like at Oakland. "I remember climbing up that scaffolding and hanging on for dear life," Pollock said. "Nowadays, you couldn't get near the stage without all this documentation, let alone the scaffolding. We were still just cobbling together as we developed it—I don't think any of that was ever discussed. I would just do it." At Dead shows through the end of the summer, he hung his banners and then helped the road crew set up, "juggling hundred-plus-pound cabinets...trying to get it up on top of another one," he said. "Ram Rod's like, 'Can you reach that one, Courtenay?' And I'm like, 'I can kind of, but I'm on my fingertips and toes.' He's like, 'We need someone taller.' It is amazing that there was never a calamity."

Meanwhile, more people in the audience were acquiring live tapes of these summer Wall shows. That year, "taping became more serious," Bob Menke, the first-generation Dead taper, later told *Audio* magazine. Another veteran taper, Jerry Moore, recalled how reels eked out into the community and that he was "hearing stuff from the summer of '74 tour before the tour was over."

Together with advancing compact hi-fi cassette technology, the Wall boosted the burgeoning taper scene. "Fans began trading, copying, stockpiling, cataloging, and commenting on tapes, and many young people's first exposure to the Dead came through those recordings," Mark Richardson wrote in his Dead cultural history. Some Deadheads prefer audience tapes to soundboard recordings, as the only way to *really* listen to Wall shows, placed right in the soundfield.

The band was still playing back their own tapes too. "They would go into the hotel room after the show or the next day and listen for purposes of doing a better job," Latvala, the original Dead archivist, later told the Dead fanzine *Dupree's Diamond News*. Indeed, Wickersham told me, the goal of the Wall project—or at least one of them—was to make better recordings. By that point, "I was less intimately involved with stuff, because the design was complete," Wickersham said. But "the soundsystem was because we didn't want to record distortion in the hall."

Back at the Oakland Coliseum, the Beach Boys were set, as specified by the Dead road and sound crews. There were lots of "Frisbees, streakers, and getting high in one way or another and sun" in the half-hour break before the surf pop band started, according to a *Rolling Stone* review of the gig, titled "The Dead Raise the Sound—26,000 amps and 400 speakers bring Dead gig alive." (That was meant to read "watts," not "amps.") By all accounts the crowd responded warmly to the Beach Boys, whose "Good Vibrations" encore "really tore the place up and struck the keynote for the afternoon."

The two California bands were no strangers. In April 1971 at the Fillmore East, they played some songs together, including "Help Me Rhonda." Kevin Smith, then the Beach Boys' road manager, first met the Dead at Chicago's Auditorium Theatre that autumn; Lesh was hyped on having just gotten his first "Alembicized" quad bass, Smith recalled—the same one he played in Oakland. "So I knew the Dead's crew already," Smith said, "and they showed me the ins and outs of the Wall of Sound concept. Amazing! No monitor console, they each mixed their own monitors onstage! Which is why the Beach Boys had their own PA system." Their production manager, moreover, "didn't trust the concept of the Wall of Sound." In gig photos, the Beach Boys' foldback speakers lined the stage lip.

At the set change, Bear approached Smith and asked why the Beach Boys hadn't used the Wall. "He told me he had designed the PA himself and was a bit upset by our decision not to use it," Smith claimed. "I explained to him it was not my call." Once they tore down most of their gear and loaded into their own truck, Smith clocked an ambulance pulling up backstage. It was dispatched for Bear, who was in the scaffolding helping disassemble the Beach Boys' PA, when he took a wrong step and fell.

"Ope, we lost Bear!" said Cantor, now primarily visiting pressing plants to ensure quality control of the Dead's studio albums. Then pregnant with her and Jackson's child, she recalled how Bear "took a dive" from one of the scaffolds that afternoon. "Not a huge ways," Cantor told me. "Just one segment up. Watch your step, dude!" Bear walked away with a broken arm, the only known instance of someone falling off the Wall.

The changeover was otherwise prompt. But some in the crowd apparently pelted the stage. As the Dead tuned up, Lesh, seen earlier "kicking back" high up on a speaker, took the mic. "Do us a favor," he said. "Save the plastic bottles and anything else for your friends out there."

Then the Dead hit. "Not a corner of the open, 55,000-seat stadium wanted for loud, clear sound, primarily due to the Dead's incredible soundsystem," *Rolling Stone* reported. "The clarity is amazing, and in combination with the volume could probably fill Death Valley with sound." The steep admission price was "justified by the high level of quality in the production and music."

The gig checked all the right boxes. "Out-of-this-world soundsystem, sunshine, thick smoke, loud, loud music," said one tripping head, who recalled Garcia giving "a kick of his leg as the shivering electricity jolted through the Coliseum." Lesh, for that matter, was "shaking the temple walls."

Corry Arnold, creator of Lost Live Dead, a career-spanning collection of press clippings, original analysis and essays, and scene reports, also attended that Saturday gig. "Most rock soundsystems in the day were loud enough, but had all sorts of holes in them—you couldn't hear the piano, or the highs were fuzzy, or the bass sounded different all over the house," Arnold later said. But standing at centerfield, "I really felt I was peering into the Future of Sound. The band played loud enough that I could hear every note, yet at the same time I could carry on a conversation in a normal tone of voice with my friend." At one point, Arnold watched Kreutzmann snap a drumstick. "But I could hear the audible 'click' on the mic as it broke," he said, "and I was absolutely amazed."

June 16, 1974. The Dead were back in Des Moines for another Graham-promoted gig at the State Fairgrounds. That humid Sunday kicked off the rest of the Dead's summer Wall run. But already there was financial stress behind the scenes.

"We really appreciate the deposit for this show prior to embarking on a long tour, as it would extremely help the cash flow," Loren, the band's new tour manager, wrote to Graham ahead of that show. The gig contract covered fifteen thousand tickets at $6 a pop ($6.50 at the door) and a $35,000 guarantee for the Dead—around $225,000 today—plus 60 percent of all gross receipts after the band had been paid. Graham's FM Productions was guaranteed $15,000.

The band's rig towered over the high-stakes proceedings. A "stage and scaffolding addendum" to the Dead's production packet called for an acoustic treatment-style "sound wall," eight feet tall and forty-eight feet wide, set on the stage floor eight feet behind the scaffolding towers. The addendum also stated that the promoter needed to provide eight stagehands at the venue by 8:00 a.m., "to help set up stage and scaffolding." These local crew "shall be available to help the Grateful Dead equipment and PA crew on day of engagement, and in fact should not be the same men to do both jobs requiring rested and alert bodies and minds." The document required that a pair of forklifts, each capable of lifting five thousand pounds, be waiting for the Dead on arrival.

Yet there was a problem, as they realized during load in. "I had to fix a bunch of amps or some shit before we packed out" for the drive to Iowa, Raizene told me. "I got everything done but I forgot the microphones—the noise-canceling jobs." He called home and said, "Shit!" Bonnie Parker, one of the Dead's accountants, ended up flying out with the microphones, arguably the component a custom system like theirs most relied upon. They might not have been "totally fucked" if Parker hadn't pulled through, Raizene added, but they would've had to scramble to buy a bunch of omnidirectional mics locally and wire them up. Parker "loved it because she never went on the road—hardly at all," Raizene said.

In the meantime, unconfirmed reports of a man dying from "bad acid" while waiting for gates to open began circulating. The crowd was "fairly rough looking, more biker types than hippies," one head recalled. Fans arriving that afternoon reportedly could hear the Dead's soundcheck from nearly a mile out, clean and clear. My mom, twenty, was again present in some capacity, and was issued a backstage pass. Before the show began, once a few trash cans behind the Wall were filled with ice and Heinekens, a now routine announcement was made through the just-arrived mics: "Please don't throw Frisbees at the speakers."

The Dead played three sets—the second year running in Des Moines—over five hours, including short breaks. Obligatory technical difficulties ran through opener "Bertha," mostly in Garcia's vocals and guitar volume. Then came an extended pause and restless audience noise as the crew fixed a blown cone. "If there's anybody out there who can't see what's happening," Lesh said, "we're replacing a bad speaker. And as you all know these things take . . . *time.*"

But the audio problems kept coming. "Can't remember which band member it was," one witness claimed, "maybe Jerry, that joked he thought there was a tweeter at the top of the Wall that was acting up." During between-song tuning, PA feedback pierced the air. "That was the wind whistling through the microphones," Weir told the audience. But nearing the end of set one, a scorching "China Rider" jam took over. (The Dead typically segued "China Cat Sunflower" into "I Know You Rider," hence the oft-used shorthand.)

"Des Moines 6/16/74" produced a "pristine soundboard recording of the Wall of Sound," Deadhead Howard Weiner, who did not attend the show, wrote in *Deadology: The 33 Essential Dates of Grateful Dead History*. "Sonic brilliance and terrifying energy are unleashed hand in hand," Weiner said of that "China Rider" jam. "Guitars growl and grind against jackhammer bass patterns as Billy's drumming blends jazz and rock, propelling the jam forward and filling the soundscape."

Then came the jolt. "Around and Around," the set one closer—another Chuck Berry cover—modulated up mid-guitar solo, which "sent an electric surge through the crowd," remembered one head. The swell is audible on the tape.

The *Des Moines Register* highlighted the "new PA" backing the band. "It's about the same size as the old system, which is to say huge," the paper reported. "But the speakers are set up above and behind the band instead of off to each side of the stage." Placing monitors behind microphones "generally has caused severe feedback, but the Dead have overcome this for the most part." The PA tone quality, the *Register* added, "was excellent and the mix on instruments was good.... But the vocals, always the main hassle, weren't quite out front. From the grandstand, in fact, they were buried." Lesh partially blamed that on the "good" mics being "inadvertently left behind." In gig photos, the Dead clearly used more rudimentary phase-canceling units. Parker had seemingly grabbed an earlier version of the microphones by mistake.

But according to one twenty-year-old attendee, the soundsystem was still so amazing their jaw dropped at the first notes: "It sounded like the best McIntosh home stereo that you ever heard except BIGGER!" Another head in the crowd that afternoon spoke of "the crystal clear Wall o' Sound," and wondered what anyone living a mile away thought of the show, "as they had to've had a pretty good listen." Really, "the acoustical sweet spot was the whole stadium, with the Wall."

Seemingly regardless of age, experiencing the system could change a person. "THE WALL OF SOUND MADE ME HEAR THINGS THAT YOU'RE NOT SUPPOSED TO," one Iowa head later recalled in a written memory. "Even to this day I am just going, *huh*, when nothing is being said."

The band again performed psychic-sonic weather control through the Wall that day, or at least it appeared that way to some. "Big puffy white clouds marched across the sky," yet another head remembered. "When a cloud covered the sun, the band would go into a modal scale. The crowd would all sit down and the dancing would nearly cease. Then the sun would come back out and the band would switch back into a 12-tone scale. The crowd would rise back up and the dancing would begin again." This apparently carried on all afternoon, "almost like the band was playing the crowd."

The audience was rapt. By the end of the performance, "the crowd responded warmly, apparently charmed by the subtle differences," the *Register* reported. A "Casey Jones" encore "left the fans quite satisfied."

After the encore, Lesh, whose "Mission Control" bass, considered a part of the Wall, made its onstage debut that day, took the mic. "Thanks a billion, folks," he said, almost ecstatic. "See ya all next year."

The Dead wouldn't play Iowa again until 1978.

The following day, back in Marin County, Chesley Millikin, a Dead management confidante, mailed a letter to a promoter in Guadalajara, Mexico. The organizer was trying to get the band to perform there.

"We need certain information prior to any serious discussion," Millikin wrote. "Please advise the name of the facility, photographs from various angles, capacity, ticket prices, expected attendance, and what tie-in you plan through your 13 radio stations. Naturally, we are most concerned with the safe transportation of our equipment as well as requiring legal guarantees of its passage from and to San Francisco."

The Dead now mandated a raft of such venue and promoter assurances. The Guadalajara show never materialized but spoke to the tedious advancing done for prospective dates, especially international ones, like the upcoming early fall European tour. The overseas trip was discussed at a meeting in San Rafael on June 17. Garcia's longtime friend Alan Trist and others addressed shipping a slimmed-down, though no less massive rig to London. "The band have 30 tons of equipment made up mostly of JBL Studio Monitors (approx. 460 of them) amps., etc.," read the meeting minutes, "which is estimated will cost $29,000 to air freight one way." That's over $372,000 today, round trip.

Meanwhile, on June 18, the Dead ripped a Tuesday nighter at the nineteen-thousand-capacity Freedom Hall in Louisville, Kentucky. No known photographic record of the gig exists, so it's unclear if the "good" mics had arrived from the West Coast by then. Turnout was poor, but "all I can say is you had to have been there to appreciate what that humongous monstrosity could spew and spray in gorgeous color-layered display," recalled one head, who claimed they saw a dozen Wall shows. Others wouldn't have considered themselves Dead fans, but "went mainly to see the 'Wall of Sound.'" Decades later, discovering a soundboard recording of the gig on the Archive was "like finding treasure in the attic." Selections from Candelario's Des Moines and Louisville tapes were officially released in 2009 as part of the Dead's short-lived *Road Trips* live series. The artwork featured a detailed illustration of the PA with a stylized cable plug whipping serpent-like, above the billing: WALL OF SOUND.

The Dead then made for the East Coast, booked for a June 20 gig back at the Omni in Atlanta. Muldaur again opened for the band and used their system, but technical difficulties delayed the Dead. Those kinks were resolved after a lengthy break, during which a few stage-left amps reportedly "blew up," sparking and smoking.

When the Dead then played "Jack Straw," a Weir-Hunter track from *Europe '72*, and hit the first A chord after the "share the wine" lyric, the sound "rolled like a peaceful tidal wave across the Omni," one head recalled. "And with the power of the Wall behind them, that's something that you just can't capture on tape, no matter how hard you try."

Set two went truly "beyond" in Atlanta, now that the system was fine-tuned. "I have never heard such a pure sound in concert," admitted another fan, who described the Omni as "a truly great—if concretey echoy [*sic*]—venue." That year, they saw the Who, the Kinks, and the Moody Blues, "and NOTHING compared to the amazing sound that The Wall produced. No distortion whatever, and mind-bending volume." During show closer "One More Saturday Night," Weir lunged backward for a last-minute amp adjustment, then ran to his mic to hit the final chorus. That "Saturday Night" cap, in one memory, "blew the roof and doors off the place."

Like so many others who caught Dead shows in this era, those present would one day boast, *I was there.* "Pretty good outfit," as still another head said of "Atlanta 6/20/74," their first Dead gig. "And what was up with that PA? Never seen anything like that. Later, I could brag about seeing a Wall of Sound show."

June 22, 1974. At the 6,500-capacity Jai Alai Fronton in Miami, booked for two nights, the Dead's crew again swung the sledgehammer during load in. The clusters "were so big there were buildings we couldn't even get those through the door!" Parish told me. For defacing the Fronton's white cinder-block exterior, making room for all their gear to enter the hall, the Dead "kicked back some money" to the venue to repair the blocks they knocked out, Parish said.

But Miami '74 became known for another wall-shaking force. The second show marked the first "Seastones" performance through the Wall. The Lagin-Lesh piece of abstracted electronic music blended pink or white noise with "bleepblorp" tones in a mini-set—the intermission between sets one and two—at twenty-three gigs that summer and fall.

At the band's early January meeting, they discussed how $27,500—around $185,000 today—was "needed for Phil & Ned's computer (the tax situation is being checked out for the computer)." Meanwhile, Lagin and Lesh visited Deadhead researchers at the Stanford Artificial Intelligence Lab, to talk "Seastones"-y Wall features like frequency-to-voltage synths and quadraphonic joysticks. And at the March meeting, held before the Sound Test, minutes noted that Lesh and Lagin "would like to play during G.D. breaks. Dave [Parker] said the cost for one extra person for the summer tour (May-August) costs $5,000 excluding hotels," or over $30,000 today. "It was decided Ned won't be going out on the May tour and 'when' would be discussed later."

"When" ended up being that late June weekend in Florida. "We had known since March that we were going to play and that we were going to start in Miami," Lagin told me. His parents came to the gig, and standing around near the Wall being set up, only had one question for Garcia and Lesh: "What's that smell?"

"Seastones" was an exploration of sound's effects on the mind. The project represented the farthest-out and most challenging application of the Wall, an outgrowth of Russian River noise hijinks, "Feedback," and an experimental predilection for always embracing, and funneling money back into, bleeding-edge audio technology. "The way they describe it is 'recorded drugs, electronic drugs,'" Garcia once said of "Seastones." "When they play it live and it's real loud, you hear these incredible things—subharmonic thumpings... below what the ear can register as pitch, and it starts to turn into a physical thing." They also deployed "super high-frequency" effects that sounded "as if they're originating in your head."

Even by open-minded Dead standards, audiences did not know what to make of the two musicians unleashing unhinged noises on a darkened stage. Lesh, on bass, had his own sky-high stacks to throw signal, while Lagin, on computer-controlled analog synthesizer, played the Wall's vocal system like an instrument unto itself, pumping out 9,600 watts in quad.

He is now one of only three "living instrument players who performed through their own dedicated part of the full Wall of Sound, and the only person who performed their own music, not just Grateful Dead, through the Wall," said Lagin, who occasionally sat in on Dead sets beginning in late 1970. "I had unique opportunities to play and listen to the Wall of Sound in many different venues, crowd sizes, hall architectures when empty and when full of bodies, and performances both inside and outside under different conditions." Every one of those places, he added, "had its own peculiarities, or specificities, or geometries." The Fronton, for one, was long and narrow, and being a jai alai facility had foot-thick granite walls, which surrounded the Wall. The Dead's engineers needed some time to dial in the rig, which explained why "Seastones" was performed only the second night.

When Lagin onboarded, "Phil convinced us to spend a ton of money on his equipment, way more than we had spent on any instrument before," recalled co-manager Scully. "An incredible array of shit that we had to cart around, a ton of keyboards and electronics, and all of it very high-tech." Scully called the result "excruciatingly dissonant electronic *musique concrète*," informally dubbed "Warp Ten." (He also referred to "Seastones" as the "Insect Fear Interlude" and "Assault of the Grisly Outer Space Noises.") The performances extended set breaks and were an "excuse for everybody to go off and get high and drink and party and have a sandwich," Scully said. "But, dear God, it was driving the audience nuts." Lagin "would be playing this bone-chilling stuff! For a bunch of high hippie people that just want to boogie, this *nouveau* noise was frightening. You could see people's faces crumbling: '*What* the *fuuuck* was *thaaaat?!?*'"

The first through-the-Wall "Seastones" clocked in just under thirteen minutes and segued into the second Dead set. "I don't mean to sound like I'm bragging," Lagin told me, "but it was so natural to play with them, and I had spent so much time in particular with Jerry, playing at home with him, and I love the music, that it just fit." But Lagin was instructed to not get *too* out there: "I was told frankly by the Grateful Dead management that they wanted to make sure that I didn't make the Grateful Dead too strange and weird," Lagin has said. "There was a real desire for the long stuff to get shorter and the short stuff to get more popular."

Yet "monumental things occurred," said Lagin. "Huge stacks of speakers were filling a very large space. Anything that could go wrong could be very catastrophically wrong." While the trouble of the musicians hearing each other eventually got sorted (thanks, again, to the band's feedback-canceling mics), "they weren't resolved the day they started using newer and larger equipment. Their ability to control the equipment grew over time. There were a lot of frustrations and anxiety involved in that. There was a sincere desire to put on the best show they could for the public."

Besides eliminating distortion and helping the musicians hear each other, the Wall also helped them be in tune. And "it's ironic that the 'guest,' the half member—me—got to play through the largest, most powerful system of all," Lagin told me. "I appreciate it then and now, the challenge of me doing that and the crew setting up for that." After it was determined that Lagin was going to be playing, they had to figure out a way that he would be played, or what he would play through. "It was very natural at that point in time for it to be the one piece of equipment, or collection of equipment that wouldn't be used most of the time that I was playing, which was the vocal system," he said. "There was no other system, anyway."

Lagin's digital and analog synthesizers "could go miles in depth and miles in height, way beyond what normal instruments and voices could do," he added. That's another reason why he played through the vocal component. "The guitar systems were all to make guitar sounds great, not to make vocal sounds great. And the vocal system was meant to make vocal sounds great, which had a range of different voices and complexity and tonality much different from guitars or drums," Lagin said. "I was really happy, pleased, and honored to play through that system."

During setups, he sometimes climbed into the scaffolding with the crew, simply "to be a brother." But the engineers behind the Wall were concerned about whether Lagin himself would "hurt" the rig. "I was very careful in that regard," he said. "I could create notes onstage, when we were setting up, that would create a wind. I also could bounce the stage and the whole system . . . like an earthquake." The techs would look at him and say, *Don't do that!* "It was me doing it—*causing* it," Lagin said. "But it was the system itself doing it. As the vocal system, it was like a living organism."

Lesh was less enthusiastic about the "Seastones" live trip. He was reluctant to attempt "performing" the piece at gigs, in part because his advanced and electronically processed rig couldn't keep up with the nearly infinite range of computerized sounds Lagin could create. Lesh later called the album-version *Seastones*, released in 1975, "a horrible bummer for Ned both aesthetically and financially—it was a rip-off. It was the lowest priority project for Round Records," the Dead's boutique label. *Seastones* was still arguably a forerunner to the entire noise and electronic ambient genres as we know them today, and has gained cult status.

Back at the Fronton, they had passed another test, one that demonstrated that "part of the Wall of Sound's ability was to express *more* than the Grateful Dead," Lagin told me. Latvala will one day earmark "Miami 6/23/74" for potential release as part of the Dead's Vault series. Lesh had initially encouraged Latvala to be the band's founding archivist, and the bassist did his best to review tapes Latvala brought to him from the band's recording archive. But "after so many months of submitting things," Latvala later told *Dupree's* fanzine, "Phil was giving me feedback that was not always based on careful analysis, like the rejection of Miami 6/23/74." The gig might not have been the greatest in Dead history, "but it's one of the best in '74."

June 26, 1974. At the Providence Civic Center, yet another venue where the Dead arrived two years running with increasing mounds of gear, the box was in the soundfield, three school bus lengths from stagefront.

A defining Wall attribute was eliminating the need for a front-of-house mixer. But the band's 1974 contracts sometimes required promoters to provide a mixing station of sorts for both lights and sound. As the Providence rider detailed, the promoter had to make available an eight-foot-wide, eight-foot-deep, four-foot-high control booth, centered on the arena floor eighty to one hundred feet out.

"Somebody still had to represent the band in what it sounded like," said Pechner, back in San Rafael making cabinets. Healy "would be attenuating the levels for this, that, and the other, and basically mixing it so people would hear a complete package," Pechner told me. What Healy did "was absolutely indispensable and he was pretty good at it. If he wanted something to happen, it usually would happen. The musicians would rely on him...because he was the number one sound guy. Always."

Healy himself is more understated. "The Wall of Sound sort of mixed itself," he told me. He would listen out in the audience, and then come back and make tweaks. Like flying an airplane, "you trim the altitude and you trim the direction and all that; you don't really manipulate it," Healy said. Instead, "we could set the soundsystem up and adjust it accordingly so that it most enhanced the requirements of the hall, and what's best suited for listening in that environment. You can't really do that in real time a whole lot, like you can when you're mixing."

That Wednesday night in the Civic Center, the "Big System" nearly reached the steel rafters. "We're experiencing the evening's first blown speaker," Weir said, to shouts and applause, shortly into set one. "That poor speaker gave its life for you. We're gonna send it back home to our little speaker graveyard. In the middle of that speaker graveyard is this great big tomb where they have the Tomb of the Unknown Speaker." A couple of songs later, while the band tuned and another equipment issue got sorted, Weir announced: "Technical malady time."

On June 28, twenty-four hours after the release of *Mars Hotel*, the Dead plugged into the Wall at the 15,900-capacity Boston Garden, a venue with crummy acoustics that Lesh referred to as a "garbage can." Another day, another opening set full of extended technical fixes.

"The first equipment casualty of the evening has just occurred," Weir told the audience a few songs in. "Another candidate for rock and roll speaker Heaven. They get gold-plated re-coning up there." Later in set one, as the band tuned, Weir again spoke to the crowd: "The drum system's all broken, but we're going to fix it." Kreutzmann "would have to change the batteries." Meanwhile, Lagin (presumably) pumped massive metronomic ticking noises through the PA as the Dead's techs worked under pressure. The remainder of the gig was fairly smooth, sound-wise. Select Candelario recordings of the Providence and Boston shows were later immortalized as *Dick's Picks Volume 12.*

By June 30, at the seven-thousand-capacity Civic Center Arena in Springfield, Massachusetts, McNally, still a few years out from becoming the Dead's publicist, was present. How could he forget that Sunday night?

"When you walk in from the lobby through the rear of the hall, you see the Wall at the other end, and it's not that far away because it's not that big of a building," he told me. McNally described the Wall "as some kind of rocketship, like one of those gigantic spaceships, as though you could fly it to the moon," and has previously spoken of entering any venue that year and taking in the full system as if confronting the mysterious lunar monolith in Stanley Kubrick's *2001* (1968). "The visual of it was astonishing," McNally said. Photographer James Anderson's set break shot of the dramatically uplit Wall at Springfield, cast in magenta and yellow, might possibly be the only known in-color image of the full system indoors.

"Obviously the sound was truly remarkable," McNally said. The lack of intermodular distortion, because no two sounds went through any one particular speaker, was crystalline. For someone who saw an "embarrassing" number of Dead shows, "the sequence that ended the first set," McNally explained, "was among what I thought was one of the best-played moments I'd ever heard from them, in terms of being in the room." That would be the "Playing in the Band" into "Uncle John's Band" into "Playin'" block that McNally and others consider "some kind of a high point." On audience recordings, firecrackers audibly popped after the "Saturday Night" closer.

From there, all twenty-seven travelers in the Dead's touring party headed home to rest and work on the PA ahead of a pair of West Coast shows, followed by still more Wall road dates back in the Midwest and East Coast through August. The band needed to stick to its summer itinerary to make money to pay for the rig. "The Dead's new system is but a mere $350,000," *Creem* reported that July. "That's a price!"

Which brings the story around to my artifact, specifically the clues that got me going after I'd first stuck my head inside the unit. The cabinet originally housed two of the 174 total 12-inch JBLs and six of the total 288 five-inchers within the Wall. The handwritten abbreviation and stamped date on the back of the monitor's remaining 12-inch cone grabbed me:

G. DEAD

JUL 17 1974

In the Wall's life, "the summer tour of 1974 showed the addition of curved arc-segment arrays for, first, the vocals and shortly thereafter, the piano system," Mark Gander, a former longtime employee and historian emeritus of JBL, told me. "The date," he said, "corresponds to their working on completing both low, mid, and high arrays, though you will notice utility monitor boxes using two of the 2202As with six 2105 five-inch upper midranges."

My speaker was ready for its moment.

July 19, 1974. On a Friday night at Fresno's Selland Arena, the band jacked into the Wall. By all accounts, the thinly attended show was "out there" and "spacey." Decades later, the system inspired the artwork of *Dave's Picks Volume*

17, pulled from Candelario's recording of the Fresno gig. The cover featured a stylized illustration of the Wall's center array and innermost stacks. Two dapper skeletons atop the cluster control the hoists like roadies.

The next gig, at the Hollywood Bowl on July 21, produced a more widely seen image of the Wall in all its imposing glory. This one took the form of another of Mayer's lovingly meticulous schematics. The electronic monster at the heart of this story is captivating, even by modern standards. There's the massive latticework of scaffolding; Grainger winches, suspending the center cluster; dozens of McIntosh power amps; and hundreds of 15-, 12-, and 5-inch speakers stacked LEGO-like in each instrument's dedicated array. Mayer even got the side fill monitors, including what has to be my cabinet. Perhaps the only thing missing were the tie-dye banners Pollock hung from the top of the scaffolding that hot, sunny Sunday, when the stage covered the pool at the mouth of the Bowl to accommodate the "monster" PA.

Mayer's rendering also included Bear's recently completed curved piano array, based on the big vocal cluster and likewise flown using Graingers. "If you look at the earlier photographs, the piano cluster was all wooden cabinets lined up" and stacked on a wooden platform, Pechner told me. "What he did is took that schematic and built a mini PA center cluster, so it was all in a box." The piece was made of a laminated sandwich material produced by Hexcel, then an East Bay company fabricating sheets of the stuff for the aviation industry. "It was lighter weight and he had it manufactured to his specs and put the speakers in it," Pechner said. But then Bear powered it up, for the first time, in Hollywood.

"It was a dud," Pechner recalled. "It had this rattling sound that he couldn't figure out. Everybody goes, 'Yeah, we're not doing that.'" Meanwhile, Bear "had convinced everybody that this new material was going to revolutionize the speaker world. It didn't work. And nothing happened—there was no repercussion. It was just like, 'Oh yeah, write that off.'" By then, everyone "kinda had their finger in the pie, it wasn't like you'd call somebody out because maybe you had something. There was kind of this honor among thieves." That's part of the reason the system cost what it did. As for Bear, who Pechner said was a smart guy and instrumental in the Wall project, "he lost a little credibility on that." "Hollywood 7/21/74" was the only occasion Bear's new piano cluster was ever plugged in live.

Two familiar openers made the bill: Commander Cody and Muldaur. Sully, the old neighborhood friend of the McKernans, made the trip down with Kevin McKernan, who was taken in by the Dead camp while grieving the loss of his older brother. Scully issued them passes, so they got inside before doors. "I liked Maria Muldaur more than the Dead," Sully admitted. "She had this incredible voice." He went slack-jawed when Muldaur and her band ran their noon soundcheck.

Later in the afternoon, after Cody's and Muldaur's respective sets, the Wall hit the customary audio bump as the Dead began. The rig was soon dialed in, and no other equipment issues hampered the rest of their performance to a crowd of nearly eighteen thousand. But at the "Seastones" intermission, the timing couldn't have been more impeccable.

"I don't personally think that the middle of a Grateful Dead concert is the best place for this music, although in some places the response has been amazing," Lesh said at the time. At the Bowl, "there were some security people who were getting pretty violent, so we went out and did our thing—everybody was pretty high in Hollywood [and] they just sort of relaxed, got into the zone, in the space of long, slow changes, which, if you're pretty high and feel like killing, it just might change your thinking," said Lesh. "I really don't know exactly what it will do to a person, but the vibe was totally different after we finished." As Lagin later told me, "The Hollywood Bowl was designed to be good for music."

One head, seated six boxes back from center stage, could attest to that effect. "Phil and Ned about blew the top of my head off," they remembered, "and the Wall was something to see." In a nearby box Conroy, the photographer Bear had recently accosted in Santa Barbara, likewise took in the scene. "That's when I got more of a chance to hear and see what was going on," Conroy said. "It was amazing clarity with the PA." The sound "didn't blast you out at all. It was so crystal clear that there was no distortion. No super loudness to it. Of course, we were up pretty close. The PA was probably going over my head." The Wall represents "the most incredible soundsystem I think I've ever experienced, or anyone has ever experienced."

Same for those farther out. "Even though we were way at the back, way high up, the sound was coming through clean and clear," another attendee recalled. "I remember hearing the signals for the [second set] reprise of 'Playin'' and being amazed at how well defined the various instruments were." That's still more proof that the Dead's embracing the linear array principle, whereby speakers are stacked on top of and thus propagate one another, had paid off.

The band's "innovations in the realm of live sound reproduction, especially, outstrip any in contemporary music, but more importantly have added a new dimension to the Dead," the Santa Cruz alt-weekly *Good Times* reported days later.

Bill Kirchen, Commander Cody's guitarist, moreover, was tripping on LSD in Hollywood, and apparently each of Lesh's notes was "moving" him, as if one was pitch and another yaw. The sound seemed to carry his body up and down, or back and forth, in different directions. Experiencing the Wall was as much in the ears as the inner visions and body of the beholder. A physical reality and a state of mind.

July 25, 1974. At 8:00 a.m., the Dead's trucks rolled back into Chicago's barn-like International Amphitheater. Crew call was 9:00 a.m., followed by load in and setup in time for 3:00 p.m. soundcheck. Doors at six, show at seven, wrap by midnight. They had it down.

My mom was present yet again, and still has her pass, courtesy of promoter Triangle Productions. At a time when men dominated stages, that Donna Jean, pregnant with her and Keith's child, stepped to her phase-canceling vocal mic that night to deliver the range of human emotion was a bit of a revelation and empowering for my mother to witness. Her memories are otherwise hazy, but by other accounts, in the darkened, cavernous hall, the sound was all over the place when the band hit. One head, seated stage-left about halfway back and up a level, remembered nothing but "swirling noise." Yet the sound "gradually improved," and once the Dead were into "Mexicali Blues" and "El Paso," the so-called cowboy songs preferred by Weir, it "was excellent." By "Row Jimmy," a reggaefied Garcia/Hunter tune, the sound "became staggering, otherworldly, and totally liquid."

Then Lagin and Lesh were on. For some, that "Seastones" was "mind numbing," though that likely had to do with the ultra-clean LSD blotters consumed for the occasion. "During the break, I heard something like incredibly beautiful birds twittering in the rafters," one fan later reported. As the lights came up for set two, they realized Garcia, facing his amps, had been gently so-loing. (Other times, Garcia contributed to "Seastones" seated behind the Wall, or in the racks, out of view.) "The Wall of Sound was flat-out the finest use of electricity I've ever witnessed," the fan said.

The only real auditory nuisance that evening might have been fans who heckled the musicians during a delicate "Dark Star" passage in the second set. "And yes, the place sucked," yet another head recalled, "but where else around here could have held that magnificent Wall of Sound????" Only after the gig, the Dead again confronted prickly Midwest union crew, who reportedly put their forklifts into some of the speaker cabinets.

The caravan continued east. On July 27, the Dead took the stage at the 10,500-capacity Civic Center in Roanoke, Virginia, a more out-of-the-way stop in the Blue Ridge Mountains. The Dead were reportedly unable to load the entirety of the system into the venue that Saturday, perhaps loath to continue defacing buildings when gear outsized loading doors. Yet even if some equipment really didn't fit inside the Civic Center, that likely made little difference to those assembled.

"The Grateful Dead as corporeal beings fade into their 25 tons of scaffolding and 7-foot high stage," the *Roanoke Tribune* reported. "It set those who didn't already come spaced out... to feel zonked by a battery of speakers and the magnetic musicians who so unobtrusively played on stage." And given "what is perhaps the most flawless speaker system a rock concert in the civic center has ever had, there was no need for people to stay in one spot." But a more negative review of the gig noted how "a group member tried to divert the audience's attention with a clumsily orchestrated [M]oog presentation." Lagin "was unsuccessful, and the crowd became bored, vocal, and at times, rowdy."

But what really "zinged" one's mind that night was Garcia's spacey mid-"Playin'" jam. Standing in front of his speaker stack, one would have perceived the guitarist short-circuit a blown amp "and turn into a brain splitting alchemist," as one head recalled. Roanoke "was a great show, though, with the Wall of Sound," another attendee reported. "When it was over, Ram Rod kept tellin' us to leave as the crew took down the Wall."

On to the Capital Centre in Landover, Maryland, for a Monday night gig on July 29. "The sound was amazing, especially after leaving so many shows with my ears ringing," recalled one head. Another Landover attendee self-reported a trippier effect: "A Jerry solo would start stage right down low [where Garcia stood] and then move around the speakers, often ending up high stage left," they claimed. "It was like you could 'see' the notes."

More likely, that fan mistook Lesh's bass notes, which could be "seen" going "around" the system, for Garcia's. But the reality is just as mind-bending, tracing back to Bear's insistence on shifting the Dead's PA to point-source, producing an audiovisual continuity that was a Wall signature. All of Garcia's sound, "except for a couple of fill-in speakers that only the band could hear, came from *that*," Leonard, the Alembic recording tech, once told me, speaking of the cabinets stacked in columns behind each respective player. "You localized on it—you saw Jerry on the stage—and the sound was coming from where he was."

This very sound localization tapped a powerful chord, being one of our oldest and highly tuned hearing mechanisms. "It's one of those things that as hunter-gatherers we depended on for survival," said Leonard. In the human inner-ear and neck muscles, precognitive connections fire when we detect transient sounds such that we instinctively turn toward auditory stimuli. "The essence of the Wall of Sound," Leonard said, "was that the panorama was real, and uncorrupted."

Two days later, the Dead and their rig leveled Dillon Stadium in Hartford, Connecticut. The band put on yet another marathon outdoor three-set daytime gig that hot Wednesday, July 31, "and the Wall of Sound, wow!" one head remembered. "Hearing THAT was a never-to-be-forgotten experience."

During the epic performance, crew scurried across the system's face, between the speaker fronts and the hanging scrim, listening for and replacing blown cones. "Some roadie climbed the Wall of Sound behind Phil and covered one ear and stuck the other six inches from each speaker all the way up to the top," another attendee recalled. "I wonder how loud that was?"

Ask any surviving Dead crew and tech about their hearing post Wall, and the answer is clear. "What do you think 120 decibels, like, three feet away would do?" Pechner said. At one gig in this era, a city official notified them of a noise ordinance. "None of us really knew what that meant," Pechner said. "Healy went out and bought a sound pressure level meter. Sure enough, it was 120 [dB]," above the approved threshold. Now, wherever they went, they had to look up the local limit and adjust the Wall's volume accordingly. Though the system was effectively only set to level "2," they were still "over a hundred [dB] almost all the time, easily," said Pechner.

That was loud enough to make one's bones vibrate "pleasantly," the sound was *that* clean, according to still another "Hartford 7/31/74" head. The Wall reportedly was heard miles away that day. That was not enough to stop the crowd from talking. During the second set break, during "Seastones," Garcia told the audience to "shut up."

Decades later, when Candelario's Hartford recording was released as *Dave's*

Picks Volume 2, the album art once again paid tribute to the Wall. The cover is a close-up illustration of a squawking crow perched atop the center cluster.

August 2, 1974. A full moon hung over Roosevelt Stadium. The Dead had returned to the crumbling Jersey City ballpark, where they would bear "one of the worst moments of their history," McNally wrote in his biography.

That Friday afternoon, blue skies gave way to gray clouds. Then "a deep, dark impending black," reported Jay Saporita, who covered the band's next few shows for Jersey-based alt-weekly *The Aquarian*. By the 7:00 p.m. showtime, "rain looks imminent and the road crew doesn't waste a second. Large plastic sheets are drawn over the drums, the piano, the amplifiers. The soundsystem... is covered with one gigantic sheet made up of what appears to be a muslin"— the black sharkstooth scrim. "Three or four men hang from scaffolding high above the audience, racking up the muslin and covering the lights." Within a half hour, "everything is covered and reasonably protected."

Lightning flashed. The clouds opened and soaked the stage. Thirty thousand eager fans watched and waited, expecting a show "rain or shine," as printed on tickets for the event. (The band maintained they weren't privy to that guarantee.) In one memory, Lesh emerged wearing a clear plastic poncho that draped over his bass, and "when he tried to play sparks flew." The crowd, one head recalled, "went nuts." That's when Weir came out to explain that the speakers were getting wet and the Dead were postponing the gig. A bottle flew from the audience and hit him.

The crowd was now on the brink of rioting. Brown, out in the soundfield at the FREE STUF stand, frantically broke down before upset fans descended. "We had to run away with the whole booth before they started destroying it," Brown told me. Onstage, ensconced behind the Wall, manager-turned-crew-member Rifkin remembered waiting for the tensions to ease, in what was the only instance their crowd ever made him fearful. The incident left the Dead somewhat embittered. The show ended up rescheduled for the following Tuesday, breaking the pattern of exactly-every-other-day, evenly spaced runs for the Wall.

"In the stark glare of the huge overhead lights and the strange silence of the emptied stadium," Saporita reported later that evening, "the equipment people start in on what will be an all night task, breaking down the set and packing it." One of the tractor-trailers that hauled the Dead's custom stage let out a "fierce, rumbling noise," and "with careful, sure maneuvering," Saporita wrote, "is eased out and heads for the Turnpike, going south," part of a convoy of gear pushing eighty tons. They were headed for the 13,500-cap multiuse Civic Center in Philadelphia for shows on August 4 and 5.

By midafternoon that Sunday, the first Philly gig, "a few minor details need attention, a few lights anchored and some work speakers replaced, but the major work is long since done," Saporita continued. The whole setup "is a carefully thought-out, rehearsed process." The roadies "know their jobs and the equipment goes up and comes down like a well-oiled machine." Saporita was somewhat taken aback by the Wall's electronics, saying, "The boards through which it is all unscrambled look amazingly like the instrument panels of a spaceship in a grade B Saturday matinee movie." During soundcheck, the system "worked well." The sound was even throughout the space, "loud but nowhere near overbearing and clear as a bell," a cliché by then. "As the bugs slowly got worked out, it could prove to be THE new soundsystem of the rock world."

Closer to showtime, Haller made final adjustments to the large spots, rigged sixty feet in the air at a thirty-degree angle, illuminating the stage. As the band members congregated behind the Wall, "the sound people ... get ready," Saporita reported. They don headphones, and the intercom system, "linking the light people to the master board and the master board to the monitors, etc., is given a final check."

Camped on the floor before showtime, one Philly '74 head recalled a dicier scene. The Wall "started rocking back and forth," they claimed, "and everyone on the stage and close to the stage scattered, and it eventually settled down, but it was pretty scary for a little while there." Given how precise the speaker cabinets had to be measured and cut, if one was a mere fraction of an inch off, that compounded moving up the stack. Ten or twenty feet up, a whole column may be a few inches off, susceptible to list or sway. Look closely at Wall photos and clearly shims got placed between certain speaker tops and bottoms, accounting for anomalies.

Haller killed the house lights and the first set in Philly began. "The sound is excellent," Saporita reported, "with no one instrument overbearing and a clear, sharp tone." Indeed, "featuring their new $750,000 soundsystem, which is really a 60-foot-tall home stereo ... the Dead could make the clarity of their musical and instrumental thoughtfulness come through such giant ozone filters as the Civic Center," read a *Philadelphia Inquirer* review. Yet here came Weir after opener "Bertha," during a tuning break: "We're making a couple of adjustments up here, as you'll notice."

The jams stretched as the show transpired. "Everyone is pushing for that new sound, that new piece of music that hasn't been played yet," Saporita added. Covered by the scrim, the rig "with its hundreds of lights and knobs and dials seems to be a gigantic instrument panel where the source is set, the fuel injected, and the rest left to the pilot and crew."

By "Seastones," they hit cruising altitude through Lagin and Lesh's "spacey" atmosphere. "Sudden eerie pitches followed by what seems to be a series of explosions but—better—sounds like a spaceship being launched," Saporita wrote. Twenty minutes into "the flight," he continued, "with a loud burst of noise, the landing gears are locked in place and all is silent. Everywhere I look people are standing rocking back and forth on their heels, or sitting in the lotus position, eyes closed and swaying." One head fabulously claimed the exercise in computerized feedback vibrated the venue floorboards into a sine wave, or S-shaped motion.

Later in set two, Weir again addressed the people between songs. "If we get started here before we get tuned up it's gonna sound just awful," he said. That was before the closing song, "Sugar Magnolia," ahead of a "Casey Jones" encore. The Wall, in full "globe hanging from ceiling mode," lived up to the hype that first evening in Philly, remembered yet another head. "The show was good," enhanced by "a mix that had each musician controlling their own levels with some help from the FOW [front of Wall] engineer."

Night two with the rafter-scraping Wall at the Civic Center was still another achievement. The gig "is excellent," Saporita reported, "with just the right amount of surprises and a few new songs thrown in for good measure." But now early Tuesday morning, the whole thing had to be disassembled, packed up, and loaded out, en route *back* to Jersey City, for the makeup gig later that day. Fortunately, "this road crew is still up from these two fabulous nights," Saporita wrote, "and, along with a good dose of cocaine, have enough energy left to move things right along."

August 6, 1974. At the Roosevelt Stadium do-over, the Dead's road-tight crew hustled all day getting the Wall up and lit. By around 6:00 p.m., they took a deserved breather.

Days prior, before the original Jersey City date got rescheduled, Weir and Gary Lambert, a writer and Deadhead who later worked for Graham and the Dead organization, had beheld the system stacked above them.

"Did you think it would come to this?" Lambert asked.

Gazing upward, Weir said, "there were times we had to cancel a show because we couldn't find an extension cord." The project had been a natural progression.

So when the makeup gig got going, "even outside the overall sound is precise and sharp," wrote Saporita, nearing the end of his week following the band. That was when Silberman, the *Skeleton Key* co-author, who was present at "Jersey City 8/6/74," *really* became a Deadhead. He could remember speaker towers in three dimensions around the crowd that day, "so it was not even *just* the Wall of Sound," he told me. "It was even more elaborate, or site-specific."

Three songs into set one, mid-"Eyes," Lesh took a bass lead. The effect wasn't just a sound but a *tactile presence*, Silberman explained, becoming more obvious when Lagin and Lesh performed. "It felt like you could see around the notes and there were times when Phil, in the process of moving the notes around, a note would pass through you," he said. "You could feel it in the hollow spaces in your thorax, as if something was on its way somewhere. That was fucking awesome."

Other firsthand accounts also center that low-end presence. "The ground shook when Phil hit a few chord bombs during many songs," one head later recalled. Still another individual present at that gig called the Wall a "monolithic wave of clarity and power."

Fan anecdotes can be so gobsmacked and consistent as to become repetitive, but they accentuate how epochal the Wall was for the time. "I don't think I have heard to this day a better soundsystem," wrote another fan of the experience at the Roosevelt. "Even close to the stage, you didn't get blasted, there were no 'ringing ears.'" The sound was evenly distributed, no matter where one took in the show: "Sitting half-way up in the stands center stage was a great way to experience the all-powerful Wall," remembered one attendee.

Leonard got an even farther afield sense of the system's capabilities. "It was a true line array," he once told me. What that produces, in a word, is *intelligibility*. That day in Jersey City, "the band was pretty much set up in what would've been home plate, and over the bleachers were where the parking lots were," Leonard said. He walked to the end of the lot; the space between him and the stage could've held over a hundred thousand people. "Although the wind was playing with the sound—it would kind of blow it away—it was crystal clear all the way out there. The coherence of the waves as it propagated was really incredible."

Select recordings of Candelario's from the Philadelphia and Jersey City shows were later released as *Dick's Picks Volume 31*. "Some sonic anomalies remain, particularly some over-exuberant piano-related sounds, but we have done as much as possible to bring the Wall of Sound into your living room," read a "caveat emptor" label on that offering. "Enjoy."

Many hold this time with reverence. "It's probably no coincidence that the music we created playing through the Wall of Sound is regarded by most Deadheads as the pinnacle of our live performances," Lesh later said. This stretch "remains to this day the most generally satisfying performance experience of my life with the band." Working Dead tunes through the Wall "was both exhilarating and terrifying; the combination of the collective risk-taking inherent in our music and the knowledge that one's slightest move was being scaled up to almost godlike omnipotence was humbling (but rarely daunting, thank goodness)."

What *had* become daunting, once the Dead were back home in San Rafael that August, needed to be confronted: the endless travel, enormous production scale, and the size and state of the crew, now comprising nearly forty people. As co-manager McIntire told the *San Francisco Chronicle* that month, in a story addressing rumors of the Dead disbanding, "We cannot continue as we have been."

A band meeting was called days after the East Coast tour, at a Marin County hotel.

"We now employed twice as many stage crew and truckers as before, meaning we had to play larger venues, sell more tickets, and play more often to be able to support the system," Lesh said. "Luckily, our audience was continuing to expand; even so, the financial strain would eventually prove untenable." Decades later, speaking with *Rolling Stone*, Weir doubled down on the band's predicament in 1974: "We were playing hockey halls, and we'd have to go in a day early to set it up," Weir said. "And we were down for a day while that was happening, so economically it wasn't a viable solution. We were selling out the hockey halls but barely breaking even."

Meanwhile, the ravages of cocaine had chilled the groupmind into an "us against the world" mentality. If an unwritten don't-ask-don't-tell policy governed tracking individual sound-related gear expenses, then the same could be said for their collective drug taking: Nobody wanted to rat anyone else out, because that would lead to all of them having to come clean. This alone reinforced a negative camaraderie and working environment.

Many crew members were overindulging and distracted, ground down and cantankerous. "The bigger we got, the more powerful, but the more headaches," Winslow later said of this era. "I was really rude a lot." The band itself, by contrast, had begun to bubble off. "At that point," claimed Lesh, "I wasn't drinking or using drugs; to avoid the onslaught of backstage acquaintances, I would find a quiet room and read before the show."

Back at the Marin hotel, Rifkin spoke first. Swanson was in the room that fateful day. "I remember that meeting when they took the hiatus, because Rifkin was the one who stood up and sort of said, 'Ehh, let's take a break—this isn't any fun anymore,'" Swanson told me. "Danny was shaking and I was sitting next to him. I was holding his hand to give him strength. That's all they'd ever done, right? That was quite a departure from what was going on. But he was right."

Separately, Loren had told Garcia that the Wall spelled financial doom for the Dead. "They had to stop," Loren later said. Garcia grudgingly came around to the idea of breaking the system down and moving on. By the hotel gathering, he apparently had made up his mind.

Band meetings "were always kinda fun and exciting," Pechner, another head in the room that day, told me. "But this particular one was speaking to the cost and how it wasn't working out. I didn't know that Jerry was gonna come up with this idea but apparently it had been bothering him for a while," Pechner said. The organization kept taking people on, and not like today's start-ups assigning an Employee 1, Employee 2, and so on, with a Human Resources department hiring qualified people. "Everybody had a friend who wanted to work for the band and somehow you try to get them in," Pechner said. "Jerry realized that as this thing was growing he was obligated to perform because he felt responsible for their income."

So when Rifkin shakily said the fun was gone and they should stop, an idea Garcia backed, the roadies expressed support. The Dead would position themselves for a hiatus, such that particular crew members had no reason to wait around for work to resume, but to go and look for jobs elsewhere. "The band told us, 'You guys gotta figure out who's who in the zoo, and get rid of the bull-shitting and hangin' things up,'" Parish told me. "Because some people couldn't do it anymore. They were burned out."

The crew was told at that meeting to register for unemployment, which the Dead had been deducting from employees' checks. Pechner, for one, "kinda got burned out." He would move on after his full-time status ended that summer. The writing was also on the wall for Quality Control Sound Products.

"Alembic was there before," Pechner said. "But that was more of an engineering design." He and Jackson, Ram Rod, and others "took that information and made something." A soon-to-be-in-house cabinet company named after the Dead road crew's self-appointed moniker, Hard Truckers; and later UltraSound, the Dead-adjacent soundsystem provider of choice for the band's tours in the '80s and '90s (that my dad did occasional work for), "owed their lineage to what we did," Pechner said. With Quality Control, "we basically were hippies that formed a legitimate corporation." By late August, Pechner, Jackson, Ram Rod, and Cardinalli all took modest partner draws and closed their business account with the Bank of Marin. "Once they took time off," Pechner said, "kinda everything fell apart."

But the Dead had one last Wall caper in them.

According to Scully, the "depraved" plan for the 1974 European tour appeared when one Tom Salter, a London-based promoter, knocked at the Dead's San Rafael office one day that summer. The "middle aged Cockney suffering from cocaine dementia" had a pitch, and arrived toting "a briefcase full of blueprints, wads of five- and ten-pound notes, and more blow than we had ever seen," Scully claimed.

"Wait til you see the Ally Pally, lads!" Salter hooted, referring to Alexandra Palace, a proposed venue in North London to host the kickoff shows. "Blow your bloody little hippie minds, it will."

The Dead gave in to Salter's scheme. "We agree to do it (whatever it is)," Scully said. The tour included only seven dates, and a dogged atmosphere would affect the quality of the performances, leading to underwhelming ticket sales, smaller crowds, and lukewarm press. Preparations "are going to be complicated," Scully added. "After all, we are carting around the 38-ton Wall of Sound," a streamlined version, though still gigantic, considering shipping costs and the logistics of trucking the rig around the continent. While the band was still recuperating in California, Scully was already advancing the tour in London. He was then "followed at regular intervals by crew and equipment."

Internal figures counted twenty-seven "travelers," including band, crew, and associates. By other accounts, the entourage included thirty-four band and crew members, plus six additional crew and truck drivers and four scaffolding handlers. Their meticulously detailed gear manifest was thirteen pages long. On top of the instruments, there are the expected hundreds of variously sized JBL cones housed in custom cabinets and dozens of McIntosh power amps in heavy-duty racks. The document held manifests for items "arriving under separate cover," including dimmer boards, intercoms and headsets, bulbs, and the nine-piece scrim, for lighting; "computer music," or the green case containing

Lagin's Interdata 7/16 computer and Datel D/A system; additional PA components, namely two-dozen-plus mics and cases of assorted spare parts, tools, cords, and cables; and wood planks, beams, and piping for staging and scaffolding. They also packed a coffee maker.

Not noted in the manifest? Kilos of dank West Coast weed, sealed inside the back compartments of Candelario's special "speakers."

September 9, 1974. The Alexandra Palace, a repurposed Victorian-era train station, houses one of Europe's finest pipe organs. Ahead of the first of three Dead shows at that hilltop venue, their sixteen-strong crew erected the scaffolding and stacked the Wall in front of the massive bellows. The symbolism and sonic lineage were clear.

But Scully called the London run a "disaster waiting to happen." Band and crew had begun to arrive days prior, in "an event of unparalleled anticipation—like the arrival of Halley's Comet," Scully said. Touching down at Heathrow, Jackson briefly quit over the increasingly coked-up and out-of-control conditions.

The band itself hadn't performed in weeks. "Garcia says if he's off for three days he gets rusty," Scully said. "Everyone is out of practice and dislocated and wrecked." They had toured "almost nonstop" since 1967, Scully reflected, "and the schedule for the last few years...has been just brutal." Worse, "not only is the equipment never where it is meant to be, we are now beginning to lose *people*," Scully continued. "Everyone is torn and frayed, bickering and fighting over nothing," while also dosing LSD "at all hours," Scully further claimed. "Crew members are threatening to go home."

Traveling with the Wall, the ultimate manifestation of their collective project, made the 1972 European excursion look innocent. Parish likened hauling the rig to herding bull elephants into places they did not want to go, venues and theaters ill-equipped to accommodate such an array of gear and ragged roadies. "It presented some real challenges to bring that to Europe," Parish told me. "That was a big deal, flying it over there and going through all the customs stuff in those days. All the racks that held all the amps were *so* heavy. You couldn't lift anything by yourself anymore."

Certain anxious, hostile, and paranoid party members, abdicating their responsibilities, "got lazy out there," said Parish, who claimed that he and Rifkin sometimes handled the entire system themselves. "Set the whole frickin' thing up with very little participation from people, because the European crews were getting so crazy about it. They were trying to sabotage us. It got dangerous." Local crews "weren't helping us and they were doing things to fuck us up, even." As the Dead had already learned, rickety wood ramps across Europe posed safety threats.

"We had to be on our toes," Parish explained. "Nobody ever got hurt but came *close*, man. That was the amazing thing about it, because when you were putting speakers up that high, you're working and they're *heavy*, and we were so able to do it." To let outsiders assist would've been impossible, anyway. European crews typically moved at a slower pace and weren't as fussy about their work, according to Parish, and couldn't comprehend why the Dead's people carried themselves as such, especially how the Americans always rushed and shouted at them. "If we tried to wait for somebody else to help us it was a hang up," Parish said. The racks, for instance, had to be forklifted: "They were tricky to put—each one different. The casters, the wheels were different. We had to stay on so much hardware we were working on. Constant work."

Their death-defying load ins and setups were immortalized by Brown. He packed the Dead's FREE STUF promo materials and his own camera, to make unofficial color home movies of the band and crew. (Lesh, for one, later thanked Brown for having the foresight to document their travels.) "They had to go up *really* high and pull themselves up and pull the stuff up and get it way up there, and go out on a limb on those things to hook up stuff," Brown told me. "I was like, *this all needs to be filmed*. It was just something I couldn't resist. It was the most interesting thing going on there." In one of Brown's setup shots, a crew member barebacks a rafter, stretching to secure a support line, while others share a joint behind the Wall. Brown has called the system at Ally Pally a "remarkably far out" experience, in that they were "in this historic building that never would have seen this kind of thing coming."

But on the eve of opening night, their collective stimulant intake boiled over. "A shouting match erupts during soundcheck," Scully claimed. Only band and crew were present, and Jackson delivered an "impassioned speech," daring the group to ditch their individual drug stashes. "We're tearing each other apart," Jackson said, as Scully remembered. "It's too dangerous to be carrying around contraband, anyway. And after the Ally Pally we're going to fucking Germany, mates. We can't be carting this stuff across borders." If they didn't stop, Jackson pleaded, it would kill them.

Ram Rod seconded, saying something to the effect of, "if you sorry sons of bitches think you can quit, let's see your stash on the floor!"—quite the outburst from someone so soft spoken. Ram Rod reportedly emptied his first, then others followed. "The stuff pours out, baggies full," said Scully, who emptied his own glass vial. Before long, "people start denouncing those who haven't come forward or those who they feel have just made a token contribution to the pile."

In Scully's questionable and spotty memory, a couple of ounces of cocaine hit the Wall's stage. "Rex sweeps it all together and then Ram Rod puts lighter fluid on it and sets it on fire," according to Scully's memoir. (By other accounts, the drugs were dumped into an onstage garbage can, then set ablaze.) Jackson reportedly threatened to walk, but Ram Rod talked him back. Garcia is said to have then made a crack to a friend, calling them "the *clean* Grateful Dead."

That's when the fire department arrived. "They are trying to unplug us," Scully said, "and if they succeed everything will really blow sky high." Scully enlisted the diplomatic Healy, who "shows them the state-of-the-art circuit breakers, our monster transformers. Everything has to be by the book and it takes forever, looking up the bylaws and codes and regulations."

The following night, the band hung backstage, waiting to start the show. Officials with the Greater London Council, an organization that was like a combination fire marshal and electrical inspector, who had arrived with the fire brigade, were reportedly "in awe of our equipment," Scully said, though "it comes down to Healy greasing the fire brigade captains with their hard hats and their slickers." In the end, "the act of burning the stash and finally playing together... has broken the tension."

Yet the gig didn't begin until 9:00 p.m. Doors opened at six, meaning a majority of the crowd of 4,300 had been waiting for hours. "Sorry for the delay," Weir said after two songs. "The generator that runs the PA broke down."

Not much had changed since their last trip through Europe, when they first encountered century-old theaters with insufficient power supplies and sockets. Earlier that August, amid tour preparations, McIntire wrote a note to Scully: "Here is generator info for Europe from Healy," it read. Number one: "for band equip *only* (not for lights too); Brushless induction, 220–3 phase; 50 to 100 kw (no smaller, no bigger)." Number two: "for lights, SCR," or silicon controlled rectifier, a kind of switching device, "is OK, or hall power for lights, use whenever possible."

They ended up using three transformers belonging to the Who, presumably to cut costs. Before the first Ally Pally gig, this borrowed power station gave Raizene the shock of his life behind the stage—the explosive scene of the snafu to which Weir alluded.

Raizene was no stranger to being jolted. Years prior, at a Dead gig in St. Louis, he received some advice from a local electrician, after Healy had asked if anyone had grounded the transformers together. The electrician had been watching Raizene, and offered "a couple tricks, otherwise you're gonna kill yourself," Raizene recalled. When hooking up "live," the electrician said, "take your left hand and rub your thigh, so you know where it is and don't put it on the case of where you're hookin' shit up." And make sure, the electrician added, "you have about a foot worth of lead away from you, so that when you put the pieces together, if anything goes wrong, you don't get it full on."

At another gig leading into the Wall proper, "we're hookin' up live hot wires down in this vault," Raizene told me. He couldn't recall exactly where in the US that was, but "you had to go through this little tube—crawl through this space—to get in there." Rubbing his leg with his left hand, he held a new twelve-inch Snap-on screwdriver in the other. "Healy is coming through the other side and it goes off," Raizene recalled. "I go, *Fuck!*" For some reason, the wires arced, "but I'm not dead because I'm rubbing my hand on my thigh." All that remained of the foot-long screwdriver in his hand was the handle. "It zapped me pretty good," Raizene said. For about three years after, he claimed, he couldn't straighten his arm fully.

The thigh-rubbing trick had saved him a couple of other times, too, so Raizene again used the technique while hooking up the transformers at Ally Pally. He took the heavy solid copper wire and stripped the plastic insulation back about a foot, and held the wire itself with what he thought was enough lead. He'd wired the first two transformers and was now going from the second to the third. All of a sudden, "*BOOM!*" Raizene recalled. "It blew up the whole damn hall. Everybody thought for sure I bought it. But I hadn't. There was nothing left of the fuckin' wire!" The flash was so big and bright "that it really didn't blind me because it went right past me."

The band played only one set that opening night, given the hour-plus late start due to the blasted transformer. The risk was that the shock could go back up through the vocal mics, "and if Weir touches it while he's playing, it could've electrocuted his ass. Or Garcia, or whoever's singing." In Raizene's hazy memory, it didn't take too long to fix. "I forgot what we did about it," he said. "We had the three but we might've just switched over to the two, so we could figure out what the fuck was wrong with the other one."

Still, hum emitted from the PA. After *Mars Hotel*'s "Ship of Fools," Weir again updated the audience. "Our team of highly skilled, readily trained technicians is taking care of the problem right now," he said.

Meanwhile, the rig stood in near-total gloom. "They have bought themselves some new hardware, massive amplification equipment, and a Rolling Stones-style lighting rig with reflecting mirrors, but on Monday night they had problems with it and the stage remained in almost perpetual darkness," *The Guardian* reported. (Other firsthand accounts that evening did report "unusual lighting" bouncing off the overhead mirrors.) The hum, at least, eventually resolved. The Dead played an abbreviated three hours, "rather like a lumbering machine that starts slowly and gradually begins to gain momentum," *The Guardian* noted.

A muted review of that gig, published in *Melody Maker*, blamed the then nonmodernized Ally Pally, built in 1875, itself. "If the Grateful Dead, with their 700-piece PA, probably the most sophisticated in the world, can't get a good sound in this God awful barn, what hope is there?" asked the reporter, Steve Lake. "I'd hazard a guess that the Dead themselves were pretty brought down by the general lack of clarity."

No matter. One head said the European debut of the Wall proper "made my eyes water." Another attendee, Gren Nation, told me his memories are fragmented, "but I do remember, after a lengthy 'technical' delay on the first night, the sound was astonishingly clear and balanced."

September 10, 1974. That afternoon, Healy and Hagen shopped John Dudley & Co., an audio electronics supplier in London. They bought £48—or around $580 today—worth of plugs, adapters, and a mini drill stand and foot control. Parts and tools always needed to be sourced locally to maintain the Wall on the road. Anything for the sound.

Dates like this second London show, on a warm Tuesday evening, "are good," Robertson wrote in his Dead-in-fifty-gigs book. "The rock-and-roll songs rock, the country songs *boom-chicka-boom* burn, the ballads all build to moving climaxes, and the longer, jammy stuff gets comprehensively jammed out." As far as "top-shelf" Dead shows go, "all of the boxes for 9/10/74 would be checked."

The roadies had pulled a familiar trick. They hung parachutes from the Ally Pally's cathedral-style ceiling, though by some accounts the hard surfaces still slapped the music back at the band. But to most any old head in the hall, the crew's on-site servicing of the system and venue acoustic treatments paid off. A "Jake from Newport" said it was clear from just the first few minutes that the night was going to be memorable, as "the sound was superb and completely different from the wobbles of Monday evening."

The Lagin-Lesh intermission, in particular, seized the crowd of just over 4,100. Slowly, "strange sounds started to come through the system," Newport Jake remembered. "The sounds got louder, and feedback was pouring out at me," rendering him speechless, "until the notes started to form into solid shapes and something was being built, created out of weird electronics." It was as if time didn't exist: "I seemed to be standing there for eons. Then the lifeforce/ feedback started to alter flow, change direction, complete the tour of the galaxy, and gradually came to an end."

Later in the second set, the Dead segued into "Dark Star." "I just lay on the floor and let the monster take me over," Jake wrote. He could feel Lesh's "notes eat their way through the floorboards and emerge underneath me, and then vibrate the whole of my body."

Lesh was in the zone—and as Garcia has said, if Lesh was "on," so was the band. Enhancing the low-end effects were the flashing lights on the neck and body of his custom bass. "Phil was on top form that night," recalled yet another head, who also could not believe the size of the Dead's rig. "The top speakers had snow on them, I swear." The PA, in still another memory, was "one ginormous wall of voodoo."

By September 11, the third and final Ally Pally night, the Dead readied to play what would be their last show in London until the '80s. Lagin (and others) later pinned the drug-ditching episode to that Wednesday afternoon, claiming it involved flushing their stashes down the hotel toilet. In Lagin's recollection, all the crew surrendered their contraband. "I believe that Jerry had flushed his stash, too," Lagin said. "And maybe he did, but twenty minutes later he had a new stash. It became evident later that he hadn't flushed his stash." Most of the rest of them simply re-upped their own supplies as the tour continued.

Lagin still recalled a transcendent gig. The entire band was tripping on LSD during that performance, and the receptive crowd of around 7,500 responded in kind. Garcia, moreover, contributed to "Seastones" that evening. "You could see the people in the front... were embodied in the sound," Lagin told me. "It wasn't that they were hearing it. It was an ocean for them. They were swimming in the ocean of sound."

The Wall lived up to the hype. "It really did come across like a giant hi-fi system," remembered one head at the third Ally Pally show. "Phil in particular had a huge and beautiful sound."

But reporters gathered at a nearby press bar weren't as sold on what sprawled into a three-set show. After set one, "all the smart journalists" retreated to the pub, and hourly sized up the state of the crowd, Robin Katz reported for *Sounds*. Set two, which "Seastones" kicked off, "started out sounding like a bad sound-check," Katz said. Their electronic music "had the overall sound of one of those 'Monster arising from the Swamp' movies. After an hour of watching the Dead's sound equipment... and listening to the hundredth variation on the Goola monster theme," Katz wrote, "we headed for the door along with dozens of other migraine-struck humans."

More "hip" studious sonic heads still witnessed the Dead in London. Members of Pink Floyd, as well as a representative of Apple Records, the Beatles-founded label, were present at Ally Pally. Electronic musician Brian Eno, who soon coined the "ambient" genre, is rumored to have also attended one of the London shows. To suggest *Seastones* had any direct influence on Eno's foundational *Ambient 1: Music for Airports* (1978) might be a stretch, but that Eno and other contemporaries were peeping speaks to what was in the air around the Wall back then.

The *New Musical Express*, a British music magazine, called that elephantine rig "the Bear-Healy-Raizene-Wickersham-Turner-Curl-Alembic-PA-system." *NME* marveled at how the musicians could individually control their instrument and vocal levels directly from the stage. Yet "Scully and his road crew have to be out there checking and leaking bits of delicate hint back to the band." In the same piece, Scully gave a version of a familiar Wall-ism: If you compare the system to "your average hi-fi with a volume control that has a dial with one to 10 on it," *NME* reported, "then you are only playing it between three and five."

After the Ally Pally shows, Garcia sat on the floor of Salter's drug-filled apartment, the Dead's London basecamp. He spoke with Lake, the *Melody Maker* reporter covering the band's time in the UK. Despite reaching a level of success that Garcia despised, Lake wrote, the group still really wasn't making money. "Our expenses are immensely high," Garcia explained, "because we're into doing it as good as we can, and as the resources and the desire of people to see the group grows, our plan has been to improve aesthetically the quality of the trip itself. Which is the reason for the PA." Lake's piece included another early use of the phrase "wall of sound" to describe the Dead's rig.

But now that the band and their fancy, expensive PA had gone mega, they became an even bigger target. "You'll have to compromise a lot until you reach the stature of the Grateful Dead and can afford the $350,000 system they're now using," Michael Brooks wrote for *Creem* that October. In a letter from Britain published in that same magazine, journalist Ian MacDonald claimed that the Dead barely registered a blip in London. "The real Big One was Wembley," MacDonald said, referring to an outdoor stadium show that featured the Band, Joni Mitchell, and Crosby, Stills, Nash, and Young. The Dead's Ally Pally appearances the preceding week "went almost unnoticed."

So, too, did the supposed absconding of some of the topmost speakers of the Dead's Wall in London. According to unconfirmed reports, thieves purloined the cabinets through the roof.

September 14, 1974. The caravan rolled into Munich, for a gig at the 15,500-capacity Olympiahalle. In such a huge, canvas-sack-like, tented-roof venue, "the soundcheck is crucial," Scully recalled of that Saturday afternoon. "Balancing the instruments, checking the power surges and so on, not to mention greasing the usual officials." Plus, by this point "the band doesn't even know what city they're in," claimed Scully, who himself hadn't slept in days.

Tensions were flaring between certain band members, namely Kreutzmann and Lesh, and management. Scully and Loren were temporarily expelled from their roles, while McIntire, "after plenty of abuse ... had had enough" and quit, McNally reported. Kant, who previously helped straighten their finances and now served as band attorney, and Millikin would manage the remaining four European dates.

So when Weir spoke to the crowd after opener "Bertha" that evening at the Olympiahalle, as feedback whined through the Wall, his announcement was fitting. "We're making a couple of adjustments," he said.

Crowd reactions were mixed. "Loved the Wall of Sound, felt every note," one head said. That was especially true whenever Garcia, or whoever, happened to take a lead, fading in and out of the darkened scrim. "The 'Wall of Sound' was exciting," another attendee recalled, even if the vocals were "mostly lost."

But that night's "Seastones" precipitated what Brown later called "a massive mental riot in the Germans' minds." Lagin and Lesh "started playing these whistling kind of weird sounds and it then got into these booming sounds and it sounded like it was the Allies bombing Germany," Brown told me. "Boy, did the audience get mad and crazy!" Unruly fans—likely American GIs, Lagin later informed me—began whistling displeasure. And as they whistled louder,

Lagin and Lesh further turned up their sonic bombardment. "It turned really ugly," Brown said. "That big soundsystem didn't help them out either. It was one of those incidents that surprised everybody. They played the wrong tune, as it were." The crowd ended up trashing the place. Nobody was injured, "and we made it out of Germany alive."

On to Dijon, France, for a September 18 gig at the Parc des Expositions. That Wednesday evening, the Dead were on from the top. But there was that hum again. "If you notice that we have the sound of divine wind blowing through our speakers," Lesh said between songs in set two, "that means there's moisture in the microphones. Please, this will only take a minute to correct." The vocal mics continued to act up that night, dropping out during a few other songs.

And yet, "in the face of equipment breakdowns and backstage politics, the band persevered," Olsson wrote of that gig in his book about the Dead's improvisation. The show "unfolds with each listening, transforming as it progresses into one of those performances that really meant the Dead were *happening*, not just reproducing themselves." As that show went on, the crowd gradually came alive, as if the atmosphere inside warmed. "The sound was quite bad," one head remembered, "but never mind. It was such an emotion to see them that it remains a great souvenir for us." After all these years, "fresh."

The show was still bad for business. Dijon was a "total flop," McNally later reported, drawing only a few hundred people. Gigs *had* to make money to pay for the Wall. But they were practically burning it, and dealing with at least one sketchy show organizer who tried withholding their bag. That night, Kreutzmann intimidated the promoter to give them their pay by running a knife down the guy's attaché case.

By the time the Dead arrived at the Palais des Sports in Paris, for the final two shows of the Europe '74 run on September 20 and 21, more darkness descended. The Paris gigs would be "only marginally better" than Dijon and Munich, McNally wrote, and "the group continued to experience social problems." In the shadow of the Wall, the promoter introduced the Dead's camp to Persian white, an especially pure and potent heroin. Garcia, already heavily into cocaine, and Scully both would especially take to the drug.

But the Parisian crowds were treated to all the sights and sounds of the Dead at their most *Wall*. The bank of speakers "impressed me so much!" one head said years later. "The quality sound was outstanding with a true balance!" The effect was powerful, they said, but "not noisy." Another head in the crowd that night, observing the phalanx of gear, figured they were in for a blasting. "When

I saw it, I thought, 'My God, that will get loud,'" they remembered, "and was surprised that it was not so, but instead the finest sound that I have ever heard in a live concert."

One more to go.

September 21, 1974. An uncredited black-and-white film of part of the band's Saturday night performance missed Lesh's signal to the band and crew after opener "Bertha."

"Hey," Lesh said, "what the fuck is feeding back?"

By then, the crew, barely seen through cracks in the Wall, had rigged up a signal light system for this exact kind of situation. If Lesh, say, was unhappy or needed something, he could step on a trigger and light up the bulb behind the Wall. So whatever was feeding back that night, seemingly then got fixed.

Whoever operated that Panasonic camera rolled from a fixed, elevated vantage point Garcia-side, looking down on and across the stage. That final European Wall gig proved another three-set endurance test; the footage opened after set two began with "Seastones," to which Garcia again contributed. The tape is murky even after recent digital restoration efforts, so despite its looming presence, the rig remains eerily shrouded. But there are flashes of the dual-mic system, the Wall-facing lighting rig, and the computerized setup of Lagin, who later said they had all dosed heavy.

At least one head in the crowd that night claimed that seeing and listening to the Dead and the Wall inspired them to become a sound engineer. Someone integral to the Dead's yearslong audio project was also present that evening. Curl took the train in, after being away from the scene for months. He and Meyer had moved to Switzerland earlier that year to research soundsystem innovations, from audio-transducer tech to speaker modularization and phase-correction. That September, Curl received a note from his old friend Healy.

"Come to Paris," Healy offered. "We'll take care of you."

When Curl arrived, after paying his own way, he told me, "I realized I wasn't *really* invited—not by the band." He was given a backstage pass, "like a visitor," not a full-time touring laminate. Security wouldn't let him near the PA, so he was stuck in his sports coat in the green room, where the catering—and Curl himself—got dosed. "I couldn't even go to the front to listen to it," he said. "I've heard mixed reviews of the sound. Some people liked it. Some people didn't. It was all so experimental." The Wall, Curl added, has a kind of "magical power" that can take one over, "but it wasn't *that* big a success. It was just big. We went all out. We tried our best. But we didn't have all the knowledge that was really necessary."

Post show, the band and crew headed to the Paris Hilton for the afterparty. Curl, who can now recognize his naivete at the time, figured he had earned his place. He helped engineer earlier iterations of the soundsystem, was instrumental in actualizing the phase-canceling mics, and occasionally toured as part of the tech crew. And so he followed them to the hotel.

Yet it quickly dawned on Curl that while the Dead did appreciate his technical abilities and contributions made as a "hired consultant," Curl himself "really wasn't that appreciated by the group," he told me. His presence especially upset Kreutzmann, who was on a wine-LSD-blow bender, and had gone out on his own earlier that evening, raging through the streets.

"I remember the night, but not the tour," Kreutzmann wrote in his memoir. Looking back at those dates, "not much rings a bell," he admitted. "That's a short tour and it was scaled down considerably from the extravagance of 1972. That must have been a business decision—it costs a lot of money to bring everyone you know on a six-week European vacation."

Now in the Hilton party room, Curl *really* got the impression Kreutzmann took offense to his presence. Curl, considering himself "in," set off the brawny drummer. "Kreutzmann, he's a bully," Curl told me. "When he feels like he can pound on somebody and get away with it, he will. And he was gonna pound on me. Jerry stopped him, thank God."

But Garcia turned to Curl and said, in no uncertain terms, that he was out of line and had to go.

"Why do I have to leave?" Curl asked.

"Because he's family," Garcia said, "and you're not."

"Well, fuck you," Curl said, turning to walk out. That was the last time he spoke to a member of the Grateful Dead.

Homesick and miserable.

That's how Parish later described the overall vibe by the end of Europe '74, in large part due to cocaine. "Everybody was having problems," Parish told me. "Once we got through that tour, it was time for big changes."

In the days following the last show, after the band—save Lesh, who stayed another week in Paris to "recharge"—had flown home and the gear was getting ready to be shipped back, various managers, crew, and drivers closed out. A handwritten receipt dated September 26 covered £83, or around $1,000 today, for truck rentals. Well into 1975, the Dead paid for the trip, with outstanding accounts for at least one overseas hotel.

That October, *MIT Tech Review* ran a foreboding review of *Mars Hotel*. The band's "sound changed, becoming less regional and more widely appreciated," the *Tech Review*'s Mitchell Lazar wrote. "With this appreciation came far more revenue…which revealed itself in the form of an amazing assemblage of audio equipment, enabling the Dead to have more control over their live sound." One of the Dead's strengths, after all, "is the ability to exert complete control over their music and…their audience," Lazar said. "Perhaps, though, the Dead reached their musical peak."

West Coast media outlets had also begun saying the quiet part out loud. Writing in the *San Francisco Chronicle* around this time, columnist Herb Caen reported on what felt like a bittersweet inevitability. The Dead, Caen wrote, were about "to rest, recuperate, rethink, and one hopes, regroup."

But there was one final stand in store for the Wall. This time, for good.

Graham had booked the Dead for five consecutive nights at Winterland later that October. The shows would be filmed and eventually released as *The Grateful Dead Movie* (1977), a groundbreaking live concert documentary co-directed by Garcia and filmmaker Leon Gast. In the meantime, the band took umbrage with Graham's billing the final show of the stand, which they claimed to have not approved. As seen stamped on tickets for night five, Graham, so key to giving the Dead and their soundsystem space and a platform over the years, elevated the drama and pomp.

He called it THE LAST ONE.

October 16, 1974. The sun shone on the Dead crew during one final Wall load in the morning ahead of night one at Winterland, their every move followed. "The movie folks were a bit of a distraction as they seemed to be everywhere and we were not used to that," Pechner, returning to work these era-capping shows, told me.

Pechner himself appears in the footage, notably in the "Goin' Down the Road Feeling Bad" sequence, which offers the finest behind-the-scenes glimpse of a Wall production. He helped roll the center cluster out of the truck and onto the forklift, which Candelario drove into the venue, where the scaffolding and cabinets were up. From there, Ram Rod and Winslow walked the cluster onto the stage. Then Raizene, all smiles and with remote-control paddles in hand, hooked in and readied to hoist the array. Healy scaled the scaffolding to spot the piece into place.

"Hey, Healy, you up there?" Raizene asked, as heard in the film's soundsystem assembly scene. "OK, one, two, three!" he shouted, flipping the switch. The Grainger winches turned, and the cluster lurched off the ground. The crew had everything down pat, moving and passing the baton seamlessly like a relay team.

Meanwhile, at stage right, Garcia spoke with Boots Jaffee, an acquaintance of the band who performed DIY pyrotechnics at these (and other) Dead shows. (Brown was awkwardly wedged between them.) Presumably flamethrower angles were in question, as they craned their necks and talked about "covering that whole front there," Jaffee said.

"I think it might even be better if we dart around behind all the stuff," Garcia replied.

"That's pretty hard, man," Jaffee said. "Ain't many holes."

"Well, I know, but that's how few there are," Garcia said. "Try and get 'em up on the top. Think about it! That would be the hippest. Then you'd have the throw…"

"But the scrim is so high!" Jaffee interjected.

"Hey, man, I know," Garcia said, "you'll just have to get stuff to happen down here in the middle somewhere, like timing it."

At stage left, Lesh chatted up a member of the film crew. "This has lots of different filters on it," Lesh said, showing off "Mission Control" and speaking direct-to-camera. "And a capability of switching from one kind of sound, like the same sound coming from all the speakers, to one string coming from half of one of these stacks," he explained, gesturing at the huge line arrays behind him. "In other words, each string from four different sets, so it bounces around depending on how I play."

Lesh slid on the bass and fingered a few notes that boomed through the empty hall, but then was met with a mysterious noise. "I'm not trying to do that on purpose," he said. "The camera!" Lesh realized excitedly. "Yeah! Bring it back," he continued, motioning at the operator to come closer. The camera interfered with the bass signal, creating an unsettling "Seastones"-y drone. Lesh, laughing, rolled the dials. His reaction is so pure. This is what it was about. Having fun. A sellout crowd later filled the hall.

The following night at Winterland, October 17, started off with a bigger bang. Arnold, of Lost Live Dead, was present that night, and "besides being very clear," Arnold recalled, "the Dead's monster system was also extremely loud." During opener "Promised Land," the raised lid of Godchaux's grand piano dropped. "There was a moment of anticipation and then an enormous boom," Arnold said. "How loud was it? You had to be there."

Once the song was over, Weir marked the first equipment snag of the evening. "You'll grow to know and love them, as we have," he said. Later, during an additional pause for adjustments, Weir dropped another line he'd been work-shopping: "It's technical difficulty time, which is kind of like Grateful Dead Standard Time," he said, over feedback. "Our prized system is chirping at us."

Beneath the Wall during set breaks on October 18, night three at Winterland, a victory lap of hijinks ensued. "There's a scene in *The Grateful Dead Movie* where everyone is sucking on the nitrous octopus," Scully wrote, referring to the gas tank outfitted with tentacle-like tubes. "That's belowdecks at Winterland."

Up above, the rig remained cloaked in black cloth. That was "mildly disappointing" for at least one head, who previously goggled at the Wall outdoors. Another attendee remembered Lagin and Lesh coming out for "Seastones," which kicked off set two of three that Friday. "It felt like my mind/body/soul was being tuned to the universe of possibilities," the fan recalled. "Once tuned in it all turned into a 'Dark Star' > '[Morning] Dew' sonic adventure." In yet another memory, the Winterland's walls breathed, "and blood dripped from the ceiling during that most transcendent 'Dark Star.'"

But in set three, as the Dead tuned between songs, Weir again addressed the crowd. "You guessed it," Weir said. "We've got another equipment difficulty." Some things never changed.

Still another head, Evan S. Hunt, can remember watching Bear record that performance "from his little, just-offstage submix feed." (Bear was reportedly stationed at stage right.) Years later, Hunt believes Bear's October 18 recording "actually sounds better than it sounded that night in Winterland … an everliving representation of Bear's prowess recording this band."

The next night, October 19, the band's original soundperson remained in his element. "At first the floor wasn't very crowded," recalled Mike Dolgushkin, who helped create the *Deadbase* guide. "Bear was down there holding a microphone toward the stage and coaxing weird noises from the PA." The Dead finally appeared after three hours. This fourth gig made a good portion of the *Dead Movie*.

Heads were *not* about to miss the Sunday show on October 20, either. For the last time, the Wall powered up and the Dead plugged in. "What a wonderful sound invention it was, it sounded so sweet, so quiet and then so loud but clear with each instrument so clearly in the mix," one attendee, who claimed to have caught all five Winterland shows, said years later. "I loved the Wall of Sound. I feel totally blessed to have heard it many times in my youth."

Before the encore, Graham brought out the crew. "There are men, for years and years, who've worked with the Dead, who made it always possible, to put all this equipment up," the promoter told the crowd, pointing back at the Wall. "They're shy, they're very, very crazy—the Grateful Dead crew! Will you all come out here, please? Come on!" The roadies began emerging into the spotlights. "Ram Rod, Steve," Graham said, "get your asses out here! Healy. Jackson. Joseph [Winslow]. Everybody! Get 'em all out here! There's the man, right there—Ram Rod! Come on, Sparky!"

Raizene, towel around the neck, pulled Graham in around the shoulder. "Here he is," Raizene told the crowd, "one of the best guys in the business— Bill Graham."

"This is the crew for ten fucking years," Graham said. "They've done it, really. Once again, for the crew."

The crowd roared. "You're a damn good audience," Parish said.

Separately, Jackson schemed to have Hart's drums ready at the break. Hart rejoined the band during the final set. "The Grateful Dead need the rolling thunder of sound that the two [drummers] generate," Scully recalled. Yet the band was "at the end of its tether, a whirlpool of inner events is swirling, our nerve endings are close to the surface," Scully added. "The band is stagnating, we don't have any new songs, we're worn out, it's been ten years without *one* break."

After the closing notes rang out, Garcia lovingly tousled Rifkin's hair as he walked off, while Lesh climbed into the chamber-like space behind the center cluster. He took a hit of DMT and zoned out—so much for any ban on smoking that psychedelic around the gear. They had blasted through the Wall. The Dead, and their burdensome rig, were entering new and different territory. They pulled the plug.

9

The Other Side (1975)

Postmortems rolled in.

In an interview after the final Wall shows, Jerry Garcia spoke about the band's path. "We can only go to bigger rooms if we sound good in them, and that led to our whole PA thing, which is expensive," he said. "Our rationale was, 'We'll divert the income into developing the resource,' because, really, we have a relationship with our audience." Since the Acid Tests, the sound and crowd interaction were priority number one.

That November, Garcia again gestured at an ultimate Dead sonic power-spot. On the average two- or three-week tour, "every gig there's the same series of adjustments, and it doesn't give us a chance to get past a certain point," he told the *Boston Phoenix*. "The first half we're trying to psych out the room, we're trying to understand what's happening acoustically, which is purely mechanics. By the second half we're starting to develop a sound in the room...where you can hear everybody clearly and any new idea has potential weight." What Garcia desired "is eventually for us to build a permanent place to perform in that would be like a whole theater," only "small and tasty."

As the second half of the 1970s proceeded, Garcia was further asked about the Dead's scheme to make "a modular, or permanent, acoustically perfect hall." Such a fantasy was "a sound one," albeit "with an element of unreality," Garcia said. "We just always function at a loss." At the moment, "our projects to date have been done and are out," Garcia said. "We're starting on a different leg."

What became of the Wall? The Dead, Garcia admitted, "dumped it." The system, he said, "was a physical model of the size of the sound we were trying to create." If the height of a standing bass wave is thirty-two feet, then "nothing that's any smaller than that can produce a soundwave that is that big in the air. So nothing really produces that thirty-two-foot bass sound except things like a thirty-two-foot organ pipe, or a thirty-two-foot column of speakers," Garcia said. The physical sound model they built worked, yet "it's the wrong direction for what the world is involved in right now. You can't use that much stuff. You can't use that much power. You can't try to brute-force information out." And so the Dead's "small in-house technical wing" was working on an altogether different model, "the problem solving level of 'How do you get a sound out that works?'" Garcia said. "Fundamentally, our model would be: As little as possible having the greatest possible effect."

Garcia's bandmates held more pointed assessments. "The Wall of Sound worked just fine," Bob Weir later said. "It was just a logistical near impossibility.... It was insane." Bill Kreutzmann, moreover, has described the PA as "Owsley's brain, in material form. It was his dream, but it spawned a monster that rose from the dark lagoon of his unconscious mind. Owsley let it out of the cage so that it could sprawl out on the stage with us, night after night—a creature that was supercool to look at, but impossible to tame." The Wall "sounded fucking awful," Kreutzmann has claimed, a not completely unfair assessment given his positioning as drummer, first boxed in by huge stacks and a two-ton cluster overhead, then moved a few feet in front of the backline. Bear himself was matter-of-fact about the overwhelming Wall. The '74 system, he later said, "was too fucking much."

The Dead took a twenty-month touring "hiatus," but played four Bay Area gigs in 1975 through rented, downsized systems provided by the likes of McCune Sound. The break, Rock Scully later wrote, "enables us to extricate ourselves from a $100,000-a-month overhead for trucking around the Wall of Sound, paying a crew of forty people to maintain it, and meeting a monster payroll."

The Wall was a victim of unfortunate bad timing. The system requiring two stages doubled the crew size *and* the number of trucks as gas prices skyrocketed. One of the few times the Dead "fibbed," Dennis McNally told me, was when they talked about the break. "I'm not even sure, right now, I could tell you to what they attributed the hiatus. But the real reason was to fire half the crew," McNally said. "They didn't do this in public. In fact, they were chickenshits about doing anything emotionally difficult."

Core crew, including Ram Rod, Steve Parish, and Bill Candelario, remained. Others were fully cooked, after giving up and sometimes risking their lives to build and run the PA, despite never taking a raise. "A good guy like Joe Winslow, he burned out on that work," Parish told me. "He never came out again, on his own volition." John Hagen, too. Yet others in Deadworld couldn't square why some were let go, "because it all seemed to be peaking then," as Eileen Law, keeper of the mailing list, later said. "The mail got really voluminous around the time of *Wake* and *Mars*. I could understand why they wanted time off, but we were swamped."

A story published around this time in the *Village Voice* dug in. "There are any number of reasons why the Dead are going into hibernation, and one of them is that they tried to run their revolution as if it were a celebration," the *Voice* reported. "It didn't work."

Something less radical about the Dead's enterprise *had* worked: The Wall was a financial deduction. Giving their audio engineers and crew funding had been easier than giving the organization's money to the state.

"They just used us as a big tax write-off," John Curl, who went on to design amplifiers for leading audiophile manufacturer Parasound, later claimed. "That was cool for them," until they called a break. What Curl was told back then "is the reason the Dead could, or would, do this—a lot of the other groups did not—is they found that the tax structure at the time was such that if they were making all kinds of extra money, which they were but from tours and stuff, that they actually were throwing away most of that money into the government." In those days, the Internal Revenue Service "could take all your money away, almost."

In his limited scope of the Dead's financial workings, the band was not losing anything significant, and was also getting "something that was good to play with," Curl said. "Something that made them feel good." For a while, at least, "the Wall of Sound was a really good thing, because it gave them that technical advantage, and of course, it was just overpowering as far as looks."

Yet the Dead were still cash-strapped. "We could use the three cents," Phil Lesh said at the time. In a radio spot on WVOI/Martha's Vineyard that year, Garcia likewise spoke to the financial strain that had been working against them: "Past a certain point, we were really working to keep the thing going rather than working to improve it or working because it was joyful," he said. The Dead's way, Garcia said elsewhere that March, "has always been to plow back the proceeds from our gigs back into expanding the quality level of the equipment." But as the oil-related economic recession ground on, "we're scuffling just like everybody else is."

They weren't doing tax planning, in other words. "We were poor," Ron Rakow told me. In late 1973 or early 1974, Rakow had even leaned on a Boston-area weed dealer he called "Cousin David," explaining that he "was broke and we needed money to finish the soundsystem." Cousin David loaned Rakow an ammo box stuffed with $40,000. (Rakow personally paid him back.) "We were just getting by," said Rakow, who was still running the Dead's label and now producing the movie with Garcia and Dan Healy. "We didn't do anything because it was tax deductible. Nothing. Everything was tax deductible—everything we did." The IRS test was simple: Was the expenditure "ordinary and necessary"? What difference, asked Rakow, who received calls at the Dead's office about IRS meetings as of late 1974, does tax deductibility have on a soundsystem? And why should, or could, it be any different than guitar strings?

So while the tax component was certainly in play, it was not the Dead's prime motivator. "They were on a quest," McNally told me. "The write-off just helped." But after the hiatus hit and the Wall was dismantled, the hardware then fell into different buckets. A half century later, we know definitively where only some surviving bits rest.

Initially, dozens of amps and hundreds of speakers went into the San Rafael warehouse, before being repurposed into Dead studio gear and also loaned out. "We took care of it and we used it, and we gave it to people when they needed things," Parish told me. Every upstart band that wanted to truck some of that around, "we could give 'em cabinets, we could give 'em amps, we could give 'em all this stuff, including instruments," Parish said. "That came from Jerry and his way of giving and spreading it out later." Today, not much remains. "It's purposely like that," he said. "There's not a lot of those cabinets around now. There were at one time—*everybody* who came to visit us got one." The Dead "shared it all."

The Wall, then, comprising many thousands of individual parts and pieces, big and small, partly got allocated to sponsor young musicians. "It went in a good direction and a good thing happened to it," Healy told me. Bequeathing gear to smaller groups ensured that even in its afterlife, the Wall was a valuable resource.

Sully, who overheard electrified proto-Dead sessions, remembers sliding into the orange truck Kevin McKernan inherited from his older brother. "Give me a hand," he asked Sully one day around this time. "Let's take my brother's Studebaker up to San Rafael and get some band gear." They pulled into the Dead's spot and found Garcia smoking a cigarette in the upstairs office. Garcia told them to pull the truck around back, where the two friends loaded up with McIntosh amps and "the speakers I ended up with," Sully said. The cabinets date back to 1972 and were later incorporated into the Wall, before being re-purposed by the short-lived Osiris, Kevin McKernan's psych rock band.

Other portions of Wall gear the Dead sold. Most of the custom scaffolding got flipped for some $30,000, Mark Raizene claimed, a $17,000 markup. "We got as much as we paid for the whole damn thing, for the scaffolding and the wood, just for the steel," Raizene said. "It was brand-new!" He said he also found a buyer for *the* defining Wall element: "I sold the center cluster to some guy who wanted to do a stereo for gigs around the Bay Area," he said. Raizene could not recall that individual's name, only that someone allegedly "smacked him upside the head with an iron skillet—we called him Half Brain." Raizene also can't recall how much he sold the unit for, but did not include the amps that powered the cluster. "You gotta buy your amplifiers, man," Raizene told Half Brain.

The remaining scaffolding, Raizene told me, formed the foundation of a cement patio at Ram Rod's Bay Area barn. Ram Rod, for his part, eventually stripped some of Lesh's bass array cabinets of their 15-inch speakers, stacking them as a chicken coop. As Healy told me, "There's pictures of hens living in the speaker cabinets." (Ned Lagin, who left the scene to do his own thing by 1976, and even asked Lesh and Garcia to not talk about him in interviews, said he also later saw some of that repurposed Wall equipment at Ram Rod's.) Kreutzmann and Weir, meanwhile, each took the lumber from the staging, to build their own stuff, Raizene told me.

Raizene then peeled off, never again returning to the Dead's immediate realm. That was despite the Hard Truckers speaker cabinet shop he created with Winslow, electronics whiz John Cutler (no relation to Sam), and others, proper spinning-up post Wall. Hard Truckers eventually transformed into UltraSound, the Dead-adjacent touring audio provider. UltraSound's co-founders, Howard Danchik and Don Pearson, even purchased, and repurposed, old Wall parts in the mid-'70s, into a touring system for Hot Tuna, a band featuring Jefferson Airplane members. Pearson was working for Tuna, and eventually linked up with Healy, who stayed with the Dead until 1994.

"UltraSound got cultivated and it became the Grateful Dead's sound company," Healy told me. "I got support from Jerry Garcia... and I fashioned the soundsystem of my dreams. That was when the sound really took a quantum, *quantum* leap."

As one era closed, another opened.

The Dead reverted to renting sound-reinforcement systems for post-Wall touring, trying experimental setups made by various providers through the remainder of the decade. These rigs were humble in size and not as expensive, but still high quality, as the Dead maintained their standards and the technology advanced—in no small part due to some of their breakthroughs with the Wall.

The Dead returned to the road with a lean six-person crew and used Healy-adjusted rental gear. "On that first tour of theaters in June '76, the Dead stayed true to their old hi-fi roots," Blair Jackson wrote in his Dead gear overview. They married two systems—one, for mostly vocals, designed by musician and audiophile Jeff Cook, and the other, for the instruments, by New York provider Bearsville Sound. (No relation to Bear.) The system's clarity and power were remarkable. Healy later called the Cook component "an incredibly interesting and obscure soundsystem that was sort of like the Wall of Sound. It was sort of styled after it." Yet way smaller and, like the Dead's pre-Wall stage plots, based on a traditional right/left PA and wedge monitors at the musicians' feet.

From there, the Dead rented equipment from FM Productions, Bill Graham's business, before switching to Clair Brothers in 1978. That's the prominent East Coast audio company that previously rented the band kit in the early '70s.

The following year, the old Wall center cluster crossed paths once more with the Dead, during a two-show run at the indoor Oakland (later Henry Kaiser) Auditorium in August. The cluster, sitting in an undisclosed area warehouse, got retrofitted with all 12-inch speakers and patched into the PA. By then, the Dead were also touring with the honeycomb aluminum piano cluster, with a special rubber damping, that Bear made for the Wall—the one that had failed at the Hollywood Bowl. Bear's mini cluster, now in working order, was being used as a left-right midrange component to the small Clair Brothers PA "that was doing, like, three-thousand-capacity venues," Dennis Leonard once told me. Kaiser was perfectly suited, a not-to-be-missed event for "everyone in the Bay Area that had ever done anything with PA." The one-off configuration was supplemented with sixteen custom subwoofers originally built for Francis

Ford Coppola's *Apocalypse Now* (1979), to which Mickey Hart and Kreutzmann provided drum and percussion music.

The Oakland shows were momentous not only because they marked significant experimental jumps forward in sound design technology by Healy and his newly assembled confidantes. The shows also centered another familiar face from the Dead's past, someone who was influential during the formative Wall days. Featuring gear by Meyer Sound, the company John Meyer founded that same year, the gigs stand out as the first major leveling-up, since the Wall, in live audio performance tech.

Sometime in that late-'70s stretch, newly onboarded Dead monitor mixer Harry Popick said he assembled his own "huge" monitor system using 12- and 5-inch Wall speakers, before he shifted to Clair Brothers gear for the Dead and the actively gigging Jerry Garcia Band. That same year—1979—some of the old Wall is also rumored to have been stored in San Rafael at Marin Recorders studio.

A slimmed-down PA partly comprised of repurposed Wall gear was assembled yet again at Kaiser in Oakland, this time for the Dead's run of New Year's shows. That was when "the sound experiments peaked," McNally reported. "They combined equipment from several different sound companies with Ultra[Sound]'s crossovers and got a five-way time-corrected stereo image that was perfect, among the best soundsystems ever."

The time-alignment method behind Meyer's new speaker-amp design, Lesh, ever the sound geek, later said, "bordered on the inexplicable." The gear gave them access to two pillars in the Dead's soundscape moving forward: the gigantic "earthquake" subwoofers that drew certain fans into the "Phil Zone," the area in front of Lesh's stage position, where his bass frequencies were most felt and heard, followed by "a full-range system delivering sound that approached the transparency of the Wall," Lesh said. Over the next half decade, "that system was able to be packaged in a way that made it practical to use for touring, even in this era of lowered expectations."

But as far as resurrected Wall parts went, the Dead's final shows of the 1970s were a bookend. "I think that was the last time any of that stuff saw life," Leonard told me of the New Year's run. Now in his seventies, Leonard has been mixing blockbuster and Academy Award–winning movies at Skywalker Sound for nearly four decades.

The rest is history. Not long into the 1980s, the Dead ended their relationship with Clair Brothers and went all in on an UltraSound-provided Meyer PA. There were occasions, for certain Midwest and East Coast dates, where the band rented Clair equipment, though before long Healy had pushed for them to fully switch. (When my dad started doing occasional stagehand work with the band's Midwest local crew in the early '80s, he can recall the Dead's UltraSound plot.) By the '90s, the Dead's computer-assisted soundsystem cost $3.5 million. To the last note Garcia ever played with the Dead, Ultra-supplied Meyer loudspeakers remained key to their ongoing post-Wall sound journey. That's another book.

In the meantime, back in early 1975, the lyricist Robert Hunter talked about the hiatus in a letter published in *Crawdaddy*. The Dead were headed for a "vacation just to cool out and survey what we've been up to," Hunter said. "Building and carting that soundsystem is, in my head, akin to building a pyramid. It is the world's greatest hi-fi system, and there's no one that would deny that."

As Healy later explained, until the system was realized the industry standard was largely based on Western Electric ideas for film sound that came out of the mid-to-late 1920s; horn and speaker cabinet designs predated the Great Depression. But as they saw later, a lot of the Dead's ideas, forged through their PA, "stuck and were influential."

The Wall represents "a milestone," Healy told me. "It was a departure from all conventions. It wasn't the best-sounding soundsystem there ever was but it served its purpose, to awaken the world and bring consciousness to the concept of sound reinforcement." The project required "backbreaking, mindbreaking work," he said. Often, he and others would spend more than twenty hours a day on the system, Healy claimed. "The preparation, and keeping it running, and keeping it all in the air, and keeping it working, was just continuous." Then again, "I guess I was crazy. A bunch of us were. It took a bunch of crazy people to do something like that. Crazy intelligent, crazy creative people."

Sure, there were some individual squabbles, as in any family. "I think I've seen the roadies punching it out together a few times, and had to pull 'em apart," Healy said. "But that's over stupid stuff—the same reason you fight with your brothers and sisters, over dumb family shit. But I don't remember there ever being any big rifts at all." Really, the Wall only worked because they made it go. "It was *us* that worked. It wasn't the soundsystem," Healy said. "It was us that the audience was listening to. It was the endless, endless, endless commitment by all of those who were involved in it. Everybody's name who comes up played some kind of a role. I'm grateful for everyone."

And then there was Alembic.

May 1975. Ron Wickersham was preparing for the biggest show of his life. But this Wall demonstration took the form of a presentation the Alembic cofounder was slated to give at the 51st Convention of the Audio Engineering Society in Los Angeles. The main ballroom at the hotel hosting the conference was standing room only for Wickersham's demo.

The presentation drew from a technical paper he co-authored with the late Don Davis, who had been working at Altec. "He was on the management team," Wickersham said of Davis. "He had a high position." When Davis split off to do his own thing, he caught the Cow Palace Sound Test, arriving in his Porsche to hear the band's magnificent system. Davis and Bear, Wickersham noted, used the same listening test technique, of going into the audience area and dashing around. Walk from one spot in the soundfield to another, and the sonic changes, like comb-filtering effects, occur too slowly to be acutely observed and then corrected. "But if you run as fast as you can, and listen around to what the sound is," Wickersham told me, "that's a real powerful education."

When the Dead began developing "some bit of notoriety" with their soundsystem, Davis wanted to learn more. "We kept him informed," Wickersham recalled. "He thought we should do the paper, so it was his suggestion." After all, "we were the only ones doing a coordinated array—everybody else was just piles of speakers." Through his connections, Davis got the article, dryly titled "Experiments in the Enhancements of the Artist's Ability to Control His Interface with the Acoustic Environment in Large Halls," published in the audio engineering journal *dB*.

Reactions to the paper, and the in-person conference demo, floored Wickersham. "It was astounding," he said. "I'm a nervous speaker, but when I got started it went pretty smoothly." He had slides made and played live Dead music.

The whole point of the Wall, according to Wickersham, had been to make recordings like those he showcased. Sixteen-track tapes, specifically, of full shows with no edits. This went back to Bear's mandate from day one, to improve the quality of live recordings. "It's a concept of doing accurate documentaries of what happens to get the full enthusiasm," Wickersham said. "Since it's loud rock and roll, we didn't need any mic preamps. The signals coming out of the mics are really huge, so it just split off," he said, using a "pile" of ultra-limited transformers that weighed four or five pounds each.

"We went in, in a line input, through transformers that we also built and plugged in the back where you could plug in a preamp," Wickersham explained. "We just plugged in a matching transformer so we had a balanced input. Then the only level control was the level control right on that channel of the recorder." That was based on the philosophy that the most authentic, uncorrupted sound quality can be achieved by *not* running through equipment. "Run through the minimum number of stages, you get the most accuracy," Wickersham told me. "That's how the recordings were made." Then, using the 16-track of one of the shows, "I made a two-track that had a mono mix of everything and the vocals isolated."

Wickersham coordinated with the technician running AES sound. "I don't know if he was just extra enthusiastic because it was the Dead," he said, "but it came out perfectly." Wickersham could wave the music off, leaving just the vocals, say, and only a tiny bit of leakage. "The people got to really hear what the microphones sounded like in the soundfield. That got received very well. And then the other aspects of describing it were pretty great." He can't recall which specific tape he played, "because not every show was recorded on the 16-track. It was just whatever one I had access to." But the recordings were all Wall, most likely of the October 1974 Winterland shows, believed to be the only multitracks made that year. "It was those microphones," Wickersham said.

Any immediate Alembic-Dead connection scaled down while adjusting to an off-road interim in 1975 and into 1976. The band's longtime in-house company might have provided (and then sold) its prototype Wall system to the Dead in the not-distant past, though the hiatus had Alembic pivot from the sound reinforcement space almost entirely. The company put focus more onto just instruments and electronics.

But as Wickersham's demo concluded, the crowd rose, an unusual sight at a conference like AES. They gave a standing ovation.

While Alembic moved on and the Dead entered their next chapter, there was still another bucket for more old Wall parts. As it turns out, Garcia saying they "dumped" the system was likely as much a figure of speech as literal truth.

Chasing down Wall relics and ephemera, and speaking to the keepers of these artifacts, yielded a credible lead that a not insignificant chunk of the rig that the band no longer wanted to store or deal with was eventually consigned to a more final resting place: the Marin County landfill.

"If it wound up in the dump it probably deserved to be in the dump," Healy told me. "It might have been stuff that was water damaged from being on Ram Rod's ranch or farm. It might have been garbage. It might have been time for the landfill." Garcia, Healy claimed, "couldn't care less about that shit." Some of that gear "probably went into the ground ... and just rotted and wasted and melted."

Decay. "I hear the rumors," Rick Turner, who broke off from Alembic in the late '70s to start his own guitar company, once told me. "There's a warehouse here, there's a warehouse there. There's a pile of this, there's a pile of that. Who knows? I don't know. Entropy, you know?"

The Dead were known to trash decommissioned kit from time to time. "Some things went to the dump, for sure," said Betty Cantor, who told me about her pair of mic splitters that got water damaged in the early '80s. The Dead then "just threw it in the dump." When she asked for the gear back, she claimed to have been told that she could not have it; they had trashed it. "It was like, what the hell?" Logistically, off-loading at the trash-processing facility would have been convenient. San Rafael is the site of one such county dump on Jacoby Street, not far from the Dead's space. Though that facility opened in 1987, it is not at all implausible to think the band fated certain damaged-beyond-saving gear to the heap.

The marked Wall stuff—cabinets, most likely—got trucked over to the dump, or so the story goes. (They removed and saved all the speakers.) But then the Dead balked. If they left the stuff there and word got out, then hard-core Deadheads would traipse around the dump, trying to recover the artifacts. The Dead's concern was not that devout fans would get any of it but rather that someone would get hurt scouring the junkyard. So using a couple of fork-lifts, they bashed up all the stuff. Yet it occurred to them that Deadheads are committed enough that they would *still* try to come and find the splintered materials, which would have made adventuring through the heap even *more* dangerous.

The Dead then reportedly did what feels unthinkable now, but would've made perfect sense at the time. They torched it. Apparently, a bonfire was made out of the material, bringing one version of the story of the Wall to an end in a blaze of glory.

Throughout my own journey researching this book, I was told to be on guard for these kinds of "rumor dreams" and "audience fantasia," in Healy's words. "You gotta watch out for that. There's really a lot of that around." I was cautioned about the cognitive fuzziness that comes with age, even (especially) for those who were there working for the Dead: "Some people, their memory now? They're getting old," Parish told me. "They forget stuff. You remember things in a halcyon way where the bright light was on you for a minute there in different ways, so you think things are more important in different ways." I was warned, too, of others making things up about the Wall, just to mess with me.

Numerous Dead insiders expressed shock, sometimes bordering on anger, when I mentioned the landfill and the alleged blaze, asking if they could recall anything of the sort. "That's none of your business, man," Parish told me. "So we won't talk about that." Rakow was even more heated: "Does that sound plausible to you?" he asked. "That's complete and utter nonsense. It's what people who have no information say. They can't say, 'I don't know shit.' They say something that they pull from their stupid ass. It just didn't happen."

And yet, a bonfire of old Wall wood is not beyond the realm of possibility. "I wasn't part of that," Raizene told me. "It'd be pretty stupid to me," but "who the hell knows." The former roadie qualified that, by explaining how "the amount of bullshit going around now compared to the amount of bullshit going around then makes it look like there was nothing happening back then." He still didn't rule out a fire: "Could be," he said. Steve Brown, who stayed on with Grateful Dead Records through 1976, similarly could not give me an on-site bonfire story about the "blazing death of the Wall of Sound." But he does remember Garcia mentioning that it was "not a good idea to leave a bunch of it piled on a garbage heap."

The source who tipped me is legit. Jason Scheuner is a collector of stage-played Dead instruments, from four of Lesh's basses (including "Mission Control") to both of Garcia's post-Wall Travis Bean TB500 guitars. Since the early '90s, Scheuner also happened to have been best friends with Rudson Shurtliff, Ram Rod's eldest kid, and often hung out at the longtime Dead roadie's house, listening to his stories. Ram Rod, who by then also served as president of the Dead organization, and his partner Frances saw Scheuner as a good influence on Rudson, and welcomed him in. One day at the farm, Ram Rod, still "spry" at that point, gifted Scheuner a pickup from Garcia's Wolf guitar.

It was there, on a separate occasion in the early to mid-2000s, that Scheuner claimed he heard firsthand "from Ram Rod," nearing the end of his life, about the landfill-to-bonfire pipeline. "It was kind of a matter-of-fact story," Scheuner said. "It wasn't like, 'Sit down boys and girls, I'm gonna tell you a story.'" But in the normal course of conversation that day, prompted by the sight of a Hard Trucker cabinet sitting in Ram Rod's kitchen, "It was like, *What happened to all this stuff?*" That's when Ram Rod explained. "I was like, *What?!*"

Could Ram Rod have been blowing smoke? Potentially. But it's a stretch to think the consummate Dead roadie, who presided over an enterprise that grossed $33.5 million in its final year of touring alone, would have had any reason to lie to Scheuner, or anyone else. Doing so would have only devalued the band's brand and muddied their lore. Plus, Ram Rod had always been an individual of few words—when he spoke, he meant it, and people listened. Why had he waited so long to tell someone about the fire? I'd ask Ram Rod, but Ram Rod is dead.

That some of the old Wall was taken by flames has kept me up at night. The visual is a powerful metaphor for an operation burning out, hot and bright, and is a reminder of the impermanence of things, including those we imbue later with meaning. "At this point we're like, *Oh my God,*" Scheuner said. But post Wall, no one in the Dead camp necessarily knew how the system would go down in history. "I guess that's also one of the reasons that those things are particularly valuable," Scheuner said, speaking of surviving Wall pieces, "because if they hadn't done that there would be a lot more of this stuff floating around."

My artifact, for that matter, followed a far different path. Post 1974, "that thing had a second life, a third life, fourth life, used for all kinds of different bands and different coordinations," Parish told me. "The history of your cabinet there… was something very useful. People needed a quick monitor, or whatever, for rehearsals—there it was." But at a certain point, the cabinet was among those Wall parts mothballed in the band's storage, where spiders moved in.

Decades went by before the artifact surfaced in New York City.

10

The Keepers

October 14, 2021. Seconds ticked down. The starting bid was $800, which I placed remotely the night before. I was now locked in a series of escalating offers on Lot 148. But once the digital auction expired, I had won. The artifact cost me $4,000.

When the unit arrived, it was as if the wooden crate had been built around the cabinet. "The shippers we ended up using are used to packing million-dollar paintings," Richard Austin, global head of books and manuscripts at Sotheby's who shepherded that Dead-themed auction, told me. "You'd hate that it made it through the Wall of Sound tour, a warehouse up in Marin County, wildfires, and God knows what else, only to be damaged on the doorstep by DHL."

Steve Parish got Austin and the Sotheby's team into that Marin County warehouse pre-pandemic. "It was north of San Francisco, chock full of equipment and stage gear," Austin recalled. The space contained "decades of accumulation, some in good shape, some in bad shape." Much of the information gathering around the items was dependent on Parish "knowing the stories for everything."

What did the auctioneers seek out first? Wall speakers. "The Wall of Sound stuff I thought was particularly interesting," Austin said, as the Dead "had modified everything as much as they could to make it tougher." Anyone even remotely familiar "knows how innovative it was when they had it going, with the big McIntosh amps and the clear sound, not just being loud."

That's when Parish mentioned something "in passing," according to Austin, about assorted Wall parts eventually being dumped. "What they couldn't give away," Austin told me, "he said, 'Oh, we just got rid of a lot of it—it ended up getting trashed.'" Austin added, "Nobody knows how things are going to be viewed in the future."

Sotheby's put preliminary estimates on items once the selection narrowed. Almost like tour prep, the sale had to be inventoried and live by a specific date. For Wall part provenance, especially, Austin "was depending on Steve's recollection of the cabinets themselves." In high-end auctions, "you don't want to say something 'is' that's not," Austin said. "If we said, 'Steve, this looks like two others that were in the Wall of Sound; was *this* in the Wall of Sound?' If he said, 'Maybe, probably, but I can't be a hundred percent sure—there's a lot of cabinets we used, we gave some away, got some back—not sure about that one,' then I didn't want to put it in unless he was sure."

Moving the load coast-to-coast, from Northern California to Sotheby's Manhattan showroom, was then also not unlike a Dead show. "It was Steve and a couple guys packing up a big truck and sending it back East to be unpacked and photographed and cataloged," Austin said. "That was the thing I was least worried about because if there's one thing Steve Parish knew about it was getting musical equipment from A to B."

But Sotheby's ran into delays. Then COVID hit—followed by a wildfire. The sale was a long time coming when lots opened in fall 2021. Touchstones from across this story's past surfaced in the high-profile sale of 228 total items, which brought in over $3 million and represents the largest sell-off of certified decommissioned Dead property to date. That included the mother rig.

"The more that we can get from every era the better," Austin had told Parish. Austin imagined probably nothing remained of the equipment from prior to the big '70s tours. "There's very little," Parish replied. Yet there was this Hells Angels set—the Klipsch speakers the band long ago gifted the motorcycle club, who used the kit at their Richmond clubhouse until 2019. Parish was delighted to find that it had been taken care of by the Angels. "Hadn't seen it in years and it was in really good shape," Parish told me. "They didn't travel. They just were sittin' down there." That humble soundsystem, originally purchased by Jerry Garcia's mom and containing what are likely the earliest surviving Dead speakers, was the opening signal in the band's yearslong audio project. They sold for over $15,000.

The Wall proper was also well represented. The electrical distribution box Bob Matthews built sold for $10,710. The "used in the Wall of Sound" shell from Garcia's Fender Twin sold for $17,640. That's the same amp Dan Healy gave an "enormous" boost to using the guitarist's beloved "Budman" McIntosh 2300, which sold for an eye-watering $378,000. Still more Wall-worn Mac 2300s went: One of the first of those units the Dead ever owned, used initially for midrange vocals and then in Garcia's extension speakers, sold for $94,500. Other Wall 2300s—for the midrange vocal cluster, the piano cluster, Bob Weir's guitar rig, and variously used for guitars, etc.—sold for a combined $250,000. Some of the empty purple and orange road cases, custom built to hold assorted other Wall 2300s, sold for a combined $13,000.

Explicitly noted in the auction, too, was Wall wood. Various 2x12s (JBL cones not intact), including some used by Weir and Garcia, sold for a combined $53,928. A cone-less 15-inch bass cab used in one of Phil Lesh's stacks went for $8,820, and yet another 1x15 sold for $17,640. There was also some aluminum for grabs: The first attempt at a pair of curved enclosures for the 5-inch cones in the Wall's vocal cluster—indeed, "what survives" from that centerpiece—sold for $15,120.

Previously, an authorized Bonhams sale of items from Ram Rod's personal collection in 2007 brought in a total of $1.1 million, and included a few bona fide Wall artifacts. Bonhams ran another Dead-themed auction in 2012, again featuring Wall parts.

Yet even these strong showings of surviving parts and components constitute a fraction of the Wall in its full splendor. Each artifact bears a unique signature and story, and might well remain out of public view forever. But every so often, a piece of the Wall slips into the light.

My cabinet was hardly labeled. "[Stage Monitor] Used on stage with the Dead," is all the description read. But inspecting the condition and vintage of the unit based on official Sotheby's photos pre-bidding, I had a hunch it came from the Wall. And my suspicions proved correct. "It sounds like you got a sleeper there," Austin said.

Reactions to my splurging on a cabinet that clocked miles with the band in the Wall era were about as high, and as low, as a Dead concert. "You have a band or an artist or something that touches you throughout your entire life, that you enjoy, and this is a seminal part of that," Austin told me. "If you had a chance to get a piece of it, why wouldn't you?"

Why not, right?

"If it's meaningful to you, hell yeah," Betty Cantor-Jackson told me. "I have my own souvenirs, as it were." (She has one of Garcia's MuTron Fuzz pedals and Waylon, the tape machine used to record many of her iconic Dead reels.) Mark Raizene was similarly pragmatic. After a year of unreceived direct messages, phone tag, and at least one canceled Bay Area plan to meet in person, Raizene and I finally stuck the landing at a dive bar in Chicago, when he was visiting family. "If that's what you want, you go for it," he told me.

The artifact, and its lore, is a piece of history. "But it's still a small group of people that would appreciate it like yourself, because you're writing a book about it," Parish told me. "You're obviously obsessed with the era and the time and the place."

In this light, $4,000 is a steal. Then again, "I would think that if you dropped a couple of thousand dollars on a cabinet you have a tendency to pay too much," said Ron Rakow, who wrote himself a check for a quarter of a million dollars and exited the Dead's scene when their in-house label folded in 1976. Besides, the artifact is busted. "It looks like a beat-up speaker," Dennis McNally said. "I realize it's a treasure to you." Bill Candelario, whom I met in 2023 while the longtime Dead roadie recovered from a stroke, was even more brusque. As Candelario, who stayed with the band to the end and started his own guitar cable company, Kidds Kables, told me, "Maybe you're crazy."

The artifact is a haunted object, housing the ghosts of sounds and lives past, present, and future, and a portal into the greater continuum the Dead tapped. "Jesus, that speaker is wonderful," Candace Brightman, who rejoined the Dead after the hiatus and remained the band's lighting designer through the end, told me. Not long after the piece arrived, I could swear I saw, in my peripheral vision, a light flash within. My rational brain knew it was playing tricks. But I can't help but feel the artifact's energy.

"Late at night," Healy asked me, "does it emanate Grateful Dead music?"

No two keepers are alike. But those in possession of Wall parts carry the weight of these artifacts, preserving the long-lasting impact of a grand experiment. They form yet another bucket for old, sometimes-but-not-always-repurposed Wall kit, and include various former Dead crew and techs who took, or "inherited," parts of the system.

Healy, for instance, has open-back 2x12 guitar cabs from the Wall, and uses them to this day. "I love the sound of them," he told me. Dennis Leonard has also previously told me about holding onto an original pair of three-way cabinets with 12-inch drivers and speakers from the Wall. "It's kind of cool to have that," Leonard said.

Meanwhile, in an East Bay storage locker, Raizene keeps original Wall JBLs. "I've got tons of speakers," he told me. Parish, too, has some Wall artifacts, including original engineering plans for the scaffolding. He is arguably the most public-facing of the surviving Dead crew, and speaks freely on *The Big Steve Hour*, his weekly Sirius XM radio program. But Parish doesn't give many outside interviews, especially about this era, and is another character I chased down through months of unanswered media requests and direct messages. Until one day in 2023, my phone rang.

"I don't know how far along you are," Parish told me. "I imagine you might be closer to your finishing of it, because I held out so long." Yet he decided to talk with me, hoping something good would come of it. The next day, Parish said he had plans to spend time with remaining Wall items currently in Dead storage. "I'm going down to visit those," Parish said. "I'm the only one that sits with that stuff, now."

Even someone like Rakow, who Lesh said "ripped the band off," is a keeper. "There was a lot of people, and a lot of good stuff, and it wound up in home hi-fi gear and barn soundsystems," Rakow told me. "I still have speakers from the Wall of Sound. I have four 4311s," the kind that were in Garcia's cabs. "I had them re-coned twenty years ago. And I made sure all of the wires ... are the same length," just as Bear would have. Rakow planned to install the gear in the barn owned by Mountain Girl, Garcia's former wife. "I'm moving the speakers out of the place I used to live at to her place, so that they're around for future use," said Rakow, who told me about recently completing intensive cancer treatment. He claimed Mountain Girl "has 4311s in her living room as well."

But other original Wall parts "inherited" by Dead insiders have since been lost to time. Richie Pechner told me about acquiring a couple of Garcia's 2x12s, used in his home stereo until he upgraded his system at the end of the decade— and traded the old gear with his landscaper. "In the late '70s, they're just speaker cabinets," Pechner said. "It didn't have that mystique. That came later, when people realized what happened. We didn't know, per se, how historic or how iconic any of that was at the time." The Wall speakers he had "were just two boxes that sounded pretty good," Pechner added. "But unless you had 100 watts going into them, a good size amplifier, they didn't produce the quality sound. You had to know what was going on." For all he knows, the landscaper used the boxes for plant stands. "Had I known then what I know now," Pechner said, "I guess I would've kept them."

Janet Furman told me a similar story about a speaker cabinet from that era.

Though she can't recall if it was part of the Wall proper, it was of the same construction and came from the Alembic woodshop. There were takeaways from the greater Wall project, Furman said, "but the main lesson was: This was a great experiment but is not really the path forward to the future." Furman parted with the piece for $25 in a local AES chapter sale. "Maybe that was a big mistake," she said, "but it was just gathering dust."

Keith Lowe, a Seattle-based bass player, first contacted me in 2015, and said he had long been interested in the Wall and was loosely searching for any part of it to own. "It's a pipe dream," thought Lowe, who plays in the Pearl Jam–affiliated grunge supergroup Brad and a Dead cover band. "But maybe something will fall from the sky."

Something did. A couple of years ago, an acquaintance sold Lowe a 15-inch speaker and cabinet sourced from an unnamed though reputable collector. "If he says it's from the Wall of Sound, it's from the Wall of Sound," Lowe was told. Rick Turner confirmed as much when Lowe ran the piece by him. "Real deal," replied Turner, who helped design those boxes. Lowe paid $100. "It's really fucking amazing," he told me.

A neat part of this quest has been connecting with far-flung keepers like Lowe. But in 2024, I got a lead on one artifact that resides mere miles away in Chicago's Jewelers Row: a unicorn McIntosh 3500 amp from Lesh's Wall rig. The photo-matched unit, purchased at auction by collector Robert Tseitlin, was used extensively in 1972 and 1973 in the Alembic PA, and in 1974 as one of only a few 3500s within the Wall proper. The artifact helps fill in the story of power, a key component of the system still being reverse-engineered fifty years on. The amp carries a small red "JOE" sticker, presumably placed by Winslow.

I've also spoken with keepers of exceedingly rare cabs clearly inscribed "Cosmic." For instance, "Cosmic Bear 5–9–74 for G. Dead," visible in faded pencil on the front of a re-coned 2x12 cab from Garcia's Wall stack, owned by guitarist and collector Mark Perlson. That May date likely corresponded with the unit's assembly days before the Reno gig, when high winds tested the Wall. The box is intriguingly also marked "#1 set of 4" by the same hand. Who knows where the others from that batch are buried?

Another 2x12 cabinet that came out of the woodwork during my reporting bears a similar tag: "Cosmic 6–72," written in red ink on the front left bottom corner of the box, part of the early Alembic PA. The piece is owned by collector and Deadhead Richard Davis, who possesses what he claims are other additional Wall cabinets, like a "PIANO"-stenciled 2x12. Davis obtained the pieces through a former UltraSound employee.

The same hand likely scrawled "Cosmic" on these artifacts; the curl at the top of the C is a tell. I have reason to believe that individual wrote "G. Dead" on the back of the remaining 12-inch cone in my artifact, too, as it matches the "G. Dead" on Perlson's cab. (On both units, the G is written soft, like a 6. When I showed the markings to both Gissen and Starfinder, Bear's former partner and son, respectively, they both ruled out Bear's hand.) These sorts of legend-like inscriptions link keepers. They mark so many of the objects and are reminders of stage plots and stacks, but also of impermanence.

"I ain't got time," Sully told me. "This stuff needs to be preserved." He was referring to the two 2x12 speaker cabinets, cones intact, in his possession, and others like it. "I'm not saying it gives me chills, but this is important shit."

I visited Sully in the Bay Area in 2023. The boxes bookend the McKernan family piano, which Pigpen first learned on and likewise fell into Sully's stewardship. The cabs are pure Alembic PA—heavy-ply, banana jack ports, and dented aluminum domes. One has the unfinished look of a Garcia-side box, while the other, featuring a black-painted front panel, has "Bob 2" written on the side. A faded "Osiris" tag is also visible, from when the gear had been retooled for that band, for whom Sully briefly roadied. Kevin, who fronted Osiris, died in the late '90s.

On that same reporting trip, I visited 2338 Santa Catalina in East Palo Alto, the former McKernan home and site of early rumblings. Despite a slight language barrier, I told the owner, an older woman, that I was writing a book about the Grateful Dead and that her house holds cultural and historical significance. "I've never heard of that," she said. "I know nothing about that." She shooed me away.

Later that year, I visited another former Dead powerspot: the pink house, where the band lived briefly in LA under Bear, then developing the next version of their soundsystem. Another spectacled older woman came to a heavy wooden door and parted the curtain, eyeing me suspiciously. She knew of the history. After purchasing the house in 1997, a neighbor informed her of the Dead connection. She asked me when exactly the band was there. "Early 1966," I said, when some of the foundational principles behind the Wall were first put into practice. She smiled when I told her the band piled their gear in the den.

Uncovering decades-old signals had become an all-consuming fixation. The day after the pink house stop, my partner Lex and I encountered even more Wall-era parts for grabs at yet another auction, on display in the Glendale showroom of Analogr, a seller of rare and one-of-a-kind studio gear and memorabilia.

The selection included four fully functioning 2x12 cabs, plus four McIntosh 2300 amps from the Wall. Another McIntosh Wall amp was featured, this one in Garcia's last stage rack; the amp was originally designated for Weir's Wall stack, but got repurposed years later in Garcia's rig. Analogr also presented a vintage wooden trunk for Wall speaker and microphone cables, and a pair of early Wall "cube" speakers, complete with Courtenay Pollock screens. The cubes came from the collection of Scheuner, who was close with Ram Rod's eldest son and now owns Lesh's "Mission Control" bass. Scheuner also owns an F2-B preamp from the Wall, and nabbed one of the four 2300s in the Analogr sale.

But the showstopper wasn't even part of the Wall. That was the quarter-scale version of the mini Wall of Sound project, for which Anthony Coscia has been on a largely self-funded mission since the pandemic to create a to-scale working replica. Just like the original rig to which it pays homage, the mini Wall works both for playback—a glorified stereo—and as a live music platform, en-abling each musician to run through their own separate stack. Coscia's quarter-scale sold for just over $70,000.

Many Dead insiders unfairly dismiss Coscia, who did not experience the Wall but saw the band in the '80s and '90s. "He needs to get a job, or get a life," Healy told me. (Coscia does have a thriving business, making his own Alembic-style cabinets and instruments.) Moreover, Coscia "thinks he knows everything," Candelario said. "If he wants to learn more about it he should load his mini PA into a truck and drive it around and unload it and set it up, and do that for about a couple months." Parish has also pooh-poohed Coscia's project on air, calling it an "aberration" and saying no one will ever re-create the Wall.

"I'm a big boy—I can get over that," Coscia told me. "And people keep call-ing in and asking, and [Parish] said, 'I'd like to talk to him.' Well, I reached out twice and never heard back. I kind of gave up on that conversation."

As someone who likewise did not catch the Wall, because I wasn't alive, standing before the closest approximation since, albeit in miniature, was sur-real. Of course it's not the "real Wall." Yet an appreciation for the rig's massive footprint comes through at even a quarter of the full size. And like the Wall, the full 110-plus-dB effect of Coscia's line arrays, composed of hundreds of speak-ers, grows more apparent farther out from the backline. In that zone—about fifteen feet back—the sound was loud enough to rumble my insides, but clear such that I could hold a normal conversation.

Despite original Dead roadies and techs throwing shade, Coscia is a formi-dable yet open source of information about the system he is resurrecting. "It's good you got a genuine Wall speaker," he told me. There were two stacks of this kind of cabinet, one each at stage left and right. The stacks were split in two banks of five and three. The bottom three were vocal monitors—this would explain the other handwritten tag on the back of my artifact's 12-inch speaker, *R-LVM*, likely short for *right-lower vocal monitor*—and the top five were for the drums, or high end. These speakers, Coscia said, "are really the biggest mystery of the Wall." His hunch is the crossovers were external, meaning outside the box. "It's cool you got one of those because it'll shine a light onto how they wired those up."

In my years of research, I've amassed hundreds of hours of interview tape with dozens of former crew, techs, employees, and assorted insiders (and outsiders). Yet many principal characters from this story are no longer around. Who knows what Wall insights went with them?

Rex Jackson, the first Dead crew member promoted to road manager, who also made cabinets with early Wall spin-off company Quality Control Sound Products, died in a cocaine-fueled auto wreck in September 1976. He was thirty. Cantor-Jackson was left to raise their son, Cole.

In 1980, Keith Godchaux, who left the Dead with Donna Jean in 1979 over increasing drug problems, died of injuries from yet another auto wreck. (Pollock was driving under the influence and survived; he did occasional tie-dye backdrop work for the band through the early '80s.) "The irony was undeniable," Lesh later said. "Drugs had helped us to create our group mind and fuse our music together, and now drugs were isolating us from one another and our own feelings, and starting to kill us off." Godchaux was thirty-two. Donna Jean was left to raise their son, Zion.

Four years later, after leaving the Dead's scene and moving home to Pendleton, Clifford Heard, who had been crew muscle more than anything, got into dealing, and was shot in the chest during a home invasion. He bled out holding a fencepost on his property.

But the greatest blow came in late summer 1995, when Garcia died of a heart attack after checking into rehab. "I guess not much can be said about that, except that perhaps it's a big loss for the world," said Weir, announcing his bandmate's death. Garcia was fifty-three.

For nearly three decades leading up to the guitarist's passing, Ram Rod had performed "the walk." He only departed a venue after a Dead show once he watched the drum riser—the very last piece of equipment—load into the truck. But given a late-stage lung cancer diagnosis in 2006, he died suddenly. Ram Rod was sixty-one. His surviving son, Strider, later shared on social media a picture of three road-worn speaker cabinets, cones intact, temporarily displayed in the driveway. "Thought I would stack them up," he wrote in a caption. "Made me appreciate how monstrous the Wall must have been."

The scene then lost an original driving presence. By the late '70s, Bear no longer had an active role in the Dead's sound but remained friendly with them. After moving to Australia in the 1990s, he threw an annual "Capricorn party." The year Rhoney Gissen attended, Bear had local musicians play on a stage and through a soundsystem he set up; one of the bands was then being managed by Cutler, who resided in Brisbane. A tech from Meyer Sound flew in for the event. To the end, Bear was after the best audio.

Bear died in 2011 in still another automobile accident. He was seventy-six. At Bear's funeral, Starfinder drew the skull and lightning bolt Dead logo atop a wooden coffin, "as if it were a piece of equipment Bear had marked for identification," Gissen said. During the service, Robert Hunter, the band's former lyricist, read from "An Anthem for the Bear," a poem he'd written. Deaf in one ear, Bear "pronounced stereo to be a distraction affording only one perfect seat in the house upon which to work its elusive illusion," Hunter said, "setting himself to design the world's most powerful hi-fi system to prove it."

Former Dead insiders continued passing as the 2010s rolled on. The last of the Pendleton unit went when John Hagen died, also in a car crash, and Winslow, who co-founded Hard Truckers and later worked for UltraSound, died in 2012. Jon McIntire, another of the Dead's co-managers in the Wall era, died that same year. Scully checked out not long after. The band had fired him in 1984 for being complicit in Garcia's worsening cocaine and heroin habits. Scully died in 2014 of lung cancer, after he himself had gotten clean. He was seventy-three.

Matthews, the band's first equipment manager and Alembic co-founder, died in 2021. Turner died the following year, days before he and I were meant to catch up. He was seventy-eight. Turner wasn't the only source I was communicating with who died during my reporting, either. Cutler, road manager during the grinding years leading into the Wall, had terminal lung cancer and died shortly after we spoke in 2023. He was eighty. Steve Silberman, the *Skeleton Key* co-author and science writer who became a Deadhead at a Wall show, died in August 2024. He was sixty-six. Raizene, the roadie who ran the Wall vocal system—among other things—died in early 2025. He was seventy-four.

Then there was the wall of silence I met from other key figures. Danny Rifkin, the Dead's former longtime manager turned roadie, currently lives in Thailand and is not known to speak publicly about the past. A request to talk with me, plus a set of my questions, got shared with him in person in 2024 through an intermediary. Rifkin declined to comment. Dave Lemieux, the Dead's current archivist, likewise could not be reached for comment despite numerous requests, seemingly not given approval to speak with me by Rhino Records. (Rhino owns the Dead's catalog.)

That silence extends to the other "Big Three" Dead members who played through the Wall. I hoped to catch any of their thoughts on what the system represents today. Weir, who played a role in the decision to port some of the speakers in his Wall stacks, declined despite repeated requests for comment. "He isn't available," Weir's handler told me. Lesh likewise did not respond to repeated requests; he died in October 2024, shortly before this book went to press. He was eighty-four. He died on October 25, 2024. I was similarly unable to reach Bill Kreutzmann, who has recently experienced respiratory health issues, despite numerous attempts.

Though their Wall did not last, its impact on the entertainment industry is undeniable. By learning from their innovations and mistakes, the Dead's willingness to push themselves and their crew to new heights left an enduring legacy with a lifetime of labor compressed into a few years. This is a distinct and timely signal in a sea of noise surrounding the Dead, a juggernaut in a seemingly endless renaissance. Musicians, performers, fans, consumers, Deadheads, and people who don't even *like* the band, all occupy a zone opened through the Wall, at the welding point of culture, technology, and creativity. It's a Dead world. We're just living in it.

June 10, 2023. On my thirty-seventh birthday, Lex and I entered Wrigley Field. In a sea of bootleg merchandise, we spotted at least one guy wearing a Wall shirt. Taking our seats, the two individuals behind us spoke about previously seeing the Dead and the Wall at the International Amphitheater, a show my mom had also attended. Synchronicities.

We had come with our friends, Doug and Meg, to see Dead & Company, at the second of two sold-out nights at Wrigley, a forty-one-thousand-plus-capacity outdoor venue, on what was billed as the band's "final tour." The summer run, which grossed $115 million, was made possible by an UltraSound-provided Meyer Sound rig, the PANTHER large-format linear loudspeaker array. This compact audio technology can push upward of 150 dB with unequaled clarity and "headroom."

Twenty or so yards out from our spot in the first horseshoe level stood one of the handful of digital delay towers, a fitting sight fifty years to the day since the Dead fine-tuned that practice at RFK Stadium. On this Saturday night, time bent back on itself in the vibrating air around Wrigley.

Meyer Sound had been the sound reinforcement provider of choice for Dead & Company since that offshoot project began in 2015. (That year, at the Dead's fiftieth-anniversary Fare Thee Well shows, featuring all four then surviving members of the band, Meyer also provided sound.) Since 2022, the band's system for these huge shows had comprised four primary PANTHER arrays, a front and a side pair, which each featured fourteen "long-throw" and four "wide coverage" loudspeakers, respectively.

Every stop presented unique acoustic challenges, as with any tour. "Each venue type required significant adaptations of the base system," read a tour-closing statement from Meyer. That kind of adaptability, and likewise the durability required of the gear, is a direct Wall descendant. "The equipment has to sound great yet also reliably withstand the rigors of the road," said Derek Featherstone, Dead & Company's now long-serving tour director and front-of-house mixer, who happens to also be CEO of UltraSound.

The sound was indeed spectacular, something I would never otherwise say about a stadium show. But the gigantic Dead & Company operation lays bare the reality that the carbon emissions of touring with something like the modern Wall equivalent is not a sustainable means of live music presentation. Weir previously justified the band's touring by saying that it is "a lot less detrimental to the planet" to bring the show to the people, not vice versa. Dead & Company has partnered with green initiatives to reduce their footprint on the road.

On night two in Chicago, during a cover of Dylan's "All Along the Watchtower," a few songs into the opening set, the full-scale Wall projection appeared. It's not the first time. In 2012, on what would've been Garcia's seventieth birthday, Weir, Lesh, Donna Jean Godchaux, and others performed Dead songs in front of a similar, static backdrop. But this is the moment Chris Coyle, Dead & Company's lighting designer, had told me about, when, from his vantage point at the control booth in the soundfield, he can see phones go up. Mine did. There was my artifact's likeness, reflected back at all of us.

"This final tour closes an important chapter in the story of the Dead in its many forms," said Helen Meyer, executive vice president of Meyer Sound, who was at the closing shows in San Francisco with her longtime partner and early

Wall consultant, John. "But it's not the end of the book. There's still more to come, with the people and the music."

In all things Dead, there is no "last."

June 14, 2024. On a Friday night in Las Vegas, Doug and I watched "the Wall" get built. We were two heads in the nineteen-thousand-capacity Sphere, the new $2.3 billion performance venue. The gig was number fourteen of a thirty-show residency Dead & Company booked that spring and summer. But not every show featured the animated soundsystem homage.

Before even entering the space, I got signs. Greeting tens of thousands of visitors at an official on-site experiential exhibit, which included a Wall photo gallery, was Coscia's mini system. At the time, Coscia said his replica project was in a holding pattern, as he sought additional funding to continue building the quarter-scale version. His end goal is a functioning full-size version of the Wall permanently installed at an East Coast venue, near his home, and for bands to be able to book time to play through it. Coscia hoped the Sphere-adjacent showing would be good exposure.

At a nearby Sirius XM broadcast booth, I briefly chatted with Parish, who has been harsh in his comments on Coscia. That was the first time we had met in person. I told Parish about finishing this book. Throughout the process, I said, I looked at my artifact and thought of him and others who once handled all those cabinets and the rest of the system, to which, he reminded me, they had given their lives. "You'll be OK," Parish said.

Taking in the Sphere at our seats, I also flashed on the ultimate, if elusive, Dead sonic powerspot. In the early to mid-'70s, they considered constructing a space to permanently install and perfectly dial in their system, in the form of a Buckminster Fuller–style geodesic dome. A sphere. Now here we were, inside one.

Once the show started, the sound was a physical presence, coming from everywhere (even the speaker under your haptic seat) within the 366-foot-high by 516-foot-wide dome. The effect was loud and clear. Crisp, not harsh. That's a direct sonic lineage between the Dead's Wall and the Sphere's rig, which German electronics manufacturer Holoplot calls "the world's largest, fully integrated, yet invisible, concert-grade audio system." Technologically, a line extends, in a fifty-year arc, from one to the other. The Wall walked so the juiced-up Sphere could run.

Notably, both of the PAs are behind the musicians. Like the Wall, the

Sphere's Holoplot X1 uses gobs of individual speakers and amps in one single sound-reinforcement system. But whereas the Wall had something like six hundred speakers arranged in an early line array, the Sphere's system uses roughly 167,000 total speakers, distributed across 1,578 Holoplot X1 Matrix Arrays. (The whole apparatus weighs over 197 tons.) The arrays use state-of-the-art "beamforming" and wave-field synthesis technology that throws sound spatially throughout the orb, theoretically providing each seat with a consistent mix and volume; the technology can also deliver independent spatial effects anywhere inside, by digitally aiming sound at particular points. As my friend Josh Terry, a music journalist, cracked, whoever decided to call it the Sphere should've named it the "Ball of Sound."

The system itself, similar to the Wall, may be obscured behind the Sphere's sprawling interior LED display, but the roughly three-minute, Pixar-quality tribute sequence certainly was elevated. The visual came in the second set, during "Help on the Way," a track from the Dead's first post-Wall studio record, *Blues for Allah* (1975). It was part of a stream of animations and projections cast over four acres' worth of wraparound screen surface. The sequence depicted the Wall's stage, scaffolding, amps, and speakers being set up, in face-scorching 16K resolution.

But if the Sphere is a kind of time machine, transporting attendees back to the "Winterland Arena," for instance, then a calculated decision was made to display the Wall as non–place based. This could be any outdoor stage, in any town, in any year, backed by blue skies and wispy clouds. Phones went up; the crowd cheered once the center cluster was "raised," completing the cycle. The animation was a real highlight of the show—people went nuts—and as clear an indication as ever that the band understands the Wall's importance in Dead history.

The experience was more than I expected, absolutely worth it, and melted away my skepticism. Does every show need to be at this sensory-overloaded, four-dimensional level? No. But for a one-off immersive, almost out-of-body trip, giving into total escapism was sublime. I teared up. As I stepped out into the hot night air, my body vibrated after the show, but my ears did not ring. I took the clarity of the sound, and those that came before, for the road.

Acknowledgments

It takes a whole crew to write a book on the Wall.

Thanks to my parents for showing the way and always being there. Your support means everything. Love to my partner Lex for reading early versions of the proposal and manuscript, keeping me sane, and always helping me put my best self forward. This book is for you, too. Thank you as well to my sister and Jacob Zawa for listening to me go on and on. And to Todd Berko, the funniest audiophile I know, keep playing it loud.

Hugs to the fellas—Chris O'Coin, Derek Mead, Ryan Freeman, Sean Yeaton, Jason Koebler, Sameer Naseem—for gassing me up on the journey and for the laughter.

Shout-outs (MWOnline) to my Chicago and Region people: Josh Terry, Sam Sacks, Alan Huck, Alana Osterling, Jerry Cowgill, Brooke Kalvaitis, Mark Byrnes, Gina Dickinson, Tucker Taylor, Deirdre Nieto, Laura Jane Grace, Mike Matias, Cat Balbini, Bobby Markos, Lindsay Davison, Tim Chamberlain, Chris Walenga, Doyle Martin, and Luca Cimarusti. This book is a not-so-secret love letter to Chicago and the Midwest, so my extended shouts to Dead Inside, Mitch Borkowski and Thunder Express (ask a punk), Andrew Ladd and Mirrorball Card Co., and Lindsey Dorr-Niro, my earliest Deadhead friend. It's a gift to share this with you all.

A big thanks to Harrison Taylor and Christine Montes for letting me crash at your place; Doug Cody and Meg Rooney for our times together and always being down; and Kay Rubino (and Hayes and Hanly), Laura Feinstein (and Goose), Sarah Mallory Mead (and Tommy), and Louise Matsakis (and Mango) for the hospitality, energy, and good vibes along the way.

My gratitude to Evan Ratliff for the introduction—I owe you—and my agents at Aevitas, Nate Muscato and David Kuhn, for seeing the vision and holding my hand. I could not have done this without my editor, Marc Resnick, whose enthusiasm, wisdom, guidance, and encouragement kept me going. Props to Lily Cronig for helping move the project over the finish line.

Cheers to David Gans, Blair Jackson, and Dennis McNally for paving the way and offering advice, and to Steve Silberman, may the four winds blow you safely home. Nods to Corry Arnold and Dave Davis for the attention to detail, Jesse Jarnow and the *Deadcast* for always digging deep, and the Grateful Dead Studies Association for fighting the good fight for legitimacy.

Additional thanks to Annabelle Walsh and the Deadhead Style Archive, tape collector Mark A. Rodriguez, and the Mini Wall of Sound's Anthony Coscia for the early support. I'm grateful for Paul Ruffino and Rattleback Records, for always welcoming me and getting me out of the house when I was stir-crazy, and Pete Barker for our conversations at the shop. My extended thanks to Jason Scheuner and Robert Tseitlin for sharing information about your own Wall instruments and artifacts.

My regards to the folks at the UC Santa Cruz Archive and the Chicago Public Library.

Finally, to everyone I spoke with: Thank you for your time and insights, putting up with my calls, helping me get to know your old friends who I never met, and trusting me with the story. This is yours.

Notes

1. THE ARTIFACT

5 *"From a musician's standpoint"* Phil Lesh, *Searching for the Sound* (New York: Back Bay Books, 2005), 216.

6 *determined* Charles Perry, "A New Life for the Dead," *Rolling Stone*, November 1973.

6 *measured seventy-six feet wide* Dennis McNally, *A Long Strange Trip* (New York: Broadway Books, 2001), 472.

6 *A rig of such magnitude* Ibid., 472.

6 *about four hours* Ken Wardell, *BAM*, June 8, 1974, www.youtube.com/watch?v =nTAHRpJieFk&t=293s.

6 *price of the equipment* Blair Jackson and Dennis McNally, *Grateful Dead: The Illustrated Trip* (London: DK Adult, 2003), 166.

7 *projecting the sound* Gauthier Giacomoni and Allen Peng, "'Dead Sound': The Grateful Dead and the Evolution of Modern Concert Sound," CBS News, May 24, 2019.

7 *"the voice of God"* Amir Bar-Lev, *Long Strange Trip* (Amazon: 2017).

7 *"to get loud, clean sound"* David Gans and Blair Jackson, *This Is All a Dream We Dreamed* (New York: Flatiron Books, 2015), 223.

7 *"the monster"* Bob Weir and Dennis Leonard, "Are We Really Listening?" TedX Talks, October 23, 2014, www.youtube.com/watch?v =aoMlSVvS7Kc.

7 *pay rent at two venues* Giacomoni/Peng.

7 *"that's the thing about it"* Wardell.

8 *"The stresses and strains"* Lesh, 218.

8 *"drowning in mountains of blow"* McNally, *A Long Strange Trip*, 475.

8 *top forty biggest corporations* Rock Scully, *Living with the Dead* (Lanham: Cooper Square Press, 1996), 276.

10 *technological underpinnings of noise-canceling headphones* Lesh, 216.

11 *"rocket gantry system"* David Gans, "The Grateful Dead: A Continual Development of Concert System Design for 20 Years," *Recording Engineer Producer*, June 1983, www.worldradiohistory .com/Archive-All-Audio/Archive-Recording -Engineer/80s/Recording-1983-06.pdf.

12 *rugs couldn't hold* McNally, *A Long Strange Trip*.

13 *primitive pre-war technology* David Gans, *Conversations with the Dead* (Cambridge: Da Capo, 1991), 319.

15 *"They'll tear your flesh off"* McNally, *A Long Strange Trip*, 215.

2. THE MOTHER RIG (1964–1966)

17 *auditoriums and movie theaters* Garrett Hongo, *The Perfect Sound* (New York: Vintage, 2022), 202.

warship's tuba-shaped ventilation ducts Ibid., 202.

18 *plugged in his ear* Dennis McNally, *Jerry on Jerry* (New York: Hachette, 2015), 52.

18 *"textures"* Ibid., 68.

18 *"That sound is very present"* Mark Richardson, *No Simple Highway* (New York: St. Martin's Griffin, 2014), 14.

18 *"tuned to an open tuning"* David Shenk and Steve Silberman, *Skeleton Key: A Dictionary for Deadheads* (New York: Bantam Doubleday Bell, 1994), 100.

18 *"the key to heaven"* McNally, *Jerry on Jerry*, 80.

19 *"what is that sound?"* Shenk/Silberman, 101.

19 *"that incredible clarity"* McNally, *A Long Strange Trip*, 44.

19 *shoddy PA sound* Ibid., 50.

19 *May 24, 1964* Jackson and McNally, *The Illustrated Trip*, 19.

19 *electronic hum* McNally, *A Long Strange Trip*, 72.

19 *"bluegrass music freak"* Steve Marcus, at the second "Night of the Living Deadheads," *The Golden Road*, Fall 1986.

19 *known to record* Richardson, 47.

19 *Garcia's friends and musical collaborators* McNally, *A Long Strange Trip*, 35.

20 *playing "free"* Ibid., 52.

20 *first gig* Ibid., 67.

20 *Garcia family's garage* Gans, 192.

20 *easily adapt* McNally, *A Long Strange Trip*, 76.

21 *"no stage, no nothing"* David Browne, *So Many Roads* (New York: Da Capo, 2015), 61.

21 *"The first night"* Gans/Jackson, 13.

21 *"The music was so loud"* Lesh, 45.

21 *"Some say that it was Garcia's"* Ibid., 54.

21 *"Pig was our first lead player"* Rock and Rock Hall of Fame induction, 1994.

21 *"a very exciting development"* Lesh, 42.

21 *"Amplification of instruments"* Ibid., 45–46.

21 *"had progressed"* Ibid., 43.

22 *Dana Morgan Sr.'s local music store* Bill Kreutzmann, *Deal* (New York: St. Martin's Press, 2015), 30.

22 *"One cool thing"* Ibid.

22 *"hated the noise"* McNally, *A Long Strange Trip*, 83.

22 *"Jerry turned on the lights"* Lesh, 50.

22 *"It felt as though the electricity"* Ibid., 52.

23 *"most endearing quality"* McNally, *A Long Strange Trip*, 83–84.

23 *"no shortage of meth"* Kreutzmann, 34.

23 *earned the band around $800* McNally, *A Long Strange Trip*, 89.

23 *"developed a whole malicious thing"* Dead Heads Newsletter, January 1972.

23 *"see right through people"* Per former In Room bartender Sam Salvo; from the UCSC archive, 2001 email from Connie Mosley to McNally.

23 *"barbaric"* McNally, *A Long Strange Trip*, 88.

23 *turn up even louder* Ibid., 90.

23 *"We learned to trust each other"* Lesh, 58.

24 *locomotive lurch* Barry Barnes, *Everything I Know About Business I Learned from the Grateful Dead* (New York: Hachette, 2011), 13–14.

24 *"love at first sound"* Michael Nash, "Grateful Tapers: An Informal History of Recording the Dead," *Audio* 72, no. 1, January 1988.

24 *first fan to tape record* Mark A. Rodriguez, *After All Is Said and Done: Taping the Grateful Dead 1965–1995* (New York: Anthology Editions, 2022), 268.

24 *each side of the stage* Blair Jackson, *Grateful Dead Gear* (San Francisco: Backbeat Books, 2006), 41.

25 *acoustics were often bad* Barnes, 130–131.

25 *longer than it was wide* McNally, *A Long Strange Trip*, 98.

25 *"Even their crew"* UCSC archive, 2001 email from Connie Mosley to McNally.

25 *hit the studio* McNally, *A Long Strange Trip*, 97.

25 *Fender Showman amps* Ibid.

25 *these other Warlocks* Ibid., 100.

25 *"It's just a loaded phrase"* Gans/Jackson, 21.

26 *plugged into speaker columns* Lesh, 65.

26 *pay the electricity bill* Richardson, 55.

26 *"When the Dead were playing"* Jackson, 26.

26 *"a great training ground"* Rock Scully, 28.

26 *"professionalism"* Ibid., 29.

27 *"gain mastery"* McNally, *A Long Strange Trip*, 118.

27 *Jay Stevens later wrote* Shenk/Silberman, 213.

27 *Scully saw the Dead* Rock Scully, 10.

27 *"scurries around"* Ibid., 15.

28 *future Alembic employee* Rosie McGee, *Dancing with the Dead* (California: TIOILI Press & Bytes, 2013), 39.

28 *"You guys sure played pretty"* Rock Scully, 19.

28 *"He's our patron"* Ibid., 30.

28 *Scully passed out* Ibid., 20.

28 *"piled in with their equipment"* Tom Wolfe, *The Electric Kool-Aid Acid Test* (New York: Bantam Books, 1968), 214–215.

28 *"The Dead's weird sound!"* Ibid., 216.

28 *"to go to work"* Robert Greenfield, *Bear: The Life and Times of Augustus Owsley Stanley III* (New York: St. Martin's, 2016), 54–55.

29 *"as above, so below"* Ibid., 43.

29 *Five minutes* Interview with Howard Rheingold, June 27, 1990, www.youtube.com/watch?v=I_D0E2rrLvc.

29 *Garcia's guitar that night* McNally, *A Long Strange Trip*, 118.

3. THE LEAD SLED
(OR, OWSLEYSTEIN) (1966)

30 *"this is new Owsley"* Kreutzmann, 43.

30 *"Extremely loud distorted tones"* Lesh, 71.

30 *"the roof was lifting off"* McNally, *A Long Strange Trip*, 134.

31 *"the most fantastic gear"* Rock Scully, 36.

31 *"I should have seen"* Note of provenance to Bonhams, 2012.

31 *In his living room* Greenfield, 64–65.

31 *"listening to music at Bear's"* Rhoney Gissen Stanley, *Owsley and Me: My LSD Family* (Rhinebeck: Monkfish Publishing, 2013), 18.

31 *"The concept of a stereo PA"* Rock Scully, 37.

31 *he was their soundman* Greenfield, 61.

31 *shaped like an umbrella* McNally, *A Long Strange Trip*, 95.

31 *a "great" Test* Kreutzmann, 43.

31 *estimated six thousand heads* Lesh, 96.

31 *"All helplessly stoned"* McNally, 125.

32 *more people tripping* Ibid.

32 *"very vividly"* Interview with Gans, 1993, www.gdhour.com/transcripts/latvala.931005.html.

32 *"The mothers of it all"* Wolfe, 223–224.

32 *"He was a bright kid"* Interview with Gans, 1991, www.youtube.com/watch?v=T-OxAEjXaaU.

33 *Scully later wrote* Tim Scully, "Time with the Dead: The LA Acid Tests," *Dead Studies* 3 (2013), 41.

33 *finest audio gear imaginable* Greenfield, 59–60.

33 *"The Ouroboros of sound"* Lesh, 73–74.

34 *"arachnoid rubber band"* Ibid., 74.

34 *power cords surged* McNally, *A Long Strange Trip*, 125.

34 *"The amps are working"* Lesh, 74.

34 *"almost as wild"* Gans/Jackson, 37.

34 *local and regional publications* McNally, *A Long Strange Trip*, 127.

34 *"some sort of machine"* Gissen Stanley, 14–15.

34 *"more famous"* Kreutzmann, 43.

35 *especially delay prone* McNally, *A Long Strange Trip*, 129–130.

35 *Dead had embarked* Ibid.

35 *"The idea was"* Lesh, 81.

35 *"in captivity"* McNally, *A Long Strange Trip*, 133.

35 *"benevolent dictator"* McGee at TRI Studios, December 6, 2012, www.youtube.com/watch?v=f56DrJ3ereA.

35 *tended to look down on* McGee, 47.

35 *"excursions or materials"* Ibid., 48.

35 *"about the ugliest hi-fi system"* Interview with Gans, 1991.

36 *metal handles were affixed* Tim Scully, 47.

36 *"to bulge out"* Lesh, 82.

36 *"His ideal was musical sound"* Ibid., 77.

36 *"building the perfect soundsystem"* Kreutzmann, 47.

36 *nearly shattered an eardrum* Interview with Gans, 1991.

36 *"interacting waves of color"* Jesse Jarnow, *Heads: A Biography of Psychedelic America* (New York: Hachette, 2016), 20.

37 *"This is not what I expected"* Greenfield, 71–72.

37 *"I've got to remember"* Jackson, 132.

37 *"original vision"* Kurt Torell, "Makin' the Seen: Synesthesia, the Grateful Dead, and the Total Work of Art," *Dead Studies* 4 (2019/2020), 86–106.

38 *"beliefs that were questionable"* Kreutzmann, 41.

38 *"talk to these machines"* Ibid., 49.

38 *"inanimate equipment"* Interview with Gans, 1991.

38 *"some bad karma"* Steve Parish, *Home Before Daylight: My Life on the Road with the Grateful Dead* (New York: St. Martin's, 2003), 104.

39 *banned smoking DMT* Rock Scully, 115.

39 *"scuzziest place"* Lesh, 78–79.

39 *"I looked around"* Wolfe, 245.

39 *Fender amps* Tim Scully, 44.

39 *"put together the beginnings"* Ibid., 47.

40 *"All their amplifiers"* Jackson, 33.

40 *"Baron Frankenstein"* Rock Scully, 46.

40 *out in the audience* Jackson, 33.

40 *"Voice of the Theater speaker boxes"* Greenfield, 68–69.

40 *"logistics of packing"* Tim Scully, 47.

41 *"None of us understood"* Ibid., 47–48.

41 *"Bear and Tim's ambitions"* McNally, *A Long Strange Trip*, 136–137.

41 *"better sound"* Browne, 101.

41 *"My instrument was the last"* Lesh, 78.

41 *crouching* Greenfield, 68–69.

41 *"Polish sausage"* Lesh, 78–79.

42 *"I'd wanted to play"* Ibid.

42 *playing stoned* McNally, *A Long Strange Trip*, 129–130.

42 *the cops* Lesh, 80.

42 *guest at the pink house* Kreutzmann, 48.

42 *"tight"* Interview with Gans, 1991.

42 *"focus of attention"* Gans, 325.

43 *Owsleystein* Weir to Jackson, 39.

43 *out of his own pocket* Tim Scully, 49.

43 *"do the technical work"* Ibid., 46.

43 *provided monitors* Ibid.

43 *A few of Bear's ideas* Ibid., 44–46.

43 *"Even mildly distorted sound"* McGee, 52.

43 *first proper media interview* Steve White, "UCLA Acid Test Canceled: Grateful Dead Cry 'Foul!'" *Los Angeles Free Press*, March 25, 1966.

44 *"Otis on the Shake Down Cruise"* Jarnow, 86.

44 *pants seat* McNally, *A Long Strange Trip*, 138.

44 *monitoring for clipping* McGee, 52.

45 *cool $75* Ibid., 55.

45 *Bear and his controlling ways* Lesh, 83.

45 *"a burden at shows"* Kreutzmann, 48.

45 *"so much paraphernalia"* Jackson, 38.

45 *"barn-burning trips"* Lesh, 87.

45 *too archaic* Jackson, 39.

45 *"separate pilot"* Gans, 317.

45 *"make you cringe"* Gans/Jackson, 55.

45 *"absolutely disastrous"* Shenk/Silberman, 214.

46 *"my personality and the sound"* Greenfield, 79.

46 *"a bust waiting to happen"* Gans/Jackson, 57.

46 *time to move on* Don Douglas, "'Are You in Control of All This?' The Folk Scene, the Acid Tests, and Witnessing the Birth of the Dead," *Dead Studies* 3 (2013), 60–61.

46 *"amplifying and manipulating"* Torell, 97.

46 *"cleanest and most powerful"* Jackson, 34.

47 *"improving the state-of-the-art"* Ibid., 39.

47 *tape deck* Tim Scully, 47.

47 *"best sound equipment"* Greenfield, 79.

47 *"hurt my back"* Jackson/McNally, 19.

47 *"it was really good"* Ibid., 56.

47 *addressed the problem* McNally, *A Long Strange Trip*, 139.

47 *left California* Gans/Jackson, 56.

4. THE GOOD, OLD RELIABLE SOUNDSYSTEM (1966–1967)

51 *half ton of equipment* For more on the size and shape of the Dead's early rig, see the weight/year breakdown in the June 1973 Dead Heads Newsletter.

51 *Garcia demand* McNally, *A Long Strange Trip*, 153–154.

51 *"very complex light show"* Jackson/Gans, 52–53.

52 *"walked up to the loudspeakers"* Joe Hagan, *Sticky Fingers: The Life and Times of Jann Wenner and Rolling Stone Magazine* (New York: Vintage, 2017), 59.

52 *Rancho Olompali* McGee at TRI Studios, 2012.

52 *"All our gear"* Rock Scully, 56.

52 *"Topsy-like" soundsystem* Interview with Gans, 1991.

52 *gradual transition* McGee, 59.

52 *"acid and a PA system"* Kreutzmann, 54.

52 *"crawled into the amplifier"* Gissen Stanley, 24–25.

52 *met you with his eyes* Ibid., 122.

53 *proper recording experience* Gans/Jackson, 52.

53 *humping their gear* McNally, *A Long Strange Trip*, 153.

53 *"Knobs"* Browne, 119.

53 *"I'm the guy"* Gans/Jackson, 51.

53 *"Bear had some great ideas"* Ibid., 55–56.

53 *"It never quite worked"* Greenfield, 78–79.

53 *"muddy sound"* Lesh, 92.

53 *"Pick out whatever you want"* Greenfield, 78–79.

54 *outgoing act of generosity* Lesh, 92.

54 *Fender and some Sunn equipment* Jackson, 39.

54 *"regular single-minded equipment"* Greenfield, 78–79.

54 *"Good, old reliable"* Jackson, 39.

54 *Altecs got repurposed* McNally, *A Long Strange Trip*, 154.

54 *"we had special tapes"* Gissen Stanley, 52–53.

54 *world's loudest band* Ibid., 56–57.

54 *without a soundperson* Greenfield, 79.

54 *"not good sound"* Jackson, 41.

54 *Garcia challenged Healy* Gans/Jackson, 96.

55 *"a few different companies"* Ibid.

55 *Bob Cohen* Jesse Jarnow, "Call Them Hippies, But the Grateful Dead Were Tech Pioneers," *Wired*, July 3, 2015.

55 *"commands attention"* McNally, *A Long Strange Trip*, 149.

56 *"huge" soundsystem* Jackson, 41.

56 *"horrible-looking monstrosity"* Gans/Jackson, 96.

56 *a new soundperson in Healy* McNally, *A Long Strange Trip*, 155.

56 *forced the Altecs and JBLs* Bear in conversation with Gans, 1991.

56 *"Healy is a fantastically good teacher"* Gans, 222.

56 *"the rest is history"* Jackson, 41.

56 *hundreds gathered* McNally, *A Long Strange Trip*, 167.

56 *Federal Bureau of Investigation came looking* Ibid., 174.

56 *occasionally dropped by* Rock Scully, 87.

56 *agents knew* McNally, 174.

57 *Circlephonics* Ibid., 211.

57 *"almost any gig we're offered"* Rock Scully, 70.

57 *$25 weekly allowance* Barnes, 170.

57 *domestic roles* Lesh, 93.

57 *advocate for their fair share* McGee, 72.

57 *shared in the wealth* Barnes, 170.

57 *tens of thousands of dollars* Ibid., 191.

58 *"voracious appetite for gear"* Rock Scully, 85–86.

58 *Grant's pickup* Rock Scully, 82.

58 *"Jerry may be tribal elder"* Ibid., 81.

58 *change the band's mind* McNally, *A Long Strange Trip*, 168.

58 *the band's primary goal* Ibid., 165.

58 *"sound and lights and musical instruments"* Barnes, 129.

58 *money remained in the pot* McGee, 187.

58 *first record deal* McNally, *A Long Strange Trip*, 165.

58 *no mention of publishing* Ibid., 173.

58 *"famous or rich"* For more on the Dead gaining artistic control of their records, see Garcia's spring 1967 interview at 710: www.youtube.com /watch?v=NuSGHiQf-n0.

58 *Rifkin made the free model palatable* McNally, *A Long Strange Trip*, 164.

58 *the Diggers* Ibid., 162–164.

59 **pure** *in the streets* Ibid., 167.

59 *"divine intervention"* Kreutzmann, 66–68.

59 *cobbled into a soundsystem* Lesh, 97.

59 *"Bear had freely distributed"* McGee, 88.

59 *the generator* Lesh, 97.

59 *"Dexamyl"* Rock Scully, 85.

60 *road tested* Gans/Jackson, 71.

60 *"production aids"* Shenk/Silberman, 230.

60 *playing quietly* McNally, *A Long Strange Trip*, 180.

60 *"hyper"* Lesh, 99.

60 *"speedy" and "crude"* Shenk/Silberman, 231.

60 *"one of our good sets"* Gans/Jackson, 71.

60 *electronic sounds and devices* Ibid., 72.

60 *"loud and clear"* Barnes, 131.

60 *"somebody can steal our equipment"* Spring 1967 interview with Randy Groenke, www.youtube .com/watch?v=NuSGHiQf-n0.

60 *1,300 pounds* Dead Heads Newsletter, May 1973.

60 *safe and sound* McNally, *A Long Strange Trip*, 187.

61 *lack of gear* Ibid., 236.

61 *"hiring a couple of Hells Angels"* Spring 1967 interview with Randy Groenke.

61 *"equipment got stolen"* Gans/Jackson, 80.

61 *"hard-drive drugs"* Rock Scully, 131.

61 *"bringing our gear"* Lesh, 100.

61 *the Dead set up their equipment* Rock Scully, 120.

61 *"just subliminal enough"* Lesh, 100.

61 *110 decibels* Kreutzmann, 70.

62 *"Space"* Shenk/Silberman, 266.

62 *Insect Fear Device* Rock Scully, 127.

62 *"Seastones"* Shenk/Silberman, 255.

62 *"Dark Star"* Ibid., 51.

62 *"travel" together* Ibid., 336.

62 *crowd murmured* Rock Scully, 94.

62 *"hard-and-fast rule"* Ibid., 95.

63 *"Lethal doses"* For more on Garcia's and Lesh's mindset ahead of the Dead's first trip to New York City, see their appearance on Tom Donahue's Bay Area radio program, April 1967, www.youtube.com/watch?v=58vDRlPDYFo.

63 *"painfully loud"* Lesh, 103.

63 *"We didn't really need a PA"* Ibid., 104.

63 *rough acoustics* Ibid.

63 *"jerk"* Rock Scully, 95.

63 *"piercing right to the blood"* McNally, *A Long Strange Trip*, 199.

63 *"blowing the Big Ones"* Lesh, 106.

63 *Tens of thousands* McNally, *A Long Strange Trip*, 204.

63 *dosed* Rock Scully, 110.

63 *dozen Twin Reverb amps* Ibid., 108.

63 *"highlight of the afternoon"* "Free Sounds, Free Snacks, Free Sun Highlight Be-In," *Stanford Daily*, June 4, 1967, http://lostlivedead.blogspot .com/2015/06/july-2-1967-el-camino-park -palo-alto-ca.html.

64 *"What if"* McNally, *A Long Strange Trip*, 208.

64 *arranged for a drop* Rock Scully, 110.

64 *but for one amp* McNally, *A Long Strange Trip*, 208.

64 *Kustom and Sunn* Jackson, 55.

64 *band played poorly* McNally, *A Long Strange Trip*, 210.

64 *"Jerry and I started grumbling"* Lesh, 109.

64 *target of frequent dosings* Rock Scully, 163.

64 *"ready to fire Weir"* McNally, *A Long Strange Trip*, 210.

64 *"jet taking off"* McNally, *A Long Strange Trip*, 210.

64 *"sound horrible"* Rock Scully, 114.

64 *twenty-five to thirty thousand* Lesh, 109.

65 *bouncing between the walls* Ibid.

65 *"reached over the walls"* McGee, 104.

65 *"the feedback loop"* Gissen Stanley, 39.

65 *he quit* Jackson/McNally, 12.

65 *arrived at the Dead's door* McNally, *A Long Strange Trip*, 217.

65 *bushy blond hair* Parish, 43.

65 *"Name's Ram Rod"* Per Mickey Hart, via Sotheby's description of Ram Rod's Prankster jumpsuit, 2021, www.sothebys.com/en/buy /auction/2021/from-the-vault-property-from -the-grateful-dead-and-friends/laurence-ram -rod-shurtliff-ram-rods-merry.

66 *calloused hands* Parish, 43.

66 *immensely compassionate* Ibid.

66 *longest-serving employees* McNally, *A Long Strange Trip*, 213.

66 *"high-water integrity marker"* Ibid., 57.

66 *fourteen thousand residents* https://pdxscholar .library.pdx.edu/cgi/viewcontent.cgi?article =1077&context=populationreports.

66 *"They invented themselves"* Gans, 231.

66 *opening a box of new speakers* Browne, 119.

66 *first issue of* **Rolling Stone** November 9, 1967.

66 *Winterland Arena* Shenk/Silberman, 323.

66 *"audio evidence"* Ray Robertson, *All the Years Combine: The Grateful Dead in Fifty Shows* (Canada: Biblioasis, 2023), 24–27.

67 *first time as road crew* Gans/Jackson, 87.

67 *"bone-marrow-chillingly cold"* Lesh, 118.

67 *Village Theater* Shenk/Silberman, 90.

67 *"The crew built a fire"* Lesh, 118.

67 *"Matthews is fired"* McNally, *A Long Strange Trip*, 233.

67 *refusing to set up* Gans/Jackson, 87.

67 *sound was "oceanic"* Lesh, 115.

67 *"this amazing wall of sound"* Browne, 124.

68 *"whipped into a jet stream"* McNally, *A Long Strange Trip*, 224.

68 *approach to making a record* Jackson, 66.

68 *blocked by heaps of sound equipment* Gans, 93.

68 *"that elusive sound"* Rock Scully, 128.

68 *"undying belief"* Ibid., 306–307.

68 *"All over the fucking place"* Jackson, 70.

68 *jump cuts and montages* Ibid.

68 *subterranean parking garage on Boylston Street* McNally, 234.

68 *acoustics of a cinder block* Jackson/McNally, 81.

69 *Ross Laver* Steve Grant, "Talking Rock," *MIT Technology Review*, December 12, 1967.

69 *loud trebles* User "davela," www.dead.net/show /december-29-1967.

5. THE RIGHTEOUS PA (1968–1969)

70 *advance man* McNally, *A Long Strange Trip*, 249.

70 *"see and feel the music"* Ibid.

70 *six thousand pounds* Dead Heads Newsletter, May 1973.

70 *the crew waited and watched* McNally, *A Long Strange Trip*, 249.

70 *"kind of harassment"* Rock Scully, 136.

70 *"unwritten rule"* Parish, 212.

71 *2,800-capacity* Shenk/Silberman, 91.

71 *"Grateful Dead quippies"* Gissen Stanley, 117.

71 *"announced his praise"* Ibid., 118.

71 *"You play, motherfucker!"* Lesh, 122–123.

72 *"the Grateful Dead's finest hour"* Ibid., 124–125.

72 *"loud and long"* Ibid., 130–131.

72 *using in a rock context* McNally, *A Long Strange Trip*, 258.

72 *"wall of sound"* Ron Baylor, "Grateful Dead Drummer Trips Through Wall of Sound," *Daily Emerald*, January 31, 1968.

73 *"set up the soundsystem"* Gissen Stanley, 129.

73 *"Recording live music"* Ibid., 100.

73 *the Carousel's rig* McNally, *A Long Strange Trip*, 255.

73 *"work on the soundsystem"* Ibid.

73 *the Dead's sonic pursuits* Jarnow, 32.

73 *"way beyond rational thought"* Gans/Jackson, 96–97.

73 *"build the best soundsystem"* Gissen Stanley, 122.

73 *Bear's audio equipment* Ibid., 124.

74 *"made them laugh"* Ibid., 126.

74 *"working on the Dead's electronics"* Ibid., 122.

74 *"The sound was wonderful"* Ibid., 132–133.

74 *"eager"* Ibid., 152.

75 *"jealous and insecure"* Ibid., 123.

75 *"ulterior motives"* McNally, *A Long Strange Trip*, 255.

75 *Alembic* Shenk/Silberman, 5.

75 *"I did recording and PA"* For more on the early days of Alembic, see an interview with Bob Matthews from March 17, 2014, www.youtube.com/watch?v=MNVNbTZUBlI.

75 *"drive to express some spark"* McNally, *A Long Strange Trip*, 217.

75 *"can-do energy"* Gans/Jackson, 100.

75 *cowboy sentiment* Shenk/Silberman, 47.

75 *"devotional type of roadie-ism"* Gans/Jackson, 99–100.

75 *band and crew* McNally, 393.

76 *"coked out"* Gans/Jackson, 111.

76 *"psychedelic prank"* Kreutzmann, 109.

76 *downright ornery* Jackson/McNally, 82.

77 *"by osmosis"* Gans, 222.

77 *"united in some great cause"* Parish, 10–11.

77 *acid distributor and weed smuggler* Sam Cutler, *You Can't Always Get What You Want: My Life with the Rolling Stones, the Grateful Dead and Other Wonderful Reprobates* (Toronto: ECW Press, 2010), 100.

77 *"booze and dope"* Ibid., 268.

77 *"cops versus us"* Jake Feinberg Show (Set I), October 18, 2021, www.youtube.com/watch?v=8ZSJANh3OuI&t=3151s.

77 *"trailed by Feds"* Cutler, 101.

78 *"generalissimo in chief"* Lesh, 111.

78 *"Rakow's first leadership role with us"* Kreutzmann, 91.

78 *wary of outsiders* McNally, *A Long Strange Trip*, 287.

78 *"waste of money"* Gissen Stanley, 126.

78 *"get-rich-quick schemes"* Kreutzmann, 94.

78 *Black Panthers* Barnes, 110–111.

78 *"community playground"* McGee, 118.

78 *behind the amp line* Ibid.

78 *brick wall* Lesh, 133.

79 *sight of a powerful PA* McNally, *A Long Strange Trip*, 261.

79 *"one look at our soundsystem"* Rock Scully, 149.

79 *tell off* Gans/Jackson, 109.

79 *"odd situation"* McGee at TRI Studios, December 6, 2012.

79 *cut power to the soundsystem* For more on the Dead at Columbia, see the Bahr Gallery's scene report: https://www.bahrgallery.com/links/grateful-dead-columbia-university-1968-yeah/.

79 *"turn off the power"* McNally, *Jerry on Jerry*, 166–168.

79 *"Boom"* Ibid., 168.

79 *"like they drove us to it"* Ibid.

79 *Dead roused* McGee, 130.

79 *"won them over"* McGee at TRI Studios, December 6, 2012.

80 *big "prank"* Lesh, 133.

80 *two hours* Ibid.

80 *"probably fared better"* Kreutzmann, 97–98.

80 *"extremely driving, amplified, and hirsute"* McNally, *A Long Strange Trip*, 262.

80 *"collective transformation program"* Lesh, 112.

80 *financial disarray* Shenk/Silberman, 32.

80 *leave his equipment set up* Gissen Stanley, 165.

80 *"Everything was primitive"* Gans/Jackson, 112.

81 *"undeclared leader"* Lesh, 135.

81 *"everybody is the leader"* Shenk/Silberman, 31.

81 *feedback as a musical element* Gans/Jackson, 106.

81 *"Enough!"* Shenk/Silberman, 87–88.

81 *"feedback is a counter-signal"* Ulf Olsson, *Listening for the Secret: The Grateful Dead and the Politics of Improvisation* (Oakland: University of California Press, 2017), 132.

82 *get the band's affairs in order* McNally, *A Long Strange Trip*, 276.

82 *"That took quite a while"* Gans/Jackson, 102–103.

82 *the FBI* For more on late '60s government surveillance of the Dead, see the Bureau's now-public band files, which stated that "LSD originates from San Francisco, California, through a renowned rock group known as Grateful Dead."

82 *"sinister acid-making cartel"* Rock Scully, 162.

82 *"chasing the sound"* Gissen Stanley, 181–182.

82 *"purely transparent musical sound"* Lesh, 143–144.

82 *Bear himself went down* Joel Selvin, *Altamont: The Rolling Stones, the Hells Angels, and the Inside Story of Rock's Darkest Day* (New York: Dey Street, 2016), 40.

83 *that path* Lesh, 143–144.

83 *delayed gig start times* McGee, 142.

83 *patent on stereo* Selvin, 41.

83 *Prototype #2* McNally, *A Long Strange Trip*, 284.

83 *"sonic frontier"* Kreutzmann, 114.

83 *"throw money at it"* Lesh, 143.

84 *"true communal fashion"* Ibid., 146.

84 *"group unconscious"* Ibid., 141.

84 *money got spent on gear* Ibid., 146.

84 *relocated* McGee, 143–144.

84 *"pack rat"* Gissen Stanley, 183.

84 *"compatible signs"* Gans, 325.

84 *low-end notes* McNally, *A Long Strange Trip*, 309.

85 *quad pickup* Lesh, 144.

85 *Veterans Memorial Hall* Ibid., 138.

85 *"feedback from the PA"* Ibid.

85 *a matter of amplification* McNally, 281.

86 *"they built upward"* Constanten on *The Good Ol' Grateful Deadcast*, April 13, 2023, www.youtube.com/watch?v=eqDpWRjiJEk.

86 *"hanging from the walls"* McNally, 281.

86 *Fillmore East PA* Grateful Dead X account, September 27, 2023.

87 *hundred-plus shows* McNally, *A Long Strange Trip*, 284.

87 *eight thousand pounds* Dead Heads Newsletter, May 1973.

87 *the rig* Jackson, 257.

88 *"the Dead's equipment"* McNally, 286.

88 *traffic citation* Ibid., 289.

88 *paid off* Jackson/McNally, 95.

88 *bribery* McNally, 289.

88 *16-track live tapes* Ibid., 299.

88 *"cobbled together"* Lesh, 142.

88 *fourteen microphones* Jackson, 257.

89 *"We turned on Bear"* Lesh, 142.

89 *Live/Dead's recording setup was "simple"* Jackson, 80–84.

89 *"I see the sound"* For more on Cantor's synesthetic sensibilities, see her response to a question from user "dank_fetus" during a 2020 Reddit Ask Me Anything session about the effect of psychedelics on her ability to perceive sound, www.reddit.com/r/gratefuldead/comments/gnn5q4/hello_everyone_i_am_betty_cantorjackson_please/.

90 *Cantor* For more on Cantor's thoughts on *Live/Dead's* "Dark Star," see her 2013 discussion with Gans and Donna Jean Godchaux, www.youtube.com/watch?v=hR7w5soIC8M.

90 *Garcia* Gans/Jackson, 126.

90 *Next to Hellund* Ibid., 144–145.

91 *"concept of the vessel"* Jackson, 86–97.

91 *Bear usually serving as catalyst* McNally, *A Long Strange Trip*, 309.

91 *"Garcia would come in"* Shenk/Silberman, 6.

91 *partnering with the new company* McNally, *A Long Strange Trip*, 309.

91 *"especially with Lenny Hart"* Gans/Jackson, 122.

91 *"Bear's thing"* Jackson, 88.

91 *"better live soundsystem"* Ibid., 90.

91 *"respected every piece of gear"* Gans/Jackson, 222–223.

91 *"crates of tubes"* Jackson, 90.

92 *in-house from scratch* Barnes, 135.

92 *prototypes* McGee, 144.

92 *confronted the band's management* Ibid.

92 *"not a paycheck"* Gans/Jackson, 122.

92 *billed the Dead* McGee, 144.

92 *first-ever invoice* Gans/Jackson, 122.

92 *"forced to be founded"* Jackson, 87.

92 *"somehow it worked"* Constanten on *The Good Ol' Grateful Deadcast*, April 13, 2023.

93 *Noise complaints* McNally, *A Long Strange Trip*, 309.

93 *"righteous"* Ibid., 310.

93 *"end of the world"* Greenfield, 122.

93 *turned and walked away* McNally, *A Long Strange Trip*, 310.

94 *"punched him in the chest"* Gans/Jackson, 122.

94 *"promoter burn and Dead incompetence"* Greenfield, 119–120.

94 *"alien features"* Lesh, 147–148.

94 *"pack up the equipment"* Gissen Stanley, 193.

94 *"our luck"* Lesh, 149–150.

94 *never one for psychedelics* Ibid., 117.

94 *"the grooves get fatter"* Ibid., 150–151.

94 *Howard Stein* McNally, 321.

95 *"wild and crazy guys"* Parish, 33.

95 *"work for the band"* Ibid., 39.

95 *"unprecedented number of PA speakers"* Cutler, 50.

95 *"Blue Cheer traveled with a soundsystem"* Ibid., 237.

95 *"Boss"* Ibid., 238.

96 *"testosterone/cocaine obnoxiousness"* McGee, 165–166.

96 *"crew got more protective and exclusionary"* Ibid., 166.

96 *"gristle"* McNally, 214.

96 *"ultimate calamity"* Shenk/Silberman, 330.

96 *thirty-foot-high stage* Rock Scully, 167.

96 *warnings* McNally, *A Long Strange Trip*, 331.

96 *"hired hand"* Parish, 38.

96 *after midnight* Lesh, 152.

97 *electrical grounding issue* McNally, *A Long Strange Trip*, 331.

97 *Orbs of blue lightning* Lesh, 154–155.

97 *jolted* McNally, *A Long Strange Trip*, 332.

97 *"incredible shocks"* Shenk/Silberman, 330.

97 *"the PA is so loud"* Lesh, 154–155.

97 *"damn near impossible"* Kreutzmann, 116.

97 *delays* Ibid.

97 *Without saying a word* Gissen Stanley, 203.

97 *giant sail* Lesh, 155–156.

97 *"they become fearful"* Rock Scully, 167.

97 *"demented ten-ton insect"* Lesh, 155–156.

97 *cornered Lesh* Gissen Stanley, 203.

98 *unholy trifecta* Lesh, 156.

98 *"the PA we need"* McNally, *A Long Strange Trip*, 337.

98 *stereo PA* Jackson, 91.

98 *"speaker towers"* Gans/Jackson, 134.

98 *"feeling of collaboration"* Kreutzmann, 118.

99 *pull off the show* Cutler, 159.

99 *"It's your problem"* McNally, *A Long Strange Trip*, 338.

99 *banana-shaped bass cabinets* Selvin, 126.

99 *by truck and helicopter* Cutler, 159.

99 *airlifted from the Novato warehouse* Selvin, 126.

99 *stuck with the tab* McNally, *A Long Strange Trip*, 345.

99 *worked all night* Selvin, 127.

99 *unpacked* McGee, 194.

99 *"We needed some kind of security"* Kreutzmann, 119.

99 *power lines and generators* McNally, *A Long Strange Trip*, 344.

100 *order and calm* Cutler, 133.

100 *"a loose kind of deal"* Kreutzmann, 119–120.

100 *worked through the night* McNally, *A Long Strange Trip*, 345.

100 *"less than thirty hours!"* Cutler, 163.

100 *"circadian rhythm"* Gans/Jackson, 135.

100 *ant in a colony* Gissen Stanley, 219.

100 *"no LSD"* Gans/Jackson, 135.

100 *lugging all the cables* Selvin, 138.

100 *Alembic's 16-track recording console* Jackson, 96.

100 *baffled* Cutler, 171.

100 *"the bands can't hear themselves"* Cantor interview on *Mime Talk!*, May 10, 2023, www.youtube.com/watch?v=3t1eO8gMsO0.

101 *"watched in shock"* Selvin, 219.

101 *bid inside* Gans/Jackson, 135.

101 *"the very truck"* Rock Scully, 184.

101 *bailed* Kreutzmann, 122.

6. THE TIE-DYE RIG (1970–1971)

102 *"responsibility on the Dead's part"* Cutler, 213–214.

102 *ten thousand pounds* Dead Heads Newsletter, May 1973.

102 *"their own light and sound"* Gans/Jackson, 138–139.

102 *500 percent* Grateful Seconds X, July 14, 2023.

102 *"needed for the soundsystem"* Gans/Jackson, 214.

102 *"the apex"* Cutler, 207.

103 *"Grateful Dead family"* Ibid., 228–229.

103 *"5,000 pounds"* John Bilby, "Grateful Dead on Way Here," *Honolulu Advertiser,* January 22, 1970.

103 *his first real working gig* Cutler, 240.

103 *"wall of sound"* Robert W. Neubert, "Airplane Had a Great Party and Everyone Will Be Invited," *Yonkers Herald Statesman,* April 3, 1970.

103 *"good equipment guy"* Cutler, 231.

104 *lips curled inward* Gissen Stanley, 122.

104 *"he was heard"* Cutler, 233.

104 *ballooning load of people and equipment* Ibid., 234.

104 *"massive array of sound equipment"* Harper Barnes, "Grateful Dead Make Rock Fans Come Alive," *St. Louis Post-Dispatch,* February 3, 1970.

105 *"cash and a smile"* Parish, 83.

105 *"brick shithouses"* Cutler, 34.

105 *"thousands of feet of cables"* Ibid., 236.

105 *"army surplus cases"* Per Parish, via Sotheby's description for Wall of Sound amp road cases, 2021, www.sothebys.com/en/buy/auction /2021/from-the-vault-property-from-the -grateful-dead-and-friends/wall-of-sound -purple-road-case-custom-built-for-a.

105 *"full-range band"* McNally, *A Long Strange Trip,* 366.

106 *142 gigs in 1970* Lesh, 173.

106 *free shows* Rock Scully, 194.

106 *fed a PA* McNally, 367.

106 *"career-oriented band"* Parish, 49.

106 *"they knew it"* Ibid., 39.

106 *feared right punch* Cutler, 34.

106 *took in Parish* Parish, 43.

106 *"built a massive public address system"* Ibid., 50.

106 *"something of a guru"* Ibid., 59.

106 *"escalating legal problems"* Ibid., 51.

106 *"routinely worked while we were high"* Ibid., 57.

107 *"all that shit"* Gans/Jackson, 169.

107 *"crystal clear"* Variety, February 18, 1970.

107 *"Legendary Marty" Weinberg* John Brackett, *Live Dead: The Grateful Dead, Live Recordings, and the Ideology of Liveness* (Durham: Duke University Press, 2023), 75.

107 *"the first person"* Rodriguez, 285.

107 *"keystone"* McNally, *A Long Strange Trip,* 355.

108 *shared among Deadheads* Jackson/McNally, 113.

108 *"in the mouth"* Shenk/Silberman.

108 *pace the aisles* Browne, 301.

108 *5,500 hours of live music* Howard Weiner, *Deadology: The 33 Essential Dates of Grateful Dead History* (Independently published, 2019), 82.

108 *"advertisement for our live shows"* Lesh, 192.

109 *"waves of energy and colors"* Harry Jackson, "On Tour with the Dead," *Zygote,* July 1970.

109 *"Waves of sound"* Rosa Schwartz, *Zygote.*

109 *Davis manipulated silence* Weiner, 72.

110 *"wave after wave"* Paul B. Grushkin, *Grateful Dead: The Official Book of the Deadheads* (New York: William Morrow, 1983), 180.

110 *"restructuring of the band's management"* McNally, *A Long Strange Trip,* 363.

110 *wanted to move on* Barnes, 17.

110 *world champion poker player* McNally, *A Long Strange Trip,* 422.

110 *"money for instruments and recording equipment"* Gans/Jackson, 148.

111 *"pretty good musical picture"* McNally, *A Long Strange Trip,* 321.

111 *five days* Selvin, 280.

111 *recording engineers Cantor and Matthews* Rock Scully, 192.

111 *"common wash"* Kreutzmann, 153.

112 *Pleasure Crew members* Ibid., 128.

112 *center of social life* Parish, 48.

112 *"loading this old silver Metro"* Parish, 44–45.

112 *"You can do our speaker fronts"* Gans/Jackson, 420–421.

113 *McGee worked* McGee, 242.

114 *"ripped apart to reveal"* Torell, 97.

114 *"well-like hole or tunnel"* Ibid.

114 *"collectively worked together"* Ibid., 99.

116 *"very hi-fi"* Jackson, 113.

116 *"grease"* Rock Scully, 302–303.

117 *"Feedback" one last time* Shenk/Silberman, 87.

117 *FBI's Dead file* McNally, *A Long Strange Trip*, 379.

117 *"liberal racial views"* Ibid., 367.

117 *all-time worst Dead audience recordings* For more on Wesleyan 1970, see this Dead Essays guide: http://deadessays.blogspot.com/2013/02/may-3-1970-wesleyan-university.html.

117 *"remarkable"* Gans/Jackson, 427.

118 *Lagin got invited to California* Ibid., 428–429.

118 *"eight-foot coffin woofers"* Michael Feirtag, *MIT Technology Review*, "The Strike!: Fantasies?" May 12, 1970.

118 *"terrible sound"* Kreutzmann, 56–57.

119 *"musical/community statement"* Miller Francis Jr., *Great Speckled Bird*, May 18, 1970.

119 *"wall of Marshall stacks"* Kreutzmann, 150.

119 *one-shot promotional UK gig* McNally, *A Long Strange Trip*, 368–369.

119 *"the real work"* Grateful Dead England 1970, The Lost Film, https://www.youtube.com/watch?v=3H-CW12fBNA.

119 *tie-dyed rig* Jonathan Green, "Ron 'Pigpen' McKernan: As Long As He's Been Doin' It Right," *International Times*, March 22, 1973.

119 *"jet plane bifurcates the sky"* McNally, *A Long Strange Trip*, 368–369.

120 *"can't compete with the outdoors"* Dick Lawson, "What Will Be the Answer to the Answer Then?," *Friends*, June 12, 1970.

120 *"delicately balanced sound machines"* Joe Fernbacher, "Swinging Rock Music Redeems Festival's Synthetic Atmosphere," *Spectrum*, July 2, 1970.

120 *"tying down sound equipment"* John Gillespie, "8,000 Young People Groove to Rock Marathon," *Winnipeg Free Press*, July 2, 1970.

121 *"solid layers of sound"* Bill Musselwhite, "Everyone Became Involved as Rock Festival Grooved," *Calgary Herald*, July 6, 1970.

121 *the PA and recording capabilities* McGee, 204.

121 *"experienced road warriors"* Ibid., 209.

122 *"they were ready to go"* Jackson, 106–107.

122 *"craziness begins"* Rock Scully, 194.

122 *sustain the Dead* Jackson, 107.

122 *"Dead financial front"* Cutler, 261.

122 *in-house sound and lights* Ibid., 300.

123 *best possible experience* Richardson, 175.

123 *"Magic"* Grushkin, 158.

123 *reconciled with his mom* McNally, *A Long Strange Trip*, 377.

123 *Matthews mixed front-of-house* Jackson, 108.

123 *"the Dead's whiz kid"* Alan Meerow, "Round Things Are . . . Boring," *Spectrum*, November 6, 1970.

123 *"overwhelmed by all the sound"* Hank Teich, *The Statesman*, October 30, 1970.

123 *"rip off your head"* McNally, *A Long Strange Trip*, 381.

124 *"new horizons in sound"* Lisa Robinson, *Creem*, December 1970.

124 *middle finger* Chip Crossland, *East Village Other*, December 1, 1970.

124 *"our music will be clear"* McNally, *A Long Strange Trip*, 577.

124 *the Syndrome* Wayne Crawford, December 1, 1970, via *Official Book of the Deadheads*.

124 *booked by the promoter Stein* University of California, Santa Cruz, Special Collections, MS332, ser. 3, Box 1:12, GDR: Show Files: Contracts October 1970–1971.

124 *"closest possible thing to Nirvana"* George Knemeyer, *Cincinnati Billboard*, December 12, 1970.

125 *except Garcia* McNally, *A Long Strange Trip*, 398.

125 *"open-backed amplifiers"* Rock Scully, 355.

125 *"momentous financial decision"* Lesh, 195.

125 *point source* Jackson, 132.

125 *six independent ones* Dead Heads Newsletter, 1974.

126 *"sound was perfect"* Gans, 333.

126 *handwritten note* UCSC SpecColl, MS332, ser. 3, Box 1:12, GDR: Show Files: Contracts October 1970–October 1971.

126 *responsible for provisioning a "soundsystem"* UCSC SpecColl, MS332, ser. 3, Box 1:18, GDR: Show Files: Contracts—Rhode Island Auditorium.

127 *"finest presentation of your show"* Ibid.

127 *"happy for life"* User "Stephen T. Marksberry," *Deadcast* "Bear Drops #1," July 14, 2020, www .youtube.com/watch?v=6AtVX6kUOJ0.

127 *Dead's road party solidified* McNally, *A Long Strange Trip*, 395.

127 *equipment team* Jackson/McNally, 128.

127 *came on full-time* Parish, 74.

127 *"all the money in the world"* Ibid., 78.

127 *first proper tour* McNally, *A Long Strange Trip*, 396.

128 *"block and tackle"* Parish, 82.

128 *nude fan* McNally, 214.

128 *"the Wall of Sound"* Parish, 125.

128 *fragile "bubble"* McNally, *A Long Strange Trip*, 214.

128 *Dead owned the Alembic PA* Jackson/McNally, 128.

128 *"make the job safe"* Parish, 154.

128 *"speed"* Ibid., 152.

128 *"mass of band and sound equipment"* McGee, 243.

128 *106 individual pieces* Ian Samwell, "Dead Weekend in Paris," *Zigzag* #22.

129 *"130-pound McIntosh amp road cases"* McGee, 245.

129 *pulled up to the château* McGee, 247–249.

129 *"one of the most amazing events"* Samwell.

129 *"hell of a time"* Garcia interview in *Rolling Stone*, 1971.

130 *"began to assemble the 'wall of sound'"* Cutler, 304.

130 *jumped Bear and broke his nose* Gissen Stanley, 235.

130 *standard-issue felon* Ibid., 241.

130 *smuggled in* Greenfield, 139.

130 *"walled prison"* Gans, 340.

130 *Armed guards* Gissen Stanley, 241.

130 *sneaking in live soundboard tapes* 2013 interview with Gans and Donna Jean Godchaux.

130 *"our friend Owsley"* Shenk/Silberman, 92.

131 *"free range"* Gissen Stanley, 242.

131 *the stage and the system* Greenfield, 137.

131 *chat with Bear* Browne, 217.

131 *"hero"* Greenfield, 138.

132 *"cranked it up"* Gans/Jackson, 167.

132 *"heroes"* Jack Haffercamp, "Grateful Dead Limp to Finish," *Chicago Daily News*, August 24, 1971.

132 *fifteen thousand heads* New York *Variety*, September 1, 1971.

133 *"electro-chemical process"* Carman Moore, "Good Lovin', Good Preachin'," *Village Voice*, September 2, 1971.

133 *budget for promoting the live record* McNally, *A Long Strange Trip*, 410.

133 *donated blood* Ibid.

134 *"play really loud"* Lesh, 201.

134 *"cut our teeth"* Shenk/Silberman, 324.

134 *Dead's main Bay Area performance center* Ibid., 325.

134 *"building the sound"* Marshall Fine, "Grateful Dead Broadcasts Its Power," *Minneapolis Star Tribune*, October 21, 1971.

135 *"invented the technique"* Kreutzmann, 163.

135 *"Grateful Dead has become incredibly popular"* Gans/Jackson, 184–185.

135 *bootleg records* Ibid., 184.

135 *"soundsystem has fallen into sad repair"* Rock Scully, 212.

135 *"Grateful Dead Standard Time"* Browne, 67.

135 *"I was appalled"* Rock Scully, 212.

135 *"restaking my old turf"* Shenk/Silberman, 142.1

7. THE ALEMBIC PA (1972–1973)

136 *"last scene of* Citizen Kane*"* Rock Scully, 217.

136 *"screw it"* Ibid.

136 *longest yet* McNally, *A Long Strange Trip*, 430.

136 *"as big as a wall"* Rock Scully, 217.

137 *forty-nine people* Ibid.

137 *"Everybody goes"* McNally, *A Long Strange Trip*, 425.

137 *"first in, last out"* Parish, 168.

137 *"greatest lighting director"* Jake Feinberg Show (Set I), October 18, 2021.

137 *"they* need *a wall of sound"* Rock Scully, 213.

137 *"backbreaking precision work"* Ibid.

138 *"mountain of scaffolding"* Ibid., 214.

138 *"out of hand"* Ibid., 217.

138 *"massive gantry"* Chris Welch, "Dead Men's Grip," *Melody Maker*, April 15, 1972.

138 *"playing in the shower"* Gans/Jackson, 187.

138 *"a brilliant stroke"* Ibid.

138 *"PA was tuning into the building"* September 1972 interview with Andy Kale, *Crawdaddy*.

138 *"waist-deep in monitor speakers"* Mick Farren, "Grateful Dead in London," *International Times*, April 20, 1972.

138 *"blew my head"* Gans/Jackson, 187.

138 *"35 speakers"* R.T., "So Difficult to Be Grateful for This," *Shields Gazette*, April 12, 1972.

139 *"clarification spread"* J.R.J., "Concert in Aarhus," *Aarhus Stiftstidende*, April 17, 1972.

139 *"big fist"* Rock Scully, 220.

139 *drenched the band's equipment cables* Browne, 179.

141 *"nightmare"* Rock Scully, 221.

141 *"have a clue"* Ibid.

141 *"wall of sound behind the band"* Tinner on *Deadcast*, April 21, 2022.

141 *entrance was too small* Rock Scully, 222.

142 *"spectacular acoustics"* Gans/Jackson, 188.

142 *"leap tall speakers"* Cal Posner, "The Cult of the Dead," *Stars and Stripes*, May 9, 1972.

142 *"they were totally cool"* McNally, *A Long Strange Trip*, 430–431.

142 *"musical chaos"* Wilfried Lilie, "Grateful Dead in Hamburg," *Flash*, no. 12, July 1972.

143 *"insufficient electricity"* Rock Scully, 222.

143 *EUROPEAN ELECTRICITY* UCSC Spec-Coll, MS332, ser. 3, Box 1:25, GDR: Show files: Europe Tour 72.

145 *"triumph"* Hervé Muller, "The Dead in Concert," *Best*, no. 47, June 1972.

145 *Parish was on a mission* Parish, 168.

145 *"keep your dignity"* Ibid., 222.

145 *"electric rush"* Ibid., 187.

145 *"talking to you"* Gans, 224.

146 *truck seized up* Parish, 168.

146 *"French revolutionary type"* Kreutzmann, 174.

146 *foreign substance into the gas tank* McNally, 432.

146 *"Equipment never leaves Paris"* Rock Scully, 223.

146 *"do the right thing"* Lesh, 207.

146 *"thank you very much!"* Gans/Jackson, 195.

146 *four and a half hours* Rock Scully, 224.

147 *"out of tune"* Keith Altham, "Dead Grateful," *New Musical Express*, May 27, 1972.

147 *"bell tone and uncertain symmetry"* Roy Hollingworth, Andrew Means, and Chris Welch, "The Day the Music Drowned," *Melody Maker*, May 13, 1972.

147 *"soundsystem stacked towering high"* Peter de Vries, "Grateful Dead Musically Overrated," *NRC Handelsblad*, May 12, 1972.

147 *"roll up yards of gold leaf"* Rock Scully, 224.

147 *"monumental proportions"* Shenk/Silberman, 52.

148 *"certainly psychedelic"* Kreutzmann, 175.

148 *million and a half watts* Andy McKale, "Bob 'Ace' Weir: Inside Straight on Dead's Full House," *Crawdaddy*, September 1972.

148 *the event organizer* Rene Thill, "The Grateful Dead: Riots at the Entrance of Villa Louvigny," *Luxemburger Wort*, May 19, 1972.

148 *brief scuffle* Michael Watts, "The Dead in Luxembourg: A Sign of Hope," *Melody Maker*, May 27, 1972.

148 *"single largest radio transmission"* Rock Scully, 225.

148 *"our amps aren't listed"* Ibid., 244.

149 *"multimillion-dollar electronic Pyramid of the Dead"* Ibid., 244–245.

149 *warrants* Ibid., 243.

149 *"blacking out half of Munich"* Ibid., 246–247.

150 *"plunged immediately into darkness"* Cutler, 309.

150 *"superb soundsystem"* Miles Palmer, *London Times*, May 25, 1972.

150 *"music floated over in waves"* Martin Hayman, "Dead: One of the Best," *Sounds*, June 3, 1972.

150 *"loud enough to be life-threatening"* Cutler, 306.

150 *Bear was being released from prison* Lesh, 209.

150 *relinked with the Dead* Greenfield, 140–141.

151 *"effortless"* Ralph Gleason, "Full Circle with the Dead," *Rolling Stone*, August 1972.

151 *similar kind of synesthesia as Bear's* Shenk/Silberman, 275.

151 *"wanted some of the other's turf"* Lesh, 209.

151 *drawings greatly improved the acoustics* McNally, *A Long Strange Trip*, 446.

151 *"isolated"* Gans, 328.

151 *laser-like single vision* Greenfield, 144.

151 *"compartmentalized"* McNally, *A Long Strange Trip*, 440.

152 *"piece of your job back"* Ibid., 440.

152 *"the union and the management"* Gans, 328.

152 *"most difficult thing for Bear"* Greenfield, 141.

152 *"design the Wall of Sound"* Ibid., 230.

152 *alcohol and cocaine* McNally, *A Long Strange Trip*, 440.

152 *"maze of hallways"* Rock Scully, 318.

153 *"our big downfalls"* McNally, *A Long Strange Trip*, 215.

153 *"hard for him"* Browne, 218.

154 *"It was a weird time"* From Gans interview, used with permission.

154 *first to institute on-stage monitors* Gans, 331.

155 *noising* McNally, 244.

155 *"everyday component"* Lesh, 209–210.

155 *control of every aspect* Ibid., 211.

155 *"alternative power base"* McNally, *A Long Strange Trip*, 437.

156 *"whirlpool of sound"* Chris Hosford, "Grateful Dead: Inventive, Exciting Music," *Los Angeles Herald-Examiner*, June 20, 1972.

156 *four-thousand-seat theaters to small stadiums* McNally, *A Long Strange Trip*, 439.

156 *monthly overhead* Dead Heads Newsletter, May 1973.

156 *colossal act at Roosevelt Stadium* McNally, *A Long Strange Trip*, 439.

156 *"We missed Pigpen"* Robert Christgau, "The Dead Make It Real in Jersey City," *Newsday*, July 30, 1972.

156 *out of tune* Browne, 93.

156 *"peak era Good Ol' Grateful Dead"* "Grateful Dead: Springfield Creamery Benefit, Veneta, OR-8-27-72," *Aquarium Drunkard*, July 30, 2012, https://aquariumdrunkard.com/2012/07/30/grateful-dead-springfield-creamery-benefit-veneta-or-8-27-72/.

157 *"nobody got electrocuted"* Greenfield, 145–147.

157 *"peeled back like magic"* McNally, *A Long Strange Trip*, 441.

157 *equipment setup delays* UCSC SpecColl, MS332, ser. 3, Box 1:23, GDR: Show files, dated September 16, 1972.

157 *half the band's system* Gans, 329.

157 *Bear regarded himself* McNally, *A Long Strange Trip*, 440.

157 *"I didn't steal it"* Gans, 329.

158 *"loud and clear"* Jake Feinberg Show, June 28, 2022.

158 *"my soundsystem"* Dinky Dawson, *Life on the Road: The Incredible Rock 'n' Roll Adventures of Dinky Dawson* (New York: Billboard Books, 1998), 222–223.

159 *"deserves major credit"* Ibid.

159 *"they went for it"* Greenfield, 149.

159 *"things were going okay"* Gans/Jackson, 172.

159 *"resources that were actually available"* Ibid., 201–202.

159 *all-male committee* Jackson, 123.

160 *"eureka" moments* Ibid.

160 *"approach it differently"* Ibid.

160 *"destroys the clarity"* Ibid., 134.

160 *"build the Wall of Sound"* Jake Feinberg Show (Set I), October 18, 2021.

160 *vacuum tube advancements* Jon Gertner, *The Idea Factory: Bell Labs and the Great Age of American Innovation* (New York: Penguin, 2012), 33.

160 *development of the transistor* Gertner, 105.

160 *digitization of sound* David Byrne, *How Music Works* (San Francisco: McSweeney's, 2012), 118.

160 *"whole renaissance"* Jake Feinberg Show (Set I), October 18, 2021.

161 *Dead were at the forefront* Giacomoni/Peng.

161 *"smooth" response* "The Grateful Dead's Sound," Alembic brochure, July 1973.

162 *"tech meeting"* UCSC SpecColl, MS332, ser. 2, Box 137:12, GDR: Business-meeting minutes, January 28, 1974.

165 *"backbone of the Dead's system"* Jackson, 114.

165 *power the Wall's midrange vocals* Per Parish, via Sotheby's description for one of the Dead's first MC 2300s, www.sothebys.com/en/buy/auction/2021/from-the-vault-property-from-the-grateful-dead-and-friends/wall-of-sound-one-of-the-deads-first-mc-2300s.

165 *"All amps have personalities"* UCSC SpecColl, MS332, ser. 3, Box 4:7, GDR: Business: Sound System, 1973–1974.

165 *willingness to explore* Jackson, 120.

165 *Garcia played* Ibid., 136.

165 *"ate the pie"* Dead Heads Newsletter, May 1973.

166 *better pay, accommodations, and treatment* Parish, 162–165.

166 *"like a single person speaking"* Gans.

166 *heart of the system* McNally, *A Long Strange Trip*, 445.

166 *distortion-free sound on the level* Jackson/McNally, 152.

167 *this specific experiment* Jackson, 136.

167 *"some technical difficulties"* Jay Harlow, "Despite PA Problems, Dead Brings Audience to Its Feet," *Stanford Daily*, 1973.

167 *"state of flux"* Jackson, 135.

167 *homegrown world-building project* Jarnow, 80.

167 *Rug padding* Alembic brochure, July 1973.

168 *"own record company"* Lesh, 212.

168 *"not interested in competing"* McNally, *A Long Strange Trip*, 427.

168 *"insurance purposes"* Deadcast, "Here Comes Sunshine: Des Moines, 5/13/73," S07 E07, May 11, 2023.

168 *"GRATEFUL DEAD EQUIPMENT INVENTORY"* UCSC SpecColl, MS332, ser. 2, Box 137:7, GDR: Business—General.

168 *"loud and clear"* Barnes, 142.

168 *"each string to a different stack"* Jackson, 130.

169 *"mass of electronic equipment"* Robert LaBrasca, "'Dead' Set Long, Languid Tone," *Capital Times*, February 16, 1973.

169 *26 terabytes' worth* x.com/signoutdk/status/1682311423316164609?s=46.

169 *most downloaded Dead show* User "Chris U.," via Archive, https://archive.org/details/gd1973-02-15.sbd.hall.1580.shnf.

169 *"starter tape"* Shenk/Silberman, 272.

170 *"not without its problems"* Mike Anthony, "Music Review," *Minneapolis Star Tribune*.

170 *first ever live performance* User "Punny2404," via Archive, https://archive.org/details/gd1973-02-17.sbd.miller.32580.sbeok.flac16.

170 *"Grateful Dead concert"* Marshall Fine, "Grateful Dead Alive in St. Paul Concert," *Minneapolis Star Tribune*, February 20, 1973.

170 *"Chicago was an important gig"* Cutler, 117.

170 *mic-split feed* https://forums.stevehoffman.tv/threads/the-grateful-deads-wall-of-sound.145294/page-6.

170 *Reels might go unflipped* Shenk/Silberman, 302.

170 *"cassette of Bear's"* https://deadessays.blogspot.com/2009/12/from-incomplete-show-files-february.html.

170 *"Best of '73" listening notes* www.agitators.com/gd/dick_1973.html.

171 *clear standout* Tom Kuipers, "Grateful Dead Descend on Assembly Hall," *Urbana Free Library*, January 7, 2022.

171 *"sound was very good"* Dave Hellund, "In Concert: the Dead," *Daily Iowan*, February 26, 1973.

172 *"purer sounds"* Kandra Hahn, "Concert Draws Mixed Appraisals," *Lincoln Journal*, February 27, 1973.

172 *"soundsystem was elaborate"* David Proctor, "Rock Show Rolls 'Em into Aisles," *Salt Lake Tribune*, March 1, 1973.

172 *died of a gastrointestinal hemorrhage* McNally, *A Long Strange Trip*, 447–448.

172 *"magnitude of the hole"* Lesh, 213.

172 *"Grateful Dead's rising success"* Kreutzmann, 184.

172 *financial umbrella* Browne, 50.

172 *"something far out and different"* McNally, 452.

173 *lines of communication* Barnes, 54.

173 *letters from upset fans* Jarnow, 81–82.

173 *Dead Heads organization* Rodriguez, 281.

173 *"essential moral position"* McNally, *A Long Strange Trip*, 419.

174 *grew to forty thousand* Barnes, 54.

174 *million-plus people* McNally, *A Long Strange Trip*, 214.

174 *Steal Your Face* Jarnow, 88.

174 *varying by venue* Jackson, 136.

174 *convened to talk* UCSC SpecColl, MS332, ser. 2, Box 137:12, GDR: Business-meeting minutes.

174 *still a stereo system* Jackson, 137.

175 *"Clear as a bell"* Comment under February 2024 Dead social post for Wall stories.

175 *"person in the backseat"* Barnes, 53.

176 *camping space* Deadcast S07 E07.

176 *country's number-one-grossing live act* Ibid.

176 *error on the venue's marquee* Ibid.

176 *moved at the door* Ibid.

176 *Total profit* UCSC SpecColl, MS332, ser. 3, Box 1:32, GDR: Show files: Gig earnings—May 13–26, 1973.

176 *"the sound was pretty amazing"* Deadcast S07 E07.

176 *divisions of road crew labor* Charles Perry, "A New Life for the Dead," *Rolling Stone*, November 22, 1973.

176 *obstructed views* Deadcast S07 E07.

177 *flying debris* McNally, *A Long Strange Trip*, 628.

177 *"world's largest home stereo"* Deadcast S07 E07.

177 *one of the longest gigs* Ibid.

177 *weather largely held* Ibid.

177 *"the subject of the jam"* Jon Van, "The Dead's Fans Mellow, But Milling," *Des Moines Register*, May 14, 1973.

177 *Garcia experienced electrical shocks* Deadcast S07 E07.

178 *"ovation"* Larry Kasperek, "Deadicated," January 14, 2013, www.pixellarry.com/pixellarry /2013/1/14/deadicated.html.

178 *initial feature story* Brian Anderson, "The Wall of Sound," *Motherboard* (*VICE*), July 5, 2025, www.vice.com/en/article/the-wall-of-sound/.

179 *"make that rainbow come out"* Deadcast S07 E07.

179 **double** *rainbow* Ibid.

179 *taken by the moment* Ibid.

179 *stage edge* Per user "acehigh53," via dead.net, www.dead.net/show/may-13-1973.

179 *"didn't know we could do that!"* Per user "Cowboy Burt," ibid.

180 *"it was so clear"* Jackson, 137.

180 *"beam" of sound* Deadcast S07 E08.

180 *uniform directivity across frequencies* Deadcast S07 E09.

181 *"seemed OK"* Per user "salde," via Archive, https://archive.org/details/gd73-05-20.sbd .weiner-warner.19564.sbeok.shnf.

181 *"busting up"* Per user "srfnsom," via dead.net, https://www.dead.net/show/may-20-1973.

181 *"knife held in his teeth"* Per user "rafterman," ibid.

182 *"culmination of the stereo PA"* Deadcast S07 E09.

182 *windy day* Philip Elwood, "Kezar's 8-hour folk rock concert—a joyous day—return of S.F.'s Grateful Dead," *San Francisco Sunday Examiner & Chronicle*, May 27, 1973.

182 *phase-canceling differential microphone setup* Jackson, 138.

182 *"di-pole microphone"* Ibid., 139.

183 *noise-canceling headphones* Giacomoni/Peng.

183 *eliminating leakage* Gans.

183 *fit the full system* Jackson, 139.

183 *"managed to transcend that"* Deadcast S07 E09.

183 *"Superb Sound"* Richardson, 207.

183 *"huge amplified sound"* Elwood.

184 *"ocean of loud music"* Betty Golden, "Kezar Rocks as the Dead Arise!" *San Francisco Phoenix*.

184 *"years of electronic fiddling"* Patrick Carr, "The Grateful Dead Makes a Real Good Hamburger," *New York Times*, March 11, 1973.

184 *"He liked it and encouraged me"* Gissen, 248–249.

184 *"learned to solder"* Ibid., 269.

184 *half dozen new audio projects then underway* Dated May 29, 1973: UCSC SpecColl, MS0332, ser. 2, 0004, 0007.

185 *"floating galaxies in the retina"* UCSC SpecColl, MS332, ser. 2, Box4:7, GDR: Business: Sound system . . . 1973–1974.

185 *eighty-three thousand heads* Deadcast S07 E10.

185 *"A day of tests"* Ibid.

185 *"Owsley Stanley design"* Ibid.

186 *"delay towers that were tilted up"* Ibid.

186 *"could've gone up in flames"* Ibid.

186 *longest Dead show* Ibid.

186 *"remarkably good quality sound"* Michael Hill, "Garcia's Guitar Was Singing As It Flew Away at RFK," *Baltimore Evening Sun*, June 11, 1973.

186 *reportedly was raped* Deadcast S07 E10.

187 *"reputation"* Don Stanley, "Grateful Dead Are Alive," *Vancouver Sun*.

187 *"towering ranks of speakers"* Jeani Read, "The Grateful Dead are best seen alive," *Vancouver Province*, June 23, 1973.

187 *"new soundsystem was excellent"* Bruce Micklus, *Oregon Daily Emerald*, June 13, 1973.

187 *"they played an atmospheric music"* Per Mark Weber, via dead.net, www.dead.net/show/june -29-1973.

188 *"they sound like The Grateful Dead"* Cameron Crowe, "Summer 1973: New Label, New Albums—Grateful Dead Flee Big Business," *Circus*, October 1973.

188 *"it didn't matter"* Per user "Mtn Minor," via dead.net, www.dead.net/show/june-30-1973.

188 *"big stacks of amps and speakers"* Per Lloyd Thomas, ibid.

188 *"sound was perfect"* Per user "stuporsession," ibid.

188 *"disappointing at best"* Sandi Schneider, *Daily-News Post*, July 6, 1973.

189 *"playing with fire"* McNally, *A Long Strange Trip*, 455.

189 *"quadramped"* Charles Perry, "Sound Wizards to the Grateful Dead," *Rolling Stone*, September 1973.

189 *monitor system* Ibid.

190 *controlling amplifiers and the soundsystem* For more of Bear's thoughts on sound, psychedelics, and telekinesis, see his 2009 talk at the Entheogenesis Australis Conference in Victoria, www.youtube.com/watch?v=geRXSVuPRhU.

190 *"when I'm gone"* Ibid.

190 *"now industry standards"* Kreutzmann, 188.

190 *staging and backstage fencing* McNally, *A Long Strange Trip*, 458.

190 *"monster stage"* Deadcast S08 E01.

190 *rental for the digital delay line* UCSC SpecColl, MS332, ser. 3, Box 1:35, GDR: Show Files: Grand Prix Racecourse, Watkins Glen, NY.

191 *traced that delay system's path* Perry.

192 *"last of its era"* McNally, *A Long Strange Trip*, 458.

193 *"beginning of the Wall of Sound"* Deadcast S08 E01.

193 *"speaker cones soft and soggy"* Lesh, 214.

194 *"our only reality"* McNally, *A Long Strange Trip*, 458.

195 *$5 million in tickets in 1973* Per Dave Davis, *Grateful Seconds*.

195 *tallying earnings* Gans/Jackson, 238.

195 *"we made money"* Ibid., 213.

195 *"follow the band around"* Jarnow, 88.

196 *burgeoning free tape exchange network* Charley Rosen, "Mr. 'Tapes' of Brooklyn: He Rules the Grateful Dead Tape Empire," *Rolling Stone*, October 11, 1973.

196 *half dozen US cities* Deadcast S04 E04.

196 *"faithful to the Dead's PA ambience"* Shenk/Silberman, 12.

196 *"they can have it"* Jerry Garcia Instagram: www.instagram.com/jerrygarcia/p/Cy6Vsc8JH5s/?img_index=1.

196 *"self-regulating community"* Barnes, 80.

196 *"our main product"* Ibid., 79–80.

196 *fan club mailers* Ibid., 118.

196 *next decade* McNally, 454.

196 *heavy police presence* Richardson, 182.

196 *"sound never has a chance"* David Marsh, "A Dead Echo," *Newsday*, September 9, 1973.

197 *"reproduction of their distinctive sound"* Roger Williams, "New Life from the Grateful Dead," *Richmond Mercury*, September 12, 1973.

197 *"understanding of the band's mission"* McNally, *A Long Strange Trip*, 421.

198 *"the Dead's soundsystem"* Donald Davis, "Grateful Dead Truck Up to Syracuse," *The Press*, September 21, 1973.

198 *ultimate sonic powerspot* Jonathan Takiff, "Dinner Date with the Grateful Dead Is Less Than a Trip," *Philadelphia Daily News*, September 21, 1973.

198 *"band's huge soundsystem malfunctioned all night"* Jonathan Takiff, "The Grateful Dead Do ½ Show on Thursday," *Philadelphia Daily News*, September 23, 1973.

198 *flying discs* Weiner, 225.

199 *"listening to your stereo"* Pete Bishop, "Grateful Dead: Versatility with New Twists," *Pittsburgh Press*, September 25, 1973.

199 *"newest and most modern sound equipment"* "Some New Facts About the Grateful Dead," *Spectrum*, 6, September 17, 1973, www.instagram.com/p/CxqyJngPK9r/?img_index=2.

199 *"wonderful intricacies of The Dead's lighting"* Dale Anderson, "Chill Prevails Despite the Grateful Dead," *Buffalo Evening News*, September 27, 1973.

199 *economic engine of the Dead* UCSC SpecColl, MS332, ser. 3, Box 155:4, GDR: Show Files: 1973–1974 tours in connection with albums.

199 *burned through those earnings* McNally, *A Long Strange Trip*, 459.

199 *began the final two-month haul* Weiner, 19.

200 *"winter of 1973 forever"* Jarnow, 361.

200 *breakdown of event expenses* UCSC SpecColl, MS332, ser. 3, Box 155:4, GDR: Show Files: 1973–1974 tours in connection with albums.

200 *"cast of characters"* Charles Perry, "A New Life for the Dead," *Rolling Stone*, November 23, 1973.

200 *feud with Jackson boiled over* Parish, 214–215.

202 *"moments of pure fear"* Per user "Candayman53," via dead.net, www.dead.net/show/october-19-1973.

203 *"overcome the arena's notoriously bad acoustics"* Steve Jordon, "Grateful Dead Treat 7,000 with New Chapter of Music," *World-Herald*, October 22, 1973.

203 *perfect for match striking* Alembic brochure, July 1973.

203 *"most impressive array of equipment yet"* Peter Citron, "Dangerous Fans," *Omaha World-Herald*, October 24, 1973.

203 *crowd of 9,100* Michael Vena, "Grateful Dead Lives, and 9,100 Love It," *Wisconsin State Journal*, October 26, 1973.

203 *"out-of-this-world kind of shows"* Dick Latvala, "Best of '73" listening notes, www.agitators.com/gd/dick_1973.html.

203 *crisp power of the system* Comment (Kevin McDaniel) under February 2024 Dead social post for Wall stories.

204 *"experimentation in far-out sounds"* Dick Richmond, "Grateful Dead Plays at Kiel Auditorium," *St. Louis Post-Dispatch*, October 30, 1973.

205 *"piles of amplifiers and speakers"* Dani Ruby, "On the Road with the Grateful Dead," *Daily Illini*, November 3, 1973.

205 *"gentleness of the group's sound"* Judy Singler, "'Dead' Captivated Audience with Mellow Style," *The Current*.

206 *electricity behind the forty-by-eighty-foot stage* "Grace Sets Stage for Freaks' Gala," *Daily Northwestern*, October 31, 1973.

208 *band's two-inch-thick technical rider* Gans/Jackson, 220.

208 *mounted behind them* Jackson/McNally, 162.

208 *"common ground with the amp line"* Gans/Jackson, 220.

208 *sound at the band's back* Jackson, 140–141.

208 *"the birth"* Gans/Jackson, 220.

208 *"sound towers and banks of amps"* Stephen Foer, "Grateful Dead Alive," *Straight Creek Journal*, December 3, 1973.

208 *their standard 85-foot-wide stage plot* Jackson, *Road Trips Vol. 4 Denver '73* liner notes.

209 *tarps got draped* Hardy Price, "Versatile Grateful Dead," *Arizona Republic*, November 27, 1973.

209 *"Looked like serious rain"* Per user "zygster," via dead.net, www.dead.net/show/november-25-1973.

210 *"didn't hurt your ears"* Per user "slipangle," via Archive, https://archive.org/details/gd73-11-25.sbd.sacks.2213.sbeok.shnf.

210 *reportedly jumped from the sound tower* Per user "hifiguytn," via dead.net, www.dead.net/show/november-25-1973.

210 *early version of "Space"* Andy Kahn, "The Mickey Hart & Jerry Garcia Concert That Helped Birth Grateful Dead's 'Space' Jams," *JamBase*, September 11, 2023.

210 *"We started late"* Gans/Jackson, 220.

210 *constructing the stage out front* Ibid.

210 *way past due* McNally, *A Long Strange Trip*, 238.

210 *"scaled down 'Wall of Sound'"* Michael J. Sanditen, "Baked in Beantown," *Dick's Picks Vol. 14.*

211 *hung from wires over the audience* Browne, 195.

211 *began around midnight* McNally, *A Long Strange Trip*, 238.

211 *feedback jam* Sanditen.

212 *"clearest audio reproduction"* William Howard, "Grateful Dead Hold Court," *Boston Globe*, December 12, 1973.

212 *"sandwitch plans"* UCSC SpecColl, MS332, ser. 3, Box 1:37, GDR: Show files: Cincinnati Gardens, Cincinnati, OH.

212 *set up the Wall of Sound* Per user "Campburt," via Archive, https://archive.org/details/gd73-12-04.s1-sbd.miller.30656.sbeok.flacf.

213 *"I think this is getting ridiculous"* Comment ("Tony Tone") under February 2024 Dead social post for Wall stories.

213 *"river of colorful notes"* Per user "uncle mickey," via dead.net, https://www.dead.net/show/december-4-1973.

213 *"it seemed that it was moving"* Per user "zibman," via Archive, https://archive.org/details/gd73-12-04pt.sbd.elliot.11799.sbeok.shnf.

213 *"blew out a row of speakers"* David M. Herd, "'Dead' Not Moribund, Just into Changes," *Dayton Daily News*, December 6, 1973.

213 *echo chamber–like hall* Jeff Sumskis, "'Dead' brings life to crowd in Cincy," *The Lantern*, December 6, 1973.

213 *"Pity all the good equipment"* *Cincinnati Enquirer,* December 4, 1973.

214 *brandished their piece at Parish* Parish, 126.

215 *"expend as much energy"* Holly Hemsworth, Letter to Editor ("More tree"), *Duke Chronicle*, November 27, 1973.

215 *Garcia chatted up a carpenter* Per user "Peter," via dead.net, www.dead.net/show/december-8-1973.

216 *"surprised the band"* Per user "McBraar," via dead.net, www.dead.net/show/december-10-1973.

216 *"multi-purpose rooms"* Gans/Jackson, 224.

217 *"nearing perfection"* Kathy Tilley, "Rock Musician Trips on Music," *Atlanta Journal Constitution*, December 14, 1973.

217 *"crisp licks"* Per user "Big Willy," via dead.net, www.dead.net/show/december-12-1973.

217 *"custom soundsystem and cosmic improvisations"* Bob Ross, "'Grateful Dead' Rise at Custis Hixon," *St. Petersburg Times*, December 19, 1973.

217 *more wattage* Rick Norcross, "'Grateful Dead' Lives to Play Music," *Tampa Times*, December 19, 1973.

218 *"electrical potential into memorable music"* Ross.

218 *"raise the hair on your arms"* Latvala interview with Gans, October 5, 1993, https://www.gdhour.com/transcripts/latvala.931005.html.

218 *$73,590* UCSC SpecColl, MS332, ser. 3, Box 1:39, GDR: Show files-Gig financial reports.

8. THE WALL (1974)

221 *Minutes* UCSC SpecColl, MS332, ser. 2, Box 137:13, GDR: Business-meeting minutes, 1974.

221 *"final element"* McNally, *A Long Strange Trip*, 470.

222 *formal "tech meeting"* UCSC SpecColl, MS332, ser. 2, Box 137:12, GDR: Business-meeting minutes, January 28, 1974.

222 *forty-footer with air-ride suspension* Browne, 194–195.

222 *120-degree arc* Lesh, 216.

223 *shouted out Raizene* Gans.

223 *Cutler got fired* McNally, *A Long Strange Trip*, 468.

223 *10 percent cut* Browne, 216.

223 *Cutler had supported their soundsystem plans* Browne, 194.

223 *Garcia's personal manager* Ibid., 224.

224 *requisite for paying for itself* McNally, *A Long Strange Trip*, 469.

224 *booking agent* Gans/Jackson, 271.

224 *"as good as can be made"* Ibid., 222.

227 *gift to Garcia* McNally, *A Long Strange Trip*, 481.

228 *"secret weapon"* http://alembic.com/club/messages/393/125947.html?1331821475.

228 *Furman preamp* McNally, 481.

230 *eardrum-rattling "POP!"* Comment (Topher Schram) under February 2024 Dead social post for Wall stories.

230 *"try out this new rocketship"* Per user "drchampagne," via dead.net, www.dead.net/show/february-22-1974.

231 *"always playing somewhere"* Grateful Dead Instagram, www.instagram.com/gratefuldead/p/BuZyZ2sB1-s/.

231 *"cuts through the body"* Olsson, 1–2.

231 *"depended on superior soundsystems"* Theodore Gracyk, *Rhythm and Noise: An Aesthetics of Rock* (Durham: Duke University Press, 1996), 39.

231 *$29,567* UCSC SpecColl, MS332, ser. 3, Box: 1:42, GDR: Show Files: Gig reports—Earnings & Expenses; February–December 1974.

232 *$22,779* Ibid.

232 *$452,237* Ibid.

233 *"group of killer bees"* Browne, 196.

233 *dozen-plus columns* Ibid.

233 *forty-five feet above the stage* Jackson, 141.

233 *nearly fifty-foot-tall notes* Browne, 201.

233 *yet another band meeting* UCSC SpecColl, MS332, ser. 2, Box 137:12, GDR: Business-meeting minutes.

234 *left a message* UCSC SpecColl, phone logs: 2/26/74–5/8/74.

234 *"cult"* Richardson, 252.

234 *left a message for Rakow* UCSC SpecColl, phone logs: 2/26/74–5/8/74.

234 *tensions were also building* Rock Scully, 233.

234 *"filling up almost all thirty tracks"* Steve Brown, "If I Told You All That Went Down: The Saga of Grateful Dead Records," *The Golden Road*, 53.

234 *"limited by recording"* Gans/Jackson, 227.

234 *"an ongoing study"* John L. Wasserman, "The Dead: Committed to Sound Perfection," *San Francisco Chronicle*, March 22, 1974.

235 *"Band and Crew" list* UCSC SpecColl, MS332, ser. 3, Box: 1:44, GDR: Show Files: Cow Palace, San Francisco, CA—March 23, 1974.

235 *"Employees and Wives"* www.dead.net/show/march-23-1974.

235 *dummy Wall speaker* Per user "Dizz Quixote," via dead.net, www.dead.net/show/march-23-1974.

235 *"loud and clear and rich"* Robertson, 120–121.

236 *"brand new toy"* Ibid.

236 *"just exactly perfect"* McNally, *A Long Strange Trip*, 596.

236 *"an impressive event"* Comment ("jwstewball") under February 2024 Dead social post for Wall stories.

236 *"audible musical magic"* Per user "Grateful Bill," via Archive, https://archive.org/details /gd1974-03-23.aud.connors.hughey.gems.78599 .flac16.

236 *"cloud of hazy smoke"* Dizz Quixote.

236 *"embedded in my soul"* Per user "pkpotter," via dead.net, www.dead.net/show/march-23-1974.

236 *"oiled sardine"* Grushkin, 164.

237 *turning point* Rodriguez, 185.

238 *"unable to fit"* Delbert Gee, "How EB Picks Concert Performers," *California* Aggie 90, no. 45, December 5, 1975.

238 *"huge beehive"* Jack Stevenson, "The Grateful Dead Were There But, There Wasn't A ...," *Nevada State Journal*, May 13, 1974.

238 *tech meeting* May 7, 1974—UCSC SpecColl, phone logs: 2/26/74–5/8/74.

238 *"I was scared"* Gans/Jackson, 223.

238 *ran out from underneath* Kreutzmann, 189.

238 *specific forklift brands* UCSC SpecColl, MS 332, ser. 3, Box 2:4, GDR: Show Files: Providence Civic Center, R.I.

239 *"people would have died"* Browne, 195.

240 *"the sound problem"* Phil Barber, "New rock concert fear: Super powerful sound," *Reno Evening Gazette*, May 9, 1974.

240 *hour and a half late* Browne, 200.

240 *reportedly singled out* Comment ("aceyou60me") under February 2024 Dead social post for Wall stories.

240 *test notes fluttering* Browne, 193.

241 *"a brilliant stroke"* Ibid., 201.

241 *appeared to come out* Per user "Deaddad," via dead.net, www.dead.net/show/march-23-1974.

241 *"the pinnacle"* Kreutzmann, 47.

241 *"much room for fault"* Ibid., 189.

241 *"transparency"* Per user "martabassy," via dead .net, www.dead.net/show/may-12-1974.

241 *ironed out* Robertson, 215.

241 *"audible to the very last seat"* "Grateful Dead to Perform in Missoula May 14," *Montana Kaimin*.

241 *"huge bank of speakers"* "In the Strangest of Places: Celebrating the 45th Anniversary of the Grateful Dead in Missoula," Sue Balter-Reitz, *Yellowstone Public Radio*, May 14, 2019.

242 *"The Book"* McNally, *A Long Strange Trip*, 472.

242 *twenty-six road members and fourteen hours* Jackson/McNally, 166.

242 *followed a routine* Gans/Jackson, 223.

242 *writing sea shanties* Parish on *Comes a Time* podcast, March 2, 2023.

242 *"community and the equipment guys"* UCSC Archive, MS332, ser. 2, and George's "Rap-Up," *Oakland Tribune*, June 23, 1974.

243 *"carry the show"* McNally, 573.

243 *dissolved any barriers* Shenk/Silberman, 29.

243 *"wall of speakers"* Steve Shirley, "Music Review," *Missoulian*, May 16, 1974.

243 *wasn't a bad seat* Per user "mknyc," via Archive, https://archive.org/details/gd74-05-14 .sbd.murphy.1823.sbeok.shnf.

243 *"Awed by the Wall of Sound"* Milo Miles, "Fight Sound with Sound: Grateful Dead's Arena Combat," *NPR*, March 31, 2014.

243 *"Best sounding show"* Per user "jerryandtheinvisibles8637," via YouTube, www.youtube.com /watch?v=D_RiiRe2sns.

243 *perceived across campus* Per user "marciapolo," via Archive, https://archive.org/details /gd74-05-14.sbd.murphy.1823.sbeok.shnf.

243 *"Wall of Sound really starts here"* Per user "apniles," via Archive, ibid.

245 *"fickle and unreliable Wall"* Per user "Mind Wondrin," via Archive, https://archive.org/details /gd1974-05-17.sbd.miller.89972.sbeok.flac16.

245 *fifteen minutes late* Per user "gotgopher2," via dead.net, https://www.dead.net/show/may -19-1974.

245 *pulling the power* Ibid.

245 *"got what they came for"* Robertson, 122.

245 *"so clean and clear"* Comment ("sustainablebill") under February 2024 Dead social post for Wall stories.

246 *sprinklers turned on* Per user "wolfbat," via dead.net, www.dead.net/show/may-25-1974.

246 *"island"* McNally, *A Long Strange Trip*, 472.

246 *"reached up to Heaven"* Per user "LonotheOno," via dead.net, www.dead.net/show/may -25-1974.

247 *"giant Martian hieroglyphic"* Per user "jacksondownunda," ibid.

247 *"literally move the crowd"* Comment (Chuck

Nagel) under February 2024 Dead social post for Wall stories.

247 *moving images* www.youtube.com/watch?v =HYt8RQQoMjA.

247 *"dead center"* Per user "TeadHead," via dead .net, www.dead.net/show/may-25-1974.

247 *"clarity of the sound"* Comment (Mark R. Breeland) under February 2024 Dead social post for Wall stories.

247 *"crystal clear sound"* Per "jacksondownunda," via dead.net, www.dead.net/show/may-25-1974.

247 *early June band meeting* UCSC SpecColl, MS332, ser. 3, Box 2:2, Show Files: Iowa State Fairgrounds, IA—June 16, 1974.

248 *"taping became more serious"* Nash, "Grateful Tapers."

248 *"before the tour was over"* Rodriguez, 191.

248 *Wall boosted the burgeoning taper scene* Richardson, 214–215.

249 *"hotel room after the show"* Rodriguez, 198.

249 *"struck the keynote"* Phil Sherwood, "The Dead Raise the Sound—26,000 Amps and 400 Speakers Bring Dead Gig Alive," *Rolling Stone*, August 1, 1974.

249 *Beach Boys hadn't used the Wall* "Update 2: Another Backstage Report," https:// lostlivedead.blogspot.com/2011/05/june -8-1974-oakland-coliseum-stadium.html.

250 *"kicking back"* Per user "UpTil4," via dead.net, www.dead.net/show/june-8-1974.

250 *"Dead's incredible soundsystem"* Sherwood.

250 *"shivering electricity"* Per user "CatchColt," via dead.net, www.dead.net/show/june-8-1974.

250 *"peering into the Future of Sound"* Corry Arnold, May 31, 2011, https://lostlivedead .blogspot.com/2011/05/june-8-1974-oakland -coliseum-stadium.html.

250 *"help the cash flow"* UCSC SpecColl, MS332, ser. 3, Box 2:2, GDR: Show files: Iowa State Fairgrounds.

251 *"bad acid"* Per user "DeepWoodsOff," via Archive, https://archive.org/details /gd1974-06-16.sbd.fink.15781.shnf.

251 *"rough looking"* Per user "lystok5," via dead .net, https://www.dead.net/show/june-16- 1974.

251 *nearly a mile out* Per user "TechGuru1," via Archive, https://archive.org/details /gd1974-06-16.sbd.fink.15781.shnf.

251 *"Please don't throw Frisbees"* Ibid.

252 *"joked"* Comment (Chuck Coleman) under February 2024 Dead social post for Wall stories.

252 *"pristine soundboard recording"* Weiner, 125.

252 *"electric surge"* Per user "MST," via Archive, https://archive.org/details/gd74-06-16.sbd .cribbs.26452.sbeok.shnf.

252 *"above and behind the band"* Delbert Gee, "How EB Picks Concert Performers," *California Aggie*, Vol. 90 No. 45, December 5, 1975.

252 *"best McIntosh home stereo"* Per user "lystok5," via dead.net.

252 *"acoustical sweet spot"* Per user "fishman," ibid.

253 *change a person* Per user "Darkstarlsd," via Archive, https://archive.org/details /gd74-06-16.sbd.cribbs.26452.sbeok.shnf.

253 *"band was playing the crowd"* Per user "Deep-WoodsOff," via Archive.

253 *"quite satisfied"* "The 'Dead': Casual Yet Still Mellow."

253 *letter to a promoter in Guadalajara* UCSC SpecColl, MS332, ser. 3, Box 155:5, GDR: Show files: Europe tour 1974—receipts.

253 *meeting in San Rafael* UCSC SpecColl, MS332, ser. 3, Box 155:6, GDR: Show files: Europe tour 1974—receipts.

254 *"humongous monstrosity"* Per user "Evan S. Hunt," via Archive, https://archive.org/details /gd74-06-18.sbd.sacks.209.sbefail.shnf.

254 *"finding treasure in the attic"* Per user "tweat," ibid.

254 *used their system* UCSC SpecColl, MS332, ser. 3, Box 2:2, GDR: Show files: Iowa State Fairgrounds.

254 *technical difficulties delayed* Per user "Will Shine," via Archive, https://archive.org/details /gd74-06-20.sbd.clugston.2179.sbeok.shnf.

254 *"blew up"* Per user "fudoki," ibid.

254 *"power of the Wall behind them"* "Will Shine," ibid.

254 *"never heard such a pure sound"* "fudoki," ibid.

254 *last-minute amp adjustment* "Will Shine," ibid.

254 *"blew the roof and doors off"* Per user "Byrd," via dead.net, www.dead.net/show/june-20-1974.

255 *"I could brag"* Per user "oydave," ibid.

255 *"bleepblorp"* McNally, *A Long Strange Trip*, 474.

255 *twenty-three gigs* Gans/Jackson, 228.

255 *"Phil & Ned's computer"* UCSC SpecColl,

MS332, ser. 2, Box 137:13, GDR: Business-meeting minutes, 1974.

255 *frequency-to-voltage synths and quadraphonic joysticks* Jarnow, 93.

255 *March meeting* UCSC SpecColl, MS332, ser. 2, Box 137:13, GDR: Business-meeting minutes, 1974.

256 *"originating in your head"* McNally, *A Long Strange Trip*, 474.

256 *"incredible array of shit"* Rock Scully, 284.

257 *"strange and weird"* Gans/Jackson, 229.

257 *"monumental things occurred"* Ibid, 229–230.

258 *"horrible bummer"* McNally, *A Long Strange Trip*, 486.

258 *"one of the best in '74"* Rodriguez, 197.

258 *control booth* UCSC SpecColl, MS332, ser. 3, Box 2:4, GDR: Show Files: Providence Civic Center, R.I.

259 *nearly reached the steel rafters* Per user "Fulcanelli," via dead.net, www.dead.net/show/june-26-1974.

259 *"garbage can"* Per user "ScubaGeek," via Archive, https://archive.org/details/gd74-06-28.moore.weiner.gdADT18.16038.sbeok.shnf.

259 *mysterious lunar monolith* McNally, *A Long Strange Trip*, 471.

260 *twenty-seven travelers* UCSC SpecColl, MS332, ser. 3, Box 155:4, GDR: Show Files: 1973–1974 tours in connection with albums; September 1973–July 1974.

260 *"That's a price!"* Michael Brooks, "Custom Machines: What's Your Favorite Guitar Fantasy?" *Creem*, July 1, 1974.

260 *"out there"* "Interstices of Grateful Dead Performance," *Hooterollin' Around*, June 24, 2011, https://hooterollin.blogspot.com/2011/06/interstices-of-grateful-dead.html.

261 *"spacey"* https://lostlivedead.blogspot.com/search?q=Selland.

261 *"monster"* Per user "jacksondownunda," via dead.net, https://www.dead.net/show/july-21-1974.

262 *"it just might change your thinking"* Gans/Jackson, 228–229.

262 *"the Wall was something to see"* Per user "IslandSavage," via Archive, https://archive.org/details/gd74-07-21.bertrando.weiner.8241.sbeok.shnf.

262 *"clean and clear"* Per user "Myshkyn," via

dead.net, https://www.dead.net/show/july-21-1974.

263 *"realm of live sound reproduction"* Alan Shapiro, "The Grateful Dead: Closing the Gap Between Art and Life," *Good Times*, July 24–August 8, 1974.

263 *sound "gradually improved"* Per user "072574," via Archive, https://archive.org/details/gd74-07-25.sbd.fink.1072.sbeok.shnf.

263 *"mind numbing"* Per user "paisley," via dead.net, https://www.dead.net/show/july-25-1974.

263 *"finest use of electricity"* Per user "072574," via Archive.

264 *"where else around here"* Per user "paisley," via dead.net.

264 *reportedly unable to load* Per user "kaptainkopter," via dead.net, www.dead.net/show/july-27-1974.

264 *"most flawless speaker system"* Donna Shoemaker, "Grateful Dead Turns 'Em On," *Roanoke Tribune*.

264 *"crowd became bored"* Ron Brown, "Grateful Dead Aloof, Boring," *World News*, July 29, 1974.

264 *"brain splitting alchemist"* Per user "fishnwhistle," via Archive, https://archive.org/details/gd74-07-27.sbd.kaplan.2420.sbeok.shnf.

264 *"crew took down the Wall"* Per user "SteveMaruti," via Archive, https://archive.org/details/gd74-07-27.sbd.kaplan.2420.sbeok.shnf.

264 *"sound was amazing"* Per user "lawrencegeusz4890," www.youtube.com/watch?v=D_RiiRe2sns.

264 *"move around the speakers"* Comment (Morgan Broman) under February 2024 Dead social post for Wall stories.

265 *"never-to-be-forgotten experience"* Per user "treegarden," via dead.net, www.dead.net/show/july-31-1974.

265 *"roadie climbed"* Per user "Cosmic.Wimpout," ibid.

265 *vibrate "pleasantly"* Comment (James Faulkner) under February 2024 Dead social post for Wall stories.

265 *heard miles away* Comment (Tom Piazza), ibid.

265 *"shut up"* Comment ("bobby_bake07"), ibid.

266 *clouds opened and soaked the stage* Jay Saporita, "We used to play for silver, now we play for life," *The Aquarian*, 8/28/74–9/11/74.

266 *"sparks flew"* Per user "atomicon," via Archive, https://archive.org/details/gd74-08-06

.merin.weiner.gdADT.5914.sbefail.shnf
/gd74-08-06d1t07.shn.

266 *postponing the gig* Per user "voxrock," ibid.

266 *somewhat embittered* McNally, *A Long Strange Trip*, 475.

266 *"heads for the Turnpike"* Saporita.

267 *"clear as a bell"* Ibid.

267 *"given a final check"* Ibid.

267 *"rocking back and forth"* Comment (Lynette Milanese) under February 2024 Dead social post for Wall stories.

267 *"giant ozone filters"* Bill Mandel, "'Grateful Dead' Runs the Whole Repertoire," *Philadelphia Inquirer*, August 5, 1974.

268 *sine wave* Per user "mcleary," via dead.net, www.dead.net/show/august-4-1974.

268 *"FOW"* Per user "guit30," ibid.

268 *took a deserved breather* Saporita.

269 *"couldn't find an extension cord"* Browne, 224.

269 *"precise and sharp"* Saporita.

269 *"ground shook"* Comment (Jeff Taylor) under February 2024 Dead social post for Wall stories.

269 *"clarity and power"* Per user "jbowne," via dead.net, www.dead.net/show/august-6-1974.

269 *"you didn't get blasted"* Per user "pchasmar," ibid.

269 *"all-powerful Wall"* Per user "essanjay," via Archive, https://archive.org/details/gd74-08-06 .merin.weiner.gdADT.5914.sbefail.shnf /gd74-08-06d1t07.shn.

270 *"pinnacle of our live performances"* Lesh, 217.

270 *enormous production scale* Richardson, 216.

270 *nearly forty people* Browne, 224.

270 *"cannot continue as we have been"* Joel Selvin, "Is the Dead Going to Die?" *San Francisco Chronicle*, August 25, 1974.

270 *Marin County hotel* Browne, 224.

270 *"financial strain"* Lesh, 218.

270 *"barely breaking even"* Browne, 224.

270 *"us against the world"* Lesh, 218.

270 *overindulging and distracted* McNally, 475.

270 *ground down and cantankerous* Richardson, 216.

271 *"rude a lot"* McNally, *A Long Strange Trip*, 472.

271 *bubble off* Lesh, 218.

271 *Rifkin spoke first* Browne, 224.

271 *"They had to stop"* Ibid.

271 *look for jobs elsewhere* McNally, *A Long Strange Trip*, 475.

272 *"depraved" plan* Rock Scully, 235.

272 *"Ally Pally"* Ibid., 236.

272 *"carting around"* Ibid.

272 *twenty-seven "travelers"* UCSC SpecColl, MS332, ser. 3, Box 155:4, GDR: Show Files: 1973–1974 tours in connection with albums; September 1973–July 1974.

272 *thirty-four band and crew members* UCSC SpecColl, MS332, ser. 3, Box 2:15, Show files: Europe Tour 1974.

272 *detailed gear manifest* UCSC SpecColl, MS332, ser. 3, Box 155:5, GDR: Show files: Europe tour 1974–receipts.

273 *Kilos* Browne, 225.

273 *sixteen-strong crew* UCSC SpecColl, MS332, ser. 3, Box 155:6, GDR: Show Files: Europe Tour 1974—receipts.

273 *"disaster waiting to happen"* Rock Scully, 237–238.

273 *Jackson briefly quit* McNally, *A Long Strange Trip*, 475.

273 *"Everyone is torn and frayed"* Rock Scully, 240.

273 *abdicating their responsibilities* Parish, 172.

274 *Americans always rushed and shouted* Ibid.

274 *"remarkably far out"* Gans/Jackson, 231.

274 *Jackson delivered an "impassioned speech"* Rock Scully, 241.

274 *it would kill them* Parish, 174.

275 *couple of ounces of cocaine* Rock Scully, 141.

275 *"the clean Grateful Dead"* Browne, 225.

275 *"burning the stash and finally playing"* Rock Scully, 241–242.

275 *4,300* UCSC SpecColl, MS332, ser. 3, Box 2:16, GDR: Show Files: Alexandra Palace— London, England, September 9–12, 1974.

275 *McIntire wrote a note* UCSC SpecColl, MS332, ser. 3, Box 2:15, GDR: Show Files: Europe Tour 1974.

277 *"unusual lighting"* Comment (Tom Graham) under February 2024 Dead social post for Wall stories.

277 *"lumbering machine"* Robin Denselow, "The Grateful Dead at Alexandra Palace," *The Guardian*, September 11, 1974.

277 *"700-piece PA"* Steve Lake, "Keep On

Truckin'-Steve Lake Reviews Live Dead,"
Melody Maker, September 14, 1974.

277 *"made my eyes water"* Comment (Tom Graham) under February 2024 Dead social post for Wall stories.

277 *Healy and Hagen shopped* UCSC SpecColl, MS332, ser. 3, Box 155:5, GDR: Show files: Europe tour 1974—receipts.

277 *"top-shelf"* Robertson, 128–129.

277 *slapped the music back* Robin Katz, "Dead? No Just Snoozing," *Sounds*, September 21, 1974.

278 *just over 4,100* UCSC SpecColl, MS332, ser. 3, Box 2:16, GDR: Show Files: Alexandra Palace—London, England, September 9–12, 1974.

278 *"vibrate the whole of my body"* Per user "Incornsyucopia," via dead.net, www.dead.net/show/september-10-1974.

278 *"top speakers had snow on them"* Per user "Cliffski," via Archive, https://archive.org/details/gd74-09-10.sbd.samaritano.18806.sbeok.shnf.

278 *"wall of voodoo"* Per user "nevilleh," via dead.net.

278 *7,500* UCSC SpecColl, MS332, ser. 3, Box 2:16, GDR: Show Files: Alexandra Palace—London, England, September 9–12, 1974.

278 *"like a giant hi-fi"* Per user "JeanSteinmann," via dead.net, www.dead.net/show/september-11-1974.

279 *retreated to the pub* Katz.

279 *"hip"* Gans/Jackson, 231.

279 *Members of Pink Floyd* Brown, "If I Told You All That Went Down: The Saga of Grateful Dead Records," *The Golden Road*, No. 11, Summer 1986.

279 *"the Bear-Healy-Raizene-Wickersham-Turner-Curl-Alembic-PA-system"* Rex Anderson, *New Musical Express*, September 14, 1974.

279 *"the reason for the PA"* Steve Lake, "Rock 'n Roll Misfit," *Melody Maker*, September 14, 1974.

280 *"compromise a lot"* Michael Brooks, "Jack It Up & Jam It Tight: A Future Perfect Guide to Musical Artillery," *Creem*, October 1974.

280 *"almost unnoticed"* Ian MacDonald, "Letter from Britain," *Creem*, December 1, 1974.

280 *purloined the cabinets* Comment (Colin Goble) under February 2024 Dead social post for Wall stories.

280 *"soundcheck is crucial"* Rock Scully, 5–7.

280 *"had enough"* McNally, *A Long Strange Trip*, 476.

280 *band attorney* Ibid., 422.

280 *manage the remaining four European dates* Jackson/McNally, 174.

280 *"felt every note"* Per user "birdsonthebat," via dead.net, www.dead.net/show/september-14-1974.

280 *vocals were "mostly lost"* Per user "darkstar90," via dead.net, ibid.

281 *"made it out of Germany alive"* Brown, *The Golden Road*.

281 *on from the top* Weiner, 216.

281 *"band persevered"* Olsson, 129.

281 *"sound was quite bad"* Per user "john-tizi," via dead.net, www.dead.net/show/september-18-1974.

281 *intimidated the promoter* McNally, *A Long Strange Trip*, 477.

281 *"experience social problems"* Ibid.

281 *heavily into cocaine* Parish, 174.

281 *"not noisy"* Per user "frenchy," via dead.net, www.dead.net/show/september-20-1974.

282 *"finest sound"* Per user "deedindeed," ibid.

282 *uncredited black-and-white film* www.youtube.com/watch?v=Bx92zPPDpzQ.

282 *inspired them* Comment (Christophe Rossi) under February 2024 Dead social post for Wall stories.

282 *research soundsystem innovations* Jackson, 143.

282 *got dosed* McNally, *A Long Strange Trip*, 477.

283 *raging through the streets* Ibid.

283 *"not much rings a bell"* Kreutzmann, 179.

283 *Homesick and miserable* Parish, 174.

283 *"recharge"* Lesh, 219.

284 *paid for the trip* UCSC SpecColl, MS332, ser. 3, Box 155:5, GDR: Show files: Europe tour 1974—receipts.

284 *"Dead reached their musical peak"* Mitchell Lazar, "Ugly Rumors from the Dead," *MIT Technology Review*, October 15, 1974.

284 *quiet part out loud* McNally, *A Long Strange Trip*, 478.

286 *"You had to be there"* www.gratefulseconds.com/2019/12/the-final-five-at-winterland-october-16.html.

286 *"sucking on the nitrous octopus"* Rock Scully, 318.

286 *"mildly disappointing"* Per user "jackson-downunda," via dead.net, www.dead.net/show/october-18-1974.

286 *"tuned to the universe of possibilities"* Per user "Grateful Bill," ibid.

286 *"transcendent"* Per user "sugarmagkauai," ibid.

286 *"Bear's prowess"* Per user "Evan S. Hunt," via Archive, https://archive.org/details /gd1974-10-18.BEAR.gems.110558.flac24.

287 *"blessed to have heard it"* Per user "nitecat," via dead.net, www.dead.net/show/october-20-1974.

287 *"ten years without* one *break"* Rock Scully, 253–254.

287 *took a hit of DMT* McNally, *A Long Strange Trip,* 479.

9. THE OTHER SIDE (1975)

288 *"divert the income"* Gans/Jackson, 236–237.

288 *"small and tasty"* Peter Herbst, "Message from Garcia: Nothing Exceeds Like Success," *Boston Phoenix,* November 19, 1974.

288 *"acoustically perfect hall"* Adam Block, "Garcia on Garcia 77," *BAM Magazine,* December 1977–January 1978.

288 *"a different leg"* Brackett.

289 *"logistical near impossibility"* Greenfield, 151.

289 *"impossible to tame"* Kreutzmann, 188.

289 *"sounded fucking awful"* "A Relix Conversation with Bill Kreutzmann and Benjy Eisen" (Episode 3, Part 5), *Relix,* June 23, 2015, www .youtube.com/watch?v=4tZgA30fG_k&t=143s.

289 *"too fucking much"* Gans, 334.

289 *downsized systems* Jackson, 151.

289 *"monster payroll"* Rock Scully, 254.

290 *never taking a raise* Jesse Jarnow, "The Story of the Grateful Dead's Gear Is the Story of Rock 'n' Roll," *GQ Magazine,* October 5, 2021.

290 *"we were swamped"* Gans/Jackson, 237.

290 *"going into hibernation"* McNally, *A Long Strange Trip,* 479.

290 *"three cents"* For more on Lesh's thoughts on the Dead's finances, see the "Louisville 6/18/74" tape.

290 *"it was joyful"* Mike B., "Jerry Garcia Interview–1975 w. Peter Simon (originally on WVOI; Martha's Vineyard)," March 13, 2021, www.youtube.com/watch?v=ZVBmhw3MDzs.

291 *"we're scuffling"* "Jerry Garcia Interview ~1975 SNACK Benefit (Grateful Dead & Friends)," October 12, 2021, www.youtube.com/watch?v =shCRg0mQEJE.

291 *IRS meetings* UCSC SpecColl, Dead office phone logs, from 8/30/74 to 11/20/74.

292 *Hard Truckers* Jackson, 152.

292 *UltraSound* Ibid., 203.

292 *Hot Tuna* Ibid., 202.

293 *post-Wall touring* Ibid., 165.

293 *humble in size* Barnes, 140.

293 *lean six-person crew* Jackson/McNally, 192.

293 *wedge monitors* Jackson, 166.

293 *East Coast audio company* Barnes, 140.

294 *experimental jumps* McNally, *A Long Strange Trip,* 529.

294 *major leveling-up* Jackson/McNally, 234.

294 *"huge" monitor system* Jackson, 183.

294 *rumored to have been stored* Comment (Jerry Davis) under February 2024 Dead social post for Wall stories.

294 *"among the best soundsystems ever"* McNally, *A Long Strange Trip,* 529.

294 *practical to use for touring* Lesh, 249.

295 *Healy had pushed for them* Jackson, 218–219.

295 *computer-assisted soundsystem* Barnes, 140.

295 *"building a pyramid"* Jackson/McNally, 176.

295 *"stuck and were influential"* Jackson, 165–166.

297 *the hiatus had Alembic pivot* Ibid., 152.

300 *an enterprise that grossed $33.5 million* Barnes, 23.

10. THE KEEPERS

302 *sold for over $15,000* Sotheby's, "[Hells Angels] Party stereo system—including the earliest Grateful Dead speakers," www.sothebys.com/en /buy/auction/2021/from-the-vault-property -from-the-grateful-dead-and-friends/hells -angels-party-stereo-system-including-the, 2021.

302 *sold for $10,710* Sotheby's, "Grateful Dead | AC Distribution Panel, used by the Dead for live shows," www.sothebys.com/en/buy /auction/2021/from-the-vault-property-from -the-grateful-dead-and-friends/grateful-dead -ac-distribution-panel-used-by-the, 2021.

302 *sold for $17,640* Sotheby's, "Jerry Garcia | A veteran of too many gigs to count…," www .sothebys.com/en/buy/auction/2021/from-the -vault-property-from-the-grateful-dead-and -friends/jerry-garcia-a-veteran-of-too-many -gigs-to-count, 2021.

303 *sold for an eye-watering $378,000* Sotheby's,

"Wall of Sound | The amp that made Garcia's Twin 'sound huge,'" www.sothebys.com/en/buy /auction/2021/from-the-vault-property-from -the-grateful-dead-and-friends/wall-of-sound -the-amp-that-made-garcias-twin-sound, 2021.

303 *sold for $94,500* Sotheby's, "Wall of Sound | One of the Dead's first MC 2300's," www.sothebys .com/en/buy/auction/2021/from-the-vault -property-from-the-grateful-dead-and-friends /wall-of-sound-one-of-the-deads-first-mc-2300s, 2021.

303 *midrange vocal cluster* Sotheby's, "Wall of Sound | MC 2300, for the vocal cluster," www.sothebys.com /en/buy/auction/2021/from-the-vault-property -from-the-grateful-dead-and-friends/wall-of-sound -mc-2300-for-the-vocal-cluster, 2021.

303 *piano* Sotheby's, "Wall of Sound | MC 2300 for the piano cluster," www.sothebys.com/en /buy/auction/2021/from-the-vault-property -from-the-grateful-dead-and-friends/wall-of -sound-mc-2300-for-the-piano-cluster-2, 2021.

303 *cluster* Sotheby's, "Wall of Sound | MC 2300 for the piano cluster," www.sothebys.com/en /buy/auction/2021/from-the-vault-property -from-the-grateful-dead-and-friends/wall-of -sound-mc-2300-for-the-piano-cluster, 2021.

303 *Weir's guitar rig* Sotheby's, "Wall of Sound | Bob Weir's MC 2300," www.sothebys.com/en /buy/auction/2021/from-the-vault-property -from-the-grateful-dead-and-friends/wall-of -sound-bob-weirs-mc-2300, 2021.

303 *variously used* Sotheby's, "Wall of Sound | MC 2300," www.sothebys.com/en/buy/auction /2021/from-the-vault-property-from-the -grateful-dead-and-friends/wall-of-sound-mc -2300, 2021.

303 *guitars* Sotheby's, "Wall of Sound | MC 2300," www.sothebys.com/en/buy/auction/2021/from -the-vault-property-from-the-grateful-dead-and -friends/wall-of-sound-mc-2300-2, 2021.

303 *purple* Sotheby's, "Wall of Sound | Purple road case, custom built for a McIntosh amp," www.sothebys.com/en/buy/auction/2021 /from-the-vault-property-from-the-grateful -dead-and-friends/wall-of-sound-purple-road -case-custom-built-for-a, 2021.

303 *orange* Sotheby's, "Wall of Sound | Orange road case, custom built for a McIntosh amp," www.sothebys.com/en/buy/auction/2021 /from-the-vault-property-from-the-grateful -dead-and-friends/wall-of-sound-orange-road -case-custom-built-for-a, 2021.

303 *Various 2x12s* Sotheby's, "Wall of Sound | Alembic speaker cabinet," www.sothebys .com/en/buy/auction/2021/from-the-vault -property-from-the-grateful-dead-and-friends /wall-of-sound-alembic-speaker-cabinet, 2021.

303 *some used* Sotheby's, "Wall of Sound | Weir's cab," www.sothebys.com/en/buy/auction/2021 /from-the-vault-property-from-the-grateful -dead-and-friends/wall-of-sound-weirs-cab, 2021.

303 *by Weir* Sotheby's, "Wall of Sound | Hand- made speaker cabinet," www.sothebys.com/en /buy/auction/2021/from-the-vault-property -from-the-grateful-dead-and-friends/wall-of -sound-handmade-speaker-cabinet, 2021.

303 *and Garcia* Sotheby's, "Wall of Sound | One of Garcia's cabs," www.sothebys.com/en/buy /auction/2021/from-the-vault-property-from -the-grateful-dead-and-friends/wall-of-sound -one-of-garcias-cabs, 2021/

303 *went for $8,820* Sotheby's, "Wall of Sound | Bass cab," www.sothebys.com/en/buy/auction/2021 /from-the-vault-property-from-the-grateful-dead -and-friends/wall-of-sound-bass-cab, 2021.

303 *sold for $17,640* Sotheby's, "Wall of Sound | Speaker cabinet, handmade at Alembic," www .sothebys.com/en/buy/auction/2021/from -the-vault-property-from-the-grateful-dead -and-friends/wall-of-sound-speaker-cabinet -handmade-at-alembic, 2021.

303 *"what survives" from that centerpiece* Sothe- by's, "Wall of Sound | From the centerpiece vocal cluster," www.sothebys.com/en/buy /auction/2021/from-the-vault-property-from -the-grateful-dead-and-friends/wall-of-sound -from-the-centerpiece-vocal-cluster, 2021.

303 *brought in a total of $1.1 million* Associated Press, "Grateful Dead Auction Brings in $1.1 Million," *TODAY*, May 8, 2007.

303 *included* Bonhams, "A Wooden Speaker Box from the Wall of Sound, Early 1970s," www .bonhams.com/auctions/15537/lot/40/, May 8, 2007.

303 *bona fide* Bonhams, "A Wooden Speaker Box from the Wall of Sound, Early 1970s," www.bonhams.com/auctions/15537/lot/41 /?category=list&length=12&page=4, May 8, 2007.

303 *Wall* Bonhams, "A Tie-Dyed Speaker Box, Early 1970s," www.bonhams.com/auctions /15537/lot/37/?category=list&length=12 &page=4, May 8, 2007.

303 *artifacts* Bonhams, "A Fabric and Suede Speaker Box, Early 1970s," www.bonhams.com /auctions/15537/lot/38/?category=list&length =12&page=4, May 8, 2007.

303 *another Dead-themed auction* Bonhams, "Two Jerry Garcia monitor speaker cabinets from the line array of Grateful Dead sound reinforcement system known as the 'Wall of Sound,' 1972–74," www.bonhams.com/auction/20158 /lot/3060/two-jerry-garcia-monitor-speaker -cabinets-from-the-line-array-of-grateful-dead -sound-reinforcement-system-known-as-the -wall-of-sound-1972-74/, May 8, 2012.

303 *again featuring Wall parts* Bonhams, "An owned and used Phil Lesh amp from the Grateful Dead's Wall of Sound with original Courtenay Pollock artwork," www.bonhams .com/auction/20158/lot/3059/an-owned -and-used-phil-lesh-amp-from-the-grateful -deads-wall-of-sound-with-original-courtenay -pollock-artwork/, May 8, 2012.

305 *"ripped the band off"* Lesh, 227.

308 *"aberration"* For more on Parish's comments, and to hear responses from Lambert and Gans, listen to "Dead Forever LIVE," Grateful Dead Channel—SiriusXM, May 17, 2023.

309 *raise their son, Cole* McNally, *A Long Strange Trip*, 494.

309 *"drugs were isolating us"* Lesh, 251.

309 *bled out* Parish, 214–215.

309 *He only departed a venue* McNally, *A Long Strange Trip*, 599.

310 *"Thought I would stack them up"* Strider Shurtliff, Instagram, April 9, 2019.

310 *flew in for the event* Gissen Stanley, 256.

310 *"marked for identification"* Ibid., 265.

310 *"world's most powerful hi-fi system"* Ibid., 266.

312 *"less detrimental to the planet"* CBS Sunday Morning, "Extended interview: Grateful Dead co-founder Bob Weir," www.youtube.com /watch?v=chmE7JglAKo, November 27, 2022.

312 *similar, static backdrop* Qello Concerts, "Move Me Brightly: Celebrating Jerry Garcia's 70th Birthday," www.youtube.com/watch?v =Bk3fDgkZmfI&t, March 18, 2024.

313 *"There's still more to come"* Meyer Sound, "Meyer Sound PANTHER Carries Dead & Company Through the Final Chapter of a Musical Epic," https://meyersound.com /news/dead-company-final-tour/, August 16, 2023.

314 *"beamforming"* Comment ("joe.u.know") under February 2024 Dead social post for Wall stories.

Index

About the Author

Alan Huck

BRIAN ANDERSON has been a Webby Award–winning senior features editor, writer, and producer at *Vice*. More recently, Anderson did a stint as science editor at *The Atlantic*, where he was part of the Pulitzer Prize–winning team for early pandemic coverage, and was later an editor at *Vox*. He lives in Chicago with his partner (and a piece of the Wall of Sound), and teaches journalism at Northwestern University. *Loud and Clear* is his first book.

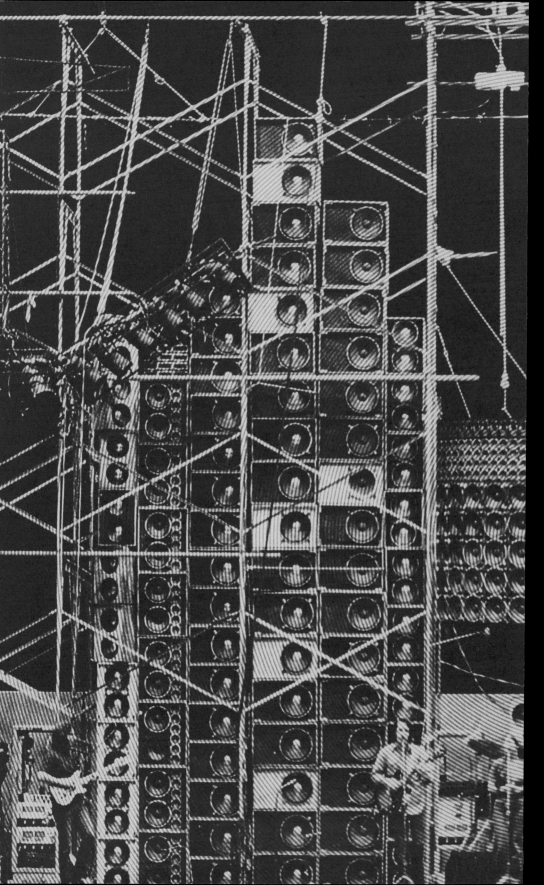